W9-CUW-548

ANNALS OF COMMUNISM

Each volume in the series Annals of Communism will publish selected and previously inaccessible documents from former Soviet state and party archives in a narrative that develops a particular topic in the history of Soviet and international communism. Separate English and Russian editions will be prepared. Russian and American scholars work together to prepare the documents for each volume. Documents are chosen not for their support of any single interpretation but for their particular historical importance or their general value in deepening understanding and facilitating discussion. The volumes are designed to be useful to students, scholars, and interested general readers.

The Diary of
Georgi Dimitrov
1933–1949

Introduced and edited by
Ivo Banac

German part translated by Jane T. Hedges,
Russian by Timothy D. Sergay, *and*
Bulgarian by Irina Faion

Yale University Press
New Haven & London

All photographs are courtesy of Boyko Dimitrov.

Designed by James J. Johnson and set in Sabon Roman type by The Composing Room of Michigan, Inc.
Printed in the United States of America by Vail-Ballou Press.

Library of Congress Cataloging-in-Publication Data

Dimitrov, Georgi, 1882–1949.
 [Diaries. English. Selections]
 The diary of Georgi Dimitrov, 1933–1949 / introduced and edited by Ivo Banac ;
German part translated by Jane T. Hedges, Russian by Timothy D. Sergay, and Bulgarian by Irina Faion.
  p. cm. — (Annals of Communism)
 Written in Russian, Bulgarian, and German. Published in Bulgarian in 1997 under the title: Dnevnik. Some material has been omitted from the English translation.
 Includes bibliographical references and index.
 ISBN 0-300-09794-8 (alk. paper)

 1. Dimitrov, Georgi, 1882–1949—Diaries. 2. Statesmen—Bulgaria—Diaries.
3. Communists—Bulgaria—Diaries. 4. Bulgaria—History—Boris III, 1918–1943.
5. Bulgaria—History—1944–1990. I. Banac, Ivo. II. Title. III. Series.
DR88.D5 A3 2003
949.903′1′092—dc21
[B]   2002190765

A catalogue record for this book is available from the British Library.

The paper in this book meets the guidelines for permanence and durability of the Committee on Production Guidelines for Book Longevity of the Council on Library Resources.

10 9 8 7 6 5 4 3 2 1

Yale University Press gratefully acknowledges the financial support given for this publication by the John M. Olin Foundation, the Lynde and Harry Bradley Foundation, the Historical Research Foundation, Roger Milliken, Lloyd H. Smith, Keith Young, the William H. Donner Foundation, Joseph W. Donner, Jeremiah Milbank, the David Woods Kemper Memorial Foundation, the Daphne Seybolt Culpeper Foundation, the Milton V. Brown Foundation, the National Endowment for the Humanities, and the Open Society Fund.

For Wolfgang Leonhard
friend and comrade
with a bottle of vinho verde

Contents

Illustrations

PHOTOGRAPHS

following page 98

Georgi Dimitrov among the agitators and leaders of the miners' strike, Pernik, Bulgaria, summer 1906.

Georgi Dimitrov and Dimitŭr Blagoev among members of the Central Committee and Control Commission and delegates to the Sixteenth Congress of the Bulgarian Workers' Social Democratic Party, Varna, Bulgaria, July 1909.

Report No. 12889, dated 1 March 1918, to the head of the military-judicial section of the War Ministry on Dimitrov's revolutionary activity during his visit to the front in January 1918.

Dimitrov, delegate to the Third Congress of the Comintern, Moscow, June–July 1921.

Bulgarian-French dictionary inscribed by Dimitrov to Lenin, "our beloved teacher and irreplaceable leader of the world's proletarian revolution," Moscow, 5 March 1921.

Dimitrov speaking at the Sixth Congress of the Comintern, Moscow, 25 July 1928.

Georgi Dimitrov.

Dimitrov's Profintern card, No. 4., Moscow, 1928.

Dimitrov's file with the Prussian criminal police, Berlin, 10 March 1933.

Dimitrov's police mug shots, 10 March 1933.

Georgi Dimitrov, Vasil Tanev, and Blagoi Popov, police photo, 10 March 1933.

Dimitrov at the Leipzig trial, 1933.

Photomontage by John Heartfield: "You are scared of my questions, Mr. Chairman of the Council of Ministers."

Dimitrov's final speech at the Leipzig trial, 16 December 1933.

Open letter from the German antifascists to Dimitrov: "Dimitrov! The Bulgarian working class can be proud of you. Long live world revolution!" Stuttgart, 20 December 1933.

Stalin and Dimitrov, attending the 1935 May Day parade in Moscow.

following page 356

Dimitrov in the Comintern office, Moscow.

Dimitrov's membership card for the Executive Committee of the Communist International, Seventh Congress of the Comintern, Moscow, 1935.

Marcel Cachin and Georgi Dimitrov, Moscow, 1935.

Dimitrov and the Comintern leaders: Palmiro Togliatti, Wilhelm Florin, Wang Ming, Otto Kuusinen, Klement Gottwald, Wilhelm Pieck, Dmitry Manuilsky, Moscow, 1935.

Dimitrov with the Kostroma voters, 19 December 1937.

Tito and Dimitrov in Meshcherino, 15 April 1945.

Mikhail Kalinin, chairman of the presidium of the Supreme Soviet of the USSR, awards Dimitrov the Order of Lenin for his struggle against fascism, Moscow, 27 June 1945.

G. Dimitrov, with S. S. Biriuzov and Marshal F. I. Tolbukhin, commander of the Third Ukrainian Front, which entered Bulgaria on 8 September 1944, at the Sofia railway station, 22 February 1946.

Traicho Kostov and Georgi Dimitrov, 26 May 1946.

Dimitrov, chairman of the Council of Ministers of Bulgaria, in his office, 30 April 1948.

Dimitrov, general secretary of the BKP, delivers a report at the fifth party congress, Sofia, December 1948.

Georgi Dimitrov.

Dimitrov with wife Rosa and children Fania and Boyko in Meshcherino, 1948.

Dimitrov and son Boyko in Barvikha, 1948.

Georgi and Rosa Dimitrov in Barvikha, 18 June 1949.

Inauguration of a monument to Dimitrov (sculpted by K. and M. Merabishvili), Moscow, 16 June 1972.

Preface

The editing of this volume has been an arduous task, interrupted by frequent changes in setting—New Haven, Moscow, Budapest, Zagreb, Dubrovnik—almost a match for Dimitrov's record. If this task were offered to me again, I am not certain that I would agree to undertake it. The reason is not the lack of historical insight to be found in the diary of Georgi Dimitrov. On the contrary, this is the single most important new source on the history of the international Communist movement in Stalin's time. Rather, the collective character of this effort has been somewhat off-putting to an historian of my solitary disposition.

Dimitrov wrote his diary in nineteen separate notebooks that are now kept in the former Communist Party archive in Sofia, Bulgaria. A typescript of eighteen of these was made in 1960 for the purposes of the Central Party Archive in Sofia, with a copy for the Marx-Engels-Lenin Institute in Moscow, currently the Russian State Archive of Social and Political History (RGASPI). An integral version of the manuscript was published in Bulgarian in 1997.[1] The Yale University Press Annals of Communism series obtained access to these materials in 1993, thanks to Boyko Dimitrov, Dimitrov's adopted son and literary executor. Since the diary is multilingual, the Press entrusted the translation to three translators—Jane T. Hedges, Timothy D. Sergay, and Irina Faion. I then significantly reduced their translation, whereby the text was cut to a third of its original size, and frequently translated various passages myself, especially in the Bulgarian part, and equipped it with the requisite introduction, explanatory footnotes, bibliographies, and abbreviations. It should be noted that the bibliographies include information on the most significant figures in the diary, whereas the less prominent figures are accounted for in the footnotes.

The reader is entitled to an explanation of the criteria that governed the reduction of the text. Since the diary is full of mere chronology, simply noting the procession of visitors received by Dimitrov, much of this material was excluded. The only exceptions, unless otherwise noted, were encounters that appear to be meaningful in their own right. I also excluded various documents that Dimitrov occasionally attached to his diary and which are otherwise available. This is especially so in the Bulgarian part. No significant information, however, even when seemingly obscure, was omitted. In any case, scholars with knowledge of Bulgarian will be able to double check by comparing the present translation with the Bulgarian volume, which was enormously helpful to me in various ways, not least of all in negotiating certain biographical mysteries.

In completing this volume I incurred many debts that I would like to acknowledge. I am grateful to Jonathan Brent, the executive editor of the series, for inviting me to undertake this project. Thanks are due to the diary translators, especially Timothy D. Sergay, who facilitated the early work on the project, and to his successor Vadim Staklo, who brought the project to a successful conclusion. I am grateful to my former student, Paul Jukić, for his enormous help in Moscow in 1993, and for his work on reducing the manuscript and marking the appropriate areas of explanation. I profited from the valuable advice of Fridrikh Firsov, the former curator at the RGASPI, with whom I originally hoped to undertake the editorial work. My Yale colleagues Beatrice S. Bartlett, David Montgomery, and Piotr S. Wandycz, as well as my student Soner Çağaptay and my colleague from Southern Connecticut State University John O. Iatrides, were quite helpful in solving some of the identity problems with the enormous international cast of characters in the diary. I acknowledge the cooperation of Mr. Panto Kolev, of the Main Archival Administration at the Bulgarian Council of Ministers, in obtaining the microfilms of the diary. I am indebted to the grant from the National Endowment for the Humanities that facilitated my research at RGASPI in 1993. Tanja Lorković, the curator of the Slavic collection at Yale, and her assistant William J. Larsh, as well as Mr. Wenkai Kung of the East Asia collection, are not the least of my creditors. But there are others, too, that I do not care to mention. As with the dying debtor in the story by Danilo Kiš, my indebtedness is askew.

I.B.
New Haven, Connecticut,
All Souls Day 2001

NOTE

1. Georgi Dimitrov, *Dnevnik (9 mart 1933–6 februari 1949),* ed. Dimitŭr Sirkov, et al. (Sofia, 1997), 794 pp.

Introduction
Georgi Dimitrov and His Diary:
The Rise and Decline of the Lion of Leipzig

IN THE SUMMER OF 1995, when the expatriate Bulgarian artist Christo (Javacheff, Hristo Yavashev) completed his "Wrapped Reichstag" project, in which some $10 million were expended on covering the old German Parliament in Berlin with a million square feet of aluminum-colored fabric, most of the amused commentators had forgotten the other noted Bulgarian whose name will forever be tied to the Reichstag—Georgi Dimitrov, who stood at the helm of the Third (Communist) International (Comintern) in its final years (1935–1943) and who headed the Bulgarian Communist Party (BKP) and the government of Bulgaria from 1945 until his death in 1949.

On 27 February 1933, in the midst of a violent election campaign, the Reichstag building was partially destroyed by fire. The police captured a Dutch laborer—Marinus van der Lubbe—in the gutted edifice. On 9 March 1933, ten days after the torching of the Reichstag and in the sixth week of Adolf Hitler's chancellorship, the Nazis arrested Dimitrov and ultimately charged him with participating in a plot to burn the Reichstag. The arrest, which was vaunted as a victory against Communist terrorism, was helpful not only to the Nazi campaign in the Reichsrat elections of 5 March 1933, but in initiating a series of measures that gave full dictatorial powers to the Nazis. After the passage of the Enabling Act (23 March 1933) they had a mandate to centralize the German government, impose Nazi control over the civil administration and the judiciary, ban or dissolve all political parties except the Nazi Party (NSDAP), begin a series of anti-Jewish measures, and outlaw all strikes and free unions.

Meanwhile, Dimitrov, two other Bulgarian Communists (Blagoi

Popov and Vasil Tanev), as well as the principal defendants—van der Lubbe and Ernst Torgler, the latter a Communist deputy in the Reichstag and the president of the Communist Party of Germany (KPD) parliamentary group—awaited trial in a Germany that was in the throes of Nazi revolution. They became the subjects of a vast defense campaign, whereby the Communists and the other antifascists took up cudgels for the defendants.

It was this trial—the Leipzig fire trial, which lasted from 21 September to 23 December 1933—that gave Dimitrov the status of an international celebrity. His audacity in cross-examining and confronting his accusers and the prosecution witnesses, among them the Nazi leaders Hermann Göring and Joseph Goebbels, anticipated the resistance to fascism that the Communists squandered in the ultra-leftist atmosphere of the "Third Period" (1928–1935). Now that the Nazis were entrenched, the slogan "After Hitler, our turn!" lost all of its sectarian appeal. Dimitrov, himself suspected as a "Right deviationist,"[1] had won the day and rescued a party vocation that had been in doubt for a decade.

Georgi Dimitrov was born on 18 June 1882 (o.s.) in the village of Kovachevtsi, near Radomir, some sixty-four kilometers west of Bulgaria's capital, Sofia. His parents were from Pirin Macedonia—the northeastern part of Macedonia, which the Ottomans had recognized in 1878 as part of the autonomous Principality of Bulgaria, under the Ottoman sovereignty. This concession, part of the Treaty of San Stefano (3 March 1878), was the consequence of a military defeat that Russia had inflicted on the Ottoman Empire in a war waged in the support of Bulgarian insurgents (1877–1878). At the ensuing Congress of Berlin (June–July 1878) the European statesmen reduced Russia's gains and the territory of autonomous Bulgaria. Macedonia was restored to the Ottomans, its Pirin area having been subdued after an uprising centered in the towns of Kresna and Razlog. Many Macedonians then fled to the Principality of Bulgaria, among them the twenty-seven-year-old Dimitŭr Mikhailov Trenchov of Razlog, who settled in Kovachevtsi, on a tributary of the Struma River. The family of the seventeen-year-old Parashkeva Doseva from Bansko, a town on the Pirin Range, had settled in Kovachevtsi a few years earlier, having fled, too, from Ottoman repression. Mikhailov and Doseva were married three years later. Georgi Dimitrov was their oldest son. The family soon moved to Radomir and then to Sofia.

Dimitŭr Mikhailov learned the hat-making trade from his brother-in-law, who, like Doseva, belonged to a small group of Bulgarians that had been won over to Protestantism by American missionaries. The Protestant ethic evidently determined the life of the hatter's family, which drew a modest income from Dimitŭr's fur-hat shop. That ethic also figured in Georgi's initial rebellion. His mother wanted him to become a pastor and in 1892 had him attend Sunday school classes at the missionary chapel.[2] Expelled two years later, Dimitrov then became an apprentice in the printing house of Ivan Tsutsev. Soon afterward he printed an anti-religious broadsheet titled *Kukurigu* (Cock-a-Doodle-Doo) and distributed it by stealth at the church after the Sunday service.[3] Still, an echo of a youthful allegiance remained. After the acquittal at Leipzig, Dimitrov attended the prison Christmas services—Protestant on Christmas Eve and Catholic on Christmas Day 1933. "If I were a believer," he wrote in his diary, "I would definitely be Prot[estant] rather than Cathol[ic]."

The Dimitrovs, a family of working-class militants, seem to have had an affinity for printers' ink. Konstantin, like his older brother Georgi, was a printer by trade and a union activist. Nikola, who moved to Russia, was a member of the Bolshevik Odessa organization and died in exile in Siberia in 1916. Todor, an underground activist of the BKP Sofia organization, was arrested and killed by the royal police in 1925. The elder of his two sisters, Magdalina (Lina), was married to the printer Stefan Hristov Barŭmov. The younger, Elena (Lena), followed Dimitrov into exile, where she married another exiled Bulgarian Communist, Vŭlko Chervenkov, Dimitrov's successor at the helm of the BKP.

As a young printers' union activist, whose heroes were Hristo Botev (1848–1976) and the other principals of the Bulgarian national-revolutionary movement, as well as the self-denying Russian revolutionaries from N. G. Chernyshevsky's novel *What Is to Be Done?* (1863), Dimitrov soon fell under the sway of Bulgarian Social Democracy. He read the works of Dimitŭr Blagoev (1856–1924), the leading Bulgarian Marxist, who as a student at St. Petersburg founded the first Marxist organization in Russia—the Party of Russian Social Democrats, in 1883–1884. Dimitrov then graduated to G. V. Plekhanov's *The Development of the Monist View of History* (1895) and the works of Marx and Engels, Karl Kautsky, and V. I. Lenin.[4]

The Bulgarian Social Democratic Party, established in 1901, soon became a battlefield for fractional interests. The pursuit of purely proletarian class politics was difficult in an agrarian country whose margin of industrial workers would rise to no more than twenty thousand by 1909. Yet this was precisely the wish of Dimitŭr Blagoev's Narrows (*tesniaks*), who confronted the more adaptable Broads (*shiroki*) of Yanko Sakŭzov. Three issues separated them. First, unlike Sakŭzov, Blagoev distrusted the peasantry as a dangerous petit bourgeois influence on the party, even when the turbulent countryside brought the Social Democrats some useful electoral support. Mistrust of the peasantry in a land of countless peasant smallholders became the mark of the Narrows—members of the Bulgarian Workers' Social Democratic Party (Narrow Socialists), or BRSDP(t.s.)—and of their Communist successors. Second, Blagoev opposed the idea that the trade unions could be independent of the party and pursue purely economic goals. He argued for the political nature of trade union struggle and party control. Third, Blagoev rejected the idea of coalitions with nonsocialist parties, including the newly formed Bulgarian Agrarian National Union (BZNS).[5] Dimitrov was received into the party in the spring of 1902 and from the beginning identified with the tesniak faction.

Dimitrov's rise among the Narrow Socialists followed his trade union career. Dimitrov was a delegate to the BRSDP(t.s.) congress (July 1904) at Plovdiv, where it was decided to form the party-affiliated General Federation of Trade Unions (ORSS). He was a secretary at the ORSS founding congress, served on its General Workers' Council, and in August 1904 became the secretary of its Sofia council. A protégé of Georgi Kirkov, Blagoev's closest associate, who was responsible for the work of the trade unions, Dimitrov was soon elected secretary of the BRSDP(t.s.) Sofia organization. Active in the tesniak operations against the "anarcho-liberals"—the party faction that resisted Blagoev's "bureaucratic centralism"—he was arrested in the course of the Pernik miners' strike (June–July 1906). At this time he married Ljubica (Ljuba) Ivošević (1880–1933), a Serbian seamstress, proletarian poet, and trade union activist, whom Dimitrov met at Sliven in 1903. She came to Bulgaria after a sojourn in Vienna and introduced him to the German language and various cultural pursuits.

In October 1908 Bulgaria proclaimed its independence from the Ottoman Empire. Prince Ferdinand, who used the occasion to assume the title of tsar, felt threatened by the Young Turk revolutionary regime that had overthrown the autocracy in July 1908 and established a parliament in Istanbul, to which the Bulgarian deputies, too, were invited. This was the overture to a series of Balkan conflicts that would reflect the interests of regional mini-imperialisms and their sponsors among the Powers. In 1912, Serbia and Bulgaria joined Greece and Montenegro in a war against the Turks (October 1912–May 1913). The Balkan allies scored a convincing victory but then fell out among themselves over the division of Ottoman possessions in Europe. In the Second Balkan War (June–July 1913), the bulk of the allies, now joined by Romania and Turkey, attacked Bulgaria and, after a series of debilitating defeats, wrested from it portions of newly acquired territories in Macedonia and Thrace, as well as parts of Bulgarian Dobruja. In these two wars Bulgaria lost 58,000 soldiers, an additional 105,000 being wounded. The period is rightly regarded as the first national catastrophe. One of the victims was Dimitrov's brother Konstantin, who perished in 1912 at the approaches to Istanbul.

The tesniaks put up a determined campaign for peace and a Balkan federation. Their antinationalist attitude stood them in good stead after the wars, as the Bulgarians settled down to a tranquil assessment of their losses. Dimitrov, who had been admitted to the BRSDP(t.s.) Central Committee (CC) in 1909 and to the secretaryship of the ORSS in 1910, having been subjected to several arrests and a brief prison term afterward, now entered the parliament along with practically the whole tesniak leadership in the elections of 1913 and 1914. He served as the secretary of the tesniak parliamentary group. In May 1914 he also became a member of the Sofia municipal council. But the greatest challenges still lay ahead, beginning with the war crisis of 1914.

At the beginning of the First World War the Bulgarian government carefully weighed the prospects of the warring alliances, in hopes of siding with the winner and thereby regaining the territories lost in the Second Balkan War and, if possible, to increasing them. In September 1915 Tsar Ferdinand finally became convinced that the Central Powers would prevail. Bulgaria mobilized and attacked Serbia within a month. The BRSDP(t.s.) took a consistently antiwar stance throughout the hostilities. Dimitrov and the other tesniak deputies repeatedly voted against the war credits. The party joined the Zimmerwald movement and sided with Lenin on everything except on demands for a new International. Dimitrov's personal commitment to internationalism was expressed in his parliamentary speeches in which he condemned the Bulgarian army's savage repression of the Serbian insurgents in the Toplica district, west of Niš, in February 1917.[6] During the summer of 1917, at Tŭrnovo, Dimitrov defended a group of wounded soldiers, who had been set upon by a raging colonel in an officers' railway compartment. Dimitrov was prosecuted for inciting disobedience, stripped of his parliamentary immunity, and imprisoned on 29 August 1918.

The second round of warfare, after a respite of less than twenty-seven months, weighed heavily on Bulgaria. The mobilization of able-bodied men and the significant war losses (101,000 dead and 300,000 wounded), as well as food deliveries to the Central Powers, induced shortages, price hikes, and war-weariness. Mutinies stirred up by the tesniaks and members of the Agrarian Union (BZNS) became frequent. By September 1918, as soldiers started agitating for the cessation of hostilities, the Allies breached the Salonika front and crushed the Bulgarian defenses in Macedonia. In the ensuing stampede the retreating soldiers, calling for peace and a new government, proceeded to Sofia. Ferdinand called upon the Agrarian leader Aleksandŭr Stamboliski (1879–1923), whom he released from prison, to pacify the approaching mutineers. Taking on the assignment, Stamboliski nevertheless formed a common cause with Blagoev, on the argument that the tesniaks and the BZNS, the leading Bulgarian opposition party, could jointly establish a democratic republic. True to his anti-peasant stand, Blagoev turned down the offer. Stamboliski wavered, proceeded to the insurgent camp at Radomir, argued for an end to the insurrection, and then, on 28 September, accepted the presidency of the insurgent republic and the resumption of the march to Sofia.

The Radomir republic ended almost as soon as it started. On 28 September Bulgaria sued for peace, armistice was signed, and Ferdinand was obliged to abdicate, to be succeeded by his son, Boris III (1894–1943). Within a few days, the loyalist troops, made up largely of pro-war Macedonians, having inflicted three thousand casualties on the host of some ten thousand to fifteen thousand men, repelled the insurgents in the suburbs of Sofia. The rest simply went home, leaving Stamboliski in the lurch. The tesniaks, however, who had by then acceded to Leninism, had a lot of explaining to do.[7] Their subsequent explanations to effect that their forces were meager and scattered, the pro-regime side aided by the Germans too strong, and the Entente troops near, tended to obscure the fundamental anti-peasant prejudice that had been the trademark of the Narrows.

The imprisoned Dimitrov was uninvolved in these decisions. It was later claimed that he had transmitted a written recommendation to the BRSDP(t.s.) CC that favored unwavering involvement in the uprising.[8] Not that the Radomir error hurt the tesniaks. The party renamed itself the Bulgarian Communist Party (Narrow Socialists), or BKP(t.s.), in May 1919 and then made its peace with the Comintern. (Dimitrov was elected to the Communist CC.) The party's program, for all its Leninist overtones, remained remarkably Blagoevist—particularly in its intransigence toward peasant views.[9]

In the parliamentary elections of August 1919, the BKP(t.s.) emerged as the second largest party—immediately after Stamboliski's Agrarian Union—with 119,000 votes (18 percent of the total) and forty-seven deputies. Their showing was better than that of the competing Broad Socialists, who had graduated to the Social Democratic Party. But the Communists would not agree to Stamboliski's invitation to join the coalition government. Nor did they support the Treaty of Neuilly (27 November 1919), the peace agreement signed by Stamboliski that deprived Bulgaria of considerable territory (Thrace, pivots on the Yugoslav border) and imposed heavy reparations on the country. Moreover, the Communist-led railway strike of 24 December 1919, which the BKP and ORSS tried to turn into a general strike, tested the strength of Stamboliski's cabinet and—after a harsh application of repressive measures by Stamboliski—ended in defeat in January 1920. Nevertheless, it helped raise the BKP's prestige, contributed to an increase in its membership (36,600 in 1920), and became a factor in the parliamentary elections of March 1920, in which the Communists won 182,000 votes (20.31 percent of the total) and fifty-one deputies. Although Stamboliski's BZNS won the plurality of votes, the BZNS majority could be reached only by the invalidation of thirteen opposition deputies, among them nine Communists.

After the strikes of 1919–1920 and Stamboliski's electoral high-handedness, the Communists eyed his government with increased distaste. The Agrarian reforms, which included plans for village cooperatives and a government grain consortium, were denounced as the artifice of a grasping village bourgeoisie. Stamboliski, who admittedly relied on a club-wielding peasant paramilitary force, the Orange Guard, was called the Balkan Mussolini.[10] Nor were his attempts, in cooperation with the Yugoslav authorities, to curb the Macedonian guerrillas much appreciated. In short, the Communists hardly differentiated between Stamboliski and the reactionary forces (royalists, militarists, Macedonian émigrés) that were already plotting against the Agrarian government. When, on 9 June 1923, the anti-Stamboliski coalition of right-wing officers moved against the government to overthrow it and then murdered the prime minister, the Communists hardly demurred. The BKP CC, in an official proclamation, called the putsch "an armed struggle . . . between the urban and rural bourgeoisies."[11] Attempts at counteraction with the Agrarians, notably at Pleven, Plovdiv, and Tŭrnovo, were stopped by the Communist leadership. In fact, the BKP seemed encouraged that the putschist cabinet of Aleksandŭr Tsankov, which was persecuting the Agrarians but tactically (and briefly) cozying up to the Communists, might strengthen the constitutionally guaranteed rights and freedoms.[12]

Dimitrov's position on these events was hardly audacious. During the strike action of 1919–1920 he went underground with the BKP leadership. In June 1920, together with Vasil Kolarov (1877–1950), Blagoev's second-in-command, he attempted to reach the Soviet Union in a fishing boat that lost its way in a storm and was captured by the Romanian border guards in Dobruja. Released in July, he made a second attempt in December 1920, this time by way of Vienna. Obliged to wait for passage to Moscow, he went to Livorno, Italy, to attend the congress of the Italian Socialist Party (15 January 1921), where he observed the Comintern's splittist strategy against the Socialist leadership. Dimitrov's colleague Hristo Kabakchiev (1878–1940), the leading intellectual of the BKP, represented the Comintern at Livorno. His efforts and those of the Italian leftists produced a split and the emergence of the Italian Communist Party (PCI).

In February 1921 Dimitrov finally made it to Moscow, where he met Lenin and represented the BKP at the Fourth All-Russian Trade Union Congress (May 1921) and the Third Congress of the Comintern (June–July 1921). Back in Bulgaria in November 1921, he returned to Moscow a year later for the Second Congress of the (Red) International of Trade Unions (Profintern) in November–December 1922. Having been elected to the Executive Committee of the Profintern, his primary preoccupation continued to be the Bulgarian Communist trade unions, which he helped build to a force of thirty-five thousand by April 1924. During the June 1923 putsch he shared in the party's "historical error" by arguing for neutrality between the "two wings" of the Bulgarian bourgeoisie. In fact, given Blagoev's illness and advanced age and Kolarov's absence in Moscow, it was Kabakchiev and Dimitrov who shared the greatest responsibility—together with the BKP secretary Todor Lukanov—for the neutrality policy of 1923. The subsequent argument, that Dimitrov's support of "neutrality" obtained as long as resistance to the putsch failed to develop, is hardly convincing.[13]

The Comintern's reaction to the BKP's failure was first disbelief, then pressure. In his report (23 June 1923) to a plenum of the Executive Committee of the Communist International (ECCI), Karl Radek condemned the spinelessness of the BKP that had led to "the greatest defeat ever suffered by a Communist Party."[14] When the BKP continued to defend its position,[15] the ECCI sent Kolarov to Bulgaria with orders to effect a change of policy and plan an insurrection. Kolarov prevailed at the BKP CC meeting on 5 August 1923, against considerable opposition. But that was the extent of his success. With but a few exceptions, notably among the fringe Agrarian elements, the BKP failed to win any non-Communist support for a "worker-peasant government" and an uprising. Moreover, after news of the planned insurgency was leaked to the Tsankov government, it ordered the arrest, on 12 September, of some two thousand Communist officials, mainly among the middle cadres. Operating from the underground, Kolarov and Dimitrov ordered an uprising for 22–23 September (it was ill prepared), and then proceeded to Ferdinand, in the Vratsa district of northwestern Bulgaria, where they established the supreme military-revolutionary committee together with their comrade Gavril Genov and two Left Agrarians.

The uprising ended in disaster. The insurgents succeeded only to an extent in northwestern Bulgaria (Vratsa district) and in the central districts of Stara Zagora and Plovdiv. There were less important stirrings elsewhere, notably in the Petrich district (Pirin Macedonia). The uprising had a predominantly rural character and was especially notable in the areas of BZNS strength, the capital, Sofia, having remained largely dormant and the BKP leaders of Ruse and Burgas having ignored the call to rise up. The control that the Bulgarian army maintained over the railroads permitted it to transport troops to the various foci of insurgency, as the occasion warranted. The authorities also relied on the White Russian émigrés (Wrangelites) and the Macedonian irregulars. By 28 September Kolarov and Dimitrov ordered a retreat into Yugoslavia, where they led some two thousand Communist insurgents. Perhaps as many five thousand perished in the uprising and the Tsankovite "white terror" that followed in its wake.

The defeat of the September uprising contributed to the growing fractionalism in the BKP but did not unduly harm Communist standing in Bulgaria. Moreover, the exiled leadership of Kolarov and Dimitrov—the Foreign Committee, which soon removed to Vienna—gained significant prestige out of this Comintern-managed affair, which was subsequently dubbed the first organized antifascist uprising. In February 1924 the Comintern endorsed the conduct of Kolarov and Dimitrov, and in May 1924 the underground BKP conference at Vitosha seconded the Comintern's endorsement.

During this period Dimitrov traveled to Moscow on several occasions. He represented the BKP in the ECCI delegation that escorted Lenin's coffin from Gorky to Moscow in January 1924. Back in Vienna at the end of February 1924, he headed the émigré BKP apparatus, directed the work of the Balkan Communist Federation (BCF), the coordinating body of the Comintern Balkan sections that cultivated the various Balkan national-liberation and minority movements, and served as the ECCI emissary to the Communist Party of Austria (KPÖ). He represented the BKP and the Balkan Communist Federation at the Fifth Congress of the Comintern and the Third Congress of the Profintern in Moscow, during the summer of 1924, where he became a candidate-member of the ECCI and a member of the Profintern's Executive Committee. From 1925 on, he was increasingly in Moscow, although he attended to assorted Comintern business in Vienna and Berlin.

In April 1925, the BKP underground operatives in Bulgaria, part of the party's underground military organization, staged a spectacular terrorist attack at Sofia's Sveta Nedelia Cathedral. They detonated a bomb on the roof of the edifice at a start of a state funeral attended by Tsar Boris and most of Bulgaria's leading political figures. The explosion claimed the lives of 123 mourners, among them fourteen generals and the mayor of Sofia. The authorities responded with great severity, arresting thousands of suspects, imposing dozens of death sentences, and murdering hundreds of detained Communists. One of the victims was Dimitrov's brother Todor. In one of the trials that followed the explosion, Dimitrov was tried and sentenced to death in absentia. In fact, the exiled Communist leader had nothing to do with the Sveta Nedelia disaster.

The terrorist incident, however unauthorized, demonstrated the growing desperation of the underground Communists in Bulgaria. Weakened by the defeat of the September uprising in 1923, isolated from potential Left Agrarian partners, they were now exposed to growing repression, which was somewhat mitigated after the Tsankov dictatorship gave way in January 1926 to a moderate government. Operating through the legal front party (the Labor Party) they recovered by the early 1930s, precisely at the point when their internal unity was increasingly challenged by a younger and more leftist generation.

Already in December 1927 and January 1928, at the BKP conference at Berlin, the delegates of the Young Communist League—Georgi Lambrev, Iliya Vasilev, and Petŭr Iskrov—started attacking the 1923 leadership. By May 1929, following the Sixth Congress of the Comintern (July–September 1928) with its ultra-leftist line of "class against class," the leftist youth leaders started taking over the BKP. When the Foreign Bureau of the BKP was reconstituted in Moscow, in August 1930, Dimitrov was effectively demoted, having been appointed its candidate-member. Admittedly, Dimitrov and Kolarov bent with the wind and offered no doctrinal alternative to the new line. As their influence waned and as their behavior in 1923 came to be attacked as "defeatist," they stood guard and waited for better times. Particularly disturbing to Dimitrov was the new leadership's renunciation of the whole tesniak heritage.[16]

It was under these circumstances that the ECCI sent Dimitrov to Germany, where he acted as the political secretary of the BCF and, after April 1929, as the leading member of the Comintern's West European Bureau. Frequently sent on various Comintern missions from Berlin to Moscow, throughout Germany, and in many other West European countries, Dimitrov was in Berlin when Hitler assumed the chancellorship in January 1933. Paradoxically enough, Popov and Tanev, who were arrested with Dimitrov in March 1933 in the Reichstag fire case, were his factional opponents and belonged to the "left sectarian" wing of the BKP leadership. It was this arrest and Dimitrov's performance in the dock that revived the influence of the increasingly marginalized revolutionary.

The history of the Communist International is usually divided into six periods. After the optimistic period of the "red wave," from the Comintern's inaugural congress in March 1919 to the bungled attempt at uprising in Germany (October 1923), when the Bolsheviks and their sympathizers expected the imminent victory of world revolution, there followed a more cautious period of "partial stabilization of capitalism" (1923–1928), when the Communists declared a temporary halt to the revolutionary upsurge in Europe and Asia. This "right turn," occasioned, too, by the failed September 1923 uprising in Bulgaria, was evident in the Communist-Guomindang alliance in China (1923–1927).

By 1926, J. V. Stalin triumphed against the Trotskyist and Zinovievist opposition in the USSR. His alliance with N. I. Bukharin, who assumed the leadership of the Comintern in November 1926, was still firm. The latter, under the pressure of oppositionists and the impatient Comintern apparatus, announced "a new, third period" at the end of 1926, signaling a more militant posture of the Communist movement. But it was Stalin, at the Fifteenth Congress of the All-Union Communist Party (Bolshevik)—the VKP(b)—in December 1927, who introduced the idea of a "new revolutionary upsurge." The Sixth World Congress of the Comintern (July–September 1928) initiated a new "left turn" that assumed its familiar Stalinist contours after the purge of the Bukharin faction in 1929. During this Third Period, which coincided with Stalin's drive for collectivization and industrialization—the vaunted Stalinist "second revolution," "right deviations" were portrayed as the greatest danger to the Communist movement. The Communists carried out a purge of the "right deviationists" (Heinrich Brandler in Germany, Jay Lovestone in the United States) and carried out a total break with the Social Democrats, who were now consistently besmirched as "Social fascists."[17]

The real Fascists, who were decidedly on the rise in the early 1930s, profited significantly from the new round of Communist–Social Democratic warfare on the Left. In 1929, in Berlin and Paris, the Communists refused to join hands with the Social Democrats even in the traditional May Day parades. After the September 1930 Reichstag elections in Germany, in which the Nazis scored significant gains, the Communist Party of Germany (KPD) declared that the Nazi showing was a favorable development, because it weakened the Weimar Republic. Moreover, the KPD joined the Nazis in undermining the Social Democratic government of Prussia (summer 1931) and, in November 1932, the Communist trade unionists cooperated with their Nazi counterparts against the Social Democrats in the Berlin transport workers' strike.

The Communist attitude, though indefensible, emerged from the early Communist view that fascism was evidence of capitalism's decay and hence that it was not an entirely unwelcome development. The defense of the capitalist order through terror was evidence of the coming revolutionary dawn. This policy was pursued even after Hitler banned the KPD, Communist statements continuing to portray Nazism as a passing phenomenon well into the fall of 1933. And when armed resistance against fascism commenced—in Austria (February 1934), it was the Social Democrats, not the Communists, who took up arms against Chancellor Dollfuss's fascist dictatorship. In this context, Dimitrov's militancy in the Leipzig dock represented a significant departure from the simplicity of the Third Period and the symbolic inauguration of a new coalition of forces in the battle against fascism.

Dimitrov's defense had four important elements. First, despite enormous obstacles placed in his way by the judges, he was consistently on the offensive, in intimating that the Nazis had set the Reichstag aflame—or directly accusing them of having done so. Dimitrov repeatedly stated that van der Lubbe—"a déclassé worker, a rebellious member of the scum of society"—was a "miserable Faustus," while "Mephistopheles has disappeared" (an allusion to the club-footed

Goebbels).[18] Second, Dimitrov boldly defended "Communist ideology, my ideals," as well as the Communist International and its program of proletarian dictatorship and the "World Union of Soviet Republics."[19] Third, he presented himself as a patriotic Bulgarian Communist who resented the racialist Nazi charge that he hailed from a "savage and barbarous" country: "It is true that Bulgarian fascism is savage and barbarous. But the Bulgarian workers and peasants, the Bulgarian people's intelligentsia are by no means savage and barbarous."[20] Finally, although he criticized the Social Democratic leaders, Dimitrov exacted from Goebbels the admission that the Nazis "do not share the bourgeois viewpoint that there is a fundamental difference between the Social Democratic and the Communist parties [. . .] When, therefore, we accused Marxism in general and its most acute form—communism, of intellectual instigation, and maybe even of practical implementation of the Reichstag fire, then this attitude by itself meant that our national task was to destroy, to wipe off the face of the earth the Communist Party and the Social Democratic Party."[21]

The fact that this admission was exacted from Goebbels, that Dimitrov paid compliments to the Anarchists (while disclaiming that van der Lubbe could be a "genuine" Anarchist),[22] that he provoked Göring into making threats once Dimitrov was "out of the courtroom,"[23] still received far greater attention in the West than in the councils of the Comintern. Despite the obligatory cheers for the "courageous Bolshevik" Dimitrov, the Thirteenth Plenum of the ECCI (November–December 1933) paid scant attention to the Leipzig trial and ignored Dimitrov's emergence from the courtroom as the most attractive Communist *massovík* in years, moreover on the crest of a growing antifascist protest in Western Europe against the Hitler dictatorship.[24] When the court sentenced van der Lubbe to death on 23 December 1933, after having simultaneously acquitted Dimitrov, Popov, Tanev, and Torgler for lack of evidence, it took the Soviet government another two months to secure the release of the Bulgarians. They were granted Soviet citizenship after Bulgaria, where Dimitrov could face execution for the earlier death sentence, refused to recognize them as Bulgarian subjects.[25]

Slowly, however, the Soviet leadership itself started changing its posture. At the Seventeenth Congress of the VKP(b), known as the Congress of Victors (January 1934), Stalin emerged unchallenged after two bitter years of famine and disarray. He used the congress podium to announce the improvement of Soviet relations with France, Poland, and the United States, these developments having been instigated by "certain changes in the policy of Germany which reflect the growth of revanchist and imperialist sentiments in Germany."[26] Dimitrov's return to Moscow on 27 February 1934 came in the wake of the significant distancing that Stalin achieved in regard to the Third Period. In fact, by 1 April Stalin was already encouraging him to strike against the "incorrect" views of the Comintern leaders on the nature of the Austrian "insurrection." By the end of May Dimitrov was nominated to make a report at the forthcoming Comintern congress. There remained the uneasy task of dispersing, by argument or constraining influence, the array of reservations among the hardened veterans of the Third Period about cooperation with the Social Democrats and the other antifascists.

Germany's growing strength and aggressiveness—her denunciation of the disarmament clauses in the Versailles treaty and Hitler's policy of remilitarization—prompted departures from the Soviet policy of unremitting hostility toward the Western democracies. The Franco-Soviet alliance (May 1935) and the earlier entrance of the USSR into the League of Nations represented an important success of M. M. Litvinov's Foreign Commissariat over the revolutionary aspirations of the Comintern. In this decisive change—which increasingly transformed the Communist International from the headquarters of world revolution to an auxiliary in the struggle against fascism—Dimitrov played a leading role[27]—hence his central function at the Seventh World Congress of the Comintern (July–August 1935).

There is little doubt that the Comintern's about-face of 1935 represented the most momentous change in the history of Stalinized communism. Still, Dimitrov's keynote speech, usually titled "The United Front Against Fascism and War," was novel in emphasis, not in content. Dimitrov stressed that fascism was a "*substitution* of one state form of class domination of the bourgeoisie—bourgeois democracy—by another form—open terrorist dictatorship."[28] Hence, it was not a matter of indifference whether the bourgeois dictatorship took a democratic or a fascist form. The task at the moment was to create a "*wide anti-fascist Popular Front* on the basis of the *proletarian united front.*"[29] In fact, although Dimitrov proposed new negotiations with the Social Democrats, his aims (and those of the Soviet leadership and the Comintern) were significantly broader. He was proposing an opening to all enemies of fascism, beyond the working class and its parties—including peasants, liberal elements, and the confessional groups. Nor did he fail to chastise the Communists for their inattention to the motifs of patriotism and national pride, which became successful recruiting themes for the fascist upsurge in many countries. Dimitrov dominated the congress so thoroughly that his elevation to the position of the Comintern's secretary-general at the end of the proceedings came as no surprise. Other secretaries of the ECCI elected at the Seventh Congress were D. Z. Manuilsky, Otto Kuusinen, Palmiro Togliatti (Ercoli), Wilhelm Pieck, André Marty, and Klement Gottwald.

Dimitrov's speech had the effect of cadence breaking on a militant organization whose rank and file clearly craved some way out of their isolation. Ironically, the Popular Front strategy, with its stress on combat against fascism and its war preparations, necessarily softened the struggle against capitalism and hence diluted the Comintern's raison d'être of class war and world revolution: "Dimitrov's 'popular front' was designed to keep the proletarian revolution in abeyance in order to deal with the pressing emergency of Fascism."[30] But the emergency was defined in terms of Soviet state interest, not necessarily that of the Comintern member parties that were now obliged to abandon the search for revolutionary opportunities. As a result, the Comintern, never a favorite of Stalin's, commenced its self-marginalization. The middle ground between the sectarianism of the Third Period and the expediency of the Popular Front was exceedingly hard to negotiate, especially under the circumstances of Stalin's terror, which was in full swing more than half a year before the opening speeches at the Hall of Pillars in Moscow.

One of the curiosities of Georgi Dimitrov's diary is an enormous hiatus that extends from 1 February 1935 to 18 August 1936, that is, the period of his meteoric rise in the councils of the Comintern, including his role in the preparations, work, and immediate consequences of the Seventh World Congress. (There are a number of smaller hiatuses in the diary, most notably for the period between 18 March and 15 August 1938. It is entirely possible that these sections were lost or destroyed.) This is not the only peculiarity in the diary, which generally requires some explanation.

Diary writing is highly atypical for revolutionaries. Dimitrov was seemingly an exception. His diary is also unusual because of its structure and the variety of moods, which mask an array of intentions. He kept a diary from June 1916 to November 1916,[31] apparently during his imprisonment in Sofia (1918) and perhaps until September 1923, and certainly while with Kolarov in the military prison in Constanța, Romania (1920).[32] In a certain sense his diaries were associated with his imprisonment. Dimitrov started making diary jottings after his arrest in the Reichstag fire case, his first entry, dated 9 March 1933—the day of his arrest—evidently having been written after the event. This first section, which was written in Dimitrov's sturdy but inelegant German, originally was probably no more than a laconic chronological reminder for the purpose of preparing his defense. Although personal details mounted in due course, the German part of his diary is on the whole hurried, terse, and structurally vastly different from the rest of the copious manuscript.

The Russian part, which was penned in Russian beginning 17 September 1934, represents the bulk of the diary—some two thirds of the text. It is more detailed, provides accounts of conversations, telephone calls, and meetings, and includes frequent attachments of various documents, speeches, and proclamations. The focus throughout is on Stalin, who is unsurprisingly the most important character among the dramatis personæ in the diary. In fact, were it not for a very rare portrayal of Stalin's less admirable side ("Called J. V. [Stalin]. Soon as he recognized my voice, he hung up!" 21 October 1939), Dimitrov's diary could be read as a form of private correspondence with Stalin. Dimitrov certainly expresses all sorts of oblique messages via his jottings. He cajoles and protests. He enters into preventive actions against possible threats. But most often he praises Stalin. The concluding part, from 11 November 1945, the day after Dimitrov's return to Bulgaria, to the last entry, on 6 February 1949, with exceptions, is written in a sort of a Russified Bulgarian.

It is important to note that it is possible to detect Dimitrov's priorities whenever the diary can be corroborated with parallel evidence. One of the best examples is the account of the Kremlin meeting of 10 February 1948 at which Stalin lashed out at the Bulgarian and Yugoslav delegations over a series of differences on Balkan policy. One of his points was that the Chinese Communist leaders, too, carried out policies contrary to Moscow's wishes, but at least they had the decency to do so on the sly, without challenging Moscow. Here is how the key passage emerges in Dimitrov's diary and in Djilas's *Conversations with Stalin*. Dimitrov quotes Stalin as saying:

> I also doubted that the Chinese could succeed, and I advised them to come to a temporary agreement with Chiang Kai-shek. Officially, they agreed with us, but in practice they continued mobilizing the Chinese people. And then they openly put forward the question: Will we go on with our fight? We have the support of our people. We said: Fine, what do you need? It turned out that the conditions there were very favor-

able. The Chinese proved to be right, and we were wrong. Maybe in this [Balkan] case it can also turn out that we are wrong. But we want to be certain about what we are doing.

Here is Stalin according to Djilas, by contrast:

Here, when the war with Japan ended, we invited the Chinese comrades to reach an agreement as to how a modus vivendi with Chiang Kai-shek might be found. They agreed with us in word, but in deed they did it their own way when they got home: they mustered their forces and struck. It has been shown that they were right, and not we. But Greece is a different case—we should not hesitate, but let us put an end to the Greek uprising.[33]

Dimitrov's account includes the passage where the Chinese ask for approval after they prepared the ground for the answer they preferred.

Dimitrov's diary is the history of the demiurge Stalin, the creator and destroyer. There are several remarkable things about this portrait. Perhaps most important, Stalin is not lacking in self-awareness. He is aware that the European workers think that the conflict with Trotsky is a result of Stalin's "bad character" (11 February 1937). He is aware that Trotsky "as we know, was the most popular man in our country after Lenin" and that "Bukharin, Zinoviev, Rykov, Tomsky were all popular." He identifies his group (Stalin, Molotov, Voroshilov, and Kalinin) as "fieldworkers [*praktiki*—literally, practical workers] in Lenin's time." But the middle cadres nevertheless supported Stalin and his friends, whereas "Trotsky completely ignored those cadres" (7 November 1937).

Nor is Stalin unaware of the Soviet Communist reputation: "It would be better to create a workers' party of Poland with a Communist program. The Commun[ist] Party frightens off not only alien elements, but even some of our own as well" (27 August 1941). He urges the leading German Communists from the Soviet Zone of Germany not to "speak so glowingly of the Sov[iet] Union" (7 June 1945). And he can be droll about the Soviet hypocrisies: "You are the 'chairman of the C[ommunist] I[nternational],' you know. We are only a section of the CI!" (26 April 1939). But that is no safeguard against personal claims to virtue: "The root of all wisdom: 1) acknowledgement of one's own mistakes and deficiencies; 2) correction of those mistakes and deficiencies" (28 July 1941).

Dimitrov demonstrates the personal nature of Soviet power, which in the time frame of his diary was Stalin's dictatorship. Stalin's ruthlessness and extremism belie the Thermidorian interpretation of the regime. The revolutionary goal brooked no obstacles. And since all alliances were conditional, the vast loneliness of the great dictator was preordained. It turns out that Soviet aircraft can stay aloft for only thirty-five minutes, whereas German and British aircraft can stay up for several hours: "I summoned our designers and asked them if our aircraft, too, could be made to stay aloft longer. They answered, '*Yes, they could, but no one ever set us a task like that!*' And now that deficiency is being corrected. Our infantry is being reorganized now; the cavalry has always been good—now it is time to tackle aviation and anti-aircraft defense. I am busy at this every day now, meeting with designers and other specialists. But I am the *only* one dealing with all these problems. None of you could be bothered with them. I am out there *by myself*" (7 November 1940). His entourage offers confirmation of Stalin's singular qualities. After days of preparations for the theses on war Zhdanov rebukes Dimitrov: "By this time Com[rade] Stalin would have written a whole book!" (24 September 1939).

Many vignettes also show the familiar scheming Stalin. He warns Dimitrov about Manuilsky's "Trotskyism" and "toadyism": "Don't leave him to his own devices! He could ruin things!" (26 April 1939). Dimitrov should also watch Rákosi: "All of them wavered at one time or another. *They did not understand our business*" (6 November 1940). His mistrust becomes a job description: "An intelligence agent ought to be like a devil: believing no one, not even himself" (20 February 1941). Or he can rage and threaten: "We have united the state in such a way that if any part were isolated from the common socialist state, it would not only inflict harm on the latter but would be unable to exist independently and would inevitably fall under foreign subjugation. Therefore, whoever attempts to destroy that unity of the socialist state, whoever seeks the separation of any of its parts or nationalities—that man is an enemy, a sworn enemy of the state and of the peoples of the USSR. And we will destroy each and every such enemy, even if he was an old Bolshevik; we will destroy all his kin, his family. We will mercilessly destroy anyone who, by his deeds or his thoughts—yes, his thoughts—threatens the unity of the socialist state" (7 November 1937). "But I will show you, if I ever lose my patience. (You know very well how I can do that.) I shall hit the fatsos so hard that you will hear the crack for miles around" (7 November 1940).

The casuistic side of Stalin was evident in the period of the Soviet-Finnish war (November 1939–March 1940). Surprised by the vigor of the Finnish defense, he argued that "Finland was prepared for a major war against us" (21 January 1940). To counter the criticisms of the deputy people's commissars of defense against the commissar, his favorite K. Ye. Voroshilov, Stalin argued that the Red Army was superb, the reversals that it had sustained being attributable to bad officers: "A good commander can manage even with a weak division; a bad commander can demoralize the best division in the army. [...] We brought not only the White Finns to their knees, but their instructors, too—the French, English, Italians, and Germans" (28 March 1940).

Perhaps the most revealing aspect of Dimitrov's Stalin is the latter's belief in Russian exceptionalism. Stalin's Russia apparently had specific circumstances and characteristics not relevant to Europe. The Soviet leader repeatedly expresses the idea that "European workers are historically linked with parliamentary democracy." Sometimes this means that explanations are in order to demonstrate why "parliamentary democracy can no longer have any value for the working class" (7 April 1934). Sometimes it means that for historical reasons the European working class cannot be expected to be engaged in a revolution against the bourgeoisie. (Stalin's distance from Lenin is clear in his statement of 7 November 1939 claiming that Lenin's First World War slogan of turning the imperialist war into a civil war was appropriate only in Russia, and not in the European countries, where the working class was "clinging" to the democratic reforms.) In any case, the Soviet form of socialism, although the best, is by no means the only form: "There may be other forms—the democratic republic and even under certain conditions the constitutional monarchy" (28 January 1945). On other occasions Stalin acknowledged Marx and Engels's idea that the "best form of the dictatorship of the proletariat" was the "democratic republic," which they "saw as embodied in the Paris Commune": "They meant a democratic republic in which the proletariat had a dominant role, rather than the republics in America or Switzerland." Moreover, such republics had a "parliamentary form" (6 December 1948). They were *people's democracies*.

As for Russia, its uncritical emulators in the Comintern, Stalin believed, "do not understand that in fact we had no parliamentarianism. The Russian workers received absolutely nothing from the Duma [parliament]" (7 April 1934). Moreover, the Russian workers were "tied to the peasants and under tsarist conditions could engage in an assault on the bourgeoisie" (7 November 1939): "We deprived the kulaks and the bourgeoisie of the right to vote. In our country, only the working people had this right. We had to relocate two million kulaks to the north, and when we abolished the kulaks as a class, we granted suffrage to all people. The capitalists and the landowners fought against us for four years during the Intervention, whereas in your country they just fled and surrendered without fight. In our case, there was no other country that could help us the way we are helping you now. [. . .] The advantage of the Soviet system is that it solves the problems quickly— by shedding blood" (6 December 1948). In Bulgaria, the transition to socialism could occur without the dictatorship of the proletariat. In any event, the "situation since the outbreak of our revolution has changed radically, and it is necessary to use different methods and forms, and *not copy the Russian Communists,* who in their time were in an entirely different position. Do not be afraid that you might be accused of *opportunism.* This is not opportunism, but rather the application of Marxism to the present situation" (2 September 1946).

Stalin's harsh view of Russia was the reverse of Russian touchiness over Western criticism, but also a pragmatic program—a preventive. In this context, the much-disparaged concept of *people's democracy,* as practiced in Eastern Europe and several Asian countries, takes on a somewhat less redundant resonance. Stalin evidently believed that—in the words of Otto Kuusinen—"it is possible to make the transition from capitalism to socialism without a direct dictatorship of the working class. But this is only a possibility, and the possibility is desirable" (23 October 1948). This was thanks to the protective influence of the Soviet Union and the strength of the Communist parties in the countries concerned. But, should "countervailing internal and external forces" develop, the option of proletarian dictatorship was always available. According to Stalin, "As long as there are antagonistic classes, there will be dictatorship of the proletariat. But in your country it will be a dictatorship of a different type. You can do without a Soviet regime. However, the regime of the people's republic can fulfill the major task of the dictatorship of the proletariat, both in terms of abolishing the classes and in terms of building socialism. The people's democracy and the Soviet regime are two forms of the dictatorship of the proletariat" (6 December 1948). The opposite of Russian exceptionalism did not ultimately remove the problem of dictatorship. Or was Stalin, unlike Mephistopheles, part of that power which ever seeks the good and ever does evil?

Stalin's thinking on Russia's international role, too, was marked by nationalism. Moreover, the period of the nonaggression pact with Germany, one might say the fifth period in the history of the Comintern, internalized many of the nationalist sentiments that emanated from fascist national survivalism. This led to the promotion of "healthy national feelings" (Zhdanov, 27 February 1941) and of "healthy nationalism." According to Zhdanov, "Com[rade] St[alin] made it clear that between nationalism properly understood and proletarian internat[ionalism] there can be no contradictions. Rootless cosmopolitanism that denies national feelings and the notion of a homeland has nothing in common with prolet[arian] internat[ionalism]. Such cosmopolitanism paves the way for the recruitment of spies, enemy agents" (12 May 1941).

Stalin freely expressed a hierarchy of nationality preferences. He argued that the destruction of Poland in 1939 was justified because Poland was a "fascist state" that oppressed the Ukrainians and Belorussians (7 September 1939). His Georgian reference point is evident in his anti-Turkish statements: "We shall drive the Turks into Asia. *What is Turkey? There are two million Georgians there, one and a half million Armenians, a million Kurds, and so forth. The Turks amount to only six or seven million*" (25 November 1940). After the German attack on the USSR, when Slavism became an important theme of Soviet propaganda, he promised to "give East Prussia back to Slavdom, where it belongs. We'll settle the whole place with Slavs" (8 September 1941).

Under the circumstances, it is not unusual to encounter certain lesser Communists promoting specific national aspirations and territorial demands. Hungarian leader Mátyás Rákosi hoped that after the war Hungary would retain Transylvania and Carpatho-Ukraine. Czech Communist Zdeněk Nejedlý probably was not pleased to learn that his Polish comrades wanted to retain Tetschen. Nor was it pleasing that the Czechoslovak leadership evidently wanted to expel the Hungarian minority after the war: "The Czechs are really going overboard," writes Dimitrov. "Sent Molotov for coordination an encoded telegram to [Czechoslovak party chief Klement] Gottwald indicating the need for a *different* approach to the Hungarian question in Czechoslovakia" (30 July 1945). In fact, Stalin understood war as an agency of national homogenization. His remark on Bulgaria's persistent claims to western Thrace is telling: "Another war is needed to solve such matters completely" (2 September 1946). It also points to the Stalinist roots of the recent cases of wartime ethnic cleansing in the Balkans and the Caucasus.

Dimitrov's diary also closely chronicles the Comintern's decline. It will come as a surprise to many that the decision to dissolve the Comintern was taken as early as April 1941, when the USSR was still treaty bound to Nazi Germany. In fact, the Comintern was the principal victim of the "healthy nationalism" that Stalin increasingly promoted after the passing of the Popular Front. Stalin took advantage of the CPUSA's formal withdrawal from the Comintern, whereby the American Communists satisfied US legal requirements while remaining in close contact with Moscow, to note that the "International was formed in Marx's time in the expectation of an imminent international revolution. The Comintern, too, was formed in such a period in Lenin's time. Today the *national* tasks of the various countries stand in the forefront. But the position of the Com[munist] parties as sections of an international organization, subordinated to the Executive Committee of the CI, is an obstacle" (20 April 1941).

Dimitrov immediately took Stalin's idea "of discontinuing the activities of the ECCI as a *leadership body* for Communist parties for the immediate future" to Maurice Thorez and Palmiro Togliatti. Both found the idea "basically correct" (21 April 1941). By 12 May 1941 Zhdanov told Dimitrov that the resolution on discontinuing the activities of the Comintern, which was being prepared, "must be grounded in principle," as hostile interpretations would have to be parried. In any case, "our argumentation should evoke enthusiasm in the Com[munist] parties, rather than create a funereal mood and dismay," but again, the "matter is not so urgent: there is no need to rush; instead, discuss the matter seriously and prepare."

The German attack on the Soviet Union appeared to give the Comintern a new lease on life. In fact, despite the growing demands of the emergency, the dissolution was merely postponed. Moreover, the Comintern was marginalized in another way. On the very day of the attack (22 June 1941) Stalin told Dimitrov that "for now the Comintern is not to take any overt action," but also that the "issue of socialist revolution is not to be raised. The Sov[iet] people is waging a patriotic war against fascist Germany. It is a matter of routing fascism, which has enslaved a number of peoples and is bent on enslaving still more."

Dimitrov felt these changes quite directly after the removal of the Comintern staff to Kuibyshev and Ufa in the fall of 1941. He noted that the Comintern and he himself were not in evidence at public occasions. For the first time in many years he was not on the Moscow honor presidium on the anniversary of the revolution. Generally, he accepted that there was "*no need* to emphasize the Comintern!" (7 November 1941). Meanwhile, the Soviet agencies were taking over parts of the Comintern operations, Stalin initially being more worried about the vanguardism of specific Soviet services (for example, the Red Army intelligence) than about the subordination of the CI (27 August 1941). But by 11 November 1941 Dimitrov agreed to combine the Comintern operations in Belgium, France, and Switzerland with Soviet military intelligence. Joint actions with the "neighbors" (the People's Commissariat for Internal Affairs, the NKVD) also increased. Yet when Dimitrov tried to use foreign commissariat personnel abroad, Molotov protested (21 February 1941).

The figure of P. M. Fitin, the chief of the Fifth (Intelligence) Directorate of the NKVD (1940–1946), increasingly loomed large in Comintern operations, not only because his network serviced (and controlled) many of the Comintern's communications. In 1943, when Stalin finally dissolved the Comintern, Fitin went to see Dimitrov "about using our [Comintern] radio communications and their technical base in the future for the needs" of the NKVD (11 June 1943). Likewise, the Red Army Intelligence Directorate took its cut a day later. But the unkindest cut of all was the decision to continue the Comintern operations within the Department of International Information (OMI) of the VKP(b) CC: "In order not to let enemies exploit the fact that this department is headed by Dimitrov, it was decided to appoint *Shcherbakov* head of the department and Dimitrov and Manuilsky his deputies. This decision is not to be announced; rather, organize and conduct the department's work *internally*" (12 June 1943). The Communist International became a secondary department of the Soviet CC, and Dimitrov a subaltern of Stalin's chief political commissar in the armed forces, whom N. S. Khrushchev once characterized as a "poisonous snake."[34]

Stalin's decision to dissolve the Comintern came at the end of the organization's steady decline. The purges played an important part, Dimitrov himself having offered no resistance to Stalin's suggestions that he lure the "Trotskyist" Willi Münzenberg back to Moscow or to the arrests of Moskvin, Knorin, and the other leading Comintern officials. In fact, although Dimitrov protected various foreign Communists after 1939—for example, his secretary Kozovski—he certainly cooperated with Yezhov and Beria during the purges. Nor was he more than an intermediary in Spanish policy. As for China, where Stalin systematically enforced the alliance between the Chinese Communists and the Guomindang against the wishes of the Chinese Communist leadership, Dimitrov occasionally protected Mao's enemy Wang Ming, whose daughter he adopted, but he certainly did not encourage Wang's opposition ("Intervening from here [Moscow] is for now inexpedient," 13 December 1943).

The Comintern's China policy was to support Chiang Kai-shek's Nationalists. During the Xi'an Incident, a disenchanted Nationalist general kidnapped Chiang in order to compel him to abandon the anticommunist course, so that the Chinese, Nationalist and Communist, could concentrate on resisting the Japanese invaders. Stalin saw the incident as inimical to the aims of the united front. Moreover, Stalin was furious at a suggestion, supposedly made by Wang Ming, to kill the captured Chiang (14 and 16 December 1936). Stalin's approach is summed up in his instructions to Wang Ming, Kang Sheng, and Wang Jiaxiang on 11 November 1937: "1) *The fundamental thing* for the Chinese Communist Party at present: to merge with the common national wave and take a leading part. 2) *The main thing now is the war,* not the agrarian revolution, not confiscation of land." Dimitrov merely echoed this stand in his warnings to Mao Zedong against the politically mistaken "tendency to wind down the struggle against China's foreign occupiers, along with the evident departure from a united national-front policy" (22 December 1943). Hence, the constant tension with the policy of the Chinese Communists that it was necessary to move forward rapidly.

But there was also a bureaucratic pettiness in the Comintern operations that was more telling than political expediency. The Comintern's trade union organization was a "soulless, dead organization" (26 January 1942). Ana Pauker, a leading Romanian Communist, made decisions about abortions for pregnant Romanian students at Comintern schools. All-important decisions—from financing to cadre changes, required the approval of Stalin and the VKP(b) Politburo. At the end, there remained only a pious thought, expressed by Stalin on 11 May 1943: "Experience has shown that one cannot have an internat[ional] directing center for all countries. This became evident in *Marx's* lifetime, in *Lenin's* and today. There should perhaps be a transition to regional associations, for example, of South America, of the United States and Canada, of certain European countries, and so on, but even this must not be rushed." This was perhaps the germ of the postwar Cominform.

As the Comintern declined and acquired new camouflage, Dimitrov increasingly concentrated on the Balkan questions. Although he did not return to Bulgaria until November 1945, more than a year after the Soviet takeover, he was deeply involved in the affairs of his native land, which he would soon dominate as the de facto party leader and prime minister.

The growing success of Tito's Partisans in Yugoslavia created new conditions in the Balkan region, favorable to Yugoslav solutions for such thorny issues as that of Macedonia. Precisely because under the Stalinist dispensation nationhood was the decisive element in territorial claims, it was very important to decide whether the Macedonians were a separate nationality or simply a Bulgarian regional group.

Dimitrov's approach to this issue went through several phases. In Dimitrov's letter to Tito (1 June 1942), Macedonians were not mentioned among the Yugoslav peoples, then defined as Serbs, Croats, Montenegrins, and Slovenes. During the same period, Macedonian Communists Dimitar Vlahov and Vladimir Poptomov were cited by Dimitrov among the Bulgarian Communist activists in Moscow (15 June 1942). And after Tito formed the Antifascist Council of People's Liberation of Yugoslavia (AVNOJ) at Jajce, Bosnia, Dimitrov instructed Tito that the inclusion of Vlahov and Tomov [Poptomov] among its members was a mistake, although the former was recognized as a "Macedonian publicist" (26 December 1943).[35] Soon thereafter Dimitrov discussed "framing the question of Bulgaria's nation[al] unification in connection with Macedonia, Thrace, and Dobruja" (14 January 1944). The Foreign Bureau of the BKP took up the question on 2 March 1944.

In the spring of 1944 Dimitrov maintained that the Macedonians were a populace (*naselenie*), an ethnic conglomerate made up of "Bulgars, Mac[edonians], Slavs, Greeks, Serbs," but not a nation (*natsiia*), there being no evidence of Macedonian national consciousness (*natsional'noe soznanie*). Practically, this meant that Macedonia could not exist as a "*separate* state," but only as a unit in a South Slavic federation made up of "Bulgars, Serbocroats, Montenegrins, Slovenes, and Macedonians" (22 April 1944). This was Dimitrov's preferred solution, as evidenced in his negotiations with Tito on the "formation of a union between Bulgaria and Yugoslavia that actually amounts to a federation of South Slavs (consisting of Bulgars, Macedonians, Serbs, Croats, Montenegrins, and Slovenes) extending from the Adriatic to the Black Sea," as he formulates it in the entry of 27 September 1944.

Since Dimitrov envisioned the "ethnic" federation only within the dualist scheme, and since Bulgaria, as a defeated Axis country, really needed Yugoslavia's international sponsorship, his thinking on Macedonia evolved following 27 October 1944, when he was still entreating Tito "to explain to the Maced[onian] comrades that to all intents and purposes they ought not to raise the question of annexing Bulg[arian] Macedonia." By 21 December 1944, he recognized the Macedonians as a people (*narod*) with full right to self-determination and argued that in compensation for "annexation of the Macedonian territories belonging to [Bulgaria] since 1913 to Macedonia within the limits of Yugoslavia if its population desires it," the districts of Bosilegrad and Caribrod that had been ceded to Yugoslavia in 1919 by the Treaty of Neuilly might be restored to Bulgaria.

Stalin, however, was opposed to the "ethnic" federation, which he saw as a Yugoslav attempt at "absorption of Bulgaria." He favored a dualist federation, "something along the lines of the former Austria-Hungary." In any case, being increasingly suspicious of Tito's intentions, he saw Yugoslav policy as excessive: "The Yugoslavs want to take Greek Macedonia. They want Albania, too, and even parts of Austria and Hungary. This is unreasonable. I do not like the way they are acting." Implicit in this criticism was disapproval of the Yugoslav position in Greece, where the Communists were pursuing a collision course with the West that was based on the assumption that the Red Army would come to their aid. "We cannot do that," Stalin concluded, his resentment of Greek "foolishness" being tempered by his growing irritation with the "inexperienced" Tito (10 January 1945).

The federative schemes soured thereafter. Dimitrov quickly detected the prevailing mood and remonstrated with Stalin against the "unhealthy sentiments" of the Yugoslavs, who were subject to a "certain degree of 'dizziness with success' and an inappropriate, condescending attitude toward Bulgaria and even toward the Bulg[arian] Com[munist] Party" (8 April 1945). And by the fall of 1945 there were irritations with the Yugoslav introduction into Pirin Macedonia of the new Macedonian linguistic standard, which was regarded as "Serbianization"—and in part certainly was. The Yugoslavs kept pursuing the exchange of Pirin Macedonia for the "western borderlands," that is, the Bosilegrad and Caribrod districts (15 and 22 April 1946). But at the Bled conference, held in Yugoslavia in early August 1947, Dimitrov and Tito agreed that "we should not work for a dir[ect] joining of the Pir[in] region to the [Yugoslav] Mac[edonian] republic" (1 August 1947). Ultimately, state interests and Stalin's interventions prevented any resolution of the Macedonian question or the attendant issue of Yugoslav-Bulgarian union. Still, it cannot be argued, as some have attempted to do, that Dimitrov, almost alone among the BKP leaders, had a particularly pro-Macedonian position.[36]

The Macedonian question was a contributing factor in the early stages of the Soviet-Yugoslav rift, as Dimitrov's diary displays with remarkable accuracy. Stalin's problem with Tito had nothing to do with "revisionism," as the subsequent ideological smokescreen would have it. Tito was dangerous because he was providing arguments to the Western enemies. Hence the great importance of Dimitrov's entry for 10 February 1948, which provides a detailed account of a meeting at the Kremlin over which Stalin presided, which important leaders of the USSR (Molotov, Zhdanov, Malenkov), Bulgaria (Dimitrov, Kolarov, Kostov), and Yugoslavia (Kardelj, Djilas, Bakarić) attended, but which Tito refused to attend.

At the meeting, Dimitrov was the whipping boy in Stalin's outbursts against Tito. On 24 January Stalin sent Dimitrov a sharp letter questioning his statements at a Bucharest press conference, where Dimitrov had spoken about the inevitability of a federation that would unite all East European people's democracies, including Greece. The Soviet party organ *Pravda* publicly disavowed Dimitrov's remarks on 29 January. Stalin now argued, albeit inconsistently, that all schemes for an Eastern federation—Yugoslav-Bulgarian or otherwise—were harmful; that is, that these measures played into the hands of the "founders of the Western bloc," especially because everybody assumed that Moscow backed the initiatives of Belgrade and Sofia. Worse still, the Yugoslavs were bringing an army division to a base close to the Greek-Albanian border. Stalin considered this move tantamount to providing a pretext for American intervention. Moreover, he was convinced that the ploy had excited exaggerated hopes in the Greek Communists, who, in his view, could not win the civil war in their country. Under the circumstances, the Yugoslavs were duty-bound to "restrict" the Greek partisan movement. "We are not bound by any 'categorical imperatives,'" Stalin argued. "The key issue is the balance of forces" (10 February 1948).

Dimitrov certainly smarted from Stalin's lashes of February 1948. This was the lowest point in his relations with Moscow. Stalin chided him for giving too many interviews, for trying to impress the world, and speaking as if he were still the "general secretary of the Comintern giving an interview for a Commun[ist] newspaper." Taking aim at Tito, Stalin charged Dimitrov with carrying on "like the Komsomol activists who fly like butterflies right into the burning flames." Milovan Djilas wrote later, in his account of the meeting, that he "glanced sidelong at Dimitrov. His ears were red, and big red blotches cropped up on his face covering his spots of eczema. His sparse hair straggled and hung in lifeless strands over his wrinkled neck. I felt sorry for him. The lion of the Leipzig Trials, who had defied Göring and fascism from his trap at the time of their greatest ascendancy, now looked dejected and dispirited."[37]

Georgi Dimitrov, like Odysseus, was polytropic—a man of many moves, capable of turning to various expedients. His most obvious human failing was a curiously discreet sort of vainglory that promoted his historical accomplishment at Leipzig. He commemorated each Leipzig anniversary and was evidently delighted when the *Evening Standard* included him among "the Great People of 1934" (31 December 1934). He counted the slogans containing his name and the portraits of him that appeared in official parades. On May Day 1939 his portrait was among those of the Politburo members. From the tribune they sounded the slogan "Long live the helmsman of the Comintern Dimitrov!"—which he rightly saw as "complete elimination of the various rumors about D[imitrov], here and abroad!" But on 7 November the same year they were bearing *one* portrait of Dimitrov and *several* portraits of the German Communist leader Thälmann. In 1941 he was not elected to the honor presidium on International Women's Day. That was no accident—the omission was due to foreign policy considerations and the work of his enemies (8 March 1941). On May Day 1942 his portrait was once again among those of the Politburo members. But on his sixty-first birthday he received birthday greetings from Maurice Thorez, La Passionaria, and Togliatti, from Spaniards, Bulgarians, Germans, and co-workers—but not from the Soviet leaders (18 June 1943). Kremlinology was apparently not only a Western art.

Dimitrov could be petty, and he had a talent that was not entirely negligible at Stalin's Kremlin: he could read the nuances of statements and gestures. He detects ambiguity in A. I. Mikoyan's toast on 7 November 1938. He fears that he is in disfavor because his name does not figure as part of the honor presidium at a meeting of musicians in Moscow (24 April 1939). He resents an upstart like Tito and incites Stalin against the Yugoslav leader on the day of their meeting in Moscow. After the meeting he writes a scathing account of Tito: "General impression: *underestimation* of the complexity of the situation and the impending difficulties, *too arrogant,* heavy dose of conceit and sure signs of 'dizziness with success.' To hear him talk, of course, you would think everything was under control" (8 April 1945). He was also capable of playing the toady, as he did in his toast to Stalin on 7 November 1937, the twentieth anniversary of the Bolshevik Revolution.

Dimitrov was a deeply emotional man. He gloried in natural beauty, as during his treatments in southern Crimea in 1938. His personal life was complicated and full of tragedies. His first wife, Ljubica Ivošević-Dimitrova, who suffered from incurable mental disease, committed suicide in Moscow on 27 May 1933, while he was in the Moabit prison in Berlin. After he visited her resting place at the Moscow crematorium on 28 May 1934, he wrote, in a *cri de coeur,* that he felt "so lonely, so terribly *personally unhappy*" (28 May 1934). During his incarceration he relied on Any Krüger, with whom he evidently had a personal relationship. Back in Moscow in 1934, he seems to have broken up with Kiti Jovanović, an émigré Serbian Communist. During the same year he married Rosa Fleischmann (Rozi), a Sudeten Jewish Communist from Boskovice in southern Moravia, whom he had met in Vienna and courted since 1927. Their only child, Dimitŭr Dimitrov (Mitia), named after Georgi Dimitrov's father, was born in 1936. The child died on 3 April 1943 from diphtheria, which was diagnosed too late. Dimitrov was mourning for him precisely at the time when the Comintern was being dissolved: "Such a remarkable little boy, a future Bolshevik, reduced to nothing" (5 April 1943).

Illness accompanied Dimitrov in his last decades. He suffered from diabetes, chronic gastritis, a diseased gall bladder, and a variety of other ailments. Although he had to go to hospitals and health spas at some very trying periods of Soviet history, these were no mere political illnesses—"*No luck!*" he wrote after another painful bout of illness on 11 October 1943—but his chief malady was the inability to offer resistance to Stalin. Dimitrov was not immune, wrote Milovan Djilas, "to that typically Communist weakness, the fear of 'falling out,' of separating from the party. Enormously decisive toward the 'class enemy,' Dimitrov, like all such true-believing Communists, was fainthearted and at a loss when facing Stalin, who, through purges and a personality cult, had come to be the movement incarnate. Yet, since Dimitrov was no careerist, no *apparatchik,* but a self-made made man who had risen through turmoil and pain, his vacillation now must have had deeper roots. He belonged to that class of Bulgarians—the best of their race—in whom rebellion and self-confidence fuse in an indestructible essence. He must at least have suspected that the Soviet attack on Yugoslavia would entail the subjugation of Bulgaria, and that the realization of his youthful dream of unification with Serbia would be projected into the misty future, thereby reopening the yawning gulf of Balkan conflicts, and unleashing a tumultuous flood of Balkan claims. Today, after so many years, I still think that even though Dimitrov was ailing and diabetic, he did not die a natural death in the Borvilo [*sic* for Barvikha] clinic outside Moscow. Stalin was wary of self-confident personalities, especially if they were revolutionaries, and he was far more interested in Balkan hatreds than in Balkan reconciliations."[38]

Djilas's conclusion is buttressed by Dimitrov's covert sympathies for the Yugoslavs in 1948. Djilas recalled that on 11 February 1948, after the fateful showdown at the Kremlin, Dimitrov hosted the Yugoslavs at a lunch in his dacha. This was at Meshcherino, but Dimitrov's diary notes only the event. Djilas's version is ampler: "From that lunch emanated a closeness we had never before experienced with the Bulgarians—the closeness of the oppressed and tyrannized. It was then that Dimitrov told us in confidence that the Soviet Union had the atomic bomb. Kostov made an effort to be friendly toward us, but neither then nor later did we show any understanding of him—not even when he was tried and shot [in 1949 . . .]. As for Dimitrov, without a doubt he felt as we did. Talking to us in front of the dacha, he said, as if in passing: 'Criticism of my statements [by Stalin] is not at issue here; something else is.' "[39] And on 19 April 1948, before the split became final, the Bulgarian state delegation, headed by Dimitrov, passed through Belgrade on the way to Prague. Djilas greeted the Bulgarians at the Topčider railroad station and jumped into Dimitrov's wagon, where Dimitrov greeted him in the corridor and, squeezing Djilas's "hand in both of his, he said, emotionally, 'Hold fast! Hold fast!' "[40]

Yet a terrible event, one of the many in the blood-soaked history of Balkan politics, mars this somewhat romanticized picture. It is clear from the diary that it was Dimitrov, more than anybody else, who insisted on the execution of Nikola Petkov, a leader of the Aleksandŭr Stamboliski Peasant Union, better known as the *Pladne* Agrarians, after their organ *Pladne* (Noon). Although this group, after two splits, remained in Bulgaria's Communist-dominated Fatherland Front (OF) government, the Petkov faction had became the most important opposition to the BKP after May 1945. The Communists had proceeded to shut down Petkov's newspaper in April 1947 and then, in June, to have him tried for treason.[41]

Dimitrov's letter to Traicho Kostov and Vasil Kolarov of 17 September 1947 makes it clear that Dimitrov considered the execution of Petkov a test of strength with the Western powers. Moreover, he was not swayed by the invidious comparisons between the treatment that the Nazis had extended to him at Leipzig and his own treatment of Petkov: "In an attempt to defend Petkov, foreign journalists would quite often refer to the Leipzig trial and the verdict proclaiming Dimitrov not guilty. It is necessary to find a suitable strategy to do away with this manipulation of the facts by pointing out the basic difference between the Leipzig trial and the trial against Petkov. We could do this when we mark the fourteenth anniversary of the Leipzig trial, September 1933" (24 September 1947). Perhaps Dimitrov's old Macedonian adversary Dimitar Vlahov was onto something when he claimed, arguing against the prevailing trend, "Georgi Dimitrov was a man, if it is permitted to use this term, who was vengeful."[42]

As Bertold Brecht had it in his apologetic poem *An die Nachgeborenen* (To Posterity, 1934–1938), "Ach, wir / Die wir den Boden bereiten wollten für Freundlichkeit / Konnten selber nicht freundlich sein" (Alas, we / Who wished to lay the foundations of kindness / Could not ourselves be kind).[43] Brecht's plea that the revolutionary generation not be judged too harshly should be read in tandem with the letters of Sofka Petkova, the sister of Nikola Petkov. On 12 January 1949, more than a year after the hanging of her brother, she wrote the following from internal exile in Svishtov to a friend in Sofia: "He who was born and died on the cross out of love for us and for our salvation, He cannot abandon us. Of that I am certain! If He wishes, with only a little spark of His love, He can capture human hearts and change the hatred that rules today into mutual love. In this alone is our genuine salvation, and the hour has come when He must give us the heart that He did not give us on the day when He was born. That is our faith and our life."[44]

Georgi Dimitrov died in Moscow on 2 July 1949. He was succeeded in his duties by Vasil Kolarov and, when Kolarov died in 1950, by Dimitrov's brother-in-law Vŭlko Chervenkov, the chief Stalinizer of Bulgaria. He, in turn, was eased out of office after Stalin's death by Todor Zhivkov, with whom the Communist regime ended in 1989. There were thus forty years from Dimitrov's death to the transition. Dimitrov's embalmed body was removed from his mausoleum in the center of Sofia in 1990 and cremated, his ashes being laid to rest next to the graves of his parents in the family plot at the city cemetery. In August 1999 the new authorities tried to demolish the mausoleum with explosives. The initial effort failed. The cube-shaped marble building merely leaned leftward.

NOTES

1. This is an assessment of the Swiss Communist leader Jules Humber-Droz, as cited in E. H. Carr, *Twilight of the Comintern, 1930–1935* (New York, N.Y., 1982), p. 88, n. 20.

2. Joseph Rothschild, *The Communist Party of Bulgaria: Origins and Development, 1883–1936* (New York, 1959), p. 51.

3. Magdalina Barŭmova, "Zhivot za naroda," in Ruben Avramov, ed., *Spomeni za Georgi Dimitrov,* vol. 1. (Sofia, 1971), p. 27.

4. David Elazar, ed., *Georgi Dimitrov: biografiia* (Sofia, 1972), pp. 19–21.

5. Lucien Karchmar, "Communism in Bulgaria, 1918–1921," in Ivo Banac, ed., *The Effects of World War I: The Class War After the Great War: The Rise of Communist Parties in East Central Europe, 1918–1921* (Brooklyn, N.Y., 1983), pp. 234–35.

6. On the crimes of the Bulgarian occupiers during the Toplica uprising, see Radoje Kostić, "Zločni bugarskih okupatora u Toplici za vreme Topličkog ustanka," *Leskovački zbornik,* vol. 28 (1988), pp. 61–69. Rodoljub Čolaković, a noted Serb Communist, recalled that when Dimitrov fled Bulgaria in 1923 he was welcomed at the rail station at Niš not only by the local Communists but also by the Orthodox bishop of Niš with his clergy. Rodoljub Čolaković, *Kazivanje o jednom pokoljenju* (Sarajevo, 1968), vol. 2, p. 35.

7. Kabakchiev's unconvincing attempt at an explanation to Lenin, in 1920, is retold in Hr[isto] Kabakchiev, "Lenin i bolgarskie 'tesniaki,'" *Istorik marksist* (Moscow), vol. 1:35 (1934), p. 184.

8. Elazar, p. 114.

9. Karchmar, pp. 248–50.

10. Ibid., p. 262.

11. Cited in Rothschild, p. 120.

12. Ibid., p. 126.

13. Elazar, p. 160.

14. Cited in Rothschild, p. 122.

15. "The Communist Party of Bulgaria and the Recent Coup d'Etat," in Helmut Gruber, ed., *International Communism in the Era of Lenin: A Documentary History* (New York, 1972), pp. 359–61.

16. Rothschild, p. 291.

17. On the origins of the Third Period, see Theodore Draper, "The Strange Case of the Comintern," *Survey* (London), vol. 18, no. 3 (84), pp. 91–137 (1972).

18. Georgi Dimitrov, *Selected Works* (Sofia, 1972), vol. 1, p. 379.

19. Ibid., pp. 362–63, 384.

20. Ibid., p. 364.

21. Ibid., pp. 350–51.

22. Ibid., p. 380.

23. Ibid., p. 347. Dimitrov's ironical response to Göring "Ich bin sehr zufrieden mit der Antwort des Herrn Ministerpräsidenten" (I am highly pleased with the reply of the prime minister) made the rounds among leftists. For the Communist presentation of the trial in the West, with the large point that the Nazis set the Reichstag aflame, see *Dimitroff contra Goering: Enthüllungen über die wahren Brandstifter* (Paris, 1934).

24. Carr, pp. 114–15. The situation among the Bulgarian Communists was even worse. As Franz Borkenau points out, "The man upon whom the whole world looked as a model of heroism was regarded as half a traitor by the Communist Party of his own country! But precisely on account of the enmity of the extreme left he was the right man for carrying through a more moderate policy." Franz Borkenau, *World Communism: A History of the Communist International* (Ann Arbor, 1962), pp. 384–85. For an example of unconvincing attempts to create a more active account of Bulgarian Commu-

nist efforts on behalf of Dimitrov see Nediu T. Nedev, *Otrazhenie na laiptsigskiia protses v Bŭlgariia* (Sofia, 1962), pp. 97–197.

25. Marinus van der Lubbe was executed in 1934. A West Berlin court set the sentence aside on 15 December 1980, without addressing the question of who set the fire. See "1933 Verdict in Reichstag Fire Is Canceled," *New York Times,* 30 December 1980, p. A3. Still, the postwar assessments of evidence, most notably by the German investigator Fritz Tobias, demonstrate that van der Lubbe acted alone. See Fritz Tobias, *The Reichstag Fire* (New York, 1964). Paradoxically, the Nazi thesis that van der Lubbe had accomplices helped strengthen the Communist thesis that the accomplices were Nazis. Still, the failure of the court to sentence the Communist defendants gave rise to various speculations spurred especially by Ruth Fischer, a leading German ex-Communist. In 1948 she claimed that, back in 1933—that is, seven years after her expulsion from the KPD—she had received information from a KPD leader Wilhelm Pieck and Maria Reese, a KPD Reichstag deputy, to the effect "that before Dimitrov stood up in the courtroom to make his courageous peroration, he knew of the secret arrangement between the GPU and the Gestapo that he would leave it a free man." See Ruth Fischer, *Stalin and German Communism: A Study in the Origins of the State Party* (Cambridge, Mass., 1948), p. 309, n. 2. This hearsay account, augmented by more hearsay from a Bulgarian ex-Communist exile and Babette Gross, the widow of German Communist propagandist Willi Münzenberg, was repackaged without any significant new proof—but a great deal of innuendo—as no less than "the Dimitrov Conspiracy" in Stephen Koch, *Double Lives: Spies and Writers in the Secret Soviet War of Ideas Against the West* (New York, 1994), pp. 107–22.

26. J. V. Stalin, *Works,* vol. 13 (Moscow, 1955), p. 308.

27. For a Bulgarian Communist view of Dimitrov's contribution to the changes in the Comintern's course, see Doncho Daskalov, *Georgi Dimitrov i noviiat politicheski kurs na Kominterna, 1934/1936* (Sofia, 1980), *passim.* See also B. M. Leibzon and K. K. Shirinia, *Povorot v politike Kominterna: Istoricheskoe znachenie VII kongressa Kominterna* (Moscow, 1975), *passim.*

28. Dimitrov, *Selected Works,* vol. 2, p. 10.

29. Ibid., p. 35.

30. Carr, p. 426.

31. Nadezhda Krŭsteva, "Belezhnikŭt na Georgi Dimitrov ot iuni 1916 do novembri 1917 g.," *Nauchni trudove na VPSh pri TsK na BKP* (Sofia), vol. 26 (1966), pp. 377–413.

32. "Belezhki na Georgi Dimitrov ot zatvora—iuli 1920 g.," *Izvestiia na Instituta po istoriia na BKP* (Sofia), vol. 14 (1965), pp. 373–78.

33. Milovan Djilas, *Conversations with Stalin,* trans. Michael B. Petrovich (New York, 1962), p. 182.

34. *Khrushchev Remembers,* trans. and ed. Strobe Talbott (Boston, 1970), p. 183.

35. The matter came up again in Dimitrov's letter to Stalin and Molotov (16 April 1944) after Tito evidently retained Vlahov as the deputy chairman of the AVNOJ.

36. That is precisely the argument of Boro Mitrovski and Tomo Ristovski, *Georgi Dimitrov za makedonskoto nacionalno prašanje i jugoslovensko-bugarskite odnosi* (Skopje, 1979), *passim.*

37. Djilas, *Conversations,* pp. 176–77. Djilas's account of the meeting is far more dramatic and detailed in areas that cast Stalin in a bad light; for example, that he did not know that Holland was part of the Benelux. Djilas also includes Kardelj's detailed

discussion, which is almost entirely missing in Dimitrov. But he excludes or significantly abbreviates those parts of Stalin's remarks which cast light on Stalin's fear of Balkan entanglements with the West, especially with regard to the Yugoslav division. Still, although Djilas admits that he wrote from memory—his *Conversations* would appear some fourteen years after the fact—he provides significant corroborating evidence, saying, for example, that Stalin used the Russian verb *svernut'* (roll up) to indicate what must be done with the Greek partisan movement (p. 181). Dimitrov uses the equivalent Bulgarian verbal construction: *da se svie.*

38. Milovan Djilas, *Rise and Fall* (San Diego, 1985), pp. 190–91.

39. Ibid., p. 171.

40. Ibid., p. 189.

41. For a recent reappraisal of the Petkov case, see Nikolaj Poppetrov, "Nikola Petkov—nach erzwungener Vergessenheit erneut aktuell," *Südosteuropa* (Munich), no. 6 (1990), pp. 368–80.

42. Dimitar Vlahov, *Memoari* (Skopje, 1970), p. 365.

43. Bertolt Brecht, *Selected Poems,* trans. H. R. Hays (New York, 1947), pp. 176–77.

44. Zdravka Rakova, . . . *Vse Kol'u Sŭnuvam: Pisma na Sofka Petkova—sestrata na Nikola Petkov, oktomvri 1947–ianuari 1952 g.* (Sofia, 2000), p. 59.

Abbreviations

agitprop	agitation and propaganda (section)
ANL	National Liberation Alliance (Brazil)
AVNOJ	Antifascist Council of People's Liberation of Yugoslavia
BCF	Balkan Communist Federation
BKP	Bulgarian Communist Party, 1919–1927, 1948–1989
BRP	Bulgarian Workers' Party, 1927–1944
BRP(k)	Bulgarian Workers' Party (Communist), 1944–1948
BRSDP(t.s.)	Bulgarian Workers' Social Democratic Party (Narrow Socialists), 1903–1919
BZNS	Bulgarian Agrarian National Union
CC	Central Committee
CCC	Central Control Commission
Cheka	Extraordinary Commission for Combating Counterrevolution and Sabotage, 1918–1922: secret police, predecessor of the GPU, OGPU, and NKVD
CI	Communist International, 1919–1943
Cominform	Communist Information Bureau, 1947–1956
Comintern	Communist International, 1919–1943
Comparty	Communist Party
CP	Communist Party
CPC	Communist Party of China
CPGB	Communist Party of Great Britain
CPUSA	Communist Party of the United States of America

DKP	Communist Party of Denmark
EAM	National Liberation Front (Greece)
EC	Executive Committee
ECCI	Executive Committee of the Communist International
ELAS	People's Liberation Army (Greece)
FND	National Democratic Front (Romania)
GDR	German Democratic Republic
GMD	Guomindang (Chinese Nationalist Party)
Gosplan	State Planning Commission
GPU	State Political Directorate, 1922–1923: secret police, successor to Cheka and predecessor of the OGPU and NKVD
GRU	Main Intelligence Directorate
GUGB	Main Administration for State Security
ICC	International Control Commission
IMRO	Internal Macedonian Revolutionary Organization
Informburo	(also Informbureau) *See* Cominform
JCF	Young Communist League (France)
JNA	Yugoslav People's Army
KIM	Communist Youth International
KKE	Communist Party of Greece
KPD	Communist Party of Germany
KPH	Communist Party of Croatia
KPJ	Communist Party of Yugoslavia
KPÖ	Communist Party of Austria
KPS	Communist Party of Serbia
KPSS	Communist Party of the Soviet Union, 1952–1991
KRN	National Home Council (Poland)
kolkhoz	collective farm
Komsomol	All-Union Leninist Youth League (VLKSM)
Krestintern	Red Peasant International
KSČ	Communist Party of Czechoslovakia
KUNMZ	Communist University for Western National Minorities
KUTV	Communist University for Eastern Workers
MOPR	International Red Aid
Narkomindel	People's Commissariat for Foreign Affairs (*See* NKID)
NKGB	People's Commissariat for State Security

NKID	People's Commissariat for Foreign Affairs
NKOJ	People's Committee for the Liberation of Yugoslavia
NKP	Norwegian Communist Party
NKVD	People's Commissariat for Internal Affairs, 1934–1946: secret police, successor to the OGPU
NSDAP	Nazi Party
oblast	Region
OF	Fatherland Front (Bulgaria)
OGPU	Unified State Political Directorate, 1923–1934: secret police, successor to the GPU and predecessor of the NKVD
OMI	Department of International Information of the VKP(b) CC
OMS	Department of International Relations
ORSS	General Federation of Trade Unions (Bulgaria)
PB	Political Bureau
PCB	Brazilian Communist Party
PCC	Cuban Communist Party
PCE	Communist Party of Spain
PCF	French Communist Party
PCI	Italian Communist Party
PCR	Romanian Communist Party
PKI	Indonesian Communist Party
PKSH	Communist Party of Albania
PMR	Romanian Workers' Party
Politburo	Political Bureau
POUM	Workers' Party of Marxist Unification (Spain)
PPK	Polish Communist Party
PPR	Polish Workers' Party
PPS	Polish Socialist Party
PRA	People's Revolutionary Army
PRC	People's Republic of China
Profintern	Red International of Trade Unions
PSI	Italian Socialist Party
PSP	Socialist People's Party (Cuba)
PSUC	United Socialist Party of Catalonia
PUR	Red Army Political Directorate

PZRP	Polish United Workers' Party
RKI	Worker-Peasant Inspection
RKKA	Workers' and Peasants' Red Army
RKP(b)	Russian Communist Party (Bolshevik), 1918–1925
RMS	Workers' Youth League (Bulgaria)
RSDRP	Russian Social Democratic Labor Party
RSDRP(b)	Russian Social Democratic Labor Party (Bolshevik), 1912–1918
RSFSR	Russian Socialist Federative Soviet Republic
SED	Socialist Unity Party of Germany
SKJ	League of Communists of Yugoslavia
SKOJ	League of Communist Youth of Yugoslavia
SKP	Finnish Communist Party
SNK	Council of People's Commissars
STO	Council for Labor and Defense
TASS	Telegraphic Agency of the Soviet Union
UGT	General Workers' Union (Spain)
USPD	Independent Social Democratic Party of Germany
VKP(b)	All-Union Communist Party (Bolshevik), 1925–1952
VTsSPS	All-Union Central Council of Trade Unions
ZPP	Union of Polish Patriots

Notes on Transliteration and Usage

In transliterating from Russian and Bulgarian to English, we have used the modified Library of Congress system—hence, "Trotsky" and not "Trotskii," "Yugov" and not "Iugov." For individual Russian and Bulgarian words and titles of books and journals, however, we used the Library of Congress system. Chinese names, with notable exceptions (Chiang Kaishek) are rendered in the pinyin version. All native names in the languages that use the Roman script were spelled in the respective standard version. Hence, "Ernő Gerő" and not "Ernö Gerö."

We have not attempted to duplicate every peculiarity of the original. Dimitrov's punctuation, including ellipses, underlines (represented here as italics), and breaks between sections of text, is largely reproduced, but not every indent and line space. Nor, for the sake of convenience, have we tried to warn the reader where Dimitrov is using German, Russian, or Bulgarian. Dimitrov's frequent and irregular abbreviations for the surnames of his colleagues are filled in. Common and recurring pseudonyms ("Ercoli" for Palmiro Togliatti, or "Walter" for Josip Broz Tito) are explained in brackets. The exceptions are pseudonyms that have acquired currency. Hence, "Moskvin" and not "Moskvin [Trilisser]," "Kang Sheng" and not "Kang Sheng [Zhang Shaoqing]." In a similar fashion, Dimitrov's shorthand renderings of words and phrases, which can nearly always be reliably determined from the context, are simply filled in the brackets: "adv[iser]" or "part[isan]."

Common abbreviations for official bodies or bureaucracies ("CP" for "Communist Party," "CC" for "Central Committee," "PB" for Politburo, and so on) are standardized throughout the text and explained initially in brackets. Such acronyms also appear in the list of abbreviations in the front matter to the book. For references to foreign Communist parties, Dimitrov's standard usage is usually preserved: "American CP," "CP of Germany," "Yugoslav CP," "CP of Finland," and so forth, without regard to the original English, German, Croatian, Serbian, or Finnish renderings.

Unfamiliar and cumbersome Russian acronyms (such as "Narkomindel" or "Narkomvneshtorg," for the People's Commissariat for Foreign Affairs and the People's Commissariat for Foreign Trade, respectively) are given in full English translation whenever they occur. The same pattern is followed for the title "narkom," which is given simply as "people's commissar"; however, better-known acronyms or abbreviations (such as that for the dreaded NKVD) are given in their familiar form. Try as we might, it proved impossible to find dates of birth or death for some of the vast cast of characters in this book. Like human lives, diaries, even when edited, can seldom be brought to perfection.

CHAPTER ONE

GERMANY

THE GERMAN portion of Dimitrov's diary, written in Nazi detention from 9 March 1933 to 28 February 1934, is extremely dry and elliptical, and occasionally obscure. Dimitrov was well aware that his jottings would be subject to examination by his captors. Hence the notes have the character of a bare record—of a chronology that can be elaborated, if necessary, containing important reminders that could be useful in his battle of will with the Nazis. The diary begins with his arrest, early encounters with the investigating magistrates, and a shrewd record of Nazi thoughts on objectivity (an obstacle in the war against national enemies), the necessity of serving "national thinking" (der nationale Gedanke), and fighting against "Marxist criminals and their Jewish intellectual instigators."

Dimitrov recorded the humiliation of being handcuffed by order of the investigating magistrate on 5 April 1933 and his almost five-month struggle to have the manacles removed. Thus fettered, he continued recording various events, confrontations with the witnesses, the receipt of letters and parcels, correspondence and meetings with his uncooperative lawyers ("Official counsel for the defense = saboteur of the defense!"), and letters to and from the investigating magistrates, various relatives, including his sister Yelena Dimitrova in Moscow, and sister Magdalina Barŭmova and mother, Parashkeva, in Sofia, various German friends, journalists, and foreign Communists, notably the writer Henri Barbusse and Jacques Doriot; the latter, ironically, later became the leader of a French fascist faction. It was during the early months of uncertainty in detention that he learned about the death of his wife Ljubica Ivošević-Dimitrova, who committed suicide in Moscow on 27 May 1933. The nature of his relationship with Any Krüger, a frequent correspondent (15 August 1933: "'engagement announcement'—she made it herself! Oh, poor, dumb Any!"), and her daughters is not clear. From August on, he corresponded with Rosa Fleischmann, a Sudeten Communist, who became his second wife.

Dimitrov was transported to Leipzig on 18 September 1933 for the trial proceedings that began on 21 September. Portions of the trial that was held in Berlin, from 10 October to 18 November, included the testimony of such Nazi chieftains as Göring and Goebbels, with whom Dimitrov clashed dramatically. The trial was concluded on 23 December 1933 in Leipzig with the acquittal of Dimitrov, his two Communist Bulgarian fellow defendants, Blagoi Popov and Vasil Tanev, and the German Communist Ernst Torgler. But unlike the other accused Communists, who defended themselves, Dimitrov turned the trial into an attack on Nazism. (Principal defendant Marinus van der Lubbe was condemned to death and later executed.) During the trial and after, he had meetings with his mother and sister Magdalina, who came to visit him from Bulgaria, and he was encouraged by various defense efforts. Kept in protective custody after the verdict, Dimitrov attended the 1933 Protestant and Catholic Christmas services after his acquittal ("If I were a believer, I would definitely be Prot[estant] rather than Cathol[ic]") but soon had to contend with the prolongation of his detention, for Bulgaria refused to acknowledge his citizenship. Finally, on 15 February 1934 the USSR granted citizenship to all three Bulgarian veterans of the Leipzig trial. Deported from Germany on 17 February, they reached Moscow the same evening, to official greetings.

The excerpts that follow contain only a few fragments that record Dimitrov's changing moods during the ordeal.—I.B.

· 5 APRIL 1933 ·
(WEDNESDAY)

[...]

7. *Handcuffs, by order of the investigating magistrate!*
(Perhaps in response to my request to ease my personal situation in prison!
—Or—as a method of interrogation?)

· 6 APRIL 1933 ·
(THURSDAY)

1. Wrote to the judge about the handcuffs (if this is a punishment, [I] do not deserve it; if it is intended as a security measure, then it is not necessary, because as a well-known Bulg[arian] political personality I think not at all of the responsibility of withdrawing or fleeing, on the contrary I have my own interest and my political honor, which has been damaged through this current accusation, to defend and rescue).

[. . .]

· 26 APRIL 1933 ·
(WEDNESDAY)

1. To the investigating magistrate:

Please allow me to remind you that I still await *information* about:
1. *Discussion* with my lawyer
2. Transfer to the cashier of the remand prison the 5 M. of my seized money that was *derequisitioned*
3. Letter to Miss Kaiser *that was not sent*
[in handwriting: "Again no answer."]
4. *German textbook* from Mr. Interpreter

In addition, I have just ascertained that I often receive the correspondence addressed to me with *great delay*.

Only yesterday, for example, I received a letter from Mrs. Krüger[1] dated 19 April—that is, on the *sixth day!*

I understand completely, that *some time* is needed for inspection, but this cannot explain, and even less justify, *a delay of almost a week.*

Mrs. Krüger also complained that she hadn't received a letter from me for an *entire week.*

I request that you authorize my correspondence, as a prisoner awaiting trial, *to be delivered more regularly* whenever possible.

1. Any Krüger, German sympathizer; friend of Dimitrov.

Finally, I remind you, that I am *still handcuffed* day and night! With these handcuffs on, I must *write* and *read, sit* and *sleep!* Isn't it enough for you that I have endured this *moral* and *physical torment* for almost a month? Isn't it *time* that this barbaric measure *be removed?*

———

[. . .]

· 1 MAY 1933 ·
(MONDAY) — DAY OF "NATIONAL WORK"

—*Moscow—Berlin*—two historical antipodes!
And I sit in "Moabit"—handcuffed!
—Dreadful and deplorable!

[. . .]

· 4 MAY 1933 ·
(THURSDAY)

1. To the *investigating magistrate:*

Naturally I do not need to thank you for notifying me that you refuse to release the money seized from me. And yet by this [action] you have freed me from a fleeting illusion. I assumed, for a moment, that at least in this connection I would be treated as a political person who is actually not guilty of arson and who is in jail only because of his convictions and his acceptance of his Communist duty, no worse than a robber or murderer, and that I can count on a few marks from my money for a textbook and newspaper.

Now I see that this was an illusion. I may not recover any of my money; I may not receive any visitors and, at the same time, I must be handcuffed day and night, although the most dangerous murderer in the prison is not placed in such a position.

Yes, this is just and logical. I mustn't forget for one minute that [I] am in the hands of class enemies who also strive to take advantage of justice as a weapon to exterminate communism, that is, in fact, to destroy its confident, determined, and reliable representatives, independent of the personal views of the individual judge. Excuse me please, Mr. Counselor of the Supreme Court, for openly expressing my opinion, my perception. Unfortunately, I cannot say these things to anyone else.

[. . .]

· 6 MAY 1933 ·
(SATURDAY)

—*A day* without *anything!* No letter, no news, no "prison event["]—
nothing! not even the *usual shave*
—I also did not write to anyone, owing to a *shortage of postal fees* (not
a penny do I have!).

[. . .]

· 10 MAY 1933 ·
(WEDNESDAY)

1. To the *lawyer:*

With my letters from 27 April and 2 May I have repeatedly requested an
interview. I am still waiting for this, in my opinion, important interview or
for an answer from you.

In the meantime, I have received a letter from my sister and mother in
Sofia, in which they told me they have undertaken the necessary steps to be
granted a *foreign currency authorization* and that the money will be sent 'in
these days' (the letter is from 25 April). Since, however, various formalities
must be taken care of in this matter, it may be a while before I receive the
money.

At the moment, I have no money even for *postage.* For this reason, I also
cannot respond to the letter from Sofia. The day before yesterday I was no-
tified that a parcel had arrived for me from Bulgaria (clearly from my sister)
and I could not receive this parcel because I couldn't pay the duty (sixty-five
Pf.!)! Not to mention that I still cannot order a newspaper or buy something from the canteen (to smoke, etc.)—Can't you, Mr. Lawyer, pay the
prison cashier a *few marks* for me, until the [crossed out: money] *promised
money arrives?* If that is possible, I would be very, very grateful to you. In
addition, you can expect to receive some money from Sofia, sent directly to
your address.

I believe that you could have such an elementary trust in me and want to
help me.

[. . .]

· 9 JULY 1933 ·
(SUNDAY)—15TH SUNDAY HERE

—Difficult, gloomy! Outside—fabulous weather!

[. . .]

· 16 DECEMBER 1933 ·
(SATURDAY)

[…]

5. My speech—one is not allowed to speak about the situation in Ger[many] at the time of the Reichstag fire; not about the legal proceedings; nor about the actual necessity of the fire for the National Soc[ialists]—and so on. My petitions: 1) not guilty because of insufficient guilt and not because of insufficient proof; 2) Lubbe as tool misused by the enemies of the working class to present their view of communism; 3) to hold accountable the person responsible for our being drawn into this trial; 4) damages for the time lost and the harm done to the health of these people.

After advice of the Senate, decision—further closing remarks from D[imitrov] not allowed—the right to speak withdrawn.

[…]

· 5 FEBRUARY 1934 ·
(MONDAY)

With Detective Superintendent *Heller.* Almost all officials known from the "fire commission." An American correspondent. He wants to inquire about my "health."

—The world is very interested. In America a film is even being made, and so forth. Are you healthy and being treated well?

—I give no interviews, no explanation, for I am not a free man. I am a prisoner of war; I am a hostage. It is no wonder that my health has deteriorated—five months of handcuffs, three-month-long trial, two months—acquitted but not yet released.

—But you aren't tortured?

—Moral torture, day in, day out! I hold the view that if my destruction is necessary for the government, then the government should carry it out, but [the authorities should] give their reasons and accept the responsibility before the world. And not stage an unworthy game.

—Yes, they do that in Russia.

—Permit me: in Russia it is impossible that innocent persons who have been acquitted by the court should remain in prison one hour longer.

—You understand that the government has political considerations. The campaign abroad; questions of prestige, and so on.

—I do not believe that it is a rational policy to hold us in prison.

—Do you believe that you will be released?

—To look at the situation in a politically rational way, I should already have been released. But reason does not always govern the world.

—Have you given up your Bulg[arian] citizen[ship]?

—No! I will never give it up!

—If you return to Bulg[aria], you will be shot—they say.

—That is a problem for the government.

—I will live another twenty years and fight for comm[unism] and then die peacefully.

—You must now be patient. The government cannot capitulate to foreign countries.

—I have enough patience, but, if matters should continue, then I have one last weapon for self-defense—the hunger strike.

—Yes, but you want to live another twenty years.

—That is a matter of opinion.

To conclude: If you are a conscientious correspondent,

—That I am!

—I would like to think so. Then convey to the public my decisive protest against this barbarity, that I and my Bulg[arian] comrades are still held in prison, as hostages.

———————————

—"Tomorrow visit from Mother and Sister," Heller announced.

———————————

—Suitcases in my cell; money—downstairs. Various other promises . . .

———————————

———————————

"Have you spoken with *Lubbe?* What do you think of him?["]

—No. What an idiot! He remains a riddle as a person. I have already given my opinion of him in court.

[. . .]

· 27 FEBRUARY 1934 ·
(TUESDAY) — BERLIN — MOSCOW!

—*Raben* at 5:30 a.m.: "Get up; pack up!" *Diels*—Written "Release and deportation." Accompanied to airport. "We want good relations with the S[oviet] U[nion]. If that were not the case, we would not send you to Moscow!" As far as *Königsberg*—Heller, Morovsky, Raben. Heller: "I hope that you will be objective. And not say such dreadful things as others have done." "I hope that I will again come to Germany, but then as a guest of Soviet Germany." "As long as I am here, that will not be the case." With another airplane, direct to *Moscow.*

At 7 o'clock—at "home." *Manuilsky,* Knorin, and others—large crowds at the airport. Enthusiastic reception. Lux! Kuusinen. *Kitty* [Kiti Jovanović].[2] Conference with foreign correspondents. Questions by telephone from editors in London, Paris, and Berlin—

—Flowers and greetings from *Ulianova*[3] and Krupskaia![4]

It is difficult to imagine a more grandiose reception or more sympathy and love.

How everything has changed!

Letter *B. Kun!*

Radi [Petŭr Iskrov][5]—*My picture*—as a badge . . .

[. . .]

2. Kiti Jovanović, Serbian Communist; émigrée to the USSR; friend of Dimitrov.

3. Maria Ilinichna Ulianova (1878–1937), Soviet Communist; Lenin's younger sister; elected member of the Soviet control commission at the Seventeenth Congress of the VKP(b) ("Congress of Victors") in 1934.

4. Nadezhda Konstantinovna Krupskaia (1869–1939), Soviet Communist; Lenin's wife; deputy people's commissar for education (1929) and theoretician of the Soviet educational system; member of the VKP(b) CC (from 1927 on) and head of the Library Department of the People's Commissariat for Education (beginning in 1934).

5. Petŭr Iskrov (1891–1938), Bulgarian Communist leader. At the second conference of the BKP (Berlin, December 1927–January 1928) he was elected (with Dimitrov and Vasil Kolarov) to the BKP's new Foreign Bureau. A member of the ECCI (beginning in 1928), he represented the BKP in the Comintern during the ultra-leftist Third Period (1928–1935); targeted by Dimitrov in 1934 as a representative of "leftist sectarianism" in the BKP, he was slowly eased from a position of leadership before his arrest and execution during the Stalinist purges.

CHAPTER TWO

THE SOVIET UNION

FROM 28 February to 1 September 1934 Dimitrov became reacquainted with the Soviet Union. From the first triumphal days packed with interviews, welcome meetings with the Soviet leaders, and little satisfactions ("Talk with [I. A.] Piatn[itsky]! Finally he is *'satisfied'! Knorin* what changed behavior"), he was quickly being drawn into struggles for a change in the Comintern's Third Period line, marked by anti–Social Democratic sectarianism. The Schutzbund "insurrection" (or "armed resistance," as Stalin put it), in which the Austrian Social Democratic armed units fought the fascists, was an issue on which Stalin tested Dimitrov's willingness to develop a more flexible policy, Stalin evidently having decided that the old one was "incorrect."

On 6 April 1934 Dimitrov became a member of the political commission of the ECCI, a member of its political secretariat, and the head of the Anglo-American secretariat. Stalin and Molotov were preparing him to reject the leadership of the "foursome" (Manuilsky, Piatnitsky, Kuusinen, Knorin), and on 23 April Stalin put him in charge of the Central European secretariat, in the process replacing Knorin and weakening Knorin's ally Béla Kun. Increasingly the opposing sides had been drawn up. Manuilsky backed Dimitrov. Piatnitsky and Knorin were the most notable holdouts. Dimitrov increasingly had Stalin's ear.

During this period Dimitrov was frequently subjected to various medical treatments. He expressed great personal unhappiness. He mourned Ljubica Ivošević-Dimitrova, quarreled with Kiti Jovanović, and carried on a long-distance courtship with Rosa Fleischmann by mail. He spent most of July and the entire month of August 1934 resting in Georgia.—I.B.

[. . .]

· 1 APRIL 1934 ·

—At the Comintern (with Manuilsky).
Conversation with Stalin ([by] teleph[one]) about the *Austrian letter.*[6] "About your letter to the Aust[rian] wor[kers]. We were outside fighting; nevertheless, we had no luck. I (. . .) ["]
—You view the fighting in Austria as *insurrection.* We Bolsheviks have always understood insurrection to mean an armed struggle for power. Seizing power in Austria is not the goal. Therefore what is occurring there is armed resistance or an armed struggle and not an insurrection. To call it an insurrection is not scientific, not Bolshevik. Think about this matter, and if you are in agreement with such a correction, then the other parts of the letter must also be changed, spec[ifically] where you speak about the rules of insurrection.
—In my letter I have presented the views of the Comintern in this matter, views that were developed before my arrival.
—These views are incorrect, however.
—You know that Otto Bauer[7] himself called the Aust[rian] events armed insurrection.
—Yes, Bauer wants to praise himself for having led an insurrection. But that is not the case. We must tell the truth and not allow any confusion.
—I ask you to formulate basic corrections yourself, and then I will edit the entire letter accordingly.
—Good, I will try to do that in the next few days.

6. Dimitrov wrote "Letter to the Austrian Workers" in March 1934. The published version, with the endnote dated April 1934, evidently took into account Stalin's criticism. Still, its main point was that the blame for the failure of the February "armed struggle" in Vienna lay with the Social Democrats, who had "failed to grasp that it was not enough to resist the attack of fascism, but that they should have turned their armed resistance into a fight for the overthrow of the bourgeoisie and for seizure of power by the proletariat."

7. Otto Bauer (1882–1938), foremost Austrian Social Democrat and leading theoretician of the Austro-Marxist school. He clashed with the Bolsheviks over his nationality program, which ruled out secession and called for a democratic federal state based on ethnic autonomy (*Nationalitätenbundesstaat*); he took an active part in the work of the Second International and the Vienna-based International Union of Socialist Parties ("$2^{1}/_{2}$ International," 1920).

—It would be good if this matter could be dealt with promptly, because right now there is a lively discussion among the Social D[emocratic] workers in Aust[ria] and among other Social D[emocratic] workers. And it is very important to get the letter into their hands quickly.

—We will try. I will send back the letter tomorrow or the day after tomorrow.

—I will reedit the letter.

—Well, good-bye. Good-bye!

—Thank you very much! Good-bye!

[. . .]

· 3 APRIL 1934 ·

Letter to *Stalin*. [Notation in margin: Not sent, because he summoned me himself.]

Dear Com[rade] Stalin!

In my view, what I managed to achieve in Leipzig constitutes political capital for the Communist International that ought to be exploited comprehensively and entirely rationally, as well as opportunely.

However, all of this is in addition equally connected with my future work, its arrangement, its nature and form, its scope. Since I formally became a Soviet citizen, the settling of that work no longer appears to be such a simple matter. Various considerations will probably have to be taken into account.

I would very much like to consult with you personally concerning a variety of concrete issues and questions of principle connected with this situation. I believe that this will undoubtedly be extremely useful in moving business forward.

I have therefore resolved to request that you find an opportunity to receive me for at least half an hour for such a personal conversation.

I am still in treatment, but since I am capable of leaving the premises, I can stop in to see you whenever that would be most convenient for you.

You need only send word here ('Arkhangelskoe')[8] a day in advance concerning the time of meeting, in order to avoid any misunderstandings.

With comradely regards.

Your G[eorgi] Dim[itrov]

[. . .]

8. Arkhangelskoe, country estate some twenty kilometers from Moscow that had been the property of Princes Golitsyn and Yusupov. In addition to serving as a museum, it was also a clinic and sanatorium in Soviet times.

· 6 APRIL 1934 ·

[…]

Manuilsky, Piatnitsky:
("Member of the Political Commission, member of the Political Secretariat, and . . . head of the Anglo-American Secretariat!")

[…]

· 7 APRIL 1934 ·

With St[alin]—(Kremlin)
—*About Austr[ian] letter:*
Following observations:
1. Shortened!
2. Don't scold, but explain, persuade. European workers are historically linked with parliamentary democracy. One must show that the bourgeoisie has now abandoned democracy and proceeded to fascism (in one form or another), because it cannot govern otherwise. For the worker, unlike in the past, to struggle now for parl[iamentary] democracy is nonsense.
3. Armed struggle, not insurrection. Insurrection occurs when the task of seizing power is posed. In Austria, this was not the case.
4. Do not put a call through directly to the Aus[trian] CP [Communist Party]. This will be perceived with prejudice by Social D[emocratic] workers. They will think that in M[oscow] D[imitrov] is compelled to say so. In addition, to join the CP as an illegal party, that is very dangerous for them. [They] must accept the revolutionary path. We also had a small party but great following.
5. In the letter, don't develop the conclusions to the end. The Social Democr[atic] workers should draw these conclusions themselves.

Don't speak as mentor to the workers.

It must be patiently and intelligibly explained to the European workers why parliamentary democracy can no longer have any value for the working class. Earlier in their struggles with feudalism, the bourgeoisie brought the working masses along with it through democracy and made certain concessions to this end. Now that they have conquered feudalism and face a new enemy—the proletariat—and must overcome great difficulties, given the crisis of capitalism, they can no longer govern using the methods of parliamentary democracy. They are on the way to fascism. And in all countries the bourgeoisie will proceed to fascism. In England also, although in different forms.

Our people in the Comintern apply everything that was right for Russian workers to European workers. They do not understand that in fact we had no parliamentarianism. The Russian workers received absolutely nothing from the Duma.[9] This is not the case in Europe. If our bourgeoisie had had another thirty years, it would certainly have linked itself with the masses through parliamentarianism, and then it would have been much more difficult for us to topple.

Don't grumble about parliam[entary] democracy, but explain this development to the working masses!

D[imitrov]: In prison, I thought a lot about why—since our teaching is correct—millions of workers in decisive moments do not join us but stay with social democracy, which has behaved so treacherously or, as in Germany, even become National Socialists.
St[alin]: And your conclusion?
D[imitrov]: I believe that the main cause lies in our system of propaganda, in [our] incorrect approach to European workers.
St[alin]: No, this is not the main cause. The main cause lies in historic development—the historic connection that the European masses have with bourgeois democracy. Then in Europe's special situation—European countries do not have enough of their own raw materials, coal, wool, etc. They are dependent on the colonies. Without colonies, they could not exist. The workers know this and fear a loss of the colonies. And in this connection they are inclined to go with their own bourgeoisie. Internally, they are not in agreement with our anti-imperialist policy. They are even afraid of this policy. And for just this reason it is necessary to explain patiently and approach these workers correctly. A constant struggle for every worker is necessary. We can't immediately and so easily win millions of workers in Europe.

The millions of masses have the psychology of the herd. They only deal through their representatives, through the leaders. When they lose trust in their leaders, then they feel powerless and as though lost. They are afraid of losing their leaders. And therefore the Social D[emo-

9. Duma, Russian representative body. In the parliamentary organization of 1906 it constituted the lower house, which was elected by an indirect system of suffrage.

cratic] workers, although not satisfied with their leaders, still follow them. They will abandon these leaders when other, better ones are already at hand. And this takes time.

M[anuilsky] doesn't understand this. Each year he prophesies proletar[ian] revolut[ion] and it does not happen. He once reported insurrection in a place where there was none . . .

People do not pay attention to the details. And the details usually clinch matters. They do no Marxist analysis. For my report, I called [Jenő] Varga and demanded numbers on the crisis. Astounded and shocked, [he] asked me: Which numbers? Such numbers as exist, I said to him. Correct numbers?

—Yes, of course—correct!

He brought me the numbers. And breathed a sigh of relief. Thank goodness, he said, there are still people who love the truth!

Just imagine, he was afraid to give the correct numbers in the CI [Communist International], because [he] would be immediately classified as [a] right opportunist . . .

He couldn't decide to publish this report without my approval!

Molot[ov]: Yes, Varga is a good scholar, but a coward!

St[alin]: People do not like Marxist analysis. Big phrases and general assertions. This is still the legacy from the time of Zinoviev.

Ah, in this connection Ilich [Lenin] was very accurate, and how accurate!

St[alin]: And who there (in CI [Communist International]) is now *the first?* Who has prevailed?

D[imitrov]: For me this is now very difficult to ascertain.

St[alin]: No, *don't dodge!*

D[imitrov]: Earlier, I knew that M[anuilsky] appeared to be the polit[ical] leader. Now I know (. . .) only that when P[iatnitsky] is not there, chaos arises. He is the pillar, so to speak!

Mol[otov]: Yes, we are therefore involved only with Piatn[itsky] the entire time.

St[alin]: Ku[u]s[inen] is good, but an academic. M[anuilsky]—agitator; Kn[orin]—propagandist. P[iatnitsky]—narrow!

D[imitrov]: In prison I often thought that, finally, the administration of the CI [Communist International] had historically crystallized under their leadership (M[anuilsky], P[iatnitsky], Ku[u]s[inen], Kn[orin]).

St[alin]: Who says, that this "foursome" must remain so? You speak about history. But one must sometimes correct history.

D[imitrov]: I believe that, as our first leader, you must indeed bear the responsibility for leading the CI [Communist International], and although [you are] frightfully busy, you must participate in important questions.

St[alin]: Yes, here at this table, we have discussed the theses for the plenum, and what has happened? When they go away from here, everything remains as before.

You see how we are occupied.

The best of our people go to the construction sites.

. . . So begin with some comrades—we will help you.

M[olotov]: You have looked the enemy in the face. And after prison you [should] now take the work into your hands.

―――――――

D[imitrov]: How will it be with my Soviet citizenship? Won't that pose certain obstacles concerning my conduct[?]

St[alin]: You can calmly respond to all questions when necessary. "After all," we do not take responsibility for the behavior of every Soviet citizen.

―――――――

(Voroshilov, Kuibyshev, Mikoyan, among others)

[. . .]

· 23 APRIL 1934 ·

—Man[uilsky] and Piatnitsky with me.

—St[alin] recommended transferring to me the leadership of the Central European Secr[etariat] (Kn[orin]—another job).

Discussion about the Seventh Congress: main question—the revolutionary unity of the proletariat against fascism and war (Man[uilsky]);

Report mass work, struggle against the war *Piatn[itsky]*

—Man[uilsky's] proposal—main reporter Dim[itrov]! Oh my God, what a peculiar lot!

[. . .]

· 24 APRIL 1934 ·
(NONWORKING DAY)

[. . .]

—*Discussion* with Man[uilsky]—we have not taken advantage of the greatest crisis in the world.

—Isolation from St[alin]. Happened first before Thirteenth Plenum. Must rely solely on himself. Demanded a member of the PB [Politburo] with us. Came to nothing. P[iatnitsky] said to St[alin]: "I have heard that you are not satisfied with our leadership of the CI. I ask you please to receive us." St[alin]: "No! It concerned only the Austr[ian] letter."

—I am suffering dreadfully with this situation in the CI—you must take over the main report. Your situation in public must be brought into accord with your role in the CI!

[. . .]

· 25 APRIL 1934 ·
[. . .]

Man[uilsky]. "I have thought a lot about your discussion with *St[alin]*. It is not a chance conversation. Instead [it] has extremely great political significance. He should have said that some years ago. Conclusions must be drawn from this discussion. In the Communist International we need a "boss." History has placed you in the forefront through the Leipz[ig] trial. You have enormous popularity among the masses. Your voice has colossal resonance. You must take over the leadership. On my honor, I will help you 120 percent in everything. You must select people and bring them together. This will not be easy. Many things must be rearranged. There is horrible routine and bureaucratism here. For a long time I have tried to change that, but I have lacked the necessary authority. You have this authority. And even if you should be unsuccessful, then everything would be as it was before—and I must tell you, there is no point in working in the CI. . . . Contact with St[alin] is necessary. That will be easier for you. He will count on you. Get well and prepare seriously for work . . .

[. . .]

· 28 APRIL 1934 ·
[. . .]

—Met *Fritz* [Heckert]: "How are you?["] "Horrible, horrible!" Things will get better. Immediately disappeared. Curious! that he has not yet felt the need to discuss with me in detail (about Germany, trial, etc.)—completely inexplicable!

· 29 APRIL 1934 ·
[. . .]

—At Leninist School—My talk (two threads at the trial—Torgl[er]-Dim[itrov] opportunist thread and Bolshevik thread. One must draw the lesson. Especially with regard to the education of our cadres.)[10]
—Speech by Manuilsky (. . . You have captured the leading position in the CI. You are our leader (?!) . . .)

[. . .]

· 1 MAY 1934 ·
(LAST YEAR AND NOW!)

—On Red Square (with Grand[ma] and Lina).[11]
—*M[aksim] Gorky:*[12] "We need no compliments, but I must tell you that your behavior was splendid. There has never been such a trial. You were actually the judge there. . . . It cannot be compared to the trial against [name unclear] or the Cologne trial against Marx.[13] This was something special. . . ."

Stalin, Molotov, Kalinin, Ordzhonikidze, Mikoyan, Zhdanov, and others on the platform (mausoleum). No one from the CI? I am on the ground in front of the mausoleum with Grand[ma] and Lina. There (. . .), Shvernik, Felix Kohn, and others.

St[alin] calls from above: "Dimitrov!" and gives a sign to come up to

---

10. Ernst Torgler (1893–1963), German Communist; member of the KPD CC, president of the KPD fraction in the Reichstag (1932–1933), expelled from the party after the Leipzig trial. Dimitrov offered the following harsh verdict of his co-defendants at a gathering at the Leninist School (Moscow) in 1934: "At the trial there were three lines: first, treacherous—Torgler; second opportunistic, defend yourself—Tanev and Popov; and, third, Bolshevik, defend the party—my own." Cited in Rodoljub Čolaković, *Kazivanja o jednom pokoljenju,* vol. 2 (Sarajevo, 1968), pp. 168–69.

11. Parashkeva Dimitrov (Babushka, Grandma, 1861–1944), Dimitrov's mother; Magdalina Barŭmova (Lina, 1884–1971), Dimitrov's sister; Bulgarian Communist activist.

12. Maksim Gorky (real name: A. M. Peshkov, 1868–1936), Russian writer and playwright; leading representative of critical realism in modern Russian literature; Bolshevik sympathizer.

13. In February 1849 the public prosecutor in Cologne initiated court proceedings against Karl Marx and two associates, who were charged with incitement to armed resistance against the Prussian authorities. Marx's brilliant speech at the trial swayed the jury to acquit the defendants. The foreman of the jury thanked Marx for his instructive lecture.

where he is standing. Greetings from St[alin], Kal[inin], Molotov, and others—Grandmother and Sister.

Voroshilov—on the platform. The speech, swearing in of the new Red Army soldiers . . .

Bukharin also on the platform: "You have accomplished an enormous amount. Held the banner aloft in every respect. It was excellent. And about the pederasts. . . . This was very successful. Your behavior from beginning to end was completely correct in principle. It was an enormous success! . . . And Torgl[er]—dirt!["]

I: to St[alin]: "We need to discuss Comintern matters again."

St[alin]: "Good, come to see me. When do you want to?"

I: "When it is convenient for you. I have noticed some confusion among the people in the CI."

He: "No, this is nothing dreadful. We will settle everything . . . "

· 2 MAY 1934 ·

At the Kremlin—with Red Commanders (Stal[in], Molot[ov], Voroshilov, Kalinin, Ordzhon[ikidze], Mikoyan and others)—Turkish flyers.

. . . *St[alin]:* Relations with Turkey [are] not bad. Now they want to conclude a military treaty with us. We refuse. We say: Our alliance has greater significance than a written treaty. Having such an ally (as Turkey!) is always good. But if Turkey should come into the complications of war, it is not convenient for us to fight for her.

Bulg[aria]—a little country. What can one do there? The Bulgarians are building six-thousand-kilowatt electric stations. And we . . .

Vor[oshilov] From the Chekists[14] no one has come. Neither Yagoda[15] nor anyone else.

St[alin] Yesterday I somewhat offended them. They arrested people for nothing . . .

---

14. Chekists, members of the Soviet secret police, the Cheka (from the Russian initials of *Chrezvychainaia Komissiia,* Extraordinary Commission), the repressive postrevolutionary agency "for combating counterrevolution and sabotage."

15. Genrikh Grigorievich Yagoda (1891–1938), Soviet Communist; veteran of the secret police; people's commissar for internal affairs and chairman of OGPU (1934–1936); people's commissar for information (1936–1938); defendant in the trial of the "bloc of Rights and Trotskyites" in March 1938. He was condemned to death and executed.

St[alin] to the commanders:
"Leaders are worth nothing *without* such assistants, co-workers . . .
["]

St[alin] (in reference to chapter "With Stalin"): I do not agree to your writing about me in such a way. That also damages your reputation. Such language between equals is not advisable. . . . Select *yourself where* and *how* to appear and what to write. Don't let yourself be talked into anything. Select only the key questions. Things went well with the Austrian letter. Otherwise, you say: I am busy, sick, or something like that. I have saved myself in this way. I have had cases where certain workers from the Donbas have turned to me. I have enlightened them. It turned out, however, that such workers do not even exist . . .

—Speak with the Schutzbundists.[16] It is not good to require of them that they join the Com[munist] Party now. Let them just be honest workers. And as they finally are convinced that communism is right, then—into the party!

—[Heinz] *Neumann*—does not understand Marxism. He is a political degenerate. He asked me what he should learn in order to be a good Marxist.

I said to him that *Das Kapital*—that is an examination of human thinking. (As Marx taught.)

He was not satisfied. *Das Kapital* was *boring* for him. He thought it would be better to study "Class Struggle in France" and "18 Brumaire."

—*Thälm[ann]* has not understood the national question. I spoke with him in 1930. He has not understood . . .

16. Members of the Austrian Socialist Defense League who in February 1934 fought against the forces of the Dollfuss dictatorship and its attempts to overrun banned socialist organizations. The Schutzbundist uprising was defeated after four days of intense fighting in the working-class districts of Vienna. Despite the socialist defeat and the persecution of the Left that ensued, the uprising constituted the first armed resistance to fascism. Many hundreds of Austrian Schutzbundists escaped to Czechoslovakia. From there they were invited to the USSR, the first sign of change in the Comintern line toward the Social Democrats, who had been reviled as "social fascists" during the Third Period.

Proletarian internationalism and nationalism.
Through social liberation—national independence.

[. . .]

· 17 MAY 1934 ·

—Blagoev evening—Bulg[arian] section together with "Old Bolsheviks."

(Ten years since the death of [Dimitŭr] Blagoev.)[17]

—*Anton* [Ivanov][18] (reporter); from *Old Bolsh[eviks]:* Kab[akchiev],[19] Blagoeva,[20] and others.

—My appearance: "Three peculiarities of Bl[agoev] (and Narrow Socialism [*tesniachestvo*]).["][21]

17. Dimitŭr Blagoev (*Diadoto* [Grandpa], 1856–1924), founder of the Bulgarian Social Democratic Party, the Bulgarian Workers' Social Democratic Party (Narrow Socialists), and the Bulgarian Communist Party (BKP).

18. Anton Ivanov (1884–1942), Bulgarian Communist leader; deputy in the Bulgarian parliament; member of the BKP CC (beginning in 1922). He headed the Sofia revolutionary committee during the abortive September 1923 uprising, was imprisoned from 1923 to 1925, and emigrated to the USSR. Member of the Red Trade Union International (Profitern) Executive Committee (1928–1930) and Comintern emissary to France and Spain (after 1935), he returned to Bulgaria in 1940 as head of the BKP internal organization (as CC secretary). He was arrested by the police and executed.

19. Hristo Kabakchiev (1878–1940), Bulgarian Communist leader; old Narrow Socialist; member of the BKP CC (from 1919 on); Comintern delegate to the Halle congress of the USPD (October 1920) and the Livorno congress of Italian socialists at which the PCI was founded (January 1921); political secretary of the BKP (January 1923). Imprisoned from 1923 to 1926, he emigrated to the USSR, where he served as member of the Comintern's international control commission (ICC, 1924–1928), taught at the Leninist School and worked at the Marx-Engels-Lenin Institute. He was arrested during the Stalinist purges in 1937 but released in 1938.

20. Stela Blagoeva (1887–1954), Bulgarian Communist; daughter of Dimitŭr Blagoev, the founder of the BKP; political émigrée to the USSR from 1926 to 1946. Starting in 1927, she worked in the ECCI apparatus, the foreign bureau of the BKP, and the Slavic Committee; after her return to Bulgaria in 1946 she served in various capacities, including the post of Bulgaria's ambassador to the USSR from 1949 to 1954.

21. The Bulgarian Social Democratic Party (1891) split once in 1892, was reunited in 1894, and split for good in 1903. The orthodox, or "narrow," faction, headed by Dimitŭr Blagoev, determined to build a purely proletarian party in a peasant country, resisted the peasant support that appealed to the "broad socialists" of Yanko Sakŭzov. The Narrows also wanted to press the nascent trade unions into political action and resisted joint activities with the nonsocialist par-

1. Class irreconcilability with the bourgeoisie and its Menshevik agen[ts.]

2. Party of the proletariat above all (everything is subjected to the inter[est] of the proletariat).

3. Steadfast belief in the power and the future of the working class.

This is why the Bulg[arian] prolet[ariat] is united as a class; Social D[emocrats] won the majority of the workers.

—The time spent as Narrow Socialists [*tesniaks*] not a *minus,* but a *plus;* but boiled in the "Bolshevik cauldron."

—Bold bearing and struggle—are qualities of Narrow Socialism [*tesniachestvo*].

—As a Narrow Socialist [*tesniak*] I would have presented myself in just as dignified and courageous a manner before the Leipzig court, but I would not have been in a position to wage and win such a battle against fascism.

—Only *Bolshevik* methods and Bolshevik heroism provided the opportunity for successfully conducting such a battle.

—In Leipzig, as I held in my left hand the code of criminal procedures of the German Reich and in my right hand the program of the Communist International and as I took advantage of the weapons in the arsenal of Lenin, I was behaving not as a Narrow Socialist, but as a Bolshevik.

———————

. . . I have committed enough errors in my long revolutionary political activity. Two errors, however, I will never be able to forget and set aside—9 June "neutrality"[22] and the fact that I, like our party, failed to perceive the fundamental difference between Narrow Socialism and Bolshevism and to draw, in the years 1918–1923, the necessary conse-

---

ties. Although Blagoev's Narrows were more Kautskyite than Leninist, Narrow Socialism left its mark on the BKP, which viewed itself as continuing the Narrow Socialist legacy.

22. Conservative officers aided by the Macedonian guerrilla organization overthrew the Agrarian government of Prime Minister Aleksandŭr Stamboliski on 9 June 1923. After several days' fighting, during which Stamboliski was killed, the putschists established a new regime headed by Aleksandŭr Tsankov. Despite the rightist nature of the coup, the forty-thousand-strong BKP declared its "neutrality" in the struggle. After finishing off the Agrarians, the Tsankov regime turned against the Communists, a decision that led to the ill-fated September uprising (1923) and a major defeat for Bulgarian Communists.

quences in a timely manner. The latter error has, to a certain extent, made the bolshevization of our party longer and more painful . . .

[. . .]

· 20 MAY 1934 ·
[. . .]

—Lunch at Kremlin cafeteria ("separate chamber")—with Mann [Manuilsky]—then thorough discussion. His letter to P[iatnitsky] about reconstituting the leadership of the ECCI—discussion with St[alin] about the Fren[ch] question (very unsatisfactory!)—in Fran[ce]—united front also "from above" . . .

[. . .]

· 27 MAY 1934 ·

—*Piatn[itsky].* Final suggestion about agenda for the congress. Speak[ers]: Pieck, Dim[itrov], Ercoli [Palmiro Togliatti], Man[uilsky], Wang Min[g], Pollitt.

(Commission about my report: Dim[itrov], Piatn[itsky], Ko[stan-yan],[23] Šmeral, Heckert)

—Disagreements with Man[uilsky]. (Austrian presidential election; (. . .); Doriot;[24] Spanish labor union question, etc.) Sharp disputes in open session of the political secretariat.

—Letter from Man[uilsky] to Piatn[itsky] ("sad letter!")—

"I am for collective leadership—decisively against a single leader." . . .

[. . .]

23. A. A. Kostanyan, secretary of the Armenian CP CC.

24. Jacques Doriot (1898–1945), French Communist leader, later fascist, who was active in the Communist youth movement; member of the Executive Committee of the Communist Youth International (KIM) beginning in 1922; secretary-general of the French organization of young Communists (from 1923 on); member of the PCF CC (from 1924 on); alternate member of the ECCI (from 1924 on); parliamentary deputy (1924) and mayor of St.-Denis (1932). After the Parisian riots of 6 February 1934, following the Stavisky affair, Doriot clashed with Thorez and refused to heed a summons to Moscow; expelled from the party in June 1934, he organized the Parti populaire française, which evolved toward fascism. Collaborator during the German occupation of France, Doriot was killed in an Allied air raid, after his withdrawal to Germany with the Nazi forces.

· 10 JUNE 1934 ·
[. . .]

—[Jacques] *Sadoul*[25] with me. (Threatening fascism in France. United front with social democracy [. . .].)

[. . .]

· 15 JUNE 1934 ·

—*Piatnitsky—Smoliansky*[26] (about Point 3 of the agenda for the congress)—with *Piatn[itsky]*.
as though absolutely *nothing new* had happened! And nothing new to say! . . . "Some want to *change* the revolutionaries!" . . . Dreadful.

[. . .]

· 18 JUNE 1934 ·
[. . .]

—*In crematorium!*
So lonely and personally unhappy! It's almost more difficult for me now than last year in prison.
—Letter to Rozi[27] and her mother.
What will come of it? In any case it is impossible to live so alone!

[. . .]

· 21 JUNE 1934 ·

—Knorin—long talk (Germ[any], Aust[ria], Czechoslov[akia], etc.; preparations for the congress, my report).

25. Jacques Sadoul (1898–1945), French Communist. As pro-Entente socialist, he participated in a French military mission to Russia in August 1917; turned Communist and founded a French Communist group in Russia; attended the founding congress of the Comintern and participated in the early ECCI; returned to France in 1924. Although he remained a lifelong member of the PCF, he never held any leading positions in the party.

26. Georgy B. Smoliansky (1890–1937), Soviet Communist who served on the staff of the Profitern and ECCI. He was liquidated in the Stalinist purges.

27. Rosa Fleischmann (Rozi, Roza Yulievna, 1896–1958), Sudeten Jewish Communist from Boskovice, southern Moravia; journalist in Vienna; second wife of Georgi Dimitrov. Dimitrov first met her in Vienna on 10 May 1927.

—Tanev[28]—with me (returned from Kislov[odsk]).[29]
—[unclear] (about [unclear])—everything is all wrong!

[...]

· 29 JUNE 1934 ·

—Plenum CC.
St[alin]: I never answered you. I had no time. On this question, there is still nothing in my head. Something must be prepared!

[...]

· 2 JUNE 1934 ·
WITH MOSKV[IN] (TAN[EV])

—Meeting of the commission about my report.
(Big discussion—Šm[eral], Piatn[itsky], Loz[ovsky],[30] Kn[orin], Kuus[inen], (...), Heckert, Maddalena.)[31]

[...]

· 4 JULY 1934 ·

—With Stal[in]—thorough discussion!

[...]

28. Vasil Tanev (1897–1941), Bulgarian Communist; founding member of the BKP who participated in the September uprising (1923). Subsequently, as a political émigré to Yugoslavia and the USSR, he was sent on various secret missions, including to Bulgaria. The Comintern sent him to Germany in 1932 to work alongside Dimitrov in the West European Bureau. Arrested in 1933 with Dimitrov, Tanev was tried by the Nazis for complicity in the Reichstag fire. Released with Dimitrov and deported to the USSR, he subsequently had to undergo self-criticism, was barred from the leading positions in the BKP, and was deported to Kolyma. In 1941 he was parachuted into Bulgaria on an ECCI mission. Apprehended by the authorities, he was killed the same year.

29. A spa and rehabilitation center near Stavropol, in the Caucasus area of the RSFRS, close to the border with Georgia.

30. A. Lozovsky (real name: Solomon Abramovich, 1878–1952), Old Bolshevik, secretary-general of the Profitern until 1937, active afterward in various publishing ventures, the Ministry of Foreign Affairs, and the Soviet Information Bureau (Sovinformbureau). He was liquidated in 1952.

31. Max Maddalena (1895–1943), leading German Communist and a Reichstag deputy. He emigrated to the USSR after the Nazi takeover, worked in the apparatus of the Profitern, and represented the KPD in the ECCI. Designated a member of the KPD clandestine leadership, he returned under cover to Germany in 1935. He was soon arrested and died in Nazi confinement in 1943.

The Russian portion of the Dimitrov diary begins in September 1934 with his return to Moscow. The only noteworthy development during the early fall was his pointed reference to the presence of the "Class against class!" slogan in the program of the French CP on 17 September: "*Before* and *now!*" he writes, evidently disappointed in the sectarian wing of the French party.

After 7 November 1934 Dimitrov started a household with Rosa Fleischmann (Rozi), who had joined him in the USSR. From 21 November to 31 January 1935 Dimitrov and his new wife were recuperating in Crimea, where he was diagnosed with latent malaria, chronic gastritis, and several other ailments. During this period he discussed assorted literary themes with Gorky (for example, Tolstoy as "not a fighter, but a believer!") and others. In a conversation with the artist P. D. Korin on 27 November, Dimitrov called for "a new *Don Quixote* (the degenerating bourgeoisie). We need a Cervantes of our own against fascism." The Kirov "murder" was duly noted on 1 December without comment.

There is a hiatus in the diary between 31 January 1935 and 19 August 1936. This period corresponds to the preparations and work for the Seventh Congress of the Comintern (July–August 1935), as well as to the beginning of the purges.—I.B.

· 19 AUGUST 1936 ·

Evening—Barvikha.
The trial of Zin[oviev,] Kam[enev,] et al. (beginning).[32]

· 20 AUGUST 1936 ·

—Man[uilsky]—Moskvin (pasquinade against Man[uilsky]).
—Pritt's[33] letter (requesting a ticket to the trial).

· 21 AUGUST 1936 ·

—Letter by Kagan[ovich] on "subversive activities" (anonymous letter against M[anuilsky or Moskvin?]).

---

32. Reference to the trial of G. Ye. Zinoviev and L. B. Kamenev ("Trotskyite-Zinovievite Terrorist Center"), which commenced on 19 August 1936.
33. Dennis Noel Pritt (1887–1972), British Labourite; president of the International Committee of Inquiry on the burning of the Reichstag (1933); president of the British Society for Cultural Ties with the USSR.

· 22 AUGUST 1936 ·

—Arrival of Šmeral (for the peace congress). Man[uilsky] and he at my place.

· 23 AUGUST 1936 ·

—Arrival of Kuusinen (he and Man[uilsky] at my place).

· 24 AUGUST 1936 ·

—Kuusinen—Man[uilsky] (article on the trial and Citrine).[34]
—Sentence carried out.[35]

· 25 AUGUST 1936 ·

—Council: Kuus[inen], Man[uilsky], Moskv[in], Shvernik, Kolarov, Smol[yanski], Šmeral (principles and directives on the peace congress).

· 26 AUGUST 1936 ·

—Man[uilsky]—Moskv[in] (decoding by the enemy—the English of our encoded communications!).
—Editors of *Pravda* (concerning the article in *Populaire*).[36]

· 27 AUGUST 1936 ·

—Sent Com[rade] Stalin Manuilsky's account of Thorez's statement.

34. Walter McLennan Citrine, first Baron Citrine (1887–1983), British trade unionist; general secretary of the Electrical Trades Union (1920–1923); general secretary of the British Trades Union Congress (1926–1946); chairman of the International Federation of Trade Unions, the socialist (Amsterdam) trade union international (1928–1945); president of the World Federation of Trade Unions (1945–1946); leader of the conservative wing in the British trade union movement. Close to Clement Attlee during the latter's ministry, Citrine was made a baron in 1946.
35. Reference to the execution of Zinoviev and Kamenev.
36. The "French front" was a specifically French version of the Popular Front, promoted for a while by the French CP (PCF).

· 28 AUGUST 1936 ·

—Ercoli [Togliatti] returned from leave.
—Meeting of the Pol[it]buro.
　—Question of aid to the Spanish (poss[ible] organiz[ation] of an internat[ional] corps).[37]
　—Subversive work of Kun and others.
　—Trial materials in foreign languages.

· 29 AUGUST 1936 ·

—Spiner [Ivan Genchev]—Kon Sin have taken off for Paris.[38]
—In the evening—Erc[oli], Man[uilsky], Moskvin.
—Got new dentures.
—Prof. Vinogradov, Dr. Barsky.

· 30 AUGUST 1936 ·

—Telegram from Thorez: "I protest against the attempt by the Soviet embassy to exert pressure on our line concerning the Spanish question" (?!).
—My article printed in *L'Humanité* (28 Aug. 36).
(Rozi and Mitia[39] came to see me!)
—Sergeev[40] and Heimo[41] (gave a variety of assignments).

37. In 1936 the Comintern initiated the International Brigades to assist the Spanish Republic. Made up largely of Communist cadres, especially from the fascist-ruled countries, it brought thousands of volunteers to Spain, an enormous propaganda victory for the Comintern's Popular Front.

38. Reference to a meeting of Chinese emigrants resident in Western Europe, which was held in Paris under Comintern auspices. The principal organizer was Kang Sheng (pseudonym: Kon Sin).

39. Dimitŭr Dimitrov (Mitia, 1936–1943), Dimitrov's son.

40. Svetoslav Kolev (pseudonym: Sergeev, 1889–1950), Bulgarian Communist; member of the BKP CC (from 1926 on); political émigré to the USSR (1926–1949); aide to Dimitrov employed in the ECCI apparatus.

41. Mauno Heimo (1894–1937), Finnish Communist who served on the staff of the ECCI, where he performed numerous services, especially on missions to the Scandinavian and Central and West European countries. He was liquidated in the Stalinist purges.

· 31 AUGUST 1936 ·

—Man[uilsky], Moskv[in], Mand[alian],[42] Ponomarev (edited the article on the fifteenth anniversary of the Chin[ese] Com[munist] Party).
—Materials for the journal.
—Heimo's sent to Norway and Denmark.
—Send Spanish émigrés from Amer[ica] and other countries to Spain (pilots, material assistance for Spain).
—Opening of the international youth congress in Geneva.

· 1 SEPTEMBER 1936 ·

—Young people's demonstration (Lukianov's[43] speech).
—Moskv[in]—Johnson[44] (J.'s trip to America—aid for the Spanish).
—Kuusinen—Ponomarev (materials for the journal).

· 2 SEPTEMBER 1936 ·

—At the Kremlin (at the PB [Politburo]—Mol[otov], Kag[anovich], Vor[oshilov], Ordzhonikidze).
—Question of the Spanish government.
A directive was agreed upon (with Stal[in] as well—by tel[ephone]): "Seek the transformation of the Giral government into a government of national defense, headed by Giral with a majority of Republicans, participation of Socialists and two Communists, as well as representatives of the Catalans and Basques."[45]
The question of aid will be additionally discussed in the PB.

[. . .]

· 3 SEPTEMBER 1936 ·

—Was at the Comintern.
—Situation in Spain critical.
—(Send a special man to Paris to help the French with purchase and transport of arms and airplanes.)

42. Reference to a member of Dimitrov's secretariat.
43. V. V. Lukianov, member of the ECCI staff.
44. Johnson, American Communist (identity unclear).
45. Reference to the government of José Giral, a liberal Republican (Izquierda Republicana) leader; prime minister of Spain July–September 1936.

—Scandalous article by Thorez in *L'Humanité* (30 Aug.) on Poland—occasioned by the arrival of Gen[eral] Rydz-Śmigły[46] in Paris.

· 4 SEPTEMBER 1936 ·

—At the Comintern in the evening (Spain!).
—Meeting about publishing matters (Janson).[47]
—Eberlein[48] (to assist Moskvin!).
—(With Rozi and Mitia.)

· 5 SEPTEMBER 1936 ·

—Session of the secretariat.
Got[twald]'s report on the Rom[anian] plenum.
Commission report on *B[éla] Kun.*
Kun's statement (repentance!).
Resolved: a) Take the conclusion of the commiss[ion] into account. b) Grant B[éla] Kun's request for mitigation of the formula following the paragraph (delete the word "harmful"). c) Relieve Kun of work in the HCP [Hungarian Communist Party] and in the ECCI [Executive Committee of the Communist International] apparatus.

[. . .]

· 7 SEPTEMBER 1936 ·
AT THE KREMLIN.

—On the Chin[ese] question.
Motion: Consider it possible to agree with the draft plan of the Chinese Commun[ists] (the direction of Ningxia and Xinjiang)—render assistance in the form of arms, and so forth.

46. Edward Rydz-Śmigły (1886–1941), Polish statesman and close associate of Marshal Józef Piłsudski, upon whose death in 1935 Rydz-Śmigły became the inspector general of the Polish army and virtual dictator of the country.

47. Reference to a German Communist on the publications staff of the ECCI.

48. Hugo Eberlein (1887–1944), German Communist leader who belonged to the Spartakusbund; founding member of the KPD and member of its leadership until 1928, when, as one of the five "conciliators," he supported the removal of Ernst Thälmann as party leader; member of the ECCI Secretariat (from 1922 on) and the ICC (1928–1937). Arrested in the Stalinist purges, he was slated for extradition to Nazi Germany (1940) but fell ill and remained imprisoned in Soviet custody until his death.

· 8 SEPTEMBER 1936 ·

—Vassart[49] arrived. Discussion with him.
—Decided to summon: Thor[ez], Togl[iatti], Gottwald, Marin. [Cuban Communist]
—Postponed the session of the presid[ium].

· 9 SEPTEMBER 1936 ·

—Clément [Fried][50] arrived.
—Discussion with Clément.

· 10 SEPTEMBER 1936 ·

—Listened to Goebbels's speech at the Nuremberg party rally over the car radio (monstrous incitement!).

· 11 SEPTEMBER 1936 ·

—Our directives concerning Chinese affairs are confirmed:
   1. Agree to the Chinese Red Army's plan of action—namely, occupying the Ningxia region and the western part of Gansu Province, at the same time categorically ruling out further movement by the Chinese Red Army in the direction of Xinjiang, which could tear the Chinese Red Army away from the basic Chinese regions.

49. Albert Vassart (1898–1958), French Communist leader and trade unionist; member of the PCF CC (from 1926 on) and its Politburo (from 1929 on); one of the four PCF CC secretaries (from 1932 on); representative of the PCF to the ECCI (1934–1935); mayor of Maisons-Alfort (beginning in 1935). He opposed the Soviet-German nonaggression pact but was arrested after the beginning of the war. Freed in 1941, he resumed the mayoralty. As a result, the PCF declared him a traitor and attempted to assassinate him. He was an active anticommunist after the war.

50. Pseudonym of Eugen Fried (1900–1943), Jewish Communist of Hungarian culture from Slovakia, who served as a liaison between the Hungarian and Slovak Council republics in 1919; member of the Communist Party of Czechoslovakia (KSČ) from its foundation (1921); member of the KSČ CC (from 1923 on) and Politburo (from 1929 on). He was criticized in 1930 for leftist deviations. He served as the representative of the Comintern in Germany, Belgium, and France and as head of the permanent Comintern delegation to the PCF (1931–1939). He was killed by the Germans in Brussels in August 1943. Some ex-Communists claimed that he was liquidated on orders from Moscow.

2. Decide in advance that after the Chinese Red Army takes the Ningxia region, aid will be rendered in the form of arms on the order of fifteen-to-twenty thousand rifles, eight cannon, ten mortars and a commensurate quantity of ammunition of foreign make. Concentrate the arms on the southern border of the MPR [Mongolian People's Republic] by December 1936 and sell them through a certain Ur[umqi?] foreign firm, after making provisions to transport them to Ningxia.

———————————

—Meeting of the journal's editorial staff.
—Kuusinen—politically responsible. (Secret editorial staffs are necessary. Those responsible for the German, French, and English editions.)
—Meeting of the [Bulgarian CP] FB [Foreign Bureau] (Kol[arov], Iskrov, Spir[idonov],[51] Bogdanov).[52]
    1. Popular Front policy
    2. Relations between the CP and the Workers' Party[53]
    3. Politburo: Mar[ek],[54] Radenko,[55] Encho Staikov,[56] Stamat Ivanov,[57] Kamenov (Damian[ov] is leaving!)[58]
—Proposed: Staikov for the Workers' Party and mass organizations; Grozdanov[59]—to help in organizational work.

· 12 SEPTEMBER 1936 ·

—The delegation from Málaga arrived (headed by Commun[ist] deputy Bolívar[60]—only three persons) by steamer in Batum (seeking

51. Spiridonov, pseudonym of Traicho Kostov.
52. Bogdanov, pseudonym of Anton Ivanov.
53. The Workers' Party was the legal front of the Bulgarian CP (BKP).
54. Marek, pseudonym of Stanke Dimitrov.
55. Radenko Vidinski (1899–1974), Bulgarian Communist; member of the BKP PB and the CC secretary (1936–1941).
56. Encho Staikov (1901–1975), Bulgarian Communist; member of the BKP PB (from 1936 on).
57. Stamat Ivanov (1896–1968), Bulgarian Communist, member of the BKP PB (1935–1937).
58. Kamenov (Damian[ov]), Bulgarian Communist, identity unclear.
59. Bulgarian Communist, identity unclear.
60. Cayetano Bolívar, Communist deputy from Málaga and political commissar for the Málaga sector.

oil and mainly to request arms). The steamer had a crew of forty-one (Commun[ists] and Anarch[ists]).

Ercoli [Togliatti] spoke with him. They're asking for eighteen-to-twenty thousand rifles, five hundred machine guns and gear.

—*Pollitt arrived.* Talk with him leaves a disturbing impression (anxiety, confusion, and so forth, in connection with new difficulties with the United Front in Spain!).

· 13 SEPTEMBER 1936 ·

Thorez arrived.

—Discussion. (Com[munist Party] in Spain has not accomplished its mission. Unorganized and uncoordinated work. [André] Marty gave orders on his personal authority alone. Conclusion: joint work by T[horez] and Marty inadvisable.)

—The Socialists want to derail the Popular Front and heap the blame for it on the Communists. Grounds: the Spanish campaign.

· 14 SEPTEMBER 1936 ·

—At the Kremlin.

(Mol[otov], Kag[anovich], Andr[eev]. Yagoda, Slutsk[y],[61] Moskv[in], Uritsk[y].)[62]

—Organization of aid to the Spanish (via a smuggling scheme).

—France: We are not seeking to overthrow the Blum[63] government; we are, however, criticizing Blum (his statement on noninterference: "No country interferes").

—The position of the Sov[iet] government and the position of Commun[ists] in France need not be identical!

—Difficulties with the united front; does it follow from this that the

61. Abram A. Slutsky (d. 1938), head of the International section of the NKVD (1934–1938). He was liquidated in the Stalinist purges.

62. Semyon Petrovich Uritsky (1895–1937), head of the intelligence administration of the Red Army who directed Soviet military aid to the Spanish Republic. He was liquidated in the Stalinist purges.

63. Léon Blum (1872–1950), French Socialist leader; leader of the French Popular Front, which brought together the Socialists, Communists, and Radicals to win an electoral victory in 1936; premier (1936–1937, 1938) and vice premier of the Popular Front government (1937–1938). Arrested by the Vichy authorities in 1940, he was imprisoned until 1945. In 1946 he served as head of the Socialist cabinet. Blum was also a noted writer.

united front policy is counterproductive? (Mol[otov]: "The answer is there in your report to the congress.")[64]

· 15 SEPTEMBER 1936 ·

—Meeting of the secretariat. (Also participating: Thorez, Pollitt, Koplenig, Hathaway[65] (Am[erican]), Clément [Fried], Vassart.) Discussion of the new aspect of the international situation in connection with Spain, and so forth. Further pursuit of Popular Front policy. Correcting the mistake of the French comrades (the "French Front," Thorez's article on the arrival in France of the Polish general Rydz-Śmigły).

· 16 SEPTEMBER 1936 ·

—Meeting of the presidium.
Agenda:
1. Information on Spain and on the Popular Front in France
2. On the campaign in connection with the trial of the Trotsky[ite]-Zinovievite Center and the lessons of these trials for the Communist parties and the entire workers' movement
3. Information on the peace congress in Geneva and Brussels
—Kosarev gave a report on the Sixth Congress.[66] Very satisfactory results (he proposes among other things convening an international congress of Catholic youth).
—Thorez's report. Speeches by Florin, Pollitt, Koplenig (meeting adjourned to 17 September 1936).
—At Kaganovich's (with Thorez).
Question of arms smuggled from France to Spain. Everything necessary for that aim will be provided.
"Com[rade] Stal[in] thinks very highly of Thorez. Affairs are going well in France, and Thorez is leading the party well. His popularity in the ranks of our party and in our country is growing rapidly."

64. Reference to Dimitrov's report to the Seventh World Congress of the Comintern (1935).
65. Clarence Hathaway (1894?–1963), member of the CPUSA CC, editor of the *Daily Worker.* Expelled from the CPUSA in 1940.
66. Aleksandr Vasilievich Kosarev (1904–1939), secretary-general of the Komsomol, the Soviet youth organization (1929–1939), who was liquidated in the Stalinist purges. His report was on the Sixth Congress of the Communist Youth International (KIM).

—"The achievements of the Pop[ular] Front, those are thanks to you. You brought the *European* spirit with you when you came here."

· 17 SEPTEMBER 1936 ·

—Meeting of the presidium.
Shvernik's report (on the peace congress).
Codovilla's[67] report (on Spain).
Ercoli's [Togliatti's] report (on the trial and campaign).
Motion: creation of two commissions (in the center and in the localities).
—Thorez left by plane the morning of 17 September 1936.

· 18 SEPTEMBER 1936 ·

—Meeting of the secretariat.
Discussion of the Spanish party's policy and activities.
Internat[ional] campaign. Material assistance.
Initiative for a foreign conference of internat[ional] prolet[arian] organizations. (With Šmeral's participation as well.)
(Special discussion of the technical situation with Pollitt, Fried, and Codovilla.)
—*Marty* summoned from Madrid.

· 19 SEPTEMBER 1936 ·

—Meeting of the secretariat.
(*Gottwald* also participates.)
—On the Spanish party's policy.
—On the French party's line.
—Yugoslav question (leader[ship] of the party within the country, abroad Gork[ić]).[68]

67. Victorio Codovilla (Medina, 1894–1970), Italian Socialist and Argentinean Communist leader who emigrated to Argentina in 1912; founding member of the Argentinean CP and member of its CC and Politburo (1921–1970); member of the Comintern apparatus and delegate on various ECCI missions to Latin America and Spain; secretary-general (1941–1963) and president (1963–1970) of the Argentinian CP.

68. Milan Gorkić (pseudonym: Sommer; real name: Josip Čižinski, 1904–1938?), preeminent leader of the Yugoslav Communists beginning in 1932, con-

—English party issues (prep[aration] for discussion with the Engl[ish] delegation in early December).
—Publishing sector (Janson and Krebs!).[69]

—In the evening at my place (Man[uilsky], Mosk[vin], Ercoli [Togliatti], Kuu[sinen], Vassart, Pollitt, Fried, Codovilla, Arnott).[70]
—Agreed upon with Pollitt—discussion of the English question in December with the delegation: Pollitt, Kerrigan,[71] Campbell,[72] Gallacher,[73] Palme Dutt,[74] Horner,[75] Ferguson![76]

· 20 SEPTEMBER 1936 ·

—To the *crematorium!*
—Conference with *Uritsky, Agranov,*[77] and others on Chinese aid. (Memorandum to the PB on credit and so forth)

---

firmed as the secretary-general of the KPJ at this meeting, arrested in 1937 as a spy, and liquidated in the Stalinist purges. Gorkić was primarily responsible for the organizational revival of the KPJ in the 1930s.

69. M. Krebs, German Communist, worked in the Comintern's publishing section, along with Janson.

70. Robin Page Arnott (1890–?), British Communist, representative of the Communist Party of Great Britain (CPGB) on the Presidium of the ECCI starting in 1928.

71. Peter Kerrigan (1899–1977), British Communist leader active in Glasgow; political commissar in Spain.

72. John R. Campbell (1894–1969), British Communist leader; Scottish journalist; member of the CPGB EC (1923–1964); member of the ECCI (1925–1964); editor of the *Daily Worker* (1949–1959).

73. William Gallacher (1881–1965), British Communist leader, member of the ECCI Presidium from 1926 on, alternate member after 1935; member of Parliament (1935–1950); president of the CPGB (1956–1963).

74. R. Palme Dutt (1896–1974), British Communist leader and publicist; member of the CPGB EC (1922–1965) alternate member of the ECCI beginning in 1935, editor of the *Labour Monthly,* the *Workers' Weekly,* and, from 1936 to 1938, the *Daily Worker.*

75. Arthur Horner (1894–1968), British Communist leader; Welsh miner; president of the South Wales Miners' Federation (1936–1946); general secretary National Union of Mine Workers (1946–1959).

76. Aitken Ferguson, British CP leader.

77. Yakov Saulovich Agranov (1893–1938), first deputy people's commissar for internal affairs; head of the NKVD for the Saratov region (1937). He was liquidated in the Stalinist purges.

—Conference with *Koplenig* and others on Austrian issues (fascist dictatorship in Austria or a reactionary regime preparing for total fascist dictatorship?).

—With *Gottwald* on Czech affairs and on the peace movement commission.

—In the evening at 7:55 we left for Kislovodsk!

[. . .]

From 21 September 1936 to 22 November 1936, Dimitrov and his wife were on holiday and recuperating in the northern Caucasus. During that period Dimitrov met with Ordzhonikidze, Kolarov, Ponomarev, and others at the same retreat. He noted, without comment, the replacement of Yagoda by Yezhov and the removal of Rykov (27 September). He was increasingly disturbed by the reversals suffered by the Spanish Republicans, whose "government was moved to Valencia" (8 November).

Back in Moscow on 24 November 1936, Dimitrov plunged into various Comintern tasks, connected with the developments in Spain, France, China, Poland, and the Soviet Union itself. After the Xi'an incident, where Stalin harnessed the anti–Chiang Kai-shek sentiment of the Chinese Communists, Dimitrov addressed the recruitment for the International Brigades in Spain. Stalin was at one point prepared to discontinue recruitment in the United States (2 January 1937), but the recruitment continued by decision of the Soviet Politburo (7 January 1937).

The year 1937 marked the height of the Stalinist purges, which were slowly heading in the direction of the Comintern cadres. On 11 January, Dimitrov noted, without comment, that he had read Radek's testimony. He added, "Bukharin's guilt is beyond doubt." His comments on the February–March plenum of the Soviet party, which marked the fall of Bukharin, are laconic and overoptimistic. He made relatively few diary entries from 21 March to 21 October 1937. The hiatuses suggest the pressing weight of the purges. On 26 May 1937, Dimitrov was summoned to Yezhov's quarters at 1:00 a.m. He was informed that "the major spies worked in the Comintern." Examination of staff members commenced, as did the arrests. During this period, too, China continued to absorb Dimitrov's interest. On 28 March 1937, Chiang Ching-kuo, Chiang Kai-shek's son, en route to China, sent the following telegram from Sverdlovsk: "Sending you my most heartfelt Bolshevik regards from the road. All your instructions will be carried out."—I.B.

· 24 NOVEMBER 1936 ·

—In Moscow!
(Man[uilsky], Moskv[in], and others.)

· 25 NOVEMBER 1936 ·

—Opening of the Extraordinary Congress [of the Supreme Soviet].
—*Stalin's* report.

· 26 NOVEMBER 1936 ·

—*At the Kremlin.*
Conversation with Stalin.

. . . Our stance on Chi[nese] affairs will have to be altered. This approach with soviets is not going to work. Form a national-revolutionary government, a government of national defense, defense of the independence of the Chin[ese] people. *Soviets—only in the cities, but not as organs of power, rather of organization of the masses. Without confiscations. Come up with a draft. We'll take a look!*
—With *Voroshilov* about aid to the Chinese.

· 2 DECEMBER 1936 ·

—Received PB resolution (dated 2 December 1936) . . . *1,166 tons* of freight for the "nomads."[78]
To the People's Commissariat for Foreign Trade—trucks and so forth. Fuel, amm[unition] and so forth.
To the People's Commissariat for Finance, send a telegram—in addition to the 2,000,000 Soviet rubles already issued, also: 500 thousand Am[erican] dollars, 5,000 thousand Soviet rubles (of the 150,000 Am[erican] dol[lars] for an airplane of foreign make, which has already been ordered).
—484 military servicemen with appropriate specialties (drivers, technicians, comm[anding] officers) to be enlisted in the service of the Xinjiang government.
—Head of expedition Com[rade] Col[onel] Monakhov.

78. Reference to the Chinese Communists during the period of the Long March.

· 3 DECEMBER 1936 ·

—Editorial commission on the constitution [of the USSR]. Stal[in] chairs—
  Significant additions.

—Deng Fa's report (unfinished!).
—Rozenberg[79] has already arrived in Moscow.
—Telegram to Thorez: "We advise that in criticizing government policy and in parliamentary voting you be guided by the fact that in current conditions it is not in the interests of the French working class to force a government crisis, and *still less* the overthrow of the Blum government."
—Molotov called.
  Concerning Nicoletti's[80] telegram about the funeral for *Beimler*[81] on Red Square, St[alin] and Mol[otov] recommend that he apply officially to Shvernik, and then the matter will be favorably resolved.
—Madrid informed of this.

· 4 DECEMBER 1936 ·

—Meeting of the CC plenum.
Confirmation of the final draft of the constitution.
—Yezhov's report on the counterrevolutionary activities of Trotskyites and rightist organiz[ations]. Piatakov, Sokolnikov, Serebriakov, and others, Uglanov, Kruglikov, Kotov[82] (400 arrested in Ukr[aine], 400 in Leningrad, 150 in the Urals, and so forth).
—Speeches by Bukharin and Rykov (tears and protestations of innocence!)

79. M. I. Rozenberg, Soviet envoy in Spain; liquidated in the Stalinist purges.

80. Pseudonym of Giuseppe Di Vittorio (1892–1957), Italian Communist, member of the PCI Politburo, political commissar of the First International, the Eleventh International, and the Garibaldi brigades in Spain; after 1945, trade union leader and member of most important PCI forums.

81. Hans Beimler (1895–1936), German Communist; member of the KPD Politburo. Killed near Madrid in December 1936.

82. Y. L. Piatakov, G. Y. Sokolnikov, and L. P. Serebriakov were among the defendants in the trial of the "anti-Soviet Trotskyite Center" (Moscow, 23–30 January 1937); N. A. Uglanov, Kruglikov (probably M. M. Kulikov), and V. A. Kotov proffered testimony against Bukharin and Rykov, the leaders of the "Bloc of Rights."

—Speech by Stalin—*"The word of a former oppositionist cannot be trusted"; the suicides of Tomsky and others as a final, desperate means of struggle against the party* . . .
—Speeches by Molot[ov] and *Kaganovich*.
(Molotov cites Bukhar[in]'s letter to Voroshilov, "polit[ical] cowards.")

· 5 DECEMBER 1936 ·

—Meeting of the secretariat.

[. . .]

—In the evening—the adoption of the new constitution by the Eighth Extraordinary Congress [of the Supreme Soviet].
Stalin is speaker.

· 6 DECEMBER 1936

—*Rally and demonstration on Red Square* [in favor of the new constitution].
—In the evening at our place—Lakoba[83] and his wife, Semyonov,[84] Manuilsky, Damianov.

· 7 DECEMBER 1936 ·

—*Meeting of the plenum* [of the Soviet party].
—Stalin's motion not to decide the issue of Bukhar[in]-Rykov, but instead to continue the investigation, since the confrontation between Piatakov and others with Bukharin and Rykov indicates the necessity of continuing to investigate the case to the end.

83. Nestor Apolonovich Lakoba (1893–1936), Old Bolshevik; chairman of the Council of People's Commissars of the Abkhazian SSR (from 1922 on); chairman of the Central Executive Committee of the Abkhazian SSR (1930–1936). He was posthumously accused of Trotskyite leanings and nationalism.
84. Semyonov, secretary of the VKP(b) Crimean committee.

· 9 DECEMBER 1936 ·

—Bogomolov[85] to see me.

1. Japanese aggression in China will continue.
2. Nanjing can make no further serious territor[ial] concessions.
3. China will go to war with Japan.
4. The United Front movement is growing quickly.
5. Chiang Kai-shek[86] will decide on an agreement with the Communists only on the brink of war with Japan and in connection with an agreement with the Sov[iet] Union.
6. In the northwest, Chiang Kai-shek will not persecute the Red Army.

—Soong Qingling (the wife of Sun Yat-sen)[87] is almost a Communist.
—*Bogomolov* brought *Rust's*[88] son with him.

· 10 DECEMBER 1936 ·

—Rozenberg to see me.

1. Political leadership of the Intern[ational] Brigades must be organized.
2. Strengthen the commanding officer staff.
3. Send new and better workers.
4. Send Mandalian,[89] too, for the politi[cal]-[organ]izational work.
5. Regard the anarchists as a mass workers' organization.
6. Strengthen the social aspects in the platform of struggle against the rebels. [Reaction] of the petty bourgeois strata, of the peasantry; worker control, and so forth.

85. Aleksandr Yefremovich Bogomolov (1900–1969), Soviet diplomat; general secretary of the People's Commissariat for Foreign Affairs; envoy to London (1941–1943) and Paris (1944–1950).

86. Chiang Kai-shek (1888–1975), leader of the Chinese Nationalist Party (Guomindang) and head of the Guomindang government at Nanjing after 1928.

87. Sun Yat-sen (1886–1925), Guomindang leader, father of the Chinese republican revolution.

88. Unclear—Riust in Russian original.

89. Mandalian, member of Dimitrov's staff.

· 12 December 1936 ·

—At the Vakhtangov Theater. Intervention.[90]
—With Lakoba and his wife.

· 13 December 1936 ·

—Conversation with Cogniot (mem[ber] of the French CP CC).[91]
—News of the uprising of Zhang Xueliang's troops in Shaanxi. Chiang Kai-shek arrested.[92]
—Stomaniakov[93] to see me.
—Optimistic, favorable assessment regarding Zhang Xueliang. The Sov[iet] Union needs to be restrained and to respond skillfully to the anti-Soviet campaign in connection with the events in Xi'an.

· 14 December 1936 ·

—Meeting of the secretariat.
—*Cogniot's* report on the French situation.
Exchange of opinions—not to force a govern[ment] crisis.
To prepare for a *change of govern[ment]*.
—Conference on *Chinese affairs*.
—Sent Stalin the report by Deng Fa.
Asked his opinion on the position of our Chinese comrades. Suggested: "Advise them to adopt an independent position, to come out against internal internecine strife, to insist on a peaceful resolution of the con-

90. On 12 December 1936 the League of Nations took up the question of foreign intervention in Spain.

91. Georges Cogniot (1901–1978), representative of the PCF in the Comintern (1936–1937); deputy in the French parliament before and after the Second World War; editor of *L'Humanité;* close associate of Maurice Thorez.

92. Reference to the so-called Xi'an Incident. The Manchurian Guomindang warlord Zhang Xueliang (the "Young Marshal," 1901–2001), whom Chiang Kai-shek sent to Shaanxi to fight the Communists, became convinced that the anti-communist action was not a priority at a time of growing Japanese threat. He kidnapped Chiang at Xi'an with the aim of forcing him to agree to a common front with the Communists against Japan. The Communists, represented by Zhou Enlai, mediated Chiang's release on Christmas Day 1936, after Chiang gave implicit agreement to a change in the anticommunist course.

93. Boris Stomaniakov (1882–1941), Bulgarian, Soviet official; deputy people's commissar for foreign affairs. He was liquidated in the Stalinist purges.

flict, on agreement and joint actions, on a democratic platform for all parties and groups standing for the integrity and independence of China, emphasizing the position adopted by the party in its letter to the Guomindang and in the interview [with] Mao Zedong."

—Late, at 12 o'clock, a call from Stalin:

"Are these events in China occurring with your sanction? (—No!) This is the greatest service to Japan that anyone could possibly render. (—That's how we're regarding these events, too!)

"*Who is this Wang Ming of yours?* A provocateur? He wanted to file a telegram to have Chiang Kai-shek killed.

—(I haven't heard anything of the sort!)

I'll find you that telegram!"

—Molotov, later:

"*Come to Com[rade] St[alin]'s office tomorrow at 3:30; we'll discuss Ch[inese] affairs. Only you and Man[uilsky], nobody else!*"

· 15 DECEMBER 1936 ·

—Conference on the Ch[inese] question.

(Kuus[inen], Man[uilsky], Mosk[vin], Wang Ming, Deng Fa, Ercoli [Togliatti], Mandalian.)

· 16 DECEMBER 1936 ·

—With "the Five" in the Kremlin

(Stal[in], Molot[ov], Kag[anovich], Vor[oshilov], Ordzhonikidze).

Exchange of opinions on Ch[inese] events.

The following text of a telegram to the Ch[inese] CC agreed upon:

In reply to your telegrams we recommend adopting the following position:

1. Zhang Xueliang's action, whatever his intentions were, objectively can only harm the consolidation of the Chinese people's forces into a unified anti-Japanese front and encourage Japanese aggression with respect to China.

2. Since this action has been taken and we must reckon with the real facts of the matter, the Communist Party of China vigorously supports a peaceful resolution of the conflict on the following basis:

a) Reorganizing the government *through the inclusion* of *a few representatives* of the anti-Japanese movement, supporters of the integrity and independence of China

(The suggested text in our draft: "reorganizing the government from among *the most conspicuous activists* in the anti-Japanese movement, supporters of the integrity and independence of China")

b) Ensuring the democratic rights of the Chinese people

c) Discontinuing the policy of destroying the Red Army and establishing cooperation with it in the struggle against Japanese aggression

d) Establishing cooperation with states sympathetic toward the liberation of the Chinese people from the attack of Japanese imperialism

Finally we advise not bringing out the slogan of alliance with the USSR.

—On the French question:

St[alin]: "We should continue further with our current line: criticizing Blum, but without leading to his downfall.

—*Blum is a charlatan. He's no [Largo] Caballero.*"[94]

—From the investigation of Piatakov, Sokolnikov, Radek, and others:

Interrogation of Sokolnikov, 12 December 1936:

Question: Thus, the investigation concludes that Trotsky abroad and the center of the bloc within the USSR entered into negotiations with the Hitlerite and Japanese governments with the following aims:

First, to provoke a war by Germany and Japan against the USSR;

Second, to promote the defeat of the USSR in that war and to take advantage of that defeat to achieve the transfer of power in the USSR to [their] government bloc;

Third, on behalf of the future bloc government to guarantee territorial and economic concessions to the Hitlerite and Japanese governments.

Do you confirm this?

Reply: Yes, I confirm it.

Question: Do you admit that this activity by the bloc is tantamount to outright treason against the motherland?

Reply: Yes, I admit it.

· 17 DECEMBER 1936 ·

—Meeting of the secretariat.

—Leński's[95] report. Discussion postponed till 20 December.

94. Francisco Largo Caballero (1869–1946), Left Socialist leader and secretary of the executive of Unión General de Trabajadores (UGT), the Spanish Socialist trade union federation; prime minister and minister of war of the Spanish Republican government (September 1936–May 1937).

95. Julian Leński (real name: Julian Leszczyński, 1889–1937), participant in

· 18 December 1936 ·

—*Feuchtwanger* and Maria Osten to see us.[96]

On the trial [they say]:

1. It is incomprehensible why the accused committed such crimes.

2. It is incomprehensible why all the accused are admitting everything, knowing that it will cost them their lives.

3. It is incomprehensible why, apart from the confessions of the acc[used], no sort of evidence has been produced.

4. It is incomprehensible why such severe punishment is being applied to political opponents, when the Soviet regime is so powerful that it has nothing to fear from people sitting in prisons.

The records of the trial are carelessly compiled, full of contradictions, unconvincing.

The trial is conducted monstrously.

· 19 December 1936 ·

—Conference on Indonesian issues. *Musso*[97] must go to Amsterdam, discuss the directive on work in Indonesia with the PB and return here for the final decision.

· 20 December 1936 ·

—Meeting of the secretariat on the Polish question.

---

the October Revolution; secretary-general of the Polish CC (1929–1937); and member of the ECCI presidium from 1929 on. He was liquidated in the Stalinist purges.

96. Lion Feuchtwanger (real name: Jacob Arje, 1884–1958) and Maria Osten (real name: Greßhöner, 1908–1942), German antifascist writers. Feuchtwanger's booklet *Moscow, 1937*, which was published in the West after his visit to the USSR, presented a useful counterpoint to André Gide's critical *Return from the USSR*, published after Gide's visit to Russia in the summer of 1936. Unlike Gide, Feuchtwanger wrote sympathetically about the Soviet achievements and took a pro-Stalinist stand on the issue of Trotskyism and the Moscow trials. His booklet was published in translation in the USSR in the edition of two hundred thousand copies, which were snapped up in weeks. Despite its apologist nature, *Moscow, 1937* contained unvarnished references to Stalin and the oppositional objections to his rule. As a result, the booklet was withdrawn from the Soviet libraries a year after its publication.

97. Musso (pseudonym: Manavar, 1897?–1948), Indonesian Communist leader, member of the ECCI presidium after 1928. In Moscow from 1936 until Indonesian independence in 1948. Assumed the leadership of the Indonesian CP on 1 September 1948, he was killed by the government troops in October 1948 after a failed Communist uprising.

Basic issues:

1. Special forms and methods of the Popular Front movement

2. Organizat[ional] leadership of the party to emphasize resolving current work issues within the country, rather than abroad

3. Strengthening the party as a *Polish* party. A commission has been selected: D[imitrov], L[eński], Kol[arov], Moskv[in], Ercoli [Togliatti], Loz[ovsky]

—A conference of fem[ale] Red Army commanding and noncommissioned officers at the Kremlin.

—The following telegram sent to Thorez, Cachin:[98]

In view of the extreme intensification of intervention in Spanish affairs by the fascist states and the increased threat to the proletariat and Republican Spain, we consider it imperative that you meet in the capacity of Comintern delegates with de Brouckère[99] and advise them to form a coordinating committee between the Second and Third Internationals to deal with problems of assisting the Spanish people, such as

1. Taking measures against the transport and landing of German and Italian troops in Spain

2. Assistance with foodstuffs, medicines, the organization of field hospitals, evacuation of the civilian population, provision of means of transport (trucks), technical assistance through qualified forces that will contribute to the defense of Republican troops, and so forth

3. All manner of assistance to the volunteer movement for the benefit of the Spanish Republic

4. Sponsorship of the International Brigades

5. Joint political campaigns in defense of the Spanish people

To this end, recommend the formation of a coordinating committee dealing with individual countries.

We are also willing to discuss any other proposal that they may have for coordinating actions by the two Internationals for the benefit of the Spanish people.

· 21 DECEMBER 1936 ·

—*At Stal[in]'s (fifty-seventh birthday).*
Molotov, Vorosh[ilov], Kagan[ovich], Ordzh[onikidze], Andr[eev],

---

98. Marcel Cachin (1869–1958), French Communist leader, publisher of *L'Humanité,* and parliamentary deputy; member of the PCF CC (beginning in 1920); member of the ECCI (1923–1943) and of the ECCI presidium (beginning in 1935).

99. Louis de Brouckère (1870–1951), Belgian Socialist; one of the leaders of the Second (Socialist) International.

Mikoyan, Yezhov, Rudzutak,[100] Shkiriatov,[101] Bubnov,[102] Mezhlauk,[103] Liubimov,[104] Khrushchev, Bulganin, Budenny,[105] Bliukher,[106] Yegorov,[107] Tukhachevsky,[108] Sovarisian,[109] Gamarnik,[110] Manuil[sky] and Fr.[?]

100. Jan Ernestovich Rudzutak (1887–1938), Latvian Communist; Bolshevik organizer in the textile trade union; candidate-member of the Soviet CP PB; people's commissar of transport; chairman of the Soviet CP Central Control Commission. He was liquidated in the Stalinist purges.

101. Matvei Fyodorovich Shkiriatov (1883–1954), Soviet Communist leader; deputy head of the Party Control Commission (1939–1952).

102. Andrei Sergeevich Bubnov (1883–1940), Old Bolshevik, secretary of the Soviet CP CC (1925); people's commissar of education (1929–1937) of the Russian Socialist Federative Soviet Republic (RSFSR). He was liquidated in the Stalinist purges.

103. Valery Ivanovich Mezhlauk (1893–1938), Bolshevik leader in Kharkov (Ukraine) during the Revolution; member of the VKP(b) CC (from 1934 on); chairman of the State Planning Commission of the USSR (Gosplan, 1934–1937); people's commissar for heavy industry (after 1937). He was liquidated in the Stalinist purges.

104. Isidor Yevstinievich Liubimov (1882–1939), Soviet party activist. He was liquidated in the Stalinist purges.

105. Semyon Mikhailovich Budenny (1883–1973), marshal of the Soviet Union (1935); first deputy people's commissar for Defense (from 1940 on); commander of the Red Cavalry.

106. Vasily Konstantinovich Bliukher (1889–1938), marshal of the Soviet Union (1935); commander of the Southern Ural Partisan Army and the Perekop Division in the Civil War; commander-in-chief, war minister, and chairman of the Military Council of the Far Eastern Republic (1921–1922); Soviet military adviser in China (1924–1927); commander of the Red Banner Army of the Far East (from 1929 on). He was liquidated in the Stalinist purges.

107. Aleksandr Ilich Yegorov (1883–1939), marshal of the Soviet Union (1935). He commanded the Kiev and Petrograd military districts, the Caucasian Red Banner Army, and (from 1927 on) the Belorussian military district. Chief of general staff of the Soviet Army (1931–1937); first deputy people's commissar for defense (after 1937); candidate-member of the VKP(b) CC (after 1934). He was liquidated in the Stalinist purges.

108. Mikhail Nikolaevich Tukhachevsky (1893–1937), marshal of the Soviet Union (1935). He held numerous command posts in the Civil War. Member of the Military-Revolutionary Council (MRC) and commander of the Western Military District (1924); chief of staff of the Red Army (1925); deputy chairman of the RMC (1931); deputy people's commissar for defense (1935) and first deputy people's commissar (1936). He was liquidated with a number of other Red Army commanders in the Stalinist purges.

109. Identity unclear.

110. Yan Borisovich Gamarnik (1894–1937), Ukrainian Bolshevik; political commissar in the armed forces; head of the political administration of the Red

(Stalin's children not there. No one from the Narkomindel [People's Commissariat for Foreign Affairs]. Mekhlis[111] not there either.)

—(Till 5:30 in the morning!)

· 22 DECEMBER 1936 ·

—Polish commission.

(Dim[itrov], Man[uilsky], Moskv[in], Leński, Bronk[owski],[112] Skulski)[113]

—Resolution of the secretariat.

—*New—the course toward fully fledged leadership in the country!*

—Razumova[114] and Gerő—on Spanish affairs.

Internat[ional] Brigades—up to 9,500 men have been sent.

[. . .]

· 16 JANUARY 1937 ·

—Sent Com[rade] Stalin the draft telegram to the Chin[ese] Comm[unist] Party. (Correction of the party line toward joint action with the Guomindang.)

Army and member of the RMC (1929), editor of the *Krasnaia zvezda* (1929); deputy people's commissar for defense and deputy chairman of the RMC (from 1930 on); member of the Soviet CP CC from 1927 on. He committed suicide during the Stalinist purges.

111. Lev Zakharovich Mekhlis (1889–1953), Soviet Communist leader who worked in the apparatus of the VKP(b) CC and in the party daily *Pravda*. He headed the main political directorate of the Red Army (1937–1940). People's commissar for state control (1940–1941, 1945–1953); member of the VKP(b) CC (1939–1953). He did political work for the Red Army during the war.

112. Bronisław Bortnowski (pseudonym: Bronkowski, 1894–1937), member of the PPK PB (from 1930 on), member of the ECCI presidium. He was liquidated in the Stalinist purges.

113. Stefan Skulski (real name: Stanisław Martens, 1892–1937), Polish Communist leader. In USSR from 1928 on, he studied at the Institute of Red Professors and worked on the Kuibyshev regional VKP(b) committee. Member of the PPK CC (from 1923 on) and its PB (from 1935 on). He was liquidated in the Stalinist purges.

114. Anna Lazarevna Razumova (1899–1973), Soviet Communist on the ECCI staff.

· 17 JANUARY 1937 ·

—Instructions for the campaign connected with the coming trial of Piatakov, Radek, and others.

[. . .]

· 19 JANUARY 1937 ·

—At the Kremlin (Stal[in], Molot[ov], Andr[eev], Zhdanov, Yezhov).
—Directive for the Chin[ese] CC—
1. Course in support of all measures taken by the Guomindang and Nanj[ing] gov[ernment] aimed at cessation of civil war and unification of all forces of the Chin[ese] people in the struggle against Japanese aggression
2. Inquire of the CC: Does it not now consider it timely to shift from the soviet system to the popular-revolutionary system of administration with all its attendant implications?

· 20 JANUARY 1937 ·

—Meeting of the secretariat.
Report by Humbert-Droz[115] (Swiss party).
Information on China (the secretariat directive).
On the campaign connected with the trial of Piatakov, Radek, and others.

· 21 JANUARY 1937 ·

—Publication of the report by the USSR prosecutor [general] on the trial of Piatakov-Radek, and the others. (Trial set to begin 23 January.)
—Evening at the Bolshoi Theater.
(Evening in commemoration of the thirteenth anniversary of Lenin's death.)

115. Jules Humbert-Droz (1891–1971), Protestant pastor, founding member of the Swiss CP, member of its CC and PB; member of the ECCI presidium (1921–1922), ECCI secretary (1921–1929), member of the Comintern's political secretariat (1926–1928), and head of the Latin secretariat. After the German attack on the USSR he joined the work of the Soviet espionage network (Rote Kapelle). Expelled from the Swiss CP in 1943, he joined the Swiss Social Democrats and became their secretary-general (1947–1958).

· 22 JANUARY 1937 ·

—Evening at the Vakhtangov Theater.
Performance of *Florisdorf*.
(For the most part a favorable impression. A strong piece. Some superfluous moralizing and overheated agitation. A number of political elements rang false.)

· 23 JANUARY 1937 ·

—The [Piatakov-Radek] trial began.
—Responsible troika formed for administering information and the campaign (Ercoli [Togliatti], Shubin,[116] Ponomarev).
—Cachin, Gottwald, Linderot,[117] Andersen-Nexö,[118] and others summoned.

· 24 JANUARY 1937 ·

—Examination of the defendants.

· 25 JANUARY 1937 ·

—Wieden,[119] his wife, Uritsky.

· 26 JANUARY 1937 ·

—Conversation with Gottwald and Zápotocký.[120]

---

116. Pyotr Abramovich Shubin (1878–1937), Dimitrov aide in the Comintern apparatus. He was liquidated in the Stalinist purges.

117. Sven Linderot (1889–1956), founding member of the Swedish CP (SKP); chairman (secretary) of SKP (1929–1951); member of the ECCI (from 1935 on); member of the Swedish parliament (1938–1949).

118. Martin Andersen-Nexö (1869–1954), Danish Communist writer; member of the DKP CC.

119. Pseudonym of Ernst Fischer.

120. Antonín Zápotocký (1884–1957), founding member of the Communist Party of Czechoslovakia (KSČ) and member of its CC from 1921 on; head of the Communist trade unions in Czechoslovakia (1929–1939); candidate-member of the ECCI from 1924 on. Confined by the Germans in the Sachsenhausen concentration camp during the occupation. After the Communist coup in Czechoslovakia he became the country's prime minister (1948–1953) and president (1953–1957).

· 27 JANUARY 1937 ·

—Meeting of the secretariat [of the ECCI] on Czech trade union issues (formation of a commission).

· 28 JANUARY 1937 ·

—Meeting of the commission on the Czech question.
—In the evening Zápotocký departed.
—Conversation with Gottwald.
—Vyshinsky's[121] indictment.

· 29 JANUARY 1937 ·

—Final version of the directive on Czech trade union issues.
—Gottwald departed.
—Final words of the defendants.

· 30 JANUARY 1937 ·

—(Morning.)
The sentencing: Radek, Sokolnikov, Arnold, Stroilov—prison terms.
The rest—the death penalty.

· 31 JANUARY 1937 ·

—The secretariat (expanded meeting).
On the campaign in connection with the trial of the anti-S[oviet] Trotskyite Center. (Cach[in], Cout[urier]-V[aillant],[122] Humbert-Droz, Linderot, Shakhler.[123])

---

121. Andrei Yanuarievich Vyshinsky (1883–1954), Soviet jurist, professor of law at Moscow State University and rector of the university (1925); procurator-general of the USSR (1935–1939), prosecutor at the Moscow trials; deputy people's commissar for foreign affairs (1940–1949); foreign minister (1949–1953); permanent representative to the United Nations (1953–1954).

122. Paul Vaillant-Couturier 1892–1937), jurist and founding member of the PCF; member of the PCF CC (from 1920 on); member of parliament; editor of *L'Humanité* (1926–1937).

123. Shakhler, member of the Comintern staff.

· 1 FEBRUARY 1937 ·

—Meeting of the commission to work up the resolution [on the trial].

· 2 FEBRUARY 1937 ·

—Feuchtwanger to see me (Comintern).
(He was accompanied by Maria Osten.)
What had impressed him the most was a) the training of our young people and their thirst for knowledge, b) the plan for the construction of Moscow.

On the trial:

1. Diversionary actions, espionage, terror—proved.
2. Also proved: that Trotsky inspired and directed.
3. Trotsky's agreement with Hess[124] and the Japanese is based only on the confessions of the defendants.

—No evidence whatsoever!

4. The fact that Radek and Sokolnikov were not sentenced to be shot will be exploited abroad as evidence that they furnished such testimony deliberately in order to save their lives.
5. The abuse hurled at the defendants leaves a disturbing impression. They are enemies, deserving of destruction. But they did not act out of personal interest, and they should not to have called them scoundrels, cowards, reptiles, etc.
6. Why such a great fuss over the trial. Incomprehensible. An atmosphere has been created of extreme unrest among the population, mutual suspicion, denunciations, and so forth. Trotskyism has been killed—why such a campaign?

—Short pamphlet with factual materials on achievements in the USSR, without ignoring the deficiencies.

—Antifascist Day with a half-hour strike.

· 5 FEBRUARY 1937 ·

—Reply to teleg[ram] from the CPC [Communist Party of China] (concerning the Guomindang's appeal to the plenum).

---

124. At the trial Piatakov and Radek testified that Trotsky had negotiated with Hitler's deputy, Rudolf Hess, the transfer of Ukraine to Germany, and of the Amur and Far Eastern regions to Japan.

—Molotov (by secure telephone)—the Chinese CC proposal is acceptable. (He altered the draft of the reply in that sense.)

· 7 FEBRUARY 1937 ·

—Discussion with Cachin and Vaillant-Couturier on French and Spanish affairs.
(They departed.)

· 8 FEBRUARY 1937 ·

—Meeting of the secretariat.
Report by Ulbricht on German affairs and election of commission.

· 10 FEBRUARY 1937 ·

—The German commission.

· 11 FEBRUARY 1937 ·

—At the Bolshoi Theater tonight. (An evening of Pushkin.)
—Conversation with Stal[in] about the resolution by the presidium [of the ECCI] on the anti-Trotskyite campaign.
Stal[in]—
1. You are not taking into account that the Europ[ean] workers think that everything is happening because of some quarrel between me and Tr[otsky], because of St[alin]'s bad char[acter].
2. It must be pointed out that these people fought against Lenin, against the party during Lenin's lifetime.
3. Quote Lenin on the opposition: "Any opposition in the party under Sov[iet] power that insists on _____ is slipping directly toward whiteguardism."
4. References to the stenographic report of the trial. Quote the defendants' testimony.
5. Play up their politics and their working for the defeat of the Sov[iet] Union.

The resolution is nonsense. All of you there in the Comintern are playing right into the enemy's hands . . .

There is no point making a resolution; resolutions are binding. A letter to the parties would be better.

· 13 FEBRUARY 1937 ·

—Report by Relecom[125] on Belgium.
Commission has been elected.

· 14 FEBRUARY 1937 ·

—Discussion with the Italian comrade Boci [?].
—Instructed Razumova (trip to Paris).
—Informational radio communications have been discontinued.
—Discussion with the new diplomatic representative in Spain Raikis [?].

· 15 FEBRUARY 1937 ·

—Ill (at home).
—In the evening: Man[uilsky], Kuus[inen], Ponomarev.

· 16 FEBRUARY 1937 ·

—Edited the final text of the letter on the Trotskyite Center trial at home.

· 17 FEBRUARY 1937 ·

—Discussion of the Belgian resolution (Man[uilsky], Relecom, B[arsky?]).[126]
—Sent Stal[in] the draft letter.

· 18 FEBRUARY 1937 ·

—*Sergo* [Ordzhonikidze] is dead! (17:30)
Found out at 12 o'clock.

125. Xavier Relecom (1901–1977), Belgian Communist leader; member of the Belgian CP CC and PB after 1929; secretary-general (1936–1941). He spent most of the occupation (1941–1945) in a German concentration camp and was eased out of the leadership after the war. In 1963 he joined the pro-Chinese faction led by Jacques Grippa, from which he was expelled in 1967.
126. Barsky, Comintern staff member.

Wrote the Comintern obituary from the ECCI for *Pravda*.
—Was at the Kremlin [to see] the late Sergo. (I found Kag[anovich], Mikoyan, and others, still there.)

· 19 FEBRUARY 1937 ·

—The secretariat.
(Honor guard for Sergo. The House of Soviets.)

[. . .]

· 20 FEBRUARY 1937 ·

—Meeting of the German commission (resolution on political and practical issues).

[. . .]

· 22 FEBRUARY 1937 ·

—German commission.
—On the political resolution.

· 23 FEBRUARY 1937 ·

—German commission on the organizational questions.
—[Soviet CP] CC plenum in the evening.
Yezhov's report on *the Bukharin and Rykov case*.[127]

—*Bukharin's* speech (disgusting and pathetic spectacle!)
—During a pause Karakhan tells the following: "Last year I rode in the same train with Tsar Boris.[128] The Turkish minister introduced

---

127. The February–March Plenum of the Soviet CP CC was entirely devoted to the case of Bukharin and Rykov. For the documents of the plenum, see J. Arch Getty and Oleg V. Namov, *The Road to Terror: Stalin and the Self-Destruction of the Bolsheviks, 1932–1939* (New Haven, 1999), pp. 364–419.

128. Lev Mikhailovich Karakhan (real surname: Karakhanian, 1889–1937), Soviet Communist leader of Armenian nationality; member of the RSDRP(b) from 1917 on; member of the Military-Revolutionary Council in October 1917. He served as secretary of the Soviet delegation at the Brest-Litovsk peace talks, deputy people's commissar for foreign affairs (1918–1920, 1927–1934), and Soviet envoy to Poland (1921), China (1923–1926), and Turkey (1934–1937). His appointment to Ankara annoyed the Turkish government because of his ethnic origin

us. Tsar Boris announced that 'we Bulgarians are proud of Dimitrov.' During [his] trial I was invited to visit Germany. But I stated: 'I can make no official visit to Germany until Dimitrov is released. And I acted to bring about his release.'"

—Karakhan: But by doing so you did the Communists a favor, since Dimitrov is now general secretary of the Comintern.

—Tsar Boris: Despite that, I am glad I stood up for him. There was an earlier incident, too, when some people in Bulgaria wanted to kill him, but I did everything to prevent it.

("Wily" tsar!)

· 24 FEBRUARY 1937 ·

—Meeting of the plenum (6 o'clock in the evening). Discussion of the Bukh[arin]-Ryk[ov] case.

· 25 FEBRUARY 1937 ·

—Two meetings—continuation of the discussion.

· 26 FEBRUARY 1937 ·

—Discussion. Election of the commission.

· 27 FEBRUARY 1937 ·

—Discussion with the Danish writer Andersen-Nexö.
—Zhdanov's report on democracy.
—Resolution on the Bukh[arin]-Ryk[ov] case. (Expulsion from the party; turn the case over to the NKVD.)
—Marty arrived!

· 28 FEBRUARY 1937 ·

—Report by Molotov.
—Report by Kaganovich.
Discussion.

---

and abrasive style. He was liquidated in the Stalinist purges. Boris III of Saxe-Coburg and Gotha (1894–1943), tsar of Bulgaria (1918–1943). He established a personal dictatorship in 1935.

· 1 MARCH 1937 ·

—Discussion of report.

· 2 MARCH 1937 ·

—Report by Yezhov.
Discussion.

· 3 MARCH 1937 ·

—Report by Stalin.
   (On Point 4.)[129]
—"Things got better after the report!"

· 4 MARCH 1937 ·

—Discussion.
—Concluding speech by Stalin (invaluable instructions).
—Closing of the plenum.
   (Truly a historic plenum!)

· 6 MARCH 1937 ·

—Looked over Molotov's old dacha (in Meshcherino).
   Suitable!

· 7 MARCH 1937 ·

—Marty's report on Spain.
—Commission (in the evening).

129. Stalin reported to the February–March CC plenum of the commission on the affair of Bukharin and Rykov. According to a recently published collection of sources (J. Arch Getty and Oleg V. Naumov, *The Road to Terror,* pp. 409–11), the report was made on 27 February 1937). Here it is dated 3 March 1937. It is not clear what Point 4 was, for the resolution of the plenum, which is dated 3 March 1937, has no Point 4, unless the conclusion, calling for the expulsion of Bukharin and Rykov from candidate-membership in the CC and from the party, and the turning over of their case to the NKVD for further investigation, is taken as such. This was ostensibly more lenient treatment than that accorded to the Trotskyite-Zinovievite opposition.

· 8 MARCH 1937 ·

—International Women's Day—the Bolshoi Theater.
—Spanish writers—Alberti and María de León.[130]
—Manuilsky in the Barvikha.

· 9 MARCH 1937 ·

—Commission on German issues.
—(Defense apparatus, etc.)

· 10 MARCH 1937 ·

—Chinese affairs.
(Chiang Kai-shek's son to be summoned and sent to China.)[131]

· 11 MARCH 1937 ·

—Discussion with the women's delegation on raising the women's question in the presidium.
—Bogoliubov[132] to see me.
(Vŭlko [Chervenkov].)

· 12 MARCH 1937 ·

—At Manuilsky's (the Barvikha).
—Evening at our place—Foster,[133] Marty, Ercoli.

---

130. Rafael Alberti (1902–1999), and his wife, María Teresa León (1904–1988), Spanish Communist poets, founders of the review *Octubre* (October). They rendered various cultural services to the Republican side in the Civil War, then lived in exile in France, Argentina, and Italy until their return to Spain in 1977. Alberti was one of the most important twentieth-century Spanish writers—"bucolic poet of the revolution."

131. Chiang Ching-kuo (1910–1988), future president of the Republic of China (1978–1988). He studied at Sun Yat-sen University in Moscow and the military academy in Leningrad. In 1936 he referred to his father as an "enemy of the people."

132. Bogoliubov, most likely a reference to A. Ye. Bogomolov.

133. William Z. Foster (1881–1961), president of the CPUSA (1929–1938); member of the Central Council of the Profintern (1922–1937), of the ECCI (1924–1943), and of its presidium (1935–1943).

· 13 MARCH 1937 ·

—At [M. S.] Andreev's[134] (with Moskv[in]).
We examined the CI [Communist International] budget.
(A tendency to cut subsidies to the parties—greater reliance on the masses!)

· 14 MARCH 1937 ·
[. . .]

—Evening at the Kremlin (PB).
Stalin, Voroshilov, Molotov (later Kag[anovich]).
—With Marty and Ercoli [Togliatti].
—Discussion on Spanish affairs.
—Merge the Com[munist] and Socialist parties into a common Socialist Workers' Party. (If the Socialists insist, the combined party is not included in the CI, and then it need not be included in the Second International either.)
—The slogan "They shall not pass!"—a slogan of resistance!
   (An offensive is what is needed!)
—No need to overthrow Caballero.
   (There is no more suitable figure to serve as head of government.)
—Get Caballero to renounce the post of minister of war (and appoint someone else commander in chief).
—During a possible reconstruction the Communists can demand greater participation by the party in government.
—If there is a decision for foreign forces to leave Spain, the Internat[ional] Brigades are to be disbanded and left in the rear, as production workers, and so forth.
—Continue the recruitment—
(a special Catalonian Internat[ional] Brigade).
(St[alin] motions to gather at his dacha on 16 March 1937.)

· 15 MARCH 1937 ·

—Discussion with the departing Chinese (to Shanghai).
—Cogniot departs for Paris on 16 March 1937 (assignment).

---

134. Soviet Communist; head of the Cadre Department at the ECCI.

· 16 March 1937 ·

—At Stalin's (dacha).
Stal[in], Mol[otov], Kag[anovich], Vor[oshilov], Mikoyan.
  (Marty, Ercoli [Togliatti] and I.)
    —until 2:30 in the morning.
—Cordially received, especially Marty. St[alin] joked: "All the same, Ercoli has his detachment, Marty has the organization of the International Brigades, but you do not see any Bulgarians; there aren't any; the Academy of Sciences has been told to get to the bottom of it!"
  —Several times he made jokes to that effect (not by chance, perhaps?).

· 17 March 1937 ·

—Meeting of the secretariat.
Report by Koplenig.
Report by Hardy[135] on the South African Party.
Browder arrived.

· 18 March 1937 ·

—At our place: Manuil[sky], Ercoli [Togliatti], Marty, Browder, Moskvin.
—Information from Browder—
—Discussion of issues relating to Marty's trip.
(Watched a film, *Paris Dawns.*)

· 19 March 1937 ·

—Meeting of the Austrian commission.
(Koplenig, Honner,[136] Fürnberg, Wieden [Fischer].)

135. George Hardy (1884–1966), British Communist leader; secretary of the International Workers of the World (IWW) maritime workers in Canada and the United States; trade union activist; member of the Central Council of the Profintern (1928–1930). He was in China (1927–1930) on trade union work. Instructor to the CP of South Africa (1936).
136. Franz Honner (pseudonym: Neudel, 1893–1964), Austrian Communist, member of the KPÖ CC from 1927 on; member of the ECCI staff (1939–1943). He was sent in 1944 to Yugoslavia, where he helped organize an Austrian battal-

—Party conference in mid-June.

CC—(approximate composition).

—Marty departed.

· 20 MARCH 1937 ·

[. . .]

—*Stalin* received the Spanish writers Rafael Alberti and María-Teresa León.

Gopner[137] translated. As she tells it, the highlights of Stalin's discussion were

a) *The nature of the revolution in Spain*—

The people and the whole world must be told the truth—*the Spanish people are in no condition now to bring about a proletarian revolution*—the internal and especially the international situation do not favor it. (Things were different in Russia in 1917—[geographic] expanses, wartime, squabbles among the capitalist countries, in the bourgeoisie, and so forth.) In Spain the proclamation of the Soviets—to unite all capit[alist] states and defeat fascism.

b) On the global scale Spain is now the vanguard. The vanguard is always inclined to run ahead of events—and herein lies a great danger. Victory in Spain will loosen fascism's hold in Italy and Germany.

c) Communist and Socialist parties must join forces—they now share the same basic aims—(a democratic republic). Such a union will strengthen the Popular Front and have a great effect on the anarchists.

d) Caballero has demonstrated his resolute character and his will to fight against fascism. Caballero must be preserved as head of government. It would be better to leave commanding to someone else.

e) The general staff is unreliable.

There has always been betrayal on the eve of an offensive by Republic[an] units.

The Republican Army wins its offensives when the general staff has no knowledge of them!

---

ion within the Partisan army. Undersecretary of the interior in the provisional government of Austria (1945); deputy chairman of the KPÖ (1945–1951); member of the Austrian parliament.

137. Serafima Ilinichna Gopner (1880–1966), representative from the Ukrainian CP organization to the Comintern; candidate-member of the ECCI (1928–1943); member of the ECCI secretariat staff.

—The battle on the Guadalajara front makes that perfectly clear![138]
f) Madrid must under no circumstances be surrendered. The fall of Madrid would be followed by recognition of Franco by England, would cause complete demoralization among the Republic[ans], and would lead to a final defeat.
g) A fascist coup in France cannot be ruled out. But conditions in France are different.
—The French bourgeoisie is better armed against fascism.
h) He believes in the victory of the Spanish Republic. After overt intervention by the Italians and Germans, the Spanish Republic will fight harder, as defenders against foreign conquerors.

[. . .]

· 26 MAY 1937 ·

—At Yezhov's (1 o'clock in the morning)
(The major spies worked in the Comintern.)

· 27 MAY 1937

—Examination of the apparatus [of the ECCI].

· 13 JUNE 1937 ·

—*Manuilsky has taken sick with scarlet fever.*

· 17 JUNE 1937 ·

—Leński arrived.
—Rilski, Skulski, and Próchniak[139] have also been summoned.

138. In March 1937 the Republican army defeated Franco's Italian allies at Guadalajara, on the outskirts of Madrid.
139. Edward Próchniak (1888–1937), Polish Communist leader; member of the PPK CC (from 1918 on) and candidate-member of its Politburo (1933–1937); member of the ECCI (1922–1924, 1928–1935); member of the ICC (1924–1928); candidate-member of the ECCI (1935–1937). He was liquidated in the Stalinist purges.

· 20 JUNE 1937 ·

L[eński] at "Yezhov's."

· 21 JUNE 1937 ·

Walecki, too.[140]

[. . .]

· 7 NOVEMBER 1937 ·

—Parade and demonstration.
—From a conversation with Stalin:

> Explanations concerning the instances [that have been] uncovered of counterrevolutionary activities (arrests and so on) in the Soviet CP [VKP(b)] and the CI will have to wait a bit longer, until all the necessary materials have been worked up. There's no point in furnishing piecemeal information.
>
> *Knor[in]* is a Polish and German spy (for a long time, and until recently).
>
> *Rakovsky*[141] has been working for the intelligence service (English intelligence) since before the Revolution and until recently. He recruited Bogomolov, too, for English intelligence.
>
> *Piatnitsky* is a Trotskyite. Everyone's testimony points to him (Knor[in] and others).

140. Henryk Walecki (real name: Maksymilian Horwitz, 1877–1938), participant in the Zimmerwald movement during the First World War; founding member of the PPK and member of the PPK CC (1920–1925); member of the Comintern apparatus after 1925; assistant head of the Balkan secretariat (1928–1935); editor of *Communist International.* He was liquidated in the Stalinist purges.

141. Christian Rakovsky (1873–1941); Bulgarian physician from Kotel, Romanian subject active in the Bulgarian, Romanian, and Russian socialist movements; secretary of the Central Bureau of the Revolutionary Balkan Workers' Social Democratic Federation (1915); participant in the Zimmerwald movement and in the Kienthal conference (1916). He was arrested in Romania after its entry into war, then freed by the Russian troops in Iași (1917); after going to Russia, he joined the Bolsheviks in Petrograd. Chairman of the Council of People's Commissars of Ukraine (elected in March 1918); member of the Russian and Ukrainian CP CC (1919–1924); member of the Soviet delegation at the Genoa conference (1923); Soviet envoy to Britain (1923) and France (1925); member of the Trotskyist opposition. Rakovsky was expelled from the party in 1927, exiled to Astrakhan, and after having recanted, in 1934, was reinstated. He headed the Red Cross and Red Crescent societies. Arrested in 1937, he was a defendant in the Bukharin trial ("The Bloc of Rights and Trotskyites," March 1938). Sentenced to twenty years of imprisonment, he was executed in 1941.

First pages of entry dated 7 November 1937.

Kun acted with the Trotskyites against the party. In all likelihood, he is involved in espionage as well. His role in the suppression of the Hungarian revolution is very suspicious.

Antipov,[142] Vareikis,[143] and others were tsarist intelligence agents.

There are certain materials indicating that Trotsky, too, was in the tsar's intelligence service from 1904 to 1905. This is now being investigated.

Yakovlev's wife turned out to be a French spy.[144] In 1918 she betrayed the military-revolutionary committee in Odessa.

—Lunch at Voroshilov's (after the demonstration).
Present: 1) Stal[in], 2) Mol[otov], 3) Vor[oshilov], 4) Kag[anovich], 5) Kalin[in], 6) Andreev, 7) Mikoyan, (8) Yezhov, 9) Chubar,[145] 10) Shkiriatov, 11) Khrushchev, 12) Bulganin, 13) Budenny, 14) Yegorov, 15) Shaposhnikov,[146] 16) Viktorov,[147] 17) Kosarev, 18) Shvernik, 19)

142. Nikolai Kirillovich Antipov (1894–1938), Soviet Communist leader who worked in the Cheka and trade unions; member of the RKP(b) CC (from 1924 on); secretary of the Ural oblast committee (1925), of the Leningrad provincial committee, and of the Northwestern Bureau of the VKP(b) CC (1926–1927); deputy people's commissar for Worker-Peasant Inspection (RKI) from 1931 on; deputy chairman of the Council of People's Commissars (SNK) and the Council for Labor and Defense (STO); and chairman of Commission of Soviet Control at the (SNK). He was liquidated in the Stalinist purges.

143. Iosif Mikhailovich Vareikis (1894–1939), chairman during the Civil War of provincial RKP(b) organizations in Simbirsk and Kiev, deputy chairman of the Baku Soviet, secretary of the Turkestan CP CC; member of the VKP(b) CC (from 1930 on); secretary of the Stalingrad territorial committee (1935–1936), and of the Far Eastern regional committee of the VKP(b) (1937). He was liquidated in the Stalinist purges.

144. A reference to the wife of Yakov A. Yakovlev, people's commissar for agriculture.

145. Vlas Yakovlevich Chubar (1891–1939), chairman of the SNK of Ukraine (1923–1934); deputy chairman of the SNK of the USSR and of the STO (1934); people's commissar for finance (1937); member of the VKP(b) Politburo (1935–1937). He was liquidated in the Stalinist purges.

146. Boris Mikhailovich Shaposhnikov (1882–1945), Soviet military commander; marshal of the Soviet Union; colonel in the tsarist army who volunteered into the Red Army in 1918; commander of the Leningrad, Moscow, and Volga military districts after the Civil War; head of the Frunze Military Academy (1932–1935); head of the general staff of the Red Army (1941–1942); head of the Voroshilov Higher Military Academy (1943–1945); candidate-member of the VKP(b) CC (from 1939 on).

147. Mikhail Vladimirovich Viktorov (1894–1938), Soviet naval commander; tsarist naval officer who joined the Red Navy after the Revolution; participant in the suppression of the Kronstadt uprising (1921); commander of the Baltic (1921–1924) and Black Sea (1924–1926) naval forces; commander of the Baltic (1926–1932) and Pacific (1932–1937) fleets; chief of the military council of the naval forces (1937–1938). He was liquidated in the Stalinist purges.

Frinovsky,[148] 20) Redens,[149] 21) Dagin,[150] 22) representative of the NKVD in the Red Army, 23) Mezhlauk, 24) commandant of the Kremlin, 25) Vorosh[ilov's] wife, (26) D[imitrov].

Voroshilov's toast to Stalin.

Toastmaster Mikoyan proposes witty toasts for everyone in turn. Voroshilov and Mikoyan. Once more [a toast] to the great Stalin.

Stal[in]: I would like to say a few words, perhaps not festive ones. The Russian tsars did a great deal that was bad. They robbed and enslaved the people. They waged wars and seized territories in the interests of landowners. But they did one thing that was good—they amassed an enormous state, all the way to Kamchatka. We have inherited that state. And for the first time, we, the Bolsheviks, have consolidated and strengthened that state as a united and indivisible state, not in the interests of landowners and capitalists, but for the benefit of the workers, of all the peoples that make up that state. We have united the state in such a way that if any part were isolated from the common socialist state, it would not only inflict harm on the latter but would be unable to exist independently and would inevitably fall under foreign subjugation. Therefore, whoever attempts to destroy that unity of the socialist state, whoever seeks the separation of any of its parts or nationalities—that man is an enemy, a sworn enemy of the state and of the peoples of the USSR. And we will destroy each and every such enemy, even if he was an old Bolshevik; we will destroy all his kin, his family. We will mercilessly destroy anyone who, by his deeds or his thoughts—yes, his thoughts—threatens the unity of the socialist state. To the complete destruction of all enemies, themselves and their kin! (Approving exclamations: To the great Stalin!)

Stal[in]: I have not finished my toast. A great deal is said about great leaders. But a cause is never won unless the right conditions exist. *And the main thing here is the middle cadres—party, economic, military. They're the ones who choose the leader, explain our positions to the masses, and ensure the success of our cause. They don't try to climb above their station; you don't even notice them.*

148. Mikhail P. Frinovsky (1898–1940), Soviet security operative; chairman of the OGPU in Azerbaijan (1930–1933); head of the Chief Directorate for Border Troops of the OGPU (1933); deputy, then first deputy, people's commissar for Internal Affairs (1936–1938). He was liquidated in the Stalinist purges.

149. S. F. Redens (1892–1940), Soviet security operative; head of the directorate of the NKVD for the Moscow region (1935–1937); People's Commissar for Internal Affairs in Kazakhstan (1938). He was liquidated in the Stalinist purges.

150. I. Ya. Dagin (1895–1940), Soviet security operative; head of the First (Security) Department of the Main Administration for State Security (GUGB) of the NKVD. He was liquidated in the Stalinist purges.

D[imitrov]: And to the one who inspires them, shows them the way, and leads them—to Com[rade] Stalin!

Stalin: No, no. The main thing is the middle cadres. Generals can do nothing without a good officer corps. Why did we prevail over Trotsky and the rest? Trotsky, as we know, was the most popular man in our country after Lenin. Bukharin, Zinoviev, Rykov, Tomsky[151] were all popular. We were little known, I myself, Molotov, Vor[oshilov], and Kalinin, then. We were fieldworkers in Lenin's time, his colleagues. But the middle cadres supported us, explained our positions to the masses. Meanwhile Trotsky completely ignored those cadres . . .

D[imitrov]: . . . And because after Lenin you showed us the true path and carried on his cause firmly and wisely. After all, there have been cases in history where successors have ruined the causes of their precursors.

Vor[oshilov] and Molot[ov]: Dimitrov wants to propose a toast!

D[imitrov]: There is nothing I can add to what Com[rade] Stalin has said about a merciless struggle against enemies and about the significance of the middle cadres. That will be taken into account in the party, and I myself will do everything in my power to ensure that it is taken into account in the ranks of the Comintern as well. But I should say that it is not only my profound conviction, but I experienced for myself in prison, under conditions of the most severe ordeals, what supremely good fortune it is for the socialist revolution and for the international proletariat that following Lenin, Comrade Stalin has carried on his cause with such unswervingness and genius, through every sharp turning point, and has ensured the victory of our cause. There can be no speaking of Lenin without linking him with Stalin! (All lift their glasses!)

Stalin: I respect Comrade Dimitrov very much. We are friends and will remain friends. But I must disagree with him. He has even expressed himself here in an un-Marxist fashion. What the victory of the cause requires is the correct conditions, and then the leaders will always be found. It is not enough merely to point out the true path. The

---

151. Mikhail Pavlovich Tomsky (real surname: Yefremov, 1880–1936), Old Bolshevik; representative of the Petersburg party organization at the London Congress of the RSDRP (1907); chairman (1918–1929) of the All-Union Central Council of Trade Unions (VTsSPS); member of the RKP(b)/VKP(b) CP PB (1922–1930); member of the ECCI (1920–1930); after Bukharin and Rykov, the third most important member of the Right Opposition. After undergoing self-criticism, he was elected candidate-member of the VKP(b) CC (1934). He committed suicide.

English party, after all, has what we consider the correct policy, but it can accomplish nothing because the *middle* cadres are on the side of the Labourites. The French party is carrying out the correct policy, but the Socialist Party is nevertheless very strong. *The fundamental thing* is the middle cadres. That must be noted, and it must never be forgotten that other conditions being equal, *the middle cadres decide the outcome of our cause.*

Khrushchev: What we have is a felicitous combination—both the great leader and the middle cadres!

—After lunch—at the Kremlin—we watched a film about Lenin.
—Red Army maneuvers!

· 11 NOVEMBER 1937 ·

—Discussion with Stalin at the Kremlin.
D[imitrov], Wang Ming, Kon Sin [Kang Sheng], Communard [Wang Jiaxiang].[152]
—The [ECCI] secretariat resolution has become obsolete.
"That's what you get when you have people sitting in offices concocting things!"
—"Using all available means, intensify the struggle against Trotskyites!" (in the resolution). "That is not enough. Trotskyites must be hunted down, shot, destroyed. These are international provocateurs, fascism's most vicious agents."

1. *The fundamental thing* for the Chinese Communist Party at present: to merge with the common national wave and take a leading part.
2. *The main thing now is the war,* not an agrarian revolution, not confiscation of land. (A war tax is indispensable.)

152. Wang Jiaxiang (Wang Chia-hsiang, pseudonym: Communard, 1907–1974), Chinese Communist; graduate of Sun Yat-sen University at Moscow; one of the "returned students," who in 1930 took over the CPC under Wang Ming; participant in the Jianxi Soviet and the Long March; part of the CPC leadership after 1934; CPC representative to the ECCI (1937–1938); Chinese ambassador to the USSR (1949–1951); assistant minister of foreign affairs of the PRC (1951–1959?); secretary of the CPC CC (1956). He was removed from leadership during the Cultural Revolution.

—The Chinese Com[munists] have gone from one extreme to another—before the idea was to confiscate everything, and now nothing!

3. A single slogan—

—A victorious war for the independence of the Chinese people.

—For a free China against the Japanese invaders.

4. How the Chinese are *to fight* with the *external* enemy—that is the decisive issue.

—When that is over, then the question will arise of how they are to fight among themselves!

5. *The Chinese* are in more *favorable* circumstances than we were in 1918–1920.

—Our country was *divided* along the lines of the social revolution.

—In China you have a *national* revolution; the struggle for independence and freedom unites the country and the people.

6. *China* possesses *enormous human reserves,* and I believe that Chiang Kai-shek is correct when he affirms that China will win, that all it has to do is hold out in the present war.

7. That will *require* building up *its own military industry.*

—*Aviation* production.

—Aircraft are easy to build; however, they are very difficult to transport.

(*We will provide* mater[ial] for aircraft!)

—*Aircraft construction* must be set up.

—Tanks also to be made (we can give them mater[ial] for tanks!)

—If China has *its own military industry,* no one can defeat it.

8. *The Eighth Army* should have not three, but *thirty divisions.*

—That can be done *in the form of reserve regiments* to reinforce the existing divisions.

—*New regiments* have to be formed; *military* training day and night.

9. Since the Eighth Army has no artillery, its *tactics* should be not direct attack, but *harrying* the enemy, drawing him into the interior of the country and *striking* at *the rear.*

It is necessary to destroy communications, railroads, and bridges [used by] the Japanese army.

10. Neither *England* nor *America* wants China to win. They fear a Chinese victory because of their own imperialist interests.

—A Chinese victory will affect India, Indochina, and so forth.

—They want Japan to be weakened as a result of the war, but not to allow China to stand on its own two feet.

—They want to have *Japan* as a *chained watchdog*—to scare China, as they used to [scare] tsarist Russia, but they don't want to give that dog the chance to devour the victim by itself.

11. *At the Chinese party congress* it is counterproductive to engage in theoretical discussions. Leave theoretical problems for a later period, after the end of the war.

—The odds of speaking about *a noncapitalist* path of development for China are worse now than they were before.

(After all, capitalism is developing in China!)

12. The question of forming a national revolutionary league has been dragged out.

13. [Send] a reliable representative of the Eighth Army and the party *to Urumqi.*

Private conversation with Stalin.

We shall probably arrest Stasova,[153] too. Turned out she's scum. Kirsanova[154] is very closely involved with Yakovlev.[155] She's scum.

Münzenberg is a Trotskyite. If he comes here, we'll certainly arrest him. Try and lure him here.

—At turning points:

1. 1905
2. 1917
3. the Treaty of Brest-Litovsk
4. the Civil War
5. and especially collectivization, a completely novel, historically unprecedented event

153. Yelena Dmitrievna Stasova (1873–1966), Old Bolshevik; member of the RKP(b) CC (1918–1920); Comintern emissary to the KPD (1921–1926); president of the MOPR (1927–1937); member of the Comintern's ICC (1935–1943); editor of the journal *Internatsionalnaia literatura* (1938–1946).

154. Klavdia Ivanovna Kirsanova (1887–1947), Old Bolshevik; wife of E. M. Yaroslavsky (1878–1943), prominent Bolshevik leader; rector of the Comintern's Leninist School (1927–1937); head of the Comintern's Women's Secretariat in the 1930s; worked in VKP(b) agitprop (1941–1947); active in the Women's International Democratic Association (1945–1947).

155. Yakov Arkadievich Yakovlev (real surname: Epshtein, 1896–1938), Soviet Communist leader, specialist in agriculture and policy toward the countryside; people's commissar for agriculture (1929–1934); member of the VKP(b) CC (from 1930 on) and head of its Department of Agriculture (after 1934). He was liquidated in the Stalinist purges.

—various weak elements fell away from the party. Yielding to the strength of the party, they never internally accepted the party's line; in particular they could never stomach *collectivization* (when cuts had to be made across the living body of the kulak), and they went *underground*. Powerless themselves, they linked up with external enemies, promised Ukraine to the Germans, Belorussia to the Poles, the Far East to the Japanese. They hoped for war and were especially insistent that the German fascists launch a war against the USSR as soon as possible.

We were aware of certain facts as early as last year and were preparing to deal with them, but first we wanted to seize as many threads as possible. They were planning an action for the beginning of this year. Their resolve failed. *They were preparing in July to attack the Politburo at the Kremlin.* But they lost their nerve—they said: "Stalin will start shooting and there will be a scandal." I would tell our people— they will never make up their minds to act, and I would laugh at their plans.

—*Regarding certain members of our immediate circle, we really were asleep at the switch.*

—An important *lesson* for us and for all Commun[ist] parties.

· 13 NOVEMBER 1937 ·
(VOLYNSKOE)

—Last discussion with Wang Ming, Kon Sin [Kang Sheng] and Communard [Wang Jiaxiang]. (It was decided to retain Commun[ard] temporarily as the representative of the Chinese party on the ECCI.)

—Report by Thorez.
—The situation in France and the coming party congress (at the end of December).

—Our warning concerning excessive optimism and dizziness with success.
—*The fundamental thing* in foreign policy is to achieve an independent policy in France, one not subordinated to the will of the English conservatives—for peace, and a decisive opposition to the fascist aggressors.
—*The fundamental thing* in domestic policy is the preservation and

strengthening of the Popular Front for the implementation of its program.

—*The fundamental thing* for the strengthening of the Popular Front is the strengthening of the link with the Socialist Party, the Republic with its masses and organizations.

—*The fundamental thing* in the struggle for the unity of the French working class is the strengthening of our own party.

· 14 NOVEMBER 1937 ·

—Wang Ming and Kon Sin [Kang Sheng] departed.

· 15 NOVEMBER 1937 ·

—Thorez went back.

(Stalin apologized that it had been utterly impossible to receive him.)

—Discussion with González Peña.[156] (Secretary of the General Workers' Union and chairman of the Socialist Party of Spain—a miner from Asturias.) He believes a union of Communist and Socialist parties would be untimely, because the danger exists, given their union, of a reduction in assistance for the Spanish Republic from the Second International and the Amsterdam International and democr[atic] circles.

· 16 NOVEMBER 1937 ·

—*Meeting with Bulgarian comrades.*

(V[asil] K[olarov], Bogd[anov][Ivanov], Marek [Stanke Dimitrov], Vlad[imirov][Chervenkov], Belov [Damianov], Spiridonov [Kostov].)

—Eliminate the Politburo.

—Have only the CC and the secretariat. Powers of the CC. Composition of the secretariat:

1. *Simo* [?]
2. Spiridonov
3. Tacho Daskalov[157]

156. Ramón González Peña (1888–1952), miner from Asturias; president of the executive commission of the Socialist Party of Spain (PSOE) from 1936 on; national president of the Socialist trade union (UGT); minister of justice (1938–1939); exile in France and Mexico.

157. Tacho Daskalov (1898–1964), Bulgarian Communist; member of the

Withdraw *Velizarov* [?] from the secretariat; use him for literary work, and check on him.
Grozdanov [?]—send to Moscow.
—CC plenum in January–February.
—Part[y] conference in the second half of March 1938.

—Resolution on the dismissals of Kirsanova and Stasova.

—Vladimirov appointed temporary director of Leninist School.
—Pieck to replace Stasova in MOPR [International Organization for Aid to Revolutionaries—International Red Aid].

[...]

· 23 NOVEMBER 1937 ·

—In "Volynskoe."
Man[uilsky], Kuus[inen], Moskv[in], Pieck
(Resolution on the dissolution of the Polish Comparty.)
—Second discussion with Spiridonov.

The rest of 1937 was seemingly uneventful. Dimitrov stood as a candidate in Kostroma for the Supreme Soviet elections in December 1937, the first under the new Soviet (Stalin) constitution. There is a hiatus in the diary between 13 December 1937 and 17 February 1938. In the first half of 1938 only two entries appear, for 17 February (reproduced below) and 17 March at an uneventful reception. This was the period of the Bukharin trial (2–15 March) and of armed conflict with Japan, which amounted to an undeclared war along the Manchurian border (11 July–10 August).

Beginning on 16 August 1938, Dimitrov was increasingly preoccupied with the weakening front in Spain. He conferred in August with, among others, Vincente Uribe, a Communist member of the Republican government, and Togliatti, member of the ECCI and the Comintern's chief representative in Spain.—I.B.

BRP, the legal Communist front organization, and its CC (1930–1935, 1937); parliamentary deputy.

· 17 FEBRUARY 1938 ·

—Man[uilsky] and I were summoned to see *Stalin and Molotov.*
Stalin: 1. The Spanish Communists should leave the government. They have two secondary posts. If they leave the government, the disintegration of Franco's front will intensify, and the international position of the Spanish Republic will ease somewhat. Their exit should not be demonstrative, nor the result of the government's displeasure, but in the interests of facilitating the government's tasks. The grounds should be that since the syndicalists are not participating, the Communists find it inexpedient to be in the government.

2. *Support the government, but not participate in the government—* that should be our stance at this stage.

3. *China.*

—Two options:

a) A bloc of the Guomindang and the Communist Party.

b) Formation of a national revolutionary federation from the Guomindang and the CP (with the participation of various other movements). The federation is not included in the CI.

4. *Reorganization of CI organs.*

—Organize congresses, plenums on a semilegal basis. (Do not print reports, speeches.)

CP aid—five hundred thousand dollars.

[...]

· 27 AUGUST 1938 ·

—Conference with the Spanish.
(Man[uilsky], Ercoli [Togliatti], Kuusinen, Moskvin, Uribe,[158] Luis,[159] D[imitrov].)

---

158. Vicente Uribe (1902–1962), Spanish Communist, member of the PCE CC (from 1928 on) and Politburo (from 1932 on) in charge of ideology and propaganda. Member of the Cortes after the elections of February 1936; minister of agriculture in the Popular Front government of Francisco Largo Caballero (September 1936). After the collapse of the Spanish Republic, in 1939, he emigrated to Mexico, where he headed the PCE émigré center; Communist member of the Republican government-in-exile (1947) responsible for economic affairs. The last period of his exile was spent in Czechoslovakia.

159. Pseudonym of Francisco Antón (1909–1976), Spanish Communist; secretary of the PCE organization in Madrid; inspector-commissar of the Madrid front, dismissed by the Republican defense minister Indalecio Prieto in October 1937; member of the PCE CC and candidate-member of the Politburo (from 1937 on), full member (from 1945 on). He was sent on PCE missions in France (1939–1940), to the ECCI (1940–1943), and Mexico (1943–1944).

—"The question of ceasing military operations and negotiating the restoration of peace in Spain can be raised *only after the departure of German and Italian interventionist troops from Spain.* Until that time, a merciless struggle against the rebels and the interventionists."

—The struggle against capitulationists in the Republicans' camp.

—Disintegration within Franco's camp is one of the critical conditions for the victory of the Spanish people.

Two factors for victory over the fascist interventionists:

a) Our own political and military strength

b) Disintegration within Franco's camp and the population on his territory

—The issue of "fraternization" with the Spanish units of Franco's army is not to be raised.

—*International Brigades to be officially relieved.*

(Marty and the CC of the Spanish CP to be assigned the organized evacuation and further disposition of volunteers.)

[. . .]

On 25 August 1938 Dimitrov received Politburo authorization for a two-month medical leave. He busied himself with all sorts of odds and ends in Moscow until his departure on 9 September 1938. He took a hand in Spanish, French, Swiss, Portuguese, Balkan, Italian, German, and other party affairs. Before his departure a reserve leadership, headed by the troika of Manuilsky, Moskvin, and Kuusinen, was appointed to direct the CI in Dimitrov's absence.

While on leave in Kislovodsk (until 12 October) and Crimea (12–29 October), Dimitrov committed to his diary far more material than was his norm in Moscow. This was the period of the Munich crisis, which stirred up antifascist sentiment throughout Europe and the world and had significant consequences for the assessment of Western policy. Although much repetitive material is not included here, some of the most typical (parts of correspondence for 14, 16, 22, 24, and 29 September, and 3, 10, 13, 15, 16, 17, 18, and 24 October), sent to or received from Manuilsky, Moskvin, and Kuusinen, are reproduced to illustrate the outrage at the Anglo-French betrayal of Czechoslovakia.

During this period Dimitrov helped direct a conference of Communist parties in Paris charged with condemning and drawing strategic lessons from fascist aggression against Czechoslovakia, Spain, and China. He was concerned about contacts with the Politburo and reminded Manuilsky and Moskvin about the importance of seeking instructions and comments from Stalin. Moskvin admitted on 30 September, "We have not established contact with the Politburo on the current developments."

Dimitrov's was taken up with his reputation ("The fifth anniversary of the Leipzig trial has gone entirely unnoticed by the Soviet press," 23 September), and with continued experiments with the Polish party ("If the Polish Walter [Karol Świerczewski] is politically clean, he should be used for work in the Polish network"—telegram to Manuilsky and Moskvin, 28 September) and Dimitrov's concern for the cultivation of Albanian émigrés (telegram to Moskvin for Marek [Stanke Dimitrov]) should also be noted. In addition, the purge of his secretary was a source of cryptic correspondence from Maria Krylova, the ECCI cadre officer (13 October), and from Dimitrov to Moskvin (16 October). Included in this section is a perceptive letter from Manuilsky (diary entry of 24 October) in which he anticipates Soviet strategy after the German attack in 1941.—I.B.

14 SEPTEMBER 1938
[. . .]

—Sent telegram: "Apparently the Henleinists' putsch is the prelude to an attack on Czechoslovakia from without. We must reckon with the possibility of war in the immediate future and do everything to strengthen the readiness of our parties for such a turn of events. Please discuss and consult with whomever you must, and advise immediately whether it would be better to discontinue my treatment and return."

[. . .]

· 16 SEPTEMBER 1938 ·
[. . .]

—Sent telegram to Manuilsky/Moskvin:

In view of Czechoslovakia, emergency measures must be taken with respect to Poland, Romania, and Hungary. Especially Poland. Articles should be published in which the tasks of the working class and all democrat[ic] forces in those countries are indicated, and this should be made known there by radio and other means. An address should be published on behalf of the Polish initiative group to workers and peasants, to the democratic organizations of Poland against the pro-Hitler policy of the Polish government.[160] The defense of the independence and integrity of the Czechoslo-

160. The Polish initiative group was established by the secretariat of the ECCI on 16 August 1938 with the idea of reestablishing the Polish Communist party without reference to the dissolved organizational structures. Anton Ivanov (pseudonym: Bogadanov) was charged with representing the ECCI to the group.

vak Republic means the defense of the independence of Poland itself. Bogdanov's [Anton Ivanov's] departure should be expedited. And an address prepared to the working class on the dissolution of the Communist Party. Point out that with the dissolution of the Communist Party, the Communist movement in Poland is not only not eliminated, but, on the contrary, once the agents of the Defenzywa [Polish intelligence] have been driven from its ranks, the conditions will have been created for its growth and development in earnest. The resolution of the Hungarian question should also be expedited. In my view, Szántó[161] deserves political confidence. A troika could be formed: Szántó, Varga, and one other Hungarian of proven worth, to assist the movement in the country. Pedro [Ernő Gerő] should be summoned immediately and brought into this work.

[. . .]

· 22 SEPTEMBER 1938 ·
[. . .]

3. *To Manuilsky, Moskvin, Kuusinen:* "It is difficult for me to judge from here, but it seems that if a popular movement in Czechoslovakia were to reject capitulation resolutely, provided the army stands resolved to resist a German attack, then that fact ought to have an enormous effect on France and England; it should unleash a movement in those countries so powerful that the traitorous Anglo-French plan would collapse under its pressure. In any case, nothing is worse than giving up without a fight."

[. . .]

· 24 SEPTEMBER 1938 ·
[. . .]

—*Telegram to Manuilsky, Kuusinen, Moskvin:*

Arousing public opinion against Chamberlain is very important. One must, however, use all means to bring about a favorable change of govern-

---

161. Zoltán Szántó (1893–1977), Hungarian Communist; émigré to the USSR; representative of the Hungarian CP in the ECCI (1938–1939); member of the ECCI apparatus (1939–1943); Hungarian envoy to Yugoslavia, Albania, France (1947–1954), and Poland (1955–1956); head of the information service in the Nagy government (1954–1955); member of the Hungarian CP CC (1954–1956), its Politburo (1956), and its presidium (after 28 October 1956). He sought refuge in the Yugoslav embassy in Budapest with the Nagy leadership. After being deported to Romania, he served as prosecution witness in the secret trial of Imre Nagy (June 1958).

ment in England and France. The weakest area in the current situation is the absence of united action by the international workers' movement. Everything must be done to effect such united action on the European scale at the very least. I again emphasize the idea of a European workers' conference. The very fact of a mass campaign, a movement in favor of such a conference, would undoubtedly strengthen and accelerate the mobilization of the masses against the fascist warmongers and their abettors and against any and all capitulationists and would have a great effect in that regard among the ranks of the Socialist parties and the trade unions. Discuss seriously and issue a directive to our friends in Paris. More detailed instructions in this regard could be forwarded through Raymond [Guyot].[162]

[. . .]

· 29 SEPTEMBER 1938 ·
[. . .]

—2. *Telegram to Manuilsky, Moskvin:* "Have you received any advice, instructions, or comments on the part of Com[rade] St[alin] or the comrades from the Politburo concerning our work in the current situation? I hope that you are informing St[alin] of the more important measures we are undertaking."

—3. *Telegram to Moskvin:* "You will have to request that checking by Comrade Yezhov's apparatus be sped up for the persons we have envisaged for the bureau of the secretariat and for my secretariat."

—Listened to Radio Sofia-Varna–Stara Zagora.

—Report on the conference in Munich—Hitler, Mussolini, Chamberlain, and Daladier.

An accord was reached:

1. The evacuation of the Sudeten region by Czechoslovak troops and authorities

2. A plebiscite for the remaining regions of Czechoslovakia

---

162. Raymond Guyot (1903–1986), French Communist leader; secretary-general of the French Communist Youth Federation (1932–1935); secretary-general of KIM (1935); member of the ECCI and an alternate member of its presidium (1935); mayor of Villejuif (Paris, 1936); deputy in the French National Assembly (1937). He was active at Comintern headquarters from the mid-1930s to 1942, during which time he helped in the Spanish effort and instructed the PCF after the signing of the Soviet-German nonaggression pact. Beginning in 1942, he led the Communist Resistance in Vichy France. After the war he helped lead PCF youth work, served on the PCF Politburo (1945–1972), and was repeatedly elected to the National Assembly.

3. The occupation of those regions by international troops and an international commission for the plebiscite and the determination of Czechoslovakia's new borders
—Unheard-of betrayal!
4. The guaranteeing of those borders by England and France
5. The release of arrested Henleinists

[. . .]

· 3 OCTOBER 1938 ·

[. . .]

—2. Telegram sent to Manuilsky, Moskvin, Kuusinen:

In the current situation one should strongly advocate the unification of Czechoslovakia's working-class parties and trade unions. For it is first and foremost on the unity of the workers' movement that the future of the working class, of the whole Czechoslovak people and the Czechoslovak Republic itself within its new borders, depends. As a first practical step toward realizing that unity, our people should seek an agreement between the Communist and the Social-Democratic parties as regards the immediate unification of the trade unions. Next, an agreement on joint discussion and resolution by the leadership of both parties on necessary measures to be taken by the working class to reinforce the national front against the capitulationists, against internal reaction and Hitler's agents, against the fascist predators that have sunk their claws into the living body of the country, for the purpose of ensuring the national character of the army and the democratic order of the republic. Simultaneously waging the most energetic campaign among the masses in the same spirit. Relying on the workers' will to unity, our party must play the role of the bold pioneer in the cause of forming a united party of the working class on a Marxist and international basis. I consider it a serious political error that to date Czechoslovak Communists and Socialists have not come out with an appeal to convene an international workers' conference. After all, it is the Czechoslovak working class and people that have the primary and greatest interest in this. The utmost criticism must be leveled at the leaders of the Second International, the opponents and saboteurs of the united front, by pointing out their historical culpability graphically and convincingly. Other measures aside, a mass-circulation pamphlet on this issue should be published, exposing the role of those leaders as regards our proposals on unified action, beginning with Abyssinia. Their feet should really be held to the fire as never before; they should be held up to the judgment of the working public of the world.

—3. Telegram from Manuilsky, Moskvin, Kuusinen:

Concerning our proposal that Communists make a joint appeal with Czechoslovak Social Democrats for convening an international workers' conference in defense of Czechoslovakia, likewise of Spain and China, of peace and democracy, Gottwald replied that in his view it would be better if some other party, a more substantial one, came out with that sort of proposal. We shall insist on our own version. Moreover, he would like some advice concerning the unification of the trade unions and workers' parties of Czechoslovakia; in particular, the masses are now demanding this. Reasoning from the interests of reinforcing the national front against the capitulationists and from the necessity of repulsing the attack by a newly stirred reaction, aimed at isolating the Comm[unist] Party, we are inclining toward the following decision: to bring about the unification of the trade unions immediately; to prepare the unity of the party by reinforcing the United Workers' Front as a basis for national unity through the immediate formation of general committees in the center and in the localities to carry on the struggle for the independence and democracy of the Czechoslovak people against the fascism that threatens to devour it. Please give us your instructions without delay.

[...]

· 10 October 1938 ·
[...]

2. *Telegram from Manuilsky:*

In view of the fact that Browder can stay only two days, we won't be able to come out to see you the way we had planned. And so we could use your advice, right away by telegraph. We are planning to raise the following questions with him: 1) on developing a campaign for sanctions against Japan in connection with the League of Nations resolution; 2) on the struggle against Munich and the defense of Spain; [3)] on aid in matériel and food for Spain; 4) on the condition of the working class in the United States.

3. *Telegram from the secretariat:*

There has been a tremendous squabble in the Socialist Youth International; the majority is against Munich. We are inclined to think that Raymond [Guyot] and [Santiago] Carrillo[163] should make a proposal for a meeting to negotiate about a united front. Please advise.

163. Santiago Carrillo (b. 1915), Spanish Communist leader; participant in the Asturias uprising (1934); secretary-general of the merged Communist and Socialist youth organization of Spain (1936); alternate member of the PCE CC and Politburo (1937); political commissar of a battalion at the beginning of the Civil War;

4. *Telegram from the secretariat:*

Daladier is blackmailing with a threat to dissolve the parliament. Blum replied by stating that in such an event the Socialists would run for election in a bloc with the Communists, which would be a cruel blow to the Radicals. After reviewing this, [we] indicated that if the Socialists were willing to fight Daladier, then the Communist Party ought to tone down its criticism of them, concentrating its fire on the opponents of the Popular Front in the Second International, especially the Labourites.

---

5. *Telegram to Manuilsky, Kuusinen, Moskvin:*

I very much regret that I will not be able to meet with Browder. Please give him my warm regards.

In discussing matters with Browder, one must take seriously into account the changes that have occurred in the international situation since the robbers' bargain that was struck in Munich and as a result of the developing antidemocratic, counterrevolutionary bloc between German and Italian fascism and imperialist reaction in England and France. In connection with those changes and their consequences, an enormous role in the coming events in Europe and on the international scale falls on the United States, on its workers and democratic movement. This first of all obliges the working class and democratic forces in the United States to participate far more closely and actively in the struggle against fascism and reaction in the international arena and particularly in Europe. The strengthening of ideological and political connections between the American and the European workers' movements, beginning with the English and French, is extremely important in the current period. There must also be the utmost extension of fraternal ties between the working class, the popular masses, and the progressive intelligentsia of the United States and the Soviet Union, especially by means of the broadest and most systematic popularizing of the latter's socialist development, peaceful policies, and social and cultural achievements!

---

member of the Madrid Defense Junta. After the defeat of the Spanish Republic he worked as a secretary of KIM in Moscow and then worked in youth affairs in the United States, Cuba, and Mexico. A member of the PCE Politburo (from 1954 on) and secretary-general of the PCE (1960–1982), he condemned the Soviet invasion of Czechoslovakia in 1968 and, after the death of Franco, returned to Spain, where he promoted the Eurocommunist and parliamentary path of the PCE. In April 1985 he was excluded from the leadership of the PCE parliamentary group and the PCE CC after accusing his successor Geraldo Iglesias of Social Democratic deviations. He left the PCE and founded the Party of the Workers of Spain-Communist Unity (PTE-UC).

The especially important international role of the United States requires persistent and utmost intensification of the process of unifying the workers' movement and forming and strengthening a democratic front in the United States itself. The most critical [objectives] for the CP of the United States at the current juncture: 1) not to allow itself to be isolated from the working class and democratic forces; 2) to assume actual leadership of the struggle of the masses; 3) not to allow reactionary fascist forces to prevail; 4) to get Roosevelt and the government, along with the US workers and general democratic movement itself, to conduct an active foreign policy against the aggressors and warmongers, against the fascist bloc of "Germany-Italy-Japan," against the robbers' bargain struck by Hitler, Mussolini, and Chamberlain.

Along with aid to the Spanish Republic in matériel and food, public opinion should be mobilized and ruling circles influenced specifically against the vicious bartering away and destruction of the Republic of Spain that has been planned by Mussolini, Hitler, and Chamberlain.

Along with developing the campaign against the invaders, all means must be utilized (the press, radio, people, and so forth) to organize ideological and political assistance to the workers' movement and the democratic forces of Japan itself. An entire system of measures should be discussed in this regard.

In addition, there should be discussion of what means would be most effective in mobilizing émigrés of various nationalities, especially Germans, Italians, Japanese, Poles, Hungarians, and Balkan peoples, in support of the masses' struggle against fascism in their respective countries and the expulsion of fascist government agents and local reactionaries from the ranks of those million-strong masses in America.

A more specific understanding should also be worked out with Browder on liaison and assistance as regards Canada and Latin America, to a certain degree authorizing the CP of the United States (hence Browder) to act as our representative.

Among internal party matters, one that seems especially important is the Marxist-Leninist education of cadres and party members through the thorough study of the *Short Course on the History of the VKP(b)*.

It would be helpful to explain to Browder the necessity for a greater degree of principled precision in certain party slogans, and concerning the gradual retiring of the popular but non-Marxist slogan "Communism is the twentieth-century Americanism."

Finally, Browder should be asked his opinion and thoughts on convening an ECCI plenum (the approximate date, composition, and agenda).

Please share the contents of this telegram with Browder as well.

[. . .]

—A pogrom campaign is beginning against Communist parties and the workers' movement, against democratic elements and Jews in Czechoslovakia itself.

—The autonomous government of Slovakia has dissolved the Communist Party. Stormtroopers from Henlein's party have occupied the party premises.

[...]

· 13 OCTOBER 1938 ·
[...]

3. Letter from Krylova:[164]

Dear Georgi Mikhailovich [Dimitrov],

Since it is not quite clear to me what is going on, I consider it incumbent on me to inform you of the following:

a) Comrade Moskvin told me that Com[rade] Walter[165] and Com[rade] Sergeev [Kolev] will no longer be working with you in the secretariat. They are leaving for other jobs.

b) Comrade Kotelnikov[166] was summoned to the party CC today and advised to transfer to work outside the Comintern. Is it your wish that these workers be transferred or that they leave? Maybe I should also be thinking about changing jobs? (10 October.) G. M., don't be angry with me over this question. When you get here, there are some things I will have to tell you about, and I am sure that you will not blame me . . .

[...]

· 15 OCTOBER 1938 ·

—Telegrams:

1. *To Manuilsky, Moskvin, Friedrich [Bedřich Geminder]:*

In connection with the trial of the POUM [Partido Obrero de Unificación Marxista][167] members, I trust that the appropriate measures have already

164. Maria Ferdinandovna Krylova (1891–1967), Soviet Communist, worked in the Cadre Department of the ECCI (1932–1938).

165. Helene Walter was Dimitrov's personal secretary from 1934 to 1938. She was liquidated in the Stalinist purges.

166. Soviet Communist, employed in the Comintern apparatus.

167. The Workers' Party of Marxist Unification (POUM) was an anti-Stalinist Marxist party that the Communists tarred with the Trotskyist brush. The POUM was strong in Catalonia and supported the Anarchist uprising in Barcelona (May 1937), in which several hundred people were killed. Banned afterward, its leader

been taken in order to 1) publicly expose as effectively as possible the counterrevolutionary crimes of Spanish and foreign Trotskyites and their role as fascist agents; 2) expose their patrons from the Second International, particularly the English Independents and the French Pivertists,[168] as accomplices in those crimes; 3) use that trial extensively in the press and by other means on an international scale for the expulsion of Trotskyites from the ranks of the workers' movement. Ercoli [Togliatti], Luis [Francisco Antón], and Julius[169] should be given direct responsibility for conducting that campaign.

[. . .]

· 16 OCTOBER 1938 ·
[. . .]

2. *Telegrams sent:*

[. . .]

—*To Moskvin:*

Since my secretary [Walter] is free, let her furnish Krylova with inventories of all files, with [M. S.] Andreev's participation and under his control. She should be told that it is a matter of the necessary renewal of the apparatus.

Andreu (Andrés) Nin arrested and assassinated by the Communists, the remaining POUM leaders were tried in Barcelona before the Tribunal for Espionage and High Treason from 11 to 22 October 1938. Despite Communist pressures, the judges dismissed the charges of espionage and desertion but condemned most of the accused on lesser charges arising from their participation in the May uprising. Nevertheless, the outcome was seen as a slap at the Communists, the court having declared the defendants' conduct as having "a marked antifascist meaning."

168. The international supporters of the POUM, among them the British Independent Labour Party, the French left socialists of Marceau Pivert, and the Communist Party of the USA (Opposition), operated through the International Bureau for Revolutionary Socialist Unity, which, contrary to Dimitrov's assertion, was not an organ of the Second International, to mount pressure on the Spanish Republican government for fair treatment of the POUM. Several delegations visited Spain to this end, including one led by Pivert in August 1938.

169. Pseudonym of Gyula Alpári (1882–1944), Hungarian Communist; chief of press bureau at the time of the Hungarian Council Republic (1919) and assistant to Béla Kun in the Commissariat for Foreign Affairs. Starting in 1921, he edited the *Imprekorr* in Berlin and was a member of the Hungarian CP CC (1925–1928). After Hitler's rise to power, Alpári moved to Switzerland and edited the Communist journal *Rundschau*. In France after 1935, he was arrested by the Gestapo in 1940 and killed in the Sachsenhausen concentration camp.

She will also have to be provided with the appropriate salary, in accordance with her being relieved by us of her duties.

[. . .]

· 17 OCTOBER 1938 ·

[. . .]

2. Telegrams received from Moskvin:

[. . .]

Comrade Ercoli [Togliatti] reports regarding the conference in Paris that on the basic problems the conference was at first marked by a certain lack of focus (confusion), which disappeared on receipt of our guidelines and with Thorez's subsequent speech. The latter had a somewhat hurt reaction to criticisms by [José] Díaz, Dolores [Ibárruri], and Ercoli concerning the deficiency of our action in general and particularly in France. Comrade Ercoli considers it necessary on our part to "take up a public position" on problems of the struggle for unity and peace after Munich. Next Ercoli raises the following issues:

1. There is some vagueness in understanding the main reason for the impossibility of resistance by the Czechoslovak people and [the fact] that the CP of Czechoslovakia should have earlier exposed and should now more clearly expose capitulationism and betrayal.

2. The CP of Czech[oslovakia] exposed the betrayal by the French government to the masses too late.

3. The tendency of some comrades to avoid criticism and pointed statements for fear of "harming unity" or "obstructing government activities."

4. There is no clear understanding of the necessity of developing the independence of the working class in order to influence and direct democratic forces, prevent betrayal, expel traitors, and so forth.

5. The same goes for independent actions by our parties.

6. It is essential through open criticism of capitulationists and traitors to reestablish our political connections with democratic elements, pacifists, the intelligentsia, and others, who are now experiencing confusion and a sense of impotence, which can turn into hostility toward our Popular Front policy.

In conclusion, Ercoli notes that over the past two months there has been a trend toward decreasing aid to Spain, in light of which, measures have been taken by them to intensify aid, which he asks us to do as well.

[. . .]

· 18 OCTOBER 1938 ·
[. . .]

2. Telegrams received from Moskvin:

[. . .]

c) The inventory of files will have to be done without the participation of [your] former secretary, whose status found its appropriate resolution the day before yesterday.

[. . .]

· 24 OCTOBER 1938 ·
[. . .]

—*Letter from Manuilsky.*
(Received in packet no. 38, 23 October 1938.)

Dear Georgi Mikhailovich,

I received your letter and was very glad to read that despite the current tense and unnerving situation, your treatment in Kislovodsk has had favorable results. We would like to think that you will have completely recovered by the end of your leave. We can't wait to see you, for right now your advice and your direct guidance of our work are extremely essential.

We are all deeply disturbed by the blow to Czechoslovakia, but that blow has not made us despondent, for we are certain that the defeat of the Czechoslovak people will raise a new antifascist wave throughout the whole world. It is only a matter of time before the masses reconsider what has happened and see how Chamberlain's policy has led them straight off a precipice. This turning point has not yet been reached, but it undoubtedly will be; for now, there is a certain confusion even in the Comm[unist] parties. Elements of that confusion are apparent even in the concluding manifesto published by the conference of Comm[unist] parties in Paris. In our view, that manifesto turned out badly; it fails to offer the masses any way out of the current situation. Meanwhile, demonstrating a solution to the masses is now the main task. It is not enough merely to assert that the wind of European reaction is in the air, and it is still stupider to compare that reaction with reaction in the era of the Holy Alliance and Metternich. Current political combinations and agreements can hardly be called stable; they last months, not years or decades. That reaction exists is indisputable, but you have to see beyond that reaction to the regrouping of forces that is under way. Until now, fascist reaction has been developing and making advances within "national" limits, so to speak. With its offensives against Austria and Czechoslovakia, however, German fascism is transgressing the bounds of its own state; it is stifling not only the workers of its own country but other peoples as well. The struggle against fascism is becoming a struggle not only of workers and democratic forces but of peoples and nations that do not wish to be enslaved by German conquerors. And this means that if a faction of Radicals falls away from the Popular Front in France, then the anti-Hitler front will simultaneously grow by the addition of elements that until now have stayed out of the Popular Front. Even nationalist elements like Kerillis[170] are coming over to join the opposition to Munich. And in England this is manifesting itself still more clearly in the fact that a person like the Conservative Duff Cooper[171] is taking a bolder line than the "Socialist" Blum. Therefore, it seems to me that we will have to make certain corrections or certain additions, if you like, to our current Popular Front tactics. The antifascist front will have to be built on a broader base, but this entails a decisive struggle against capitulationist elements within the workers' movement and within the "democratic" elements, which are beginning in some places to speak an almost fascist language. However paradoxical it may seem, Kerillis and Churchill are now closer to the antifascist front than Daladier and certain French Socialists. This new situation calls for Communists to speak not only on behalf of the Popular Front but for the whole nation as well, the entire people, calling on them to resist. After all, a nation is not some gang of traitors willing for the sake of its class privileges to offer up its own people to be torn to pieces by German fascism. A nation is millions of workers and peasants, working people, who are being betrayed by the Chamberlains and Daladiers. This role of Communists as spokesmen for the aspirations of nations should be especially emphasized in countries like Czechoslovakia, Yugoslavia, Romania, and so forth, countries exposed to attack by German fascism. But this presupposes that Communist parties overcome their pacifist illusions, that they struggle against their own governments precisely because those governments are providing neither preparations for defense against Hitler nor that defense itself. Comm[unist] parties should demand governments standing for struggle, not capitulation, and should promise such govern-

170. Henri de Kerillis (1899–1958), French right-wing journalist and politician; leader of the National Republican Party; except for seventy-three Communists and a dissident Socialist, the only member of the French National Assembly to vote against the Munich treaty supported by Prime Minister Daladier. In the United States during the war, he attacked de Gaulle as a dictator (1945). He died on Long Island.

171. Alfred Duff Cooper, first Viscount Norwich of Aldwick (1890–1954), British conservative MP; intimate friend of Winston Churchill; anti-appeasement secretary of state for war (1935–1937); first lord of the admiralty (1937–1938). He resigned in protest over the Munich Pact. After serving as minister of information in Churchill's first cabinet (1940–1941), and then ambassador to France (1944–1947), he was elevated to the peerage in 1952.

ments popular support. No matter how devastating the current blow may be, as peoples mobilize against foreign enslavement, there will also come a new antifascist ground swell. During the World War, Lenin said that if capitalism held out for twenty or thirty years, then one could not rule out that the imperialists would go from the enslavement of colonies to the dividing up of European states, and the prospect would then arise of national-revolutionary wars in Europe. Today such a situation is at hand. Communists should be calling the masses to such a national-revolutionary defense effort.

All of this calls for thorough consideration, so that we can direct our sections accordingly, after working out each country's specific tasks for this course of action. This, of course, does not settle the issue of the struggle against internal fascism but rather intensifies that struggle, since "internal fascism" is drawing the masses into the abyss of fascist bondage. This also raises the issue of the significance of the unity of the international workers' movement. The unity of the international workers' movement will not of itself break the back of armed fascism, but it will facilitate the overthrow of capitulationist profascist governments, and in so doing it creates the conditions for a successful war against fascist Germany, Italy, and Japan. It is not enough now only to talk about mere unity. We must show that the working class, that peoples can be saved from internal fascism and foreign fascist enslavement through a united front consisting of France, England, the USSR, the USA, plus smaller peoples. But the success of such a united front depends on the removal from power of profascist elements and the creation of governments prepared to fight against Germany.

I would ask that you think hard about these issues; we are currently occupied with our day-to-day tasks. Moreover, Kuusinen and I have to edit the translation of the *Short Course on the History of the VKP(b)*. What a remarkable book! You literally study it and your soul can rest and relax.

I shake your hand firmly.

(No signature! How could he have forgotten to sign?)
19 October 1938.

[. . .]

The winter and early spring of 1938–1939 were marked by reversals in Spain and rump Czechoslovakia. During this period Dimitrov's health frequently lapsed and he was bedridden on several occasions. The purge spread to the Comintern and claimed Moskvin and several others. Manuilsky and Dimitrov himself seemed to be under a cloud. Hence, Dimitrov's efforts to improve the "cadre situation" in the Comintern and to clear various budgetary and logistical matters, such as improvements in Hotel Lux, the Comintern headquarters. (The budget for 1938 amounted to 1,342,447 gold rubles.) Another area of concern was

Comintern communications, which were clearly the unquestioned domain of the NKVD.

Throughout this time Dimitrov labored on the "questions" of various Communist parties, including those of France, Canada, Sweden, the Netherlands, Czechoslovakia, Yugoslavia, the Philippines, Norway, Spain, China, Austria, Bulgaria, Poland, and Hungary. Tito, Lin Biao, and various Spanish Communist leaders, now exiled after the Casado coup, were among those Dimitrov received during this period. Many, but not all, party visitors received monetary subsidies.

Dimitrov's health was failing during the Eighteenth Congress of the VKP(b), and his report was delivered by Manuilsky on 11 March 1939. Already at this congress Stalin stated, "the Soviet Union will not be pulling chestnuts out of fire" for the Western powers. This marked the slow shift toward accommodation with Nazi Germany, which was further signaled by the dismissal of Litvinov on 3 May. Dimitrov commented on none of these developments.—I.B.

· 7 NOVEMBER 1938 ·

—On Red Square.

—After the demonstration, a combined luncheon in the Kremlin: Stalin, Molot[ov], Kagan[ovich], Vorosh[ilov], Kalin[in], Andreev, Yezhov, Mikoyan, Beria, Budenny, Frin[ovsky], Yaroslavsky,[172] Shcherbakov,[173] Bulganin, Shvernik, Kosarev, Shaposhnikov, Kulik,[174] Smirnov,[175] the chief of aviation, two comrades from the Georgian NKVD, Mekhlis, and others.

---

172. Yemelian Mikhailovich Yaroslavsky (1878–1943), Old Bolshevik from the Baikal region; active in the revolution of 1905 in Odessa; participant in the October 1917 uprising in Moscow; member of the VKP(b) CC (1921–1923, 1934–1939), secretary of the CC (1921–1922); headed the USSR Society of the Godless and the Old Bolshevik organization; elected to the Academy of Sciences of the USSR in 1939.

173. Aleksandr Sergeevich Shcherbakov (1901–1945), first secretary of the Moscow committee of the VKP(b) (1938–1945); secretary of the VKP(b) CC and candidate-member of the Politburo (1941–1945); chief of the Main Political Administration of the Red Army; chief of the Sovinformburo; deputy people's commissar for defense (from 1942 on).

174. Georgy Ivanovich Kulik (1890–1950), deputy people's commissar for defense (from 1939 on); marshal of the Soviet Union (1940). He was deprived by the Supreme Court of the USSR (February 1942) of his rank and decorations for the loss of Kerch and reinstated with the rank of major general in March 1942.

175. Not clear to which Smirnov this refers, Aleksei Semyonovich Smirnov (b. 1917), Soviet air force commander, not being sufficiently senior at the time.

—Significant group of new people.

—Mikoyan is toastmaster. Toasts to everyone in turn.

—Crit[ical] toast especially as regards Kosarev:

Kag[anovich]: Kosarev is still not correcting his fundamental errors.

Stal[in]: Mikoyan's speech is soft [on him].

Mik[oyan]'s toast to me: D[imitrov] grappled bravely with his foes in Leipzig. When I read his courtroom statements, I said to myself: this is our Bolshevik. Our country and our party love D[imitrov]. But this also confers obligations. Great strides have been made in the workers' movement in the West. European workers have learned how to shake their fists. But that is not sufficient. D[imitrov] has accomplished a great deal, and another man might be satisfied with that. But we are certain that in future he will have people not only shaking their fists but learning to bring those fists down on the enemy, on the bourgeoisie.

—Stalin: So who is supposed to be learning?

—Mikoyan: The European workers.

—Stalin: This is not quite clear!

——————————

—Kozovski[176] was arrested this morning. Wrote Yezhov about this.

[. . .]

· 12 NOVEMBER 1938 ·

—Telegram by telephone for Friedrich [Geminder]:

Communicate specific instructions to Paris on using the latest Jewish pogroms in Germany[177] for maximal intensification of the campaign against the profascist and capitulationist policies of the bourgeois governments in Western Europe as regards German fascism.

176. Ferdinand Kozovski (pseudonym: Petrov, 1892–1965), Bulgarian Communist, political émigré to the USSR (1926–1944). He fought in the International Brigades in Spain. After being arrested in the USSR (1938–1939), he worked during the war for TASS and the Bulgarian radio program of the ECCI. Member of the BKP CC (from 1944 on); deputy minister of defense of Bulgaria and chief of the political administration of the Bulgarian army (1945–1948). He served afterward in the Bulgarian diplomatic service.

177. Refers to the Kristallnacht, the night of 9–10 November, when rampaging Nazi mobs attacked Jews and destroyed their synagogues and businesses, a fateful step on the path to genocide.

· 17 NOVEMBER 1938 ·

—Kruzhkov[178] has been appointed secretariat bureau chief.
—Tatarenko[179] has been appointed personal assistant (instead of Walter).
—Dengel[180] should be working on the editorial board and in the Control Commission.

[. . .]

· 23 NOVEMBER 1938 ·

—M[oskvin] was called in to the NKVD.
He has not come back!

· 24 NOVEMBER 1938 ·

—At Yezhov's (his dacha).
"M[oskvin] was closely tied to *all* of that crowd. It will have to be determined to what extent he had those ties in recent years. It will also be determined whether he was entrapped by any foreign intelligence service that was pressuring him."

· 25 NOVEMBER 1938 ·

—Accepted M[oskvin]'s files.
—Late in the evening at Beria's (we worked together with Vyshinsky and Merkulov).[181]

178. Vladimir Semyonovich Kruzhkov (b. 1905), Soviet Communist; chief of the bureau of the ECCI secretariat; director of the Marx-Engels-Lenin Institute of the VKP(b) CC (1944–1949).

179. Pyotr Timofeevich Tatarenko (b. 1908), Soviet Communist; personal assistant to Dimitrov in the ECCI (1938–1943); employed in the Cadre Department of the ECCI (1943).

180. Philipp Dengel (1888–1948), German Communist journalist; deputy in the Reichstag (1924–1930); member of the KPD CC (1925–1935). He was employed in various capacities in the Comintern apparatus from 1928 to 1941, when he became incapacitated, owing to illness.

181. Vsevolod Nikolaevich Merkulov (1895–1953), Soviet security operative; NKVD officer; people's commissar for state security (from 1941 on); first deputy people's commissar for internal affairs (1941–1943), people's commissar for state security (1943–1946); member of the VKP(b) CC (1939–1952). He was arrested and liquidated in the purge of the Beria group.

"Nikolaev[182] is an agent for several intelligence services at once; Volin is a German agent; Poliachek is a Polish spy!"[183]

—A number of cases [incidents] will have to be reexamined.

—"New instructions, on assignment from Stalin, to work up instructions regarding arrests."

—Wrote Com[rade] Stalin on the necessity of replenishing the delegation with a new comrade (to replace M[oskvin]).

> To Comrade Stalin, J. V. [Joseph Vissarionovich],
> Politburo of the CC of the VKP(b):
>
> As of yesterday, I have temporarily assumed all of the functions that the arrested Moskvin was to have performed as a member of the ECCI secretariat (directorship of the liaison service, supervision of management of affairs, settlement of financial matters).
>
> *However, this will be beyond my capacity to sustain for any prolonged period.*
>
> It would be essential to replenish the VKP(b) delegation to the ECCI with a suitable comrade to whom this work could be commissioned. All the more so since the arrested enemy of the people undoubtedly did a great deal of damage in the ECCI apparatus, which must now be remedied and restructured immediately, without halting current operations.
>
> *I urgently request your cooperation in rapidly appointing such a comrade.*
>
> With Communist greetings,
> G. Dim[itrov]

25 November 1938

[. . .]

· 10 DECEMBER 1938 ·

—Telegram to Spain (Negrín's[184] plan is unsuitable, fraught with tendencies toward personal dictatorship. At this stage, achieving unity among the trade unions is crucial for victory. This is what Negrín should be aiming for in the interests of eliminating the difficulties coming from the old party cliques.)

[. . .]

---

182. A. K. Nikolaev (Rybakov, b. 1900), Soviet Communist, chief of the cypher section at the ECCI and, after July 1943, at the Department of International Information of the VKP(b).

183. Volin and L. M. Poliachek were on the ECCI staff.

184. Juan Negrín (1892–1956), Spanish Socialist; professor of physiology at the University of Madrid; finance minister (1936); prime minister of Spanish Republic (1937–1939) dependent on the Communists. He died in exile in France.

—Molatin from the State Bank to see me.

—Budget Estimate for 1938: 1,342,447 gold rubles; 11,916,000 red rubles [ten-ruble bank notes, or *chervontsy*].

Indebtedness, 1937: 277,289 gold rubles.

—P[lan?]. 63/103–22 August 1938

[Hard] currency:

—Subsidy for par[ty] work and KIM—	529,529
—Subsidy for inter[national] organizations—	64,578
—Publishing—	212,000
—*Rundschau, Imprekorr*—	230,000
—Honoraria for for[eign] employ[ees]—	1,000
—ECCI apparatus expenses—	95,000
—Signals service—	140,000
—Financial aid and expenses for student travel—	20,000
—Reserve fund—	50,000

1,342,447

Payments on 1937 indebtedness— 277,989

1,619,736

Soviet [currency]—

1. ECCI secretariat

—Telegr[aph] agency

—Management, correspondence . . .

—Special payments for Group A.

6,262,000

2. Signals service (central)

—Maintenance of centr[al] apparatus

—Special assignments

—Maintenance of these points in the ap[aratus].

2,121,084

3. Signals service (facilities):

Utilization—facility no. 1

Utilization—facility no. 2

  —school

  —facility no. 3

—Maintenance of supplies department

  —Motor-vehicle transport

  —Construction

a) facility no. 1, no. 2, no. 7, no. 3, warehouse assistance
Institutes of higher education

—[Totals]—

$$3,532,916$$

$$11,916,000$$

[...]

· 11 December 1938 ·
[...]

—Merkulov called: About Julius's [Alpári's] visa (they have "certain facts" against him in the NKVD).
—I reminded about Kozovski.

[...]

· 30 December 1938 ·
[...]

—Walter (Yugoslavia) [Josip Broz–Tito]—final instructions.
—Leadership (provisional) within the country. Conference. Establishment of permanent leadership. In Paris: a man for liaison.

· 26 January 1939 ·

—Conference on Spanish events (Manuilsky, Florin, Kuusinen, Gottwald, and D[imitrov]).
—Instructions sent to Thorez, Browder, and others.
To Thorez:

> Arrange a meeting between representatives of the Popular Front and headquarters and get it to assist Spain. Talk with Herriot,[185] Kerillis, and other prominent figures to get influence over the government and headquarters.

To Thorez:

> You and Cachin immediately appeal on behalf of the Communist International to the Socialist International with a proposal for joint actions for rendering all manner of assistance to Spain through the governments of France, England, the United States, and the Scandinavian countries, for the

185. Edouard Herriot (1872–1957), French Radical leader and author; mayor of Lyon (from 1904 on), member and president of the Chamber of Deputies; member of several cabinets, prime minister of France (1924–1925, 1932); arrested during the Vichy period; president of the French National Assembly (1947–1954).

lifting of the blockade, organizing accommodation of refugees. To influence the government, propose organizing joint rallies and popular demonstrations. To that end, mobilize in France, besides workers' organizations, the radicals as well. Mobilize all Comm[unist] parties in other countries, first and foremost England, along these lines.

Send a delegation to Catalonia from the French Comm[unist] Party consisting of three persons, led by a Politburo member, for the purpose of remaining with the Spanish comrades during these trying days, counteracting attempts to capitulate on the part of certain bourgeois and socialist elements within the Popular Front. Advise the Spanish comrades to hold out for all they are worth in Catalonia. Accelerate the sending of volunteers.

To Browder:

Advise all workers and democratic organizations to undertake joint actions promoting all manner of assistance to Spain through the government of the United States and other countries, a campaign for lifting the blockade, for refugee relief. To influence the government, organize joint rallies and demonstrations with other organizations. Through democratic organizations, militate for action [*or* a declaration] by Roosevelt in defense of Spain. Pass on these instructions to Canada and the South American countries.

—Barcelona has fallen!

· 27 JANUARY 1939 ·

—Telegrams to Paris (further instructions as regards Spain).
—Letter to Com[rade] Stalin (enclosure: appeal of the Communist Party).
—We consider the political line in the appeal correct. The Spanish comrades have been advised—despite everything—to continue the fight.
—A variety of measures for intensifying aid to the Spanish Republic, including quietly sending volunteers.
(We request instructions in connection with the extremely serious situation.)

· 28 JANUARY 1939 ·

—Aleksandrov[186] to see me (asking help).
—In Czechoslovakia fascism has been imposed.

186. Georgy Fyodorovich Aleksandrov (1908–1961), Soviet Communist; head

The people are against it and are holding out.

Even Béron[187] is increasingly "leaning left."

Sentiment against pressure from Berlin is growing.

—The matter of Sudeten refugees and German émigrés in Prague.

[. . .]

· 7 FEBRUARY 1939 ·
[. . .]

—*Telegram to Paris:*

1. Pass the following on to the Spanish CC: the course of resistance must be maintained, despite the loss of Catalonia; for these purposes the front in Levante must be activated; capitulation by the Spanish government must be prevented, through replacing adherents of capitulation in the government with staunch adherents of resistance.

2. The course of continued resistance in Spain must be firmly maintained. Pressure your government to help through mobilizing the masses. Take all measures to ensure the dispatch of the Catalonian army to the central zone; avoid sinking as a result of possible provocation; immediately organize supplies of all necessary arms and food to Valencia. Mobilize all the resources of the party and the Popular Front to accommodate the refugees and not allow them to become demoralized. Furnish regular reports on the situation.

[. . .]

· 14 FEBRUARY 1939 ·
[. . .]

—Chinese comrade Lin Biao (going locally by Li Tin), commander of the 115th division of the Eighth Army; rector of the military academy in Yan'an. He brought materials from the Sixth Plenum of the CC (November 1938).

—The Seventh Congress of the Chinese Communist Party is anticipated in May.

—Forty people took part in the plenum (almost all the CC members

---

of the editorial-publishing council at the ECCI (until 1939); chief of VKP(b) CC agitprop (1940–1947).

187. Emile Béron (1896–1966), French Communist from Alsace, secretary of the PCF federation of Moselle; member of the PCF CC (from 1926 on), member of the Chamber of Deputies (beginning in 1928). He clashed with the PCF in 1932, opposed the Popular Front policies in 1938, approved of the Munich pact, and supported Pétain in 1940.

and the commanders and commissars of the Eighth and Fourth Armies).

—The Eighth Army, the Fourth Army, partisan detachments, rear units, schools, and so on—329,000 in total.

—They are receiving 600,000 Chinese dollars a month from the government.

—Needs: 1) Money, 2) Arms, 3) Cadres.

—In Yan'an (in the CC):

Mao Zedong

Wang Ming

Lo Fu [Zhang Wentian][188]

Kon Sin [Kang Sheng]

Chi Pin [Chen Yun][189]

Ren Li [Ren Bishi][190]

---

188. Zhang Wentian (pseudonym: Lo Fu, 1900–1976), Chinese Communist leader who studied in Japan and at the University of California. A student at Sun Yat-sen University in Moscow and subsequently a Comintern employee (1926–1930), Zhang was among the twenty-eight "returned students" whom the Comintern emissary Pavel Mif installed in the CPC leadership in 1930. Zhang, a deputy to Qin Bangxian, headed the party's agrarian section and edited the party organ. A member of the CPC CC and Politburo (1931), he was responsible for agitprop and organizational work. In 1934, Zhang chaired the Council of People's Commissars of the Jiangxi Soviet. Elected secretary-general of the CPC at the Zunyi conference (January 1935), he formally led the CPC until 1937, when his position was eliminated. After the Communist victory he served as the ambassador to the USSR (1951–1954) and deputy minister of foreign affairs (1954–1959). Attacked during the Cultural Revolution, he was removed from the CPC leadership at the Ninth Congress (1969).

189. Chen Yun (pseudonym: Chi Pin; real name: Liao Chenyun, 1905–1995), Chinese Communist leader; member of the CPC CC (1931–1987), its longest-serving member. He was responsible for the trade unions in the Jiangxi Soviet. Sent to Moscow in 1935 to explain the decisions of the Zunyi conference, he joined the CPC delegation at the Seventh Congress of the Comintern. After the Communist victory, Chen served as the deputy prime minister in charge of financial and economic affairs and in that capacity was the principal architect of China's first five-year plans. Critical of the Great Leap Forward, he lived in seclusion during the 1960s but returned under Deng Xiaoping as a supporter of an incentive-based economic reform program. In his last years he resisted the drift toward a market economy, in the process becoming the leader of the conservative faction among the CPC elders.

190. Ren Bishi (pseudonym: Ren Li, 1904–1950), Chinese Communist leader; secretary of the Communist Youth League (1927–1928); member of the CPC CC (1927–1950); member of the CPC Politburo (1931–1950), of the Central Bureau

Zhou Enlai

Bo Gu [Qin Bangxian][191]

· 15 FEBRUARY 1939 ·

—*[Soviet] PB resolution of 2 February:*

1. Advise [order] the People's Commissariat for Foreign Affairs to grant authorization for entry into the USSR of 250–300 Sud[eten] Communists.

2. Assign a commission consisting of comrades Mol[otov], Dekanozov,[192] Shvernik, and Bogdanov[193] to examine the list of Sudeten Communists that have been received at the People's Commissariat for Foreign Affairs, and to provide for their employment in Soviet firms and institutions.

---

1. Authorize the return entry to the USSR of three hundred persons formerly sent to Spain as volunteers by the ECCI and now located in France.

2. Assign comrades Beria and Litvinov[194] to settle all questions connected with the return of the persons designated in point 1.

[. . .]

---

for the Soviet Areas (1931), in which he headed the organizational department, and of the Central Executive Committee of the Jiangxi Soviet; secretary of the Hunan-Jiangxi border regional committee (1933); political commissar of the Second Front Army (1935–1936) and of the Eighth Route Army (1937–1938); resident in the USSR (1938–1940); member of the CPC secretariat (1940–1950).

191. Qin Bangxian (pseudonym: Bo Gu, 1907–1946), Chinese Communist leader; one of the "returned students"; member of the CPC Politburo; secretary-general of the Chinese Communist youth organization, secretary-general of the CPC (1932), and "the person with overall responsibility in the party center" (1931–1935). After being removed from the top position at the Zunyi conference (January 1935), he became director of the general political department of the Red Army; alternate member of the ECCI (1935); chairman of the northwest branch of the Soviet government at Yan'an; director of the Xinhua news agency. He was killed in a plane crash in April 1946.

192. Vladimir Georgievich Dekanozov (d. 1954), VKP(b) operative in the Caucasus; high functionary of the secret police and close associate of Beria; chief of the external intelligence administration of the NKVD (1938–1940), responsible for the Soviet takeover of Lithuania (1940); deputy people's commissar for foreign affairs; Soviet envoy to Germany (1940–1941). He was liquidated in the purge of Beria's associates in December 1953.

193. Bogdanov, chairman of MOPR for the USSR.

194. Maksim Maksimovich Litvinov (1876–1951), leading Soviet diplomat, active in the earliest Soviet negotiating teams in Estonia, Sweden, Denmark, and Great Britain, and at the conferences at Genoa (1922) and Geneva (1927); mem-

· 17 FEBRUARY 1939 ·
[...]

—Maltsev[195] from the NKVD:
The Kozovski case: espionage charges.
Testimony by Lalkov[196] (at the Blag[oev] evening, 1936); gave information to Kozovski on a munitions factory in Mukhche (?), at the suggestion of Mednikarov.[197] In late December Lalkov confirmed his testimony.
—The issue of the driver (a spy), recommend[ed] by Kozovski for Sp[anish] air force!
—Tichnikov[198] (. . . . .) refused.
—Georgiev [Atanasov].[199]

[...]

· 23 MARCH 1939 ·

—A conference of the secretariat on Kuusinen's *Pravda* article on the twentieth anniversary of the CI.
—Man[uilsky]'s sortie:
  "The political line of the article is incorrect."
—A strange attempt to disqualify Kuus[inen] politically.
—A decision to raise in the pres[idium] the issue of a campaign in connection with the twentieth anniversary of the CI.
—Prepare a draft of the main points.
—Kuusinen's article not to be carried in the journal.

[...]

---

ber of the VKP(b) CC (1934–1941); people's commissar (1930–1939) and deputy people's commissar for foreign affairs (1939–1946); Soviet envoy to the United States (1941–1943) and Cuba (1942–1943).

195. NKVD officer.

196. Bulgarian émigré to the USSR.

197. Aleksandŭr Mednikarov (1879–1938), Bulgarian Communist; political émigré to the USSR (from 1925 on). He was liquidated in the Stalinist purges.

198. Bulgarian political émigré in the USSR.

199. Shteryu Atanasov (pseudonym: Georgiev, 1902–1967), Bulgarian Communist, political émigré to the USSR (from 1925 on); resident in Spain (1936–1939); member of the BKP CC (1941–1962); employee of the ECCI; general of the Bulgarian army.

Georgi Dimitrov (first row, second from right) among the agitators and leaders of the miners' strike, Pernik, Bulgaria, summer 1906.

Georgi Dimitrov (standing, fourth from right) and Dimitŭr Blagoev (seated, center) among members of the Central Committee and Control Commission and delegates to the Sixteenth Congress of the Bulgarian Workers' Social Democratic Party, Varna, Bulgaria, July 1909.

Report No. 12889, dated 1 March 1918, to the head of the military-judicial section of the War Ministry on Dimitrov's revolutionary activity during his visit to the front in January 1918.

Dimitrov, delegate to the Third Congress of the Comintern, Moscow, June–July 1921.

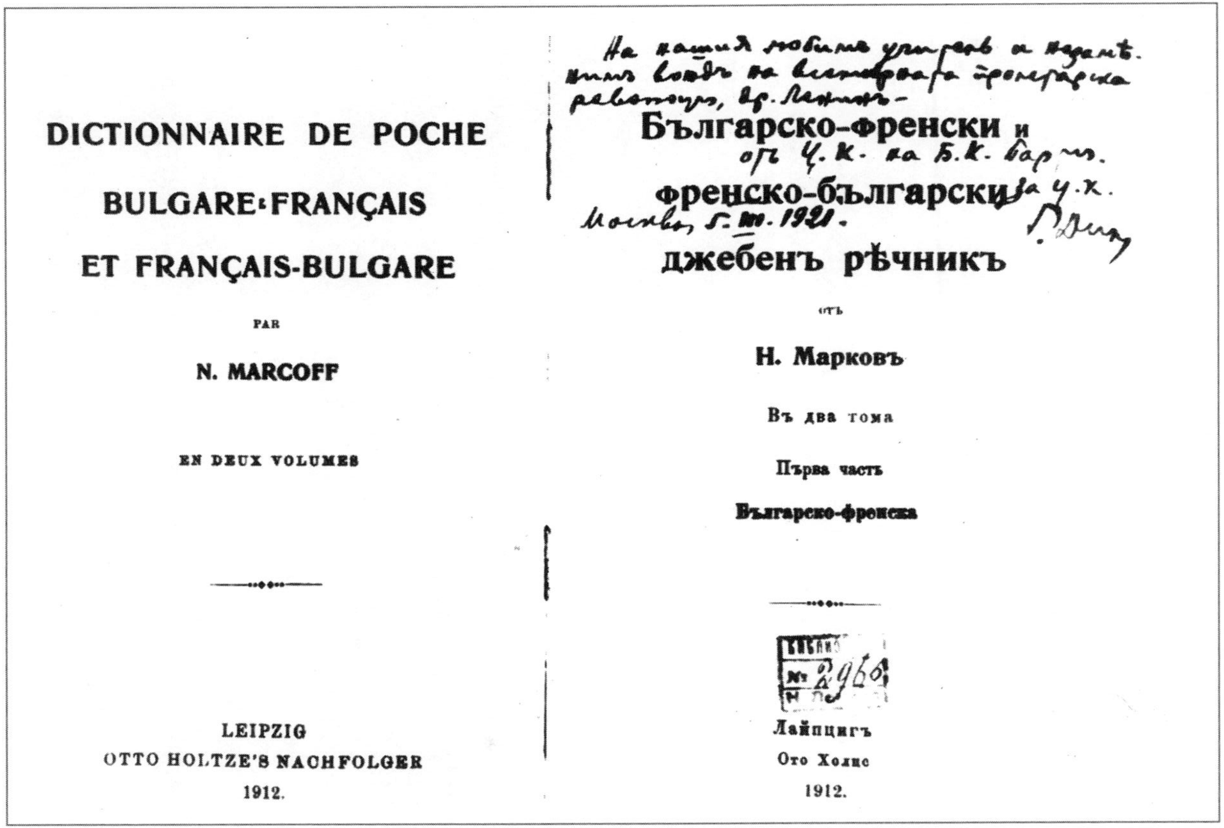

DICTIONNAIRE DE POCHE

BULGARE-FRANÇAIS

ET FRANÇAIS-BULGARE

PAR

N. MARCOFF

EN DEUX VOLUMES

LEIPZIG
OTTO HOLTZE'S NACHFOLGER
1912.

Българско-френски и
Френско-български
джебенъ рѣчникъ

отъ

Н. Марковъ

Въ два тома

Първа часть

Българско-френска

Лайпцигъ
Ото Холце
1912.

Bulgarian-French dictionary inscribed by Dimitrov to Lenin, "our beloved teacher and irreplaceable leader of the world's proletarian revolution," Moscow, 5 March 1921.

Dimitrov speaking at the Sixth Congress of the Comintern, Moscow, 25 July 1928.

Georgi Dimitrov.

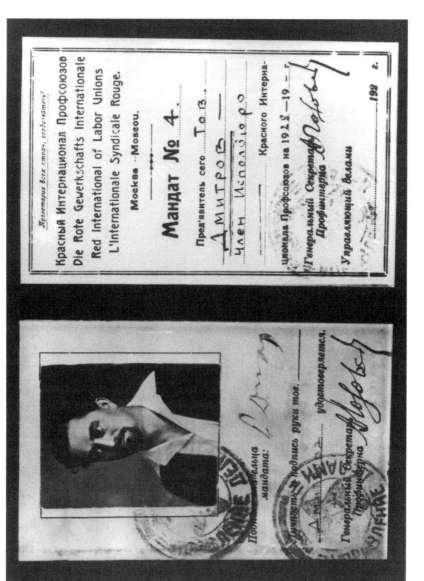

Dimitrov's Profintern card, No. 4., Moscow, 1928.

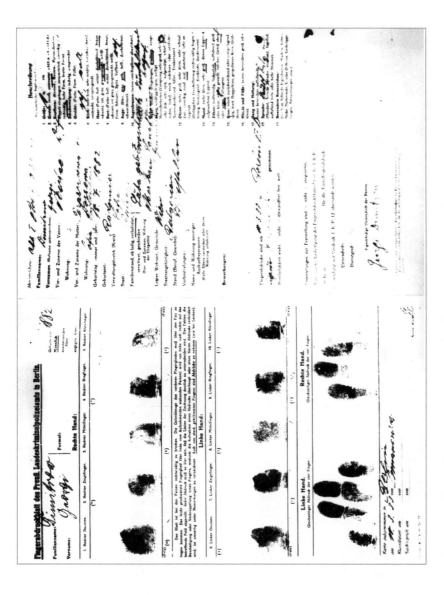

Dimitrov's file with the Prussian criminal police, Berlin, 10 March 1933.

Dimitrov's police mug shots, 10 March 1933.

Georgi Dimitrov, Vasil Tanev, and Blagoi Popov, police photo, 10 March 1933.

Dimitrov at the Leipzig trial, 1933.

Photomontage by John Heartfield: "You are scared of my questions, Mr. Chairman of the Council of Ministers." It was widely popular during the Leipzig trial of 1933.

Dimitrov's final speech at the Leipzig trial, 16 December 1933.

Open letter from the German antifascists to Dimitrov: "Dimitrov! The Bulgarian working class can be proud of you. Long live world revolution!" Stuttgart, 20 December 1933.

Stalin and Dimitrov, attending the 1935 May Day parade in Moscow.

· 7 APRIL 1939 ·

—At the Kremlin (José Díaz, Man[uilsky], Dim[itrov], trans[lator] Krylova).

—Stalin, Molotov, Beria. Transferring the party's Spanish valuables through French comrades. (Transfer directly to the Spanish CC according to inventory, deed, and so forth.)

—*Stal[in]:* The Spanish are brave, but careless. Madrid was all but in the hands of the Communists, and then suddenly other forces seized power and began killing Communists. It is not clear how it worked out that way. It appears that the Communists somehow quietly slipped away, leaving the masses to themselves, leaderless. The object is not to fight under any circumstances, even when your forces will not allow it. If the situation were insupportable, the party could announce that it considers it possible to replace the government with another one, more acceptable for the present moment, and then proceed to end the war.

But the party is obliged to say so clearly to the masses!

There are times when you have insufficient forces to continue the fight.

There are times when you suffer defeat.

"We have been beaten," Lenin said in 1905.

We are not obliged to maintain an offensive *no matter what,* but the party must tell the masses explicitly what they must do, rather than withdraw and leave the masses to themselves, disoriented.

The party should have explained why the government withdrew without a fight. Adopt a clear position as regards the Madrid junta.

The greatest failure was that Miaja,[200] and the others, were already covert conspirators and had been operating as such.

---

200. José Miaja (1878–1958), Spanish Republican general; member of the right-wing Unión Militar Española, who joined Diego Martínez Barrio's "government of conciliation" as commander of Madrid military district at the beginning of the Civil War, in belief that the government would conciliate the military insurgents. Before its withdrawal from Madrid, on 6 November 1936, Miaja received orders to create a defense council (Junta de Defensa), with himself as president, and to defend the capital "at all costs" against the advancing Nationalists. This seemingly impossible task, which Miaja greatly resented, became a source of his overnight prominence, as the Republican forces successfully defended Madrid. Despite Miaja's weak record and mediocre strategic grasp, the Communists promoted his image for their own self-serving purposes, recruited him into the PCE, and controlled him. Nevertheless, in the final days of the Republic, in March 1939, he joined the anticommunist junta of Colonel Segismundo Casado, who wanted to negotiate a favorable peace with the Nationalists, and he served as its figurehead president. He died in exile in Mexico.

They dug themselves in in Madrid while battles were under way in Catalonia.

Madrid became *different!*

The Communists failed to see that!

How to fight the enemy is something the Spanish Communists demonstrated well, and they provided enormous experience.

How to yield power and withdraw they were unable to demonstrate.

A conference of Spanish Communists should be convened to clear up all these questions, to draw lessons for other parties as well.

One must learn from negative experiences, too.

Regarding the remark in Ercoli's [Togliatti's] letter that the junta could not be overthrown because it had been impossible to open the front, Stalin related an incident in 1918 in Stalingrad (Tsaritsyn), when our forces were surrounded on all sides, and counterrevolutionaries stirred up a rebellion in the city. Stalin and Vor[oshilov] took seventy men from each of the regiments and suppressed the rebellion.

[. . .]

· 13 APRIL 1939 ·

—Last discussion with Løvlien,[201] with Trachtenberg,[202] with Airoldi[203] (CP of France).

—Airoldi specially furnished with instructions to correct the mistake in the direction of regarding the CI separately from the VKP(b). Dimitrov is "leader" of the CI.

—All three of them departed!

—Julius [Alpári] remained working for *Rundschau,* but under the observation of an ECCI representative, Clément [Fried].

---

201. Emil Løvlien (1899–1966), Norwegian Communist; editor of NKP organ *Arbeideren;* secretary of the NKP CC (1934–1940); alternate member of the ECCI (1935–1943). After spending the war in Moscow, he served as deputy in the Norwegian parliament (1945) and chairman of the NKP (1946–1965).

202. Alexander Trachtenberg (1884–1966), born in Russia, where he was a member of the RSDRP. He was imprisoned for revolutionary activity; he then emigrated to the United States in 1906, where he studied at Yale and New York University. Founder of International Publishers; founding member of the CPUSA. He was arrested for Communist activity in 1953 and 1956.

203. Julien Airoldi (b. 1890), French Communist; candidate-member (1937) and member (1945–1949) of the PCF CC; PCF representative to the ECCI (1939); deputy representing the Rhône district in the French National Assembly (from 1945 on).

—Ulbricht: an assignment supposedly from the NKVD to furnish information on him (so he is a "dubious" element).
—Marat[204] (connections with the Turkish party).

· 14 APRIL 1939 ·

—Gottwald, Szántó, Šmeral, Julius [Alpári]. They have been assigned to investigate the problem of freeing Rákosi and to contribute specific proposals.
—Evening at the Barvikha with Díaz.
—Discussion with Líster[205] (just arrived from Paris). Líster reports:
1. The Casado[206] coup in Madrid occurred on 5 March 1939 (Líster believes that Miaja is not a traitor, but was deceived into involvement in the conspiracy).[207]
2. Negrín, [Álvarez] del Vayo,[208] and other ministers were in Elda (a village in the vicinity of Alicante), closer to the Campa airfield. This is where Dolores [Ibárruri], Moreno,[209] Alfredo [Togliatti], Hernán-

204. İsmail Bilen (pseudonym: Bostancı Marat, 1902–1983), Turkish Communist; secretary of the Turkish CP CC (1927–1929, 1936–1937) and Politburo (from 1935 on); representative of the Turkish CP to the ECCI (1937–1943).

205. Enrique Líster (1907–1994), Spanish Communist; student at the Leninist School in Moscow (1934–1936); commander of the Fifth Regiment in the Battle of Madrid (1936); member of the PCE CC (from 1937 on); commander of various other Republican units in the Civil War, including an army corps; spent the war in the USSR; member of the PCE Politburo (1946–1970). After the Eurocommunist leadership expelled him from the PCE in 1970, Líster founded the pro-Soviet Communist Party of Spanish Workers (PCOE) and served as its secretary-general.

206. Segismundo Casado (1893–1968), Spanish general; liberal opponent of the Primo de Rivera dictatorship. He supported the Republican cause and fought in the defense of Madrid and the principal battles of the Civil War. Having been made a general in 1938, he commanded the People's Army of the Center; once the outcome of the war was certain, he rose against the Negrín government and established an insurgent National Council of Defense (March 1939), in hopes that negotiations with the Franco side would produce a fair deal for the professional Republican officers; he later clashed with the Communists. In exile from 20 March 1939 on, he lived in Britain, where he worked for the BBC, and then in Latin America. Returned to Spain in 1961.

207. As mentioned (n. 200), Miaja had joined the anticommunist junta of Colonel Segismundo Casado.

208. Julio Álvarez del Vayo (1891–1975), Spanish Left Socialist; economist and writer; pro-Communist foreign minister of the Spanish Republic (1936–1937, 1938–1939).

209. Stoian Minev (Stoïan Mineff, pseudonyms: Moreno, I. I. Stepanov, Boris Stefanov, 1893–1959), a native of Bulgaria who spent most of his life in the USSR

dez,[210] Checa,[211] Uribe, Modesto,[212] Líster, Castro,[213] Melchor,[214] Claudín,[215] Tagüeña,[216] and a number of commissars and army com-

---

or on various Comintern missions (1919–1943); head of the Comintern's Latin section (1926–1933); worked in Stalin's personal secretariat (1927–1928) and after the end of the Spanish Civil War in the secretariats of Dimitrov and Manuilsky (1939–1942). After a serious illness that incapacitated him during the war, he worked at the Institute of Economics of the Academy of Sciences of the USSR.

210. Jesús Hernández (1907–1971), Spanish Communist; member PCE CC (from 1931 on); student at the Leninist School in Moscow; member PCE Politburo (from 1932 on) in charge of agitprop; editor of *Mundo Obrero*. Cortes was deputy for Cordova (1936); minister of education, fine arts, and health in the Republican governments (1936–1938); chief political commissar of the central-southern region. After the collapse of the Republic he represented the PCE in the ECCI. On a mission to Mexico in 1943 he broke with the PCE, which expelled him in 1944, and in 1953 he wrote an exposé (*Yo fui un ministro de Stalin; The Great Betrayal* [Engl. trans.]) on the Communist role in Spain. During the same year he supported the establishment of a pro-Yugoslav international Communist group. He died in exile in Mexico.

211. Pedro Checa (1910–1942), Spanish Communist; member of PCE CC (from 1932 on) and Politburo (from 1935 on); party secretary (after 1935); in France, the USSR, and Mexico after 1939.

212. Juan Modesto (1906–1969), Spanish Communist; student at the Frunze Military Academy in Moscow (1930); leader of Antifascist Militia of Workers and Peasants (MOAC), a paramilitary organization that the PCE founded before the beginning of the Civil War; colonel (later general) of Republican army; participant in all the main battles of the Civil War (Jarama, Guadalajara, Brunete, Belchite, Teruel); chief of the Army of Ebro (1938–1939); member of the PCE CC (from 1937 on). He died in exile in Czechoslovakia.

213. Enrique Castro Delgado (1907–1965), Spanish Communist, member of the PCE regional committee in Madrid, director of party organ *Mundo Obrero;* founder of the Fifth Regiment during the early days of Civil War and its commander until September 1936; member of the PCE CC (from 1937 on), director of the Institute on Agrarian Reform, chief of the operations section of the Madrid junta, subcommissar of war in the General Commissariat of War. After the fall of the Republic, Castro represented the PCE to the ECCI; he went to Mexico after 1945 and returned to Spain in 1963.

214. Federico Melchor, Spanish Communist; leader of Unified Socialist Youth (JSU); director of *Mundo Obrero;* director general of propaganda.

215. Fernando Claudín (1913–1990), Spanish Communist leader and dissident; student of architecture; leader of the Young Communists; member of the PCE CC (1937–1947) and its Politburo and Executive Committee (1947–1956) and secretariat (1956–1964). After spending years in exile in Mexico, Cuba, Chile, Argentina, and France, he served as the PCE representative in Moscow (1954–1964), but the PCE expelled him in 1965. He was the author of several books on Communist history.

216. Manuel Tagüeña Lacorte (1913–1971), Spanish Communist; lieutenant colonel in the Spanish Republican army who acquired the rank of general in the USSR.

manders were also, arriving here after the fall of Catalonia to get new appointments in the army on the central front.

3. On 6 March, in the afternoon, Negrín, del Vayo, and the other ministers (minus Uribe) departed by plane, after declaring that it was impossible to stay longer, for Elda was surrounded by Casado's followers and there was the danger of being arrested.

(Líster asserts that everyone believed that that was correct. There was nothing else to do.)

4. On the same day (6 March) at 10:00 p.m. a meeting of CC members was held.

Checa gave a report on the situation. Alfredo [Togliatti] made a speech.

Matters discussed:

a) Attitude toward Casado

b) Whether part of the party leadership ought to remain

c) Whether it would be possible for all to remain

It was concluded:

a) To regard Casado as a traitor

b) It was necessary to leave

c) To leave a CC delegation consisting of several comrades to organize party leadership and to transport out cadres unable to remain in the country

Afterward, a meeting of the Politburo was held.

The night of 6–7 March (at 3:00 a.m.) Toboso[217] read out the list of comrades who were to board planes (three party planes).

Thirty-six people flew out!

Alfredo [Togliatti], Checa, and Claudín (Komsomol) remained.

5. On 6 March at 9:00 a.m. (before Negrín and the other ministers had departed) Dolores [Ibárruri], Moreno [Minev], Monsen,[218] and others flew to Oran (evidently by decision of the Politburo).

6. Líster believes that in the given conditions on 6 March this departure of the government and party leadership was necessary, for otherwise they would have been arrested by the "Casadoists."

But he also affirms that if Negrín (as head of government) had gone to Madrid together with Modesto and Líster on 5 March (immediately after the coup), it would have been possible to overthrow Casado and restore the Republic's position.

[In margin:] But Negrín had no intention whatever of acting against Casado!

217. Irene Falcón (pseudonym: Toboso, b. 1907), Spanish Communist; secretary to Dolores Ibárruri.

218. Monsen, secretary to Dolores Ibárruri.

· 15 April 1939 ·

· 24 April 1939 ·

—In Kuntsevo. (At D[mitry] Z[akharovich] [Manuilsky]'s: the May Day appeal of the CI, editing of draft.)

—My apprehensions regarding displeasure in the CC (occasioned by the surname D[imitrov] not appearing in *Pravda* on the honor presidium [of those] at the meeting in Chita and in *Izvestiia* [of those] at the meeting of musicians in Moscow). Consulted with D[mitry] Z[akharovich]. "What should I do?" "What conclusions to draw from this?" "They've decided to wait a bit and think things over!"

· 25 April 1939 ·

—Final draft of the May Day appeal. D[mitry] Z[akharovich] himself sent it to Com[rade] Stalin, to avoid further delay. I did not look over this version of the draft.

· 26 April 1939 ·

—At the Kremlin: regarding the appeal. (Stalin, Molotov, Kagan-[ovich], Voroshilov, Mikoyan, Zhdanov.)

—J. V. [Stalin] (to me): Did you see that appeal?

—D[imitrov]: Not the latest version. But this is a collective work, with Com[rade] Man[uilsky] as chief editor.

—J. V. [Stalin] (regarding the passage in the appeal praising Stalin, especially:

"Long live our Stalin!

Stalin means peace!

Stalin means Communism!

Stalin is our victory!")

—Manuilsky is a toady!

He was a Trotskyite! We criticized him for keeping quiet and not speaking out when the purges of Trotskyite bandits were going on, and now he has started toadying!

There is something suspicious here.

—That article of his in *Pravda*—"Stalin and the World Communist Movement"—is harmful and provocative!

(Molotov: Yes, a provocative article, and published at the precise moment when we are engaged in negotiations with England!)

—Did you know about this article?

D[imitrov]: I knew about it. He wanted to include a polemical passage against Kuusinen's article in *Pravda* on the twentieth anniversary of the CI, to which I objected, and he threw that part out. He believed that Kuusinen's article had been incorrect politically, because it pointed up D[imitrov]'s role at the Seventh Congress (setting new tasks).

J. V. [Stalin]: Which D[imitrov] did at the Seventh Congress—why not write about it?—And so whoever writes about D[imitrov] is an opportunist, and whoever keeps mum about him isn't an opportunist? That's a fine how-do-you-do!

Kuusinen is so much more *honest* than Manuilsky.

—We know Manuilsky! He is a man of moods: goes from one extreme to the other. Strictly a lightweight!

—He's kept you "under his thumb," hasn't he?

D[imitrov]: It's not that he's kept me "under his thumb," but he takes advantage of my illness, of the fact that I am in no condition to be at my post the way I should be.

J. V. [Stalin]: He certainly knows how to dodge and intrigue.

D[imitrov]: He always leaves the impression that he is acting with CC clearance.

J. V. [Stalin]: What CC clearance! You should be keeping a tight rein on him! Don't leave him to his own devices! He could ruin things!

After May Day we shall consider sending a different comrade of ours as well into the CI.

D[imitrov]: We are interested in your opinion on the French issues we have raised.

J. V. [Stalin]: We are very busy just now. Resolve those issues yourself. (Joking)—You are the "chairman of the CI," you know. We are only a section of the CI! . . .

J. V. [Stalin] would not allow "under the banner of Marx-Engels-Lenin-*Stalin*" to remain in the appeal but insisted on simply "Marx-Engels-Lenin."

(Although in CC slogans "M.-E.-L.-S." has already been published.)

J. V. [Stalin]: It is not a question of *prestige,* but a question of *principle.* Slogans are our own "national business," and in this case we slipped up; there was no call to write them like that! But this is *an international appeal:* here we have to put things more precisely!

Vor[oshilov]: Comrade Dimitrov often appeals for various forms of aid to the Chinese comrades. Granting such aid would make difficulties for us with Chiang Kai-shek.

J. V. [Stalin]: We have to bear in mind that we are as a state assisting the Chinese state. And we shall have to keep that up; otherwise we shall do harm to the struggle of the Chinese people.

· 27 April 1939 ·

—D. Z. [Manuilsky] is flustered, but he is trying to carry on as if nothing whatever were the matter!

(He is writing explanations to J. V. [Stalin].)

· 28 April 1939 ·

—Completely busy with this May Day article for *Pravda!* (Ponomarev and Kuusinen are not much help!)

· 29 April 1939 ·

—Late at night (actually toward morning!) finished the article. D. Z. [Manuilsky] helped with the final editing.
—Kokkinaki's flight: Moscow to North America![219]

· 30 April 1939 ·

—Terribly down. Awful headache, vomiting!

· 1 May 1939 ·

—Fine weather. Wonderful parade and demonstration!
—Along with the Politburo portraits there were portraits of D[imitrov] too.

219. Reference to the polar flight of Soviet test-aviator, Gen. Vladimir Konstantinovich Kokkinaki (b. 1904), from Moscow to USA in 22 hours and 56 minutes.

—The slogans pronounced from the tribune included "Long live the helmsman of the Comintern D[imitrov]!" (The 1 May slogans included D. Z. [Manuilsky], too!)
—Complete elimination of the various rumors about D[imitrov], here and abroad!
—J. V. [Stalin] left early, owing to the flu. The customary 1 May group dinner was consequently not held.
—The reception for parade participants at the Kremlin is postponed from 2 May to 5 May.

[. . .]

The remainder of 1939 was marked by a radical shift in Soviet policy, as Stalin rejected the diplomatic overtures of Britain and opted for the nonaggression treaty with Germany. This opened the road to the European war and the division of Poland, in which the Soviet Union participated. The Communist movement was shocked by these events and had to be browbeaten into accepting the new line of the "second imperialist war," according to which Germany and the Western countries were treated as equally predatory. Moreover, by the fall of 1939, as a result of unequal treaties, the USSR acquired bases in the Baltic countries and then made similar demands on Finland, which rejected them. This led to the Winter War with Finland (30 November 1939–12 March 1940), which further isolated the Soviet government and the Communist movement.

Throughout this period, Dimitrov, who was ailing, kept his thoughts to himself. None of his entries on these dramatic events betray any emotion or resistance, but they are also devoid of any excessive approval. Dimitrov continued to work on myriad party affairs and to deal with the "questions" of the Communist parties of Spain, France, Poland, Hungary, Germany, Bulgaria, Britain, Czechoslovakia, Belgium, the Netherlands, Canada, Denmark, China, Yugoslavia (he met with Tito on 11 November 1939), the United States, Japan, Finland, and Sweden. He continued his analyses of the Spanish collapse and busied himself with Comintern duties (entrance visas for Spanish refugees, building projects, schools, and finances: "*22 July 1939:* Resolution of the [Soviet] Politburo, 20 July 1939): 'Open a line of credit for the ECCI against the 1939 estimate in the amount of three hundred thousand gold rubles and two million *chervonnie* rubles.'"

Sections of the diary detail Stalin's thinking on the new Soviet posture and show the growing role of Andrei Zhdanov, the rising Politburo star, responsible for the Comintern. There is a hiatus in the diary between 29 September and 16 October 1939.—I.B.

· 19 MAY 1939 ·

—Discussion with Díaz on Spanish affairs ([Stela] Blagoeva translates). On the subject of party leadership Díaz says:

A homogeneous Politburo and secretariat must be formed (the current membership does not qualify as such!).

—Uribe (considers himself superior to the other members except for Díaz and Dolores [Ibárruri]; possesses insufficient authority).

—Delicado[220] is unsuitable for organizational work.

—Giorla[221] shows irresponsibility and unhealthy ambition.

—Current secretariat membership: Dolores [Ibárruri], Delicado, Uribe.

—Checa is still in Oran.

—Dolores has Monsen as secretary (he is a lawyer, in Spain he was always a governor).

—Unsuitable for Dol[ores]'s sec[retary].

[. . .]

· 20 MAY 1939 ·
[. . .]

—In the evening: Chang Li and Li Tin [Lin Biao]. On Chinese affairs! (Advice for the meeting of the CC of the Chinese CP at the end of May:

Concentrate your fire against the capitulationists. The persecution of Communists should be regarded and represented to the Chinese people as a constituent part of capitulation plans.

The essential thing is to strengthen the Communist Party—Guomindang bloc.

Better to link up with the party elements in the Guomindang, and—supported by the masses—isolate the capitulationist elements in the Guomindang.)

[. . .]

· 23 MAY 1939 ·

—Discussion with Díaz, Dolores, and Checa. (Checa reported on the final weeks of the Spanish Republic.)

220. Manuel Delicado (1901–1980), Spanish Communist; member of PCE Politburo; in exile in France and Latin America; returned to Spain in 1976; president of the PCE party control commission.

221. Luis Cabo Giorla, Spanish Communist; member of PCE Politburo; in the Americas after 1940 working with the Spanish exiles.

On the night of 6 March, Checa and Ercoli [Togliatti] left the airfield for the countryside . . . They were arrested [by the Casado military police]. Freed on 9 March in Albasade [Albacete!]. In Valencia the night of 10 March. On 11 March: conference with Hernández, Uribe, Palau,[222] Claudín. On 17 March, Hernández sent to Kirt. Checa until 20 March: Valencia; 21 March: Mufsid; 24 March: they flew out!

[. . .]

· 24 MAY 1939 ·

—Stepanov (Moreno) [Minev]. Reported on Spanish events. (He is to write a detailed report.)

—He reports that the Spanish CP archives have fallen into the hands of the French "Second Bureau."

—Marty has done good work, in Spain and now in France.

—Legros [Tréand][223] asserted that he has suspicions as regards Darnarre, Péti, and Sampé—agents of the "Second Bureau" . . .

—Legros reports:

1. The Republican government has given Legros's apparatus valuable property worth an estimated four hundred million francs for sale and storage. The transfer occurred in such circumstances and in such a manner that the government does not know what it has transferred.

2. No one except Legros knows where that property is being stored and how its sale is proceeding.

3. Without the appropriate instructions from the Spanish CP secretariat, Legros will not give up a single centime.

4. In view of the fact that the transfer occurred without verification and without any knowledge of the contents of the crates, it is possible without the slightest difficulty or risk to allocate 150 to 200 million.

5. If doing so is permissible, then to which reserves should the funds be directed, and how should they be disposed of?

—Duties refunded by the customs authorities amounted to over fifteen million francs. What should be done with these monies?

[. . .]

222. José Palau, Spanish Communist.

223. Maurice Tréand (pseudonym: Legros, 1900–1949), French Communist in charge of PCF leadership security and underground operations (beginning in 1932) and in charge of PCF CC cadre commission (beginning in 1934); member of PCF CC (1937–1945); ECCI operative in Western Europe.

· 28 May 1939 ·
[. . .]

—D. Z. [Manuilsky]: reported on the CC plenum:

Report by Andreev, "On measures for preserving public collective farm lands from squandering" (reporting a whole series of incidents where individual homesteads have been displacing collective farms). A number of secretaries spoke and gave quite a pessimistic view of the situation. *J. V. [Stalin] spoke, saying that the collective farm system is holding firm. Sixty percent of collective farm personnel are honest, hardworking, staunch supporters of the collective farm. Ten percent are loafers and profiteers.* It will now be easier to correct the situation if measures are taken to eliminate such elements from the collective farms. *The panicky talk coming from certain comrades smacks of Menshevism. That's not our stance.* Individual homesteads cannot displace collective farms, but if things are allowed to drift along the way they are going now, then after a few years and at great cost the situation will be corrected—*which could be easily accomplished now without such a cost.* In the process, one must keep the long term clearly in view and forestall any notion as crazy as rejecting the *combination* of the personal interests of collective farm personnel with the general interests of the collective farms.

—Viacheslav Mikhailovich [Molotov] gave a report on the international situation (on the negotiations with England and France).

—The English proposed that the Soviet Union guarantee freedom from aggression for Poland, Romania, and other states, while not undertaking any obligations themselves as regards the Soviet Union. *Litvinov advised accepting this. We rejected it.* We requested concluding a defense pact between England, France, and the Soviet Union, with subsequent inclusion of Poland and Romania. Romania is to reject the pact with Poland that is directed against the Soviet Union. Also the formation of a pact with the Baltic states.

The English, after long hesitation, announced that they accepted our proposals, but they formulated them in such a way that the pact was to be concluded on the basis of Article 16 of the League of Nations, which meant that the League of Nations (i.e., Bolivia and other such states) is to determine whether aggression is taking place and which party is the aggressor. Naturally, we rejected that. We favor the formation of a front for peace on behalf of all peace-loving states, against aggression. We are willing to conclude the appropriate pacts on the basis of reciprocity, but *we are conducting and will conduct our own independent line.*

—We regard the conclusion of the Anglo-Polish and Anglo-Turkish pacts as positive developments.

—Litvinov was furnishing explanations, but J. V. [Stalin] found them unsatisfactory (he made some ironical remarks about Litvinov, who as a "specialist" on international affairs considered the Politburo insufficiently informed on these issues!).

[. . .]

· 29 MAY 1939 ·
[. . .]

—A letter has been received from two Macedonians in Sofia, via the Fifth Directorate of the Red Army (Proskurov),[224] containing a proposal to re-create a foreign center for Macedonian operations. Who are they ("Apostle" and Arthur)—I sent for answers from Vlahov[225] and Gromov.[226]

[. . .]

· 8 JUNE 1939 ·

—Ercoli [Togliatti] and Sergeev [Kolev].
Discussed Spanish conference work with Ercoli [Togliatti] and Díaz.
—Comorera[227] raises the following issues:

224. Chief of intelligence administration at the Red Army general staff.

225. Dimitar Vlahov (1878–1953), Macedonian revolutionary, born in Kukuš (Kilkís), in Aegean Macedonia; a founder of the Internal Macedonian Revolutionary Organization (United), or IMRO (United), the pro-Communist wing of the Macedonian national movement (1925). He was in the USSR from 1935 to 1944, was elected to the presidency of the Antifascist Council of People's Liberation of Yugoslavia (AVNOJ) in 1943, and was active in the Macedonian branch of KPJ from 1944 on. Deputy in Yugoslavia's Federal National Assembly and its vice president; president of the People's Front of Macedonia.

226. Vladimir Poptomov (pseudonyms: Gromov, Tomov, 1890–1952), Macedonian revolutionary from Pirin Macedonia; a founder and political secretary of IMRO (United) from 1925 to 1933; councilman of AVNOJ (1943); member of the BRP(k) Politburo (1944); minister of foreign affairs of Bulgaria (1949). Whereas Vlahov opted for Yugoslavia and Macedonian identity, Poptomov opted for Bulgaria and Bulgar identity.

227. Joan Comorera (1894–1958), Catalan Socialist, later Communist; president of the pronationalist Socialist Union of Catalonia (USC), the largest compo-

1. The "Catalan Republic."[228]
2. Admit the "United Socialist Party" [PSUC] to the Comintern as an independent section.
—Discussions by the Spanish comrades among themselves are dragging on. Documents are still not ready.

[. . .]

· 22 JULY 1939 ·
[. . .]

—Resolution of the [VKP(b)] P[olit]-buro, 20 July 1939:
"Open a line of credit for the ECCI against the 1939 estimate in the amount of three hundred thousand gold rubles and two million *chervonnye* rubles."

[. . .]

· 22 AUGUST 1939 ·

—Meeting of the secretariat.
—Directive for the parties in connection with negotiations between Germany and the USSR.

· 23 AUGUST 1939 ·

—(Ribbentrop[229] and his entourage arrived in Moscow to negotiate the nonaggression pact.)

[. . .]

---

nent of the United Socialist Party of Catalonia (PSUC), formed in July 1936 with Comorera as its secretary-general. The PSUC, which was connected with the Comintern through its Communist component, had pro-Catalan and middle-class instincts, but it was effectively controlled by the PCE. Comorera himself became a member of the PCE CC and opposed the influence of the Anarchists and the POUM in Catalonia. In exile after 1939, Comorera was expelled from the PSUC (1949). He secretly returned to Spain and was arrested (1954) under unclear circumstances. A military tribunal in Barcelona sentenced him to thirty years' imprisonment. He died in prison.

228. Comorera evidently hoped to obtain the support of the ECCI for Catalan independence.

229. Joachim von Ribbentrop (1893–1946), German foreign minister (1938–1945).

· 24 AUGUST 1939 ·

—Nonaggression treaty between the USSR and Germany published. (Photo in *Pravda* and *Izvestiia:* Molotov, Stalin—Ribbentrop, and Gaus!)[230]

· 25 AUGUST 1939 ·

—Meeting of the secretariat on the nonaggression pact. A directive has been drafted and sent to the parties.

[...]

· 28 AUGUST 1939 ·

—Opening of the extraordinary session of the Supreme Soviet of the USSR. The agenda:
1. Agricultural tax
2. Universal conscription law
3. Ratification of the nonaggression treaty between the USSR and Germany

· 29 AUGUST 1939 ·

—*Beno's wife (Herta) has arrived.*[231] She traveled from Warsaw to Moscow with an employee of the Soviet embassy in Prague, Tkachun.
—Took sick and could not go to the session of the Supreme Soviet.

· 30 AUGUST 1939 ·

—Vŭlko [Chervenkov], Lena,[232] Beno, and Herta here with us. Saw *The Parade of Youth* and *Courage.*

230. Friedrich Gaus (1881–1955), German official; specialist in international law; director of the Foreign Ministry Legal Department; undersecretary (from 1939 on); adviser to foreign minister Stresemann at Locarno (1925); member of Ribbentrop's party at the signing of the nonaggression pact in Moscow.

231. Herta Fleischmann was the wife of Beno Fleischmann, Dimitrov's brother-in-law.

232. Elena Dimitrova (Lena, 1902–1974); Dimitrov's sister; wife of Vŭlko Chervenkov; Bulgarian Communist; political émigrée to the USSR (1925–1945); employed by the ECCI and the OMI; member of the BKP CC (after 1945); director of the central party school (1945–1949).

—Doctor arrived, advised staying home on 31 August so the infection would not develop complications.
—Disturbing reports from all countries.
—Military preparations in England and France.
—Mobilization in Holland, Belgium, and Switzerland.
—Germany and Poland have assumed fully military postures.
—All the same, there is still a chance of coming to a compromise solution about Danzig and the corridor.
—In the USSR, calm assurance about the future.

· 31 AUGUST 1939 ·

—Report by Voroshilov on conscription legislation.
—A report by Molotov on the Soviet-German nonaggression treaty. Ratification of the treaty by the Supreme Soviet of the USSR.

· 1 SEPTEMBER 1939 ·

—*War has begun between Germany and Poland.*
—Meeting of the secretariat on the current situation. Exchange of opinions is to be continued tomorrow.
—The following telegram has been sent to *Thorez:*

We think that you ought not to announce your unqualified support for the Daladier-Bonnet government. You would do best, in our view, to take something like the following position:

By its betrayal of Czechoslovakia, Spain, and Munich and its violation of collective security, the Daladier-Bonnet government has strengthened fascist Germany; following the policy of the English warmongers against the USSR, this government has alienated the USSR and led the French people to the brink of war. Such a government cannot be entrusted with the defense of the country. There must be a government to which the people will rally, and not one that divides popular forces through its criminal persecution of the party of the working class. Inform Pollitt that the English Communist Party's position is according to our information correct, and that it should continue to be consistently maintained. Confirm your receipt of this, and report your opinion.

· 2 SEPTEMBER 1939 ·

—Meeting of the secretariat. Continuation of the exchange of opinions.

—Commission formed (D[imitrov], M[anuilsky], Kuus[inen]) to draft a document.

· 3 SEPTEMBER 1939 ·

—England has declared war against Germany. France has announced that it is commencing to fulfill its obligations as regards Poland.
—French comrades—Guyot and Airoldi—have been given instructions. They're leaving tomorrow by plane. (Letarge, too.)[233]

[. . .]

· 7 SEPTEMBER 1939 ·

—At the Kremlin (Stalin, Molotov, Zhdanov).
Stalin:
—A war is on between two groups of capitalist countries—(poor and rich as regards colonies, raw materials, and so forth)—for the redivision of the world, for the domination of the world!
—We see nothing wrong in their having a good hard fight and weakening each other.
—It would be fine if at the hands of Germany the position of the richest capitalist countries (especially England) were shaken.
—Hitler, without understanding it or desiring it, is shaking and undermining the capitalist system.
—*The position of Communists in power is different from the position of Communists in the opposition.*
—We are the masters of our own house.
—Communists in the capitalist countries are in the opposition; there the bourgeoisie is master.
—We can maneuver, pit one side against the other to set them fighting with each other as fiercely as possible.
—*The nonaggression pact is to a certain degree helping Germany.*
—*Next time, we'll urge on the other side.*
—Communists in the capitalist countries should be speaking out boldly against their governments and against the war.
—*Before the war, opposing a democratic regime to fascism was entirely correct.*
—*During war between the imperialist powers that is now incorrect.*
—*The division of capitalist states into fascist and democratic no longer makes sense.*

233. Activist in the Young Communist League (JCF) of France.

—*The war has precipitated a radical change.*

—Yesterday's United Popular Front served to ease the position of slaves under a capitalist regime.

—*Under conditions of an imperialist war, the prospect of the annihilation of slavery arises!*

—Maintaining yesterday's position (the United Popular Front, the unity of the nation) today means slipping into the position of the bourgeoisie.

—That slogan is struck.

—Formerly (in history) the Polish state was a nat[ional] state. Therefore, revolutionaries defended it against partition and enslavement.

—*Now [Poland is] a fascist state, oppressing Ukrainians, Belorussians, and so forth.*

—The annihilation of that state under current conditions would mean one fewer bourgeois fascist state to contend with!

—What would be the harm if as a result of the rout of Poland we were to extend the socialist system onto new territories and populations?

We preferred agreements with the so-called democratic countries and therefore conducted negotiations.

—But the English and the French wanted us for farmhands [*v batrakakh*] and at no cost!

—We, of course, would not go for being farmhands, still less for getting nothing in return.

The working class must be told:

—A war is on for mastery of the world.

—The bosses of the capitalist countries are waging war for their own imperialist interests.

—This war promises workers and toilers nothing but suffering and privations.

—Speak out boldly against the war and its perpetrators.

—Expose the neutrality, the bourgeois neutrality, of countries that, favoring neutrality for themselves, are in fact supporting the war in other countries in the interests of gain.

—Principal points of the ECCI presidium must be prepared and published.

· 8 SEPTEMBER 1939 ·

—A directive for the Communist parties has been prepared [in German]:

This war is an unjust, imperialist war, and the bourgeoisie of all the belligerent nations share equally in the guilt. In no land may the working class, much less the Communist Party, support the war. The bourgeoisie is fighting the war, but not against fascism as Chamberlain and the leaders of social democracy claim. The war is being fought between two groups of capitalist countries for control of the world. The international working class can certainly not defend fascist Poland, which has rejected the help of the Soviet Union and suppressed other nationalities.

The Communist parties have fought against the supporters of Munich because they wanted a true antifascist front that would include the Soviet Union, but the bourgeoisie of England and France have repudiated the Soviet Union in order to pursue a predatory war.

The war has materially altered the situation. The division of the capitalist states into fascist and democratic [camps] has lost its former significance. Strategy must be altered accordingly. The strategy of Communist parties in all warring lands at this stage of the war is to oppose the war, to expose its imperialist character; where Communist deputies are available, to vote against war credits, to explain to the masses that the war will not bring them anything but adversity and ruin. In the neutral countries, one must expose governments that seem to favor their own country's neutrality but support the war in other countries in order to make a profit—as the government of the United States of America does with regard to Japan and China. Everywhere, Communist parties must undertake a decisive offensive against the treacherous policy of social democracy.

Communist parties, especially those of France, England, Belgium, and the United States of America, which have proceeded in opposition to this view, must immediately correct their political line.

[. . .]

· 17 SEPTEMBER 1939 ·

—Report by Molotov over the radio about the Red Army's crossing the border into western Belorussia and western Ukraine.
—Discussion with Springhall[234] (English CP): he departs on 18 September 1939.

[. . .]

234. Douglas Springhall (1901–1953), British Communist; member CPGB CC; in the International Brigades in Spain (1936–1937); representative of the CPGB to the ECCI; head of the CPGB organizational section (1939–1943). He was expelled from the party in 1945.

· 18 SEPTEMBER 1939 ·

—We saw a film, *A Night in September*—the Donbas, Sergo [Ordzhonikidze].

· 19 SEPTEMBER 1939 ·

—The secretariat was shown a draft of theses regarding the war.

· 20 SEPTEMBER 1939 ·

—We worked (M[anuilsky], K[uusinen], D[imitrov]) at Government House on editing the theses.

· 21 SEPTEMBER 1939 ·

—Work continued.

· 22 SEPTEMBER 1939 ·

—We decided to make fundamental revisions in the second part of the theses.
—We requested comments and proposals by the other secretaries.

· 23 September 1939 ·

—Members of the secretariat shown the draft of the theses.

· 24 September 1939 ·

—Zhdanov called from Stalin's dacha about the theses—"By this time Com[rade] Stalin would have written a whole book!"

· 25 September 1939 ·

—We worked at the government house on the final version of the theses.

· 26 September 1939 ·

—Work continued.

· 27 September 1939 ·

—Finished the theses and sent them to Stalin, Molotov, and Zhdanov.

[...]

· 21 October 1939 ·

—J. Vis. [Stalin] called. Soon as he recognized my voice, he hung up!

[...]

· 24 October 1939 ·

—Zhdanov called about the article:[235] "I talked with Com[rade] St[alin]. He read the article. Corrected it. The article is good. He wanted to go over the corrections with you tonight, but he did not have the text with him. Said he would call you!"

· 25 October 1939 ·

—*At the Kremlin (Com[rades] Stalin and Zhdanov)* regarding the article.
1. *Not to get ahead of ourselves!*
    —Not to put out every slogan at once.
    —Slogans must be brought out that are appropriate for the given stage of the war.
    —Slogans must be put out that have ripened, that are understandable and acceptable to the masses.
    —The masses must be led to revolutionary slogans gradually!
    —Slogans must be brought out that will help the masses to break with Social D[emocratic] leaders!
2. *For now the main thing is negative slogans!*
    —Down with the imperialist war!
    —End the war, end the bloodshed!

235. Refers to Dimitrov's article "The War and the Working Class in the Capitalist Countries," which was published in *Kommunisticheskii Internatsional*, nos. 8–9, 1939.

—Drive out governments that support the war!

—(We will not come out against governments that favor peace!)

—Raising the issue of peace now, on the basis of the destruction of capital, means helping Chamberlain and the warmongers,

—means isolating oneself from the masses!

3. *During the first imperialist war the Bolsheviks overestimated the situation.*

—*We all got ahead of ourselves and made mistakes!*

—*That can be explained by the current conditions, but not justified.*

—*There must be no copying now of the positions the Bolsheviks held then.*

—*We have learned a few things since then and gotten smarter!*

—It should also be remembered that the current situation is different: at that time there were no Communists in power.

Now there is the Soviet Union!

4. *The Com[munist] parties should be not propaganda groups, but the political parties of the working class.*

—*This is no time for theories!*

—The masses must be *mobilized for the struggle!*

—We believe that in our pacts of mutual assistance (Estonia, Latvia, Lithuania)[236] we have found the right form to allow us to bring a number of countries into the Soviet Union's sphere of influence.

But for that we will have to maintain a consistent posture, strictly observing their internal regimes and independence.

—*We are not going to seek their sovietization.*

—*The time will come when they will do that themselves!*

[. . .]

· 7 November 1939 ·

—Parade and demonstration.

(People were bearing a portrait of D[imitrov] and several portraits of Thäl[mann].)

---

236. The Soviet Union concluded a treaty with Estonia that gave the Soviets naval and air bases on Estonian territory (29 September 1939) and concluded similar treaties with Latvia (5 October 1939) and Lithuania (10 October 1939). The treaty with Lithuania, a mutual assistance pact, involved the transfer of Soviet-occupied Polish Wilno (Vilnius) and the surrounding areas to Lithuania.

—Luncheon at Stalin's (Kagan[ovich], Molot[ov], Andreev, Mikoyan, Budenny, Kulik, D[imitrov].)

—*Stalin:* The slogan of "the United States of Europe" was mistaken. Vladimir Ilich [Lenin] caught himself in time and struck that slogan . . .

—*I believe that the slogan of turning the imperialist war into a civil war (during the first imperialist war) was appropriate only for Russia, where the workers were tied to the peasants and under tsarist conditions could engage in an assault on the bourgeoisie.*

—*For the European countries that slogan was inappropriate, for the workers there had received a few democratic reforms from the bourgeoisie and were clinging to them, and they were not willing to engage in a civil war (revolution) against the bourgeoisie. (The European workers had to be approached differently.)*

—These peculiarities of the European workers should have been taken into consideration, and the question put differently; different slogans should have been brought out for them.

In Germany, the petty-bourgeois nationalists are capable of a sharp turn—they are flexible—not tied to capitalist traditions, unlike bourgeois leaders like Chamberlain and his ilk.

—*Bureaucratism* means holding to established rules, routines, *not thinking independently, contributing nothing new* that might be dictated by changed circumstances . . .

[. . .]

· 10 November 1939 ·

—Meeting of the secretariat. (Propaganda Department, Stalin's sixtieth.)

—Kuusinen met with Jos. V. [Stalin] regarding Finnish affairs.[237]

---

237. After the Baltic successes, in October the Soviet government proposed a similar arrangement to Finland, whereby Finland would agree to border adjustments near Leningrad and would lease to the USSR a naval base at Hanko on the Gulf of Finland. The Finns' demurral led to the Soviet attack on 30 November. The Soviets justified the clumsy aggression, which was entirely improvised, by citing a call for "fraternal assistance" from a (bogus) Finnish people's government, which the Soviets had set up in the border town of Terijoki—and which was headed by Kuusinen.

· 11 November 1939 ·

—Walter [Tito] (Yugoslavia): last discussion before his departure.
—Thorez is here at my dacha.[238]

· 12 November 1939 ·

—Thorez, his wife and son, are here with us.
—*Kozovski has been released.*
—Invited Kozovski and his wife and Belov [Damianov] and his wife to see me.

[...]

· 1 December 1939 ·

—Appeal by the CC of the CP of Finland.
—Formation of the people's government of Finland (Kuusinen).
—Establishment of diplomatic relations with the new government.

· 2 December 1939 ·

—Declaration of the people's government.
—Conclusion of treaty of mutual assistance and friendship between the Soviet Union and the Finnish Democratic Republic.

[...]

· 21 December 1939 ·[239]

—At the Kremlin: "Comradely dinner."

[...]

—Stalin: To the pilots, to the tank crews, to the fighters, to the workers, peasants, intelligentsia, to the young people!
[In margin: It's gotten pretty crowded—Finland, Bessarabia, Chernovtsy!]
—Molotov: *Stalin has surpassed Len[in]. By his participation in all*

---

238. Thorez deserted from the French army in October and, together with his wife, Jeanette Vermeersch, and son, made his way to the Soviet Union. For this he was sentenced in absentia to five years in prison and loss of citizenship.

239. Stalin's sixtieth birthday.

the practical leadership work, he is entirely bound up with the practical life of the party and the Soviet Union.
—Until 8:00 a.m.
An unforgettable night!

[. . .]

Dimitrov's diaries in the winter and spring of 1940 were marked by the consequences of the nonaggression treaty with Germany and of the Finnish war, the latter assessed by Stalin in an entirely too favorable fashion. By April, Hitler struck at Norway and Denmark, and in May at France and the Low Countries. Dimitrov's taciturnity and lack of comment on these events is remarkable. Throughout, he busied himself with the party affairs of Argentina, Sweden, Hungary, China (the Chinese commission in which Zhou Enlai participated), Romania, France, India, Bulgaria, Norway, Denmark, Lithuania, and New Zealand. There is a hiatus in the diary from 12 May to 13 September 1940, during which the Allies rescued the troops at Dunkirk, Italy entered the war, the Vichy government was established, the Germans commenced terror bombing of Britain, and a defense agreement was concluded between Britain and the United States. In the Balkans, the USSR gained Bessarabia and northern Bukovina. In addition, Romania was forced into territorial concessions to Hungary and, by September, to Bulgaria. Dimitrov took ill again and was directed for treatment to Sochi, to which he removed on 22 September 1940.

Dimitrov stayed on the Black Sea coast until 30 October 1940 and continued his treatment afterward in Moscow. This trip, unlike the previous stays at the southern Russian resorts, was marked by almost total political inactivity. He even declined to write the usual October Revolution anniversary article for *Pravda*. The important exceptions to that lack of activity are included below. It is as if Dimitrov concealed his thoughts and turned his pen to the incidental—the beauty of the Black Sea region. Still, he noted with sentiment the passing of the old Bulgarian revolutionary Hristo Kabakchiev ("I was told by telephone from Moscow that Kabakchiev died on the night of 6 October. The poor man did not live to see Bulgaria again, only under our rule!"). Strikingly, Kabakchiev was among the very few of the purge victims to be released after the investigation (1937–1938).—I.B.

· 9 JANUARY 1940 ·
[. . .]

—Letter sent to Com[rade] Andreev in connection with the hard currency estimate: advance needed for 1940, four hundred thousand gold rubles.

[. . .]

· 21 JANUARY 1940 ·
[. . .]

—*Evening at the Bolshoi Theater.*
Report by Shcherbakov.
In the Politburo office.
Friendly atmosphere.
—Stalin, Molotov, Voroshilov, Kaganovich, Kalinin, Andreev, Beria, Shvernik, Bulg[anin], Shkiryatov, Shcherbakov, Budenny, D[imitrov].

—*Molotov (regarding document on the tactics of the German CP):* Yes, I noticed. You have not made up your mind to call the war imperialist as far as Germany is concerned!" "We shall have to exchange views on the tactics of the German party."

—*Stalin: World revolution as a single act is nonsense. It transpires at different times in different countries. The Red Army activities are also a matter of world revolution.*

—*Stalin:* It is clear now how Finland was prepared for a major war against us. They readied every village for that aim. Hangars for thousands of aircraft—whereas Finland had [only] several hundred of them.

There are 150,000 Finnish *Schutzkorpists*—that's where the White Finns are strongest. We have killed sixty thousand of them; we shall have to kill the rest, and that will be the end of it.

There should be nothing left but the bare bones of a state.

We have no desire for Finland's territory. But Finland should be a state that is friendly to the Soviet Union.

—*Stalin:* A toast: "To the fighters of the Red Army, which was undertrained, badly clothed, and badly shod, which we are now providing with [proper] clothing and boots, which is fighting for its somewhat tarnished honor, fighting for its glory!"

(Kulik arrived and reported bad news.)

—*Stalin:* You're lapsing into panic. I shall send you Chelpanov's book on the foundations of psychology.[240] The pagan Greek priests were intelligent people. When they would get disturbing reports, they would adjourn to their bathhouses, take baths, wash themselves clean, and only afterward would they assess events and make decisions.

—The human being takes in through its organs various impressions and sensations and all kinds of shit.

[But] there are inhibiting centers. (Those centers are underdeveloped in Kul[ik]'s case!) You have to throw out all the garbage and make decisions on the basis of the fundamental facts, and not under the influence of momentary moods or terrifying, nonexistent things!

—*Stalin: Mayakovsky was the finest proletarian poet.* (He had received several letters from Demian[241] and others objecting to that assertion.)

———————

—I questioned Stalin about relations between Bulgaria and Yugoslavia, about the significance of the Yugoslav Cvetković.[242]

———————

—In connection with Turkey he said: "It is not we but the Turks who stand to lose. We are even glad that we shall be free of certain ties of friendship with Turkey."

[. . .]

· 3 FEBRUARY 1940 ·

—Discussion with Vokshin and Sork[in] (center in Yugoslavia).[243]

[. . .]

240. Refers to the works of Georgy Ivanovich Chelpanov (1862–1936), Russian psychologist and philosopher who adopted aspects of Marxism during his long career as a researcher and instructor.

241. Demian Bedny (real name: Yefim Alekseevich Pridvorov, 1883–1945), Soviet revolutionary poet and propagandist.

242. Dragiša Cvetković (1893–1969), prime minister of Yugoslavia (1939–1941).

243. Josip Kopinič (pseudonyms: Vokshin, Antun Kadić, Vazduh, Mali, 1911–1997), Yugoslav Communist, who fought in the International Brigades in Spain. Together with G. Z. Sorkin (b. 1899), a Soviet signals service operative at the ECCI, he coordinated the Comintern center in Zagreb, which Kopinič and his wife Stella, a Greek Communist, led from 1940 to 1944. The center connected the CPs

· 23 FEBRUARY 1940 ·
[. . .]

—Sent letter on financial assistance ($350,000) to the CP of China and to Comrade Stalin.

[. . .]

· 24 FEBRUARY 1940 ·

—Zhou Enlai, Ren Li [Ren Bishi], and their wives are here with us.

· 25 FEBRUARY 1940 ·

—Continuation of conference on Indian issues.

—*Spoke on the telephone with Comrade Stalin:* Cannot see me about Chinese affairs. Very busy. Has not read the material he was sent. "There is a lot of paperwork I am not finding time to read. Decide for yourself. We shall give the assistance (three hundred thousand American dollars)."

[. . .]

· 1 MARCH 1940 ·

—Prasolov (adv[iser] at the Soviet legation in Sofia) and Sergeev [Kolev].

Letters from our people. Reports.

T[odor] P[avlov]:[244]—*"There is a traitor in the party leadership!"*

[. . .]

---

of Italy, Switzerland, Austria, Hungary, Bulgaria, Greece, and Yugoslavia with Moscow, and Tito used it extensively in the early stages of the war. Kopinič, himself Slovene by nationality, was involved in two important party matters in Croatia. In 1941, after the establishment of the Croatian collaborationist state, he attempted to usurp power in the Communist Party of Croatia and to effect the escape of a large group of imprisoned Communists, held in Kerestinec, near Zagreb. Both attempts ended in failure. He continued his intelligence activities on behalf of the USSR after the war in Turkey, under cover of being a Yugoslav trade attaché. He sided with Tito during the Cominform split of 1948 and returned to Yugoslavia to serve as the director of two major firms. After Tito's death he was involved in several major controversies over his role in the 1940s.

244. Todor Pavlov (1890–1977), Bulgarian Communist and Marxist philosopher; member of the BKP CC (from 1924 on), political émigré to the USSR (1932–1936); elaborated Stalinist aesthetic concepts (such as the "theory of reflexes");

· 27 MARCH 1940 ·

—At the plenum [of the VKP(b) CC]. Report by Molotov on foreign policy.
—Report by Voroshilov on the lessons of the Finnish war.
   —Ignorance of the actual situation in Finland.
   —Unpreparedness for such a war.
   —A significant number of commanders were unsuitable.
   —Poor uniforming of the army.
   —Our casualties: 233,000, including 52,000 killed.
   —The Finns: 70,000 killed and 200,000 wounded.
   —We need a regular army. Ready at any moment. Increase [forces]!
   —Stop the turnover in command staff.
   —Make significant improvements in rail transportation.
   —Increase supplies.
   —Study the Mannerheim Line on site.

[. . .]

· 28 MARCH 1940 ·

—At the CC plenum.
—Lively discussion of Voroshilov's report. Contributions by *Mekhlis, Shchadenko,*[245] *Kulik (all deputies of the people's commissar). They attack the people's commissar* [Voroshilov] *and the general staff.*
—They claim that incorrect information on the strength and defensive capabilities of the enemy, his fortifications, bases, and territories, was the fundamental error in the Finnish war.
   —*Kulik:* If you are going to fight a war, then you have to provide for a) replacements of manpower and matériel; b) sanitary services.
   —The commander's authority has to be enhanced (that authority was severely undermined in 1924 and 1937).
   —Our commanders cannot be treated as officers used to be treated (the problem of the special department!)
   —Mekhlis: "Com[rade] Voroshilov will believe only his secretaries. Does not like criticism. Cannot stand Mekhlis."

---

member of the Bulgarian Regency Council (1944–1946); president of the Bulgarian Academy of Sciences (beginning in 1947).
   245. Yefim Afanasievich Shchadenko (1885–1951), Soviet Communist; member of the VKP(b) CC (1939–1941); Red Army general; deputy people's commissar for defense.

—Mushkovich [Smushkevich][246] (aviation):

In the Spanish war: 150 aircraft.

In Mongolia: 500 aircraft.

In the Finnish war: 3,000 aircraft, and losses of up to 40 percent.

—*Stalin:* Argues against the attacks by Kulik, Mekhlis, and Shchadenko. They ignored the general staff, failed to support it, and now they are putting the blame on it. The general staff began actually operating during the war under the direction of [field] headquarters.

—*The mistake was that the people's commissars like to lead via their secretaries.*

—*What Kulik said is entirely mistaken.* He himself is responsible for art[illery] guidance, and so forth.

—*Mekhlis is a good man, a hard worker, but unsuitable for army leadership.*

—*Shchadenko is responsible for cadres, but for him, no one counts except farmhands. Whoever is not a farmhand will not do, as far as he is concerned.*

—*As for Voroshilov, it does not often happen around here that a people's commissar speaks so openly about his own shortcomings.*

It is not true that the army's fighting capacity decreases in wintertime. All the Russian army's major victories were won in wintertime. Alexander Nevsky against the Swedes, Peter I against the Swedes in Finland, Alexander I's victory over Napoleon. *We are a northern country.* There are a great many good traditions in the old army that are to be used. The matter of rusks for the army and so on.

Conclusions:

1. *Our fighters are superb.*

2. *Our commanders are 60 percent good; 40 percent are slackers, weak-willed [types], cowards, and so forth.*

Good commanders: determination, will, knowledge; reasonable (do not beat their heads against a wall). They know how to attack when they should, hold back where advancing is impossible, saving their strength to strike again.

They do not take things by storm!

Everything depends on the commander. A good commander can manage even with a weak division; a bad commander can demoralize the best division in the army.

3. Artillery: the decisive role,

tanks: clear a path for the infantry,

aviation: invaluable role.

246. Yakov Vladimirovich Smushkevich (1902–1941), Soviet general; chief of air force (from 1939 on); deputy chief of supreme staff (from 1940 on).

4. We brought not only the White Finns to their knees, but their instructors, too—the French, English, Italians, and Germans.

5. If the people's commissariat performs better, we'll have the best army in the world.

[. . .]

· 28 SEPTEMBER 1940 ·

[. . .]

—A radio report of the conclusion in Berlin of a tripartite pact between Germany, Italy, and Japan!

—Exceptional significance.

—Further expansion of the war to world war dimensions.

[. . .]

· 26 OCTOBER 1940 ·

[. . .]

—*Letter to Comrade Ercoli* [Togliatti]:

Com[rade] Ercoli:

In my view, Kuus[inen] is correct. In the current national conditions, forming the expelled Social Democratic opposition, with the Communists' help, into an independent organization will allow it to speak out more decisively and plainly against the traitorous policies of the Social Democratic leadership, and in defense of truly proletarian domestic and foreign policies. This is of enormous significance from the point of view of correct political orientation for the working class, rallying the working masses and hastening the further destruction of the positions of reactionary social democracy. Meanwhile, the line of struggling to restore the opposition to the ranks of the Social Democratic Party not only promises no practical results whatever; it will in fact significantly hinder that so necessary process.

26 October 1940   G. M. [Dimitrov]

[. . .]

· 28 OCTOBER 1940 ·

[. . .]

—Instructions just now passed on from the CC: this year it is not recommended for the ECCI to make a public appeal!

—Instead of an appeal, an article!

[. . .]

· 6 NOVEMBER 1940 ·
[. . .]

—Evening at the Bolshoi Theater. Ceremonial assembly on the occasion of twenty-third anniversary of the October Revolution.

—[I] was elected to the honor presidium.

—Kalinin is speaker. (Rákosi and his brother sat in the first row.)

—During intermission: *St*[alin]: How is Rákosi?

D[imitrov]: Feeling fine, but a reaction will obviously set in after lengthy imprisonment.

St[alin]: He does not sympathize with the Trotskyites?

D[imitrov]: No. He is holding out staunchly. Even in prison, in connection with the trial of the Trotskyites, he took a firm position against the Trotskyites.

St[alin]: All of them wavered at one time or another. *They did not understand our business.*

D[imitrov]: The release of Rákosi is a great *October's* gift for the Comintern!

· 7 NOVEMBER 1940 ·

—On Red Square.

—After the demonstration, luncheon with Joseph Vissarionovich [Stalin]. Present were Molotov, Kalinin, Voroshilov, Budenny, Andreev, Kaganovich, Beria, Mikoyan, Shvernik, Bulganin, Malenkov, Shcherbakov, commander of the Moscow district Tiulenev (an army general),[247] D[imitrov] (later on Timoshenko,[248] too, was summoned).

247. Ivan Vladimirovich Tiulenev (1892–1978), Soviet general; commander of the Caucasian and Moscow military districts (1938–1940); in the war, commander of the armies at the southern front (1941), the Caucasian military district, and the Caucasian front (1942–1945); commander of the Kharkov military district (1945–1946); candidate-member of the VKP(b) CC (1941–1952).

248. Semyon Konstantinovich Timoshenko (1895–1970), Soviet marshal; commander of the North Caucasus (1937), Kharkov (1937), and Kiev (1938) military districts; commander of the Ukrainian front that occupied eastern Poland (1939); commander of the northwest front during the Finnish war (1939–1940); people's commissar for defense (1940–1941), then deputy commissar; commander of the western, southwestern, Stalingrad, and northwestern fronts (1941–1943); commander of the second, third, and fourth Ukrainian fronts (1944–1945); holder of various command posts after the war, ending with that of inspector general of the armed forces (1960–1961); member of the VKP(b) CC (1939–1952); candidate-member (1952–1970).

First pages of entry dated 7 November 1940.

—Lifted our glasses to everyone, in order of seating around the table.

—Conversation turned to the Civil War on the southern front (the disagreements between St[alin] and Tr[otsky]).

—I asked J. V. [Stalin] by what criterion leadership cadres were selected.

—*J. V.* [Stalin]: Trotsky held to old officers, specialists, who often turned traitor.

We, on the contrary, selected people loyal to the Revolution, people connected with the masses, by and large noncommissioned officers from the lower ranks, although we were clearly aware of the enormous value of honest specialists.

Vl[adimir] Ilich [Lenin] had the impression at first that I did not give a damn for specialists. He called me in to see him in Moscow. Tr[otsky] and Piatakov tried to prove that and interceded for two specialists who had been fired by me. At that very moment a report came in from the front that one of them had turned traitor and the other had deserted. *Ilich,* after reading the telegram, exposed Trotsk[y] and Piatakov and acknowledged the correctness of our actions.

———————————

—We sat over our lunch from 5:30 till 9:00. Everyone was getting ready to leave, when suddenly J. V. [Stalin] said: "I would like to speak," and took his glass in his hand:

—History has spoiled us. We have had many successes with comparative ease. This has led to complacency in many of us, a dangerous complacency. People do not wish to study, although the conditions for study here are superb. People think that since they are from worker and peasant stock, since they have calluses on their hands, then there is nothing they cannot do, and there is no sense in learning anything new or working to improve themselves. And meanwhile—they are real dolts.

We have a lot of honorable, courageous people, but they forget that courage alone is far from sufficient: you have to know something, you need skills: "Live and learn!" One must be constantly learning, and every two or three years relearn things. But around here no one likes to learn. People are not studying the lessons of the war with Finland, the lessons of the war in Europe.

We beat the Japanese at Khalkin-Gol.[249] But our aircraft proved inferior to the Japanese aircraft for speed and altitude.

249. In August 1939, after a series of vicious skirmishes between the Japanese

We are not prepared for the sort of air war being waged between Germany and England.

It turns out that our aircraft can stay aloft for only thirty-five minutes, while German and English aircraft can stay up for several hours!

If in the future our armed forces, transport, and so forth, are not equal to the forces of our enemies (and those enemies are all the capitalist states, and those which deck themselves out to look like our friends!), then they will devour us.

Only given equal mater[ial] forces can we prevail, because we are supported by the people, the people are with us.

But for that, we shall have to learn, we shall have to know, and we shall have to be capable.

Meanwhile, no one from the war department issued any warnings about the aircraft. Not one of you thought to do that.

I summoned our designers and asked them if our aircraft, too, could be made to stay aloft longer. They answered, "*Yes they could, but no one ever set us a task like that!*" And now that deficiency is being corrected.

Our infantry is being reorganized now; the cavalry has always been good; now it is time to tackle aviation and anti-aircraft defense. I am busy at this every day now, meeting with designers and other specialists.

But I am the *only* one dealing with all these problems. None of you could be bothered with them. I am out there *by myself* . . .

Look at me: I am capable of learning, reading, keeping up with things every day—why can you not do this? You do not like to learn; you are happy just going along the way you are, complacent. You are squandering Lenin's legacy.

(*Kalinin:* One has to give some thought to time management, somehow there is never enough time!)

No, that is not the problem! People are thoughtless, do not want to learn and relearn. *They will hear me out and then go on just as before.* But I will show you, if I ever lose my patience. (You know very well how I can do that.) I shall hit the fatsos so hard that you will hear the crack for miles around.

I drink to those Communists, to those Bolsheviks—party and non-

---

Kwantung Army and the Red Army under the command of General Zhukov along the Khalkin-Gol River, which marked a part of the Mongolian-Manchukuo border, the Soviets scored a decisive victory and secured the Mongolian frontier. A Soviet-Japanese agreement ending the conflict was signed by Molotov and Japanese ambassador Togo on 15 September 1939.

party (and the nonparty Bolsheviks are usually less complacent!)—who understand that you have to learn and relearn!

(Everyone stood straight and listened quietly; clearly no one ever expected J. V. [Stalin] to come out with such scolding. There were tears in Voroshilov's eyes. As he spoke, J. V. [Stalin] *addressed himself particularly to Kaganovich and Beria.*)

—Have never seen and never heard J. V. [Stalin] the way he was that night—a memorable one.

The winter and spring of 1940–1941 were dominated by the slow spread of the war toward the Soviet borders. As Germany expanded its influence in the Balkans (Bulgaria, Yugoslavia), thereby ultimately precipitating the war with Yugoslavia and Greece, Dimitrov gave vent to his long-dampened anti-Nazi sentiments. His comments were increasingly less elliptical and more direct. Generally, the Comintern apparatus, strengthened by the presence of Thorez, Rákosi, and Pauker, operated in a more optimistic atmosphere. Intelligence and strategic work intensified, as did interest in cadre education, party schools, and so on. A foretaste of the things to come can be found in Dimitrov's laconic report on Nazi behavior: "Heart-rending stories about the situation of Jews in Czechoslovakia and Austria" (29 May 1941). Throughout this period Dimitrov dealt with the affairs of Communist parties in the United States, Britain, Italy, Spain, Romania, Denmark, Norway, Greece, Germany, Mexico, Chile, Turkey, France, Palestine, China, Finland, Sweden, Austria, Japan, Belgium, Turkey, Yugoslavia, and India.

Dimitrov's health problems and those of his wife Roza continued during this period. He attended the ailing José Díaz, secretary-general of the Spanish CP, and experienced an "unpleasant surprise" from Manuilsky ("One gets the impression in the CC that I am voluntarily withdrawing from work. They are not getting anything from me any more, it is always *you* signing things and sending them. I cannot go on working with you," Manuilsky said to Dimitrov on 29 January 1941) but used his wiles to win him over in times of need. After Dimitrov's intervention with the physicians on behalf of Manuilsky's ailing wife, "he burst into tears of emotion, embraced and kissed me. 'Thank you, thank you so very much,' [Manuilsky] said through his tears. 'In three weeks I shall be back at work and I shall be of use to you.' 'You have always been of use, it is just that sometimes you get into these sour moods of yours, which you would be better off without. Get better and do not worry. Everything will be fine,'" said Dimitrov. Despite reversals, things were all of a sudden looking up.—I.B.

· 16 NOVEMBER 1940 ·

—Ercoli [Togliatti], Marty, and Gottwald to see me about the inquiry from the American CP in connection with its extraordinary congress.

—[We] decided on an answer: "If it is absolutely necessary to pass a resolution on the organization's belonging (to the Comintern), then that resolution should emphasize the party's faithfulness to Marxism-Leninism and to proletarian internationalism at a time when in the interests of preserving its lawful possibilities for working legally, the party is compelled to discontinue temporarily its formal ties to the CI."[250]

[. . .]

· 25 NOVEMBER 1940 ·

—*Meeting with Molotov:* Talked about Bulgaria. Indicated to him that immediate measures must be taken to prevent Bulgaria from falling under the exclusive influence of Germany and being used by Germany as its willing instrument.

Molotov: We are acting along those lines. This very day we shall be discussing a number of concrete measures.

In Berlin we concluded no agreement and assumed no obligations whatever with the Germans.[251] The Germans are developing Turkey right now—and that is their chief concern. What Turkey will do is hard to predict. But we are watching developments there carefully, as well as events surrounding Turkey.

The Germans want to portray us as having approved their plans in the Balkans. However, we have published a refutation regarding the addition of Hungary to the Tripartite Pact. Now everyone will know that we gave no consent whatever.

250. In response to the Voorhis Act, which required organizations under foreign control to register with the US attorney general and provide information about their officers and finances, the CPUSA requested a formal disaffiliation with the Comintern. With Comintern approval, this step was enacted at a special CPUSA convention in November 1940.

251. Molotov had returned from a two-day visit to Berlin (12–14 November 1940), where he parried Hitler's grandiloquent urging for Soviet participation in the Tripartite Pact and a carve-up of the British possessions in South Asia with his objections to the German role in Finland and guarantees to Romania. Molotov intimated that the Soviet Union might wish to protect itself in the Black Sea basin by proffering guarantees to Bulgaria. The talks, which were inconclusive, hastened Hitler's preparations for an attack on the Soviet Union.

D[imitrov]: We are following a course of demoralizing the German occupation troops in the various countries, and without shouting about it, we mean to intensify those operations still further. Will that not interfere with Soviet policy?

M[olotov]: That is of course what we must do. We would not be Communists if we were not following such a course. Only it must be done quietly.

———

—Just returned from the Comintern, when I was summoned *to see Stalin*. I found Molotov (and Dekanozov) there.

Stalin: Today we are proposing to the Bulgarians that we conclude a mutual-assistance pact. It is not a guarantee, as the Bulgarian ambassador [Ivan] Stamenov evidently misunderstood Molotov [to say] earlier, that we are offering, but a mutual-assistance pact. We are indicating to the [Bulgarian] government that the security of both countries is threatened from the Black Sea and the straits, and that joint efforts are needed to ensure that security. Historically, this is where the threat has always originated: the Crimean War—the taking of Sevastopol, Wrangel's intervention in 1919, and so forth.

We support Bulgaria's territorial claims—the Midye [Midiya]-Enez [Enos] line (the Edirne [Adrianople] region of Western Thrace, Dedeağaç [Alexandroúpolis], Drama, and Kaválla).[252] We are prepared to render aid to the Bulgarians in the form of loans of grain, cotton, and so forth, as well as [our] navy, and by other means. If a pact is concluded, we will reach concrete agreements on the forms and dimensions of mutual assistance. In concluding a mutual-assistance pact, *we not only have no objections to Bulgaria's joining the Tripartite Pact, but we ourselves in that event will also join that pact.*

If the Bulgarians decline our offer, they will fall entirely into the clutches of the Germans and the Italians and so perish.[253]

252. With the imposition on Istanbul of the Midye-Enez line, in the Treaty of London (30 May 1913), Turkey gave up all territories to the west (notably Edirne) to the states of the Balkan Alliance. Turkey recovered Edirne in the Treaty of Constantinople (29 September 1913). Bulgaria lost its Aegean coastline from Dedeağaç to the Mesta River after the First World War. Drama and Kaválla were occupied by Bulgaria from 1915 to 1918 but had belonged to Greece since 1913. Hence, Soviet diplomatic support for Bulgarian claims was highly detrimental to Turkish interests.

253. The Bulgarian government declined the Soviet offer, as Dimitrov learned on 20 December in a phone call from Molotov.

As regards Turkey, we demand a base to ensure that the straits cannot be used against us. The Germans would evidently like the Italians to become masters of the straits, but they themselves cannot fail to acknowledge our prior interests in that region. We shall drive the Turks into Asia. *What is Turkey? There are two million Georgians there, one and a half million Armenians, a million Kurds, and so forth. The Turks amount to only six or seven million.*

—The main thing at present is Bulgaria. If such a pact is concluded, Turkey will not dare make war on Bulgaria, and the whole situation in the Balkans will appear in a new light.

—*It is incorrect to regard England as beaten.*[254] It possesses great forces in the Mediterranean, and stands directly before the straits. With its seizure of the Greek islands England has strengthened its positions in that region.

—Our relations with Germany are polite on the surface, but there is serious friction between us.

—The proposal to the Bulg[arian] government has been communicated today. Our envoy has already been received by Filov.[255] Soon he will be received by Tsar Boris as well. It is important for that proposal to be widely known in Bulgarian circles.

(It was decided to summon [Bulgarian envoy] Stamenov to inform him, too, of the proposal made in Sofia.)

—I filed the following telegram to our people in Sofia:

Today the Soviet government has communicated to the Bulgarian government a concrete proposal for concluding a mutual-assistance pact.

The Soviet government considers that ensuring the security of Bulgaria and the Soviet Union and preserving peace in the Black Sea region and in the straits is of vital importance to both countries and demands their joint efforts. The Soviet Union undertakes to support Bulgaria's legitimate territorial claims, in particular, the restoration to Bulgaria of the Edirne [Adrianople] region—the Midye [Midiya]-Enez [Enos] line, Western Thrace, including Dede-Ağaç [Alexandroúpolis], Drama, and Kaválla—and to render all manner of assistance to Bulgaria. In concluding such a pact, the So-

254. This was a rebuttal of the claims made by Hitler and Ribbentrop during Molotov's visit in Berlin.

255. Bogdan Filov (1883–1945), Bulgarian archaeologist, professor of ancient art, and politician; president of the Bulgarian Academy of Sciences (1937–1944); prime minister of Bulgaria (1940–1943); member of the Regency Council (1943–1944). He was tried and executed by the Communists in 1945.

viet Union not only has no objections to Bulgaria's joining the Tripartite Pact but will itself in that event also join that pact.

This proposal was presented today to Tsar Boris and to Filov. Please take immediate and vigorous action to publicize this proposal inside Parliament and outside it, in the press and among the masses.

Mobilize our deputies, and initiate a vigorous nationwide campaign in support of this proposal; demand its immediate and unconditional acceptance. The destiny of the Bulgarian people for many years to come rests on this decision.

Please confirm receipt of this message. Keep us apprised of the progress of the campaign and of events, as well as of reactions by government and other circles.

· 26 NOVEMBER 1940 ·

—Informed St[alin]:

Last night I communicated to our Bulgarian comrades in Sofia the proposal made by the Soviet government to Filov and to Tsar Boris.

—We have already had confirmation from Sofia of receipt of that message. Simultaneously, the CC of the Bulgarian party reports that intense mobilization is under way in Bulgaria. Troops are being rushed to concentrations on the Turkish and Greek borders.

[. . .]

· 27 NOVEMBER 1940 ·

—Consul General in Prague Kulikov to see me.

—The Bat'a, Škoda, and other plants are working at full capacity making arms and equipment for the German army.

—In the environs of Prague an enormous aviation factory is being built, which is to produce up to a thousand aircraft a month.

—The patriotic, anti-German spirit of the Czechs has not been broken.

—Terrible hatred of the Czechs for the National Socialists of Germany. In that atmosphere one finds national solidarity among the Czechs. A very thin stratum of society has deliberately gone over to serve the Germans.

The chief director of "Bat'a" in the city of Zlín—Glavnička, Josef— is pro-Soviet. So are the chief director of "Škoda" Gromadko and his deputy Škvor.

—"Bat'a" is mass-producing footwear with wooden soles. (It would not hurt to try that here, too.)

—Zápotocký and Dolanský[256] are in the concentration camp at Oranienburg.

—Clément [Fried] and Kopševa are in Dachau.

—Zápotocký is suffering from sciatica and tuberculosis—they are preparing to try him for involvement in Soviet intelligence!

—Zápotocký's daughter complains that the party is providing no material assistance.

[. . .]

—All four of them had Soviet documents for travel to the USSR in their possession before their arrest!

· 28 NOVEMBER 1940 ·
[. . .]

—In the evening a call from Molotov, from Stalin's office: Our people in Sofia have been disseminating leaflets about the Soviet proposal to Bulgaria. Idiots! Sent instructions to stop that harmful stupidity.

[. . .]

· 14 DECEMBER 1940 ·

—Directive for the CC sent (to Sofia). The campaign in connection with the pact is not to be party, antibourgeois, antidynastic or anti-German in nature. It must be conducted not on a class basis, but on general national and state grounds.

[. . .]

· 20 DECEMBER 1940 ·

—Telephone conversation with Molotov on Bulgaria. (Mol[otov]: The Bulg[arian] government has declined the Sov[iet] proposal. Fears becoming involved in war, etc.)

[. . .]

256. Jaromír Dolanský (1885–1973), Czech Communist; secretary of the KSČ parliamentary group (1924–1928); member of the KSČ CC (from 1929 on) and of the Politburo (1938–1968). He was arrested by the Germans in 1939 and confined to the Oranienburg concentration camp until the liberation. After the war he served as the assistant secretary-general of the KSČ (1945), finance minister of Czechoslovakia (1946–1949), head of the state planning commission (1949–1951), and deputy prime minister (1951–1963).

· 26 DECEMBER 1940 ·
[. . .]

—Met with Timoshenko, on Chinese affairs.
(Possibilities of assisting the [Communist] Eighth Army with arms.)
[. . .]

· 3 JANUARY 1941 ·
[. . .]

—General Panfilov ([Red Army] Intelligence Directorate) to see me about party organization of party detachments in Manchuria.
[. . .]

· 4 JANUARY 1941 ·
[. . .]

—General Panfilov to see me on Chinese/Manchurian affairs.
[. . .]

· 12 JANUARY 1941 ·

—Called Molotov regarding the possible entry of German troops into Bulgaria. [He] promised to talk with Stal[in] about our meeting regarding this matter. Molotov said: "A declaration from TASS has been published saying that admitting troops across Bulgaria has not been coordinated with us. For now, we are taking no other measures."
[. . .]

· 13 JANUARY 1941 ·
[. . .]

—Sent Stalin a *personal* letter:

Dear Comrade Stalin,

I urgently request that you receive me in order to confer on the line that the Bulgarian Comm[unist] Party ought to be taking in connection with the entry of German troops into Bulgaria.

The impending entry of German troops into Bulgaria confronts the Bulgarian Comm[unist] Party with an exceptionally difficult and complicated task. With its enormous influence in the country, the Comm[unist] Party, of course, cannot pass over in silence such an action by Germany, committed with the consent or with the connivance of the Bulgarian government. But the question is how and by what means the party is to react, what concrete position is it to take?

I would submit that the Comm[unist] Party ought to come out decisively against the movement of German troops into Bulgaria, no matter the pretext under which that movement was undertaken, pointing out that such a violation of Bulgarian neutrality leads to the involvement of the Bulgarian people in a war being fought over foreign interests, threatening to turn Bulgarian territory into a theater of hostilities, and jeopardizing the independent existence of the country. Simultaneously, it ought to expose the responsibility of Tsar Boris and the government, who, in rejecting the Soviet proposal for a mutual-assistance pact, bear the full guilt for the present situation, and in this connection it ought to underscore still further the necessity of a mutual-assistance pact between Bulgaria and the USSR.

Making broad use of the declaration by TASS, the Comm[unist] Party ought to paralyze the efforts of government circles to deceive the masses, in alleging that the movement of German troops has been coordinated with the USSR.

The Communist Party ought further to deploy the mass movement against the establishment of a regime of occupation in the country and the seizure of its economic and food resources, thereby avoiding ill-advised actions, provocations, and armed clashes.

Comradely regards,
G. Dim[itrov]

—I get a call at 2:00 in the morning from Stal[in]

I read your letter. I agree with your position. It is necessary to expose, while avoiding provocations. Provocations would only make it easier for the Germans to occupy the country . . .

The party should act on its own behalf, not as the Soviet Union's auxiliary. The Bulg[arian] government is suppressing our declaration. We shall broadcast it in Bulgarian over the radio.

[. . .]

· 16 JANUARY 1941 ·

—*Golikov*[257] ([Red Army] Intelligence Directorate), Panfilov ([Red Army] Intelligence), Biriukov (member of the Far East Military Council—Khabarovsk) to see me. We conferred on Manchurian develop-

---

257. Filipp Ivanovich Golikov (1900–1980), Soviet general and marshal; commander of the Sixth Army (1939); deputy chief of the supreme staff and chief of the Red Army Intelligence Directorate (1940–1941); deputy people's commissar for defense (from 1943 on); head of the chief political administration of the Soviet army and fleet (1958–1962); member of the KPSS CC (1961–1966).

ments (part[isan] detachments and part[y] organizations). We agreed on the formation of a temporary bureau of the CC of the Chinese CP and on the direction of party work in Manchuria.

[. . .]

—Armed actions between the Guomindang and our troops in China. Disturbing reports. Danger of the renewal of internal internecine war. —Received the following encoded communication from the secr[etary] of the CC of the Chinese Comm[unist] Party:

In accordance with an order by Chiang Kai-shek, our Fourth Army, numbering over ten thousand men under the command of General [Chen Yi?],[258] is moving north from the southern Yangzi River region but was surrounded by a ring of seventy thousand troops sent by Chiang Kai-shek. Bloody fighting by both sides has been under way for eight days and nights.

In the northwest more than three hundred thousand troops are already concentrated, surrounding the border region of Shanxi-Gansu-Ningxia, around which have been erected military blockade installations stretching for several thousand versts.[259]

The danger exists that our army will be completely destroyed. Simultaneously Chiang Kai-shek has sent more than twenty divisions, which have deployed in a broad offensive against our partisan army bases in four provinces: Jiangsu, Shandong, Anhui, and Hubei. They are preparing mass arrests and mass murder on a China-wide scale. The reactionary atmosphere is extremely serious. We are preparing in political and military terms to direct an energetic counteroffensive against such a broad offensive as is being waged by Chiang Kai-shek.

[. . .]

· 18 JANUARY 1941 ·
[. . .]

—Sent a *personal* letter to *Stalin:*

Dear Comrade Stalin,

The two encoded communications we have received from the CC of the Chinese Comm[unist] Party, as well as reports coming through the Soviet

258. Probably Chen Yi (1901–1972), Chinese Communist leader; commander of the 1st detachment of the New Fourth Army; commander of the New Fourth Army after the incident described (1941–1945); commander of the Third Field Army (1948–1954); chairman of the military control commission and mayor (1949–1958) of Shanghai; member of the CPC CC (from 1945 on) and its Politburo (after 1956); one of the ten marshals of the People's Republic of China; vice premier (from 1954 on); foreign minister (from 1958 on). He died after maltreatment by the Red Guards during the Cultural Revolution.

259. A *verst* measures about 1.07 kilometers.

network, demonstrate that Chiang Kai-shek evidently considers the present moment ripe for a general blow against the Chinese Comm[unist] Party, and therefore his generals have viciously attacked and routed the Fourth Army and are undertaking further aggressive measures against the Eighth Army and the [Communist-controlled Shanxi-Gansu-Ningxia] Special Region.

No matter how grave and perilous the position of the Chinese Communists, they cannot let the criminal attack on the Fourth Army go unanswered and cannot fail to defend themselves against the armies of Chiang Kai-shek now attacking the Eighth Army and the Special Region.

Thus, if Chiang Kai-shek does not suspend the aggressive actions being taken by his generals, large-scale internal, internecine war will inevitably flare up, which, of course, could only favor the Japanese.

In the interests of avoiding such an internecine war, alongside possible means of influencing Chiang Kai-shek through the Soviet network, the appropriate campaign should be undertaken in America, England, and other countries that would be able to exert a certain pressure on the Chinese government and to a certain degree influence Chinese public opinion. I submit that that campaign ought to be conducted through two avenues:

1. By exposing the criminal actions of the Chinese reactionaries, who are disrupting the unity of the Chinese people in its struggle against the Japanese invaders, in the foreign, China-sympathizing press.

2. By directing protests to Chiang Kai-shek from friends of the Chinese people (various societies, organizations, prominent public figures) and appeals to him and to the Chinese people not to allow the unleashing of internecine war and a schism in the united anti-Japanese front, not to allow the Japanese to conquer China "by the hands of the Chinese themselves."

We can communicate instructions on organizing that campaign to our comrades through entirely secure channels.

I urgently request your opinion regarding the appropriateness of our undertaking such steps.

    With comr[adely] regards,
      G. D[imitrov]

—I was informed late at night that the letter had been conveyed to Stalin.

[. . .]

· 20 JANUARY 1941 ·

—Talked with Viacheslav Mikhailovich [Molotov] about Chi[nese] developments. "In order to consider and take the appropriate measures, we shall need to obtain more precise information about what has occurred," he told me.

From Chongqing, 17 January 1941:

> ... Chiang Kai-shek has today appealed to Moscow through General Zhang Qun[260] with a request amounting to the following: to consider the recent occurrence involving troops of the Third Region [Guomindang war zone] and the Fourth PRA [People's Revolutionary Army] as a military incident of a local order, in not attaching any political significance to it and not widely publicizing it. He declares that this "incident" will in no way influence relations between the central government and the Chinese Communist Party and will have no effect on their further cooperation in the struggle against the Japanese. The senior officer corps of the Fourth PRA will be released.[261]

· 21 JANUARY 1941 ·
[...]

—Evening at the Bolshoi Theater. Ceremony in observation of the anniversary of Lenin's death. Report by Shcherbakov. Remarkable program. While Mayakovsky's verses about Lenin were being declaimed, *Stalin* remarked: "Ten volumes of verse by Demian Bedny are not worth that one poem of Mayakovsky's. D[emian] B[edny] could never rise to such a height."

—Molotov and I talked about Bulgaria and other issues. Molotov reported that *the Sov[iet] government has declared to the German government that Bulgaria and the straits belong to the security sphere of the USSR.*

An encoded communication was brought in from Sofia (from the Fifth Directorate [Red Army Intelligence Directorate]) reporting that Tsar Boris allegedly wished to speak with the Sov[iet] envoy plenipotentiary behind Germany's back. The Germans gave a ten-day ultimatum for passage across Bulgaria. Tsar Boris supposedly attempted suicide . . .

---

260. Possibly General Zhang Qun, Chiang's intimate; foreign minister of China (1935–1937) and secretary-general of the Supreme National Defense Council (1938–1942).

261. The developments described are part of a New Fourth Army incident, a clash between the Guomindang troops and the Communist New Fourth Army in Anhui Province that lasted from 7 to 13 January 1940, after the Communists delayed implementing the Guomindang order to move north. Some three thousand Communists were killed and still more executed in captivity. The incident did not end the anti-Japanese united front but certainly soured it.

—Talked with Stalin about Chinese developments.

—"Ye Ting[262] is an undisciplined partisan [guerrilla]. We shall have to find out whether he brought that incident on himself. We, too, had some good men among our partisans whom we were forced to shoot because of their lack of discipline, and so forth."

—"The question of the Eighth Army, which has been standing on the same territory for three years now, is more complicated than it appears."

—We agreed to discuss this question specially in a few days.

—We lingered late at the Bolshoi Theater: Stalin, Molotov, Timoshenko, Zhdanov, Budenny, Kulik, Merkulov (he had come with the telegram from Sofia) and I. All the others left immediately after the commemorative ceremony.

—*Stalin:* "Voroshilov is a good fellow, but he is no military man." Regarding Meretskov:[263] "You are courageous, capable, but without principle, spineless. You want to be nice to all the military districts, but you should have a plan instead and adhere to it strictly, despite the fact that someone or other is going to be resentful."

[. . .]

· 23 JANUARY 1941 ·
[. . .]

—Soviet envoy to Yugoslavia Plotnikov to see me. He related many things of interest about the situation in Yugoslavia. Mass pro-Soviet sentiment. As for the army and the intelligentsia, in that regard things are looking better in Yugoslavia than they are even in Bulgaria.

[. . .]

262. Ye Ting (1897–1946), Moscow-trained Chinese Communist general involved in the unsuccessful Nanchang uprising (Jiangxi, August 1927); military organizer of the abortive Canton uprising (Guangzhou, December 1927). He went afterward to the USSR and Western Europe. Commander of the New Fourth Army. Having been imprisoned by the Guomindang for five years, he died in an airplane crash soon after his release.

263. Kirill Afanasievich Meretskov (1897–1968); Soviet general and marshal who was in Spain during the Civil War (1936–1937); commander of the Leningrad military district; drafter of the operational plan for Soviet attack on Finland; candidate-member of the VKP(b)/KPSS CC (1939–1956); chief of the general staff of the Red Army (1940–1941); deputy people's commissar of defense (from 1941 on); commanded the Seventh, Fourth, and Thirty-Third armies in the war (1941–1945); general inspector of the Ministry of Defense (from 1964 on).

· 4 FEBRUARY 1941 ·
[. . .]

—Evening at the Kremlin.

Celebration of Voroshilov's sixtieth. Present are members of the Politburo; Marshals; Generals Tiulenev, Meretskov, and others; people's commissars, members of the CC—Shkiriatov, Yaroslavsky, and others; Mikhailov (representing the youth)[264] with their wives. Attendance is somewhat smaller than at Molotov's jubilee.

—Toasts to nearly everyone present.

—The toast to me: To the health of the "commander in chief" of the Comintern! (Voroshilov).

—At the end, a toast "To the union of the elder and younger generations, to Shkiriatov, Mikhailov and Manuilsky!"

—We sat until 4 a.m.

—Stalin delivered toasts two or three times.

—To the Red Army and Navy.

—"With our foreign policy we have managed to take advantage of the goods of this world and to use those goods (we buy cheap, sell dear!). But the might of our army and navy has helped us to conduct a policy of neutrality and to keep the country out of the war."

—To the young cadres: —"In other countries (England and France especially) the young cadres are kept [back] for twenty or twenty-five years and then admitted to various leadership positions. That was one of the reasons for France's downfall.

—We have another approach: we promote our young cadres, sometimes even too eagerly. We promote them with pleasure, with joy.

—Old men cling to the old ways. The young go forward.

—Replacing the old men with the young at the proper time is very essential. The country that fails to do that is doomed to failure."

———————————

—To increased might.

—We have been lucky. "God" has helped us. Lots of easy victories. Risk of dizziness. Must not get cocky. Work hard and learn.

264. Nikolai Aleksandrovich Mikhailov (1906–1982), Soviet Communist leader; editor of *Komsomolyskaya Pravda* (1937–1938); first secretary of the Komsomol CC (1938–1952); member of the VKP(b)/KPSS CC (1939–1966); Soviet ambassador to Poland (1954) and Indonesia (1960–1965); Soviet minister of culture (1955–1960).

—We now have an army of four million men on their feet and ready for anything.

—The tsar used to dream of a standing army of 1,200,000 men.

—Toast to Lenin:

—"Lenin gave rise to us, created us; he's our forefather. We owe him everything. Be like Lenin. We are all 'newly hatched chicks' next to Lenin."

· 5 FEBRUARY 1941 ·
[. . .]

—Sent Mao Zedong the following telegram: "We consider that a split (with Chiang Kai-shek) is not inevitable. You ought not to be heading toward a split. On the contrary, supported by the masses favoring the preservation of the united anti-Japanese front, the Comm[unist] Party ought to do everything incumbent upon it in order to avoid a split. We request that you reconsider your current position and inform us of your thoughts and proposals."

[. . .]

· 11 FEBRUARY 1941 ·

—Conference with French comrades (Maurice [Thorez], Marty, Raymond [Guyot]), and Ercoli [Togliatti] and Stepanov [Minev] on French Com[munist] Party policies.

—Three fronts are forming:

a) Vichy (Pétain—National Council)

b) Paris ([Pierre] Laval-[Marcel] Dea and the others—National Unity)[265]

c) Popular Front (Com[munist] Party—work[ers])

—Struggle against Vichy and Paris, but concentrating fire on Paris.

—People's committees:

1. Organization for supplying and distributing foodstuffs and control

2. Elimination of barriers between the occupied and unoccupied zones

---

265. After the occupation of France, Pierre Laval was vice premier and minister of foreign affairs in the Vichy government. Dismissed by Pétain in December 1940, he moved outside of the Vichy zone to German-occupied Paris, where he backed a closer collaboration with Germany.

3. Return of prisoners of war to France
4. Return of German troops to Germany
—The Frenchman wants nothing whatever from Germany. He has no thought of revenge. He wants to be master in his own house. He is not responsible for the policies of the French bourgeoisie.

[. . .]

· 12 FEBRUARY 1941 ·
[. . .]

—Late at night, at 12:30, Poskrebyshev[266] called. He reported that instructions for the Chinese comrades could be issued in the spirit of my proposals, which St[alin] considers correct.

[. . .]

· 20 FEBRUARY 1941

—At the party conference.[267] In the morning, closing of the debate on Voznesensky's[268] report. Resolution adopted.
—Evening session—closed. (Only delegates with deciding votes or with a voice but no vote participate.)
—A number of members and members-elect of the CC and Audit Commission were withdrawn and replaced with new people. (Withdrawn: Litvinov, Merkulov (former people's [commissar of] ferrous metallurgy), Zhemchuzhina,[269] and others).

266. Aleksandr Nikolaevich Poskrebyshev (1891–1965), Soviet Communist; operative of the VKP(b) CC secretariat (from 1924 on), chief of the special and secret sector (1928–1953); member of VKP(b) CC (1939–1954); general of the Red Army (from 1939 on); Stalin's personal secretary.

267. The Eighteenth Conference of the VKP(b) convened from 15 to 20 February 1941 in Moscow. Organizational matters predominated. Malenkov and Voznesensky presented reports.

268. Nikolai Alekseevich Voznesensky (1903–1950), Soviet Communist leader; candidate-member (1941–1947) and full member (1947–1949) of the VKP(b) Politburo; first deputy premier in charge of the Council of People's Commissars Economic Council (from 1941 on); deputy chairman of the State Committee for Defense during the war; member of the Politburo Commission for Foreign Affairs (from 1947 on); author of *War Economy of the USSR in the Period of the Fatherland War* (1947); protégé of Zhdanov (Leningrad group). Voznesensky was dismissed in 1949, arrested, and liquidated.

269. Polina Semyonovna Zhemchuzhina, Soviet Communist; Molotov's wife. During the 1930s she held several functions, including deputy people's commissar for food production, people's commissar for fisheries, head of the cosmetics indus-

—What happened to Zhemchuzhina was especially striking. (She made a good speech. "The party rewarded me, gave me encouragement for good work. But I let things get out of hand; my deputy (as people's commissar of the fishing industry) turned out to be a spy, so did a woman friend. I failed to demonstrate element[ary] vigilance. I drew a lesson from all that. I declare that I will work to the end of my days honestly, like a Bolshevik . . ."

During voting, one member abstained (Molotov). Perhaps because he is her husband; even so, that was hardly correct . . .

—A number of members and members-elect were admitted to the CC, mainly military comrades.

—They (the military) were proposed by Stalin himself. He characterized them as *modern* military personnel, with an understanding of the nature of modern warfare, not old-fashioned, and so forth.

—*Stalin:* "It is a shame we failed to single out such people before. We did not know our cadres well!"

—He said of Golikov that as an intelligence agent, he is inexperienced, naïve. An intelligence agent ought to be like a devil: believing no one, not even himself.

—Kuusinen, too, was admitted into the CC. Molotov recommended him: "There is no need to speak at length about Com[rade] Kuusinen. Suffice it to say that he is among the most senior members of the Comintern Executive Committee. And has always worked for the bolshevization of the fraternal Com[munist] parties. Now he is doing Soviet work—chairman of the Supreme Soviet of the Kar[elian]-Fin[nish] Republic. There is ample justification for admitting him into the CC."

—Also elected to the CC was Maisky[270] (Soviet ambassador to London). Molotov emphasized that Maisky works well as an envoy plenipotentiary in difficult conditions, and it had to be demonstrated

---

try board, and candidate-member of the VKP(b) CC (1939). She was imprisoned from 1949 to 1953.

270. Ivan Mikhailovich Maisky (real name: Jan Liachowiecki, 1884–1975), Soviet Communist diplomat; former Menshevik; envoy to Japan and Finland (1927–1932) and Great Britain (1932–1943); deputy people's commissar for foreign affairs (1943–1946) and member of the Soviet delegations at the Yalta and Potsdam conferences; professor of history and member of the Academy of Sciences of the USSR (1946). He was arrested as a British spy in 1953, sentenced to a term of six years of penal servitude, and amnestied in 1955.

that the party values diplomats who carry out the party's will. That also served to counterbalance the expulsion of Litvinov from the CC.

———

—A motion passed to put M. M. Kaganovich and other people's commissars and CC members on notice that if they fail to correct their errors they will be dismissed as people's commissars and withdrawn from the CC.

———

—With that, the conference was closed.

[...]

· 25 FEBRUARY 1941 ·
[...]

—Golikov from the Intelligence Directorate: on Chinese affairs. Chiang Kai-shek proposes sending a Soviet adviser to the Eighth Route Army as well.

[...]

· 27 FEBRUARY 1941 ·
[...]

—In the CC secretariat (Zhdanov, Andreev, Malenkov). Discussion of our proposal for ECCI schools. In principal, all agreed. Confirm the schools individually (after working up their programs, choice of instructors, composition of student bodies, and so forth). Principal aim: to train for the most part cadres from the Slavic countries (Bulgaria, Yugoslavia, Poland, Czechoslovakia). In the curriculum: the emphasis is to be on the study of one's own country, one's own party, their problems, how to fight the enemy on one's home territory.

—Zh[danov]: "We got off track on the national question. Failed to pay sufficient attention to national aspects." A combination of prolet[arian] internationalism and the healthy national feelings of the given people. Our "internationalists" have to be trained.

[...]

· 6 MARCH 1941 ·

—D. Z. [Manuilsky] and I discussed the draft theses on the Second International.

(I offered him my observations: our intention is not evident in the theses; there is no clear orientation toward our goal: the final ousting of social democracy from the workers' movement, the establishment of a united command for the workers' movement in the person of the Com[munist] Party; not to allow social democracy to rise again and reprise the counterrevolutionary role that it played at the end of the first imperialist war, etc.)

[. . .]

· 8 MARCH 1941
[. . .]

—It could be said, for the first time on International Women's Day I was *not elected* to the honor presidium. That, of course, is no accident. Apart from foreign policy considerations, this has to be taken as a *signal* of some kind of behind-the-scenes "shenanigans."

[. . .]

· 20 MARCH 1941 ·

—*Zhdanov* gave me his comments on *the theses on social democracy* over the telephone:

—Considers the theses *unsatisfactory:*

1. The center of gravity in them is set on historical analysis (*the past*) rather than on *the present moment* in social democracy;

2. Social democracy is examined on the international scale, instead of *differentiating* the various individual major countries—*the victors and the vanquished, the combatants,* and the *"neutrals,"* and so forth.

3. The *bankruptcy* of social democracy is examined without any indication of the *shameful* predicament in which *the working class* finds itself in the face of current events.

4. In criticizing social democracy, formul[ations] are used that are no longer current (it has rejected social[ist] slogans).

5) No indication that the bourgeoisie and the fascists are adopting the *social[ist] slogans* of the working class in order to strengthen their own position and to destroy the workers' movement.

6. No concrete and effective citations and statements of Social Democratic leaders about their current positions.

The fundamental question now:

—Will the working class allow the bourgeoisie to reinforce its power for a period of several more decades? (The Soviet Union—

here—is doing its part; but *where* is the working class of the capitalist countries?)

[. . .]

· 28 MARCH 1941 ·
[. . .]

—*Received a telegram from the CC of the Yugoslav party on its position in connection with the developments in Yugoslavia.*[271]

1. The party is organizing nationwide resistance to a German-Italian invasion of Yugoslavia and of attempts by England to draw Yugoslavia into the war on its side.

2. Nationwide pressure on the new government, demanding annulment of the Vienna pact and the conclusion of a mutual-assistance pact with the USSR.

3. To adopt a guarded attitude toward the new government.

· 29 MARCH 1941 ·
[. . .]

—Spent the evening with Viacheslav Mikhailovich [Molotov] (at the Kremlin).

—We talked about Yugoslavia.

—It would be counterproductive to organize street demonstrations. The English would take advantage of them. So would the internal reaction. Cadres of the Communist movement would be beaten. At present the thing to do is to gather strength and prepare. Not raise a stink, not shout, but firmly carry out your position. The Yugoslav comrades ought to be advised to do this.

—V. M. [Molotov] has his doubts about the campaign in connection with Thälmann's fifty-fifth. If there is a conspicuous campaign

271. On 27 March 1941, the Yugoslav military staged a coup d'état against the Cvetković-Maček government, which, backed by the regent, Prince Paul, had just acceded to the Tripartite Pact (signed in Vienna on 25 March). The putschists, aided by the British, dismissed Prince Paul and the regency and declared that Peter II was of age. General Dušan Simović then assumed the premiership, taking in some ministers from the deposed government (notably Maček's Croats) but also some known antifascists. The government did not consider it prudent to repudiate Yugoslavia's participation in the Tripartite Pact, but that stance did not appease Hitler, who became determined to strike back. The Simović government needed support, among other possible sources, from Moscow.

abroad, while here we do not do a thing, that would be awkward. But having any kind of observance could hardly be politically expedient, since we are maintaining a nonhostile policy as regards the Germans. We shall have to consult with the CC, but it would be best not to intensify that campaign.

———————

—Regarding Turkey: The Germans are trying to set the Turks against us, intimidating them with the notion that we will attack them in the rear if they resist Germany. That is why we issued that statement. The Turks can now rest assured as far as we are concerned, and act more boldly. The Turks, of course, would have liked to get more from us.

———————

—This Yugoslav business is a slap in the face for the Germans. Matsuoka[272] got the same cold shower . . . (The discussion was extremely friendly.)

———————

—I wrote up [the following telegram] to send to Yugoslavia (to the Communist Party CC):

We urgently advise confining yourselves at this stage to an energetic and skillful explanation of the position you have adopted among the masses, but without organizing any street demonstrations, and taking all pains to avoid armed clashes between the masses and the authorities. Do not give way to momentary inclinations. Do not let yourselves be carried away with sensational and outwardly effective actions, but instead concentrate all your attention on explaining our principles and slogans, our Communist policies—on the strengthening of the party; on rallying and organizing the forces of the working class, of the peasant masses and the toiling urban strata, and on the thorough preparation of those forces; on strengthening the influence of the party with the army and young people. Do not get ahead of yourselves. Do not give in to provocations by the enemy. Do not expose the people's vanguard to attack and cast it too early into the fire. The time is not yet ripe for decisive engagements with the class enemy. Tireless explanatory efforts and the thorough preparation of oneself and the

272. Yosuke Matsuoka (1880–1946), Japanese foreign minister (1940–1941) and chief architect of Japanese alliance with Germany and Italy. Matsuoka had just passed through Moscow on the way to Berlin and had been received by Molotov and Stalin.

masses—those are the party's present tasks. Take this into consideration and [put it] into action. Confirm receipt. Report to us regularly.

[. . .]

· 2 APRIL 1941 ·
[. . .]

—The CC in Sofia has been sent a warning in connection with the anti-Serbian demonstrations: " . . . The involvement of Bulgaria in the war against Yugoslavia is not only an act of base treachery as regards a neighboring fraternal people; it will also mean turning the Bulgarian people itself into *warriors* for German imperialism, shedding its own blood for foreign interests and condemning its own country to terrible ruin and destruction. Develop a campaign along these lines, without giving in to enemy provocations."

[. . .]

· 6 APRIL 1941 ·

—Sunday.
—Agreement with Yugoslavia published with a photo of the Yugoslav delegation and Molotov, Stalin, and others.
—*Germany* has declared war on Yugoslavia and Greece.[273]

[. . .]

· 9 APRIL 1941 ·

—Talked with *Zhdanov* about the CI's *May Day* appeal. We both consider it inexpedient in the current situation to come out with a Comintern appeal for May Day. (To make a thorough analysis would mean showing one's cards to a certain degree, giving the enemy an opportunity he could use against us, and so forth.)

The events in the Balkans do not alter the overall stance we have

---

273. In the early hours of 6 April 1941 the Soviet-Yugoslav friendship and nonaggression pact was signed at the Kremlin. It obliged the two sides to "safeguard the policy of friendship" in case either country was attacked by a third party. Only a few hours later Germany, Italy, Hungary, and Bulgaria invaded Yugoslavia. The royal government, in stages, proceeded abroad, and the Yugoslav side signed the capitulation act on 17 April. On 8 May, Vyshinsky summoned the Yugoslav envoy in Moscow and informed him that relations between the two countries must cease. On 6 April, Germany also attacked Greece.

taken as regards the imperialist war and both of the combatant capitalist alignments. We do not approve of German expansion in the Balkans. But that does not mean that we are deviating from the pact with Germany and veering toward England.

Those among us who think it does are underestimating the independent role and power of the Sov[iet] Union. It seems to them that we have to orient ourselves toward either one imperialist alignment or the other, but that is profoundly mistaken . . .

[. . .]

· 18 APRIL 1941 ·

—Called up Zhdanov about our directive on the observance of May Day. [He] related Joseph Vissarionovich's [Stalin's] comments on the necessity of differentiating between countries (combatant, noncombatant, occupied, and so forth). Regarding the fundamental positions ("The imperialist war is the business of the imperialists; the people's peace is the business of the working class and peoples." "The war of the Greek and Yugoslav people against imper[ialist] aggression is a just war," etc.) there are no reservations.

[. . .]

· 20 APRIL 1941 ·

—Was at the Bolshoi Theater. Final evening of "Tadzhik Days." Present (in the PB box): Stalin, Molotov, Kalinin, Voroshilov, Andreev, Mikoyan, Kaganovich, Shvernik, Shcherbakov, Zhdanov, Malenkov, Dim[itrov].

—After the performance we lingered until 2:00.

—J. V. [Stalin] was telling us about his talk with Matsuoka.

"We, too, have communism—moral communism," Matsuoka was telling J. Vissarionovich. Whereupon the latter made a joke about "Japanese communism" . . .

—We drank to my health as well. In this connection J. V. [Stalin] said: "D[imitrov] has parties leaving the Comintern (alluding to the Amer[ican] party). And there is nothing wrong with that. On the contrary, the Com[munist] parties ought to be made independent, instead of sections of the CI. They should turn into national Com[munist] parties with various names—the Workers' Party, the Marxist Party, etc. The name does not matter. What matters is that they put down roots in their own peoples and concentrate on their own proper tasks. They ought to have a Com[munist] program; they should proceed on a Marxist analysis, but without looking over their shoulders at Moscow; they should resolve the concrete problems they face in the given country independently. And the situation and problems in different countries are altogether different. In England there are certain ones, in Germany there are different ones, and so forth. Once the Com[munist] parties have become stronger in this way, then reestablish their international organization."

The International was formed in Marx's time in the expectation of an imminent international revolution. The Comintern, too, was formed in such a period in Lenin's time. Today the *national* tasks of the various countries stand in the forefront. But the position of the Com[munist] parties as sections of an international organization, subordinated to the Executive Committee of the CI, is an obstacle . . .

Do not cling to what was the rule *yesterday*. Take strict account of the new *conditions* that have arisen . . .

From the point of view of the *parochial* interests (of the CI), that may be unpleasant, but it is not those interests which are decisive!

The membership of the Com[munist] parties within the Comintern in current conditions facilitates bourgeois persecution of them and the bourgeois plan to isolate them from the masses of their own countries, while it prevents the Communist parties from developing *independently* and resolving their own problems as *national* parties . . .

—The question has been formulated sharply and clearly of the further existence of the CI for the immediate future and of new forms of international connections and international work under the conditions of world war.

· 21 APRIL 1941 ·

—Raised for discussion with Ercoli [Togliatti] and Maurice [Thorez] the issue of discontinuing the activities of the ECCI as a *leadership body* for Com[munist] parties for the immediate future, granting *full independence* to the individual Com[munist] parties, converting them into authentic *national* parties of Communists in their respective countries, guided by a Communist program, but resolving their own concrete problems in their own manner, in accordance with the conditions in their countries, and themselves bearing responsibility for their decisions and actions. Instead of the ECCI, having an organ of *informational and ideological and political assistance for Com[munist] parties*.

Both found that formulation of the question basically correct and entirely appropriate to the current situation of the international workers' movement.

· 22 APRIL 1941 ·

—Meeting of the American commission. Developed the aim of independent development and action by Com[munist] parties, their performance and struggle as national Communist parties of their respective countries, and the ramifications this entails for America.

—In the evening a reception at the Kremlin for participants in the days of Tadzhik art. Remarkable evening.

At the end, *J. V.* [Stalin] proposed a toast to Lenin: "I thank you for your salutations and the sympathy you have shown me . . . People are in the habit of praising their living leaders until those leaders collapse. Then, once they are dead, they forget all about them. Such customs are unseemly; however, they are universal. We Bolsheviks, however, are in the habit of swimming against the current. And we reject those customs. We ought never to forget about the great man to whom we owe everything we have and everything we have achieved. We ought never to forget about Lenin. Lenin gave birth to us all, forged us, organized us, armed us, aimed us. He created the party of the Bolsheviks, which knows no fear before difficulties, which knows no fear in a struggle. He created a new ideology of humanity, an ideology of friendship and love among peoples, equality among races. An ideology that holds one race above others and calls for other races to be subordinated to that race is a moribund ideology, it cannot last for long . . . I propose a toast to Lenin, our teacher, our educator, our father!

—The Tadzhik people is a distinctive one, with an old, rich culture. It stands higher than the Uzbeks and the Kazakhs. We saw this especially clearly in the Tadzhik Days festival. We wish it [the Tadzhik people] to continue flourishing, and Muscovites to do their utmost to help!"

· 23 APRIL 1941 ·

—Discussion with lecturers on the international situation (sixty-five persons).

—Gave explanations:

1. Of the Soviet-Japanese pact
2. Of the situation in the Balkans and the prospect of war in the Mediterranean basin

3. Of relations between the Soviet Union and China following conclusion of the pact with Japan

—General conclusions:

a) Events in the Balkans are not hastening the end of the war; on the contrary, they are prolonging and intensifying it. World war is long and drawn out.

b) The flames of war are coming ever closer to the borders of the Soviet Union, which should do its utmost to prepare for any "unforeseen contingency."

c) The Soviet Union is being given an ever freer hand as regards the West.

—Again discussed the directive for the CP of France with Maurice [Thorez], Marty, and Ercoli [Togliatti].

[...]

· 4 MAY 1941 ·
[...]

—A telegram from Sofia (via the NKID [People's Commissariat for Foreign Affairs]).

—Todor Pavlov relates that the [Communist] Workers' Party urgently requests advice on the party's position as regards the "liberation" of Macedonia and Thrace.

· 5 MAY 1941 ·

—Text of the telegram from Sofia:

Todor Pavlov reported that the latest events have put the Workers' Party in a difficult position. The Workers' Party is unable to formulate independently its attitude to the occupation of Thrace and Macedonia by Bulgarian troops. Given the atmosphere of chauvinist intoxication that has partially affected the working masses as well, primarily the petty bourgeois, if the Workers' Party were to come out against the "liberation" of Thrace and Macedonia and the western outlying districts, it could find itself isolated from certain strata of the population. Moreover, opposition to the "liberation" of these regions ought to be accompanied by some sort of concrete demands. Agitating for maintaining Thrace and Macedonia in their former state borders after the actual rout of Greece and Yugoslavia would be futile.

Neither could the Workers' Party approve of the "liberation" of Thrace and especially Macedonia, considering the Soviet government's statement to the Bulgarian government of 3 March 1941, and the friendship agreement concluded between the USSR and Yugoslavia. The Workers' Party leadership cannot produce cogent responses to left-wing political figures and cannot provide instructions for its members who for various reasons are traveling to Thrace and Macedonia. Communications with the appropriate authority are very slow and irregular. The Workers' Party urgently awaits instructions.—1 May 1941.

—Discussion with Kolarov, Pieck, Marek [Stanke Dimitrov], Belov [Damianov] and Vladimirov [Chervenkov] on decisions and actions of the Bulgarian Com[munist] Party on the basis of the materials received.

—And also on the telegram from Sofia. There is some suspicion that Com[rade] Pavlov is not expressing the view of the CC, but has instead sent an inquiry on his own initiative.

—It was decided to send advice to the CC on the recent developments in the country.

———————————

—In the evening a ceremonial assembly in the Kremlin for graduates of the military academy, and reception afterwards.

At the ceremonial assembly J. V. [Stalin] made a speech:

—The Red Army has substantially reorganized and rearmed itself on the basis of the experience of modern warfare. But our schools are lagging behind that process in the army. They are not conducting training on the basis of the latest models of weaponry. We have to reckon with the enormous advances taking place in military science and with the experience of the current world war.

Why is it that France was routed and England is losing, while the Germans are winning? The major reason is that Germany, as a defeated country, sought and found new avenues and means of escaping the onerous position in which it found itself after the first war. It created an army and cadres, supplied itself abundantly with arms, especially artillery, as well as an air force. Meanwhile, France and England, following their victory, got dizzy with success, boasted of their might, and failed to carry out the necessary military preparations. Lenin turns out to have been correct when he said that parties and states perish from dizziness and success.

An army that thinks itself invincible and beyond the need for further improvements is doomed to defeat.

Is the German army invincible? No. It is not invincible. In the first place,

Germany began the war with the slogan of "liberation from Versailles." And it had the sympathies of peoples suffering from the Versailles system. But now Germany is continuing the war under the banner of *the conquest and subjection of other peoples,* under the banner of *hegemony.* That is a great disadvantage for the German army. It not only is losing the former sympathy of a number of countries and peoples but, on the contrary, has opposed to itself the many countries it occupies. An army that must fight while contending with hostile territories and masses underfoot and in its rear is exposed to serious dangers. That is another disadvantage for the German army.

—Furthermore, the German leaders are already beginning to suffer from dizziness. It seems to them that there is nothing they could not do, that their army is strong enough and there is no point in improving it any further.

All of which goes to show that the German army is not invincible.

Napoleon, too, had great military success as long as he was fighting for liberation from serfdom, but as soon as he began a war for conquest, for the subjection of other peoples, his army began suffering defeats . . .

Our army must be constantly reinforcing and improving itself. And our military schools must march in step with the army, not lag behind.

At the reception J. V. [Stalin] proposed toasts several times. He was in an exceptionally good mood.

. . . The main thing is an infantry, a well-supplied infantry. But the major role is played by the artillery (cannons, tanks). To perform that role the artillery needs air power. Air power does not of itself decide the outcome of the battle, but in combination with the infantry and the artillery, it plays an exceptionally important role. It is not long-range air power that matters the most (it is needed for diversionary operations deep in the enemy's interior), but short-range air power (bombers, dive bombers). Short-range air power covers the operations of artillery and other weaponry. The cavalry has not lost its significance in modern warfare. It is especially important when the enemy is beaten back from his positions, in order to give chase and not allow him to fortify new positions. Only the correct combination of all types of troops can ensure victory.

. . . *Our policy of peace and security is at the same time a policy of preparation for war. There is no defense without offense. The army must be trained in the spirit of offensive action.* We must prepare for war.

· 6 MAY 1941 ·
[. . .]

—Sobolev from the NKID [People's Commissariat for Foreign Affairs] reported that Tsvetanova-Dragoicheva[274] related to Lavrishchev[275] that the telegram sent by T[odor] Pavlov has no bearing on reality. The Workers' Party does have a position on the Macedonian and Thracian question and is issuing a special declaration-appeal.

—Sent Sobolev the following letter: "In the interests of avoiding such unpleasant misunderstandings as occurred with the tendentious message from Todor Pavlov, please inform Com[rade] Lavrishchev that Tsvetanova [Dragoicheva] is the person in our party leadership's confidence in Bulgaria and she alone is entitled to communicate the opinions and inquiries of the party leadership."

[. . .]

· 10 MAY 1941 ·

—Sent the following telegram to Sofia via Fitin:[276]

We are in solidarity with the appeal against the war and with the articles in *Rabotnichesko delo* no. 7. The chief task for the party at this stage is to explain to the people the danger of utter national enslavement and to rally the healthy forces of the nation to the struggle for national independence. An authentic national policy must be opposed to the traitorous policy of the bourgeoisie: the Bulgarian army must be the defender of national independence, and not a gendarme detachment for Germany; against involving Bulgaria in the war; defense of the state against foreign intervention and the withdrawal of German troops from the country; defense of the economic

274. Tsola Dragoicheva (pseudonym: Sonya Tsvetanova, 1898–1994), Bulgarian Communist leader who studied at the Leninist School; member of the BKP CC (from 1936 on) and Politburo (1940–1948, 1957–1982); representative of the BKP in the Fatherland Front (OF) from 1942 on; secretary of the OF after the Communist seizure of power (1944); president of the Women's National Union; minister of communications (1947–1957).

275. Soviet diplomat in Bulgaria.

276. Pavel Mikhailovich Fitin (1907–1971), NKVD general; graduate of an engineering program who was specially trained in foreign intelligence; deputy chief (1938–1940) and chief (1940–1946) of the Fifth (intelligence) Directorate of the NKVD; rebuilt the Foreign Intelligence Directorate after the purges.

independence of the country and the future of its people as an independent and full-fledged nation; friendship with the Soviet Union.

Expose servility before the imperialist dictators, bolster the people's faith in their own strength and in friendship with the USSR; bolster solidarity with the Balkan peoples in the struggle against the imperialists. There will be neither peace nor a definitive solution to the Macedonian and Thracian question as long as the imperialists are at work in the Balkans and their abettors rule.

Take account of the new difficulties—the fomenting of chauvinism, the opening of profitable services in the occupied regions, the seizure of Serbian and Greek peasants' lands, as well as the intensified attack on the working class and party. Take measures to reinforce the party and to safeguard its cadres.

[. . .]

· 12 MAY 1941 ·

—Gottwald and I edited the lead editorial for *Kommunisticheskii Internatsional* [Communist International].

—D. Z. [Manuilsky] and I discussed the grounds for the resolution to discontinue the activities of the ECCI. A great many unclear and difficult issues connected with that restructuring.

—*In the CC (to see Zhdanov).*

—We discussed the question of the Comintern.

1. The resolution must be grounded in principle, for we will have some serious explaining to do abroad as well as among our own Soviet Communists as regards why such a step is being taken. There used to be a Comintern with its own considerable history; then suddenly it ceases to exist and function as a united international center.

In the resolution, all possible blows by the enemy ought to be anticipated, for instance, that this is supposedly a mere maneuver, or that the Communists are rejecting internationalism and the international proletarian revolution.

—Our argumentation should evoke enthusiasm in the Com[munist] parties, rather than create a funereal mood and dismay.

—It should be pointed out that the essential thing at this stage is not to direct the movement in various countries from a single international center, but rather to put the primary emphasis on the movement and its leadership in each individual country, to develop fully the independence of Com[munist] parties that are themselves capable of leading the workers' movement in their respective countries, themselves capable of devising their own strategy, tactics, and organization and bearing full responsibility for the workers' movement in their own countries, of relying utterly and completely on their own strength and capabilities.

—We will have to develop the idea of combining a healthy, properly understood nationalism with proletarian internationalism. Proletarian intern[ationalism] should be grounded in such a nationalism in the individual countries. (Com[rade] St[alin] made it clear that between nationalism properly understood and proletarian internat[ionalism] there can be no contradictions. Rootless cosmopolitanism that denies national feelings and the notion of a homeland has nothing in common with prolet[arian] internat[ionalism]. Such cosmopolitanism paves the way for the recruitment of spies, enemy agents.)

—The ideas of the Communist International have penetrated deeply into the progressive strata of the working class in the capit[alist] countries. At the present stage it is necessary for the Communist parties to develop as indep[endent] national parties. It is on the basis of a flourishing national Communist movement in the individual countries that an international Communist organization will be reborn at the following stage on an even stronger and broader base.

—It must be clearly demonstrated that discontinuing the activities of the ECCI is not tantamount to rejecting internat[ional] prolet[arian] solidarity. On the contrary, it is only its forms and methods of manifesting itself that are changing—[to] forms and methods more appropriate to the current stage of the international workers' movement.

2. This step is to be entirely serious and consistent. It should not be taken in such a way that only the trappings, one could say, are being changed, but everything else remains the same—that is, the ECCI is disbanded, but in fact an international directing center continues to exist in a different guise.

3. It matters a great deal on whose initiative this is to be done: on the leadership's own initiative or on the proposal of a number of Com[munist] parties. It seems the latter would be better.

4. The matter is not so urgent: there is no need to rush; instead, discuss the matter seriously and prepare.

Three questions ought to be discussed:

a) How to ground [the resolution] in principle

b) On whose initiative the resolution is to be adopted

c) The legacy of the CI—what next?

5. In any case, the Communist movement can reap great benefits from this step:

a) All anti-Comintern pacts immediately lose all grounds.

b) The bourgeoisie's highest trump card, that the Communists are subjects of a foreign center, hence "traitors," will be taken away.

c) The Com[munist] Party in each country will strengthen its independence and turn into an authentic nat[ional] party of its country.

d) Joining Com[munist] parties will become easier for the worker activists who currently choose not to join, out of the belief that, by doing so, they alienate themselves from their own peoples.

· 13 MAY 1941 ·

—Jean Richard Bloch[277] gave us a thorough report (in the secretariat) about France. Exceptionally interesting details concerning the causes of the rout, the current moods of various French social strata, as well as the actions of the occupying authorities. The Laval group (Paris) is 100 percent traitors; the Pétain group (Vichy) is 50 percent traitors. The growing influence of de Gaulle as a figure carrying on the struggle against the Germans. Universal hatred for the occupiers among the people. National resistance, sabotage, and so on, except for a small fraction of venal capitalists and political intriguers who have cast their lot with a German victory.

—A report that Rudolf Hess has fled to England. An exceptionally important event that deals a great blow to Nazi Germany.

[. . .]

· 5 JUNE 1941 ·

—Sent the following telegram to Mao Zedong:

It is difficult for us to offer any sort of military advice from here. However, this much is quite clear to us: that you certainly ought to take all possible vigorous action to counter the Japanese offensive, no matter what difficulties you face. Not only the further course of the Chinese people's national war but the future of the Commun[ist] Party and army depends on this. We find correct and timely the proposal made to you by Zhou Enlai in his telegram dated 1 June concerning such concrete and vigorous actions.

[. . .]

277. Jean Richard Bloch (1884–1947), French writer; émigré to the USSR; secretary of the Association of French Writers.

A new era began with the German attack on the Soviet Union on 22 June 1941, a day after Chiang Kai-shek's warning. The diary is reproduced integrally for the month after the beginning of the war to illustrate the atmosphere, which was remarkably calm, given the circumstances. In this period after 22 June, quite unlike in 1940 and early 1941 during the discussions about the dissolution of the Comintern, it appeared that the Comintern had been given a new lease on life. Propaganda work, along with infiltration by Communist émigrés living in the USSR into the German-occupied countries, became primary, as did broadcasts and work among the Axis prisoners of war. The Comintern apparatus cooperated closely with the NKVD and military intelligence in various efforts, including the transport of Communist leaders and operatives to occupied or neutral countries. By the autumn of 1941 the situation had worsened at the fronts, and Moscow itself was threatened. There ensued the evacuation of the Comintern staff to Kuibyshev (Samara) and Ufa. Dimitrov was stationed in Kuibyshev from 18 October to 20 December 1941, and then in Ufa until 16 March 1942.

Dimitrov, remarkably vigorous during this period, spent long hours at the Comintern headquarters in Moscow after his family's evacuation to Kuibyshev in July. As always, he was disproportionately involved in Bulgarian affairs, sometimes to the neglect of more pressing matters. He was unhappy with his family's arrangements at Kuibyshev and with the failing health of his boy Mitia: "Spoke with Rozi. Terribly depressed [. . .] Wants to come back to M[oscow]. 'We are losing our boy,' she says, groaning. Things have taken an altogether bad turn" (2 September 1941). The atmosphere improved by the end of December 1941, but the Comintern was increasingly in the backwaters of the war effort. Communications with Moscow were rare and most of the work quite dull and routine: radio propaganda, journals, occasional missions abroad, prisoners of war. The future bloc leaders assembled in Ufa (Pieck, Ulbricht, Gottwald, Rákosi, Gerő, Pauker, Kolarov, Chervenkov, and Dimitrov himself) made no strategic contributions.—I.B.

· 21 JUNE 1941 ·

—A telegram from Zhou Enlai in Chongqing to Yan'an (to Mao Zedong) contains among other things an indication that Chiang Kai-shek is declaring insistently that Germany will attack the USSR, and is *even giving a date: 21 June 1941!*

—Rumors of an impending attack are multiplying on all sides.

—Have to be on guard . . .

—Called Molotov this morning. Asked him to talk over the situation and the necessary instructions for Com[munist] parties with Jos[eph] Vissarionovich [Stalin].

—Mol[otov]: "The situation is unclear. *There is a major game under way.* Not everything depends on us. I will have a talk with J. V. [Stalin] If anything particular comes of it, I will give a call!"

· 22 JUNE 1941 ·

—Sunday.

—At 7:00 a.m. I was urgently summoned to the Kremlin.

—Germany has attacked the USSR.

The war has begun.

—In the office I find Poskrebyshev, Timoshenko, Kuznetsov,[278] Mekhlis (in military uniform again), Beria (giving various orders over the telephone).

—In Stalin's office are Molotov, Voroshilov, Kaganovich, Malenkov.

Stalin to me: "They attacked us without declaring any grievances, without demanding any negotiations; they attacked us viciously, like gangsters. After the attack, the bombing of Kiev, Sevastopol, Zhitomir and other areas, Schulenburg[279] appeared to announce that Germany considers itself threatened by a concentration of Sov[iet] troops on its eastern border and has undertaken countermeasures. The Finns and the Romanians are going along with the Germans. Bulgaria has agreed to represent German interests in the USSR. Only the Communists can defeat the fascists . . ."

—Striking calmness, resoluteness, confidence of Stalin and all the others.

278. Nikolai Garasimovich Kuznetsov (1902–1974), Soviet admiral; military attaché and adviser in Spain (1936–1937); commander of the Pacific fleet (1937–1939); people's commissar for the navy (1939–1946) and commander-in-chief of the navy in the war; commander of the Pacific fleet after the war; first deputy minister of defense and commander-in-chief of the Soviet navy (1953–1955); member of the VKP(b)/KPSS CC (1939–1955).

279. Count Friedrich Werner von der Schulenburg (1875–1944), German diplomat; entered the diplomatic service in 1901; German envoy to Iran (1923), Romania (1931–1934), and the USSR (1934–1941); partisan of German-Russian friendship. He considered the German attack on the Soviet Union (1941) a disaster for his country; rebuffed by the Nazis, he joined the anti-Hitler opposition; intended by the 22 July 1944 conspirators for Germany's Foreign Ministry, he was arrested by the Nazis and executed.

—The government declaration that Molotov is to make over the radio is being edited.

—Orders are being issued for the army and navy.

—Measures for mobilization and martial law.

—An underground area has been prepared for the work of the CC and the staff.

—Diplomatic representatives, Stalin says, are to be transported out of Moscow and sent elsewhere, to Kazan, for instance. Here they could spy.

—We make arrangements concerning our work. For now the Comintern is not to take any overt action. The parties in the localities are mounting a movement in defense of the USSR. The issue of socialist revolution is not to be raised. The Sov[iet] people are waging a patriotic war against fascist Germany. It is a matter of routing fascism, which has enslaved a number of peoples and is bent on enslaving still more . . .

—In the Comintern the secretaries and leadership workers were summoned. Explanation of our positions and tasks at the present time.

—Instructions sent to Com[munist] parties in America, England, Sweden, Belgium and France, Holland, Bulgaria, Yugoslavia, and China.

—A variety of organizational measures were adopted.

—*Mobilization of all our forces is announced.*

· 23 JUNE 1941 ·

—Worked on organization of propaganda and especially [propaganda] over the radio.

—Measures for reorganizing ECCI work for wartime conditions.

—Permanent leadership: G[eorgi] D[imitrov], Manuilsky, and Ercoli [Togliatti].

· 24 JUNE 1941 ·

—Meeting of the secretariat. Information on the situation.

—Consideration of the declaration of the English Com[munist] Party (incorrect attitude toward Churchill, who is for continuing the war against Germany and in favor of the USSR); also the declaration of the Swedish Com[munist] Party, which is demanding that Sweden maintain its neutrality as regards all combatant countries, that is, as regards even the USSR. It is portraying fascist Germany's war on the USSR as a war between capitalism and socialism, which is playing right into the hands of the Germ[an] fascists.

—Telegrams sent to the Engl[ish] and Swedish Com[munist] parties. The text of the English telegram:

> Your declaration contains two errors that should be corrected. In the first place, the treacherous attack on the USSR by German fascism should not be portrayed as a war between two systems—capitalism and socialism. To characterize the Germano-Soviet war in such terms is tantamount to aiding Hitler in rallying the anti-Soviet elements in the capitalist countries to his cause. The Soviet people are waging a patriotic war in defense of their own country against fascist barbarism, without imposing their own socialist system on anyone. All peoples have a stake in the victory of the Soviet people, including the English, who are fighting for a just peace, freedom, and independence. In the second place, one must bear in mind that by continuing its war against Germany, England is supporting the just war of the Soviet people. Therefore your attacks on Churchill following his last speech are incorrect. The thrust of your statements should be directed against capitulationist, anti-Soviet elements. Demanding the replacement of Churchill's government with a people's government in the current situation means playing into the hands of the pro-Hitler, anti-Soviet elements of England.

· 25 JUNE 1941 ·

—Sent a letter to Stal[in] and Molot[ov], informing them of the instructions we have sent to the fraternal Com[munist] parties, and especially of the encoded communication to the English Com[munist] Party in connection with its incorrect declaration.

———————

—Discussion of further work by the Department of the Press, radio work, and so on.

———————

—Instructions sent to the CP of France concerning cooperation with the Gaullists against the German occupiers.

———————

—The French Com[munist] Party has been sent instructions concerning cooperation with the Gaullists. Regarding [our] position in view of the Germano-Soviet war, [we] indicated the following: "We insist once again on the absolute necessity of avoiding portraying Germany's war on the Soviet Union in all your agitation as a war between the capitalist system and the socialist system. For the Sov[iet] Union it is a patriotic war against fascist barbarism. Canting about world revolution only does Hitler a favor and obstructs the international consolidation of all anti-Hitler forces."

· 26 JUNE 1941 ·

—Additional instructions given to the American party.
—The essential part of the telegram:

The fundamental change in the circumstances and character of the war necessitates a change in the tactics of the Com[munist] parties. The primary task now is to risk everything to achieve victory for the Soviet people and the complete destruction of the fascist barbarians. Everything must be subordinated to this primary task. From this follows:

1. That the Communists and the working class of America, proceeding from the interests of the American people, should fully and completely support the fight against German fascism;
2. That they should demand all possible assistance, in whatever form and without condition, from the American government as well as from the Soviet people and the English people, in the fight against Hitler's fascism—the common enemy of all peoples;
3. That they should support all governmental measures that enable the Anglo-American bloc to continue fighting against fascist Germany, because this war itself provides concrete assistance to the just war of the Soviet people.

In doing this, the party should always preserve its political independence from the government. The party must direct its attack against the pro-Hitler elements of the American bourgeoisie, against all those who help German fascism under the guise of pacifism and isolationism and who oppose helping the S[oviet] U[nion]. The party must endeavor to establish a mass front against fascist barbarity for the freedom and independence of the peoples of the entire world.

In addition to these major aims, the party must continue to fight for democratic freedoms and for the daily needs of the masses.

[. . .]

· 27 JUNE 1941 ·

—The CP of England has been sent a new telegram along the lines of yesterday's telegram to the Amer[ican] Com[munist] Party.

—Discussion with the Hindu comrade Larkin (his pseudonym). Gave him instructions in the spirit of our new orientation.

· 28 JUNE 1941 ·

—Conference on foreign radio work (Ercoli [Togliatti], Gottwald, Rákosi, Friedrich [Geminder], Fürnberg, and others).
—Sent Shcherbakov and Lozovsky (Informbureau) our proposals on the organization and leadership of foreign radio,[280] in the interests of improving it as far as possible.

—Final discussion with Ryan[281] (CP of America). He is flying tomorrow on a special plane to Vladivostok in order to board a ship leaving for America.

—Gave instructions providing for the safekeeping of secret CI archives and documents.

· 29 JUNE 1941 ·

—(Sunday).
—Vŭlko, Lena, and the children, Arthur, Ella, and Beno are with us.[282]

280. The Soviet overseas radio network became a priority during the war. The Comintern helped start special broadcasts for Bulgaria (Radio Hristo Botev), Poland (Radio Tadeusz Kościuszko), Hungary (Radio Lájos Kossuth), Yugoslavia (Radio Free Yugoslavia), and Germany (German Popular Transmitter). The Comintern was also involved in various diversionary infiltrations of German broadcasts ("intruding voice").

281. Pseudonym of Eugene Dennis (1904–1961), American Communist leader who began his party work in southern California; Comintern emissary to South Africa, China, and the Philippines (1931–1935); member (from 1938 on), secretary-general (1946–1959), and president (1959–1961) of the CPUSA national committee. He was imprisoned (1951–1955).

282. Dimitrov's sister Lena and her husband Vŭlko Chervenkov were a part of Dimitrov's family circle, along with his wife's two brothers Artur and Beno, and Ella Spiglova, Artur's fiancée and later spouse.

· 30 JUNE 1941 ·

—At V. M[olotov]'s (found Beria, Mal[enkov], Shcherb[akov] and Pronin [?] there).

—The situation is extremely tense.

—The Council of People's Commissars and the CC have sent party and Soviet organizations a directive for action in the zones adjacent to the front.

—The enemy has already invaded Soviet territory—seizing a large part of Lithuania, including the cities of Kaunas and Vilnius, seizing part of Latvia, the Brest, Bialystok, and Volynsk oblasts of Soviet Belorussia and a number of regions of western Ukraine. Certain other oblasts are in jeopardy. The German air force is enlarging the territory under bombardment, striking at cities: Riga, Minsk, Orsha, Mogilev, Smolensk, Kiev, Odessa, Sevastopol, Murmansk.

The Council of People's Commissars and the CC are declaring that in the war with fascist Germany that has been forced on us, the issue of life or death for the Soviet state will be decided, whether the peoples of the Soviet Union are to be free or enslaved.

—Discussion of Moscow issues (defense, possible evacuation, and so on).

———————————

—What can the CI do to help?

—Every hour is precious. Communists everywhere should take the most decisive steps to aid the Soviet people.

—The main thing is to disorganize the enemy's rear and demoralize his army.

———————————

—Instructions along these lines have been sent to the Comm[unist] parties.

———————————

—We are preparing a variety of (concrete) proposals for individual countries.

· 1 JULY 1941 ·

—Closed meeting of the presidium. Measures for mobilizat[ion] in the ECCI network (selection of people for milit[ary] and polit[ical] work in the enemy's rear, and so on).

—New instructions have been issued to the parties. (Put everything they have into assistance for the Sov[iet] Union!)
—Sent Molotov our polit[ical] and organizational proposals.

· 2 JULY 1941 ·

—Prepared people from political emigration for combat action and political work in the enemy's rear.
—Molotov and Malenkov have been sent a proposal for rendering financial assistance to the Chinese comrades, since the military actions of our Chin[ese] army take on an exceptional significance at this time.
　—Also a request to appropriate two hundred thousand dollars for our work.

· 3 JULY 1941 ·

—Historic speech by Stalin, explaining the situation and calling for a merciless national war to smash the enemy.

———————————

—Received a report that our request to allocate one million dollars to our Chinese comrades has been granted.
—Two hundred thousand dollars has been appropriated for our current work.

———————————

—850 milit[ary] and polit[ical] workers have been selected from the volunteer Intern[ational] Brigades and political emigration (including students in the schools).

———————————

—Instructions on distribution and use of Stalin's speech have been sent.
—At 2:30 a.m. there was an air-raid alert; nothing followed!

· 4 JULY 1941 ·

—A group of Polish Communists selected for transport to Poland.
—The editorial staffs of the German and Polish newspapers have been selected.

—Instructions sent for distributing Stalin's speech everywhere.

—Yugoslavia has been sent instructions against the cowardly and traitorous position of the Croatian CC. At the present time, a united front of the peoples of Yugoslavia against the fascist enslavers must be combined with party actions aimed at disorganizing the enemy's rear.[283]

—A report from Sofia: On instructions from the Germans, mass arrests are under way in the country. Four thousand Communists have been arrested and are in concentration camps. Arrests are continuing—their total will be brought to ten thousand.

· 5 JULY 1941 ·

—Issues connected with evacuating ECCI archives.

—Issues connected with evacuating the children of ECCI workers.

—Discussion of Kolarov with Dr. Al. Girginov:[284]

—The overwhelming majority of the Bulgarian people are on the side of the Sov[iet] Union—anti-German sentiments. Tsar Boris is dictatorially issuing orders at the Germans' bidding. The government is

283. After the German attack on the USSR, the head of the Comintern center in Zagreb, Josip Kopinič (Vokshin), became critical of what he perceived to be the lack of initiative of the Communist Party of Croatia (KPH) in diversionary work. On 4 July he sent a message to Moscow charging that the KPH leadership was "not developing the initiative of the masses but instead putting a break on them." He claimed that no sabotage was attempted at the railroads and that the KPH leadership was prohibiting the cutting of telegraph and telephone wires. Kopinič aimed at usurping power in the KPH, his ambition being aided by his prestige in the Comintern, which backed him up. On 5 July, the Yugoslav CP secretary-general, Josip Broz Tito, then in Belgrade, warned Kopinič not to interfere in the work of the KPH. Nevertheless, Kopinič informed Moscow that the KPH did not recognize the Comintern directives. Moscow instructed him to create a new KPH CC, which would carry out the line of the CI. Kopinič then denounced the threesome in charge of the KPH (Rade Končar, Pavle Pap, and Andrija Hebrang) as agents of the Gestapo and established ties with the leadership of the KPH city committee in Zagreb. His aim was to have this body assume the functions of the KPH CC. A stop was eventually put to Kopinič's activities. After an investigation by a KPJ commission (23–27 July 1941), Tito and the KPJ Politburo, meeting on 10 August 1941 in Belgrade, dissolved the Zagreb KPH committee, repudiated Kopinič's claims, and asked the Comintern to have him removed from the work in the CI. The Comintern accepted Tito's arguments but did not discipline Kopinič.

284. Aleksandŭr Girginov (1879–1953), Bulgarian politician; leader of the Democratic Party; minister of finances (1931) and of internal affairs and health (1931–1934); an opposition figure.

an unwilling instrument in his hands. Boris will try to draw Bulgaria into the war against the USSR.

———

—On my return home at night, there was an air-raid alert. We ducked into the PB bomb shelter (the Kirov metro station). Splendid, solid furnishings. The alarm turned out to be false.

· 6 July 1941 ·

—Sunday.

—*At Molotov's* (with D. Z. [Manuilsky]).

—Discussion of our issues:

1. Our proposals have been accepted (with the exception of the proposal to form an Anglo-Russian trade union committee. The idea is still premature. At the present stage it could only arouse all sorts of unnecessary suspicions among the English.)

2. We must organize political work among German prisoners of war.

3. Unofficial radio broadcasting is needed in various languages. Organizing this has been authorized.

4. The proposal made to Cripps[285] to dispatch Thor[ez], Marty, and Raymond [Guyot] has met with no objections.

—*Molotov* reported that an announcement had been made to the Eng[lish] government that the Sov[iet] government supports:

1. The restoration of Czechoslovakia and Yugoslavia, as well as an independent Polish state within its national borders, with the restoration to it of certain cities and regions that are currently within USSR territory

2. The creation of national centers (Yugoslav, Czechoslovak, and Polish) on USSR territory

3. The creation of their respective national legions, with armaments from the USSR

———

285. Sir Stafford Cripps (1889–1952), British envoy to Moscow (1940–1942); left-wing Labourite, solicitor general (1930), and MP (1931); founder of the Socialist League (1932). His position favoring a popular front with the Communists led to his expulsion from the Labour Party, to which he was readmitted after the war. He served as chancellor of the Exchequer (1947–1950).

Vyshinsky called to say that the English agree to the dispatch of our Frenchmen. In this connection Cripps wished to meet with one of them. They agreed that Thorez could do that tomorrow.

—Linderot has been sent the following instructions for the Norwegians and Danes:

1. Communists in occupied countries should immediately organize a national unity front, and for this purpose they should make contact with all powers fighting against fascist Germany (including Nygaardsvold's[286] adherents in Norway). The purpose of this national front is to mobilize all classes of society to fight against the German occupation. The movement for the creation of a national front must be formed under the watchword of democracy and national freedom from fascism (Hitler's yoke). Communists do not raise the question of their hegemony in the national front.
2. In the occupied countries, it is absolutely necessary to combine the political struggle with all possible direct actions that will disorganize the enemy's rear and hinder the provision and transport of troops and materials. One must do everything in order to rouse the masses to active battle against the occupation.

· 7 JULY 1941 ·

—150 foreign Communists fit for combat duty have already been furnished. Selection and mobilization of foreign Communists is continuing.

—Discussion with Thorez about his intended meeting with Cripps.

—A general directive has been sent to New York (for the United States, Canada, and Latin American countries) and London:
1. On the nat[ional] front in the occupied countries
2. On combining the nat[ional] front with direct[ive?] activities to disorganize the enemy's rear, and with the partisan movement
3. On a campaign to create a united front of states against the Hitlerite

---

286. Johan Nygaardsvold (1879–1952), Norwegian Laborite; prime minister of Norway (1935–1945); from 1940 to 1945 head of the government-in-exile.

yoke (the USSR, England, America, and other govern[ments]) fighting against fascist Germany

——————

—A message to Mao Zedong that monetary assistance (one million dollars) has been authorized and is being sent in installments.

· 8 JULY 1941 ·

—The organization of *special* radio broadcasts in German, Polish, Serbian, Bulgarian, Romanian, Hungarian, Slovak, and other languages.

——————

—Polish comrades have arrived from Homel [Belorussia]: Kaplan[287] and three others. Talked with them about their future work.

——————

—Evacuation of the children of ECCI staff (up to eight hundred) planned for 11 July.
—Kollontai[288] asked whether Linderot should be sent out of Sweden, where he is in great danger.
—Sent a message that Lind[erot]'s departure from Sweden would be inexpedient. Take measures there to safeguard him (poss[ibly] putting him on illegal status).

· 9 JULY 1941 ·

—Our general directive has been sent to China. Discuss the proposal to the CC of the Chin[ese] Com[munist] Party and draw concrete con-

287. Regina Kaplan-Czytrin (b. 1908), Polish Communist; editor of the Polish-language radio station in the USSR (1941–1944).

288. Aleksandra Mikhailovna Kollontai (1872–1952), Soviet Communist leader; daughter of a tsarist general, Social Democrat who sided alternately with the Bolsheviks (until 1906, after 1915) and the Mensheviks (1906–1915); member VKP(b) CC (after 1917); Soviet envoy to Norway (1924–1930) and Sweden (1930–1945).

clusions for the Chin[ese] party, and inform us of your own decisions in this connection.

———————

—Our directive has been sent a second time to Sofia.
—Called up the Polish activists in Homel by telegraph.

———————

—Determined the contingent of children and mothers to be evacuated to Gorky. Staff of the children's colony has been approved.

———————

—Rozi has enrolled in Sanitary Directorate medical courses.

· 10 JULY 1941 ·

—*Rozi's birthday.* (Born 1896: forty-five years old.)
—Lena's children have been left with us (along with Mitia and Fania).
—Final determination of the composition of the *Bulgarian, Polish, and German* groups of political workers to be transported to the respective countries.
—Children's evacuation problems: 1) composition of the colony, 2) service personnel, 3) finances, 4) leadership.

———————

—Appeal to the Polish people from the Alliance for the Liberation of Poland.

· 11 JULY 1941 ·

—Sent Merkulov lists and information on the German, Bulgarian, Polish, Hungarian, and Carpatho-Ukrainian groups of Communists to be sent into their respective countries for party and partisan work.
—Wrote Beria about that, to secure his assistance in the practical organization of transport.
—Gave Molotov and Shcherbakov reports on strikes, sabotage, and the partisan movement in France, Belgium, Yugosl[avia], and Bulgaria.

—Discussion with Polish comrades (Nowotko,[289] Finder,[290] Skoczewski,[291] Wierbłowski,[292] Kaplan) about their work.
—Sent Shcherbakov a proposal for creating a reserve foreign-language printing base.

—The ECCI children's collective with mothers, pediatricians, medical nurses, nannies, and other service personnel left for Gorky this evening.
—Wrote a letter to the secretary of the Gorky regional committee Radionov about arrangements and assistance for the children's collective.

· 12 JULY 1941 ·

—Discussion of the draft appeal to the Czech people.
—Sent Malenkov a letter on providing for reserve radio communications between the ECCI and Communist parties abroad!
—Díaz reported through Stela [Blagoeva] that he does not trust Ercoli [Togliatti].
—A number of staff members from various departments were reassigned for work in radio propaganda and the Department of the Press.

---

289. Marceli Nowotko (pseudonyms: Marian, Stary, Jan Wysocki, 1893–1942), Polish Communist leader; member of the PPK (from 1918 on). He spent ten years in prison for Communist activities; lived in the USSR (1939–1941); parachuted into occupied Poland in December 1941 as part of the Polish Workers' Party (PPR) initiative group (with Paweł Finder and Bolesław Mołojec); served as first secretary of the PPR. He was killed in 1942 by the Mołojec brothers, who apparently believed that he worked for the Gestapo.

290. Paweł Finder (1904–1943), Polish Communist leader. He did time in prison for Communist activities (1934–1939); lived in the USSR (1939–1941); parachuted into Poland in December 1941 as part of the PPR initiative group; served as secretary-general of the PPR CC (1942–1943). He was killed by the Gestapo in October 1943.

291. Reference unclear.

292. Stefan Wierbłowski (1904–1978), Polish Communist who was in the USSR during the war; member of the PPR/PZPR CC (1944–1964); envoy to Czechoslovakia (1945–1948).

—Merkulov reported that Lukács[293] and Rudas[294] have been arrested because in January of 1941 a Hungarian intelligence agent who was caught at the border claimed that he had been told to make contact with Lukács and Rudas. Maintained the same thing at his trial.

· 13 JULY 1941 ·

—Sunday (Lena, Vlad[imirov] [Chervenkov], Arthur, and Ella).
—A report on the conclusion of an agreement between the USSR and England for a joint war against Hitler's Germany.

—*Molotov* called about the Icelandic Communists' protest against the occupation of Iceland by the Americans. Gave him the explanation that the Com[munist] Party leader[ship] had recently been arrested, and this action evidently has not proceeded from long-established Commun[ist] circles.

Sent the English comrades a telegram in this connection to correct the position of the Icelandic Communists.

· 14 JULY 1941 ·

—Preparations for dispatching the Bulg[arian] group by submarine, the Polish group as a partisan detachment across the front.

---

293. György Lukács (1885–1971), Hungarian Communist philosopher; people's commissar for public instruction during the Hungarian Council Republic (1919); political émigré to Vienna, Berlin, and Moscow (1929–1931, 1933–1945). Having been arrested in 1941, he returned to Hungary after the war and taught at the university. In 1956 he served as minister of culture in Imre Nagy's government; he was expelled from the party but reinstated in 1967. His main work is *Geschichte und Klassenbewusstsein* (History and class consciousness, 1923).

294. László Rudas (1885–1950), Hungarian Communist; member of the initial Hungarian CP CC; political émigré to the USSR from 1922 to 1945; instructor at the Institute of Red Professors, the Leninist School, and the KUNMZ. Arrested during the purges, he returned to Hungary after the war, headed the central party school, and served as the rector of the University of Economics. He was the author of several books, notably *Der dialektische Materialismus und die Sozialdemokratie* (Dialectical materialism and social democracy, 1934).

—Approved the restructuring of the apparatus (reassignments of staff members from various departments for work in the Department of the Press and radio).

—Approved the list of temporary use of a variety of people for foreign radio.

—Ignatoshvili [State Security] reported that families are already being resettled in Kuibyshev. R[oza] Yu[lievna] and I agreed about resettling our family.

· 15 JULY 1941 ·

—Sent Clément [Fried], Paul (Stockholm), and Bernard (Amsterdam)[295] a telegram as follows for Denmark and Norway:

> Press ahead and swiftly implement our directives using all means at your disposal. This fateful time demands decisive and effective battle tactics without consideration for the difficulties and sacrifices. Give us detailed information about such actions.

[. . .]

—Sent Molotov a letter about creating a radio studio here for illegal radio broadcasts.

—Talked with Vyshinsky about dispatching Thorez, Marty, and Guyot to London. A telegram has been sent to Maisky. A reply from the Engl[ish] government is expected.

—Had a talk with the Bulgarian comrade Denev,[296] a volunteer in Spain, about the possibility of transporting a Bulgarian group via the Burgas Bank of the Black Sea.

—Worked on problems of the next issue of *K[ommunisticheskii] I[nternatsional]*.

· 16 JULY 1941 ·

—Wrote Molotov about illegal dispatch of monetary assistance to the Com[munist] Party of China.

---

295. The identity of the Comintern contacts in Stockholm and the Netherlands is not clear.

296. Sŭbi Denev (1900–1941), Bulgarian Communist; secretary of the BRP CC; representative of the BRP CC to the PCE CC (1936–1939); member of the ECCI staff (1939–1941).

—The creation of a special radio studio here for illegal radio broadcasts has been authorized.
—Examination of lead editorial on the Soviet-English agreement for the journal.
—A new group of Polish Communists (ten people) has arrived from Homel.
—Made final arrangements with Fitin and Panfilov for dispatching our groups to individual countries for party and partisan activities.
—Sent Khrushchev a telegram by telephone about sending Polish Communists here from western Ukraine.

· 17 JULY 1941 ·

—Looked over materials for the next issue of *K[ommunisticheskii] I[nternatsional]*.
—A message from Merkulov that he is placing at our disposal fourteen French prisoners of war escaped from Germany (members of the Com[munist] Party and Komsomol of France).
—Vyshinsky reported that the Engl[ish] and de Gaulle consider it inexpedient at the present time to conduct negotiations with the leaders of the Communist Party of France.[297]

—Discussion of French business with Thorez, Marty, and Guyot.

—Foreign Literature Publishing House issues. Printing base in the city of Engels. (Author[ization] to transfer from the *Iskra revoliutsii* [Spark of the Revolution] printing house by 23 July: two printing machines, two linotypes, eight sets of matrices and sixty tons of foreign typefaces and typogr[aphical] supplies.)—CC secr[etariat].

· 18 JULY 1941 ·

—Wrote Molotov about evacuating Díaz to Kuibyshev. (Molotov replied: "Better to send him south, Sochi, for instance.")

297. Although a parliamentary deputy, Maurice Thorez was put on active duty in September 1939 at the beginning of the war. He deserted in October and fled France for the Soviet Union. He was sentenced in absentia to five years of penal servitude and stripped of his French citizenship—all before the occupation of France. The Free French regarded him as a deserter.

—Final editing of corrections for the journal (next issue), especially of the lead editorial.

—A telegram received from the CC of the CP of China reports the decision by the Chin[ese] comrades to do everything possible to oppose the movement of Japanese troops from northern China against the USSR. They request ammunition, in order to enlarge their operations.

—*Wrote to Stalin and Molotov in this connection.*

—Looked over materials for illegal radio broadcasts. Also three pamphlets intended for German soldiers.

· 19 JULY 1941 ·

—Díaz is here. He expresses political mistrust of Ercoli [Togliatti]. He bases his suspicions on his work and behavior in Spain. Dolores [Ibárruri] also states she has less than full confidence in Ercoli. She feels there is something alien about him, something unlike us, although she cannot substantiate that concretely.

—(Before, too, there was a signal in that regard from Gramsci's[298] family.)

—We agreed to use Ercoli for the time being only in radio and other propaganda, not admitting him into especially secret business.

—Sent *Molotov* and *Shcherbakov* information obtained from abroad through our network on actions against Hitler in the occupied countries.

—Sent Lozovsky the French appeal for radio [broadcast].

—In connection with the agreement between the USSR and Czechoslovakia, a directive has been issued to Czechoslovak comrades in America and England calling for collaboration with the Beneš government and participation in Czechoslovak military formations.[299]

---

298. Antonio Gramsci (1891–1937), Italian Communist leader and Marxist theoretician; a founder of the pro-Communist weekly *L'Ordine Nuovo* (1919); representative of the PCI to the ECCI (1922–1923); member of the ECCI presidium; secretary-general of the PCI (after 1926); deputy in the Italian parliament (1924) He was arrested by the fascists (1926) and sentenced to twenty years of imprisonment (1928); he died in prison.

299. Eduard Beneš (1884–1948), president of Czechoslovakia (1935–1938, 1946–1948) who headed the London-based Czechoslovak government-in-exile.

· 20 JULY 1941 ·

—Sunday.

—*Stalin is people's commissar of defense!*

—In connection with the telegram from the Chinese CC, Molotov relayed the following opinion to me: "The Chinese CP's line of conduct is accepted. As regards ammunition—make no promises for now."

—A reply along these lines was given to the CC of the Chinese CP.

—Inquired of Mao Zedong what basis there was for reports from Chongqing of renewed clashes between the Eighth Army and troops of the centr[al] government, and what measures had been taken to avert a possible exacerbation of relations with the Chin[ese] government.

—Met with Andreev (about our issues).

—"I am staying on top of military supplies right now. Not up to date on the other issues. Better talk it over with Molot[ov]."

· 21 JULY 1941 ·

—Discussion with the Chin[ese] comrades leaving for China (Li Tin [Lin Biao] and the military group).

—First raid on Moscow (five and a half hours). (Up to two hundred fasc[ist] aircraft. Seventeen shot down. No damage to important installations. Or to the Kremlin and the Comintern.)

—Was in the Politburo bomb shelter from 10:15 to 3:30. St[alin], Mol[otov], Kag[anovich], Beria, Malenkov, Shcherbakov, Shvernik, Mikoyan, Zhukov,[300] and others, were there.

300. Georgy Konstantinovich Zhukov (1896–1974), general; marshal (1943); wearer of four orders of Hero of the Soviet Union. He distinguished himself in the military operations against the Japanese in Mongolia (1939); chief of the general staff (January–July 1941); deputy commander in chief and first deputy commissar of defense (1942–1945); coordinator at the Battle of Stalingrad; commander of the First Ukrainian and First Belorussian Fronts; commander of the Soviet occupation armies in Germany (1945–1946); deputy minister (1953–1955) and minister (1955–1957) of defense; key ally of Khrushchev against Beria (1953) and the "antiparty group" (1957). He was dismissed for "Bonapartist tendencies" in 1957.

—*Stalin:* An appeal to the Bulgarian people would be inexpedient at the present time.
—*Molotov:* An agreement with the Poles is expected soon. And then the issue of the Polish legion will also be resolved.
—Arrived home at 5:30.
—Díaz's trip to Sochi has been arranged with the First Department.

· 22 JULY 1941 ·

—This evening at 10:20 Rozi, Mitia, Fania [Dimitrova], Vova [Vladimir Chervenkov], Ira [Irina Chervenkova], Rozi's mother [Henrietta Fleischmann], Dora [Liebling] and Ilza [Ilse Liebling][301] left from the Kazan Station for Kuibyshev. I accompanied them to the station. As soon as we left the station, an air-raid alert was announced. We drove to the PB bomb shelter. The alert lasted until 3:30 a.m.
—The personal effects of a downed German pilot, Franz Pock, were brought in (maps of Moscow installations and so on).
—Bogdanov from MOPR [International Red Aid] to see me: about evacuation and assistance for political émigrés and their families.

· 23 JULY 1941 ·

—Two [air-raid] alerts (daytime and nighttime).
—Once again, they did not leave a mark on the Kremlin or military installations!
—Propaganda issues. Communications issues.
—Received secr[et] letter from the [Bulgarian] CC about forming illegal party branches in threatened regions and training people for part[isan] operations.

· 24 JULY 1941 ·

—Discussion with second group of Chinese comrades leaving for China.
—Meeting of the secretariat.
1. Measures for securing our installations and people against air attack

---

301. Women and children of Dimitrov's extended family: his wife, son, adopted daughter (daughter of Wang Ming), children of his sister Elena (Vova and Ira), his mother-in-law, sister-in-law, and the latter's daughter.

2. Liquidation of "Kuntsevo" as a holiday home and resettling secretaries and other leadership personnel in "Pushkino"

—R[oza] Yu[lievna] and the others have not yet reached Kuibyshev.

—Received a resolution of the State Committee for Defense about establishing a reserve radio station for the ECCI in Ufa.

—Discussion with Rom[anian] comrade Feierstein,[302] who worked with Georgiev [Atanasov] in Kishinev and Izmail.

—Again two air-raid alerts (from 10 to 11:30 PM and from 2 to 3:30 AM).

· 25 JULY 1941 ·

—Our people should have arrived at Kuibyshev by tonight, but there is still no word.

—Kasradze[303] to see me on Publishing House issues.

—Sent a telegram to New York—in connection with the absence of actions by Amer[ican] Hungarians and Bulgarians, as well as the inadequate activity by Mexican Communists in support of the Sov[iet] Union.

—And another telegram to Stockholm, telling Linder[ot] not to show himself in front of the police authorities. If they arrest him, they will keep him in custody for the whole duration of the war. He has to live and work illegally.

—Air-raid alert from 6 to 7 a.m. Nothing during the night.

[. . .]

· 28 JULY 1941 ·
[. . .]

—An air-raid alert from 10:00 to 3:00 a.m.

Stalin: The root of all wisdom: 1) acknowledgment of one's own mistakes and deficiencies; 2) correction of those mistakes and deficiencies.

[. . .]

302. Feierstein, Romanian Communist; she studied at the ECCI school for radio operators.

303. K. M. Kasradze-Panasian, director of the Foreign Language Publishing House at the ECCI.

· 30 JULY 1941 ·
[. . .]

—A telegram from Sofia: The party is working. Leadership comrades at their posts. Sabotage and diversionary act[ivities] have begun. They ask: in an uprising what sort of assistance could they count on from the USSR?

· 31 JULY 1941 ·
[. . .]

—Letter from Beria about admitting five Germ[an] comrades into the camp for German prisoners of war.

[. . .]

· 1 AUGUST 1941 ·

—Preparation for dispatching the Bulgarian group. (The Fifth Directorate [Red Army intelligence] employee Grigoriev met with me in this connection.)

—Dolores [Ibárruri] (on Spanish business).

—Rákosi (Hungarian radio, about the arrest of Lukács and Rudas and so on).

—Means have been organized for cutting into radio broadcasts from Germany and Austria (on their wavelengths) with our announcers delivering polemical apostrophes and brief statements.

—Air-raid alert from 11:00 to 1:30 (another failure for the fascists).

—Saw Voroshilov in the bomb shelter (he had come to Moscow for the day and has already left).

—In fine spirits. Unwavering confidence in victory.

—"They will never take Leningrad!"

—Could not reach Kuibyshev and talk with Rozi.

· 2 AUGUST 1941 ·

—Conference on radio address by representatives of the Slav[ic] peoples and appeal for Slavic solidarity and a united struggle against German fascism.

—Looked over illegal broadcast materials (Bulg[arian] and French).

—Wrote Stalin about preparations for an uprising in Bulgaria and possibilities for rendering assistance from here in the event of an uprising.

[. . .]

· 4 AUGUST 1941 ·

—Sudoplatov[304] and Egenstein (?) [probably L. A. Eitingon, Soviet security operator] to see me. About problems relating to transporting people out. Sending five Germans to prisoner-of-war camps. Acceptance of ten French prisoners of war and so on.
—Dolores [Ibárruri] about the Spanish school.
—Looked over materials for illeg[al] Bulgarian radio broadcasts.
—Received a message from "Luka" [Anton Ivanov] via Fitin. Negotiations with Velchev's people.[305] The question of an uprising. Assistance with arms and ammunition, and so on.
—Air-raid alert (from 10:30 to 1:30).
—Negotiations *with Sta[lin] about Bulgaria.* "No uprising now. The workers would be smashed. For now we can render no assistance. An attempt at an uprising would be a provocation."

—Now it is a matter of the defense of socialism, and not the construction of socialism. Many tanks must be produced. Curtail the production of agricultural machinery.

· 5 AUGUST 1941 ·
[. . .]

—Air-raid alert from 10:00 to 1:00 a.m. In the bomb shelter: Timoshenko, Zhukov, Shchadenko (from the front), and others.
—*Tim[oshenko]:* We gave the Germans a good beating. Smashed a

304. Pavel Anatolievich Sudoplatov (1907–1996), Soviet secret police operative; lieutenant general of Soviet state security; head of the wartime NKVD partisan administration; head of the postwar Spetsbureau, the NKVD department that carried out foreign assassinations. He was arrested in 1953 as an associate of Beria; tried in secret by a military collegium of the Supreme Court of the USSR in 1958, he was sentenced to fifteen years and released in 1968.

305. Damian Velchev (1883–1954), Bulgarian general and politician; head of the Military League that seized power in May 1934; minister of war (1944–1946); envoy to Switzerland (1946–1947). He emigrated in 1947 and died in France.

few of their divisions. They do not come straight for me any more. They try to go around. Sooner or later we shall destroy the German fascists. I guarantee it. (Robust and energetic, good man!)

· 6 AUGUST 1941 ·
[...]

—The situation in Ukraine is alarming.

· 7 AUGUST 1941 ·

—Major General Kalganov (Fifth Directorate) [Red Army intelligence] to see me about Manchurian business. (Part[isan] detachments have been mothballed; partisan training in Khabarovsk; sending people from the Special Region on reconn[aissance] and divers[ionary] missions). Part[y] leadership is needed in Manchuria itself.

———————————

—Gudimovich (NKVD): about preparing the Polish group. Very interesting information on the situation in Warsaw through 29 June (the day Gudimovich left there).

———————————

—Examination of the Slavic appeal. Ini[tiative] committee for the Slav[ic] rally formed as follows: Gavrilović,[306] Wanda Wasilewska,[307] Korneichuk.[308]

[...]

306. Milan Gavrilović (1882–1976), Serbian politician; Yugoslavia's envoy to the USSR (1940–1941); leader of the Agrarian Party and a minister in the London-based Yugoslav government-in-exile; leader of the Serbian anticommunist emigration after the war.

307. Wanda Wasilewska (1905–1964), Polish and Soviet writer; member of the VKP(b) from 1941 on; leader of the Union of Polish Patriots (ZPP) in the USSR. She lived in Kiev after the war and participated in the work of the World Peace Council.

308. Aleksandr Yevdokimovich Korneichuk (1905–1972), Ukrainian author and playwright; president of Ukrainian Writers' Association (1938–1941, 1946–1953); staff member of the People's Commissariat for Foreign Affairs during the war; member of the KPSS CC (from 1952 on); member of presidency of the World Peace Council.

· 9 AUGUST 1941 ·
[. . .]

—Looked over the speeches of the Bulgarian and Macedonian representatives for tomorrow's Slavic rally.

[. . .]

· 11 AUGUST 1941 ·
[. . .]

—In the bomb shelter:
Molot[ov]: "As long as we are being pressed by the Germans, we should avoid any major, serious actions abroad. When things start looking up for us, that is the time to deploy everything we have."

[. . .]

· 14 AUGUST 1941 ·

—Major Melnikov (Fifth Directorate) [Red Army intelligence] reported on the training and dispatch of groups of Bulgarians to Bulgaria through their network (by air, parachute drop, Soviet armaments, and so on). Discussed issues connected with dispatching Polish and other groups as well.
—No coordinating center at all for this work (NKVD, Red Army, etc.). Arrangements for this business are still primitive.

[. . .]

· 16 AUGUST 1941 ·
[. . .]

—Air-raid alert from 12:00 to 3:30 a.m. In the bomb shelter: St[alin], Mol[otov], Beria, Mal[enkov], etc.
—Jos[eph] V[issarionovich Stalin's] conversation with Khrushchev by HF [high frequency].
—What is the CO doing? What good is he doing there? V[oroshilov] and T[imoshenko] are touring the front, helping commanders, and so forth. But B[udenny] just sits there in Poltava and does not move. Makes himself out to be a great CO but does not do a thing. How can we put up with that? Why don't you say something? Here you are, a member of the CC, a member of the PB, a member of the military council at the front. You should be ashamed of yourself! How can you

be so oblivious? What's the matter with you? [You have] given up half of Ukraine. You're ready to give up the other half, too. It's a disgrace! What measures are you taking? Why don't you say something? I'll give you nineteen divisions. You have thirty aircraft at your disposal there in your region. Organize operations. Under no circumstances let the Germans reach the left bank of the Dnieper. Do whatever it takes. If not—I'm telling you plainly—we'll make short work of you. . . .

· 18 AUGUST 1941 ·

[. . .]

—Air-raid alert from 10:30 to 2:00 a.m. Met Budenny and Khrushchev in the bomb shelter:

—For now Kiev is holding out staunchly. Odessa can defend itself. The enemy's offensive will be checked. He will not be allowed to reach the left bank of the Dnieper. However, everything depends on the initiative of the commanders. 95 percent of the Red Army is fighting well.

—Concerning Odessa, B[udenny] says: "I have issued an order to maintain the defense to the last Red Army soldier!"

—Partisans are operating in the rear, but still insufficiently. They could do significantly more.

—In the territories taken by the Germans, a portion of the population remains. In Nikolaev a consid[erable] portion has remained. The remaining collective farmers are against the destruction of grain (this is an issue of contention between the party activists and the collective farmers).

—A strict order is being issued against unauth[orized] retreats, commanders' not discharging their duty, etc.

[. . .]

· 20 AUGUST 1941 ·

—Fitin to see me. We agreed concerning contact and mutual cooperation in the area of liaisons with foreign countries in the interests of intensifying operations in all spheres.

Commissioned Fit[in] and Sorkin[309] to work up the concrete issues and make a report.

[. . .]

309. Grigory Zakharovich Sorkin (b. 1899), Soviet Communist; member of the ECCI staff (1938–1943); deputy head of the communications service; on the staff of Institute 100 of the Department of International Information at the VKP(b) CC (from 1943 on).

· 23 AUGUST 1941 ·

—Received a telegram from Walter [Tito] (Yugosl[avia]), in which he reports that the party does not trust Anton[310] (employee of the Fifth Directorate) and requests that the party personnel working with Anton be returned to the party.

I met today in this connection with Colonel Dragun and Major Grigoriev [both of Red Army intelligence]. Together we examined materials concerning this Anton. Nothing suspicious. Favorable comments. Fifth Directorate personnel who are personally acquainted with him without exception give him favorable references (on the basis of his carrying out a variety of missions, especially in Spain).

[. . .]

· 26 AUGUST 1941 ·
[. . .]

—Pieck reported that f[ormer] cavalry div[ision] commander Gorbatov (under KPD [Communist Party of Germany] sponsorship) had come to see him at his home and told his daughter, then him, horror stories about the status of the front (everything is lost, and so on). Either the man has gone crazy, or else he is a covert enemy.

—Told Mekhlis to find out who this commander is. Mekhlis called late at night and said that he had summoned Gorbatov (brigade commander). He had given muddled responses. Mekhlis requested Pieck's written report.

[. . .]

· 27 AUGUST 1941 ·
[. . .]

—From 2:00 to 3:30 in the bomb shelter.

—Spoke with J. V. [Stalin] about Polish business. "It would be better to create a workers' party of Poland with a Communist program. The Commun[ist] party frightens off not only alien elements, but even some of our own as well." At the present stage, the struggle is one of national liberation. Naturally, not a Labour Party as in England. The Hitler regime is tempering the Communists. Tsarism made us that way.

310. Pseudonym of Ivan Srebrenjak (d. 1942), Croatian Communist; operative of Red Army intelligence who was at odds with Tito from the 1930s; head of the Soviet military intelligence center in Zagreb (from 1940 on). He was arrested and executed by the Ustašas.

—Raised the question of coordinating partisan movement and sabotage operations abroad among the NKVD, the Fifth Directorate, and the ECCI. "The Fifth Directorate [of Red Army intelligence] comrades want to lead the movement. That will never do. Golikov will come here. We shall have to settle this business."

[...]

· 29 AUGUST 1941 ·
[...]

—Discussion with departing Polish group (ten persons). Provisional leadership inside Poland: Nowotko, Finder, Mołojec.[311]
—Formation of a workers' party (with Communist program). Not formally linked with the Comintern.

[...]

· 1 SEPTEMBER 1941 ·

—At the CC (meeting with Shcherbakov).
Conference on forming a permanent Slavic committee. (Aleksandrov, Khavinson [TASS], Fedeev,[312] Lozovsky.) We also agreed that nat[ional] radio broadcasts are to be directed and controlled by us. A summary of the contents of radio broadcasts goes to the Informbureau for review and appropriate comments and proposals.

—Conferred with the Polish comrades. Examination of the political declaration of the Workers' Party of Poland.

[...]

311. Bolesław Mołojec (pseudonyms: Długi, Edward, Witold Długi, 1909–1942), Polish Communist; member of the initiative group (with Marceli Nowotko and Paweł Finder) authorized by the Comintern to organize the new PPR. Together with his brother Zygmunt, he assassinated Nowotko in 1942, apparently believing that the PPR leader was working for the Gestapo. The Mołojec brothers were condemned by a PPR court and executed.

312. Aleksandr Aleksandrovich Fedeev (1901–1956), Soviet writer; member of the VKP(b) CC (1939–1956); secretary-general of the Soviet Writers' Society (1946–1954); author of three socialist realist classics—*The Rout* (1927), *The Last of the Udege* (1930–1940), and *The Young Guard* (1945). He committed suicide.

· 5 SEPTEMBER 1941 ·

—Major General Kalganov [Red Army intelligence] to see me. He passed on information from the Sov[iet] comrades in Yan'an. They are complaining of some irregularities in relations with the leadership of the CP of China.

—Initiated inquiry with Mao Zedong in this connection.

—Wrote Shcherbakov (with Marty's letter attached) [advising] against slogans included in the French radio broadcast of 3 Sept[ember] calling to arms, to an immediate uprising. This is premature. It goes against the French Com[munist] Party's current line.

[. . .]

· 8 SEPTEMBER 1941 ·

[. . .]

—At 12:00 (midnight) an air-raid] alert.

Was in the Kir[ov station] bomb shelter. Good mood. The Boss [Stalin] made wisecracks the whole time. "If we win, we'll give East Prussia back to Slavdom, where it belongs. We'll settle the whole place with Slavs."

—Königsberg is pretty well destroyed. From four to thirty-eight of our aircraft are carrying out raids on Berlin. We are now producing twice as many aircraft as before the war—outstanding new aircraft. Ten women's pilot regiments (two hundred fighter planes) will be formed.

—In reply to M[ikhail] Iv[anovich Kalinin's] remark that our men at the front are fighting bravely, J[oseph] Vis[sarionovich Stalin] said: "Any fool can be brave. What we need is for the men to know how to fight!"

—Shakhurin[313] said: "Yesterday Ibárruri made an impassioned speech at the women's rally." In this connection J[oseph] V[issarionovich Stalin] remarked: "Yes, it was a good speech. She (Ibárruri) is a good woman."

—Spoke with Molot[ov] in connection with the Yugosl[av] comrades' request to supply them with arms. He replied: "It cannot be done now. Our own need is enormous. We have to compensate for great losses."

313. Aleksei Ivanovich Shakhurin (1904–1975), Soviet Communist; VKP(b) official; people's commissar for the air industry (1940–1946).

Concerning Leningrad he said: "The situation is tough. They (the Germans) are using their last reserves. But we are also facing shortages of reserves . . . "

———————————

—The alert lasted from 12:00 to 2:30 a.m.

[. . .]

· 11 SEPTEMBER 1941 ·

[. . .]

—In connection with the deportation of Germans and Austrians from M[oscow], we have agreed with the NKVD not to touch employees of the ECCI, foreign radio, our publish[ing house] and schools, and persons registered with us for our use.

[. . .]

· 12 SEPTEMBER 1941 ·

—Major General Panfilov to see me. Reported on the transport of our people. Considers it possible to transport in a "Douglas" airplane a certain quantity of arms (machine guns, revolvers, grenades, explosives) to Yugoslavia by air.

[. . .]

· 15 SEPTEMBER 1941 ·

[. . .]

—Major Herzenstein (from [Red Army] intelligence) reported on Japan and Manchuria.

—The Japanese have seventy-two divisions (division: twenty to twenty-two thousand). Four thousand aircraft. Forty divisions in China and Manchuria. The major forces against us are in the Maritime Region and against Chita. They are forcing preparations for war with the USSR. They are awaiting results from negotiations with the Americans. The Germans are quite unhappy with the Japanese.

—There are up to 1,500–2,000 part[isan] detachments in Manchuria. Their morale is low. There is no leadership in Manchuria itself.

———————————

—No air-raid alerts.

[. . .]

· 19 SEPTEMBER 1941 ·
[. . .]

Air-raid alert: from 11:30 to 2:00. In the Kirov [station] bomb shelter. (St[alin], Mol[otov], Beria, M. I. [Kalinin], Shcherbakov, Malenkov, Shaposhnikov, etc.) The situation in Kiev is extremely serious. Around Leningrad, all clear!

[. . .]

· 3 OCTOBER 1941 ·
[. . .]

—*Met with Voroshilov:* Long talk about the situation at the fronts.

—Awful, just awful. Our artillery is better than the Germans'. Same with our air force. Our fighters are braver. But our organization is weaker than theirs. Our commanding officers are less well trained. The Germans succeed usually because of their better organization and clever tricks. They cannot sustain direct combat. We shall never give up Leningrad. But I am worried about Kharkov, and that means the Donbas, too.

—A whole series of mistakes have been made. Many troops and arms were concentrated too close to the border, while the interior defense line was still unfinished. The fact that we shared a border with Germany (with no springboard) also worked against us.

—Informed him of the situation and the movement abroad.

—No air-raid alerts.

[. . .]

· 9 OCTOBER 1941 ·
[. . .]

—*Umansky:*[314] gave a report on America. (Man[uilsky], Ercoli [Togliatti], Marty, Stepanov [Minev].)

—Roosevelt is following the gener[al] line of Amer[ican] imperialism (the destruction of Hitlerism). Assistance to the USSR will be rendered. Roosevelt is trying to put off American participation in the war until 1942. But if Hitler makes significant inroads into the USSR, that participation may come sooner. The food industry is against Roosevelt's position: it is counting on access to the European market as per

314. Konstantin Aleksandrovich Umansky (1902–1945), Soviet diplomat; counselor at the embassy to the United States (1936–1939); envoy to the United States (1939–1941) and Mexico (from 1943 on). He died in a plane crash.

agreement with Hitler. Negotiations with Japan are an attempt to gain time. Great sympathy for the USSR in America. Great advances in the working class. The main thing is the industrial unions. Decisive action is needed against Lewis.[315] The primary means of influence in America is the *cinema;* in the second place *radio,* and the *press* comes in third. The crucial problem for the Amer[ican] Com[munist] Party is a position combining nat[ional] defense with the defense of workers against encroach[ment] of capital.

[. . .]

· 14 OCTOBER 1941 ·

—Met with Shcherbakov. Since Moscow itself is becoming the front, preparations must be made for the worst possible scenario. Agreed on a number of concrete measures.

Also on a publishing and printing base outside Moscow.

—Conference with Khavinson and Rubinstein (TASS), Polikarpov (foreign radio) and Blindermann (NKVD) in my office. Organization of future radio broadcasting from outside Moscow, especially illegal broadcasts.

—Determined which personnel must immediately be sent to these broadcasting sites.

—Meeting of the troika with leadership workers: decided to send the part[y] school, radio school, the secretariat and most of the staff to Ufa on the fifteenth.

—Sent Molotov the appeal of the German CP.

—At 4:00 a.m. an air-raid alert.

· 15 OCTOBER 1941 ·

—R[oza] Yul[ievna], Arthur, and Ella left for Kuibyshev at 1:00 p.m.

—*Molotov* called about the appeal. Asked whether we agreed with the changes made by J. V. [Stalin]

315. John L. Lewis (1880–1969), American labor leader; president from 1920 to 1960 of the United Mine Workers of America (UMW); founder in 1935 of the Committee for Industrial Organizations (CIO). Despite his early support for Roosevelt and the New Deal, Lewis had a falling out with Roosevelt and supported Wendell Willkie in the 1940 presidential elections. After Roosevelt's victory, Lewis resigned from the CIO presidency. In 1942 he took the UMW out of the CIO, and he did not discourage UMW strike activity during the war.

" . . . Evacuation is necessary. I advise you to leave before the day is out."

—*Met with Stalin:* Malenkov, Molotov, Shaposhnikov and Voznesensky were there.

—Sta[lin], Mol[otov] and I were left alone afterward.

—*St[alin]:* The appeal turned out well.[316] We will publish it today. We will have to transmit it over the radio, too, as a document found among the effects of the dead noncommissioned officer Stolz . . .

. . . You have been told that you have to evacuate? It has to be done if you are to continue functioning.

—The government, foreign del[egations] and so on, are being evacuated.

—Moscow cannot be defended like Leningrad.

—And as if nothing disturbing were going on at all, [Stalin] calmly began asking about Thälmann, brought up his letters of last year and said: "It is clear that T[hälmann] is being worked on from all sides. He is not a committed Marxist, and his letters show the influence of fascist ideology. He wrote about the plutocracy, assuming that England has been smashed—nonsense! . . . They will not kill him because they are evidently counting on using him if necessary as an 'intelligent' Communist . . . "[317]

As we took our leave of St[alin] he was saying, "Have to evacuate before the day is out!"—which he said [as casually] as if he were saying, "*Time for lunch!*"

—It was already 5:00. Trains were to leave in three or four hours. Gathered my people and made hasty arrangements for evacuating and leaving a temp[orary] lead[ership] group of employees behind in Moscow.

—At 8:30 we were at the loading base. I grabbed Thorez and brought him, too.

316. Concerns the appeal, nominally by the KPD, to the German soldiers engaged in war against the USSR.

317. Ernst Thälmann, chairman of the KPD (*see* Biographical Notes), was confined by the Nazis to the Buchenwald concentration camp, where he was executed in 1943.

· 16 OCTOBER 1941 ·

—We traveled all night without stopping, although slowly. At 7:00 p.m. our train was in the Gorky station.

Traveling on the train: Kalinin, Andreev, Shvernik, Voznesensky, Shkiriatov, Saburov,[318] Zemliachka,[319] Mikhailov (Komsomol), Myshakova,[320] Mikoyan's family.

—Sent Sorkin, Guliaev,[321] Vladimirov,[322] and Tatarenko the following telegram:

1. Take every precaution against divulging the fact of the transfer of our institution and its destination.

2. Send all necessary staff out of M[oscow], beginning with foreigners and especially Germans, by all available means.

3. Send the maximum possible quantity of technical means necessary for our future work, including even radio apparatus and telephone instruments.

4. Settle accounts with the service and other personnel remaining in Moscow, and issue them their salaries through the end of December.

Draw up paperwork for residents in our institution's buildings registering them as employees of the agricultural exhibit.

Transfer those residing in [Hotel] "Lux"[323] to other buildings immediately.

---

318. Maksim Zakharovich Saburov (1900–1977), Soviet Communist leader; activist in the Donbas; head of Gosplan (the state planning administration) from 1941 on; deputy chairman of the Council of People's Commissars (1941–1944, and 1947 on); first deputy chairman of the Council of Ministers (1955–1957); member of the KPSS presidium (1952–1957). He was excluded from the KPSS Presidium in 1957 for his support of the "antiparty group" (Malenkov, Kaganovich, and Molotov).

319. Rozalia Samoilovna Zemliachka (1876–1947); old Bolshevik, member of the RSDRP from 1901 on; member of the Moscow bureau of the RSDRP(b) (1915–1916); first secretary of the Moscow RSDRP(b) committee in 1917 who was assigned to various party duties thereafter; member of the VKP(b) CC (1939–1947); deputy chairman of the Council of People's Commissars (1939–1943).

320. Secretary of the Komsomol CC.

321. Pantaleimon Vasilievich Guliaev (b. 1903), Soviet Communist; chief of the ECCI Cadre Department (1939–1941).

322. Mikhail Kuzmich Vladimirov, Soviet Communist; on the ECCI staff.

323. Hotel Lux (later Tsentralnaia), 10 Gorky Street (now Tverskaia); ECCI residential quarters in Moscow.

Send effects and papers belonging to Jean [Thorez] and the other comrades as opportunity allows.

5. Leave a small group of people in M[oscow] equipped with a radio link to us for future work in our network. There must be radio operators and cryptographers.

6. For all issues connected with our institution, maintain contact with Comrade Shcherbakov in the CC.

Andreev instructed his HF assistant to transmit this telegram by telephone to M[oscow].

———————

We were stopped at the station in Gorky until 10:00. It turned out that the train had been misdirected to Gorky in leaving Kovrov! We were supposed to pull out from Kovrov in a different direction . . . The train has turned back to Kovrov now! Thanks to this blunder we will be another twenty hours late! . . .

[. . .]

· 17 OCTOBER 1941 ·

—By 12:00 we were on this route, which we were supposed to take leaving Kovrov (Erasmus Station to Red Junction [?]). We traveled through Penza-Syzran to Kuibyshev. We have been assured we will be at our destination by 1:00 p.m. tomorrow . . .

I have been unable to determine anything about the train carrying Roza and Shvernik's wife . . .

Drafted an urgent message for *Blinov* (head of radio service) in Ufa, telling him to accept radio telegrams from our correspondents. Looks as though I will not get a chance to send it before Penza.

—Voznesensky spoke tonight with Kaganovich in Moscow. Kag[anovich] reported that nothing in particular has happened. It seems things are not too bad . . .

———————

—We were in M[ikhail] Iv[anovich Kalinin]'s car (Andreev, Shkiriatov, and I). Found him having lunch with V[iacheslav] Mikh[ailovich Molotov], Shvernik, and Voznesensky. We had tea together. Everyone is in good spirits, although quite concerned. Everyone is contemplating the imminent capture of Moscow by the Germans.

—Vozn[esensky] assures us that *industry will be reestablished* within two or three months. Crucial issue is what the prospects will be at the fronts.

—Emergency evacuation of our troops from Odessa.

[. . .]

At the present, crucial stage of the war the highest priority of the working class and above all the Communists of every country is not to give way to despondency in view of the fascist gang's temporary successes, not to lose sight of the final victorious outcome of the struggle by the anti-Hitler front, and for its own part to do everything possible not only to guard its respective peoples against such despondency, but also to bring renewed energy and still greater force and resolve to the continuation of the holy struggle for the destruction of the fascist monsters, for the victory of the just cause of progressive mankind against fascist barbarity and pillage.

17 October 1941

· 18 OCTOBER 1941 ·

—At the Syzran station we caught up with the train carrying Roza and Shvernik's wife. A great and pleasant surprise. We transferred them to our train.

—At 1:00 p.m. we arrived in Kuibyshev.

· 19 OCTOBER 1941 ·

—*With Andreev* at the station (in his car).

—Talked about our arrangements in Ufa and liaison between ourselves and the CC in Kuibyshev.

—We drove together to the CC building (the former regional soviet Executive Committee). Across from it is the building with our apartments.

—Called Ufa. Andreev gave instructions to the regional committee secretary Anushin to have our institution furnished with work facilities and dwelling space. Andreev and I agreed on cutting back the ECCI apparatus to 150 persons. Remaining staff to be put at the disposal of the CC for work in different regions or else given other jobs.

—Contacted the NKVD and other institutions.

—At 1:00 a.m. the train with the Chekists arrived. We had forty-nine of our people aboard, led by Ercoli [Togliatti], Pieck, and the other secretaries. Manuilsky did not come on this train. They brought us Lena and Vŭlko [Chervenkov]. They spent the night at our place.

—*Khavinson* called from Moscow tonight. Reported on the situation, the order by the State Committee for Defense, and so on. Moscow is mobilized for defense.

· 20 OCTOBER 1941 ·

—*I held a conference.*

—Ercoli [Togliatti], Pieck, Florin, Kolarov, Marek [Stanke Dimitrov], Dolores [Ibárruri], Gerő, Stepanov [Minev], Ponomarev, Sergeev [Kolev], Vladimirov [Chervenkov], Jean [Thorez], Toboso, Koplenig.

1. *Settled questions of our arrangements in Ufa.* Ercoli [Togliatti] acts on behalf of the secretariat. He gets a troika of assistants—Ponomarev, Sergeev [Kolev], Stepanov [Minev].

—Radio broadcasting begins immediately (special broadcasts to different countries).

—Responsible for this matter are Ercoli [Togliatti], Gerő, etc. Ercoli is in daily telephone contact with me.

2. *Political directive concerning our radio propaganda* and operations at present. Proposed a draft I had worked up. Accepted unanimously, without any comments.

—[They] left at 11:00 p.m.

—Sent my commissar Kukhiev with them to help get them settled.

· 21 OCTOBER 1941 ·

—Manuilsky arrived early this morning on the Narkomindel [People's Commissariat for Foreign Affairs] train.

—Other trains carrying our people are still en route.

—The apartment above us is being furnished as work space (offices for secretariat in Kuibyshev).

—Installed an HF telephone, *vertushka* [hotline] and so on.

—Had breakfast and lunch with Manuil[sky], his wife and daughter (from his first wife).

—*Krupin* to see me late tonight (with his colleague Ladygin).[324]

—Organized a reception for the arriving Comintern staff at the station; provided them with food and dispatched them to their next destination. Determine where the trains are.

—Reached agreements concerning finances in Ufa, retaining our foreign hard currency, and so on.

· 22 OCTOBER 1941 ·

—Viach[eslav] Mikhail[ovich] [Molotov] flew in to Kuibyshev.

—Man[uilsky] and Varia[325] had lunch with us.

—Spoke with Ercoli [Togliatti] in Ufa. They are having a hard time settling in. Dwelling space is extremely scarce. Special train led by Belov [Damianov] and Gottwald arrived in Ufa.

—Spoke with the secretary of the Ufa regional committee. Also with the NKVD—Sokolov.

[. . .]

· 2 NOVEMBER 1941 ·
[. . .]

DIRECTIVE[326] SENT TO:

London, New York (for the Latin American countries as well), Stockholm, Yugoslavia, Bulgaria, China, Holland, to Clément [Fried] (for France and Belgium)

---

324. Krupin and Ladygin were from the financial and accounting staff of the VKP(b).

325. Varvara Platonovna Manuilska (b. 1902), Soviet Communist who was on the ECCI staff; Manuilsky's wife.

326. This directive to the foreign Communist parties is a much shortened and sharpened version of the theses laid out in the journal entry of 17 October, only the conclusion of which is given here, with a somewhat more somber account of the Soviet predicament and prospects.

Hitler's military successes are temporary and precarious. They will by no means lead to a victorious outcome of the war for Germany. On the contrary, these successes have come at the cost of the colossal exhaustion of the fascist armies and the loss of millions of Hitler's finest units. Hitler has poured his last reserves into the eastern front. The fascist armies are now approaching their maximal concentration of power and offensive capabilities. Henceforth, their fortunes can only diminish.

The military difficulties Hitler faces are enormous. His rear in the occupied countries is increasingly insecure. Resistance by the enslaved peoples is increasingly active. Merciless partisan warfare is under way in the captured Soviet territories. The German people and the army are demanding an end to the war. Demoralization and internal strife have taken hold in the ranks of Germany's allies.

Meanwhile, the transfer of part of the government to Kuibyshev signifies the resolve of the USSR to wage war until final victory. The will and unity of the Soviet people are unshakable. Its hatred for the fascist invaders is infinite. The Red Army is acquiring the necessary combat experience. Its ranks are being replenished with fresh formations from our country's inexhaustible human resources. The timely evacuation of factories and skilled workers, the expansion and full utilization of industry in the Urals, and aid from England and the USA are contributing to successful resistance by the USSR and preparations for a Soviet offensive aimed at sweeping the fascist hordes from our land.

The popular masses in England and America, concerned for their own future in the face of the fascist advance, are supportive of the USSR. The forces of the anti-Hitler front are growing in every country. The real prospects for a victorious outcome in this war belong to the Soviet Union, to the anti-Hitler front. Nevertheless, Communist parties must bear in mind that in the present stage of the war, the USSR is in a difficult position. The heroic struggle of the Red Army and the entire Soviet people is in need of full and prompt support on the part of the working class and the peoples of the entire world. This will reduce our losses at the fronts and the sufferings of millions in the occupied countries and will hasten the destruction of the fascist enemy's monstrous military machine. In the occupied countries there must be more active development of sabotage, strikes, demonstrations, and, where conditions are ripe for it, partisan movements oriented toward a national war effort. There must be no despondency. Everything for the rapid destruction of Hitler, for the victory of the USSR, for the salvation of mankind from the fascist monsters.

G. Dimitrov

3 November 1941

[. . .]

· 6 NOVEMBER 1941 ·

—Ceremonial assembly in observance of the twenty-fourth anniversary of the October [Revolution]. Palace of Culture in Kuibyshev. Similar meeting taking place simultaneously in Moscow. Stalin's report broadcast from Moscow (remarkable document!).
—I was elected to the honor presidium at the Kuibyshev meeting; in Moscow I was not.

· 7 NOVEMBER 1941 ·

—Parades in Moscow and Kuibyshev.
—Speech by *Stalin* on Red Square.
—In Kuibyshev—speech by Voroshilov.
—Striking impression in the country, in the army, and abroad.

—Like yesterday, was not in the parade today.
—*No need* to emphasize the Comintern!

[. . .]

· 11 NOVEMBER 1941 ·

—*Ilichev* and Bolshakov[327] to see me.
—Agreed on combining operations in Belgium, France, and Switzerland (between their people and the party leadership).

[. . .]

· 12 NOVEMBER 1941 ·

—Molotov called about the need for Chinese Com[munist] party representatives to take part in the forthcoming session of the [Chinese] national-political council.
    —Sent directive to Mao Zedong.

· 17 NOVEMBER 1941 ·

—Received reply from Mao Zedong saying *he will participate.*

[. . .]

327. Ilichev and Bolshakov, Red Army intelligence officers.

· 7 December 1941 ·
[. . .]

—*Ponomarev and Ilichev* ([Red Army] intelligence) to see me.
—The matter of organizing Chinese CP intelligence has to be worked up concretely, with incorporation of Stal[in's] suggestion.
—About transporting arms to Yugoslavia: try to use captured German matér[iel].
—In December, transport Polish group (Nowotko, Mołojec, Finder, and others) to *Warsaw*.
—Agreed about liaison between intelligence in Kuibyshev and ourselves in Ufa.

[. . .]

· 8 December 1941 ·

—*Japan* has declared war on the USA and England.
—Hostilities have commenced in the Pacific basin.
—Agreed by telephone with Man[uilsky] and Ercoli [Togliatti] in Ufa about commentary in this connection in our *intern[al]* radio broadcasts: Hitler is responsible for extending the war to new continents, a desperate attempt to save himself from impending catastrophe. This does not fundamentally alter prospects for the outcome of the war. I recommended caution in commentary until the position of the Soviet Union is officially announced.

[. . .]

—Spoke with Vyshinsky and Lozovsky about Japan's military action.
—They still have not heard anything about Moscow's position.

[. . .]

· 9 December 1941 ·

—Sent Com[rades] St[alin], Mol[otov], Ber[ia], Kal[inin] encoded communication on *the Iranian question* (restoration of the Com[munist] Party, etc.). Proposed that the Com[munist] Party not be restored, but to work within the Peo[ple's] Party of Suleiman Mirza (democratic [political] figure) and pursue a line of
1) struggle for democratization of Iran; 2) defense of workers' interests; 3) strengthening of friendly relations between Iran and the USSR; 4) complete eradication of fascist agenc[ies] in Iran and suppression of

anti-Soviet propaganda. Communists should at the same time work for the creation of trade unions and peas[ant] organizations.

[...]

· 12 DECEMBER 1941 ·

[...]

—*Viach[eslav] Mikh[ailovich]* [Molotov] called late tonight from Moscow: "I spoke with Stalin about your telegram about Iran. We agree with the approach you suggest . . ." "Things are not so bad at the front . . . "

I: "Should we return to Moscow then?"

M[olotov]: "Not yet. The time will come!"

—Regarding arms assistance for the Yugoslav Partisans (at least captured German arms), M[olotov] said: "Cannot be done!"

[...]

· 18 DECEMBER 1941 ·

—Received Polish group (being transported to Poland): Nowotko, Mołojec, Finder, Skoniecki, Aleksandrowicz, Paplinski, Kowalczyk, Sliwa, Micał, Kamenetskaia (radio operator), Kartin (radio operator); Guliaev is accompanying the group. Held discussion and gave them instructions. The line determined for the Workers' Party of Poland remains basically still in effect at the present stage.

[...]

· 30 DECEMBER 1941 ·

—Meeting of the secretariat, including radio editors, commentators, and other polit[ical] staff.

—Critique of the nature and contents of our radio propaganda and our overall work abroad.

—Formulated our concrete tasks for the immediate future:

1. Facilitate Turkish resistance to the Germans in their attempt to seize the Dardanelles and enter the Caucasus through Turkey.

2. Oppose the use of the Bulgarian army against Turkey.

3. Bring about the formation of a powerful movement in Italy, Hungary, Romania, Slovenia [Slovakia?] and Finland [not] to furnish Hitler with new human resources to prepare for that German offensive in the spring; work for the breakup of Hitler's coalition.

4. Oppose the use of the Spanish army by Hitler.

5. As regards China, facilitate settlement between CPC [Communist Party of China] and Chiang Kai-shek, in the interests of mounting a general counteroffensive by Chinese armies against the Japanese.

6. Assist in preparing pop[ular] masses in the occupied countries for decis[ive] armed actions against the occupiers, simultaneously with the Red Army's gener[al] counteroffensive in the spring.

7. Generally demoralize Hitler's *German* home front and *Mussolini's Italian* home front.

[. . .]

· 26 JANUARY 1942 ·

—Rákosi on Hungarian business. Again he insists on petitioning the American embassy to allow him to go to America to work among Hungarian émigrés there.[328]

—Not feasible!

—Friedrich [Geminder]: about our foreign telegraph agencies.

—Operations expanding significantly.

—*Evening meeting* of trade union organization. Half the membership missing. Soulless, dead organization.

—Addressed them quite sharply!

[. . .]

· 31 JANUARY 1942 ·
[. . .]

—*Conference with French comrades* (Man[uilsky], Ercoli [Togliatti], Thorez, Marty, Stepanov [Minev], and D[imitrov]).

—Discussion of the activities of the CP of France.

—Following exchange of views, it was recommended to the French that they prepare advice for the group in their country, *activate struggle,* with the possibility of armed action against the occupiers.

[. . .]

328. On 26 December 1941, according to Dimitrov's diary entry, Rákosi had requested assignment to the United States to work among Hungarians living in America. Dimitrov called the idea "impracticable."

· 4 FEBRUARY 1942 ·

[. . .]

—Examined minutes of the party organization meeting [for] discussion of Molotov's note and German atrocities. Meeting badly organized. Party committee did not lead. Unwholesome sentiments became apparent.

—Uncertain: the extent to which the *German people,* along with Hitler, may be held responsible for these atrocities.

[. . .]

· 11 FEBRUARY 1942 ·

—Sent *Duclos* directive for the CP of France. Time has come for more aggressive actions, preparation for direct popular uprising.

[. . .]

· 12 FEBRUARY 1942 ·

[. . .]

—D. Z. [Manuilsky] and I exchanged views on certain suspicious aspects of the radio propaganda of the English and their military operations.

—They wouldn't be preparing for capitulation or compromise with Hitler, would they?

Must be on guard!

· 13 FEBRUARY 1942 ·

—*Shcherbakov* called. Agrees with all my proposals for radio broadcasting and work among prisoners of war.

I drew his attention to recent rather suspicious behavior by the English. Cripps's speech on postwar conditions also raises doubt. Who needs such speeches!

[. . .]

· 28 FEBRUARY 1942 ·
[. . .]

—Sent Stalin, Molotov, and others references on major leadership figures in the Yugoslav Partisan movement: 1) *Tito*—Walter—real surname Broz, Josip; 2) Popović, Konstantin;[329] 3) Černović, Milovan [Djilas]; 4) Žujović, D. Sreten;[330] 5) Birk, Franc Edvardović [Kardelj]; 6) Ribar, Ivan Davidović;[331] 7) General Arso Jovanović.[332]

Wrote Stalin, Molotov, and Malenkov about six Spanish commanders who have graduated the Red Army General Staff Academy, to have them admitted to the Red Army as trainee alternates [. . .]

[. . .]

329. Konstantin (Koča) Popović (1908–1992), Yugoslav Communist from a prominent bourgeois family; student in France and Surrealist writer; fought in the International Brigades in Spain; one of the leaders of the Partisan uprising in Serbia; commander of the 1st Proletarian Brigade, 1st Proletarian Division, 1st Proletarian Corps, and Second Yugoslav Army; chief of the general staff of the Yugoslav People's Army (1945–1953); minister of foreign affairs (1953–1966); vice president of Yugoslavia (1966–1967); member of collective Yugoslav presidency (1967–1972). He resigned from all functions in 1972 in protest against Tito's purge of the liberal Serbian party leadership.

330. Sreten Žujović (pseudonym: Crni, 1899–1976), Yugoslav Communist leader; student at the Comintern's Leninist School in Moscow (1933–1935); member of the KPJ Politburo (1936–1938, 1940–1948); commander of Partisan main staff in Serbia (1941); Yugoslavia's minister of finances (1945). He sided with the Soviets immediately before the 1948 break. He was imprisoned (1948–1950) but then released after his public recantation.

331. Ivan Ribar (1881–1968), Yugoslav politician; member of the Democratic Party and president of Yugoslavia's Constituent Assembly (1920–1922); opponent of the dictatorship of King Aleksandar in the 1930s; president of the Antifascist Council of People's Liberation of Yugoslavia (AVNOJ), the Partisan political representative body (1942–1945); president also of the Constituent Assembly (1945–1946) and Yugoslavia's National Assembly (1946–1953). Dimitrov could also be referring to Ivan Ribar's son—Ivo Lolo Ribar (1916–1943), member of the KPJ Politburo, secretary of the League of Communist Youth of Yugoslavia (SKOJ), who was killed in a German air raid in Bosnia.

332. Arso Jovanović (1907–1948), Yugoslav military officer; captain in the royal Yugoslav army; chief of the Yugoslav Partisan supreme staff (1942–1945) of the general staff of the Yugoslav army (1945–1946); postwar graduate of the Voroshilov Higher Military Academy in the USSR; commander of the Higher Military Academy (1948); after the Cominform resolution, he tried to flee to Romania; he was killed by Yugoslav border guards.

· 1 MARCH 1942 ·

—Sunday.
—Spoke with Viacheslav Mikhailovich [Molotov] about Walter's [Tito's] telegram from Yugoslavia about the arrival there of the English military mission seeking a meeting with Partisan supreme staff.[333]

[. . .]

· 5 MARCH 1942 ·
[. . .]

Sent Stal[in], Molot[ov], and others the telegram I sent to Walter [Tito] criticizing the narrow scope of the Partisan movement.
—Intruding German voice is encountering problems. Blinov to see me about this.

[. . .]

· 8 MARCH 1942 ·

—Sunday.
—Received telegram from Walter [Tito] (Yugoslavia): "We are short of ammunition and military supplies, owing to continuous fighting. Please send emergency assistance. Our troops are in serious difficulty, owing to lack of military supplies. We await your planes every night. Weather here is now good."

Forwarding the contents of the telegram to Beria, I wrote to him: "I urge you to take a special interest in this matter and to speak with Comrade Stalin personally about rendering any possible assistance. Even modest assistance would mean a great deal to the heroically struggling Yugoslav comrades. Please do inform me immediately whether such assistance will be possible."

[. . .]

333. Refers to the mission of Maj. Terence Atherton, a Special Operations Executive (SOE) operative, whose members were put ashore by a British submarine near Petrovac, Montenegro, in February 1942. The mission reached Tito's headquarters but, to the chagrin of the Partisans, departed mysteriously on 16 April 1942, apparently in an attempt to reach the Chetniks—royalist anticommunist guerrillas. All trace of the mission was lost after the end of May. Partisan proponents have claimed that Atherton was liquidated by a Chetnik commander.

· 10 MARCH 1942 ·
[. . .]

—Received the appeal of the supreme staff of the Partisans from *Walter* [Tito] (Yugoslavia). It is party-oriented: the Commun[ist] Party organized the Partisans—long live the Red Army, long live Comrade Stalin, not a thought for England or America, and so on.

Directed Walter to change these things, to give the appeal a broadly national character.

—*Shcherbakov* called late: he had spoken with Stal[in]; he had told him, "Have D[imitrov] and the group of Germans come to M[oscow], the sooner the better . . ."

An hour later Poskrebyshev called: "Connecting you directly with Stalin: 'It would be good if you and the group of Germans were in the city tomorrow.'"

[. . .]

· 14 MARCH 1942 ·
[. . .]

—Conference on Polish issues (Dzierżyńska, Natanson, Kasman (the Poles),[334] D. Z. [Manuilsky], Ercoli [Togliatti], Gottwald, Friedrich [Geminder], and others).

—Clarified *the positions of Polish* national radio as regards reactionary activities of the Polish government in London and, since that radio [service] is obliged to cover these issues, that it ought not to come out directly against the Sikorski government.[335]

Dimitrov was back in Moscow on 19 March 1942, where he remained, except for occasional trips of inspection (Kuibyshev-Ufa, 6–10 June 1942). This was a period of routine work, as the influ-

---

334. These were some of the senior Poles in the ECCI apparatus: Zofia Dzierżyńska (1882–1968), ECCI staff member and widow of head of the Cheka Feliks Dzierżyński; Solomon Natanson (b. 1904), ECCI staff member; Leon Kasman (1905–1984), ECCI staff member and member of the PZPR CC (1948–1968).

335. Refers to the London-based Polish government-in-exile, headed by Gen. Władysław Sikorski (1881–1943).

ence of the Comintern kept declining. Dimitrov was constantly involved in Bulgarian affairs, but the problems of Tito's forces kept interjecting themselves into his work (particularly the question of conflict with the Chetniks of Draža Mihailović), as did those of Mao Zedong. Part of Dimitrov's time was devoted to the infiltration of occupied East European countries by native Comintern-trained operatives, without exception in collaboration with the NKVD and the Soviet military intelligence. The Nowotko case in Poland was the most dramatic of these operations. Attempts were made to woo non-Communist figures to pro-Soviet positions for future reference (Mihály Károlyi in London exile), but Dimitrov seems to have been mainly unconcerned with issues of the "second front," his stance being typically unsentimental when the Western Allies were concerned.

Dimitrov's marginalization was evident from the petty work with which he was concerned, including such matters as using the CPs in the occupied countries for more exact weather reports on behalf of Soviet air force operations, continued obsession with the "intruding voice," and draft appeals from various intellectual front groups to the occupied countries. His meetings with Stalin practically ceased, Molotov being Dimitrov's sole occasional senior interlocutor—and very rarely, at that. Affairs of the Communist parties of Finland, Austria, Sweden, the Netherlands, Turkey, Cuba, Spain, Great Britain, Indonesia, Iraq, and Denmark continued to occupy him. And he endured periods of illness in the fall of 1942.

By November 1942, as the Red Army increasingly pressed the Germans, the Comintern started considering plans for the future. A series of commissions were organized with the aim of setting policy for the postwar period. Their ordering is significant. First came the German commission (Wilhelm Pieck), then the Austrian (Friedl Fürnberg), the Italian (Palmiro Togliatti), the French (Maurice Thorez), and the Czechoslovak (Klement Gottwald), but also, oddly, the Iraqi one. By the end of January 1943, with the lifting of the blockade of Leningrad and the surrender of Paulus's army group at Stalingrad, Dimitrov gave the "directive for our radio propaganda in connection with the new phase of the war!"—I.B.

[. . .]

· 19 MARCH 1942 ·

[. . .]

—Comrade Stalin called. He asked when the German comrades would arrive and whether the Chinese were on the way. "When they arrive, let me know. I am interested in the Germans and the Chinese now. We shall talk about everything else later . . . "

[. . .]

· 20 MARCH 1942 ·
[. . .]

—*Shcherbakov* called and reported that Comrade Stal[in] has advised delaying the publication of the appeal by the supreme staff of the Yugosl[av] Part[isan] army, owing to relations with the Yugosl[av] government.

· 21 MARCH 1942 ·
[. . .]

—Informed Walter [Tito] that we will delay publication of the appeal by the supreme staff of the Partisans, pending definitive clarification of certain issues in relations between the Sov[iet] government and the Yugosl[av] government in London.

[. . .]

· 26 MARCH 1942 ·

—Called *Malenkov* about Yugoslavia. Emphasized to him the necessity of immediate resolution of the question of assisting the Partisan army with arms, as well as the question of transporting our people (part[y] workers) abroad.

[. . .]

· 12 APRIL 1942 ·
[. . .]

—Disturbing reports from Yugoslavia that the Partisans are unlikely to hold their positions in Bosnia under the general offensive by German, Italian, and Hungarian [should be "Croatian"] troops—owing to lack of sufficient ammunition.[336]

[. . .]

336. This entry refers to a report of 10 April 1942 from Walter [Tito], in Foča, eastern Bosnia.

· 17 April 1942 ·

—Walter [Tito] reports (from Yugoslavia) that yesterday the English mission stationed at Partisan headquarters disappeared without a trace, along with its radio station. They left behind an outrageous letter for headquarters. Also took with them a certain Serbian general whose life our people had saved from Mihailović . . .[337]

[. . .]

· 25 April 1942 ·

—Aviation engineer *Afanasiev* (back from America) gave me an account of his impressions and observations of the United States. Overall conclusion: enormous possibilities for revolutionary movements against trusts and magnates.

[. . .]

· 28 April 1942 ·
[. . .]

—Sent *Stalin* letter about partis[an] war in Yugoslavia and the conduct of the English and of the Yugosl[av] government in London, which is obstructing the development of this war.

[. . .]

—Spoke with Molot[ov] by telephone on Yugoslav and Bulg[arian] business. [He] requested that Bulg[arian] documents be sent to him again.

[. . .]

· 5 May 1942 ·

—Wrote *Stalin* about the proposal by the Labourite Laski[338] that the Labour Party initiate negotiations with the VKP(b) for the unification

337. Refers to the Atherton mission (cf. n. 333). Gen. Dragoljub (Draža) Mihailović (1893–1946) was the leader of the collaborationist Chetnik movement, which promulgated a Great Serbian nationalist program. Formally a minister of the royal government-in-exile, Mihailović's first concern was the Communist insurgency, against which he fought with Axis weapons. Captured by the Communists after the war, he was given a show trial, condemned to death, and executed.

338. Harold Laski (1893–1950), British Labourite leader and political theoretician (1893–1950); faculty member of the London School of Economics (from

of the inter[national] workers' movement (report from Pollitt, who requests my opinion on this matter).

My opinion is that this is quite a suspicious notion. Even if the Labourites have proposed such an initiative sincerely, it would still be inexpedient and counterproductive in the current situation, and therefore Pollitt and the English CP should in no way engage themselves in this matter as regards the Labourites.

[. . .]

· 7 MAY 1942 ·

—Received report from Sofia that *Radionov,*[339] *his assistant Popov*[340] *and a number of Communist Party members were arrested at the end of April.* If this is confirmed, then the Party has sustained an extremely serious blow.

—*General Panfilov* and *Commissar Ilichev* (from the [Red Army] Intelligence Directorate) to see me along with their colleague *Kasatkin,* recently arrived from Sofia. The latter reported on the situation in Bulgaria. His information is somewhat shallow. Conclusions:

1. Growing hatred of Bulgarians for the Germans.

2. Germans are everywhere the real masters.

3. Unfriendly relations between Germans and Italians.

4. Enormous sympathies for the Soviet Union among the people.

5. The Bulgarian army is in no condition to wage war against the USSR.

6. On the other hand, it would be quite possible to lead the Bulg[arian] army against the Turks.

—*Panfilov* and *Ilichev* reported on preparations for the Germans' offens[ive] on the eastern front. Three directions: 1) against Moscow; 2)

1920 on); member of the Labour Party executive committee (from 1936 on); chairman of the Labour Party (1945–1946).

339. Tsviatko Radionov (1895–1942), Bulgarian Communist; participant in the September uprising (1923); émigré to Turkey and the USSR; fighter in the International Brigades in Spain (1936–1939). He was sent by the ECCI to Bulgaria (1941), where he was a member of the BKP CC and chief of its military commission. Caught by the Bulgarian authorities in 1942, he was condemned to death and executed.

340. Anton Popov (1915–1942), Bulgarian Communist; BKP CC associate. He was captured by the Bulgarian authorities in 1942, condemned to death, and executed.

between Moscow and Leningrad; 3) to the south: Rostov and the Caucasus.

[...]

· 13 MAY 1942 ·

—Regarding recruitment of people for Engl[ish] and Amer[ican] intelligence by Wolff's[341] American committee in the interests of supposedly using them for subv[ersive] work behind the German lines: gave instructions to the Amer[ican] CC not to engage in these activities and to break off all contacts between Amer[ican] Communists and these intelligence services, for these contacts would allow intelligence agents to infiltrate the party and jeopardize the work of the Amer[ican] and other Com[munist] parties.

[...]

· 16 MAY 1942 ·

—Held a lengthy discussion with a group of Polish comrades who are to be transported by airplane to Poland in several days. Provided them with explanations and instructions regarding the political line and practical work of the Polish Workers' Party. Group consists of eight persons, including two women. Among them are two radio operators. They are taking radio apparatus, codes, and so on. Checked preparations for transport. Evidently satisfactory.

[...]

· 18 MAY 1942 ·

—Major of State Security *Zhukov* to see me regarding the Polish army and Czechoslovak brigade. Reported on the situation in the Polish army. Forty-four thousand Poles are on USSR territory and three divisions (12,500 apiece) in Iran. Anti-Soviet sentiments predominate. The officer corps is Piłsudskiite—from the old Polish army. The commander in chief, *Anders,*[342] however, is completely loyal.

341. Refers to the activities of Milton Wolff, American leftist, member of the US Young Communist League and the PCE, commander of the Abraham Lincoln Brigade, within the International Brigades in Spain, and head of the Veterans of the Abraham Lincoln Brigade organization, who proposed that the Abraham Lincoln Brigade veterans help the American and British intelligence agencies in the war against the fascists. Wolff himself was recruited by Col. William Donovan's OSS and helped recruit other veterans until the ban from Moscow.

342. Refers to Gen. Władysław Anders (1892–1970), commander of the Polish

The Czechoslovak brigade numbers 800 men. It is planned to add 2,500 Sub-Carpathian Ukrainians from f[ormer] Czechoslovakia. We reached an agreement regarding future work and to that end furnishing certain Polish, and other, comrades of ours.

[. . .]

· 20 MAY 1942 ·
[. . .]

—Received a message from *Pollitt*. Our advice is sought regarding the Com[munist] Party's line and work in connection with the forthcoming national party conference (23 May 1942). *Beaverbrook*[343] wanted to propose to him that they make joint appearances speaking out against Churchill. Frank Owen, editor of Beaverbrook's paper the *Evening Standard,* appealed to Pollitt to support his candidacy as an "independent" running against the government candidate in the by-election in Bury. Pollitt refused to support him . . .

· 21 MAY 1942 ·

—Replied to Pollitt:

In our opinion the party should support the current leadership in England in its efforts directed at strengthening the fighting alliance with the USSR against Hitler and mobilizing all the forces and resources of the English people in offensive actions for the destruction of fascist Germany, while criticizing the manifest hesitancy and *shortcomings* in the direction of those efforts.

The party should not yield to advances made to it by anti-Churchill people. We consider it inexpedient for Pollitt to meet with Beaverbrook. Such a meeting in current conditions could be actually counterproductive.

In the interests of national unity, the party should not put forward its own candidates in the by-election. The party favors only candidacies of people standing for close alliance with the USSR and for the energetic pros-

---

army in the Soviet Union, himself a veteran officer from the interwar times, when Marshal Józef Piłsudski (1867–1935) was the inspector general of the Polish army. Captured by the Soviets in 1939, Anders was released in 1941 to head the Polish army made up of released Polish captives in the USSR; he led this army into Iran (1943) and committed it to the Italian front. Having been stripped of his citizenship by the Communist authorities in 1946, he remained abroad, a member of the Polish government-in-exile in London.

343. William Beaverbrook (1879–1964), British newspaper publisher and Conservative MP who held several ministerial posts in Churchill's wartime cabinets.

ecution of the war until the rout of Hitlerism. It is against candidates who favor the continuation (in any form) of the infamous Munich policy. The party will take full advantage of the electoral campaign to popularize its slogans.

—The Polish group landed safely in Poland during the night (in two places).

—Before the plane landed, the Polish comrades sent me the foll[owing] letter:

Dear Comrade Dimitrov,

On the day we leave Sov[iet] soil for our own country we send you our heartfelt and battle-ready regards.

We assure you that we will faithfully execute the tasks you have set before us for the benefit of the workers' cause, for our native country, and for all mankind.

We will take the path pointed out for us by our great Comrade Stalin. In our struggle and work we will regard your life and struggle as our model.

—Fornalska, Goldschlag, Dronszkiewicz, Kowalski, Stach [August Lange], Heyman, Krasicki, Gruszczyński.

19:00 hours, 20 May 1942.

[. . .]

· 24 MAY 1942 ·
[. . .]

—Received a disturbing telegram from Walter [Tito] (Yugoslavia):

Since 22 May I have been in the Montenegrin sector of the front with [my] chief of staff. The situation here is critical. Italian troops, together with Draža Mihailović's Chetniks under the command of Stanišić,[344] are advancing from all sides against our Partisan troops. The Chetniks are coming through forests and over mountains, while the Italians are motorized. The Chetniks possess enormous quantities of automatic weapons, mortars, and ammunition. They are mobilizing peasants by force; resisters are either killed or driven en masse into concentration camps in Albania. Our Partisan battalions are completely exhausted from continuous fighting; we are also out of ammunition. We must withdraw the majority of our battalions from Montenegro to prevent their destruction.[345]

344. Bajo Stanišić (1891–1943), prewar Yugoslav army colonel. He participated in the Partisan uprising in Montenegro in July 1941. In February 1942 he started collaborating with the Italians and formed Chetnik units. He was killed in battle against the Partisans in October 1943.

345. On Partisan defeats in spring 1942 in Montenegro (and elsewhere) at the hands of the Chetniks and Italians, see Jozo Tomasevich, *War and Revolution in Yugoslavia: The Chetniks* (Stanford, Calif., 1975), pp. 210–211.

The whole nation is cursing the Yugoslav government in London, which is abetting the occupiers through Draža Mihailović. Fighters and people everywhere confront me with the same question: Why is the Soviet Union not sending us aid, at least a few automatic weapons?

Our Partisans are fighting with unprecedented heroism. For instance, the commanders and fighters of the Lovćen battalion relayed the following to me: *Tell* Comrade Tito that we are going to save two comrades to come and report that all the rest of us have been killed.

Aid for us is a very serious issue. On behalf of the supreme staff we ask you to relay our request for aid to the Red Army Supreme Command. The enemy is doing his utmost to destroy us. Hundreds of thousands of lives are in jeopardy. We know that this is impossible. We are carrying on the fight despite all losses.

Is there nothing that could be done in London to oppose such a treacherous policy on the part of the Yugosl[av] government?[346]

· 25 MAY 1942 ·

—Received the NKVD specialist on Anglo-Saxon countries Gaik *Ovakimian.*[347] Reported on the status of the English CP according to their information. Pol[litt's] strange behavior. English intelligence is using him to plant its people in the party and also in the apparatus of Sov[iet] organs. So far it has been impossible to determine whether Pol[litt] is carrying out this work deliberately or whether English intelligence is taking advantage of his lack of vigilance.

—Arranged to undertake the most scrupulous study of Pol[litt] and what is generally taking place in the leadership of the English CP.

—*Ovakimian* also reported on the "cooperation" between the NKVD and English intelligence in transporting people behind the German lines. The English are of very little use in this regard. For the most part they sabotage.

[. . .]

346. The Yugoslav government-in-exile in London supported the Chetniks of Draža Mihailović. Initial claims for his leadership in the armed resistance movement in Yugoslavia were popularized in the Anglo-American press in late 1941, at a time when Hitler's forces were unchallenged in Europe and threatening to occupy the USSR.

347. NKVD operative resident in New York from 1933 to 1941. He was arrested in May 1941 and exchanged for six Americans or dependents who had been refused exit from the USSR.

· 26 MAY 1942 ·

—Fitin sent word from Sofia that on or about 1 May, *"Luka" (Anton) [Ivanov] and Donko Chernookov (Traicho Kostov)* were arrested. A serious blow for the Bulgarian CP leadership!

[...]

· 1 JUNE 1942 ·

—*Fitin* (NKVD) to see me. Discussed possible measures for determining the causes of the downfall of the CC of the CP of Bulgaria and the fates of the arrested CC members.

[...]

—Sent *Walter* [Tito] the following telegrams in reply to his latest encoded communications:

> 1. Exposing the treacherous actions of the Chetniks to the people—concretely, with documentation, convincingly—is of course necessary. But it would be politically expedient at present to do so in the form of an appeal to the Yugoslav government, emphasizing that the fighting Yugoslav patriots are entitled to expect that government's support, and not its allowing various parties acting in its name to stab the Partisan people's liberation army in the back when it is fighting against the occupying hordes. Expose, in other words, but refrain for now from turning this into a direct attack on the government itself.
>
> 2. A broad political campaign must be deployed against collaborators on the basis of a united struggle of Serbs, Croats, Montenegrins, and Slovenes against the common enemy. Conduct that campaign to divide, rather than unite, all the Chetniks against the Partisan army. In this regard your tactical line ought to be to win over part of the Chetniks to your own side, to neutralize others, and to destroy the most malicious part of them without mercy.
>
> 3. It would be very effective to organize—along with statements issued by the supreme staff and the other Partisan headquarters—statements (in leaflets and so on) by well-known Yugoslav public figures and politicians against collaborators and in favor of the Part[isan] people's liberation army, in favor of the fighting unity of Yugoslav patriots, irrespective of political convictions and former foreign-policy orientation (pro-Soviet and pro-English).
>
> 4. A national committee for aid for the Yugoslav people's war of liberation ought to be formed, consisting of well-known patriotic Serb, Croat, Montenegrin, and Slovene public figures, who would speak out at home and abroad in defense of the political platform of the struggle of the Partisan People's Liberation Army.

We request that you consider our advice and inform us of your views, as well as the concrete measures you intend to take along these lines.

———————————

Unfortunately, as we have already informed you previously, you cannot count on receiving any ammunition or automatic weapons from us in the immediate future, for reasons that you will understand. The main reason is the impossibility of transport. It is therefore necessary for you to make the maximum and most rational use of all available possibilities to supply yourselves locally (including the very slightest as well as the most difficult). Thus, despite the hellish difficulties, carry on and expand the war of liberation, hold your position, and parry the enemy's blows until external assistance becomes possible.

[. . .]

· 3 JUNE 1942 ·
[. . .]

—Manuil[sky] reported on the *special mood* of the German comrades in connection with Engl[ish] bombing of *Cologne* and Essen. They are purportedly depressed and irritable . . .

[. . .]

· 4 JUNE 1942 ·
[. . .]

—Sent *Stalin and Molotov* the foll[owing] letter (with my encoded communication to Walter [Tito] (Yugoslavia) enclosed):

In reply to Walter's latest telegrams from Yugoslavia, we have sent him the two enclosed telegrams.

The matter of the attitude of the Yugoslav government in London to the partisan war in Yugoslavia remains thus far unclarified and unsettled. Meanwhile, Draža Mihailović's so-called Chetniks, along with Nedić's puppet government[348] and the occupiers, wage battles against units of the Partisan people's liberation army with the irrefutable support of London.

I submit that since the Yugoslav government and the English are by treaty engaged with us in the fight against fascist Germany, one ought to find an

348. Milan Nedić (1877–1946), Serbian and Yugoslav officer; general of the Yugoslav royal army, chief of staff, and minister of the army and navy. He was of pro-German orientation, and after the occupation of Yugoslavia, the German occupying authorities appointed him president of the collaborationist Serbian administration on 29 August 1941. Captured by the Partisans and tried as a war criminal, he allegedly committed suicide in prison.

opportunity, in the appropriate form, to point out to them the unacceptability of such conduct and the necessity, in the interests of our common cause, of bringing about a favorable settlement of relations between the Yugoslav government and the heroically fighting Partisan army in Yugoslavia.

· 5 JUNE 1942 ·

—Meeting of the secretariat with German and Czech comrades (Pieck, Ackermann,[349] Ulbricht, Florin, Fürnberg, Friedrich [Geminder], Šverma,[350] Man[uilsky]).
—Examined positions of the CP of Germany in connection with Engl[ish] bombing of Germany and the CP of Czech[oslovakia] in connection with the assassination attempt on Heydrich.[351]

———

—In Germany we must proceed from the fact that the war has been shifted directly onto German territory.
—In Czechoslovakia fascist Germany is waging a war of extermination of the Czechs by any and all means. A nat[ional] liberation war by the Czech people must oppose this. The centr[al] problem is the organization of that partisan war.
—Our radio broadcasting should carry out these aims.

[. . .]

349. Anton Ackermann (real name: Eugen Hanisch, 1905–1973), German Communist; graduate of the Comintern's Leninist School; KPD CC member (from 1935 on); veteran of the International Brigades in Spain (1936–1937); head of the Free Germany radio station; member after the war in East Germany of the SED CC (1946–1948). He was denounced as a "deviationist" on account of his theses on the German road to socialism, reinstated on the SED CC in 1950, demoted again in 1953 after taking part in a leadership group that was in opposition to Ulbricht, and rehabilitated again in 1956. Member and later vice-president of the GDR State Planning Commission (after 1958).

350. Jan Šverma (1901–1944), Czechoslovak Communist; editor of the KSČ newspaper *Rudé pravo* (1924); graduate of the Comintern's Leninist School; member of the KSČ CC Politburo (from 1929 on); member of the executive bureau of the Profintern (1930); alternate member of the ECCI (from 1935 on); deputy in the Czechoslovak parliament (from 1935 on). Living in emigration (in Yugoslavia, the USSR, France, and Britain) after the Munich pact, he represented Czechoslovakia on the Slavic committee in Moscow. Having been sent to Slovakia in 1944 to take part in the Partisan movement, he succumbed to illness and died.

351. Reinhard Heydrich (1904–1942), Nazi functionary; deputy chief of the Gestapo (1934); Reich protector of Bohemia and Moravia (from 1941 on). He was assassinated by the Czechoslovak resisters in May 1942.

· 7 JUNE 1942 ·
[. . .]

—Called a conference of secretaries and leaders of radio editorial boards: Ercoli [Togliatti], Gottwald, Marty, Koplenig, Kopecký,[352] Appelt,[353] Bianco,[354] Stepanov [Minev], Antipov,[355] Magnus [Richard Gyptner],[356] Moltke [?], [Francisco] Antón, Toboso, Svoboda [Jaroslav Procházka],[357] Tatarenko, Natanson, Holkunen,[358] and others.

352. Václav Kopecký (1897–1961), Czechoslovak Communist; member of the KSČ CC and editor in chief of the KSČ organ *Rudé pravo* (from 1929 on); Communist deputy in the Czechoslovak parliament (from 1929 on); member of the KSČ Politburo (from 1933); after the Munich pact in the USSR, representative of the KSČ to the ECCI; member of the KSČ Politburo (1951); minister of culture and deputy prime minister of Czechoslovakia in the 1950s.

353. Rudolf Appelt (1900–1955), Czechoslovak Communist of Sudeten German background; member of the KSČ CC and alternate member of the Politburo (from 1931 on); Communist deputy in the Czechoslovak parliament. He fled to the USSR in 1938 after the German takeover of Sudetenland, where he was in charge of the Comintern's publications. After returning to Czechoslovakia in 1945, he was directed to East Germany, where he joined the SED central apparatus. He served as GDR ambassador to Moscow (1949–1955).

354. Vincenzo Bianco (1898–1980), Italian Communist arrested by the fascist authorities in the 1920s; émigré to the USSR (after 1925) and graduate of the Comintern political school; alternate member of the PCI CC (from 1931 on). He was arrested in Italy during a clandestine tour in 1931; amnestied, he rejoined the PCI apparatus and fought in the International Brigades in Spain; afterward in Moscow, he represented the PCI to the ECCI and worked in the PCI apparatus after the war. He was investigated for "deviationist" activities in 1951.

355. Aleksandr Ivanovich Antipov (b. 1913), Soviet Communist; member of the apparatus of the KIM (1941). He was responsible for the Comintern schools (1942) and was on the staff of the Cominform (after 1949).

356. Richard Gyptner (pseudonym: Richard Magnus, 1901–1972), German Communist; member of the EC of KIM (from 1922 on). He worked under Dimitrov in the Comintern's West European Bureau (Berlin) and worked in the secretariat of the Comintern (after 1939) and in the central apparatus of SED (after 1946). He headed the GDR Ministry of Foreign Affairs' Department for the Capitalist Countries and served as GDR ambassador to China (1955–1958), Egypt (1958–1961), and Poland (1961–1963).

357. Jaroslav Procházka (pseudonym: Svoboda, 1897–1980), Czechoslovak Communist; émigré to the USSR (1931–1945); member of the ECCI staff; political commissar in the Soviet-sponsored Czechoslovak Corps; member of the KSČ CC (1946–1952). He taught in various military and political schools in Czechoslovakia.

358. Head of the Finnish editorial board at the ECCI and on Soviet radio.

Explained new aspects of the situation: 1) failure of Hitler's "spring offensive"; 2) the extension of the war onto Germany's own territory as a result of mass bombing by the English; 3) bankruptcy of the puppet "German collaboration" governments in the occupied countries; 4) growth of opposition [movements] in Hitler's vassal states; 5) war of extermination against peoples in the occupied countries, *particularly* against the Czechs, and so on.

Hence the conclusions: 1) shift from resisting to attacking the Hitlerites along the entire line; 2) for the occupied countries (particularly Czechoslovakia), the central problem being organizing partisan warfare against the occupiers; 3) for Hitler's vassal states: an immed[iate] break with fascist Germany, cessation of hostilities, separate peace treaties with the Allies; 4) for Germany: immediate cessation of the war, slogans of direct, active measures against Hitler, including armed struggle, and so on.

During the discussion everyone present expressed agreement with these aims. What remains is concretizing them for each individual radio editorial board.

[. . .]

· 10 JUNE 1942 ·
[. . .]

—*Encoded communication* received from *Nowotko* in Poland. All members alive. Operating. Four thousand in the party, three thousand in the milit[ary] organization! Thank God they are not missing!

[. . .]

· 12 JUNE 1942 ·

—*Called a conference of secretaries with lead[ership of] radio editorial boards and polit[ical] workers* in connection with the Soviet-English treaty and the Soviet-American agreement.

Explained significance of these documents and provided *political* guidelines as regards their utilization in our political work and radio propaganda.

Discussion of concrete measures along these lines.

General conclusion: here is a powerful weapon in the struggle against the Hitlerite gang and its accomplices, as well as against the "fifth column" and anti-Soviet elements in America itself and England; the fundamental provisions of the pact—the parties seek no territorial gains for themselves personally and undertake not to interfere in the internal affairs of other states—represent programs for the masses in Germany and its vassal states in their struggle to end Hitler's war of pillage; the treaty and agreement provide a powerful stimulus to the further rallying of anti-Hitler forces the world over.

---

1. A blow to the fifth column and all anti-Sov[iet] elements in England and America

2. A blow to the circles in Germany and its accomplice [states] that are counting on a compromise peace treaty between Germany and England

3. Intensification within Germany itself and among Hitler's vassal states of lack of faith in the victory of Hitler

4. Encouragement of active popular offensive actions against the occupiers in Hitler's interior

5. A blow to pro-Hitler circles in Bulgaria, Turkey, Sweden, and Spain

6. A powerful stimulus to the rallying of anti-Hitler forces the world over

[. . .]

· 15 JUNE 1942 ·

—Meeting with the *Bulgarian activists* (Kolarov, Chervenkov, Belov [Damianov], Poptomov, Kozovski, Blagoeva, Kiro Lazarov,[359] Vlahov, Sergeev [Kolev], Lukanov).[360] Discussed work and party propaganda in the country and from outside.

—Set forth the following fundamental aims:

1. Transition from *resisting* the Bulg[arian] government's pro-Hitler course to *the attack,* to the liquidation of that course, that is, a break with fascist Germany, expulsion of Hitler's armed forces and agents from Bulgaria, orientation toward friendly relations with the Soviet Union and the whole anti-Hitler coalition on the basis of the Roosevelt-Churchill Atlantic Charter and the Anglo-Soviet pact; forma-

---

359. Kiril Lazarov (1895–1980), Bulgarian Communist; political émigré to the USSR (1925–1944); member of the Bulgarian editorial board at the ECCI (1941–1942); deputy editor in chief of Radio Moscow's Bulgarian program (1942–1944); part of the apparatus of the BKP CC (1945–1947); director of the Central Statistical Administration (1947–1949).

360. Karlo Lukanov (1897–1982), Bulgarian Communist; fighter in the International Brigades in Spain (1936–1937); member of the ECCI staff; director of Bulgarian radio (1944–1947); deputy chairman of the Bulgarian state Committee for Science, Art, and Culture (1947–1949).

tion of an authentically nat[ional] Bulgarian government capable of implementing such a policy.

2. *Organization of offensive:* fundamental, central task of the party. Everything must be subordinated to that task.

3. *Immediate agreement between* the Workers' Party [Communists] and the anti-German groups of the Agrarian Union, Social Democratic Party, Democrats, Radicals, and so on, in the interests of consolidating the anti-Hitler Fatherland Front—the salvation of Bulgaria from fascist enslavement. That consolidation requires a political platform for the current struggle and the basic outlines of what Bulgaria should be like following the victory of the anti-Hitler coalition over fascist Germany.

4. *A victorious offensive* requires that we orient ourselves toward three fundamental forces: a) the army; b) youth; c) Partisan detachments. Everything else must for now play a secondary role.

5. The *part[y] activists* here must turn *their own face* to Bulgaria for comprehensive aid to the struggle in the country. Organize their own operations rationally, consider themselves mobilized on that front.

6. *The next few months* are to be considered decisive for Bulgaria as well. The Bulgarian people should not yet be called on to take active part in the war; a victorious uprising against Hitler's Germany and its network of agents in Bulgaria must be brought about on the territory of Bulgaria itself, and the country must be oriented toward the anti-Hitler coalition.

—Manuilsky reported that the CC had assigned him to work mainly in propaganda among enemy troops (Seventh Department of the Red Army Political Directorate). Asked me to assist him in this area with advice and to relieve him of his regular duties in the ECCI.

[...]

· 16 JUNE 1942 ·
[...]

—Colonel Bolshakov ([Red Army] Intelligence Directorate) reported in connection with groups transported to Poland and Germany: it has been established that all are alive and have begun operating. I established working contact and collaboration between Morozov[361] and Bolshakov.

[...]

361. Ivan A. Morozov (d. 1945), Soviet NKVD operative; deputy chief of the

—Sent *Mao Zedong* the following encoded communication:

The current situation absolutely dictates that the Chinese Com[munist] Party undertake everything incumbent upon it to bring about any possible improvement in relations with Chiang Kai-shek and the strengthening of the united Chinese front in the struggle against the Japanese. We are aware that Chiang Kai-shek and the Guomindang leaders are doing their utmost to provoke the Com[munist] Party, in order to discredit and isolate it, but one cannot consider it correct policy on our part for our people to give in to these provocations instead of reacting to them intelligently. Yet there are indications that in Chongqing Zhou Enlai is overlooking this and by his own actions is occasionally playing into the hands of the provocateurs. He is organizing secret conferences with Chiang Kai-shek's enemies and foreign correspondents that are directed against Chiang Kai-shek; the latter, naturally, finds out about them and uses them to further stir up feelings against the Com[munist] Party and to justify his own provocational actions.

Please give serious attention to this situation and take immediate measures to ensure that Com[munist] Party representatives in Chongqing carry out a firm and consistent policy aimed at improving the Com[munist] Party's relations with Chiang Kai-shek and the Guomindang, for your own part avoiding anything that might strain those relations. Points of contention must be clarified with Chiang Kai-shek directly, and attempts made to settle them.

Please notify us of the measures and decisions you have taken in this regard.

· 17 JUNE 1942 ·

—Met with *Shcherbakov* at M[oscow regional] com[mittee]. Discussed and settled a variety of general propaganda and radio propaganda issues.

—Major General *Panfilov* and two [Red Army] Intelligence Directorate workers recently arrived from Yan'an (China), Col[onel] Skrynnik and Col[onel] Germanov, were in to see me. Reported on the situation in the *Special Region,* our party's policy, the condition of the Eighth Army, party and army leadership, and so on.

General conclusion: *quite a lot of trouble* in the work and in the leadership of party and army. Immediate measures for correcting the situation are indispensable.

[. . .]

ECCI business section (from 1942 on), then chief of the First Department of the ECCI (liaison and work in foreign countries); director of Institute 100 (from 1943 on).

· 20 JUNE 1942 ·

—Meeting of the secretariat with directors of radio stations and political workers on problems of covering the Anglo-Soviet pact, the Sov[iet]-Amer[ican] agreement, the session of the USSR supreme soviet on ratification of the pact and the review of the first year of the Patriotic War against the Germano-fascist hordes.

Valuable and useful exchange of views. I provided the direct[ors] with guidelines:

1. The aggressive nature of our propaganda; keep the initiative in our hands.

2. Bear in mind that the worse the enemy's position becomes, the *more furiously* he will try to save himself, using anything and everything that he thinks possible; hence, we are still faced with a severe and arduous struggle to bring about his destruction.

3. We have every possibility of destroying the enemy before 1942 is out, but these are only possibilities. The *actual* destruction of the enemy will require the persistent and intelligent exploitation of these possibilities. Victory will have to be earned.

―――――――――

4. The issue of a second front has already been raised concretely and is on the agenda. But successfully bringing about the second front requires the active participation of the peoples of the European continent as well in the struggle against the occupiers. The development of that struggle (including part[isan] warfare) is both a condition and a constituent part of the second front, that is, the invasion of the European continent by Anglo-American armed forces. It is on the basis of these points that our radio propaganda should proceed for the immediate future.

[. . .]

· 25 JUNE 1942 ·
[. . .]

—Telegram from *Mao Zedong*: reports that he fully concurs with us (telegram of 16 June 1942). Has taken steps.

[. . .]

· 2 JULY 1942 ·
[. . .]

—Sent the *Dutch party* a directive indicating that the correct line it has adopted favoring assistance to a second front is by itself insufficient. The party must simultaneously take into account that one of the most crucial conditions for a successful second front is the struggle *at the present time* by the peoples of the occupied countries themselves against the German invaders. We must assume that the destruction of the Germans' communications and military bases, the weakening of their forces, the creation of the greatest possible panic and the reorganization of occupat[ion] troops, the suppression of the fifth column, and so on—that all of these represent an inseparable, constituent element of the coming second front against fascist Germany . . .

[. . .]

· 6 JULY 1942 ·

—Our envoy to Turkey *Vinogradov*[362] to see me. Reported on the situation in Turkey. In his estimation, the Turks will not enter the war, even if the Germans take Suez. It will be another matter if the Germans succeed in reaching the Caucasus. Currently, they will not let either the Ital[ian] or the French navies pass through the straits to the Black Sea. They will try all sorts of maneuvers until the outcome of the current major battles on the Soviet-German front becomes clear. The Turks would be willing to wage war on Bulgaria, just as the latter would be willing to wage war on Turkey. Hatred for the Bulgarians is extremely strong; there is strong hatred for the Italians, too. The Turks are afraid of the Germans *now;* they are afraid of *us* as regards the *future.* Their internal sentiments could be characterized as "[Send] the *Germans* to the *hospital, Russians* to the *cemetery.*"

They are maintaining 1,200,000 men under arms. Their weaponry, however, is deficient. The majority of their troops remain on the western border. At most eight hundred planes and four hundred tanks. They are trying to obtain arms from Germany, in addition to the limited quantities they have received from England and America.

Turkish nationalism is extremely pronounced and deeply rooted in the people.

362. Sergei Aleksandrovich Vinogradov (1907–1970), Soviet envoy to Turkey (1940–1948).

—All state issues are decided by *İsmet İnönü*[363] and *Çakmak*,[364] chief of staff of the Turkish army . . .

—The Germans are hard at work in Turkey (diplomacy, propaganda, and so on); whereas we, on the contrary, are doing poorly . . .

—A part of the *Turkish army* is quite mercenary. Influential newspaper owned by [Hüseyin Cahit] *Yalçın* (an old, staunch Anglophile). Yalçın is a talented publicist and deputy in the Meclis, where he possesses enormous authority.

—The English ambassador [Sir Hugh Knatchbull-]*Hugessen* is not especially friendly toward us. He gave his consent to conducting a trial in connection with the "assassination attempt" on Papen.[365] The Amer[ican] ambassador [Laurence A.] Steinhardt is on the surface very amiable, but he, too, is not supporting us with the Turks.

—Examined a great deal of current business.

—Send Andreev a letter about immediate allocation of foreign hard currency for foreign operations.

[. . .]

· 13 JULY 1942 ·

[. . .]

—Cuban comrade Blas Roca[366] was in Brazil and with the help of the Brazilian foreign minister met with Prestes[367] in prison (cheerful, fighting spirits, complete confidence in victory over fascism).

[. . .]

363. İsmet İnönü (1884–1973), Turkish general and statesman; close associate of Kemal Atatürk; prime minister (1923–1924, 1925–1937, 1961–1965) and president (1938–1950) of Turkey.

364. Marshal Favzi Çakmak [Paşa](1876–1950), chief of general staff of the Turkish army.

365. Franz von Papen (1879–1969), German diplomat and politician; chancellor (1932); ambassador to Turkey (1939–1944).

366. Blas Roca (real name: Francisco Calderío, 1908–1987), Cuban Communist leader; secretary-general of the Cuban CP (from 1934 on); alternate member of the ECCI (from 1935 on); delegate to Cuba's constituent assembly (1939). After the victory of the 26 of July Movement, Roca's orthodox Communists joined Fidel Castro's new Cuban Communist Party (PCC). He served as a party secretary (1965–1975) and member of the Politburo (1975–1986).

367. Luis Carlos Prestes (pseudonym: Garoto, 1898–1990), Brazilian revolutionary; career military officer. From 1924 to 1927, Prestes led his battalion (the Prestes Column) in rebellion against the government. The Prestes Column led a mobile guerrilla war throughout Brazil, traversed some fourteen thousand miles, and engaged the government troops in hundreds of skirmishes. Prestes was sup-

· 14 JULY 1942 ·

—Brigade commissar *Kuznetsov* (from Sevastopol) to see me. Reported in detail on the heroic saga. Our warriors fought until the last remaining ammunition. With more ammunition they could have held out in Sevastopol even longer. Sevastopol is a heap of ruins. Nothing was left to the enemy in Sevastopol, and as it is a naval port, he will not be able to use it. Our people managed to get the surviving command and political personnel out of Sevastopol at the last minute: several thousand fighters and commanders made it into the partisan regions of the Crimea. But in the city there are still up to twenty thousand wounded, mostly severe cases, as well as many fine doctors and nurses, many women and workers who had provided for the defense of Sevastopol. The Tatars played a despicable, traitorous part. They helped the Germans. There was even a special Tatar division formed of up to fifteen thousand men, which our troops destroyed almost completely. The Russian, Bulgarian, and Greek populations in the Crimea, by contrast, acquitted themselves well. There are part[isan] divisions numbering up to ten thousand men.

[. . .]

· 15 JULY 1942 ·
[. . .]

—Informed Mao Zedong that the Soviet representative (Dekanozov) is in Xinjiang to clarify and settle relations with the Duban.[368] There-

---

ported by the rural workers and peasants of the coffee plantations and cattle ranches. The mystique of Prestes grew, so that even the official press did not dare attack the "Knight of Hope" (*Cavaleiro da Esperança*). In exile from 1927 on, Prestes traveled to Moscow in 1931 and declared himself a Communist, becoming a member of the ECCI in 1935. He returned to Brazil and led a Communist front—the National Liberation Alliance (ANL)—which launched an uprising against the Vargas dictatorship in November 1935. Captured in 1936, he was sentenced to forty-six years in prison. While in prison, he was elected the secretary-general of the Brazilian Communist Party (PCB). After his release in 1945, he was elected to the Brazilian senate. From 1947 on, when the PCB was outlawed, through several dictatorships, some of which forced him into exile, Prestes was at the helm of the PCB. Considered orthodox and rigid, he lost the support of the PCB CC in 1980. He was expelled from the PCB in 1984.

368. Gen. Sheng Shicai proclaimed himself the Duban (governor) after usurping power in Xinjiang (April 1933).

fore the Chinese Com[munist] Party people should for now remain in Xinjiang.

[. . .]

· 17 JULY 1942 ·

[. . .]

—Sent *Nowotko* (Poland) the following telegram:

1. We consider your partisan tactics entirely correct. Concentrate your attention at present mainly on destroying the Germans' communications with the eastern front.

2. The most important thing in organizing partisan detachments is scrupulous selection of cadres, provision for liaison with the populace and its support, the establishment of secure bases. Make every effort to avoid hasty actions in this regard. Count on making the second half of July and the month of August primarily a period for organizing your partisan movement.

3. As for the party, do not go after sheer quantity of organizations and members, but try instead to form strong, proven, and battle-worthy organizations in the major localities, and beware especially of provocateurs. As regards admitting PPS [Polish Socialist Party] members, maintain the strictest vigilance. A united front with PPS organizations is not the same as admitting them into the Workers' [Communist] Party.

4. Put particular effort into better protecting the party's leadership centers and its military organization from enemy attacks.

5. All in all, do not get distracted, do not dig yourselves in, do not pursue quick, momentary successes. Think things through, painstakingly gather and strengthen your party forces and your links with the masses.

[. . .]

· 24 JULY 1942 ·

[. . .]

—*Molotov:* called about our comrades' report from Yugoslavia. Their assertion that Mihailović's people are willing tools in the hands of the occupiers seems to him simplified and one-sided.

———————————

—We agreed that I would stop in to see him and we would discuss the situation of the Part[isan] troops in Yugoslavia.

[. . .]

· 29 JULY 1942 ·

—*Met with Molotov.* Agreed on *form and content* of démarche with the Yugoslav government in London concerning the partisan war in Yugoslavia, especially the role of Draža Mihailović, who is acting against the Part[isan] army and abetting the occupiers. Begin by reporting the major facts to the Yug[oslav] government, and when it starts producing its objections, then submit to it as well the statement by the conference of publ[ic] figures of Montenegro and the Sandžak and the group of Yugoslav officers.

—We discussed the situation. "The English are hardly likely to open a second front this year. But they must be pressured . . ."

—"The English and the Americans evidently intend to wage war against Hitler, but they would like to do so by our hand . . ."

—"Now they are talking about reducing the aid they are sending, in view of the Germans' submarine campaign. But one may well suspect that the English themselves are jettisoning part of their cargoes in order to demonstrate the necessity of reducing shipments. There are enemies, after all, in the Admiralty and other English bodies who want to wreck the cause of aid for us . . ."

—"Turkey's position remains uncertain. Must be on our guard. There is no ruling out that the Turks could even turn against us . . ."

[. . .]

· 5 AUGUST 1942 ·

[. . .]

—*Rákosi:* on Hungarian business. Directed his attention to certain sectarian tendencies in radio propaganda by Hungarian comrades as regards the anti-Hitler national front in Hungary, its composition and nature. A positive position must be taken as regards *Károlyi*,[369] and a

---

369. Count Mihály Károlyi (1875–1955), Hungarian liberal statesman; premier and provisional president of Hungary after the dissolution of the Habsburg Monarchy (1918–1919). After his resignation over the Allied assignment of Transylvania to Romania, Hungary went through a brief period of Communist dictatorship under Béla Kun. Károlyi emigrated from Hungary after the collapse of Kun's Council Republic. In 1943, in London, he formed Movement for Democratic Hungary as an alternative to the Horthy dictatorship. After his return to Hungary after the war, he was appointed ambassador to France (1947–1949). In growing opposition to the Communists, he resigned his position and remained in emigration in France.

platform developed for the national front upon which all anti-Hitler groups and elements in Hungary could *now* unite for a joint struggle.

[. . .]

· 10 AUGUST 1942 ·
[. . .]

—On the eighth sent Walter [Tito] (Yugoslavia) and Birk [Edvard Kardelj] (Slovenia) the following encoded communication:

Do not call your proletarian brigades proletarian; instead call them shock brigades, we repeat, shock brigades. Understand that this has enormous political significance, both for consolidating people's forces against the occupiers and collaborators within the country and for foreign countries. You are waging a people's liberation war using forces composed of workers, peasants, the people's intelligentsia, and other patriots—you are not waging a proletarian struggle. You must always proceed on this basis. Quit playing right into the hands of the enemies of the people, who will always make vicious use of any such lapses on your part.[370]

[. . .]

· 11 AUGUST 1942
[. . .]

—Received reply to encoded communication on proletarian brigades from Birk (Slovenia):

"Received your telegram. We concur entirely with your instructions, and we will immediately take steps to correct the error."

—*Pollitt,* speaking on behalf of the CP of England, has come out strongly against the repression of the leaders of the Indian National Congress.

---

370. Tito responded on 12 August by sidestepping Dimitrov's directive: "We agree with you that only the term 'shock' brigade ought to be used, and not 'proletarian.' The term 'proletarian' will be retained only by the First and Second Brigades, the majority of which are made up of workers. We stress that the term 'proletarian' was demanded by the fighters and superiors themselves, although there were peasants and adherents of other parties among them." In fact, before the end of the war, an additional ten brigades were called proletarian. Kardelj's response to Dimitrov was more docile.

—The day before yesterday I received from Fitin an encoded communication to me from *Pollitt,* contents as follows:

The general political situation in England is extremely unsatisfactory. There are growing indications that the government does not intend to open a second front but will merely intensify air raids on the Continent.

In government circles and outside them there is growing discontent with Churchill and his methods of leadership. Cripps is extremely unhappy with his position and talks of resigning on grounds of disagreements over methods of leadership and the conduct of the war, although at the same time he has no plans of his own for a positive, aggressive policy against Hitler. Certain circles supported by the Conservative Party are exploring grounds for appointing Eden[371] to the post of prime minister, should such a political crisis arise as would lead to changes in leadership.

In connection with the Soviet Union's serious position, the masses are extremely disturbed by the absence of a second front. Annual conferences of the major unions: miners, railway workers, engineers, electricians, and so on—all have come out in favor of a second front. Never before in England has there been such a broad campaign as the one now under way in favor of a second front, in the full awareness of the sacrifices that that would entail. The lack of a second front is intensifying the people's fears that the Soviet Union will be abandoned to its fate.

One cannot ignore the support for the so-called independent candidates by voters in parliamentary elections.

While directing our main fire against profascist elements and rightist Labour leaders, who are the main opponents of a second front, we are stepping up our positive criticism of the government and simultaneously stepping up our mobilization of the masses to compel the government to open a second front. We feel ourselves to be walking a knife's edge, and failing to lead the masses in the way they expect of us, *seeing* the Soviet Union carrying on the fight by itself. I believe we are approaching a most acute political crisis, in which we will be unable to lead the masses unless a second front is opened.

I would be grateful for your assessment of the situation.

[. . .]

371. Sir Anthony Eden (1897–1977), British statesman; Conservative MP (from 1923 on) of internationalist orientation; foreign minister (1935–1938, 1940–1945, 1951–1957), secretary of war (1940), and prime minister (1955–1957). He was instrumental in concluding the wartime Anglo-Soviet alliance.

· 12 AUGUST 1942 ·
[. . .]

—Our American correspondent *Janet Ross*[372] came to see me to report on the conversations she had had with Engl[ish] and Amer[ican] correspondents. The Amer[ican] cor[respondent] Parker told her that relations between the Sov[iet] Union and England are quite strained over the second-front issue. The English do not want to open a second front this year. Churchill is supposed to be negotiating precisely this question here with Stalin. The reception for correspondents at the Amer[ican] ambassador's held by [Gen. Omar N.] *Bradley* was organized in order to conceal the presence of Churchill in M[oscow].[373] Another correspondent reported that Churchill is arriving in M[oscow] *in the next few days.* All the Engl[ish] and Amer[ican] correspondents favor the opening of a second front and consider the Sov[iet] Union's position exceptionally grave.

[. . .]

· 14 AUGUST 1942 ·
[. . .]

—*Marty* reported on his meeting with *Garaux* (de Gaulle's representative). In his opinion the meeting went favorably. Garaux talked almost the whole time. Considered an uprising by the French people before the opening of the second front a hopeless cause. De Gaulle was not counting on the officers and soldiers of the Vichy army. The majority of the officers have sold out and should be shot. The upper bourgeoisie favors collaboration with the Germans. Only the popular masses are against the occupiers. De Gaulle is sending arms to his people inside France. De Gaulle is having great difficulty with the English and the Americans. Garaux favors joint actions with Communists. De Gaulle is convinced of the necessity of these joint actions.

Recommended to *Marty* that he send Thor[ez] (Ufa) information about his discussion and draft a brief report on its main points for Duclos (France).

[. . .]

372. Correspondent for the Comintern's news agency.
373. Churchill arrived for his first visit to Moscow precisely on 12 August.

· 17 August 1942 ·

—Received the *Minsk secretary* of the Komsomol (Malchavsky) who was in Belorussia on a *clandestine* basis for five months. Recounted many interesting particulars about the situation in Belorussia and about the part[isan] movement. The Germans have almost wholly exterminated the Jewish populace. In Minsk alone sixteen thousand Jews have been killed, in Borisov eight thousand. A typical fact is that Jews everywhere put up no resistance whatever. Went like lambs to the slaughter. Many of them believed it was "divine punishment" . . . Only a few Jews have joined the partisans. Even Komsomol Jews declined to flee from areas where punitive detachments were heading when our people advised them to do so. They did not wish to leave their families behind. The partisan movement is growing quickly now. There are virtually entire regions controlled by the partisans. There are almost no German garrisons in Belorussia, except for the ones in the cities. The Germans carry out their measures with the help of local *kulaks* and other anti-Soviet elements. The *kolkhoz* land is divided up. The peasants are afraid that their land will be confiscated; they sowed, and the harvest is not bad. The peasants' instincts for private property are very much in evidence. The Germans are playing on those instincts. The partisans are also preparing for winter. The populace everywhere is waiting for the Red Army to arrive.

Sov[iet] money is in the main the going currency in Belorussia. The peasants prefer having Sov[iet] money (one mark to ten rubles).

[. . .]

· 19 August 1942 ·

[. . .]

—[Caridad] *Mercader*[374] (Blagoeva int[erpreted]). At Sudoplatov's request, entered her in the party register. To date she has worked in NKVD network. Member of the CP of Spain.

From an aristocratic Spanish family. Former husband a Catalonian factory owner. Participated as a young woman and after her marriage in anarchist organizations. After being persecuted in Spain, she emi-

---

374. Caridad del Río Mercader (b. 1915), Spanish Communist; associate of the French editorial board at the Soviet foreign radio board; mother of Ramón Mercader, Trotsky's assassin; both worked in Sudoplatov's network and participated in the plot to liquidate Trotsky.

grated to France in 1930 with the children. Graduated Paris Sorbonne. Worked in Federation of Young Women. Was active polit[ically]. In 1935 was assigned to Spain. Active there in the people's war. Sudoplatov characterizes her as exceptionally faithful and devoted. Works on the foreign radio French editorial board. Gave instructions to regularize her party status in the CP of Spain and consider her one of our reserves.

[. . .]

· 20 AUGUST 1942 ·

—Marty reported on his *second* meeting with *Garaux*. Provided interesting information on relations between *de Gaulle and the Engl[ish] and Americans.* The raid on *Saint-Nazaire* was undertaken without de Gaulle's knowledge—on Madagascar, too. The negotiations in Martinique: without de Gaulle, and so on. The English are against making a base for de Gaulle in Algiers. In Garaux's opinion, the English are doing everything they can so that after Germany is defeated, they will have a French regime fully and completely dependent on them, rather than a national French government capable of conducting an independent policy . . .

[. . .]

· 27 AUGUST 1942 ·

—*Semaun* (Indonesia),[375] *Plyshevsky,*[376] *Morozov:* In connection with *Semaun*'s departure for Indonesia, I held a discussion with him on Indonesian affairs. Explained to him the errors in his theses on the tasks of Indonesian Communists, consisting in the position of temporary collaboration with Japan. Indonesian patriots (Communists and others) should carry on a determined struggle against Japanese demagogy and underhanded Japanese methods of *subjoining* Indonesia. In-

375. Semaun (1899–1971), Indonesian Communist; a railway worker from Semarang, Java, he belonged to Sereket Islam (the Islamic Association), a nationalist political party in the Dutch East Indies. After a split (1920), the organization's left-wing formed the Indonesian CP (PKI) with Semaun as its president. He traveled to the USSR (1921–1922); arrested by the Dutch in 1923, he went back to the USSR in 1924 and apparently remained there until 1956, when he returned to independent Indonesia.

376. Ivan Petrovich Plyshevsky (b. 1907), Soviet Communist; on the staff of the ECCI (1940–1943); Dimitrov's assistant at the Department of International Information (OMI) after the dissolution of the Comintern.

donesia should conduct its own *Indonesian policy* aimed at gaining nat[ional] freedom and independence. The Japanese are not the friends but the enemies of the Indonesian people. They would like to enslave Indonesia at the hands of Indonesian nationalists.

[. . .]

—*Walter* [Tito] (Yugoslavia) sent the following encoded communication:

The supreme staff of the people's army of Yugoslavia appeals to the General Staff of the RKKA [Red Army] to assist us with military equipment and especially arms. We have enormous opportunities for expanding the partisan and volunteer army. We are unable to admit thousands of patriots to the ranks of our liberation army, despite their request, owing to the lack of arms.

If a second front should be opened in the Balkans, we would be in a position to destroy all communications and also to raise an army here of at least five hundred thousand fighters. Active aid by the allies and arms assistance would make for a very difficult predicament for the fascist occupiers. Our partisan detachments would operate in the direction of Austria, Italy, Macedonia,[377] etc. The people's sympathies are 95 percent in favor of the Soviet Union and the Allies. Of course, the presence of Red Army units in the Balkans would be more desirable for our peoples than the presence of Allied units. We consider that a second front in the Balkans would have a great deal of latent force for the destruction of fascist troops. The people here do not believe in the striking power of English troops in the West.

[. . .]

· 28 AUGUST 1942 ·
[. . .]

—Sent *Stal[in]* and *Molotov* the following letter:

Our agency today received the following telegram from London:
"The Yugoslav government in London has published the following statement:

The Yugoslav government in London expresses its complete confidence in the leadership and loyalty of General Mihailović and his courageous soldiers. As a token of its confidence, the Yugoslav government in early June appointed Mihailović commander in chief of all armed forces engaged with

---

377. The reference to Macedonia was omitted from Tito's selected works. See Josip Broz Tito, *Sabrana djela,* vol. 11 (Belgrade, 1982), p. 245.

the enemy on Yugoslav territory. The government maintains continual contact with Mihailović. General Mihailović, who enjoys great popularity with the Serbian populace and throughout Yugoslavia, commands a well-organized army, the only one of its kind, numbering (depending on the character of partisan warfare) from 8 to 150 thousand Chetniks fighting under the command of regular Yugoslav army officers. With the help of his mighty army, Mihailović is inflicting heavy losses on the enemy. For more than a year now, Mihailović's army has by its operations been pinning down about thirty-six enemy divisions: seventeen Italian divisions, seven Bulgarian, four German, four Hungarian, and four of [Ante] Pavelić's[378] regular troop divisions, as well as fifteen Ustaša battalions. Mihailović's troops have rendered a valuable service not only to Yugoslavia but also to Russia.

It must be noted that this statement by the Yugoslav government is utter falsehood and effrontery, since it has actually been determined that Draža Mihailović is in command of no army whatsoever in Yugoslavia and is carrying out no military actions whatsoever against the occupiers. On the contrary, his Chetniks often attack Partisan divisions—striking at those divisions from behind—that are waging a fierce struggle against the occupiers. The partisan war in Yugoslavia, which has lately become especially intense, is fully and entirely under the direction of the supreme staff and the regional staffs of the people's Partisan army, which have nothing to do with Draža Mihailović.

Even Nedić's newspaper in Belgrade *Novo vreme* [New Time] and Pavelić's newspaper in Zagreb *Nova Hrvatska* [New Croatia], which continually publish detailed information about clashes with the Partisans, do not mention a single instance of armed struggle by Mihailović's Chetniks, but instead speak only of clashes with units of the Partisan army.

[. . .]

· 3 SEPTEMBER 1942 ·

—*Dolores [Ibárruri], Marty, Antón, Hernández* (Blagoeva inter-[preted]). Discussed Spanish business. Recommended to them that they release a Spanish CC manifesto in connection with the immediate danger of Spain's involvement in the war on the side of fascist Germany. Explain that involvement in the war will mean further destruction and millions of Span[ish] casualties, turning Spain itself into a the-

378. Refers to Ante Pavelić (1889–1959), Poglavnik (chief) of the collaborationist Independent State of Croatia (NDH) and of the Ustaša (Insurgent) movement, a Croat fascist organization.

ater of hostilities with the gravest consequences. It is a matter of the survival of the Spanish people and of the existence of Spain as an independent state. Since the beginning of the Second World War the position of Spain has changed radically: formerly, the struggle was over issues of Spain's domestic regime (the republic versus a military-fascist dictatorship); now *the fundamental issue is how to save Spain from catastrophe and the Spanish people from destruction.* Formerly the division in the Spanish people ran between those who were *for a democrat[ic] republic* and those who were *against it;* now it is between those who are *for* and *against* involving Spain in the war on the side of Hitler; *for* and *against* saving the Spanish people from the horrors of war. The need now is for nat[ional] unity of all Spanish patriots, irrespective of polit[ical] convictions (from Communists to Catholics and conservatives) in the struggle against the Falangists, who are pushing the country over the brink. A genuine nat[ional] government of unity of the Spanish people is needed on the [following] basis: against alliance with fascist countries, against involving Spain in the war, for the release of Republican polit[ical] prisoners and the return of Republican émigrés from abroad, for freedom of the press, for providing food for the people, for convening a *constituante* [constituent assembly] to draw up a new constitution guaranteeing the Spanish people freedom and independence.

[. . .]

· 4 SEPTEMBER 1942 ·
[. . .]

—Dolores [Ibárruri] in connection with change in Spanish government. She and other comrades consider these changes a defeat for Hitler. Cautioned them not to get carried away. This does not yet mean a defeat of the Falange's Hitler[ite] course. For now, it indicates only that a crisis exists in the Falange itself and that opposition to Franco is growing. Therefore, there is no need to alter the original line we have set down for the Spanish CP CC manifesto. Dolores [Ibárruri] concurred with that.

[. . .]

· 7 SEPTEMBER 1942 ·

—*Sobolev* [. . .][foreign affairs] to see me. Reported on Eden's proposal to the Soviet government to work jointly to settle relations between the Yugoslav Partisans and Draža Mihailović. Informed him of the materials we have on Mihailović's role. Asked my advice on possible grounds for an agreement. Recommended the following conditions:

1. Mihailović is to fight against the occupiers;
2. Cease the vicious attacks on the Partisans;
3. Temporarily separate the zones of military operation of Mihailović's people from those of the Partisan army;
4. Establish contact and mutual representation between Mihailović's headquarters and Partisan army headquarters;
5. The Yugosl[av] government is to revoke the demotion of officers fighting in the ranks of the Partisan army.

—Received the German writers *Weinert* and *Bredel*.[379] They reported on their work in foreign radio and the PUR [Red Army Political Directorate] directed at the demoralization of German fascist troops. Complained of difficulties in their work in the PUR. The Russian comrades in the PUR fail to account for the German mentality and often insist on propaganda that cannot produce positive effects.

—The German writer *Becher*[380] has attempted suicide (slashed his veins). Not in mortal danger. Measures taken for his recovery.

[. . .]

· 16 SEPTEMBER 1942 ·
[. . .]

—Sent *Fitin* letter with request to ascertain through his network the activities of the Hungarian group in London and the position of Károlyi and proposed to Kreibich[381] that he contact the Hung[arian] comrade Kálmán Moskv . . . [?]

[. . .]

379. Erich Weinert (1890–1953), German Communist poet; veteran of the International Brigades in Spain; consultant for the Comintern's Foreign Language Publishing House; and Willi Bredel (1901–1964), German Communist writer; Spanish veteran at work in the Foreign Language Publishing House.

380. Johannes R. Becher (1891–1958), German Communist writer; author of the play *Schlacht um Moskau* (Battle for Moscow, 1942) in which he touted the idea of "two Germanies"—a "Germany of megalomaniacal rulers" and a "Germany of the people."

381. Karel Kreibich (1883–1966), Czechoslovak Communist of Sudeten Ger-

· 21 SEPTEMBER 1942 ·
[. . .]

—The Iraqi comrade *Zoger*[382] (his local name), concerning his return to Iraq. Ascertained possibility of his working (clandestinely) in Iraq. Consented to his return. Directed him to write a pamphlet for Iraq and other Arab countries on the Sov[iet] Union and the Patriotic War against fascist Germany from the point of view of the struggle of Arab peoples for nat[ional] independence, and also his view of the Iraqi Communists' *pol[itical] line* and practical work.

[. . .]

—Sent *Larsen*[383] (Denmark) directive on organization of spec[ial] party inform[ation] service, which is to inform us and send military-polit[ical] information on the situation in Denmark and actions by the Germans.

Concerning liaison with the English, gave him the foll[owing] instructions:

We recommend particular caution as regards the English. You ought to maintain communications with them via second parties. Do not use any of the active leadership comrades for such communications. Do not give away any of your internal affairs and intentions. You may receive material [financial] assistance from them, but undertake no obligations as regards them. Under no circumstances should your newspaper, its orientation and

man origin; founder of the Sudeten German section of the KSČ (1921); member of the KSČ EC and vice president (1921–1924); member of the KSČ Politburo (1927–1929); member of the ECCI (from 1921 on); editor of the KSČ German-language organ *Vorwärts* (1933). He was elected to the Czechoslovak senate (1935); he subsequently emigrated to Britain, after the Munich pact, and participated in the council of state, part of the London-based Czechoslovak government-in-exile. He was Czechoslovakia ambassador to the USSR (1950–1952).

382. Pseudonym of Hassan Ahmad al-Shaq Qasim, Iraqi Communist; ECCI Middle East specialist responsible for Arabic broadcasts in the USSR.

383. Axel Larsen (1897–1972), Danish Communist leader; member of the EC of the KIM (1921); member of the ECCI (1924–1928); chairman of the Danish CP (DKP), 1932–1958; member of the Danish parliament (1933). Active in the Danish Resistance during the Nazi occupation, he was captured and confined to the Sachsenhausen concentration camp (1942–1945). Having served as minister without portfolio (1945), he was expelled from the DKP in 1958 for "Titoist deviation." He founded the People's Socialist Party (1959), which gained eleven parliamentary seats during the election of 1960, and twenty in 1966.

contents, depend upon the English. In all respects be independent, with a free hand. Beware of English spies infiltrating any sections of the party or recruiting party personnel. Remember that they are capable of bringing dangerous disintegration into your ranks.

· 22 SEPTEMBER 1942 ·

—*Marty* met with French air force captain *Mileros* (recently arrived from London). Expects arrival of French pilots and mechanics, who are to study methods of combating German aviation. Marty relayed the contents of his discussion with Mileros. Quite interesting military-political information. Advised Marty to maintain contact with him and to use his invitation to General Péti[384] to obtain further information, following, however, the rule of "buy the maximum, sell the minimum!" ...

[...]

· 9 OCTOBER 1942 ·

—*Vlasov*[385] about Yugoslav radio broadcasting. Recommended: 1) greater popularizing of heroes and distinguished figures in the Part[isan] army on the basis of the present fighting; 2) greater exposure of Chetnik atrocities committed against the Partisans and their families; 3) smashing the legend being promulgated abroad that Mihailović is leading the struggle of the Yugosl[av] people, by pointing out that he and his people are not undertaking any milit[ary] actions against the occupiers; on the contrary, Mih[ailović's] Chetniks are striking at the rear of the fighting Partisans; 4) smashing the malicious slander that the Partisans want to establish Soviet power and collective farming in Yugoslavia and explaining that the struggle currently under way is not

384. Representative of de Gaulle's Free French in Moscow.

385. Pseudonym of Veljko Vlahović (1914–1975), Yugoslav Communist leader; militant student at the University of Belgrade; commissar of the Georgi Dimitrov Battalion of the 15th International Brigade in Spain. After he was wounded at the Jarama front, his leg was amputated. He went to Moscow afterward (1939–1945). Member of the Young Communist League of Yugoslavia (SKOJ) CC (1939) and representative of the SKOJ to the KIM; representative of the KPJ to the ECCI and secretary of the KIM (1942); organizer of the New Yugoslavia radio station in the USSR; member of the KPJ/SKJ CC (from 1948 on) and of the SKJ presidency (from 1968 on); chief SKJ theoretician on party development and relations with the foreign Communist parties.

for that, but for driving the occupiers out of the country and winning the liberty and independence of the Yugosl[av] peoples.

[. . .]

· 1 NOVEMBER 1942 ·

—Last night received encoded communication from *Nowotko* in which he reports that in retaliation for the hanging of fifty Poles in connection with explosions at Warsaw railroad junctions, on Saturday evening our combat organization threw bundles of hand grenades simultaneously into German restaurants mostly frequented by German officers and various German scum, into cafés at the main station, and into the printing house for the Polish newspaper the Germans put out, *Nowy kurier warszawski* [New Warsaw Courier]. The number of killed and wounded was high, more than a hundred people. . . . On our side there were neither casualties nor arrests. This has made a deep impression on the populace, all the more so since this is the first combat action in Warsaw of a mass nature aimed directly at the personal security of the occupiers . . .

———————

—Submitted the foll[owing] encoded communication last night for transmission to *Nowotko:*

1. Your news is extremely valuable. Continue along these lines, meanwhile bearing in mind the instructions sent by us in this regard.

2. We are very happy to learn of intensification of your combat activities. We regard the line of your work and struggle as correct.

3. Your remarks concerning radio are correct, and the Polish comrades will take them into consideration, but bear in mind that a portion of the content of radio programming must be directed at Polish radio listeners outside Poland as well.

4. We are well aware of your difficulties and requirements. Unfortunately, for reasons beyond our control, to date we have not managed to send you what you need. We are doing everything necessary to expedite this matter. In hopes that we would be able to do so tomorrow or the day after—and this turned out not to be the case—in our recent transmissions we did not provide you with any reports.

5. We just now received your report on your first major combat action. Well done! Bravo to all of you!

6. Our greatest apprehension concerns the security of your center and of Nowotko himself. I do not doubt that you are taking serious precautions. But I ask again that you reexamine the measures you have taken to date and

consider additional measures that would secure the center from disaster and provide for uninterrupted leadership of party and military organization.

The essential requirement for further successes is the securing of your firm leadership under any conditions and despite any blows from enemies of the party.

Fraternal regards to you all. I grasp your hand firmly.

[. . .]

· 6 NOVEMBER 1942 ·
[. . .]

A ceremonial assembly tonight at the Kremlin. Report by *St[alin]*.

Second front: strongly emphasized (directed at the English).

Two coalitions: the *Italo-German* and the *Anglo-Soviet-American*. The victory of the latter is assured.

[. . .]

· 9 NOVEMBER 1942 ·
[. . .]

—Received the following telegram of greetings from *Poland:*

> Very grateful for recent telegrams. [Your] confidence in the correctness of the line of struggle we have adopted and your approval of it will help us in future to bolster our work and struggle still further. We well remember your words, dear Comrade Dimitrov, spoken to us before our departure, that this war must be the final one. We assure you that we will hold the arms taken up by the Polish masses and not release our grip on them until we have toppled the accursed capitalist order whose misshapen spawn is fascism and Hitlerism.
>
> On the twenty-fifth anniversary of the Oct[ober] Revolution we send you, beloved leader of the Comintern, and all comrades our heartfelt, Communist regards.
>
> Long live victory! Long live the Red Army! Long live the Comintern! Long live Stalin!

[. . .]

· 10 NOVEMBER 1942 ·

—*Fitin* to see me about transporting their personnel from London via Holland to Berlin. Agreed on the cooperation that our Dutch comrades are to extend. Sent instructions in this regard to Holland.

—Sent Duclos (Paris) the following encoded communication: "Report immediately on the position you have adopted in connection with events in North Africa and Hitler's occupation of the unoccupied zone, the slogans you are advancing, and the actions you are undertaking. Keep us regularly informed of current events in France."[386]

[. . .]

· 11 NOVEMBER 1942 ·

—*Meeting of the secretariat.* Discussion of events in North Africa and in France itself.

I formulated our positions as follows:

The events in North Africa and in France itself constitute a new and severe blow to the Italo-German coalition. The American action eases and hastens the opening of a second front on the Continent. Hitler's occupation of the unoccupied zone in France signifies the bankruptcy of the "collaboration" between Hitlerite Germany and Pétainist France. This act formally gives the French a free hand in their struggle against the occupiers. Pétain's protest is indicative of the mood in France. A new situation is developing in the West, one that is favorable to the Allies and extremely difficult for the Italo-German coalition. The immediate threat to Italy is evident. Hitler has reached a definitive impasse. We are on the eve of a decisive turning point in the war. We ought to act quickly and skillfully to take advantage of the evolving situation. As regards France—everything available into the fight, together with the Americans, against the Germano-Italian occupiers, for the liberation of France. As regards Italy—rupture with Hitlerite Germany, saving the Italian people from catastrophe by means of a separate peace. As regards Spain—decisively against involving it in the war on the side of Hitler's sinking ship. As regards the Hitlerite vassals—intensify in every way possible the struggle for withdrawal from Hitler's war. As regards the occupied countries—take full advantage of the weakening in the Italo-German coalition in order to drive out the occupiers, relying mainly on the development of the partisan movement. As regards Germany—transition from defense to an advance on the Hitlerite gang, taking advantage of the ruin of Hitler's plans under the onslaught of the Red Army in the East and the second front in the West, whose coming is an entirely real prospect.

On the basis of these positions we must concretize our slogans and measures for various countries.

The slogan advanced by Radio France calling for a general strike and occupation of businesses at the current stage is to be considered premature.

---

386. On 8 November 1942 an Anglo-American invasion force, commanded by Gen. Eisenhower, disembarked in French Morocco and Algeria. The Vichy forces were quickly overcome. By 11 November the Germans occupied Vichy France.

Sent directive in this spirit to *Ercoli* [Togliatti] for the Ufa bureau of the secretariat.

[. . .]

· 18 NOVEMBER 1942 ·

[. . .]

—*Rákosi:* informed him of *Károlyi's* reply from London that he agrees with the platform of the *Hungarian front of nat[ional] independence.*

[. . .]

· 19 NOVEMBER 1942 ·

[. . .]

—Sent *Marek* [Stanke Dimitrov] (Tiflis) the foll[owing] instructions:

1. According to a report from Sofia, the people's voice can be heard everywhere in the provinces. In Sofia itself it cannot be heard.

2. Since the *voice* broadcasts within Bulgaria, it ought not to give information that can be known in the USSR but is unknown (over for[eign] radio stations) in the country itself.

3. The *voice* ought to possess an *especially* patriotic nature.

4. The *voice* ought to go no further than the principal aims pursued by Radio Hristo Botev. It ought not to advance slogans more radical than those advanced by Hristo Botev.

5. In its form and argumentation the *voice* ought not to repeat Hristo Botev literally. It must act in such a way that radio listeners consider the voice independent of Radio Hristo Botev.

6. Try to avoid excesses and exaggerations.

7. It is desirable to speak more calmly.

[. . .]

· 26 NOVEMBER 1942 ·

—Received *Rákosi* regarding his reply to Károlyi about the platform of the Hungarian independence front. Gave him advice and in particular [advised him] to put this entire matter so that it appears that the initiators of the platform are inside Hungary, and that Károlyi, Rákosi, and others from abroad are subscribing to their initiative—that is, to remove any émigré associations from the formation of the Hungarian independence front.

[. . .]

· 4 DECEMBER 1942 ·

—*Meeting of the commission on German Com[munist] Party issues.*
Heard additional reports, discussed draft manifesto of the anti-Hitler conference. German comrades were directed to rework that draft *radically,* by clarifying issues of the Nationale Friedensfront [National Peace Front] and the Nationale Friedensregierung [National Peace Government]—identifying the polit[ically] organized forces we are counting on to bring about their formation—and in particular to formulate the fighting platform of the national front. Include a representative of the *opposition Nat[ional] Socialists,* as well, among the conference participants.

[...]

· 5 DECEMBER 1942 ·
[...]

—Received a report from Poland (Mołojec) that on 28 November *Nowotko* was killed on the street by the police! A terrible loss! Requested details, determination of responsibility for the breakdown, what measures have been taken to ensure the security of the leadership, and so on.

[...]

—Delayed publication of *Rákosi's* article about Transylvania in *Bolshevik* on the grounds that it is *pro-Hungarian!*

[...]

· 16 DECEMBER 1942 ·

—Our envoy to China *Paniushkin*[387] to see me. Reported on the proposal he made to [the relevant] authority regarding operations in China and for settling relations between Chiang Kai-shek and the CP of China. On the latter subject, I recommended formulating a six-point platform for negotiations and an accord between Chiang Kai-shek and the Com[munist] Party:
1. Recognition of Chiang Kai-shek's supreme command by the 18th

387. Aleksandr Semyonovich Paniushkin (1905–1974), Soviet envoy to China (1941–1944); deputy chief at the OMI (1944–1947); director of the OMI after Dimitrov's return to Bulgaria (1945).

Army Group (numbering two hundred thousand men) and its inclusion in the Chinese army while it retains its own direct command.

—Remaining CPC armed forces to be considered partisan troops under the military command of Chiang Kai-shek's main headquarters.
2. Supplying the 18th Army Group with all forms of arms and provisions.
3. Including representatives of the 18th Army Group in all military headquarters and military regions and appointing one a deputy chief.
4. Lifting the blockade of the Special Region, cessation of the persecution of Communists and the release of [General] Ye Ting and arrested personnel of the Fourth Army, the army Political Directorate, and representatives of the CPC.
5. Drafting and publishing jointly with the government of Chiang Kai-shek an agreement on the postwar democratic development of China.
6. Legalization of the Commun[ist] Party throughout China and the creation of normal conditions for production and distribution of the centr[al] organ of the Communist Party *Xinhua Ribao* [New China daily, Chongqing].

Agreed that following approval of this platform by [the relevant] authority, he (working along diplomatic lines) and I (working along ECCI lines) will cooperate to bring about such a settlement of relations between Chiang Kai-shek and the Com[munist] Party.

[. . .]

· 17 DECEMBER 1942 ·
[. . .]

—Prof. Burmin, Vinogradov, and Mayorov: examined me and determined that things are proceeding well. Blood and urine tests for sugar are satisfactory.
—*Paniushkin* telephoned, saying he had learned in his discussion with *Viacheslav Mikhailovich* [Molotov] that the CC will not now deal with relations between Chiang Kai-shek and the Com[munist] Party, and therefore the plan proposed in that regard should be temporarily *postponed*.

[. . .]

· 23 DECEMBER 1942 ·

—Our ambassador to London (with the émigré governments) *Bogomolov* was in to see me. Recounted a lot of interesting things. A rather dismaying spectacle, these émigré governments with their kings and entourages in London. Extreme reactionary inclinations and hostility toward us among the Poles. Utter disorder among the Yugoslavs. De Gaulle's entourage is repulsive and full of spies. The Czechs behave better, although you cannot trust in Beneš's sincerity either.

[. . .]

· 25 DECEMBER 1942 ·
[. . .]

—*Rákosi* to see me. Informed him that in London Károlyi let on that he had received a message from Rákosi through our embassy, and as a result our neighbors are refusing to associate with Károlyi regarding this matter.[388]

[. . .]

· 26 DECEMBER 1942 ·

—Ivanov (our ambassador to the Mong[olian] Republic) and Valfong (from the NKVD) to see me. Discussed with them establishing a permanent "road" between the Mong[olian] Republic and *Yan'an* (China). Direct liaison between the ECCI and the CC of the Com[munist] Party of China. Outlined practical measures.

[. . .]

· 30 DECEMBER 1942 ·

—Meeting of the commission on *the Czech question.*

Quite a few complex and disputed areas that will have to be clarified and resolved: 1) How to *reconcile* the contradictions between Czechs and Slovaks, between Czechs and Sudeten Germans, between Slovaks and Hungarians, and so on, in such a way as to obtain a platform for a united national front against the German occupiers that all sides will find acceptable? 2) For what sort of Czechoslovakia is a struggle under way—for the former one, with its domination by Czechs, or a different one? 3) the issue of Czechoslovakia's borders; 4) relations with Beneš and his government in London, and so on.

---

388. The "neighbors" referred to are the NKVD.

—*Gottwald's* draft is unsatisfactory. Assigned him to rework the draft on the basis of our discussion and submit it at the commission meeting on 2 January 1943.

[. . .]

· 31 DECEMBER 1942 ·

—Received Austrian prisoner of war *Angermann*.[389] Valuable activist of the CP of Austria. Was in the Schutzbund, participated in the February uprising of 1934 in Vienna. In 1936–1937 in the Leninist School. Beginning April 1942 on the eastern front. Went over to the Red Army in October. Makes a very favorable impression. Willing to work clandestinely in Austria, where he has an opportunity through acquaintances to set himself up independently and subsequently obtain a connection with the party.

—*Sudoplatov* (NKVD) to see me. Wants me to give him Angermann for transport to Austria with assignments in his network. Set him three conditions on which I granted his request: 1) sending [him] in the very near future by reliable channels; 2) [he is] to carry out our assignments as well; 3) after a few months he is to be transferred entirely to operations in our network.

[. . .]

· 6 JANUARY 1943 ·
[. . .]

—Fedichkin (Sudoplatov's dep[uty] chief of NKVD Department) brought material on the *Croatian pilots* who flew over to our side in May of 1942.

—Agreed to bring one of them in to meet me, a man named Supek,[390] claiming to have been a member of the CP of Yugoslavia.

[. . .]

389. Josef Angermann (1922–1945), Austrian Communist; worker in the ECCI. He was killed in Austria in 1945 as an underground KPÖ official.

390. Berislav Supek, pilot in the royal Yugoslav air force, then in the Croatian air force, and after the war in the new Yugoslav air force. In 1952 he repeated his feat of 1942 by defecting with his plane to Romania. He was thereafter involved in the various pro-Soviet (Cominformist) émigré groups.

· 7 JANUARY 1943 ·
[. . .]

—Since *Nowotko* was killed in Warsaw, the Polish leadership comrades have been suspicious of Mołojec, who was together with Nowotko. His strange behavior has strengthened those suspicions. Received a report today that on 29 December our people liquidated (!) Mołojec and formed a provisional leadership group: Gudar [probably Paweł Finder], Fornalska, Kowalski ... Situation extremely serious and dangerous.[391]

[. . .]

· 9 JANUARY 1943 ·
[. . .]

—Polish business examined in connection with the liquidation of Mołojec. (Encoded communication on this matter signed by *Finder* (member of troika), *Fornalska* (member of CC), *Gomułka* (member of Warsaw committee),[392] and *Jóźwiak* (People's Army chief of staff).[393] Ascertained that all of them are unquestionably honest and devoted comrades, and that party affairs can be provisionally entrusted to them.

---

391. Mołojec, Gudar, Małgorzata Fornalska (1902–1943), and Aleksander Kowalski (1908–1951), all Polish operatives with Nowotko.

392. Władysław Gomułka (pseudonym: Wiesław, 1905–1982), Polish Communist leader; PPK member and trade union activist (from 1926 on); at the Leninist School in Moscow (1933–1936); prisoner in Poland (1936–1939); first secretary of the PPR CC (1943–1948) instrumental in the creation of the Communist People's Guard (Gwardia Ludowa) and the People's Army (Armia Ludowa); deputy premier of the provisional government and the government of national unity (1945–1947); minister of recovered territories (until 1949); member of the PZRP CC (1948–1949) accused of "right deviationism" in 1948, expelled from the PZRP CC in 1949, and imprisoned (1951–1954); after his rehabilitation in 1956, first secretary of the PZRP CC (1956–1970). He followed a modified reform course after 1956 ("the Polish road") but in 1968 went along with Mieczysław Moczar's anti-Semitic campaign and in 1970 repressed the workers' strikes in the Baltic ports. He resigned his post as leader in 1970 and was expelled from the PZRP CC in 1971.

393. Franciszek Jóźwiak (pseudonyms: Witold, Franek, 1895–1966), Polish Communist; chief of staff of the Gwardia Ludowa and the People's Army; member of the PPR Politburo (1945–1948), the PZRP CC (1948–1959), and the Politburo (1948–1956), and head of the CCC. As minister of state control (NIK) he slandered Gomułka after the latter's arrest. A member of the dogmatist "Natolin" group, Jóźwiak was removed from all government posts in 1956.

—Sent the following encoded communication to Warsaw:

We direct the provisional group of four [*chetvyorka*] immediately to take all measures necessary to continue the party work begun under Nowotko's leadership and to ensure fully reliable and continuous contact with us. It is essential to preserve at all costs the fighting unity of the party *aktiv,* for the measure that was applied to Mołojec entails the risk of mutual destruction of a portion of the party cadres. Although we do not doubt the purity of your intentions, you ought to have used other means to eliminate Mołojec from the leadership and render him harmless. We await the findings of the commission investigating Nowotko's death. Keep us regularly apprised of measures you take to secure the party from strikes by the enemy and from infiltration of its ranks by enemy elements and provocateurs. Report whether Finder is aware of the directives and guidelines for the work of the troika that we regularly sent Nowotko. Confirm receipt of the present communication.

[…]

· 11 JANUARY 1943 ·

—Conference on Radio Free Yugoslavia and utilization of materials obtained regarding the *People's Council* [AVNOJ],[394] the *antifascist congress of the youth* of Yugoslavia, and so on.[395]

(Fried[rich][Geminder], Dravić,[396] Wolf,[397] Ponomarev.) Recom-

394. On 26–27 November 1943, in Bihać (western Bosnia), Tito presided over the first session of the Antifascist Council of People's Liberation of Yugoslavia (AVNOJ), the Partisan organ of political representation to which the KPJ tried to attract all willing political forces. Speaking to the fifty-four assembled delegates from Croatia, Bosnia-Herzegovina, Montenegro, and Serbia, Tito attacked "our domestic traitors—Ustašas, Chetniks, and others," and explained that although "we do not have the opportunity to create a legal government, because international relations and the circumstances do not yet permit it," the Partisans had the right to create a political body that would "gather all the popular masses."

395. On 27 December 1943, in Bihać, Tito presided over the first congress of the Antifascist Youth of Yugoslavia. In his speech to the 365 delegates, Tito used harsh language against the "traitorous exile government in London." He ended his speech by saying that he was "convinced that your hand will not tremble should your gun aim even at the closest relative who has crossed over to the ranks of the traitors."

396. Pseudonym of Djuro Salaj (Gjuro Sallay: 1889–1958), Yugoslav Communist; member of the KPJ CC (1926–1930); political émigré to the USSR (1930–1944); editor at the New Yugoslavia radio station; member of the KPJ CC (from 1948 on) and the SKJ CC EC (from 1952 on); president of the Yugoslav trade unions (1945–1958).

397. Pseudonym of Mihály Farkas (1904–1965), Hungarian Communist

mended not playing up the special declaration against the Yugosl[av] government and against Mihailović, and also [reminded them] that the Com[munist] Party alone has kept its faith with the people.

[. . .]

—*Vyshinsky,* NKID [People's Commissariat for Foreign Affairs], called. Consulted with me about using the resolution and signature[s] of the Partisans' conference in the Sov[iet] government démarche regarding Mihailović (Yugoslavia).

· 12 JANUARY 1943 ·
[. . .]

—*Marty* reported on his discussion with the French general *Péti.* The latter told him of a serious conflict that has arisen between himself and de Gaulle's diplomat[ic] representative *Garaux.* Garaux wanted to subordinate Péti's military mission to himself. Péti is sending his own man to de Gaulle to report on this matter.

—Advised Marty not to interfere either directly or indirectly in the Gaullists' internal bickering.

—Wrote *Shcherbakov* about relieving the Polish activist *Kolski*[398] of his duties in the army (political instructor) so that we can send him to Poland to take the place of Nowotko, who was killed.

· 13 JANUARY 1943 ·

—Saw *Shcherbakov* (CC). Conference on *radio propaganda over foreign radio.* In attendance: Shcherb[akov], Aleksandrov, Khavinson, Polikarpov, Kruzhkov, Manuilsky, and I.[399] Discussed reports by:

---

leader active in Hungarian and Czechoslovak Communist parties; alternate member of the ECCI presidium (1935–1943); secretary-general of the KIM (1939–1943); member of the Hungarian CP Politburo and deputy secretary-general (1948–1953); Hungarian undersecretary of the interior and chief of the political police (1945–1948); minister of defense (1948–1953); chief architect of the rigged trial against László Rajk. Farkas was expelled from the party in 1956 and condemned to sixteen years of imprisonment, of which he served part, for "violations of socialist legality."

398. Bernard Zucker-Kolski (1902–1944), Polish Communist; candidate-member of the PPK (after 1932). He worked in the Comintern apparatus. The ECCI sent him to Poland, where he was killed by the Nazis.

399. Aleksandrov was from the VKP(b) agitprop, Khavinson from TASS, Polikarpov from the foreign radio broadcasting, and Kruzhkov was the director of the Marx-Engels-Lenin Institute at the VKP(b) CC.

Khavinson (TASS) and Polikarpov (foreign radio). Determined that on the basis of the changed situation it is essential to make our radio propaganda still more aggressive; to keep the Germans and their satellites reeling from blows; to emphasize, especially in the vassal and occupied countries, the Germans' weakened condition, their inability to exert the same pressure on them that they formerly did, the increased opportunities for resisting them, and so on; and to intensify our propaganda to neutral countries. Concrete proposals will be formulated and distributed to members of the conference for their opinions and comments.

[. . .]

· 15 JANUARY 1943 ·

—Bolshakov ([Red Army] Intelligence Directorate): a report from Yan'an that Wang Ming is seriously ill. He needs treatment in Chengdu or in the USSR, but Mao Zedong and Kon Sin [Kang Sheng] supposedly do not want to let him leave Yan'an, for fear that he will give out unfavorable information about them.

—Advised against the [Red Army] Intelligence Directorate representative's interfering in these internal affairs of the Chinese Communists.

[. . .]

· 20 JANUARY 1943 ·
[. . .]

—*Pieck* and the German writer *Johannes Becher* to see me about Becher's pamphlet. I explained to Becher that it is politically inexpedient to represent the German people in its *entirety* as corrupt, with bad and dangerous qualities.

You have to differentiate and show the positive qualities to be found in the depths of the German people, on the strength of which the German people could rise up and rid themselves of the Hitlerite clique, washing away their shame and the bad and dangerous qualities.

There is a need for serious national self-criticism, but not for indiscriminate self-flagellation. Becher was grateful for my remarks and advice.

[. . .]

· 21 JANUARY 1943 ·

—At the Kremlin.

Ceremonial-commemorative meeting on the occasion of the nineteenth anniversary *of Lenin's death*. Report by Shcherbakov.

Refreshments following the meeting with Stal[in], Molot[ov], Kalinin, Beria, Malenkov, Andreev, Shcherbakov, Shvernik, Man[uilsky].

—Conversations on various topics.

—In answer to my proposal to Stal[in] that certain of our issues also be considered in the next few days, Stalin said: "No time for them. Whenever I get a little free time, I either collapse into bed for some sleep or else take up something frivolous, not serious issues."

———————

—Regarding the mood of the German working class, Stalin said: "Evidently, the majority of German workers have nothing against being the *dominant nation*. A minority of them are against it, but they have been suppressed. German soldiers are still not surrendering en masse. The Red Army will have to teach them some even harsher lessons before the process of demoralization begins."

Stal[in] made a lot of jokes . . .

He made Mindin[400] tell new anecdotes, and so on.

[. . .]

· 24 January 1943 ·

—Held final conference on political line and immediate tasks of the CP of Iraq (Marty, Salman—the Iraqi secretary, Plyshevsky, Wolf [Farkas], Belov [Damianov], Friedrich [Geminder], Morozov).

—Approved secretariat resolution and draft platform of popular-democr[atic] party, whose formation the Communist Party is to try to bring about (as orientation points for the CC of the CP of Iraq).

[. . .]

From early February to mid-August 1943 the Axis retreat continued. The period ended with the Allied invasion of Sicily and the overthrow of Mussolini. Nevertheless, Dimitrov faced serious problems, some of a personal nature. On 3 April 1943, his young son Mitia died after a struggle with diphtheria. Dimitrov recorded his pain and continued heartbreak ("Mustered all my moral strength and worked as I always do, although *sick at heart!*"). His low spirits most certainly were not lifted by

—————

400. Refers to an ECCI staffer.

the decision to dissolve the Comintern, of which Molotov informed him on 8 May 1943. For the remainder of spring and early summer the Comintern was transformed into the Department of International Information (OMI) of the Soviet party's Central Committee. Similarly, its other operations and functions were taken over by various Soviet agencies, not least of all the security apparatus. Dimitrov was installed in his new office at the VKP(b) CC on 9 July 1943, where he officially had the function of deputy head of the department (sharing the two deputy positions with Manuilsky), whereas Soviet Politburo alternate member and chief of the Soviet Information Bureau A. S. Shcherbakov figured as department head.

During this period—in addition to the overriding organizational matters and personal reversals—Dimitrov was busy with the Chinese CP, with Yugoslav and Bulgarian problems, and especially with the attempts to create national committees of prisoners of war and political émigrés for the Axis countries, above all Germany. These committees were meant to substitute for the public work of the CI, but they ran into problems as a result of Western objections. Spanish CP matters also took up Dimitrov's time, as did the affairs of fringe Communist parties in Iran and Iraq. The period ends with another of Dimitrov's numerous illnesses, in July–August 1943.—I.B.

· 1 FEBRUARY 1943 ·
[...]

—Received Wang Ming's telegram (from China) on disagreements that exist within the leadership of the Communist Party of China. He claims that Mao Zedong is carrying out a policy at odds with the Comintern line—for strengthening the united nat[ional] front against the Japanese. Asks us to intervene in order to prevent a split in the party. Telegram addressed to Stalin and me.

[...]

· 3 FEBRUARY 1943 ·
[...]

—Received disturbing telegram from *Walter* [Tito] (Yugosl[avia]) requesting assistance in connection with the enemy's general offensive against the liberat[ed] territory.[401]

401. In his message, sent from Drvar (western Bosnia) on 31 January, Tito introduced a note of reproach: "I must ask you again, is it not in any way possible for

—Received telegram from *Mao Zedong* containing accusation against Wang Ming.

[. . .]

· 4 FEBRUARY 1943 ·

—Marty reported on his discussions with *General Péti.* Warned him *once again* to be extremely cautious, because all such persons as Péti are *intelligence agents.*

[. . .]

· 8 FEBRUARY 1943 ·
[. . .]

—*Thorez and Marty* on French matters. Discussed draft agreement between the Com[munist] Party of France and de Gaulle. Recommended not concluding a formal agreement, but rather confining ourselves for now to mutual declarations of a joint struggle by Communists and Gaullists against the occupiers and on maximal intensification of that struggle in France itself.

Replied to this effect to the inquiry from Dekanozov (NKID).

[. . .]

· 10 FEBRUARY 1943 ·
[. . .]

—*Marty* reported that General Péti informed him of London's consent to Marty's trip there. Directed him to determine *precisely* how that trip is going to look, and then we shall decide whether he is to go.

———————

—Sent *Walter* [Tito] the foll[owing] encoded communication in reply to his encoded communication on mater[ial] assistance:

You must not doubt for an instant that if there had been the slightest opportunity to render material assistance to your splendid, heroic struggle, we

———————

you to render us any help at all? Death by starvation threatens hundreds of thousands of refugees. Can it be that after twenty months of our heroic, almost superhuman, struggle no way can be found to help us? [. . .] The hungry people give our fighters the last crumb of bread, although they are themselves dying of hunger."

would have done so long ago. The Soviet people along with its leaders stand fully and entirely on your side, filled with admiration and profound fraternal sympathy for the Yugoslav national-liberation army. Joseph Vissarionovich [Stalin] and I have on numerous occasions personally discussed avenues and means of rendering you our assistance. Unfortunately, to date it has proved positively impossible to solve this problem, owing to intractable technical and transport difficulties. Even now we have not ceased our efforts to discover practical possibilities for sending assistance. As soon as such possibilities are found, we shall do everything necessary. How could you doubt it? I ask you to understand the current situation correctly and explain it to your comrades and fighters. Not to lose heart, but to strain every nerve to endure even this current, extremely arduous trial. You are performing a great task, which our Soviet land and all freedom-loving peoples will never forget. Fraternal regards to you and all comrades and best wishes in your heroic struggle against the accursed enemy.

[. . .]

· 11 FEBRUARY 1943 ·
[. . .]

—Dekanozov called about treating Wang Ming in the USSR. Advised him to apply to Soviet ambassador to China Paniushkin with instructions to work up an exit authorization from Chiang Kai-shek for Wang Ming to travel to the USSR.

[. . .]

· 19 FEBRUARY 1943 ·

—*Lehtinen*[402] *and Friedrich* [Geminder]: on Finnish national radio broadcasting. Crisis in Finland is deepening. Fatigue from the war is universal. Trends favoring a separate peace are growing rapidly. Recommended putting the question to the Finnish comrades directly: 1) Finland ought to propose a truce to the Sov[iet] Union despite the resistance of the Germans; 2) enter into separate peace negotiations; 3) since the Finnish government will not do so voluntarily, a popular

---

402. Inkeri Lehtinen (b. 1906), Finnish Communist; student at the Comintern's Leninist School. Despite the fact that her husband was arrested during the Stalinist purges, she was a member of the SKP CC and minister of education in Kuusinen's Terijoki government; representative of the SKP to the ECCI; participant in the SKP leadership after the war (SKP CC Politburo) and editor of the party theoretical review *Kommunisti*.

mass movement to meet these two demands of the Finnish people must be developed by all possible means.

[. . .]

· 21 FEBRUARY 1943 ·
[. . .]

Molotov called. Expressed his displeasure at our giving certain assignments to NKID personnel abroad, in particular *Kiselev*[403] in America. Explained to him that we are not giving assignments but expressing certain requests regarding assistance in our work, without detriment to their [staff members'] NKID functions.

· 22 FEBRUARY 1943 ·

—The ECCI letter to Stalin was *published* in the press, along with his reply.

—The fact that it was published is significant: a public confirmation of the existence and activity of the Comintern under conditions of the Patriotic War against the Germ[an]-fascist invaders.

—*Kuusinen, Lehtinen, Taimi*[404] regarding Finnish Com[munist] Party and Finnish national radio broadcasting. Recommended to them the following line for the campaign in Finland:

1. Breaking off the alliance with Hitler[ite] Germany that is killing Finland
2. Immediate cessation of hostilities
3. Withdrawal of Fin[nish] troops to the 1940 borders
4. Entrance into separate peace negotiations

[. . .]

· 25 FEBRUARY 1943 ·

Marty reported on his discussion with French pilots hosted by *General Péti.*

—Garaux (de Gaulle's rep[resentative]) informed him that the passport for his trip to London (with wife) was ready and he would also see

403. Yevgeni Dmitrievich Kiselev (1908–1963), Soviet diplomat; consul general of the USSR in New York (1943–1945); chief of the Balkan desk at the NKID (1948–1949).
404. A. Taimi, Finnish Communist.

to it that he gets an Engl[ish] visa. Advised Marty to take the passport and visa, and we will decide about the trip itself after determining all technical details of the trip from the point of view of *necessary security measures.*

[. . .]

· 27 FEBRUARY 1943 ·
[. . .]

—*Kuusinen, Taimi, and Holkunen.* Discussed text of directive for radio broadcasting to Finland and the Finnish Com[munist] Party's political campaign regarding separate peace. Directed Kuusinen to reedit text to reflect a variety of substantial comments I had made.

[. . .]

· 2 MARCH 1943 ·

—*Kuusinen, Taimi, Lehtinen*
1. Discussed and passed final version of *document on the struggle for a separate peace in Finland* (for campaign over Radio Free Finland and the Communist Party in the country);
2. *Designated the following to be sent to Finland:* Kondol, Kosunen, Jouhteinen and Gostren Inga.[405] Their mission:
   a) create a *radio point* for communications with us;
   b) aid in reestablishing party leadership;
   c) forward directives on line and tactics of the party.
3. The Finnish comrade Foss (Mud) to be recalled from party school at Kushnarenkovo as consultant in Cadre Department.
4. Approved Lehtinen [as] prov[isional] representative of Finnish Com[munist] Party.
—Sent *Ercoli* [Togliatti] and others in Ufa the following encoded communication:

> We have learned from reliable sources that special school students are often getting drunk on vodka and that there have been a considerable number of instances among them of sexual promiscuity. Since the mission of the special school is to provide us with workers for clandestine operations who are sound in both moral and political respects, personnel with a healthy Communist way of life as well as good technical training, I urgently request that the situation in the school be investigated and that decisive measures be taken to put an end to all forms of social demoralization. The consumption

405. Finnish Communists.

of vodka must be entirely forbidden not only in the special school, but also in the party school and in the apparatus.

Report on the measures you have taken and their results.

—Sent *Finder* (Poland) the foll[owing] encoded communication:

In your telegram to Stalin you speak of "establishing worker and peasant power" in Poland. At the present juncture this is politically incorrect. Avoid such formulations in your polit[ical] campaign. The fundamental slogans for your struggle ought to be:

1. Expulsion of the occupiers from Poland
2. Winning nat[ional] freedom
3. Establishing people's democratic power (not worker and peasant power!)

Please bear this in mind.

· 3 MARCH 1943 ·

—Sent *Stalin and Molotov* documents on campaign for separate peace in Finland.

[. . .]

—*Molotov* called regarding our spec[ial] radio stations, particularly Radio Kościuszko (in connection with polemics with Sikorski!).

Agreed to establish personal contact with Narkomindel [People's Commissariat for Foreign Affairs] on issues of radio programming for *allied and semi-allied* countries.

[In the] *last hour:* our troops have taken *Rzhev.*

[. . .]

· 4 MARCH 1943 ·
[. . .]

—*Marty:* received passport (French) for himself and his wife, along with letter from Garaux for the Engl[ish] ambassador concerning the issuing of an Engl[ish] visa. Gave him instructions on necessary preparations for trip to London.

[. . .]

· 5 MARCH 1943 ·

—*Umansky, Palgunov* (NKID) to see me. Reported (on the instructions of Molotov) on our clandestine nat[ional] radio stations. Determined how contact ought to be established between ourselves and the NKID on issues of our radio broadcasting to Poland, Czechoslovakia, Yugoslavia, and so on, that is, the countries of our allies and semi-allies.

—*Kruzhkov* (from Informburo): regarding the very same matter.

[. . .]

· 8 MARCH 1943 ·

—Meeting of *Informburo* held by *Shcherbakov. Umansky* and *Palgunov* from the NKID took part. Discussed contact [coordination] in area of our spec[ial] radio programs with Informburo and the NKID.

Agreed on the following: 1) Establish contact with Informburo (Khavinson) concerning all programs (with the exception of Yugosl[av] and Polish programs), and with the NKID (Umansky) for Polish and Yugoslav programs.

[. . .]

· 11 MARCH 1943 ·

[. . .]

—Sent *Walter* [Tito], as well as *Birk* [Kardelj] (Slovenia) and *Vokshin* [Kopinič] (Croatia) the following encoded communication:

> —The fact that Mihailović is still able to recruit Chetniks by the thousands and to throw them against your army units and Partisan detachments undoubtedly indicates the necessity of an overall intensification of your political work among the masses in the occupied territories and particularly among the Chetniks themselves. After all, Mihailović is recruiting quite a few Chetniks from the peasantry and petty bourgeoisie. The precise demagogic devices and slogans Mihailović is using to recruit people ought to be discovered, and those devices and slogans ought to be mercilessly exposed. It is very important, along with military strikes against Chetnik bands, to demoralize them politically at the same time, to split their ranks and snatch up any errant Chetniks for your own side. Is there nothing you could do to make better use of domestic radio broadcasting and other propaganda media for these purposes? Please also inform us of your suggestions and requests for intensifying and improving this political work over Radio Free Yugoslavia as well.

· 12 MARCH 1943 ·
[. . .]

—*Morozov, Karaivanov:*[406] on Karaivanov's trip to Basra (Iraq) as leader of *center for communications* with Iraq, Syria, Palestine, and Turkey.

Gave him concrete guidelines for his work in Basra.

[. . .]

· 19 MARCH 1943 ·

—Stal[in] reported regarding the *Finnish document:*
"A stance favoring a separate peace with Finland is at the present time unacceptable."

[. . .]

—Sent *Linderot* (Stockholm) the following encoded communication (through Fitin):

I find your conduct incomprehensible. Despite numerous requests, you have still not reestablished direct and regular communications with us. What is the matter? How could you fail to understand that these communications have exceptionally critical significance at the current juncture? How could you fail to realize that the additional duty of assisting us by providing communications with Norway, Finland, and Denmark as well now falls on your party? For a number of years we have rendered you assistance, provided considerable loans. How could you not consider it necessary now, under conditions of a decisive struggle against the fascist enemy, to strain every nerve, all your own material resources, to provide at the very least the necessary communications and thus contribute to the successful prosecution of the struggle in your neighboring countries? Where else should your internationalism find practical expression, if not first and foremost in this area? I urgently request that you immediately take all measures necessary to

406. Pseudonym of Ivan Genchev (1889–1960), Bulgarian Communist; member of the BKP insurrectionary committee during the September uprising (1923). He went afterward to Yugoslavia and Austria, where he edited the BKP newspaper *Rabotnicheski vestnik* (Workers' Herald) and worked for the ECCI (from 1926 on), frequently on foreign missions (China, 1929–1934), France (1938–1939), and the Middle East (1942–1943). He returned to Bulgaria in 1944; after a conflict with some of the BRP(k) leaders, he settled in Yugoslavia, where he became naturalized and served as a member of the national Federal Assembly and member of the SKJ CC (1952–1960).

liquidate this abnormal state of affairs. Confirm receipt of the present communication.

[. . .]

· 20 MARCH 1943 ·

[. . .]

—*Molotov* called and reported that using the *Finnish document* on the separate peace campaign over Finnish nat[ional] radio would be political[ly] inexpedient at the present time.

[. . .]

· 22 MARCH 1943 ·

[. . .]

—*Umansky* called late about Yugoslav radio programs. V. M. [Molotov] was for some reason very agitated and ordered him to check the contents of these programs. Gave instructions to *Fürnberg* to provide Umansky with the materials he needs tomorrow.

[. . .]

· 24 MARCH 1943 ·

—*Marty, Thorez, and Stepanov* [Minev].
—Marty obtained an informational report from Grenier[407] (London) through Miler [?] (Gaullist). Advised not answering in detail and not giving any directives through the Gaullists.

[. . .]

· 29 MARCH 1943 ·

[. . .]

—Sent letter to *Stal[in] and Molot[ov]* (copy to Andreev) about foreign currency allocation for ECCI (up to $25,000 monthly).

[. . .]

---

407. Fernand Grenier (1901–1992), French Communist; member of the PCF CC; representative of the PCF on de Gaulle's London-based French national committee; minister in the French provisional government (1944).

· 30 March 1943 ·

—*Marty:* regarding his trip to London. The English are holding up the issuing of a visa. Advised him: 1) to be insistent with the Engl[ish] ambassador in Moscow (get an answer out of him, yes or no!); 2) to have Grenier in London make a representation to de Gaulle—for now not to raise the issue in the press.

[. . .]

· 1 April 1943 ·
[. . .]

—*Dravić [Salaj], Friedrich [Geminder], Fürnberg, Ponomarev:* on Yugoslav business, in particular Walter's [Tito's] telegram in which he reports prisoner exchanges with the Germans, and so on.[408] Sent Walter the following telegram:

We are disturbed by the fact that you are exchanging prisoners with the Germans, sending them delegates who are conducting various negotiations with the Germans, as well as by the fact that the German ambassador in Zagreb has expressed a wish to meet with you personally. What is the meaning of this? The people are waging a fierce war with the occupiers, and suddenly such relations as these arise between you and the Germans. Could this not be connected with the Germans' policy of using our people to incite an internecine struggle among the Yugoslavs themselves and thus hasten the destruction of the People's Liberation Army? Please furnish an explanation in this regard. Furthermore, the fact that displeasure with the English is growing among the entire people is understandable. But do you not think that at the present juncture the interests of the national liberation struggle are best served not by encouraging displeasure with the English, but by stirring up the utmost hatred for the occupiers, first and foremost the Ger-

408. On 30 March 1943, writing from Drače, eastern Bosnia, Tito informed Dimitrov that "three of our delegates" were in Croatia's capital Zagreb from 20 to 25 March to negotiate the exchange of prisoners with the Germans. In a detailed report he transmitted various German views, including the expectation of an agreement between Berlin and London. He noted that the German ambassador to Croatia had expressed a wish to meet Tito. In fact, the Yugoslav Partisan team in Zagreb, consisting of Milovan Djilas (member of the KPJ PB) and Dr. Vladimir Velebit (Tito's chief diplomatic troubleshooter), was of exceptionally high rank. (Earlier, Gen. Koča Popović, commander of the 1st Proletarian Division, joined Djilas and Velebit in negotiations with the Germans at Gornji Vakuf, in central Bosnia.) Moreover, the Partisans were trying to achieve a truce with the Germans and even offered, "We would fight the British if they landed." Milovan Djilas, *Wartime* (New York, 1977), p. 243.

mans? Meanwhile any links with German authorities could undoubtedly abate that popular hatred, which is now so indispensable. I await your reply.

[...]

· 3 APRIL 1943 ·

—*At 1:25 this afternoon Mitia passed away!*

Spent the whole night at the hospital. Today, too—until he died. Professor Buznikov, Professor Khachaturov, and Dr. Mayorov were there, too.

Mitia suffered terribly. The damned disease was completing its treacherous work. He kept calling for me and saying, "*Papochka,* I want to go home. I can't stand it here any more. Get us a car. Let's go to Government House," etc.

By 12:00 the injections ceased having any effect. By 12:30 he had lost consciousness, *and at 1:25, in front of our very eyes,* he succumbed. What a tragedy! What a horror, particularly for Rozi. She has spent the last fourteen days at his bedside. Superhuman efforts were made to save him—but to no avail, his heart gave out! Death conquered life . . .

———————————

—This evening (after sanit[ary] treatment at the Sanitary Point) we came home. Rozi is terribly shaken up. *Zinaida Ordzhonikidze*[409] is with her. Our closest friends have gathered here. Dm[itry] Zakhar[ovich Manuilsky] and his wife came, Dolores [Ibárruri], [Ana] Pauker, and others . . .

—I took steps to ensure that *important* current business at the Comintern is not neglected.

· 4 APRIL 1943 ·

—Sunday (Black Sunday for Rozi and me!).

At 3:00 we went to the hospital. Vladimirov [Chervenkov] and Lena, Arthur, Dora, Ella and Ilza, Kolarov, and his wife went with us.

Collected *Mitia's coffin* and at 4:00 we were at the crematorium. We found a large group of ECCI personnel waiting there.

The very worst moment came, the lowering of the body into the

409. Zinaida Gavrilovna Ordhzonikidze, the widow of G. K. (Sergo) Ordzhonikidze.

oven . . . "Thank God," Rozi took all this like a hero. There was a risk that her legs would give out—fortunately, that, too, went well.

Three fourths of the rest of our personal lives burned up along with *Mitia's coffin!* An immeasurable void has appeared in Rozi's and my personal lives. . . . Only someone who has personally experienced such profound grief can fully understand it!

We went back home with Manuilsky and his wife, Dolores [Ibárruri], the Blagoevs, Kolarov and his wife, Vladim[irov] [Chervenkov] and Lena, Belov [Damianov], our doctors. Professor Khachaturov and Dr. Mayorov, as well as Zinaida Ordzhonikidze, who has been staying close to Rozi all the time . . .

The presence of that company was a very great help to Rozi in sustaining this awful blow without any disasters . . .

· 5 APRIL 1943 ·

—This morning Rozi, Zinaida Ordzhonikidze, and I visited the crematorium. We saw his urn. All that's left of our wonderful Mitia with all his promise is a small box of bone and ashes! . . . Such a remarkable little boy, a future Bolshevik, reduced to nothing . . . What a horrible loss! . . . Poor Rozi! She is facing her terrible grief staunchly, but how will she manage to go on living and working without Mitia? . . .

The *urn* was immured. Flowers were laid out. We sensed a great, happy page in our personal lives turning over forever before our eyes . . .

I went to work in the awareness that even in the midst of the most trying conditions and trials we Bolsheviks are not supposed to lose heart and allow our cause to suffer because of personal misfortune.
—Mustered all my moral strength and worked as I always do, although *sick at heart!*
—This evening Manuilsky and other comrades stayed with us here until late.

[. . .]

· 8 APRIL 1943 ·

—*Vlasov [Vlahović], Friedrich [Geminder]:* on the line of our Yugoslav radio broadcasting in connection with King Peter's[410] interview

---

410. Peter II Karadjordjević (1923–1970), king of Yugoslavia.

in London. Gave instructions: 1) provide a summary of the king's interview for Walter [Tito] (headquarters of the peo[ple's] liber[ation] army); 2) draft a special article for Radio Free Yugoslavia on unity in the struggle against the occupiers (exposing the Chetniks), for now not mentioning King Peter's interview; 3) draft a reply to the king's interview on behalf of fighting Yugoslavia.

[. . .]

· 12 APRIL 1943 ·
[. . .]

—Colonel *Starinov*[411] returned to Moscow (he is at Khrushchev's disposal for Ukrainian work). Described the situation in the south in detail, particularly Krasnodar and Rostov. Typical facts: on the *Don* and *Kuban* the Germans successfully ingratiated themselves with the locals. They have permitted no gross excesses. The populace thought that the Soviet Union was now done for, and people started reconciling themselves with the Germans. All kinds of girls married Germans . . . The prevailing attitude—the Germans have not done anything wrong! During the German withdrawal, a lot of Don and Kuban locals withdrew along with them. The Germans played chiefly on the *kolkhozy.* The dissolution of the kolkhozy was celebrated like a major holiday . . . The Jewish populace, however, was destroyed en masse by the Germans under the guise of *resettlement.* Twelve thousand Jews were destroyed in Krasnodar . . . *Starinov* recounted terrible facts.

[. . .]

· 8 MAY 1943 ·
[. . .]

—Went to see Molotov tonight, together with Manuil[sky]. We discussed the future of the Comintern. Reached the conclusion that the Comintern as a direct[ing] center for Com[munist] parties in the current conditions is an impediment to the Com[munist] parties' independent development and the accomplishment of their particular tasks. Work up a document dissolving that center.

411. Ilia Grigorievich Starinov (b. 1900), Soviet officer; veteran of the International Brigades in Spain (1936–1937); chief of the central partisan school (1942–1943); deputy chief of the Ukrainian and Polish staffs of the partisan movement (1943–1944); chief of staff of the Soviet military mission in Yugoslavia (1944).

· 9 MAY 1943 ·

—Sunday. Came down with influenza. Could not visit Mitia's grave. Rozi went by herself.

· 10 MAY 1943 ·

—Consultation with Professors Burmin, Khachaturov, Grinar, and Dr. Mayorov. Determined an influenzal infection and reaction owing to extreme nervous tension connected with Mitia's death.

—Stayed home. This evening Manuilsky came to see me. Discussed contents of document dissolving the CI.

[. . .]

· 11 MAY 1943 ·

—Man[uilsky] and I edited *draft resolution of the ECCI on the dissolution of the Commun[ist] International.*

Sent the draft to *Stalin and Molotov.*

—This evening Man[uilsky] and I met with Stalin (Molotov was present). *Stal[in]* approved our draft. We discussed implementing the resolution. Settled on the following procedure: 1) consider the draft in a meeting of the presidium and adopt it as a proposal for sections; 2) distribute it to the sections and request their consent; 3) upon receiving consent of the sections, publish it. As for which functions are to continue henceforward and in what form—*Malenkov and I* have been commissioned to discuss and draft a concrete proposal.

In this regard, *Stal[in]* said: Experience has shown that one cannot have an internat[ional] directing center for all countries. This became evident in *Marx's* lifetime, in *Lenin's,* and today. There should perhaps be a transition to regional associations, for example, of South America, of the United States and Canada, of certain Europ[ean] countries, and so on, but even this must not be rushed . . .

· 12 MAY 1943 ·

—I acquainted the following persons by turns with the draft resolution of the ECCI presidium:

    —Marty, Thorez, and Dolores [Ibárruri]

    —Pieck, Ulbricht, Koplenig

—Rákosi and Šverma
—Pauker, Lehtinen, Vlasov [Vlahović]
—Kolarov, Wolf [Farkas]
All consider the proposal to CI sections to dissolve the Comintern as the directing center of the international working-class movement to be correctly formulated, both politically and on principle.
—Scheduled a meeting of the presidium tomorrow for discussion of the draft resolution and a final decision on this matter.

—Prepared the draft resolution to be sent to the following persons:
   —draft resolution to Pollitt (via Fitin)
   —Also through our network:
1) to Mao Zedong; 2) to Walter [Tito]; 3) to Finder; 4) to Duclos; 5) to Browder (for Latin America); 6) to Linderot (Sweden).

Rozi and I visited Mitia's grave!

· 13 MAY 1943 ·

—Restricted meeting of the ECCI presidium. Participants: Thorez, Marty, Dolores [Ibárruri], Pieck, Ulbricht, Koplenig, Rákosi, Šverma, Wolf [Farkas] (KIM), Kolarov, Pauker, Lehtinen, Vlasov [Vlahović], Manuilsky, Dim[itrov]; as interpreters: Stepanov [Minev] and Fürnberg.

Following my report, which explained and substantiated the proposed draft resolution, all participants in the meeting of the presidium expressed their views by turns. The proposed draft was *unanimously* adopted as a *basis*. A period until 17 May was given to all the members of the presidium and to party representatives attending the meeting of the presidium, for comprehensive discussion of the contents of the draft and for introducing possible amendments, alterations, or additions to it.

Before the meeting of the presidium I received the following message from *Stalin:*

> 1. Do not rush this matter. Submit the draft for discussion, give the ECCI presidium members the opportunity to consider it for two or three days and introduce amendments. He, too, will have certain amendments to make.
> 2. For now do not send the draft to foreign countries. We will decide on that afterward.

3. Do not leave the impression that we are simply driving out the comrades of the foreign leaderships. The people will work for newspapers. Four newspapers should be created (in German, Romanian, Italian, and Hungarian); separate antifascist committees of Germans and others may also be formed.

[. . .]

—[Jenő] Varga reported that *Stalin* had read his report at the academy and found it *good, Marxist*. Any criticisms of that report in the CC secretariat are no longer valid.

[. . .]

· 17 May 1943 ·

—*Second restricted meeting of the ECCI presidium.*
—Consideration of the draft resolution, point by point. Some unessential amendments were made. Their editing was assigned to an edit[orial] commission consisting of Thorez, Pieck, Dolores [Ibárruri], Manuilsky, Dimitrov. There was also discussion of two alternatives for implementing the resolution: 1) publish it with the signatures of presidium members in the USSR as a proposal to the sections for their approval (in which case notify them in advance that the proposal in question will be published); 2) forward the draft resolution to the sections for discussion, and upon receiving their consent, publish it as a document of all constituent parties of the CI.

The first alternative was adopted as *the more expedient.*

[. . .]

· 18 May 1943 ·

Meeting of edit[orial] commission
(Pieck, Thorez, Dolores [Ibárruri], Manuilsky, Dimitrov).

The amendments to the resolution adopted at the presidium were edited. Everything was approved unanimously.

—Man[uilsky] and I edited the minutes of yesterday's meeting of the presidium with brief summaries of the remarks of individual comrades.

Sent *Stal[in] and Molot[ov]:*
1. Minutes of the meeting of the presidium of 17 May 1943
2. Minutes of editorial commission
3. Draft resolution with indication of the passages that have undergone alterations

—Received encoded communication from Ufa: "[We are] in agreement with the decision of the presidium.—Ercoli [Togliatti], Gottwald."

· 19 May 1943 ·

—*Restricted meeting of the ECCI presidium.*

Discussion of organizational issues in connection with the dissolution of the Comintern:

1. National radio programs
2. Foreign bureaus of ind[ividual] parties
3. Maintaining liaison with foreign countries
4. SUPress Telegr[aph] Agency
5. Archives, library, party committee, and so on

All these functions are to be retained in one form or another. Regularizing them in the new conditions is to proceed along VKP(b) CC lines.

—Meeting *with Stalin tonight* (Molotov, Voroshilov, Beria, Malenkov, Mikoyan were present).

Stal[in] proposes certain clarifications to the draft resolution: 1) delete the final paragraph as unnecessary; 2) indicate that the issue of dissolution in wartime was raised by a number of CI sections; 3) the point on the First International: emphasize that Marx dissolved the First Int[ernational] "as a result of the acute need to create mass national workers' parties." Agreed: 1) to notify sections that the resolution in question will be published; 2) to publish the resolution in ten days' time; 3) to publish it with the signatures of presidium members (for the VKP(b), Zhdanov, and Manuilsky); 4) upon receiving decisions from the section CCs approving the resolution, publish a communiqué from the presidium signaling final dissolution.

[. . .]

· 20 May 1943 ·

—*Stalin* called: "Couldn't the presidium resolution be submitted to the press today? Publication should be hurried along."

Explained to him that I am sending an encoded radio message today in the afternoon, evening, and nighttime to the various parties. They will decipher it and discover the contents no earlier than tomorrow afternoon or evening. It would be awkward to publish before then. It will have to be submitted to the press no earlier than tomorrow evening for publication on 22 May. That is how we left it.

—Convened the editor[ial] commission. Reported on the new amendments to the resolution proposed by *Stal[in]*, *Molotov*, and others. Those amendments and the entire draft were unanimously adopted, *in the final version.*
—Sent the resolution for translation into German, French, English, and other languages.
—Assigned *Fürnberg, Friedrich [Geminder], and Glaubauf*[412] to see to the translation and to send it to foreign countries the night of 21 May.
—*Morozov:* reported on special school and First Department business.

—Rozi and I were at Mitia's grave!
This loss is becoming harder and harder for us to bear!

· 21 MAY 1943 ·

—*Politburo* meeting in Stal[in]'s office. Along with members and candidate members of the PB, Manuilsky and I also attended.

Molotov reads out the ECCI presidium's resolution dissolving the Comintern.

Kalin[in] remarks that our enemies will take advantage of this step. It would be better to make attempts to transfer the CI center to some other place—London, for instance! (Laughter.)

Stal[in] explains that experience has shown that in Marx's time, in Lenin's time, and now, it is impossible to direct the working-class movement of all countries from a single international center. Especially now, in wartime conditions, when Com[munist] parties in Germany, Italy, and other countries have the tasks of overthrowing their governments and carrying out defeatist tactics, while Com[munist]

---

412. Fritz Glaubauf (1901–1975), Austrian Communist of Sudeten German background; worked in the KIM apparatus (1923–1930); ECCI emissary in Latin America (1930–1935); on the staff of the ECCI (1935–1943); headed the SUPress news agency at the OMI (1943–1945); associate editor of the KPÖ organ *Volksstimme* (after 1945).

parties in the USSR, England, America and other [countries], on the contrary, have the task of supporting their governments to the fullest for the immediate destruction of the enemy. We overestimated our resources when we were forming the CI and believed that we would be able to direct the movement in all countries. That was our error. The further existence of the CI would discredit the idea of the International, which we do not desire.

There is one other reason for dissolving the CI, which is not mentioned in the resolution. That is the fact that the Com[munist] parties making up the CI are being falsely accused of supposedly being agents of a foreign state, and this is impeding their work in the broad masses. Dissolving the CI knocks this trump card out of the enemy's hands. The step now being taken will undoubtedly strengthen the Com[munist] parties as nat[ional] working-class parties and will at the same time reinforce the internationalism of the popular masses, [an internationalism] whose base is the Soviet Union.

The resolution is unanimously adopted.

An exchange of view follows on certain issues connected with the dissolution of the CI.

—Gathered the department leaders tonight and explained to them that the dissolution will be implemented *in an organized fashion,* and that for now it must be explained to their personnel that they should carry on their work and await further instructions.

· 22 May 1943 ·

—The ECCI presidium's resolution dissolving the Comintern was published in *Pravda.*

—Explanatory sessions in this regard were conducted in the ECCI departments, as per my instructions of yesterday.

[. . .]

· 24 May 1943 ·

—Held conference with the Germans (Pieck, Ulbricht, Ackermann), Hungarians (Rákosi, Gerő), Romanians (Pauker), Austrians (Fürnberg) on the formation of German, Hung[arian], Romanian, Italian, and other *antifascist committees* consisting of public figures and prominent antifascist prisoners of war.

—Also the creation, or rather, the conversion, of existing newspapers for prisoners of war into general antifascist newspapers (German, Ital[ian], Roman[ian], Hungarian, and Finnish).

These proposals were unanimously adopted.

I commissioned each nat[ional] group to work up these issues concretely and draft proposals.

[. . .]

· 31 MAY 1943 ·

—*Met with Malenkov* (CC) together with Sukharev,[413] Morozov, Fürnberg, Friedrich [Geminder]. Dealt with organiz[ational] problems connected with dissolution of the CI. We agreed: 1) to preserve nat[ional] radio broadcasting, in transferring ownership of the given national radio broadcasting [assets] to the foreign bureau of the appropr[iate] Com[munist] Party; 2) to preserve the SUPress Telegr[aph] Agency under CC control; 3) to preserve the liaison service (radio communications, passport technology, and so on), meanwhile leaving open the question of where and how it is to be conducted; 4) to make the library a branch of the IMEL [Institute of Marx-Engels-Lenin] library; 5) to transfer the archives to the CC; 6) Publishing House to continue operations as a separate publishing house attached to the VKP(b) CC; 7) to organize registration of cadres of the [foreign] Com[munist] parties with the VKP(b) CC; 8) to transfer economic objects to the CC business administration.

Meet with Malenkov tomorrow or the day after to work up the Politburo resolution on all these matters.

[. . .]

· 2 JUNE 1943 ·

Tonight Stalin called: "Must we wait for reports from all parties and then publish the communiqué?" I answered him that since certain parties have scheduled their conferences for 7 or 8 June, we ought to wait a few more days. That is how we left it.

[. . .]

413. Konstantin Petrovich Sukharev (b. 1899), Soviet Communist; NKVD operative; chief of the signals service and secretary of the budget commission at the ECCI (1939–1943); deputy chief of the VKP(b) business administration in charge of the former structures of the Comintern (after 1943).

· 4 JUNE 1943 ·
[. . .]

—Sent following encoded communication to France, Belgium, Holland, America, Yugoslavia, Poland, Sweden, China:

> Please report immediately:
>
> First. Were there dissenting opinions in the CC during consideration of the ECCI presidium's proposal to dissolve the Comintern, and if so, what were they specifically?
>
> Second. How was this proposal greeted by the party aktiv in the localities?
>
> Third. What effect did the proposal to dissolve have on party masses and sympathetic circles?
>
> Fourth. Have elements appeared in the party that are attempting to take advantage of dissolution for factional and disorganizational activities, and if so, which people, and who are they?
>
> Fifth. What measures have been taken to ensure that the proposal to dissolve is correctly understood in the party ranks and also to paralyze enemy propaganda portraying this matter as a maneuver, a sham dissolution, and so on?
>
> Sixth. What is the party doing to explain to the masses the Comintern's positive role over the course of its existence, particularly in the struggle against fascism and current fascist warmongers, and also to repulse the enemy's slander campaign?

[. . .]

· 5 JUNE 1943 ·
[. . .]

—Sent *Stalin* and *Molotov* additional reports of approval of the presidium's proposal that we have received. Informed them that we are convening a meeting of the presidium from 8 to 10 June and that we intend to publish the communiqué on the dissolution of the Comintern on 10–11 June, before the opening of the Labourite conference (13 June of the current year).

[. . .]

· 8 JUNE 1943 ·

—Held the final meeting of the ECCI presidium:

1. It was established that all sections (all extant sections capable of reporting their decisions) have *unanimously approved* the proposal to

dissolve the Comintern, and that not a single objection has come in from any section.

2. The abolition of the Executive Committee of the Commun[ist] Intern[ational], the presidium, and the secretariat of the Executive Committee, as well as the Internation[al] Control Commission, was announced.

3. A *commission* was appointed consisting of *Dimitrov* (chairman), Manuilsky, Pieck, Ercoli [Togliattii], and head of the Managerial-Operat[ional] Directorate Sukharev (secretary) to undertake the practical liquidation of current business, the organs of the apparatus, and CI property.

4. A *communiqué* to be published in the press to this effect.

[. . .]

· 11 JUNE 1943 ·

—*Fitin* to see me about using our radio communications and their technical base in the future for the needs of the People's Commissariat for State Security. We clarified a number of issues along these lines but have reached no definitive decision as yet.

—*Manuilsky and Pieck:* drafted a resolution on forming an antifascist German committee, Free Germany.

—Sent this draft to *Stalin and Malenkov.*

[. . .]

· 12 JUNE 1943 ·
[. . .]

—Received *Lieutenant-General Ilichev and Colonel Bolshakov* (from Red Army Intelligence Directorate). Settled questions of the further cooperation of our correspondents and communications centers abroad.

At *Stalin's* tonight (Molotov, Voroshilov, Beria, Malenkov, Mikoyan, and Shcherbakov were pres[ent]). Discussion of our draft on formation of a German antif[ascist] committee, Free Germany. Draft was on the whole approved. Stal[in] stressed that it was essential for the Germans to point out the danger of the dismemberment and destruction of Germany, a danger that can be avoided only by overthrowing Hitler. For no one is going to conclude a peace treaty with a Hitlerite Germany. The struggle to save Germany from ruin, for restoring the democratic rights and freedoms of the German people, for the establishment of a parliamentary order, and so on—these are to be the tasks of the antifasc[ist] committee of *German patriots*.

—It was decided to form a special *Department of International Information* [OMI] in the VKP(b) CC to be entrusted with directing the antifascist committees, clandestine nat[ional] radio broadcasting, liaisons with foreign countries, the SUPress Telegr[aph] Agency, and the Foreign Language Publishing House.

—In order not to let enemies exploit the fact that this department is headed by Dimitrov, it was decided to appoint *Shcherbakov* head of the department and Dimitrov and Manuilsky his deputies. This decision is not to be announced; rather, organize and conduct the department's work *internally*.

This morning Rozi and I visited Mitia's grave.

· 13 JUNE 1943 ·

—Sunday

—Splendid weather, but Rozi and I are feeling terribly depressed. Our unforgettable son is no more . . .

—Worked at home. Edited Bulg[arian] commentary for foreign radio.

· 14 JUNE 1943 ·

—Met with *Malenkov*. Worked out with Shcherbakov and Manuilsky in *concrete* terms how the *Department of International Information* is to function in such a way as to avoid the risk that the enemy will exploit it to claim that the Comintern is continuing to exist in a different form, as well as which functions that department is to assume.

After exchanging views, we agreed to meet again in three days to reach a final decision.

[. . .]

· 18 JUNE 1943 ·
[. . .]

—Received various birthday greetings (Thorez, Dolores [Ibárruri], Ercoli [Togliatti], from the Spaniards, Bulgarians, Germans, co-workers, etc.).

—People's Commissar for State Security *Merkulov* to see me. Clarified matters concerning transfer of a variety of our establishments to his People's Commissariat, and also [its] servicing the foreign bureaus of the different parties in transporting their cadres to their [respective] countries.

[. . .]

· 23 JUNE 1943 ·

—*Ercoli* [Togliatti]: regarding the Foreign Bureau of the Ital[ian] Com[munist] Party, the antifasc[ist] Ital[ian] committee, the antifascist Italian newspaper, and so on.
—*Rákosi:* regarding the antifasc[ist] Hungarian committee and the use of Hung[arian] cadres.

[. . .]

· 28 JUNE 1943 ·
[. . .]

—Sent Walter [Tito] (Yugoslavia) the following encoded telegram:

Your last telegram (concerning the successful repulse of the last German-Italian offensive) cheered all of us up immensely. Well done, Yugoslav heroes. You would do well to consider whether it might not be more expedient to preserve a limited liberated territory as a base for the People's Liberation Army, while throwing the greater part of the army's battle-ready forces into the maximum possible disruption of the Germans' and Italians' communications, until you have cut Yugoslavia off completely from the West and the Balkans. At this stage it seems that these tactics would yield more effective results in the fight against the occupiers, as well as a more rational use of your armed forces and to a certain extent a better means of preserving them for subsequent decisive battles in Yugoslavia. Please communicate your views on this matter.

[. . .]

· 30 JUNE 1943 ·

—Pieck reported on his trip and his discussions with *German generals and Paulus*[414] concerning their possible participation in the Free Ger-

414. Friedrich Paulus (1890–1957), German general; commander of the German troops in the Battle of Stalingrad. He surrendered in January 1943 and afterward joined the Free Germany national committee and appealed to his countrymen to surrender. In Soviet confinement until 1953, he spent his last years in the GDR.

many national committee now being formed. For now, none of them has given his consent. But a group of German officers is exhibiting an inclination to do so. . . .

[. . .]

· 1 JULY 1943 ·
[. . .]

—Met with *Malenkov,* along with Shcherbakov and Manuilsky. Agreed on the work of the department. Nat[ional] radio broadcasting, the foreign bureau[s], the telegraph agency, the Foreign Language Publishing House, and the radio center for radio communications have been preserved. Also distributed functions among ourselves. I get the basic functions; Manuil[sky] handles prisoner-of-war issues.

—*Marty:* regarding his trip. Reported on his conversations with the British ambassador and the French. Evidently, neither the English nor the French are inclined to authorize a trip to England or Algeria.

[. . .]

—Looked over *Zhdanov's office* at the CC, which has been assigned to me.

· 2 JULY 1943 ·

—Office at the CC. Left instructions for furnishing it. Selected a room for the crypt[ography] section.

—Summoned *Zhdanov's son* (Yur[i] Andr[eevich]) to see me regarding a job in my secretariat. He prefers active work, particularly in his own field (he is a chemist). Asked him to think it over and consult with his father, and then give me his answer.

—*Rákosi:* regarding the Hung[arian] Com[munist] Party's *action program,* especially the Transylvanian question. Advised him not to get carried away with the immediate political situation, but rather to conduct a principled policy, including as regards Hungary's territorial borders.

[. . .]

· 7 JULY 1943 ·

—*Manuilsky and Pauker* to see me. Pauker reported on her work with Romanian prisoner-of-war officers. Gave instructions regarding preparations for forming a Romanian antifascist committee. Determined that the *Romanian* committee (somewhat unlike the German committee) is to have a broader platform, one that will in fact unite all parties, both opponents and supporters of Antonescu,[415] who are speaking out against Romania's waging war on the side of Hitler and in favor of a break with Germany.

[. . .]

· 8 JULY 1943 ·

—*Sukharev, Morozov*: established the structure and staff of the First Department, which has been made over into Institute 100, attached to the business administration of the VKP(b) CC.
—*Friedrich* [Geminder]: clarified which of the First Department personnel are to be retained to provide technical support for national radio broadcasting.

[. . .]

—Received resolution of the CC secretariat concerning *Sukharev's* appointment as deputy business administration manager of the VKP(b) CC.

[. . .]

· 16 JULY 1943 ·
[. . .]

—*Rákosi*: on the Hungarian Com[munist] Party's formulation of the Transylvanian question. Explained to him that the draft declaration they have submitted is politically incorrect and inadvisable. Such a formulation of the question would play into Horthy's[416] hands and would sow disorientation and confusion in the ranks of Hungary's Communists and other democratic elements. Hungary's claims to Transylvania must certainly be linked with breaking its alliance with Germany and ceasing Hungary's participation in the Hitlerite war.

[. . .]

· 19 JULY 1943 ·

—Met with *Shcherbakov*. Determined definitively that the (modified) functions of the First Department, redesignated Scientific Research In-

415. Ion Antonescu (1882–1946), Romanian marshal, premier, and wartime dictator. He was overthrown in a royal coup in August 1944, tried for war crimes, condemned to death, and executed.
416. Miklós Horthy (1868–1957), Hungarian admiral and regent.

stitute 100, will continue in future at Rostokino; national radio broadcasting will operate as Scientific Institute 205; the library will be a branch of the VKP(b) CC library. Managerial functions are assumed by the KPSS (b) CC administration.

—The question of the SUPress Telegraph Agency remains an open one for now, pending a discussion with Shvernik about turning the agency over to the VTsSPS [All-Union Central Council of Trade Unions].

[...]

· 16 AUGUST 1943 ·

—Manuilsky reported on the progress in forming national committees of prisoners of war and political émigrés. Work has been held up, owing to unfavorable discussions in England and America regarding the German Free Germany committee. The formation of Hungarian, Romanian, and Italian committees has been suspended.

[...]

Dimitrov's health deteriorated steadily after August 1943. He suffered from several maladies—notably, acute inflammation of the prostate. At the end of 1943 he wrote resignedly, "The last four months of 1943 were especially difficult ones for me. Very nearly died." In fact, he was bedridden and had plenty of time on his hands. He read a great deal of Balkan history and concerned himself, as much as his condition permitted, with the affairs of Bulgaria and Yugoslavia, but also China, Austria, Hungary, Poland, Czechoslovakia, and Spain. Still, Manuilsky controlled most of the departmental work.

The ailing Dimitrov displayed tenderness and suspicion, obsequiousness and impatience, but for the most part he was marginalized. Hence, he was thrilled to learn that the American leftists and liberals were commemorating the tenth anniversary of the Leipzig trial with celebrations in Madison Square Garden, presided over by Paul Robeson, Lillian Hellman, George Kaufman, and Arturo Toscanini. His entries for the second half of 1943 are as interesting for their significant lacunae as for their slim contents. There is no paper trail regarding Soviet annoyance with Tito over the Jajce conference, where Tito took a harsh line against the exiled King Peter of Yugoslavia. Moreover, the queries sent to Tito in late December 1943 suggest that Moscow knew very little of the guerrilla movements in Greece or generally about the state of the Greek Communist movement.

In early 1944 Dimitrov continued the work of what he himself refers to (in quotation marks) as the Soviet CC "Foreign Department." But because of either his illnesses or something else, he was increasingly responsive to his nominal deputy Manuilsky—in effect, to Molotov. The steady decline of German power concentrated attention on the opportunities that would come with victory. Poland's fate was already being decided, as were the moves in the Balkans, particularly Bulgaria. The Chinese Communists continued feuding, but Mao was eager to demonstrate loyalty. The resolution of the CP split in the United States was suggested in exchanges with Earl Browder and William Z. Foster as early as February–March 1944, as was Stalin's thinking on postwar governments in Western Europe, in exchanges with departing Togliatti (March 1944). And there were early warnings about Yugoslav-Bulgarian contention over Macedonia.

By the spring and summer of 1944 the German retreat was increasingly dramatic. Despite some scares (such as the attack by the Germans on Tito's headquarters at Drvar in May 1944), the Nazi retreat was clearly irreversible. Balkan affairs loomed increasingly large as the Ukrainian front swung toward the Bug and the Dniester. By July Manuilsky was installed in Kiev as Ukraine's nominal minister of foreign affairs; by August the Red Army had entered Romania, and three weeks later Bulgaria. Dimitrov was not overwhelmed by the Communist takeover of his homeland during the night of 8–9 September 1944. He was busier than ever with Bulgarian, Macedonian, and Yugoslav affairs and kept in touch with Stalin and Molotov about these matters, as well as with the Bulgarian Communists and Tito (in Moscow himself in September 1944). The Communists, helped by the Soviet Army, were now in charge of Romania, Bulgaria, and the eastern portions of Yugoslavia (Serbia and Macedonia). Throughout, Dimitrov had time for Slovak, Hungarian, Romanian, Greek, Chinese, and even Spanish party affairs. But there is not a word in the diary on the Warsaw uprising or about the Soviet passivity on the right bank of the Vistula, as the Germans destroyed the Home Army insurgents.—I.B.

· 25 AUGUST 1943 ·

—Lieutenant General of State Security *Fitin, Marty, and Stepanov [Minev]* to see me. Fitin reported that *Pierre Cot*[417] is assisting Sov[iet]

---

417. Pierre Cot (1895–1977), French politician; member of the Radical Party; minister of aviation in the Popular Front government in the 1930s, as well as briefly after the war. In exile in the USA during the war, he became a Soviet intelligence asset involved on various Communist fronts and a winner of the Stalin prize (1953).

organs in New York with valuable information, but he could do a great deal more in this regard—as Cot himself has stated—if he possessed written approval for such work from Thorez or Marty. We arranged for Marty to provide Fitin a memo along these lines for Cot.

[. . .]

· 31 AUGUST 1943 ·
[. . .]

In connection with events in Bulgaria, sent *Stalin* (copy to Molotov) the following letter:

The death of Tsar Boris[418] has revealed a serious political and state crisis in Bulgaria.

On the basis of the Bulg[arian] constitution the ministerial council has declared Boris's six-year-old son the new tsar of Bulgaria, to be known as Tsar Simeon II.

According to the constitution, a Great National Assembly must be convened within a month to constitute a three-member regency council [to govern] until the new tsar comes of age. There can be no doubt that the Hitlerites and their Bulgarian agents will do everything possible to keep Bulgaria and her army in the hands of Hitlerite Germany.

However, the current situation makes it entirely possible to develop a broad national movement against Hitler's agents and Bulgaria's pro-German foreign policy.

For the Fatherland Front, which includes clandestine representatives of the largest political parties with the greatest authority for the people and army—the Democratic Party (Mushanov),[419] the Agrarian Union (Gichev)[420] and the Workers' Party (the Communists)—broad opportunities are now appearing to overthrow the Filov government with the support of the popular movement and to form an anti-Hitler Bulgarian coalition government, which would administer the constitutionally mandated elec-

418. Tsar Boris died on 28 August 1943 and was succeeded by his six-year-old son Simeon II.

419. Nikola Mushanov (1872–1951), Bulgarian politician; leader of the Democratic Party; minister in various cabinets from 1908 to 1944; prime minister of Bulgaria (1931–1934). He refused to enter the Fatherland Front and served as a minister without portfolio in the last pre–Fatherland Front government; though sentenced after 9 September 1944, he soon rejoined the anticommunist opposition.

420. Dimitŭr Gichev (1893–1964), Bulgarian politician; leader of the BZNS; minister (1931–1934, 1944). After 9 September 1944, he headed the opposition BZNS, but he finally joined the Fatherland Front. A Communist court sentenced him to life imprisonment in 1948.

tions to the Great National Assembly. All of this could deliver a crushing blow to the Hitlerites in Bulgaria and their Bulgarian agents.

The basic position of our Bulgarian party is stated in the two attached broadcasts of the clandestine people's radio station Radio Hristo Botev.

I would be most grateful if you could receive me to discuss this matter, as I urgently request.

[. . .]

· 2 SEPTEMBER 1943 ·

—*Rákosi:* consulted with me on Hungarian issues, particularly the position of the Czechosl[ovak] Com[munist] Party and the Hung[arian] Com[munist] Party as regards Carpatho-Ukraine. There are disagreements between the Czech and Hungarian Com[munist] parties over this matter. Directed him to state the Hungarian Com[munist] Party's point of view in writing and to call on the Czech [*sic*] Com[munist] Party to do the same. Then we will discuss this matter jointly.

[. . .]

· 20 NOVEMBER 1943 ·

—*Pieck, Florin, Ulbricht, and Ackermann.* Come to consult with me on German issues. Brought to their attention that they are to proceed on the basis of *the most likely prospect,* the destruction of fascist Germany under the blows of the armed forces of the Sov[iet] Union and its allies, [and] thereafter the temporary occupation of Germany, with all the ramifications of this fact. Therefore the task of the German Com[munist] party (as regards the postwar period) lies first of all in creating the sort of organized national force that, with the help of the Soviet Union, would be capable of taking upon itself the rebirth of Germany as a genuinely democrat[ic] country.

[. . .]

· 23 NOVEMBER 1943 ·

—*Manuilsky and Morozov* to see me at the dacha regarding *the breakdown* in Warsaw (the CC secretary, Finder, has been arrested; so has the radio operator Bortusziewicz; code's been broken, and so on). Gave instructions regarding precautionary measures for radio communications with Germany, Czechoslovakia, and Hungary, because these had had dealings with Finder. Assigned Morozov to obtain through Fitin any possible detailed information on the breakdown and the status of the Polish center since the breakdown.

————————

—Lieutenant General *Ilichev* with a member of his staff, recently arrived from Yan'an (China). Reported on the situation of the Eighth [Route] Army, the Special Region and the Com[munist] Party. No hope whatsoever for normalizing relations between the Guomindang and the Com[munist] Party.

[. . .]

· 13 DECEMBER 1943 ·
[. . .]

Sent *Wang Ming* (Yan'an) the following message through *Ilichev:* "Letter for Fanichka arrived.[421] She is living with us. She is growing up and developing well. Straight A's at school. Sends her papa and mama warmest regards and best wishes. A great loss has befallen us: in April our Mitia died of malignant diphtheria. As for your part[y] affairs, do your best to settle them yourselves. Intervening from here is for now inexpedient."

————————

A pact of "friendship" and so on has been concluded between the USSR and Czechoslovakia. Signatories: *Molotov* and *Fierlinger*[422] (Czechoslovak ambassador to the USSR).

---

421. Fania Dimitrova (1932–1985), daughter of Wang Ming adopted by Dimitrov (1937). She lived in Bulgaria (1947–1948), then in the USSR.

422. Zdeněk Fierlinger (1891–1976), Czechoslovak politician and diplomat; left-wing Social Democrat; envoy to the Netherlands, Romania, the USA, Switzerland, the League of Nations, and Austria (1922–1936); envoy to the USSR (1937–1945); premier of the pro-Soviet Czechoslovak provisional government formed at Košice (1945); premier of Czechoslovakia (1945–1946); chairman of the Czechoslovak Social Democratic Party of Workers (ČSDSD) in 1945–1947 and 1948 who was instrumental in subjoining this party to the KSČ (June 1948); member KSČ CC presidium (from 1948 on); president of the Czechoslovak parliament (1953–1964).

· 14 December 1943 ·
[. . .]

—*Gottwald* called; wanted me to receive him here tomorrow. Wanted to report on Czech comrades' negotiations with Beneš and to consult with me regarding those negotiations.

· 15 December 1943 ·
[. . .]

—Received *Gottwald*. Reported on negotiations with *Beneš*. To hear him talk, Beneš is quite radical. Acknowledges that the Com[munist] Party of Czechoslovakia is the strongest party and ought to assume *a leadership role* in the future government . . . Proposes that the Communists furnish a representative to the current government in London.

Advised Gottwald:

1. To bear in mind that Beneš's sole aim is to tie their hands, to ensure that they will not have freedom of action during the destruction of Germany, and if he can, even to discredit them

2. Not to take part in the current government

3. To demand the formation of a new provisional government with the active participation of the Communists

4. The formation of a bloc consisting of the Communist Party, Benešists, and Social Democrats on a democratic platform

5. The essential task currently is to use all means available to intensify the struggle against the Germans in Czechoslovakia, the part[isan] movement, and so on.

[. . .]

· 17 December 1943 ·
[. . .]

—Gave *Friedrich* [Geminder] instructions to have the *declaration* of the antifascist Council of People's Liberation [AVNOJ] transmitted over Radio Free Yugoslavia.

[. . .]

· 22 December 1943 ·

—Sent *Mao Zedong* (Yan'an) via *Ilichev* the following personal letter (encoded telegram):

1. Regarding your son: I have arranged for him to be enrolled in the Military-Political Academy; on graduating, he will have acquired a solid background in the areas of Marxism-Leninism and contemporary warfare. He is a capable young man, and I have no doubt that he will make you a reliable and fine assistant. He sends you his warmest regards.

2. Regarding matters of political nature: It only stands to reason that since the dissolution of the Comintern, none of its former leaders may intervene in the internal affairs of Com[munist] parties. However, speaking privately and as a friend, I cannot fail to tell you of my alarm at the situation in the Chinese Com[munist] Party. You are aware that I have had occasion since 1935 to deal closely and often directly with Chinese affairs. On the basis of everything known to me, I consider politically mistaken the tendency to wind down the struggle against China's foreign occupiers, along with the evident departure from a united national front policy. At a time of national war for the Chinese people, such a tendency risks isolating the party from the popular masses and is capable of precipitating the dangerous intensification of an international war in which only the occupiers and their agents in the Guomindang could have an interest. I consider politically incorrect the campaign being waged against Zhou Enlai and Wang Ming, who are being incriminated with the Comintern-endorsed national front policy, as a result of which they have allegedly led the party to schism. Persons such as Zhou Enlai and Wang Ming must not be severed from the party. I am also disturbed by the fact that among certain party cadres there are unhealthy sentiments as regards the Soviet Union. The role being played by Kon Sin [Kang Sheng] also seems dubious to me. The implementation of such a correct party procedure as the purging of enemy elements from the party and its consolidation is being pursued by Kon Sin and his apparatus in forms so misshapen that they are capable only of sowing mutual suspicions, arousing the profound outrage of the rank-and-file party membership, and aiding the *enemy* in his efforts to demoralize the party. As early as August of this year we had received utterly reliable reports from Chongqing that the Guomindang had decided to send its provocateurs to Yan'an with the aim of setting you at odds with Wang Ming and other party figures, as well as fomenting hostile sentiments against all persons who had lived and studied in Moscow. I warned you in good time about this treacherous intention on the part of the Guomindang. Their secret aim is to demoralize the Com[munist] Party from within, to crush it all the more easily. I have no doubt that by his actions Kon Sin is playing right into the hands of these provocateurs. Forgive me my comradely bluntness. But it is only my profound respect for you and my firm conviction that as the generally acknowledged leader of the party you have a stake in seeing things in their true light that allows me to speak to you with such candor.

Please reply to me by the same channel I have used to send you the present letter.

I grasp your hand firmly!

[. . .]

· 26 DECEMBER 1943 ·
[. . .]

Sent *Walter* [Tito] the following encoded telegram:

We consider it a mistake to include Vlahov and Tomov [Poptomov] in the Antifascist Council. Vlahov is an émigré lacking any connections with Yugoslav Macedonia, although he is a Macedonian publicist. Tomov [Poptomov] is a former Bulgarian Communist deputy and currently a Bulgarian commentator for Soviet foreign radio. Please consider how their inclusion could be practically annulled without incurring political cost to yourself, and inform us accordingly.

Also sent Walter [Tito] the following encoded telegram:

Please ascertain and report data on the partisan movement in Greece, the numbers of armed forces in action against the occupiers, the region of their activities, the territory they hold, which organizations are directing the activities of these partisan detachments, and whether you are in contact with them. Is it true that a partisan army known as ELAS, commanded by Colonel Sarafis,[423] actually represents a consistent democratic force fighting for the common cause of the anti-Hitler coalition? Is it likewise true that a different wing of the partisan forces known as EDES, led by Colonel Zervas,[424] is playing a role something like that of Mihailović's Chetniks in Yugoslavia, fomenting internal fratricidal war and playing into the hands of the occupiers? What sort of force do the detachments commanded by Colonel Psarros[425] represent? We would consider it highly advisable for

423. Stephanos Sarafis (1890–1957), Greek military officer of Venizelist antimonarchist orientation. Having been sent into internal exile after the restoration of monarchy in 1935, he apparently joined the KKE, becoming commander of the Communist-dominated National People's Liberation Army (ELAS) with the rank of general. Sent again into internal exile after the liberation, he was released in 1951 and thereafter belonged to the leftist EDA (Greek Democratic Left), which he represented in the Greek parliament.

424. Napoleon Zervas (1891–1957), Greek military officer of Venizelist orientation; commander of the British-backed nationalist National Republican Hellenic League (EDES), which operated mainly in Epirus and engaged both the occupiers and the Communist-controlled ELAS; founder of the National Party in 1946; minister of public order (1947) and of public works (1950–1951).

425. Demetres Psarros (1893–1944), Greek military officer of Venizelist orientation who organized Resistance bands in Aegean Macedonia in association with the republican EKKA (National and Social Liberation). In March 1943 he took command of "5/42 Regiment," which was attacked several times by the Communist-led ELAS before it was finally destroyed in April 1944 when Psarros was murdered.

you to establish liaison with those partisan detachments which are the true friends of the three allied powers and of your own heroic army. We urgently request a reply.

[...]

· 28 DECEMBER 1943 ·

—Sent *Walter* [Tito] the foll[owing] encoded telegram:

We find your replies to the three Cairo questions to be correct. It is desirable, however, to show the necessary flexibility as regards propaganda against the king, in the interests of better disorganizing his supporters abroad and in Serbia and of more easily overcoming certain difficulties on the part of the Anglo-Americans in their aid to the People's Liberation Army. One could declare, for instance, that if the king will not oppose the national committee, the latter will for its part refrain from all propaganda against the king. Furthermore, you must by all means avoid whatever could give the impression that you supposedly favor giving the Croats priority over the Serbs in the new federated Yugoslavia—that is, supplanting the former hegemony of the Serbs with the hegemony of the Croats. Bear in mind that various Anglo-American circles are taking all possible advantage of this.

———————————

—Asked *Fitin* to ascertain immediately through his network in Warsaw:

1. Which of the Ludist [Stronnictwo Ludowe, People's Party] and PPS [Polska Partia Socjalistyczna, Polish Socialist Party] activists are willing to collaborate with the League of Polish Patriots [ZPP], and whether any of them could travel to Moscow for negotiations on this issue.

2. The present whereabouts of the Ludist [Kazimierz] Bagiński and what position he is taking.

[...]

—*Manuilsky and Berman*[426] to see me regarding the composition of the *Polish national committee* being formed. The nat[ional] committee is to have the nature of a provisional Polish government.

426. Jakub Berman (1909–1984), Polish Communist leader from a bourgeois Jewish family. He graduated from the Law Faculty of the University of Warsaw and then obtained a Ph.D. in history. Member of the PPK (from 1928 on) who was in the USSR during the war; staff member of the press section of the ECCI (1941–1943); editor of the Polish edition at Institute 205; member of the PPR Politburo

—Lieutenant General *Ilichev* and Major General *Bolshakov:* on Chinese affairs, in particular as regards delivery of my letter to Mao Zedong.

[. . .]

· 30 DECEMBER 1943 ·

—Sent Walter [Tito] the following [encoded telegram]:

Additional checking has not established direct evidence confirming *Ribnikar's*[427] working for English intelligence. What has been confirmed, however, is that Ribnikar met with an authorized agent of the "Intelligence Service" and informed him concerning various issues. Checking is being continued. Please report whether you are aware of Ribnikar's meetings with a representative of English intelligence and on what issues Ribnikar supplied him information.

[. . .]

· 5 JANUARY 1944 ·

—Went in to work for the first time since 9 September 1943. Tough going, but it looks as though I shall manage . . .

—*Manuilsky* reported to me on his conversations with Molotov concerning operations of the CC "Foreign Department." (I am the department head; Man[uilsky] is my deputy. Direct link with Molot[ov]-Politburo.)

—Sent to *Molotov:*

1. A draft about establishing the Central Bureau of Polish Communists and a proposal for its personnel roster.

2. A concrete proposal to send at least twenty tons of supplies (medi-

---

(1944–1948); member of the Polish Committee for National Liberation (1944–1945); member of PZRP Politburo (1948–1956), responsible for ideology, education, culture, foreign affairs, and security; member of government presidium (1950–1952); deputy premier (1954–1956). Having been expelled from the PZRP CC in 1956 and from the PZRP in 1957, he was held responsible for the "period of errors and distortions."

427. Vladislav Ribnikar (1900–1955), Yugoslav journalist and official; director (from 1924 on) of the Belgrade daily *Politika,* which the Ribnikar family owned and which he steered in a pro-Communist direction during the 1930s. His house in Belgrade was used by Tito for various clandestine KPJ meetings before and immediately after the beginning of the war. Ribnikar joined the KPJ in 1941. Member of the AVNOJ presidency (after 1943); founder and first director of the Tanjug news agency; minister in postwar Yugoslav governments.

cines, arms, footwear, certain armaments as well) to Yugoslavia (for the People's Liberation Army).

—*Mikhailov* (sec[retary] of the Komsomol) asked me to receive him and the other CC secretaries to consult about operations of the Soviet youth antifascist committee.

· 6 JANUARY 1944 ·

—Met with *Molotov*. Showed me the text of a PB resolution on the formation of the CC Foreign Department. Spoke about Polish affairs, particularly the formation of the Polish national committee and the Central Bureau of Polish Communists.

[. . .]

· 9 JANUARY 1944 ·
[. . .]

—*Mol[otov]* called to coordinate [with me] his reply for Mushanov as regards his proposal for Bulgaria's withdrawal from Germany.

The rough text of the reply: "If Bulgaria wishes to withdraw from Germany and as a first step in that direction recalls its troops from Serbia, then the Sov[iet] Union is willing to assume the role of intermediary between England and America as regards Bulgaria's withdrawal from the war. Naturally, Bulgaria must inform the Sov[iet] gov[ernment] of its intentions."

· 10 JANUARY 1944 ·
[. . .]

Recently received *Mao Zedong*'s reply (through Ilichev's network) to my letter (encoded telegram) of 22 December 1943.

To Comrade Dimitrov:

1. We are not winding down the anti-Japanese struggle. On the contrary, during 1943 units of the Eighth [Route] Army conducted active operations against the Japanese on dozens of occasions. As a result, a portion of the territories lost in 1940 and 1942 has been regained. The Eighth [Route] Army now numbers approximately five hundred thousand. The struggle against the Japanese was waged quite fiercely in 1943.

2. Our line as regards collaboration with the Guomindang remains unchanged. In July 1943 a very tense and dangerous situation developed. The

Guomindang was planning an armed offensive against the Special Region. The comprehensive measures we undertook at the time allowed us to avert a clash. It is possible that similar tensions may develop in 1944. Our policy and our measures will be designed to avoid armed clashes.

3. Zhou Enlai and I are on very good terms. We have no intention of severing him from the party. Zhou Enlai is a great success and has made great progress.

4. Wang Ming has engaged in diverse antiparty activities. All party cadres have been apprised of this. However, we are not planning to make this known to the party masses as a whole; still less are we planning to publish this for all the nonparty masses. The examination of all of Wang Ming's errors by senior party cadres has resulted in a still greater degree of consolidation and unity among those cadres.

5. I assure you and can vouch for the fact that Comrade Stalin and the Soviet Union enjoy the love and great respect of the Com[munist] Party of China . . .

6. In my view, Wang Ming is unreliable. Wang Ming was arrested before in Shanghai. Several people have stated that while he was in prison, he admitted belonging to the Com[munist] Party. He was later released. There has also been talk of his dubious connection with [Pavel] Mif.[428] Wang Ming has engaged in extensive antiparty activities.

Kon Sin [Kang Sheng] is reliable. The checking of cadres is not being performed by his apparatus. They are responsible for dealing only with a portion of the spies. We have performed a comprehensive and thorough checking[429] of cadres.

—Mao Zedong.

—On 7 January *Mao Zedong* sent a second *telegram:*

Comrade Dimitrov:
Apart from my telegram of 2 January, in which I set forth my point of view, today I would like to inform you of the following as regards these issues: I am sincerely and deeply grateful to you for your remarks to me.

---

428. Pavel Mif (real name: Mikhail Aleksandrovich Fortus, 1901–1938), Soviet Communist; vice rector and later rector of the Comintern's Sun Yat-sen University; member of the ECCI staff (from 1925 on); adviser to the CPC agitprop section (1927); deputy chief of the Far Eastern Secretariat of the Comintern (1928–1935). He went to China in 1930 at the head of the twenty-eight returned students of Sun Yat-sen University, who were slated to take over the leadership of the CPC. Dimitrov's assistant on Chinese affairs (from 1935 on); rector of the Communist University for Eastern Workers (KUTV) beginning in 1936. He was arrested in the Stalinist purges and died in prison.

429. Mao used the term *proverka* (checking, auditing, examination) rather than *chistka* (purge), which Dimitrov used in his letter to Mao (22 December 1943).

I must study them thoroughly, bear them in mind, and take the appropriate measures. In the area of Guomindang relations our policy is one of collaboration.

I assume that the situation in this area will be better in 1944. Internal party issues: our policy in this area is aimed at unification, at the consolidation of our unity. As regards Wang Ming, precisely the same policy will be carried out. Work carried out in the second half of 1943 has resulted in significant improvement in the internal party situation and party unity.

Please set your mind at rest. All your thoughts, all your concerns are close to my heart, for my own thoughts and my own concerns are, at bottom, exactly the same.

Regards,
Mao Zedong

· 11 JANUARY 1944 ·

—*Mol[otov]* called and asked me what sort of impression is being made by the Soviet government's statement on the Polish question in today's newspapers, whether it was sufficiently convincing, and so forth.

Told him the statement is an exceptionally powerful and remarkable document.

Mol[otov]: Some of our people may believe that we are being very deferential as regards the Poles, but that does not much matter.

[. . .]

· 13 JANUARY 1944 ·

—*Man[uilsky]* and I met with *Molotov*. Discussed plans for organizing the Centr[al] Bureau of Polish Communists.

[. . .]

—Pieck to see me regarding the German question.
—Invited the Pol[ish] Communist Berman [to see me] regarding the composition of the CB [Central Bureau] of Pol[ish] Communists.
—Received Mao Zedong's son, who is studying at the military academy.

· 14 JANUARY 1944 ·
[. . .]

—*Shcherbakov* sent me the text of the All-Slavic Committee's appeal to the Bulgarian people for my review.

—Held a meeting of the Foreign Bureau (at my city apartment): Kolarov, Chervenkov, Belov [Damianov].

1. Discussed framing the question of Bulgaria's nation[al] unification in connection with Macedonia, Thrace, and Dobruja.

2. Examined draft appeal of All-S[lavic] Committee. It was approved in the main. Draft needs, however, various changes and improvements.

[. . .]

· 18 JANUARY 1944 ·

—Met with *Molotov.* Again discussed the composition of the Centr[al] Bureau of Polish Communists, as well as the reply by the All-Union Central Council of Trade Unions [VTsSPS] to the General Council of Trade Unions regarding the convocation of the World Trade Union Conference.

[. . .]

· 19 JANUARY 1944 ·

—Received *Wanda Wasilewska, Berman,* and *Minc*[430] regarding the composition of the Centr[al] Bureau of Polish Communists.

—Sent encoded telegram to *Wang Ming* in Yan'an via *Ilichev* concerning [his] relations with Mao Zedong.

· 20 JANUARY 1944 ·
[. . .]

—Received Polish comrade *Zawadski, Aleksander,*[431] concerning his work in the Polish corps and his appointment as secretary of the Centr[al] Bureau of Polish Communists.

[. . .]

430. Hilary Minc (1905–1974), Polish Communist leader who studied economics in France (1924–1927), from which he was expelled for Communist activities. After several years in the USSR (1928–1930), he became secretary of the PPK central editorial office (1930–1939). After the beginning of the war, he went to Soviet-occupied Lviv and (in 1941) to Samarkand, where he taught economics. On returning to Poland in 1944, Minc became a member of the PPR/PZRP Politburo (1944–1956) and minister of trade and industry (1944–1949). He was dismissed from his posts in 1956.

431. Aleksander Zawadski (1899–1964), Polish Communist; political émigré to the USSR (after 1939); member of the PPR CC Politburo (1944–1945; member of the PZRP Politburo and CC secretary (from 1948 on); head of the Central Council of Trade Unions (1949–1951); deputy prime minister (1951–1952); head of the Council of State (1952–1964).

· 24 JANUARY 1944 ·

—Received *Ercoli* [Togliatti]. Informed him concerning reports from Italy and issues raised by the Italian comrades. A party congress is scheduled for the twenty-sixth in *Bari,* and a conference of the national committee for the twenty-eighth.

[. . .]

—Sent *Molotov* a draft reply to *Vyshinsky* on Italian issues.
—Sent *Stal[in]* (copy to *Molotov*) proposal for composition of the C[entral] B[ureau] of Polish Communists and its function[s].

· 25 JANUARY 1944 ·

—Received CC resolution approving the composition of the CB of Polish Communists and its function[s] in accordance with my proposal.

[. . .]

· 9 FEBRUARY 1944 ·

—*Walter* [Tito] reported that he had received a personal telegram from *Churchill,* who was insisting on negotiations with the Yugosl[av] king for a joint struggle against the Germans. Walter asked our opinion, specifically Com[rade] Stalin's opinion.

After coordinating with the appropriate parties, I sent Walter the following reply:

> We have received your inquiry as regards relations toward King Peter. I report here our collective opinion, which includes the opinion of the comrade you named, to whom we ask you to refer in future telegrams as Friend (I repeat, Friend).
>
> First. The AVNOJ, too, as well as the Englishman [Churchill] whom you know, favors the unity of the Yugoslavs, but as long as there exist two governments, one in Yugoslavia and the other in Cairo, there can be no unity. Therefore the Cairo government must be eliminated, including Mihailović; moreover, it must furnish the AVNOJ government with a complete accounting of its expenditure of enormous sums of the people's money.
>
> Second. The government in Yugoslavia, that is, the AVNOJ government, must be acknowledged by England and the other allies as the sole government of Yugoslavia, while the king must submit to the laws of AVNOJ.
>
> Third. If King Peter accepts all these conditions, then AVNOJ has no objections to cooperating with him, provided that the question of the monar-

chy in Yugoslavia is decided by the people following the liberation of Yugoslavia.

That is our opinion.[432]

· 11 FEBRUARY 1944 ·

—*Browder* reported that in connection with recent decisions concerning the policy of the Com[munist] party of the United States, [William Z.] *Foster* had gone over to the CC's opposition and was planning to speak out publicly.

In this regard I sent *Browder* the following encoded telegram: "I have received your report concerning Foster. Please report in greater detail the grounds of your disagreement. Have Foster himself formulate his point of view for me. It would be desirable for the time being for him to refrain from speaking out publicly on this matter."

[. . .]

· 25 FEBRUARY 1944 ·
[. . .]

—Sent *Kasman* the following encoded telegram for the CC of the Polish Workers' Party:

> We are leery of the PPR's [Polish Workers' (Communist) Party's] sectarian course as regards the Krajowa Rada Narodowa [National Home Council, KRN], playing up the leading role of the PPR, underestimating the significance of the participation of other anti-German parties and organizations in the Rada, of political deviations that create the false impression that the PPR is heading toward the sovietization of Poland, which in current conditions could only play into the hands of various provocateurs and enemies of the Polish people. What call was there, for instance, to term the Rada's measures decrees when the Rada is not the government of Poland? Isn't the PPR being overly eager to establish its command [headquarters] when there is still no Polish army in the country?
>
> We request an immediate reply.

—Sent the following telegram to Mao Zedong via *Ilichev:*

> Dear Comrade Mao!
> I have received both your telegrams. I was especially glad of your second telegram. I had no doubt that you would give my friendly remarks the seri-

---

432. In his response to Churchill, sent from Drvar, western Bosnia, on 9 February 1944, Tito adapted Dimitrov's points almost without change.

ous attention they require and that you would take the appropriate measures as dictated by the interests of the party and our common cause. I would be most grateful to you if you would inform me of the practical results that your measures have yielded to date.

Fraternal regards. I firmly grasp your hand.

—Sent *Dekanozov* the foll[owing] letter:

I urgently request that you pass instructions through your network to Sofia to ascertain and immediately report:

1. What the political position of the Workers' Party (Commun[ists]) is in the current situation and what concrete slogans are being advanced by the party, particularly as regards the Macedonian and Thracian questions.

2. What relations obtain between the Workers' Party and other anti-German parties and organizations (Agrarians, Democrats, Social Democrats, Radicals, Populists, and the "Zvenoists").[433]

3. What parties and societies other than the Workers' Party belong to the Fatherland Front and whether there are committees in the center and in the localities.

4. What Workers' Party activists are at liberty and able to act in its name.

5. Whether the articles on Bulgaria in *Pravda* are being widely disseminated and what influence they are having in the country.

6. What concrete forms Work[ers]' Party activities are taking (propaganda, publications, polit[ical] actions, part[isan] actions, sabotage, diversion against the Germans).

[. . .]

· 28 FEBRUARY 1944 ·

—Sent Sofia (via Fitin) a political directive for the party: cautioning it against erroneously raising the issue of an armed course toward an isolat[ed] uprising and the party's independ[ently] seizing *power.*

—Sent Walter [Tito] the following encoded telegram: "We have heard from Sofia that the English have reportedly supplied Tito with arms

433. The Zvenoists were members of the political union *Zveno* (the Link), an elitist association determined to reform and modernize Bulgaria from above. They were hostile to parliamentarianism, but also to mass movements. *Zveno* came to power in May 1934 as a result of a military coup by the Military League of Col. Damian Velchev. The *Zveno* dictatorship, however, was headed by Col. Kimon Georgiev, who held the position of Bulgarian prime minister. In January 1935 Tsar Boris carried out a bloodless coup against *Zveno,* dismissed Georgiev, and took the first steps toward a personal royal dictatorship.

and uniforms for Bulgarian part[isan] detachments. Please report immediately whether this is the case and whether there is any chance at all of assisting the Bulgarian detachments with certain quantities of arms through Tito, as would of course be quite desirable and useful."

To Walter [Tito] and Georgiev [Atanasov]: "It is imperative to determine immediately what communications are available between Bulgaria and Yugoslavia. Please give this matter top priority and keep us apprised of the measures you are taking."

· 29 FEBRUARY 1944 ·

—Sent *Mao Zedong* the following encoded telegram:

Please inform us whether there have been any significant changes in relations between the Com[munist] Party and Chiang Kai-shek, and if so, what concrete form these changes have taken. Could you not provide us with a regular brief bulletin for the preceding week or ten days covering the situation in the Special Region, the actions of your army and part[isan] detachments against the Japanese, and major aspects of the Com[munist] Party's activities? In the current complex situation that would be quite useful.

· 1 MARCH 1944 ·

—*Manuilsky* and *Ercoli* [Togliatti] discussed Ercoli's draft on the Italian Communists' immediate tasks and made final corrections.

Sent this document to V. M. [Molotov] tonight with a request to receive Ercoli in person before his departure for Algeria (on 4 March).

—Sent Walter [Tito] a reply to Tito's request for reinforcements of men, arms, etc.: "It has been decided to render the maximum possible assistance. Immediate measures in this area are being taken."

—Sukharev: regarding the [budget] estimate and other CC [business] administration issues.

—Sent the following directive to Sofia via Fitin:

On the basis of the inquiries we have received from you, it appears to us that the party CC is pursuing the line of an isolated uprising for an independent seizure of power. If so, such a line is entirely erroneous and fraught with great dangers. It leads to the isolation of the party from other political groupings in the Fatherland Front and from the other anti-German groups and elements, as well as from the army, which would inevitably thwart any attempt to incite the people to an armed uprising against the German invaders and their Bulgarian agents. For that matter, this line contradicts the correct political line taken by the party organ *Rabotnichesko delo* [Workers' Cause], in 1943. An uprising must be preceded, apart from everything else, by political accord with the other anti-German organizations, at least with the Fatherland Front groups, for joint struggle. It must have a clear political aim: the creation of a national, democratic, and antifascist government to implement the avowed democratic platform of the Fatherland Front. The participation of a significant segment of the army is an extremely important factor for a successful popular uprising. Without the army [or] with the army in opposition, the Germans and the fascist government would crush the uprising. Moreover, the most essential element in preparing a popular uprising consists, on the one hand, in the carrying out of political actions that are even today mobilizing the popular masses and, on the other hand, in the expansion of the partisan movement (sabotage, diversions, and so on) against the Germans and fascist authorities.

2. One must also bear strictly in mind that in current conditions any steps and actions that create the false impression that we are supposedly dealing with the sovietization of Bulgaria can only play into the hands of various provocateurs and enemies of the Bulgarian people, and all such steps and actions must therefore be strictly avoided.

3. We strongly recommend to the party leadership the political line taken by [Radio] Hristo Botev, which is set forth in legal form in the article by D[imitrov] in *Pravda*.

4. As for arms, these must be obtained primarily within Bulgaria through all available means, especially the assistance of reliable persons in the army. Obtaining arms and uniforms for partis[an] detachments through Tito is not only acceptable; it is highly desirable. Without assuming, moreover, any political or other obligations with regard to the English.

5. Immediate measures must be taken, including the dispatch of suitable personnel, to establish at any cost a reliable channel of communications with the Yugoslav comrades. At Tito's headquarters we have a Bulgarian comrade whom we have assigned to work on establishing that channel of communications from the Yugoslav end.

6. Confirm receipt of this message. Send reply of the CC. We await a detailed report.

· 2 March 1944 ·

—*Meeting of the Foreign Bureau of the Bulgarian CP* (Kolarov, Chervenkov, Marek [Stanke Dimitrov], Belov [Damianov]).
—Determined Marek's duties as secretary of the Foreign Bureau.

—Discussed the situation in the country and outlined immediate political measures.

—Examined our *position* on the Maced[onian] question.

[. . .]

· 3 MARCH 1944 ·
[. . .]

—*Manuilsky, Thorez, Ercoli* [Togliatti]: discussed directive for French com[rades] in Algeria (Ercoli will pass it on!) and the position of Thorez, whose visit to Algeria has been rejected by de Gaulle.

[. . .]

· 4 MARCH 1944 ·

—Last night *Stal[in]* received *Ercoli* [Togliatti], in *Molotov's* presence. "At the present stage do not call for the king's immediate abdication; Communists can join the Badoglio government;[434] [our] chief efforts must be concentrated on creating and reinforcing unity in the struggle against the Germans." Carry out that line, but without referring to the Russians . . .

―――――――――――

—Regarding the difficulties being created in the PPR regional committee and the People's Guard regional command in Lublin, sent *Kasman* (Poland) the foll[owing] encoded telegram:

While observing all necessary precautions, explain to the Lublin comrades that your group does not interfere in the affairs and the leadership of the partisan detachments and does not itself organize the part[isan] struggle. Also explain, in terms that are appropriate and secure for your work, that [your] group has special assignments—in particular, the creation of a base and center for communications with Moscow to assist the PPR and the People's Guard. It requires for the execution of its assignments a guard detachment with the necessary armaments. The party regional committee and the regional command are to render your group their full cooperation. I am assigning you personally the task of dividing the new shipment between

434. On 25 July 1943, Marshal Pietro Badoglio (1871–1956), forced the resignation of Benito Mussolini, whose Fascist party was dissolved. Badoglio's cabinet accepted the terms of Italy's surrender to the Allies (9 September 1943) and declared war on Germany (13 October 1943). Badoglio resigned as Italian premier on 4 June 1944.

your detachment and the Lublin detachment. Confirm receipt of this message. Report on results.

[. . .]

· 5 MARCH 1944 ·

—Sunday.

—*Ercoli [Togliatti] to see me.* Reported on his discussion with Stal[in]:

—The existence of two camps (Badoglio-King and the antifascist parties) is weakening the Ital[ian] people. This is to the advantage of the English, who would like to have a weak Italy on the Mediterranean. If the struggle between these two camps continues, it will mean disaster for the Italian people.

—The interests of the Ital[ian] people dictate that Italy be strong and possess a strong army.

—For Marxists, *form* never has decisive significance. It is the essence of the matter that is decisive. A king is no worse than a Mussolini. If the king opposes the Germans, there is no point demanding immediate abdication. There are no kings in Germany or Spain, but Hitler and Franco are no better than the most react[ionary] king.

—Communists may join the Badoglio government in the interests of 1. The intensification of the war against the Germans, carrying out the democratization of the country and unifying the Ital[ian] people.

—The essential thing is the unity of the Ital[ian] people in its struggle against the Germans for an independent and strong Italy.

—Carry out that line, *without referring to the Russians;* of course, one may indicate that the Soviet Union as well would not object to such an Italian policy.

—Outwardly, loyal relations with the English.

—*Marek [Stanke Dimitrov], Chervenkov, and Belov [Damianov].* Invited them here to report on new information from Bulgaria.

—Assigned *Ercoli* [Togliatti] to give the following instructions verbally to the French comrades (Marty, Guyot, and others):

We recommend:

1. Not frittering away your political line in the French Committee of National Liberation on squabbles over secondary and formal questions—squabbles that turn into agitational politics that only exacerbate relations with de Gaulle (as for instance over the candidacy of Giraud, and so on)—but rather placing at the center the fundamental issues of the war:

a) The formation of a French army and its active participation in combat operations against the Germans

b) The purging of the state and military apparatus of Pétain-Lavalist agents

c) Aiding the armed partisan groups fighting in France

2. Discussion of the future constitution of France is completely premature and unnecessary. Such discussion smacks of abstract propagandism under conditions in which the need is to finish off Hitler's army by all possible means. The party must not be allowed to lapse *émigré*-fashion into parliamentary cretinism, in abandoning the struggle to destroy Hitlerite Germany in favor of constitution drafting.

3. The party must act as the leading force of the nation, expressing its aspirations as a state party capable of arguing and winning over not only its own adherents but broader strata as well, including vacillating elements and groups.

4. At the same time, the party makes no concessions to elements that are attempting to turn the policy of the French Committee of Nat[ional] Liberation toward the old, exhausted, and quite reactionary course and thus playing into the hands of Pétain-Laval.

5. The party is not to display inordinate zeal in defending the USSR, in order not to afford its opponents the chance to represent it as an agency of Moscow.

On the contrary: popularize and defend sincere friendship between France and the USSR as the basis for French foreign policy and the renewal of the French people.

6. Remarks to Marty, that he is to act more tactfully.

7. Intercede regarding Thorez's returning to Algeria.

[. . .]

· 7 MARCH 1944 ·
[. . .]

—Regarding the disagreement between *Browder* and *Foster,* received the following encoded telegram from the latter (through Ilich[ev]'s network):

I agree with the overall assessment of Teheran put forward by Browder, with the exception of [his] serious underestimation of the danger of American imperialism. I do not agree with several points as regards America, including the question of the Republicans' and Democrats' running a common candidate in the elections, which will result either in the removal of Roosevelt or in the reduction of aid.

I do not agree with [Browder's] assessment of the role of big American capital as a progressive one that minimizes the danger of reaction in the

USA. I do not agree with the assumption that employers will voluntarily double their workers' salaries in order to keep their businesses in operation. I do not agree with having the regulation of foreign trade depend on monopolists. I do not agree to monopolists' being controlled only with their own consent. I do not agree with accepting the basic slogan of the major industrialists, the freedom of entrepreneurial initiative, which will thus reduce to a minimum the necessity for social welfare, control over monopolies, and a government program of public works as a remedy for mass unemployment.

I agree with national unity following the war as well, with a well-considered strike policy, but I do not agree with extending no-strike pledges into the postwar period. I agree that America does not at present face the problem of socialism, nor will it immediately after the war; but I also cannot ignore the socialist lessons of the Soviet Union. I am drafting a full statement of my views. I will accept your advice.

Also received the foll[owing] encoded telegram from Wang Ming (Yan'an):

Dear G. M. [Dimitrov]! In the course of December and January two telegrams of yours have been forwarded to me.

I thank you for your concern for the CPC and myself. My attitude toward Mao Zedong remains the same as it was before, for I wholeheartedly support him as the leader of our party, irrespective of our personal disagreement in the past regarding particular issues of the anti-Japanese national united front policy and the very serious campaign against me that has been waged in the last year over matters of internal party life.

I have been told by a comrade that he has been systematically informing you regarding all these matters.

I do not know what interests you in this area and which issues are unclear.

Please provide me some indications, and I will reply. For the last year a campaign has been under way in the party to reexamine its entire history on the basis of the ideas and activities of Mao Zedong.

He is being represented as the chief representative of Chinese Bolshevism and sinoized Marxism-Leninism.

Recognizing that you are capable of enhancing the authority of the party, which is especially important in the absence of the Comintern, and given the accentuation of the CPC as the national proletariat party, I fully support that campaign.

To that end I have already stated both verbally and in writing to Mao Zedong and the CC that the struggle against Li Lisan-ism,[435] the promotion

435. Li Lisan (1899–1967), Chinese Communist leader; trade unionist in

of the new policy of an anti-Japanese national united front, is to Mao Zedong's credit, and not mine, as I used to believe.

I have also stated that I renounce all political disagreements.

I sincerely thank you and dear Rozi for the many years that you have
cared for and raised my daughter.

I offer my profound condolences on the death of your beloved Mitia.

· 8 MARCH 1944 ·

—*International Women's Day.*
Sent Molotov a report on the telegrams received from Poland.
—Our telegram to *Browder* regarding the telegram received from Fos-
ter:

Received Foster's telegram. Please report which leading party comrades
support his views. I am somewhat disturbed by the new theoretical, political and tactical positions you are developing. Are you not going too far in
adapting to the altered international situation, even to the point of denying
the theory and practice of class struggle and the necessity for the working
class to have its own independent political party? Please reconsider all of
this and report your thoughts. Confirm receipt of this message.

[. . .]

· 9 MARCH 1944 ·

—Sent *Molotov* the foll[owing] memo:

21 March 1944 marks the 150th anniversary of the Kościuszko uprising.[436] Reactionary Polish circles in England, the USA, and other countries
will undoubtedly attempt to make use of this occasion for anti-Soviet purposes. In order to paralyze that campaign by the Polish reaction and to

---

Shanghai; member of the Profintern Executive Committee (from 1925 on); member of the CPC CC and Politburo (from 1927 on); secretary-general of the Chinese
Trade Union Federation (1927). Effective leader of the CPC (after 1928), during
the Third Period Li called for a general insurrection against the Guomindang. He
was denounced for his failed "putschist line" by the Comintern and was removed
from the leadership of the CPC in November 1930. In the USSR (1931–1945), Li
was briefly arrested during the Stalinist purges. After going back to China in 1945,
Li was a member of the CPC CC (from 1945 on), vice president of the Trade Union
Federation (from 1948 on), People's Republic of China minister of labor (1949–
1956), and secretary of the North China bureau of the CPC CC (from 1962 on).
Persecuted and tortured during the Cultural Revolution as the leader of a "Soviet
spy ring," he died in prison.

436. The 1794 Polish uprising against the partitioning powers—Russia and
Prussia—led by the Polish patriot Tadeusz Kościuszko.

demonstrate the Soviet Union's friendly disposition toward the Polish people, we consider it politically expedient to celebrate the 150th anniversary of the Kościuszko uprising in our country as well. We therefore support the request of the Central Bureau of Polish Communists to carry out the following measures on the 150th anniversary of the Kościuszko uprising:

1. Run several articles in the Soviet press by the Centr[al] Bureau of Polish Communists over the signatures of responsible Polish antifascist activists.

2. Hold a joint commemorative meeting of the All-Slavic Committee and the Union of Polish Patriots in observance of the anniversary.

3. Organize a radio concert of Polish music.

The campaign should be based on the following fundamental propositions:

The regime that Kościuszko opposed was overthrown by the people who founded and now govern the great Soviet state, people who are the true friends of Poland. The descendants of those who did the bidding of tsarism, who betrayed Kościuszko and are now betraying Poland, have posts in the government-in-exile and through their anti-Soviet campaign are aiding the sworn enemy of Poland, Hitlerite fascism.

$$[\ldots]$$

· 11 MARCH 1944 ·
$$[\ldots]$$

—*Proposal regarding the 150th anniversary of the Kościuszko rebellion* has been approved. Assigned Manuilsky and Baranov[437] to carry out the measures we planned.

· 12 MARCH 1944 ·
$$[\ldots]$$

—Received from Sofia (via Fitin) the following messages:

I.

1. We are doing everything in our power to obtain arms locally; however, this remains difficult and time-consuming and is not meeting all our needs.

Apart from obtaining arms locally, we mainly require machine guns, for the enemy is well organized and armed.

2. Please inform us of the manner in which we are to be rendered aid via Yu-

---

437. Leonid Semyonovich Baranov (b. 1909), Soviet Communist; deputy chief of the OMI; deputy chief of the foreign policy section at the VKP(b) CC; chief of the Cominform office (after 1947).

goslavia and to whom meeting places and passwords are to be divulged in order to receive that aid.

3. Report whether it would be correct at present to propagandize your name as leader of the Bulgarian people? To date we have been speaking of you only as leader of the party.

4. Send military specialists to our main staff to direct immediate operations in the cities: Plovdiv, Sofia, Shumen, Gabrovo, Sliven, and Pleven.

5. Also send as soon as possible two radio operators and code for communications with you.

6. We have *Dramaliev*[438] and *Pashov*[439] representing us in the Fatherland Front. The work of the Fatherland Front committee has taken the form of issuing several leaflets and leading the popular struggle in the localities.

7. Radio Hristo Botev is heard in the province[s]; it is being jammed in Sofia, and therefore reception is difficult. The programming is having a good influence; the crucial information is being reproduced by organizations in their own press. The number of wavelengths carrying the programs ought to be increased, as should the power of the transmitter. Programs at 23:30 are not being heard; programming at this hour can be discontinued. It would be desirable to transmit more facts concerning the expansion of the mass popular struggle against the German invaders.

It would be desirable for you and C[omrade] Kolarov to make more frequent [radio] appearances.

8. If possible tell me news of my son Boris Petrovich Liubimov; in 1938 he was a pilot in Tambov.

—Petŭr.[440]

II.

We report data on the numerical strength of the partisan detachments:

In *Sofia Province* there are three detachments, numbering in toto up to 200 men, deployed in Dupnitsa, Trŭnsko, Botevgrad and Ihtiman.

In *Plovdiv Province* there are three detachments, numbering in toto 800 men, located in the Sredna Gora region and in the Rhodopes.

438. Kiril Dramaliev (1892–1961), Bulgarian Communist; BRP representative in the Fatherland Front (OF); member BKP CC (from 1947 on); minister of education (1947–1952).

439. Ivan Pashov (1881–1955), Bulgarian Communist; BRP representative in the OF; member of various BRP/BRP(k)/BKP leading bodies.

440. Pseudonym of Dobri Terpeshev (1884–1967), Bulgarian Communist; member and organizational secretary of the BRP CC (1938–1941); member of the BRP/BRP(k)/BKP Politburo (1943–1950); chief of Bulgariet's planning commision (1944–1950).

In *Pazardzhik Province* there are three detachments, numbering 150 men, deployed in the Panagiurishte, Peshtera, and Chepino regions.

In *Macedonia*—one detachment of 100 men, located in the region of Gorna Dzhumaia, Razlog, and Petrich.

In *Sliven Province* there are three detachments, numbering 200 men, deployed in the region of Burgas, Sliven, and Yambol.

In *Stara Zagora Province* there is one detachment of 50 men, deployed in the region of Stara Zagora, Kazanlŭk, and Gŭlŭbovo.

In *Haskovo Province* there is one detachment of 20 men; its area of operations: Haskovo, Harmanli, and Kŭrdzhali.

In *Gabrovo Province*: two detachments, numbering 200 men, located in the region of Gabrovo, Sevlievo, and G[orna] Oriahovitsa.

In *Pleven Province*: three detachments, numbering 200 men; area of operations: Pleven, Lovech, and Cherven-briag.

In *Shumen Province*: two detachments numbering 180 men; area of operations: Shumen, Omurtag, and Tŭrgovishte.

In *Varna Province*: two detachments numbering 40 men; area of operations: Varna, Dobrich, and Provadiia.

In *Vratsa Province*: two detachments, numbering 180 men; area of operations: Vratsa, Sogarina, Ferdinand, Oriahovo, Vidin, and Lom.

In all there are twenty-six detachments numbering a total of 2,320 men. The partisan detachments are constantly growing in numbers and in future will grow to be a great force.

In the partisan detachments 25–30 percent are Communists, as many again are Komsomol members, and the remaining 30 percent are nonparty.

By age group, the detachments are composed basically of youth; 70–75 percent of them are rural poor; about 20 percent are working-class, and the rest are from the intelligentsia.

The organizational structure of the partisan detachments is as follows: at the center is the main staff, next come the staffs of provinces, regions, and detachments. At the head of the detachment are the commander, the commissar, and the chief of staff. Commanders and commissars are appointed from among people (Communist[s]) from the same provinces. We are experiencing a severe shortage of military cadres.

The activities of these detachments are as follows: temporary occupation of an inhabited locality; organization of assemblies, rallies, and demonstrations; destruction of provisions and goods laid up for the Germans and the government; disarming and destruction of police and other enemies.

Several diversions have been carried out against railroads and other lines of German communications.

The partisans have through their combat operations won the warm sympathies of every stratum of the population, especially among the peasantry. —Petrov. [?]

[. . .]

· 3 1 MARCH 1944 ·

—*Manuilsky:* reported on current business.

Telegram from *Bogomolov* in Naples:

Ercoli [Togliatti] has arrived and begun working. Saw Bogomolov on 28 March, together with Thorez and Reale.[441]

· 1 APRIL 1944 ·

—Received following telegram from *Mao Zedong* through *Ilichev's* network:

Dear Com[rade] Dimitrov!

I received your telegram of 26 February. Very pleased.

In this telegram I will set out for you the situation as regards relations between the CPC and the KMT [Guomindang] in the recent period.

1. In August, September, and October of last year the KMT, taking advantage of the dissolution of the Comintern, commenced a broad campaign for dissolving the Chinese Commun[ist] Party.

Simultaneously, after assembling large armed forces at its borders, it began threatening the Special Region. Chiang Kai-shek assumed at the time that all these measures would inevitably bring about a schism within the CPC. However, our party as a result drew together and became stronger.

We assumed a firm position, both as regards the campaign he had launched for the dissolution of the CPC and as regards his military threat.

This position of ours compelled the KMT at its eleventh plenum in September of last year to pass a resolution stating the possibility of resolving all issues between the CPC and the KMT by political means.

At this point we published a declaration of our own, in which we welcomed this statement by the eleventh plenum of the KMT.

2. In December of last year at the Cairo Conference, Roosevelt conveyed to Chiang Kai-shek the necessity of maintaining unity between the KMT and the CPC and of preventing armed conflict between them.

From 3 August through December of last year various articles were published in the Soviet and American press directed mainly against schism [or] armed conflict between the CPC and KMT [and] favoring their unity.

All of this taken together was a great help to us.

3. *Chiang Kai-shek,* in conversation with our representatives in Chongqing in December of last year, made a request to send our representative Dong Biwu[442] from Yan'an to Chongqing for a meeting and negotiations with him.

441. Eugenio Reale (b. 1905), Italian Communist; member of the PCI CC; headed the PCI's southern center (1943–1944); head of the PCI's international department (after 1948).

442. Dong Biwu (1886–1975), Chinese Communist leader; founding member

4. In January of this year Chiang Kai-shek ordered Hu Zongnan[443] to ease the situation around the Special Region. Accordingly, Hu Zongnan in February issued orders to the troops under him to suspend preparations for an armed attack on the Special Region. Simultaneously, on his orders four of the most battle-ready infantry divisions were withdrawn from the borders of the Special Region and replaced with four second-rate, less battle-ready infantry divisions.

5. We elected to send a representative of the Special Region government, *Lin Boqu,*[444] to Chongqing for negotiations with Chiang Kai-shek. The latter welcomed these measures. Lin Boqu leaves in early April.

6. At a press conference in Chongqing, foreign correspondents put various questions to the KMT representative concerning the Special Region and the PRA [People's Revolutionary Army]: what their situation is, what the KMT's policy regarding them is, and so on.

In February a group of foreign correspondents addressed a letter to Chiang Kai-shek requesting his permission for a trip to the Special Region.

No matter how displeased Chiang Kai-shek may have been with that letter, he was nevertheless compelled to grant his permission for that trip. But he also ordered a group of his own people to accompany those correspondents to the Special Region.

There are representatives of America, England, Canada, and Australia in that investigative group of foreign correspondents, ten persons in all.

For our part, we welcome the arrival of this group. It should arrive in Yan'an roughly in early April.

7. Roosevelt has expressed the wish to appoint his own military representative to the Special Region to investigate the situation in the PRA.

Chiang Kai-shek is clearly displeased at being confronted with this question. It remains for now an open one, unresolved.

---

of the CPC; head of the CPC's Hubei regional committee; student at the Comintern's Sun Yat-sen University and the Leninist School (1928–1932); member of the Central Executive Committee of the Jianxi Soviet and president of the soviet's supreme court; veteran of the Long March; CPC representative in Chongqing during the War of Resistance against Japan; member of the CPC CC Politburo; chairman of the people's government of North China (1948–1949); president of the supreme people's court (1954–1959); chairman of the People's Republic of China (1968–1975).

443. Hu Zongnan (1896–1962), Chinese Guomindang general; deputy commander, acting commander, and chief of staff of Guomindang Southwest Military and Administrative Headquarters.

444. Lin Boqu (1886–1960), Chinese Communist; member of the Guomindang and the CPC; student in the USSR beginning in 1927; chairman after the Long March of the Shaanxi-Gansu-Ningxia border region government at Yan'an (1937–1948); secretary-general of the Central People's Government Council (1949–1954); member of the CPC CP (1938–1960) and its Politburo (1945–1960).

8. Throughout last year, the KMT carried out only two major operations against the Japanese by way of military actions: the first in the Yichang region, the second in the Changde region.

But even these operations were imposed on the Guomindang army by the Japanese, who initiated offensives.

The battle-readiness of the Guomindang army is deteriorating day by day. America is expressing its displeasure with this passiveness on the part of the Guomindang army.

The armed forces of the CPC have firmly engaged 58 percent of Japan's entire army in China and more than 90 percent of its marionette troops.

In view of these circumstances America wishes to use our armed forces to deliver a blow to the Japanese army during a counteroffensive.

9. We for our part strongly wish that the American government would promote a favorable resolution of the problem of CPC-KMT relations.

At the same time, we also strongly wish that America would render us assistance in arms and ammunition, for which we are experiencing an urgent need.

If there is any opportunity, please inform Browder of this and ask him to assist us in this area. China has a hope of a counteroffensive against Japan.
23 March 1944

Mao Zedong.

[. . .]

· 16 APRIL 1944 ·

—Sent *Stalin* and (*Molotov*) the following letter:

In connection with the telegram dated 13 April 1944 from C[omrade] Korneev[445] (head of the Soviet mission to Yugoslavia), please bear in mind the following explanation:

1. We did not receive from Walter [Tito] prior to the session of the Antifascist Council [AVNOJ] a roster of the composition of the council and of the national committee, and therefore he was unable to receive from us [any advice or instructions?] regarding this issue or the rejection of Vlahov's candidacy.

When it became known that Vlahov had been elected to the council presidium and Tomov [Poptomov] to the council as representatives from Macedonia, I, acting on behalf of the Bulg[arian] Com[munist] Party, indicated to C[omrade] Walter [Tito] that Vlahov and Tomov [Poptomov], members of the Bulg[arian] Com[munist] Party, are known in Bulgaria as

---

445. Nikolai Vasilievich Korneev (1900–1976), Soviet general; head of the Soviet mission to Yugoslavia (1944–1945). After the war he served in the USSR's Ministry of Defense and at the Red Army General Staff Academy.

Bulgarian Communists; Vlahov was in the civil service for many years, and Tomov [Poptomov was] a deputy in the parliament from the Bulgarian Com[munist] Party; moreover, it has been quite some time since either had any connection with Macedonia, and both live in emigration, for which reason it would be politically inexpedient to have them in the Yugoslav council, and I conveyed my request that, should he find it possible, he quietly and inconspicuously annul this unfortunate step.

Com[rade] Walter [Tito] replied that he agreed, that he considered this a chance omission, and that he would take measures to rectify it.

Recently, when Vlahov was listed in C[omrade] Korneev's information as deputy chairman of the council, I reminded C[omrade] Walter [Tito] of his assurances regarding the removal of Vlahov from the council and inquired about how matters really stood with Vlahov's participation on the council presidium.

2. As for the question of Macedonia itself, the Bulgarian Communist Party has taken and still maintains the following position:

a) The Com[munist] Party is opposed to the forced annexation of Macedonia to Bulgaria and the occupation of Macedonia by Bulgarian and German troops.

b) The Com[munist] Party advocates the cessation of all hostilities against Yugoslavia and the People's Liberation Army and the immediate recall of the Bulgarian occupation corps from Yugoslavia; while units of this corps remain on Yugoslav territory, they ought to fight against the German occupiers together with units of the People's Liberation Army of Yugoslavia.

c) The Com[munist] Party considers that the question of the future of Macedonia can be correctly settled only on the basis of a fraternal accord between Bulgaria and Yugoslavia, taking into account the interests and will of Macedonia's own populace and with the assistance of the Soviet Union, but this presupposes Bulgaria's breaking with Hitlerite Germany and joining Yugoslavia in the fight to drive the German invaders out of Bulgaria.

This is the position that I set forth in my article in *Pravda*. I have given the Bulgarian comrades directives along these lines, which are being carried out in the country. Com[rade] Walter [Tito] is of course mistaken in his suspicions of C[omrade] Kolarov, since it is not he but I who personally maintain contact with the Bulgarian Com[munist] Party, and apart from me no one gives it advice or directives.

3. I am personally entirely in agreement with C[omrade] Walter [Tito] that in the current situation it is absolutely inadmissible for Communists to argue among themselves over questions of their countries' future borders and territories, and that Communists must pursue a single line providing for their concerted struggle against the German invaders.

4. One could hardly say definitively at present just what is to become of Macedonia after the war, and I will not presume to do so myself. Everything

will depend on various still-unknown factors. The most desirable orientation for the Balkans and for the Soviet Union, in my opinion, would be the establishment of a federation of South Slavs consisting of Bulgars, Serbs, Croats, Slovenes, Montenegrins and Macedonians all on an equal footing. In such a federation, Macedonia could obtain its national freedom and statehood and would cease to be the apple of discord among the Balkan states.

However, speaking about this publicly and propagandizing such a slogan at this point is, in my view, premature and perhaps even harmful.

[. . .]

· 19 APRIL 1944 ·

—Manuilsky was in to see me. Reported on progress of our business. Informed me that in connection with Korneev's telegram, a reply was made to Tito, roughly as follows:

1. The Vlahov question was not discussed here; resolve it in whatever way you find necessary.

2. Generally, all political questions involving Yugoslavia will be settled by *Alekseev's* [Molotov's] network.

3. Bulgaria has indeed caused us a great deal of harm, but if it withdraws from the war, we have an interest in having it as an ally.

4. The Macedonian question will be discussed here. Provided it is resolved after the war, our attitude toward Yugoslavia will be most favorable.

[. . .]

· 22 APRIL 1944 ·
[. . .]

—Vlahov on the Macedonian question. Explained to him in detail:

—"The Macedonian nation" or the *Macedonian populace!* (Bulgars, Mac[edonians], Slavs, Greeks, Serbs.)

—"Macedonian *national* consciousness"? (*Where* and *how* does it exist?)

—Is Macedonia capable of existing as a *separate* state?

—Federation of South Slavs (Bulgars, Serbocroats, Montenegrins, Slovenes, and Macedonians).

—In that federation Maced[onia] could obtain its freedom and statehood, despite the ethnograph[ic] conglomeration that it represents.

[. . .]

· 24 APRIL 1944 ·

—Molotov reported that the Sov[iet] gov[ern]ment has made Bulgaria a strict démarche: put an end to the use of Bulgarian communications, and so on, by the Germans against the Sov[iet] Union.

The Bulgarian gov[ern]ment's reply is expected tomorrow. Mol[o-tov]: "What do you think?" I: "Keep up the pressure!" "Right!"

[. . .]

· 28 APRIL 1944 ·

—Morozov on liaison issues. Gave him various new instructions, particularly on reinforcing liaison with Duclos and Raymond [Guyot] in France, establishing liaison with Greece, and securing reliable air transport to Yugoslavia for Marek's [Stanke Dimitrov's] group.

· 29 APRIL 1944 ·

—Meeting of the Bulg[arian] For[eign] Bureau (Kolarov, Marek [Stanke Dimitrov], Belov [Damianov], Chervenkov). *Djilas* was asked to report on the organization of the CP of Yugoslavia and its methods and modes of operating in conditions of the national liberation struggle against the German occupiers.

Djilas recounted a great deal that Bulg[arian] Communists, too, would find interesting and useful.

· 30 APRIL 1944 ·

—*Dolores [Ibárruri] and Blagoeva to see me.*

I gave Dolores new information regarding Hernández in Mexico.

We agreed on sending the following enciphered telegram from Dolores, Líster, and Modesto:

To Uribe, Mije,[446] *[Francisco] Antón* (to be shared with *Hernández* as well):

1. We have received your message regarding Hernández.
2. Although, on the basis of recent reliable information on Hernández's dis-

446. Antonio Mije (1905–1976), Spanish Communist; member of the PCE CC Politburo and a CC secretary (from 1932 on); deputy general commissar of the Spanish Republican army (1936–1939); member of the PCE foreign center in Mexico (1939–1945).

loyal conduct while still in Moscow, we are willing to grant that he has manifested such conduct still more flagrantly while in Mexico, nevertheless we categorically advise utterly avoiding any exacerbation of the conflict pending a final resolution of the matter by the CC of the party. Everything possible must be done on your part to influence and help Hernández to refrain from any statements and actions that might compromise the unity of the party, which is so needed at present.

3. We consider Mije's coming here inadvisable in the current situation.

[. . .]

· 5 MAY 1944 ·

—*Manuilsky and Thorez* regarding *Thorez* (de Gaulle, considering him a deserter from the French army, is not letting him come to Algeria).

Advised Thorez to: 1) draft a telegram for de Gaulle with a copy to our members in the national committee; 2) write a letter to the CC bureau in Algiers debunking the myth of Thorez's desertion; 3) make regular appearances on Sov[iet] foreign radio broadcasts to France; 4) investigate the possibility of being clandestinely transported into France.

[. . .]

· 10 MAY 1944 ·

—Received, together with *Marek* [Stanke Dimitrov], four Bulgarian comrades: *Gilevich,* Tsveinski, Sitev, *Katsarov.*[447] We discussed in detail the situation in Bulgaria, the tasks of our party, the Fatherland Front and part[isan] movement. Instructed them thoroughly regarding their work in Yugoslavia, Macedonia, and Bulgaria.

[. . .]

· 20 MAY 1944 ·

—*Meeting* of the For[eign] Bureau (Kolarov, Chervenkov, Belov [Damianov]). Examined the situation in Bulgaria in connection with the resignation of the Bozhilov government.[448] Remarks over foreign radio

447. Gilevich, Ivan Tsveinski (1902–1944), Ilia Sitev; Petko Katsarov (b. 1905), all Bulgarian Communist political émigrés to the USSR.

448. Dobri Bozhilov (1884–1945), Bulgarian politician; minister of finances (1938–1943); premier of Bulgaria (1943–1944). He was tried and executed after the war.

by Bulg[arian] comrades (Kolarov, Chervenkov, Belov [Damianov], and others) were approved.

Called Molotov regarding the request from the Amer[ican] agency Associated Press for an interview with me on Balkan issues. Informed him that I did not consider it advisable at present to grant such an interview and that I would let the agency's letter go unanswered. He was of the same opinion.

Molot[ov] informed me that the Sov[iet] government had issued the Bulg[arian] gov[ern]ment a fourth note in which it insisted on the opening of So[viet] consulates in Varna, Burgas, and Ruschuk and declared that if the Bulg[arian] gov[ern]ment did not meet this demand, the Sov[iet] Union could no longer maintain its diplomatic relations with Bulgaria. "We have put up with the Bulg[arian] gov[ern]ment's aiding the Germans against us under the guise of dipl[omatic] relations for long enough. In all likelihood we will in the immediate future break off diplomatic relations and declare a state of war with Bulgaria. We are convinced that preserving these relations is hindering the development of the anti-Hitler movement in the country."

[. . .]

· 26 MAY 1944 ·
[. . .]

First time since the war began that I have not been getting a radio connection to the Yugoslav comrades (yesterday and today). Very disconcerting. Causes are being investigated.[449]

· 27 MAY 1944 ·

—*Manuilsky* to see me. Reported on Polish affairs and other matters. No radio connection, either, with Yugoslavia today (either through their own lines or through the Sov[iet] mission to Yugosl[avia]).

Rumors of a German raid at Tito's headquarters . . .

[. . .]

449. On 25 May 1944 the Germans initiated a powerful attack against Tito's headquarters at Drvar (western Bosnia). The aim was to kill or capture the top KPJ leaders. Tito managed to escape the German attack with members of the foreign missions. During the night of 3–4 June he flew on a Soviet plane from the Field of Kupres to Bari, Italy. He removed his headquarters to the island of Vis (Dalmatia) on 7 June 1944.

· 28 MAY 1944 ·
[. . .]

—It has been determined that the Germans did indeed raid Tito's headquarters. Fortunately, his staff and the Sov[iet] mission managed to retreat unharmed.

· 29 MAY 1944 ·

—Received new reports on the German raid on the territory of Tito's headquarters. All the top comrades managed to escape. A new base for a headquarters is being organized. An order by Tito for an offensive on all other sectors of the front to counter the Germans' main thrust.

[. . .]

· 1 JUNE 1944 ·
[. . .]

—*Ercoli* [Togliatti] has reported:

I am convinced that Badoglio loathes the English with a passion and that Badoglio could be effectively exploited while carrying out various measures if he were persuaded that the given measure would work against the English but be indispensable for Italy. Badoglio is more tolerant of the Americans and is not above flirting with them in order to weaken the English positions in Italy by temporarily strengthening the Americans' [positions]. Badoglio has maintained a pessimistic view of the prospects of the current Allied offensive on the Ital[ian] front from the very start. To this day he does not believe that the Anglo-Americans are soon going to liberate Rome.

In the opinion of Ercoli and Reale, the majority of the politicians with whom they come in contact believe that Rome will nevertheless soon be liberated.

According to the information of the deputy minister of war, the Communist Palermo, there are now twenty-eight thousand Ital[ian] soldiers at the front (instead of the fourteen thousand who were there until only a few days ago). Discipline in the forward units is satisfactory, [something] which cannot be said of the rear units. There is displeasure with the Anglo-Americans in the forward units, owing to their haughty attitude toward the Italian soldiers. A huge majority of the officers in both forward and rear units are former fascists. Communists enjoy great authority in the army. The Communist Palermo was met very warmly everywhere.

[. . .]

· 5 JUNE 1944 ·
[. . .]

Sent Stalin the following letter:

The Foreign Bureau of the Communist Party of Bulgaria has formulated the party's position as regards the Bagrianov[450] government, as follows:

1. It took two weeks for the German and Bulgarian fascists to agree on the composition of the new Bagrianov government. Those two-week birth pangs were the result of the profound crisis Bulgaria is experiencing, the disorder that obtains in the fascist camp owing to lack of faith in a German victory, and the growth of the anti-German movement in the country, and in the same connection, the unwillingness of every one of the more eminent Bulgarian politicians to join a pro-German government.

2. The Bagrianov government is essentially pro-German. The basic ministries (war, internal affairs, foreign affairs, railways, industry, and trade) are in the hands of inveterate Germanophiles (Bagrianov, General Rusev, Professor Stanishev, Kolchev, Vasilev). This government differs from the Bozhilov government in two characteristic particulars:

1. The leading group, headed by Bagrianov, is called on to carry out the very same pro-German policy, but more flexibly and intelligently than Bozhilov did.

2. The Bagrianov government also includes such outwardly presentable figures as Professor Arnaudov and Doncho Kostov, as well as a couple of other uncompromised Germanophiles. Their presence in the cabinet is a means of fostering illusions that the new government is not going to follow the Germans' orders blindly and that it will seek ways of preventing Bulgaria's participation in the war on the side of Germany against the Soviet Union. Thus, the Bagrianov government is better suited for carrying out a two-faced policy than was the bankrupt Bozhilov government.

3. The composition and nature of the Bagrianov government indicate an attempt to deceive the people temporarily, and if possible the Allies as well, to gain time and to paralyze as far as possible the expanding partisan movement and the growing discontent in the ranks of the army directed against the Germans. The Bagrianov government has been called on to solve an insoluble problem, namely, to sate the wolves but leave the sheep unharmed.[451] On the other hand, its existence, too, could prove only temporary and lead to further exacerbation of the crisis in Bulgaria.

4. Taking into account the anti-German sentiments among the people and in the army, the Bulgarian fascists and their German masters are desperate

---

450. Ivan Bagrianov (1891–1945), Bulgarian politician; minister of agriculture (1938–1941); premier of Bulgaria (1 June–1 September 1944). He was tried and executed after the war.

451. An idiomatic saying, equivalent to "to run with the hare and hunt with the hounds."

to have a Bulgarian government that would be able to secure the further implementation of a pro-German course, on the one hand, while preserving the mask of Bulgarian neutrality as regards the Soviet Union and maintaining diplomatic relations with it, on the other. It is better for the Germans to get what they need at the hands of Bulgaria's own rulers than to occupy Bulgaria directly, like Hungary, since the internal situation and sentiments of the people and army in Bulgaria are not what they were in Hungary before its occupation.

5. There can be no doubting that with the formation of the Bagrianov government, not only has the profound crisis Bulgaria is experiencing not been resolved, but there has not been even the slightest easing of that crisis. The causes of that crisis lie in the fact that the Bulg[arian] leaders are conducting an antipopular pro-German policy against the will of the Bulgarian people, that they have handed the country over to the Germans to the detriment of its own interests and future, that they are pushing the country toward a new and terrible catastrophe. This crisis can be resolved only through a break with Hitlerite Germany and through the consistent implementation of a Bulgarian national policy of cooperation with the Soviet Union and its allies. Such a resolution of the crisis can be promoted only by a genuinely Bulgarian national government expressing the will of the Bulgarian people and supported by the people and the army in the struggle to drive the Germans from Bulgarian territory.

6. Therefore the Com[munist] Party line calling for expansion of the partisan movement and joint struggle by partisan bands and patriots from the army against the German invaders is to remain in force even after the formation of the Bagrianov government. It is precisely now, when Bagrianov will be attempting various fraudulent and demagogic maneuvers within the country and abroad, especially as regards the Sov[iet] Union, that we must beware of playing into the hands of the Bulgarian fascists. We must safeguard the people now opposing the Germans against any illusions as regards the Bagrianov government and prevent any slackening of the people's liberation struggle. On the contrary, by exploiting confusion in the ranks of pro-German circles and the internal weakness and instability of the Bagrianov government, it is imperative to vigorously intensify the partisan movement and all other forms of the struggle for the immediate expulsion of the German bandits from Bulgarian territory.

· 6 JUNE 1944 ·

—*The Anglo-American invasion of France has commenced.* A major landing has been made between Cherbourg and the mouth of the Seine. At last—the second front! Now everything will depend on the speed and dimensions of the invasion . . .

[. . .]

· 16 JUNE 1944 ·

—*Thorez, Manuilsky, Baskakov,*[452] *Friedrich [Geminder], Stepanov [Minev]* to see me. Examined radio broadcasting to France in connection with the Anglo-Amer[ican] invasion.

Thorez was sharply criticized for being insufficiently active of late.

He was seriously advised to straighten up and provide leadership of radio broadcasting over Radio France and political liaisons with the CC of the French Communist Party and with comrades in Algeria.

[. . .]

· 20 JUNE 1944 ·
[. . .]

—Ercoli [Togliatti] reports:

Immediately after the Germans left, three thousand Communists emerged from the underground in Rome. The Com[munist] Party in Rome is growing rapidly. The large growth of the Com[munist] Party is evident everywhere (in particular, in Naples Province, including Naples, the Com[munist] Party numbers twenty-five thousand members). *Scoccimarro*[453] followed a basically correct line in Rome, but he took "a somewhat doctrinaire" approach to many issues. In Rome Ercoli [Togliatti] saw *Ermette* [Novella],[454] *Vignia* [Negarville],[455] *Platone, Massini, Di Vittorio,* and various other

452. S. Baskakov, on the staff of the VKP(b) CC.

453. Mauro Scoccimarro (pseudonyms: Silvestri, Negri, Marco, Morelli, 1895–1972), Italian Communist; member of the PCI CC (1922–1926, 1943–1972); alternate member of the ECCI (1924–1926) who was arrested on a secret mission in Italy and imprisoned (1926–1943); minister in the coalition governments of Bonomi, Parri, and de Gasperi (1944–1947); deputy and (from 1948 on) senator in the Italian parliament; member of the PCI directorate and Politburo; president of the PCI control commission.

454. Agostino Novella (pseudonym: Mario Ermette, 1905–1974), Italian Communist; member of the PCI Foreign Bureau in France (1940–1943); part of the PCI leadership after the war.

455. Celeste Negarville (1905–1958), Italian Communist; secretary of Turin's Federation of Young Communists (1924). He was imprisoned for Communist activity (1927–1934) before emigrating to France and the USSR. Member of the KIM Executive Committee and presidium (1935); member of the PCI Foreign Bureau in France. Once he returned to Italy in 1943, he was active in the Communist partisan movement. Head of PCI agitprop (from 1945 on); member of the PCI CC and PCI secretary for the Piedmont region (from 1945 on); undersecretary of state for foreign affairs (1945–1946); deputy in the Italian parliament and mayor of Turin (1946); member of the PCI directorate (1951–1956).

leadership workers. Throughout the country, but especially in newly liberated regions, large percentages of Com[munist] party members are believers. There are many believers among people newly joining the Com[munist] Party as well. Ercoli [Togliatti] is conducting his work in such a way as not to offend the religious feelings of these Communists and to ensure that work with them is conducted very tactfully, utterly avoiding any cheap agitation.

Throughout the rank and file of the Christian Democrats there are many members of that party who are close to the Communists, many so-called Christian Communists. In Rome the Christian Communists were singled out as a special group and the Christian Democratic party leadership expelled them from the party. That group never disintegrated; it is being reorganized into an independent party of Christian Communists; the group has its own newspaper. The pope has attacked the Christian Communists. He convoked delegations of workers to the Vatican and made speeches against the Christian Communists.

The number of small political parties in Italy grows with every passing day (Nenni,[456] monarchists, the Spartacists, and so on); it can be assumed that a significant number of them subsist on Anglo-American funds. The small parties are now militating for a ministerial post in a new cabinet to serve as representative of the small parties.

[. . .]

· 22 JUNE 1944 ·
[. . .]

—Spoke with Vyshinsky about the remarks of the Bulg[arian] comrades over foreign radio. I proposed *restoring* the page taken out of Chervenkov's remarks. Since I personally looked over the Bulg[arian] remarks, there is no reason for Narkomindel [the People's Commissariat for Foreign Affairs] (his staff) to alter them.

[. . .]

· 27 JUNE 1944 ·

—Manuilsky reported on Stalin's reception of a delegation from the Krajowa Rada Narodowa of Poland. The question of the future Polish

---

456. Pietro Nenni (1891–1980), Italian Socialist; veteran of the International Brigades in Spain; secretary-general (from 1943 on) of the Italian Socialist Party (PSI); deputy prime minister or minister of foreign affairs in several cabinets—in alliance with the PCI (1947–1956) and in coalition with Aldo Moro's Christian Democrats (1963–1969); president of the Italian Senate (after 1979).

government (possibly headed by Mikołajczyk,[457] who is supported by the Americans and the English, but with [the posts of] min[ister] of war, min[ister] of for[eign] affairs, and min[ister] of inter[nal] affairs filled by people supporting the Krajowa Rada [KRN]).

The delegation also met with the Amer[ican] and English ambassador[s].

[. . .]

· 10 JULY 1944 ·
[. . .]

Manuilsky to see me. We said our goodbyes. After twenty years of working together, he's transferring to a new post—in Ukraine (people's commissar of for[eign] affairs).

[. . .]

· 15 JULY 1944 ·
[. . .]

—Shtern[458] copied down the report from Sofia along with my reply to the CC of the Com[munist] Party of Bulgaria.

· 16 JULY 1944 ·

—Sent the following reply to Sofia via Fitin:

1. Received your report. I am surprised that you could let yourself be taken in by Bargrianov. You did promise, you know, that you would follow the directive programs of [Radio] Hristo Botev. And once the new government was formed, we expressed our negative view of Bagrianov over Hristo Botev the very next day. We broadcast and commented on our bas[ic] directive numerous times (the text of that directive is cited).

2. The assertion that Bagrianov intends to head toward a break with Germany, that he supposedly enjoys the confidence of the Sov[iet] government, that he has accepted the latter's demands, and so on, is all sheer bunk. While helping the Germans any way he can, Bagrianov is only using demagogic maneuvers to gain the time he needs to play out his pro-German role.

457. Stanisław Mikołajczyk (1901–1966), Polish politician; leader of the Peasant Party; premier of the Polish government-in-exile (1943–1945); vice premier and minister of agriculture of the post-Yalta Polish government. At odds with the Communists, he fled to the United States in 1947.

458. Asia Isaevna Shtern, Dimitrov's secretary.

The fact that the campaign in the Sov[iet] press has temporarily ceased indicates only that the Soviet friends of the Bulgarian people have armed themselves with a little more patience, but not any support of Bagrianov.

3. Taking all this into account, the party ought to cease immediately any and all negotiations with Bagrianov and swiftly rectify its gross political error. Expose by all available methods and means Bagrianov's demagogy and lies. Make every effort to influence our partners in the Fatherland Front as well in this regard. The essential thing is to expand the partisan movement against the Germans by all available means. Reinforce the party leadership and the leadership of part[isan] detachments and their staffs. Carry out joint combat actions with the units of Tito's army.

4. Secure a direct radio connection with us at last, and also monitor and use Radio Hr[isto] B[otev] and the people's voice over official Sofia and Skopje radio.

5. We have sent you a group of Bulg[arian] comrades from Yugosl[avia]. Their first assignment is to establish a route between Yug[oslavia] and Bulg[aria] for transport of men and arms. As soon as this difficult task has been accomplished, it will be possible to send armaments for our part[isan] detachments. Report immediately where and how these comrades of ours could get in touch [with you] in the border regions. Confirm receipt of this message. We impatiently await your reply and fur[ther] information.

—Invited Lieutenant General Ilichev and Lieutenant Gen[eral] Korneev (head of our military mission to Yugoslavia).

—Korneev reported in detail on the situation in Yugoslavia and relayed information from Tito to me.

· 17 JULY 1944 ·

—*Meeting of the Foreign Bureau of the CP of Bulg[aria]* (Kolarov, Marek [Stanke Dimitrov], Chervenkov, Belov [Damianov]).

Briefed them on Tito's letter and his critical remarks regarding the practical operations of the Bulg[arian] Com[munist] Party.[459]

[. . .]

459. Tito sent a sharp letter to Dimitrov at the beginning of July from his headquarters on the island of Vis. He charged that the BRP line "was and still remains incorrect on the question of liberation struggle." In Tito's opinion, the BRP was creating illusions about the Bulgarian army, displayed lack of initiative in the Fatherland Front, held incorrect views on Macedonia (in basically overlooking the fact that the Macedonian question was being resolved *within* Yugoslavia), and avoided armed struggle: "It is not true, as the Bulgarian comrades from the CC al-

· 25 JULY 1944 ·
[. . .]

—Received detailed telegram from *Mao Zedong* on the situation in China, particularly the Special Region.

The arrival of foreign correspondents in Yan'an. An Amer[ican] military mission is expected to be attached to Mao Zedong's army. Chiang Kai-shek was compelled to consent at last to the Americans' sending such a mission.

· 26 JULY 1944 ·
[. . .]

—Sent Tito the foll[owing] encoded telegr[am]:

Received your letter. Thank you very much, especially for the critical comments as regards the Bulg[arian] Com[mmunist] Party. In the main, your comments are completely correct. Especially concerning the expansion of the partisan movement and its growing into a general people's uprising against the German occupiers. I have often drawn the attention of our Bulg[arian] comrades to their errors, deficiencies and shortcomings. In particular, I gave the following instructions concerning the Macedonian question: 1) rigorously oppose the Germano-Bulgarian occupation of Macedonia; 2) fully support the Macedonian policy of a new federated Yugoslavia granting equality of rights to the Macedonians; 3) avoid all disputes over questions of territories and the future borders of the Balkan states; 4) follow a united line of struggle by Bulg[arian], Yugosl[av], and Greek Communists against the German occupiers; 5) bear in mind that a correct resolution of territorial issues in the Balkans following the war is possible only on the basis of a common struggle by the peoples of Yugoslavia, Bulgaria, and Greece, together with the Macedonians, for the liberation of the Balkans from the Germans, on the basis of fraternal cooperation among these peoples, first and foremost the closest possible friendship between the new democr[atic] Bulgaria and the new Democr[atic] Federated Yugoslavia as Slavic states and with the assistance of the great Sov[iet] Union.

I consider that there can be no question of taking Yugoslav Macedonia away from Yugoslavia after the enormous sacrifices that the peoples of Yugoslavia have borne and continue to bear in their war against the common enemy.

As you yourself note, the situation with the Bulgarian party is already im-

---

ways said, that there were no conditions in Bulgaria for the undertaking of a people's uprising by way of the organization of partis[an] detachments, etc."

proved. But a great deal must still be done along these lines. The chief problem is that the p[arty] leadership is rather deficient, although it is composed of very dedicated persons. You are probably aware that many of the best leaders, beginning with the secretary of the CC Anton Ivanov, were executed. As many as ten thousand party members, the majority of them valuable activists, are in prisons and concentration camps. Therefore, along with necessary advice on rectifying the party's tactics, the first order of business is to reinforce the leadership in the center and in the localities. We are sending people for the purpose, who, together with Georgiev [Atanasov] and Vinarov,[460] should make their way to the country as soon as possible. I have no doubt that you will render the necessary assistance in this regard, as well as in establishing reliable communications between the CC of the Bulgarian Com[munist] Party and your own CC. As soon as it becomes possible to do so, I would urge you to send a suitable delegate of your own, who would be attached to the Bulgarian CC, in order to assist the Bulg[arian] comrades directly with your rich experience in the national-liberation struggle.

Our delegate Marek [Stanke Dimitrov] will inform you in detail about the measures we are taking to put Bulgarian affairs in order.

I would be most grateful if in future you would regularly inform me of your views and comments on the activities of the Bulgarian Com[mmunist] Party.

I have forwarded your letters to Comrades Stalin and Molotov.

I grasp your hand firmly!

(s[igned]) D[imitrov]

[. . .]

· 15 AUGUST 1944 ·
[. . .]

—Conferred with *Molot[ov]* on the inquiries from the Politburo of the CC of the CP of Greece. They are to resolve the questions they raised themselves.

[. . .]

· 16 AUGUST 1944 ·
[. . .]

—Received *Gottwald* and *Šmidke*[461] regarding Slovakia.

—Instructions sent to Kiev not to send part[isan] detachments to Slo-

460. Ivan Vinarov (1896–1969), Bulgarian Communist; worker in Soviet intelligence; general of the Bulgarian army.

461. Karel Šmidke (1897–1952), Czechoslovak Communist; political émigré

vakia for now—pending resolution of the general question of joint action by Slov[ak] army and the Red Army against the Germans in Slovakia.

$$[\ldots]$$

· 24 AUGUST 1944 ·

—Received Pauker (with Mirov)[462] in connection with events in Romania.[463] Gave various advice for Romanian comrades.

—Regular review of int[ernational] inform[ation] with the consultants.

—Baranov reported on his meeting with Polish comrades *Bierut*[464] and *Wiesław* [Gomułka]. The latter absolutely insisted on meeting with me personally to discuss Polish affairs.

—Sent *Stal[in]* and *Molot[ov]* text of the directive to the CC of the Com[munist] Party of Bulgaria.

· 25 AUGUST 1944 ·

—At the dacha received the chairman of the Polish Krajowa Rada, *Bierut,* and Secretary of the PPR Gomułka (Wiesław) on Polish issues.

---

to the USSR (1939–1943); head of the Slovak branch of the KSČ (1944–1945); chief of staff of the partisan detachments of Slovakia (1944); deputy chairman (1945–1946) and chairman (1948–1950) of the Slovak National Council.

462. Yakov Tsodikovich Mirov-Rozkin (b. 1894), Soviet Communist on the staff of ECCI; editor and secretary (1939–1943) responsible for the journal *Kommunisticheskii Internatsional*; staff member of OMI; Dimitrov's assistant (1945–1948).

463. As the Red Army proceeded toward Romania, on 23 August 1944 King Michael dismissed the cabinet of Gen. Ion Antonescu and accepted the terms of armistice proffered by the Allies. The Red Army reached the capital, Bucharest, by 31 August.

464. Bolesław Bierut (pseudonyms: Iwaniuk, Tomasz, 1892–1956); Polish Communist leader. He was at the Comintern's Leninist School (1928–1930). He undertook various Comintern missions in the early 1930s. After being imprisoned in Poland (1933–1939), he was in the USSR for a time after 1939. President (1944–1947) of the National Home Council (KRN); president (1947–1952) and prime minister (1952–1954) of Poland; secretary-general, chairman, and first secretary of the PZRP; Politburo member (1948–1956).

—*At the* CC.

—Received Pauker on Rom[anian] affairs.

—Rákosi: on Hung[arian] affairs.

—Instructed *Marek's* [Stanke Dimitrov's] group being sent to Bulgaria via Yugoslavia (Marek [Stanke Dimitrov], Lavrov, Nikolov, Antonov, Krŭstev, Afanasiev [Gavril Atanasov], Tsveinski).

[. . .]

· 28 August 1944 ·

—Received Šmidke, Gottwald, and Šverma on Slovak and Czech affairs.

[. . .]

· 29 August 1944 ·

—Received *Gottwald* regarding recent reports from Slovakia.[465]

[. . .]

· 30 August 1944 ·
[. . .]

—Looked over *Vlahov's* article on the Maced[onian] question for the journal *Slaviane*. Made various substantive corrections.

[. . .]

· 1 September 1944 ·
[. . .]

—Received Vlahov regarding his article for *Slaviane* (it contains serious errors) and in connection with his trip to Yugoslavia.

[. . .]

—Gave Friedrich [Geminder] instructions for stepping up unoffic[ial] radio broadcasting to Slovakia in connection with the anti-German rebellion that is under way.

---

465. On 29 August 1944, in expectation of a Red Army advance, the Slovak National Council, in which the Communists participated, commenced an uprising in Banská Bystrica, central Slovakia, against the collaborationist Slovak state and its German allies. After two months of bitter struggle the insurgents were overwhelmed. Banská Bystrica fell to the Germans on 27 October 1944.

—Heard Gottwald's report on the conference with the authorized agents of the Czechoslovak government who have come to Moscow.

Directed him to write a *memo* about events in Slovakia and the position of the CP of Czechoslovakia and a *factual* article for the Sov[iet] press on the Slovaks' struggle against the Germans.

· 2 SEPTEMBER 1944 ·

—Manuilsky (in to see me wearing a colonel's uniform). Flown in from Kiev in connection with negotiations with the Romanian delegation.

[. . .]

—Sent *Molotov* a letter on the need to expedite a decision on our possibly aiding the Slovaks.

[. . .]

—Belov [Damianov]: on Bulg[arian] affairs (a new government has been formed from the bourg[eois] opposition).[466]

· 3 SEPTEMBER 1944 ·

—Sunday.

—*Kolarov, Chervenkov, Belov* [Damianov] here at Meshcherino. Discussed situation in connection with the formation of a new Bulgarian government (the Muraviev government). The directive I proposed was accepted. Dictated an article to Chervenkov (directive article) for [Radio] Hristo Botev.

—Wrote *Stal[in]* and *Molot[ov]* a characterization of the new government and formulated our directive regarding the need to form a Fatherland Front government.

[. . .]

· 5 SEPTEMBER 1944 ·

—Molotov called about the break with Bulgaria and the declaration by the USSR of a state of war. We exchanged views on the contents of the note to the Bulgarian government.

---

466. The new government was headed by Konstantin Muraviev (1893–1965), an Agrarian leader, who was a minister in prewar governments (1923, 1931–1934). He was sentenced to life imprisonment after the war.

—Sent *Stal[in]* and *Molot[ov]* the reports I had received from the party CC in Sofia.

—Sent Molot[ov] our proposal regarding tasks of the trade union delegation from the USSR leaving for Italy.

—At 9:00 p.m. Molotov's note as regards Bulgaria was proclaimed over radio.

—Called a meeting of the Foreign Bureau (Kolarov, Chervenkov, Belov [Damianov]) before the proclamation of the note.

—Drafted a directive article for Radio Hristo Botev and directives for the CC in Sofia.

—Selected personnel (Bulg[arians]) for the PUR [the Red Army Political Directorate].

—A group of Bulgarians was selected for transport to Bulgaria.

—Assigned Kolarov to write a draft appeal to the Bulg[arian] people on behalf of the Bulg[arian] publ[ic] figures here in the USSR.

[. . .]

· 6 SEPTEMBER 1944 ·

—We spent the night at Government House.

—Regular informational review with department staff.

—Sent *Stal[in]* and *Molot[ov]* [my] memo on the Muraviev-Mushanov-Gichev-Burov government considering it inadequate to the tasks currently facing the Bulg[arian] people and therefore capable of lasting a very brief period.

—Gave Radio Hristo Botev detailed instructions regarding programming at the present time.

· 7 SEPTEMBER 1944 ·

—D. Zakharych [Manuilsky] and Ana Pauker to see me regarding Pauker's departure for Romania.

—Arranged with Shcherbakov to have *Luka László*[467] (CC mem[ber]

467. Luka László (pseudonym: Vasile Luca, 1898–1963; real name: László Lukács), Romanian Communist leader; secretary of the PCR regional committees in Braşov (1924–1929) and Iaşi (1932–1933). He was imprisoned (1933–1940) but released by the Soviet troops after the occupation of Northern Bukovina (1940) and sent to Moscow for party work. Member Romanian CP CC and its Politburo (1945–1952); minister of finance (1947–1952). He was dismissed in 1952, arrested and sentenced to death in 1954; the sentence was commuted to life imprisonment, and he was posthumously rehabilitated in 1968.

of the CP of Romania) relieved of duty in the army for work in Romania.

—Director of the Diplom[atic] Academy to see me—about training of international affairs specialists.

· 8 SEPTEMBER 1944 ·

—Conference of department staff—report from *Boretsky*[468] on Turkey, its position and policy in the current phase of the war.

—Meeting of the Foreign Bureau on Bulg[arian] affairs.

—*Kolarov's lecture on Bulgaria* in the House of Unions (office of lect[ures]).

—Report from Sofia: on the demonstration, and so on. Firing on the demonstrators.

—Sent *Stal[in]* and *Molot[ov]* a proposal:

1. Transport of arms for part[isan] detachments in Bulgaria.
2. Relieving Bulg[arian] officers from duty in the Red Army for military operations in Bulgaria.
3. Sending Bulg[arian] part[y] workers to Bulgaria.
4. Mater[ial] assistance to the CP of Bulgaria of up to $50,000.

———————————

—The Red Army has occupied a line from the Danube (Ruse) to the Black Sea (Varna and Burgas).

· 9 SEPTEMBER 1944 ·

—Sof[ia] radio reported the formation of a Fatherland Front government:

1. K[imon] Georgiev: president[469]
2. P[etko] Stainov: foreign affairs[470]
3. D[amian] Velchev: War Ministry
4. Mino Neichev: justice
5. Intern[al] affairs: Anton Tanev [Yugov][471]

468. On the staff of OMI.

469. Kimon Georgiev (1882–1969), Bulgarian politician; leader of the *Zveno* group and the Fatherland Front; minister (1926–1928), prime minister (1934–1935, 1944–1946), and foreign minister (1946–1947) of Bulgaria.

470. Petko Stainov (1890–1971), Bulgarian jurist; minister (1930–1931); envoy to France (1934–1935); minister for foreign affairs (1944–1946).

471. Pseudonym of Anton Yugov (1904–1991), Bulgarian Communist; secre-

6. Finances: Petko Stoianov[472]

7. Public services and utilities: Boris Stefanov[473] [should be: Boris Bumbarov][474]

8. Education: Prof[essor] [Dimitŭr] Mihalchev[475] [should be: Stancho Cholakov][476]

9. Railways: Angel Derzhanski[477]

10. Agriculture: Asen Pavlov[478]

11. Trade: Dim[itŭr] Neikov[479]

12. Health: Racho Angelov[480]

13. Soc[ial] policy: Gr[igor] Cheshmedzhiev[481]

---

tary (1933–1934) of the procommunist IMRO (United). He was at the Comintern's Leninist School in Moscow (1934–1936). Member of the BRP CC Politburo (from 1937 on); BRP CC secretary (1941–1944); minister of internal affairs (1944–1949); deputy prime minister (1947–1949, 1952–1956). He was demoted during the Kostov affair (1949) but became minister of industry (1950) and prime minister (1956–1962). He was removed from all state and party functions during the purge of the Chervenkov group (1962).

472. Petko Stoianov (1879–1973), Bulgarian scholar; member of the Radical Party leadership; minister of finance (1944–1945) who was thereafter in the opposition.

473. Boris Stefanov (pseudonym: Ivan Draganov, 1883–1969), Bulgarian Communist from Dobruja who was active in Romania; member CC (1922–1941) and Politburo (1924–1941) of the Romanian Communist Party (PCR), and secretary-general (1934–1940). Having been imprisoned in Romania (1926–1932), he escaped and fled to the USSR, where he remained until 1944 and was a member of the ECCI presidium (1935–1941). He settled in Bulgaria after the war.

474. Boris Bumbarov (b. 1896), Bulgarian politician; leader of the BZNS; minister in the Fatherland Front government (1944–1945) who was thereafter in the opposition.

475. Dimitŭr Mihalchev (1880–1967), Bulgarian philosopher and diplomat; envoy to the USSR (1934–1936, 1944–1946); president of the Bulgarian Academy of Sciences (1944–1947).

476. Stancho Cholakov (1900–1981), Bulgarian economist; minister of education (1944–1945) and of finance (1945–1946).

477. Angel Derzhanski (1895–1964), Bulgarian politician; adherent of the BZNS Pladne group who was in the opposition after 1945.

478. Asen Pavlov (1898–1977), Bulgarian politician; BZNS leader; in the opposition after 1945.

479. Dimitŭr Neikov (1884–1949), Bulgarian politician; secretary of the Social Democratic party (1945–1948); president of the presidium of the Bulgarian parliament (1946–1949).

480. Racho Angelov (1873–1956), Bulgarian Communist; physician by profession; minister of health (1944–1946); member of the Bulgarian parliament's presidium (after 1947).

481. Grigor Cheshmedzhiev (1879–1945), Bulgarian politician; Social Demo-

14. Min[ister] of propaganda: D[imo] Kazasov[482]
15. Min[ister] without portfolio: [Dobri] Terpeshev
16)   "   "   "   : N[ikola] Petkov[483]

New regent's council:
1. Professor Ven[elin] Ganev[484]
2. Tsvetko Boboshevski[485]
3. Todor Pavlov

—Kazasov's statement over the radio containing an announcement in this regard.

—Held conference on party school issues of the Germ[an] Com[munist] Party (Pieck, Ulbricht, Ackermann, Baranov, Volkov,[486] Mirov, Korotkevich,[487] and others).

—Gave instructions to transmit over Radio H[risto] Botev in connection with the formation of the Fatherland Front government.

· 10 SEPTEMBER 1944 ·

—Sunday.
—*Sent the Sofia CC* the foll[owing] telegram:

> 1. Report immediately on each member of the new cabinet, what each one's political affiliation is, and precisely who our ministers are and the length of their party membership.
>
> 2. Have the Fatherland Front daily newspaper and our party's daily newspaper begun publication already? You may count on the necessary material assistance from us for this purpose.
>
> 3. Take immediate measures for thoroughgoing reinforcement of the party and its leadership in the center and the localities.

---

cratic deputy (1919–1934). He resigned from the Fatherland Front cabinet in 1945.

482. Dimo Kazasov (1886–1980), Bulgarian politician and journalist; minister of propaganda (1944–1945) and of information (1945–1947).

483. Nikola Petkov (1893–1947), Bulgarian politician; leader of the BZNS Pladne group; minister in the Fatherland Front government (1944–1945); afterward the leading oppositionist. He was tried, sentenced to death in a rigged trial, and executed in 1947.

484. Venelin Ganev (1880–1966), Bulgarian jurist; active in the Radical party.

485. Tsvetko Boboshevski (1884–1952), Bulgarian politician; minister (1923–1930).

486. Aleksandr Vasilievich Volkov (b. 1903), Soviet Communist; in the ECCI Cadre Department (1939–1941); afterward in the Red Army's political administration.

487. On the OMI staff.

4. Report which active personnel have emerged from prisons and concentration camps and what is their position is vis-à-vis the party.

5. The national committee of the Fatherland Front and its local organs to continue to exist and actively promote the consolidation of the popular masses and the implementation of Fatherland Front programs, without opposing themselves, of course, to the government.

6. Radio Hristo Botev will for the time being continue operating. Send your observations, proposals, and requests as regards its programming.

7. Please report regularly on all crucial developments.

—Lieutenant Gen[eral] Gundorov[488] (and wife) and Lieutenant General Kovpak[489] are here. Discussed the work of the All-Slavic Committee delegation leaving for America.

—Chervenkov and I edited a directive program for [Radio] Hr[isto] Botev.

· 11 SEPTEMBER 1944 ·

—Pauker: about her departure for Romania.

—Foreign Bureau: on Bulgarian affairs.

—Sent the CC various instructions in connection with the new situation in Bulgaria. Held conference with editorial board of [Radio] Hr[isto] Botev on its work at the present time, pending discontinuation of Hr[isto] Botev programming.

—Regular review (inform[ational]) with department staff.

———————————

—Prof[essor] Yerusalimsky[490] (from *Kr[asnaia] zvezda* [Red Star]) to see me in connection with his trip to Bulgaria. Briefed and instructed him.

—Sent (apart from others) the following encoded telegram to the CC of the Bulgarian CP in connection with its inquiry concerning the army and form[ation] of political commissars:

488. Aleksandr Semyonovich Gundorov (1895–1973), Soviet general; president of the All-Slavic Committee (1941–1947).

489. Sidor Artemovich Kovpak (187–1967), Soviet general; leader of the Ukrainian partisan movement (1941–1944).

490. Arkady Samsonovich Yerusalimsky (1901–1965), Soviet historian; staff officer of the Academy of Sciences of the USSR (1925–1941). He taught at the higher diplomatic school (1939–1941) and the University of Moscow (1944–1956).

At the present stage it would be advisable to form a polit[ical] education department in the army, but not to appoint political commissars. Your main attention should be directed toward cleansing the army of pro-German, fascist commanders and replacing them with commanders loyal to the cause of the Fatherland Front. Try to carry out all measures in this regard with the consent of our partners in the Fatherland Front government and national committee. People's tribunals must be formed to hear the cases of traitors, fascist criminals, and their punishment. Take immediate measures to establish strict democratic order in the country and discipline against provocateurs and saboteurs. Keep in mind that the fascist reaction is not yet smashed, and there are still Germans in the Balkans. Everything must be mobilized to suppress them. Why has our party not yet come out with a public statement over the radio and in other media? Confirm receipt of this message. We await your reply and further information.

[. . .]

· 24 SEPTEMBER 1944 ·

—Sunday.

—Invited Kolarov, Chervenkov, Belov [Damianov], Ganev,[491] Tomov [Poptomov], Kozovski, Stela Blagoeva, Mihailov (Ruben) [Avramov],[492] Sergeev [Kolev] to the dacha.

The Foreign Bureau and I continued our discussion of Bulg[arian] affairs, then we all had lunch together, watched a film, and so on.

—Sent to the CC, along with other telegr[ams], the following, more important encoded telegram:

We welcome your decision on the work of our ministers. It must be firmly and consistently implemented. One must bear in mind that, as the party of the government and the leading party in the Fatherland Front, our party bears an extremely great responsibility to the people and to the country, and also to the Soviet Union, upon whose military successes and for-

491. Dimitŭr Ganev (1898–1964), Bulgarian Communist active in the Dobruja Revolutionary Organization and the PCR; member of the PCR CC (1934–1940); member of the BRP CC (from 1942 on). After September 1944 he held various party and state positions in Bulgaria.

492. Ruben Avramov (pseudonyms: Ruben Levi, Ruben Mihailov, 1900–1986), Bulgarian Communist; political émigré to the USSR (1925–1944); staff member of the BRP foreign bureau and the ECCI; veteran of the International Brigades in Spain; deputy chief of the Comintern school (1939–1944); member of the BKP CC (1948–1970).

eign policy successes a great deal depends, including the current and future position of Bulgaria and all the Balkans. We must speak and act not as run-of-the-mill and irresponsible provincial agitators, but as [befits] sober, real Bolshevik politicians and statesmen. Implementing our firm line, we are to be completely loyal with our partners in the government and the Father-land Front nat[ional] committee, in honoring our obligations and reacting tactfully to hostile maneuvers. We are to regard our cooperation with them for the benefit of the people not as a temporary coalitional combination, but as a long-term fighting alliance against a common enemy and for the construction of a new democratic Bulgaria. All of this must be firmly driven home not only to Dobri Terpeshev, but to all parties and its [*sic*] activists.

[...]

· 27 SEPTEMBER 1944 ·

—Second talk with Tito.[493] Got into a lengthy discussion with him. Reached agreement on issues concerning the Bulg[arian] and Yugoslav Com[munist] parties, as well as on the basic issues of relations between new Yugoslavia and new Bulgaria. Between ourselves, naturally, there is perfect mutual understanding, but there will be difficulties to over-come in the implementation of the line that we have set down—the formation of a union between Bulgaria and Yugoslavia that actually amounts to a federation of South Slavs (consisting of Bulgars, Mace-donians, Serbs, Croats, Montenegrins, and Slovenes) extending from the Adriatic to the Black Sea. Difficulties especially on the part of the English and their Great Greek and Great Serbian agents.

—Sent the CC my thoughts concerning the base on which to seek the settlement of issues relating to the Bosilegrad and Tsaribrod areas,[494] and to the Bulgarian troops in Macedonia and Thrace.
—Also informed Sofia that at Tito's suggestion, the Bulgarian govern-ment delegation should travel to Craiova [Romania] for negotiations with the Yugosl[av] nat[ional] committee (Tito).

493. Tito visited Moscow from 21 to 28 September 1944.
494. Bosilegrad and Tsaribrod (in Dimitrov's honor—Dimitrovgrad after 1945), two Bulgarian pivots along the Serbian border, were given to Yugoslavia by the Treaty of Neuilly (1919).

· 28 SEPTEMBER 1944 ·

—Meeting of the Foreign Bureau at the CC.
—Final instructions to the departing comrades.
—Received Rákosi and Kellermann[495] on Hungarian business.
—Also various department staff.

· 29 SEPTEMBER 1944 ·

—The Chervenkov-Belov [Damianov] group took off for Sofia. A report of their safe landing came tonight.
—Sent a message to the CC:

> [Dimitŭr] Ganev's report has been presented to *Stal[in]* and *Molot[ov]*. Chervenkov and Belov [Damianov] will make a preliminary report to you concerning our discussions in connection with that report, and afterward Ganev himself will give you a detailed account. The first group of part[y] workers was sent today. The second group will arrive together with Ganev. The third soon after the first. Ganev will be detained here a couple of days more on account of his report.
>
> Immediately confirm the arrival of our comrades and your receipt from them of the articles and materials we have sent for you.

—Held regular review of department staff.

[. . .]

· 4 OCTOBER 1944 ·

—Made arrangements with *Bulganin* regarding assistance to CC of the PPR (Poland).

[. . .]

· 6 OCTOBER 1944 ·
[. . .]

—Stal[in] called:

> Bulgaria ought to withdraw its troops from Thrace and Macedonia. It is important to win back the Bulg[arian] army, which the English have de-

---

495. Alexander Kellermann (1894–1971), Hungarian Communist; staff member of the ECCI (1936–1943) and Institute 205 (1943–1944); member of the Hungarian CP CC (1945–1948).

manded be disarmed. The armistice is being held up by the English; they are demanding that Wilson[496] sign, not Tolbukhin,[497] and that the chairmen of the control commission be one of our men and one of theirs. We are insisting on and will get Tolbukhin as signatory and our chairmanship of the commission. The Red Army is staying in Bulgaria until peace is concluded and at least until the end of the war with Germany.

[. . .]

The end of 1944 was transitional for Dimitrov. His health is no longer mentioned as often as in early 1944, although he would have two relapses in the winter and spring, as well as in the summer of 1945. Balkan arrangements were being pursued with the Yugoslavs, perhaps a touch too soon for Soviet taste. He clearly discerned the difference between the popular fronts that the Soviets suggested to Thorez and the form of "shotgun wedding" that was practiced in Bulgaria. Dimitrov was occasionally impatient with the "sectarian" mistakes of Bulgarian Communists, as well as the Yugoslavs' ambitions in the Balkans, but hardly restrained the Bulgarian Communists on their path to total power. He was increasingly managing Bulgarian internal matters, as endless delegations and individuals passed through his office.

Despite the flurry of activity, Dimitrov was in fact being demoted. There is a note of jealousy when it comes to the new rising star Tito (*"too arrogant,* heavy dose of conceit"), apparently favored by Stalin. At the May Day parade in 1945, on the eve of V-E Day, Dimitrov was at the diplomats' stand. Still, he favored the Yugoslav position in Trieste, an issue that was much more contentious in the Yugoslav-Soviet relations than is apparent from the diary.

The great events of 1945 seem to have bypassed Dimitrov. There is a lot more about the difficulties with the anticommunist opposition in Bulgaria than on Yalta, Potsdam, not to mention the A-bomb, which is not even mentioned. The old comrades, now usually back in their home countries, kept sending greetings, but Dimitrov was mainly offering "detailed explanations and instructions" to the visiting Bulgarians and other Balkanites. The elections for the Bulgarian National Assembly became the occasion for his return to Bulgaria after twenty-two years of exile. The return was

496. Henry Maitland Wilson (1881–1964), British field marshal; supreme Allied commander in the Mediterranean (1944–1945).

497. Fyodor Ivanovich Tolbukhin (1894–1949), Soviet marshal; commander of the Third Ukrainian front, the Soviet Red Army group in the Balkans, and parts of Central Europe.

carefully managed by the Soviets, who provided ample security, and finally effected in November 1945.—I.B.

· 10 OCTOBER 1944 ·
[. . .]

—*Churchill and Eden:* talks between them and Stalin and Molotov.
—*Colonel General Biriuzov*[498] called from Sofia. Requested certain explanations regarding withdrawal of Bulgarian troops from Thrace and Macedonia. Explained to him that these troops are to be withdrawn as soon as possible.

[. . .]

· 14 OCTOBER 1944 ·

—Looked over a review on the Bulgarian press prepared for *War and the Working Class.*
—Sent *Stal[in]* and *Molot[ov]* a brief characterization of the staff of the Bulgarian armistice delegation, which is arriving tomorrow.
—Received the Hungarians (Rákosi, Gerő, Wolf [Farkas], Révai,[499] Magyar [?]), regarding draft platform of Hungarian Communist Party. Had long discussion; I criticized their impracticality, political speculations, and so on, gave them advice, and directed them to rework the platform; the main thing, however, was to get on with sending a party leader[ship] group to Hungarian territory for local party work.
—Kolarov: on Bulg[arian] affairs. Reprimanded him for lack of initiative and ineffectiveness in his work.

[. . .]

498. Sergei Semyonovich Biriuzov (1904–1964), Soviet general, later marshal; deputy commander-in-chief of the southern Soviet army group and deputy chief of the Allied Control Comission in Bulgaria (1945–1947).

499. József Révai (1898–1959), Hungarian Communist; participant in Béla Kun's Council Republic (1919). After being in emigration in Austria and Germany (1919–1930), he returned to Hungary, where he was captured and imprisoned (1931–1934). He headed the Hungarian CP work in Prague (1937–1939) and served on the staff of the ECCI (1939–1943) and as director of Radio Kossuth (1943–1944). Once back in Hungary after the war, he directed the party daily *Szabad Nép* (Free People) and served as minister of culture. A member of the Hungarian CP Politburo (1945–1953, 1956), he fled to the USSR during the Hungarian revolution (1956) but returned in 1957 as an unreconstructed Stalinist.

· 18 OCTOBER 1944 ·

—Molotov briefed me on his talk yesterday with the Bulgarian delegation. He pointed out to the Bulgarians that they were assessing the Bulgarian situation too optimistically. The enemies (German agents) in Bulgaria are still quite dangerous. The new government faces great difficulties. He emphasized to them that the country's economic situation could not be as catastrophic as they were representing it, for Bulgaria to all intents and purposes has not been at war. Regarding the conditions of the armistice, he said that they would not be easy, of course, but they would be no more severe than the Romanian ones, notwithstanding the urgings of the allies. The armistice conditions had to be regarded as a means for clearing the way for the favorable settlement of the Bulgarian situation in the future.

—Molotov informed me that Tito had complained of certain incorrect attitudes on the part of Bulg[arian] troop units operating jointly with the Yugosl[av] army—specifically, that they had taken most of the booty at Pirot [Serbia] for themselves, and so on. There are various sources of friction between the Bulgarians and the Yugoslavs.

—I advised the CC in Sofia in this regard and directed them to investigate immediately and take appropriate measures to eliminate all such friction.

[. . .]

· 27 OCTOBER 1944 ·
[. . .]

—Sent Tito a proposal to explain to the Maced[onian] comrades that to all intents and purposes they ought not to raise the question of annexing Bulg[arian] Macedonia, which could be done only upon determining the new borders between Bulgaria and Yugoslavia and on the basis of preliminary hearings between those states; no steps should be taken in Bulg[arian] Macedonia without preliminary clearance from the CC of the CP Bulgaria.

· 28 OCTOBER 1944 ·

—The armistice with Bulgaria was signed.

—I arranged a meeting between the Bulg[arian] delegation and *Mikoyan* on economic issues, in particular the possibility of barter between Bulgaria and the USSR.

—Thorez received a telegram from de Gaulle telling him he could return to France following the publication in an offic[ial] state press organ of a decree on amnesty of war criminals dating to 1940.

[…]

· 18 NOVEMBER 1944 ·

—Received *Thorez and Ramette*[500] in connection with their departure for France. Paniushkin, Ponomarev and Morozov took part in the discussion. Agreed on liaison and information; aid to the French Com[munist] Party, using its connections and with the cooperation of the Belgians, Italians, and Swiss. Gave them various explanations and advice on French Com[munist] Party polit[ical] and tact[ical] issues.
—Received Spanish generals (in the Red Army) *Modesto, Líster,* and *Cordón.*[501] Explained what their tasks would be in Yugoslavia (while attached to Tito) and their further travel to France and Spain.
—Examined some copy for the department bulletin.

· 19 NOVEMBER 1944 ·
[…]

—Thorez to see me tonight (after his audience with Stalin, with Molotov and Beria present). He arrived together with Baskakov and Baranov.
Thorez reported on their discussion. Emphasized that everything said had basically been in accord with what I had already told him regarding French affairs. Stal[in] had advised him:
1) to pursue a "left bloc" line in a form appropriate for France; 2) to patiently cultivate allies among the Socialists, Radicals, and others; 3) to advocate the rebirth of a militarily and industrially powerful France and the creation of a democratic regime (the Allies want a weak France as well as a weak Italy); 4) not to overestimate his resources and not to expect the party to be able to solve single-handedly all the problems facing the French people; 5) not to allow the party to become isolated

500. Arthur Ramette (1897–1988), French Communist; member of the PCF CC (from 1930 on) and Politburo (1937–1950); deputy in the French parliament (1932–1939). He emigrated to Belgium (1939–1940) and the USSR (1940–1944) and served on the staff of the ECCI and French-language radio.

501. Antonio Cordón (pseudonym: Anton Antonovich Kuznetsev, 1895–1969), Spanish Communist; undersecretary (later secretary-general) of the Spanish Ministry of Defense; general in charge of the Spanish Republican eastern army. He served in the Soviet Red Army.

from other democratic groups and the masses; 6) not to defy the de Gaulle government; to maintain a loyal stance; 7) not to insist on preserving the armed forces of the Resistance; a united army is necessary, but to try to have his own people and positions in that army; 8) that reviving the Young Commun[ist] League was not strictly necessary; it would be better to establish a general patriotic people's youth league, and so on.

[. . .]

· 21 NOVEMBER 1944 ·
[. . .]

—Received at Government House tonight: Kardelj (dep[uty] chair-[man] of the nat[ional] committee of Yugoslavia [NKOJ]), General Terzić[502] (head of the Yugoslav military mission to Moscow) and Vlasov (Vlahović).
—*Kardelj,* on Tito's instructions, reported in detail on the situation in Yugoslavia and relations between Yugoslavia and Bulgaria.

[. . .]

· 23 NOVEMBER 1944 ·

—Talked at length with *Kardelj.* He informed me of his audience with Stal[in] and Molotov. They had agreed on preparing and concluding an alliance between Bulgaria and Yugoslavia with a view to establishing a *common federation of South Slavs:* Bulgars, Serbs, Croats, Slovenes, Macedonians, and Montenegrins.

[. . .]

· 27 NOVEMBER 1944 ·

—Regarding some alarming reports from the CC (Sofia) on subversive actions by certain ministers and allies from the Father[land] Front, sent the following encoded telegram to the CC:

Naturally, every effort must be made to avoid a crisis in government at the present time, which is being provoked by enemy agents. However, the

502. Velimir Terzić (1909–1983), Yugoslav Communist; prewar military officer; commander of the Bijelo Polje (Montenegro) Partisan unit; commander of the main staff of Montenegro; deputy commander of the 5th Montenegrin Proletarian Brigade; chief of staff of the fifth operative zone and of the main staff of Croatia; head of the Yugoslav military mission in the USSR; after the war, commander of an army; chief inspector of the Yugoslav People's Army (JNA); chief of the military academy and of the military historical institute. His writings in the 1960s and 1970s anticipated some of the Great Serbian themes of the 1980s.

party must at the same time categorically demand that its allies in the government and on the national committee comply with the conditions of the agreement concluded between them and ourselves, which have by now been set forth in various published joint declarations and documents. You could propose establishing an interdepartmental commission attached to the Ministries of War and Internal Affairs for settling disputes between the military authorities and the people's militia in the center and in the localities. But under no circumstances should the Ministry of Internal Affairs be ceded. You can agree to the abolition of the Fatherland Front committees within institutions and to their replacement with trade-union plenipotentiaries, but there must be no infringing on the national committee and local committees of the Fatherand Front, which in the absence of a people's assembly and community councils are the sole existing public organs [of government]. Kimon Georgiev, Velchev, and the rest of the ministers must be put on notice that unless there is an immediate cessation of subversion and provocations vis-à-vis the Fatherland Front and the essential unity of the people against fascism, our party will address a manifesto to the Bulgarian people and will publicly expose the provocateurs of civil war. It will propose convoking a general congress of Fatherland Front committees and will declare anyone promoting schism in the Fatherland Front and jeopardizing the unity of the people to be an enemy of the people and state.

We must demonstrate in practice—firmly, calmly, without the slightest histrionics, maintaining all necessary discipline in the country—that our country will never allow the historic cause of 9 September to be defeated.

[. . .]

· 6 DECEMBER 1944 ·

—Conference with the Hungarians (Rákosi, Gerő, and Nagy).[503] Baranov, Baskakov, and Paniushkin also attended.

The Hungarians reported: 1) arranged with Hungarian bourgeois

---

503. Imre Nagy (1896–1958), Hungarian Communist; prisoner of war in Russia. He joined the RKP(b) in 1918; once back in Hungary in 1921, he infiltrated the Social Democrats. After being arrested in 1927, he emigrated to Austria (1929) and the USSR (1930), where he worked at the International Agrarian Institute. Director of the Hungarian-language radio broadcasts during the war; minister of agriculture in the provisional Hungarian government (1944–1945); minister of the interior (1945–1946); president of the Hungarian parliament (1947). In conflict with Rákosi, he was demoted in 1949. He served as deputy prime minister (1952) and prime minister (1953–1955). He was accused of "rightist deviation" and dismissed from his position in April 1955, then expelled from the party; readmitted in October 1956, he was Hungarian premier during the 1956 revolution. He was arrested by the Soviets, condemned to death, and executed.

figures, generals, and others, to establish a provisional nat[ional] assembly as the source of power in the new Hungary; 2) the prov[isional] nat[ional] assembly will establish a provisional nat[ional] government including two Communists—Nag[y] (agriculture) and Gábor[504] (education); 3) adopted the general platform of the new Hung[arian] government.

—Discussion of practical measures for implementing this line.

[. . .]

· 8 DECEMBER 1944 ·

[. . .]

—Forwarded to Molotov an inquiry from Greek Communist Party Politburo member *Petros Rousos,*[505] recently arrived in Sofia to report to the Bulg[arian] Com[munist] Party CC: can assistance be granted to the Greek Com[munist] Party in order to oppose armed intervention by England?

· 9 DECEMBER 1944 ·

—Informed Sofia that in the current situation our Greek friends will not be able to count on active intervention and assistance from here. Also advised the Bulg[arian] Com[munist] Party CC not to become directly engaged [with] the beginnings of internal struggle in Greece.

[. . .]

· 13 DECEMBER 1944 ·

—*Stal[in]* called regarding an audience for Kol[arov] and myself on Bulg[arian] issues. His answer: Very busy now, but in the next few days I shall find some time. . . . The Communists are taking too high a tone. The Zvenoists want to withdraw from the government. Now if Kol[arov] comes on the scene there too, they will go right out of their minds.

504. Andor Gábor (1884–1953), Hungarian Communist poet who was on the staff of the ECCI's Foreign Language Publishing House.

505. Petros Rousos (real name: Polychronidis, b. 1908), Greek Communist; reporter, editor, and finally publisher of the Communist newspaper *Rizospastis* (Radical); member of the Greek Communist Party (KKE) CC (1935–1973); KKE liaison in 1946 in Belgrade, together with Yiannis Ioannidis, with the Balkan CPs. Following defeat of the Communist insurgency, he lived in exile in the USSR but returned to Greece in 1974.

Better to wait a while before Kolarov leaves for Sofia. How bad can things be for him here, anyway? . . .

—Regarding recent events in Bulgaria (the provocat[ional] attempts to precipitate a gov[ernmental] crisis and suppress the Fatherland Front), sent the following encoded telegram to the CC:

> I concur with the Politburo's assessment of recent events. Bearing in mind the overall situation, however, I advise you most insistently to remain firm in your actions, but also moderate; to show the greatest possible maneuverability and flexibility as regards your [coalition] allies, particularly as regards the Zvenoists; not to take too high or aggressive a tone, not to play up outwardly the Communists' leading role in the government and in the Fatherland Front; not to take steps that are not absolutely indispensable but that could contribute to the consolidation of an anticommunist bloc. A governmental crisis must be avoided at present. It is not enough that we ourselves do not seek such a crisis. We must do everything in our power to foil the plans of foreign and internal provocateurs whose interests would be served by such a crisis precisely now. Naturally, we must take advantage of recent events to strengthen our positions in the army, in the state apparatus, and in the country, but this must be done intelligently, tactfully, never forgetting that we are by no means powerful enough to be the single decisive factor in the country and to dictate our will to our allies. We must not forget that if our opponents are yielding at present, then that is largely attributable to the presence of the Red Army in the country. Otherwise, we would already have a civil war on our hands. In my view, there is a certain fanaticism evident among us, in our party, an exaggeration of our own resources and an underestimation of those of our opponents, both internal and foreign. And that, as you know very well, is a serious danger. We must bear firmly in mind that the current situation allows only for collective management of state affairs, and this imposes a certain amount of self-denial on us, which, of course, in no way implies any display of weakness or lack of principle on our part. At the first opportunity I will write you in greater detail on this. Please consider these remarks of mine calmly and soberly, and inform me of your own views.

[. . .]

· 19 DECEMBER 1944 ·

—Received *Prof[essor] Mihalchev* at Government House.

—Reported on his mission and on the situation in Bulgaria. Passed on various reports from [Todor] Pavlov (Reg[ency] Council]) as well. Regarding the solidity of the government and the Fath[erland] Front, he stated: "Everyone understands that in the current situation there is no other way. Therefore, even our opponents are obliged to reconcile themselves with this state of affairs." In other words, the Father[land] Front is a shotgun wedding.

[...]

· 21 DECEMBER 1944 ·
[...]

—*Kolarov* to see me. We discussed terms of the treaty of alliance between Yugoslavia and Bulgaria. Sent the following encoded telegram to the CC (Sofia):

The more essential points of the treaty of alliance that ought to be discussed with the Yugoslav comrades are as follows:

1. Yugoslavia and Bulgaria, waging war jointly as allies against Germany, undertake to render one another the utmost assistance and support until total victory over the common enemy, at the same time discharging their obligations as provided for in their agreements with the United Nations.

2. All consequences for Yugoslavia that have followed from Bulgaria's participation in the war on the side of Hitler as of 9 September 1944 [and] from the occupation by Bulgarian troops of part of Yugoslav territory, and so forth, will be settled amicably between the two countries in the spirit of the present treaty of alliance.

3. For purposes of defense against aggression and the securing of national independence, Yugoslavia and Bulgaria conclude a defensive alliance and undertake not to enter into any alliances or accords whatsoever with other states that are directed against either country. They will consult one another on all matters affecting the security of both countries.

4. In the interests of the economic development and prosperity of both countries, Yugoslavia and Bulgaria conclude a customs union. In accordance with this, appropriate commercial, economic, railroad, transportation, veterinary, and police-administrative agreements for occupational safety, for the struggle against unemployment, and so on, will be drafted. The passport regime between the two countries will be abolished.

5. Yugoslavia and Bulgaria undertake to render each other mutual support and assistance in all matters concerning the construction and consolidation of people's democratic power in both countries, in accordance with the will of their peoples. Cooperating in all economic and cultural areas, they will cultivate fraternal friendship between their peoples and eradicate all remnants of chauvinism and fascism.

6. Welcoming the decision by the Antifascist Council of Yugoslavia to recognize the Macedonians as a people enjoying equal rights with the other peoples of federative Yugoslavia, both parties recognize the Macedonian people's full right to self-determination. Bulgaria agrees to the annexation

of the Macedonian territories belonging to it since 1913 to Macedonia within the limits of Yugoslavia if its population desires it. Moreover, if in future a federative state is established by the will of the peoples of Yugoslavia and Bulgaria, a united Macedonia will be included in such a federation as a member enjoying equal rights with all other members. For its part, Yugoslavia agrees to return to Bulgaria those portions of its territories that were ceded to Yugoslavia according to the Treaty of Neuilly of 1919.

The time and manner of implementing the terms of this paragraph, and likewise the settlement of all questions pertaining to territorial changes, will be specially negotiated by both governments before the end of the war. 7. Expressing their peoples' inflexible will to be factors for peace in the Balkans, Yugoslavia and Bulgaria will coordinate their efforts to consolidate friendly relations among the Balkan peoples based on mutual respect and cooperation.

8. A joint commission of representatives of both governments is established for the practical implementation of the terms of the treaty of alliance.

The preamble to the treaty ought to indicate the resolve of both states to see the present war against Germany through to a victorious conclusion, as well as the fact that the vital interests of the peoples of both countries dictate the conclusion of a permanent alliance of friendship and cooperation between its peoples, which are bound by tribal ties of kinship, a common history, an ancient struggle against foreign oppression. Such an alliance will be a critical step toward the unity of all the Balkan peoples for defense against any and all aggression and the securing of a stable peace and prosperity in the Balkans; it will be an important contribution to the cause of international security, and so on. Also, cite the agreement of 5 October 1944.

[. . .]

· 23 December 1944 ·
[. . .]

—Among other instructions for the CC (Sofia), sent the following encoded telegram to *Kostov personally:*

Yesterday received a number of issues of *Rabotnichesko delo* [Workers' Cause] and was unpleasantly struck by the lead editorial of number 59, entitled "We will carry out the directives of Comrade Traicho Kostov." Incomprehensible how the editorial board could have permitted such a politically incorrect and noxious thing. Directives for the party are given and can be given only by the CC, the party leadership, and not an individual person, even if that person is secretary of the CC. What's more, framing the issue this way puts you personally in an awkward and false position and can only hinder the necessary consolidation of your authority as political secretary of the CC among the other Politburo members. Measures must be taken to ensure that the editorial board does not permit itself such inappropriate going overboard, which borders on toadying, something that has no place in our party. I urge you to be extremely vigilant as regards such antiparty displays.

[. . .]

· 25 DECEMBER 1944 ·
[. . .]

—Sent Stal[in] (and Molot[ov]) the following letter:

I am forwarding to you the attached draft of treaty of alliance between Yugoslavia and Bulgaria, produced by delegates of the CCs of the Yugoslav and Bulgarian Com[munist] parties in Belgrade.

Both CCs firmly intend to take concrete steps to put this measure through along state lines in the immediate future, as soon as the issue of the Yugoslav government is settled.

According to the statement of the CC of the Yugoslav Com[munist] Party, the conclusion of a treaty of alliance will encounter no serious obstacles in Yugoslavia. For their part, the Bulgarian comrades state that their Fatherland Front allies look favorably upon concluding such a treaty between Yugoslavia and Bulgaria.

Personally, I believe that the current moment is entirely favorable for establishing the very closest alliance relations between Yugoslavia and Bulgaria, with the prospect of their unification in a common federative state, and that favorable moment ought not to be missed. As for the draft of the treaty, it appears correct to me.

Please provide advice and guidelines in this regard, especially considering that in bringing about a treaty of alliance between Yug[oslavia] and Bulg[aria] there may arise difficulties of a foreign-policy nature.

[. . .]

· 26 DECEMBER 1944 ·
[. . .]

Spoke with Molotov about the treaty of alliance between Yugoslavia and Bulgaria. He informed me that the Yugoslavs would like the treaty to be concluded for 1 January 1945, which he personally found entirely inappropriate, since this major issue requires very thorough preparations.

[. . .]

· 29 DECEMBER 1944 ·

—Received Slovak delegation together with Gottwald, Kopecký, Appelt. Delegates reported in detail on the situation in Slovakia and Carpatho-Ukraine and stated the Slovaks' position regarding the future organization of Czechoslovakia as a state of Czechs and Slovaks (two separate peoples) as against Beneš's position regarding a Czechoslovak people and a Czechoslovak state.

[. . .]

· 4 JANUARY 1945 ·

—At the dacha received Romanian comrades Ana Pauker, Gheorghiu-Dej[506] (Romanian minister), and Apostol[507] (chairman of Romanian trade unions).

They reported in detail on the situation in Romania and the activities of the Communist Party.

They recounted a discussion with *Stalin*. The latter had offered advice as follows:

1. Concentrate attention on *agrarian reform* (even now a division of the lands abandoned by refugee landowners and German agents is practically under way). Leave court and monastery domains alone for now.

(America developed because it had no landowners; France began developing after the destruction of the landowning class.)

2. Build farm machine and tractor stations (the USSR is providing a certain quantity of tractors).

3. The USSR can provide a certain quantity of cotton for processing in Romanian textile factories.

506. Gheorghe Gheorghiu-Dej (1901–1965), Romanian Communist leader. Imprisoned for his leadership in a 1933 strike, he was liberated in 1944 and took part in the 23 August 1944 coup. Member of the PCR CC (from 1936); secretary-general of the RCP CC (1945–1954, 1955–1965) and deputy chairman of the council of ministers (from 1945 on); prime minister (1952–1955); president of the state council (1961–1965). He pursued an independent foreign policy and the industrialization of Romania.

507. Gheorghe Apostol (b. 1913), Romanian Communist leader; president of the General Confederation of Labor (1944–1953); member PCR/PMR CC (from 1945) and its Politburo (from 1948 on); vice president of the council of ministers (1952–1954); first secretary of the PMR (1954–1955); in November 1987 one of the signatories of the "Letter of Six," signed by veteran Romanian Communists, which accused the Romanian president Nicolae Ceauşescu of discrediting socialism.

4. Do not bring up nationalizing at present. Pay attention to the development of the *oil* industry.
5. Try not to scare and not to alienate the bourgeois (anti-German) elements, particularly the Tătărescu group.[508]
6. Use the *Vladimirescu*[509] division as internal support for the national-democratic front.
7. Work toward establishing a national-democratic front government.
8. Develop the argument that if such a government comes about, the USSR will help in having North Transylvania end up Romanian.

If such a government is formed, the USSR is prepared to conclude a mutual-assistance pact along the lines of the pact with Czechoslovakia.

Among the many New Year's greetings from Bulgaria I received the following one from Petko Stainov:

Happy New Year! I will always very gratefully remember your valuable assistance to our delegation during the signing of the peace treaty. You helped clarify for the Soviet government and its Allies the nature of the activities of the Fatherland Front. You also helped win back trust in the new Bulgaria. All of that helps the Bulgarian government meet the challenge it faces for the new year of 1945: the challenge of establishing peace in the Balkans and the brotherly unification of the South Slavic peoples. We helped our younger Slavic sister Macedonia and, by encouraging our military units who waged the war against the Germans there, Bulgaria hopes to be admitted as an ally to the family of the democratic peoples once the victory has been won.

I wish you good health and good spirits in the coming New Year. On behalf of the Bulgarian people, I would like to express its gratitude to you, its son, for your efforts to strengthen the four political organizations that today make up the Fatherland Front. Our people also express their belief that with your support and through close and faithful friendship with their lib-

508. Reference to the adherents of Gheorghe Tătărescu (1886–1957), leader of the right wing of the National Liberal Party of Romania and an instrument of King Carol II. Tătărescu served as minister of industry (1933), prime minister (1934–1937, 1939–1940), and the envoy to France; after the war he was the vice premier of the National Democratic Front (FND) government and minister of foreign affairs (1945–1947). He resigned under Communist pressure.

509. Division formed from the Romanian prisoners of war in the USSR and named after the leader of the 1821 revolution in Wallachia and Moldavia. The division fought against the Germans in Moldavia, Transylvania, Hungary, and Slovakia in 1944–1945.

erator, in the coming year they will succeed in fighting for and earning a place under the Slavic and Balkan sun.

Petko Stainov, minister of
foreign affairs and religion.

[...]

· 5 JANUARY 1945 ·

—*Rákosi:* reported on Hungarian affairs (provisional national assembly, provisional national government, activities of the Com[munist] Party, etc.).

—*Pieck and Ulbricht:* on German affairs (German party school, publishing house to produce literature for Germany, etc.).

[...]

· 10 JANUARY 1945 ·

—*Stalin called:* I received the Yugoslav delegation yesterday.[510] The Yugoslavs informed me that they had proposed to the Bulgarians that Bulgaria join Yugoslavia on the same basis as the Serbs and Croats. But the Bulgarians had not agreed to this and had insisted on combining Yugoslavia and Bulgaria as equal partners in a Bulgarian-Yugoslav confederated state. I said that the Bulgarians were right, the Yugoslavs wrong. Yugoslavia and Bulgaria ought to be combined into a coequal state on a parity basis, something along the lines of the former Austria-Hungary. Otherwise, bringing Bulgaria into Yugoslavia would mean the absorption of Bulgaria. Moreover, the Yugoslavs still lack a government empowered to conclude a treaty with Bulgaria. They wanted Bulgaria to send a diplomatic representative to Belgrade. The Bulgarian government, however, is in no position to send a diplomatic representative; all it can do is have its political representative attached to the national committee. It would be better to begin with a mutual-assistance pact, and then take it from there ...

—The Yugoslavs are inexperienced; the Bulgarians are evidently more experienced.

—I advised not starting this fighting in Greece. The ELAS people should not have resigned from the Papandreou government.[511] They've

510. The delegation consisted of KPJ Politburo member Andrija Hebrang, chief of the supreme staff Gen. Arso Jovanović, and Gen. Gojko Nikoliš. The first two were received by Stalin and Molotov on 9 January 1945.

511. George Papandreou (1888–1968), antiroyalist and anticommunist Greek

taken on more than they can handle. They were evidently counting on the Red Army's coming down to the Aegean. We cannot do that. We cannot send our troops into Greece, either. The Greeks have acted foolishly.

—The Yugoslavs want to take Greek Macedonia. They want Albania, too, and even parts of Hungary and Austria. This is unreasonable. I do not like the way they are acting. Hebrang[512] is apparently a sensible man and grasped what I was telling him, but the rest of them in Belgrade are going too far.

—As for Kolarov leaving for Bulgaria, I'm afraid that his arrival there could alienate the Agrarians and others. They will write up his biography, kick up a fuss, use his presence to insinuate the sovietization of Bulgaria, and so on. Meanwhile the present government must be preserved and if possible even expanded . . .

[. . .]

· 18 JANUARY 1945 ·
[. . .]

—In connection with the CC report that the government has produced a new draft agreement between Bulgaria and Yugoslavia, sent the following encoded telegram to the CC:

---

politician; headed the Greek government-in-exile (1944–1945), which was denounced by the procommunist ELAS; minister in several cabinets (1946–1952); prime minister of the Center Union government (1964–1967) that was overthrown in a military coup. He remained under house arrest until his death.

512. Andrija Hebrang (1899–1949), Yugoslav Communist leader; Tito's ally in the Comintern-sponsored antifractional struggle in the Zagreb KPJ committee (1928). Having been arrested and imprisoned (1929–1941), he led the "right" faction in the prison disputes with the ultra-Left of Petko Miletić (1897–1939?); a member of the Communist Party of Croatia (KPH) CC (from 1941 on), he was arrested again, by the Ustašas, in 1941 and exchanged for Ustaša officers captured by the Partisans. After serving as secretary of the KPH CC and member of the KPJ Politburo (from 1943 on), he was removed from the Croatian leadership in 1944 on charges of "nationalism." Having been transferred to Belgrade and appointed minister of industry, head of the planning commission, and the economic council, he was expelled from the KPJ Politburo in April 1946, but he retained his planning post. He was arrested in 1948 on charges of supporting Stalin's positions in the early polemics with the Yugoslav leadership; the case against him, which was being prepared, was never brought to trial. Hebrang himself died in unexplained circumstances in his prison cell in 1949. Efforts were undertaken to represent him as an Ustaša agent. His wife and various associates were kept in prison and otherwise harassed long after his death.

Received the latest government draft. Can hardly believe that our own ministers approved it! This draft makes a complete hash of the whole issue. Declaring a "federation of South Slavs" now, providing for a Provisional Council of South Slavic Unity as a common federative power, and so on, at the present stage is politically inadvisable in every possible respect and could have very harmful consequences. I again recommend taking our prior draft as a basis, and on that basis reaching an agreement with the Yugoslavs. Our government's draft must be considered unworkable and premature; it fails to take into account the current Balkan and international situation, and it should therefore be voted down.

[. . .]

· 20 JANUARY 1945 ·
[. . .]

—Received Major General Davydov from the NKGB [state security] concerning his transfer to work in the CC system—as director of Institute No. 100.

[. . .]

· 21 JANUARY 1945 ·
[. . .]

—At the Kremlin tonight (ceremony commemorating Lenin). After the session, a friendly dinner with *Stalin,* Molotov, Kalinin, Voroshilov, Beria, Malenkov, Mikoyan, Bulganin, Andreev, Voznesensky, Shkiriatov, Shvernik.

—Agreed with *Stalin* and *Molotov* immediately to summon representatives of the Bulgarian government and representatives of Tito for joint consultation concerning treaty of alliance between Bulgaria and Yugoslavia.

Stalin: "We should support them (Bulgaria and Yugoslavia) if anything happens. But to that end they ought to coordinate their major actions with us ahead of time or at least keep us apprised of their affairs."

[. . .]

· 22 JANUARY 1945 ·
[. . .]

Received a report from Sofia that the following have left by plane for Moscow: Kimon Georgiev and Anton Yugov, as well as Traicho Kostov, Tsola Dragoicheva, Raiko Damianov,[513] Titko Chernokolev.[514] They're spending the night in Bucharest.

· 23 JANUARY 1945 ·

—Arrived in Moscow: *Kimon Georgiev* and *Anton Yugov* as members of government delegation, the other four as party delegation.

—Received the party delegation and held long discussion (Traicho Kostov, Tsola Dragoicheva, Raiko Damianov, Titko Chernokolev, Anton Yugov, Boris Hristov[515] and Boris Simov).[516]
—Yugov conveyed a request from Kimov that I receive him as well together with Mihalchev.

· 24 JANUARY 1945 ·

—Received *Kimon Georgiev* and *Yugov*. Talked over the draft treaty of alliance between Bulgaria and Yugoslavia.

—At the CC received *Kostov, Dragoicheva, Chernokolev, Hristov* regarding party issues.

[. . .]

—We were visited until late at night by: Traicho Kostov, Tsola Dragoicheva, Vide[nov?], Chernokolev, Damianov, Hristov, Kolarov.

---

513. Raiko Damianov (b. 1903), Bulgarian Communist; political émigré in the USSR; member of the BRP/BRP(k)/BKP CC (1935–1966) and Politburo (1945–1962); veteran of the International Brigades in Spain (1938–1939). After being arrested in 1940 in Bulgaria, he escaped and joined the partisans (1943). He was president of the Bulgarian trade union association (1945–1950).

514. Titko Chernokolev (1910–1965), Bulgarian Communist engaged in youth organizing; member BRP/BRP(k) CC (1944–1949); staff member of CC apparatus (1945–1948); deputy minister of agriculture (1948–1950).

515. Bulgarian trade counselor in Moscow.

516. Bulgarian foreign trade official and deputy chief of the planning commission.

Stalin and Molotov received Kimon Georgiev and Yugov together with Yugoslav representatives Hebrang and M. Pijade.[517]

· 25 JANUARY 1945 ·

—Received president and minister *Kimon Georgiev* and minister of internal affairs *Yugov* about finalizing a draft of the treaty of alliance between Bulgaria and Yugoslavia.

—Conference with Bulgarian party delegation (Traicho Kostov, Tsola Dragoicheva, Raiko Damianov, and Titko Chernokolev).

Sent Chernokolev to the Komsomol CC to give an informational report on RMS [Workers' Youth League of Bulgaria].

—Gave Traicho Kostov instructions on his informational report to the department (Friday).

—Molotov informed me of Comrade *Stalin's* discussion with the Bulgarian and Yugoslav government delegates on the treaty of alliance between Bulgaria and Yugoslavia and his advice not to mention any federation in the treaty.

· 26 JANUARY 1945 ·
[. . .]

—Vyshinsky and I talked over the final draft of the treaty of alliance between Bulgaria and Yugoslavia. We agreed that the Yugoslavs' desire to form a federation incorporating Bulgaria into Yugoslavia must be rejected in favor of establishing a federation of Bulgaria and Yugoslavia on equal terms.

517. Moša Pijade (pseudonyms: Janko, Šiki, 1890–1957), Yugoslav Communist; academic painter and journalist. He was arrested in 1925 and spent fourteen years in prison, where he organized party courses and translated Marx's *Capital*. He was interned in the Bileća concentration camp (1939); member of the KPJ CC (from 1940 on); organizer of Partisan uprising in Montenegro; vice president of the AVNOJ (1943); after the war president of the presidium of the Federal Assembly, vice president of the Federal Executive Council (cabinet), and president of the Federal National Assembly.

Dimitrov in the Comintern office, Moscow.

Dimitrov's membership card for the Executive Committee of the Communist International, Seventh Congress of the Comintern, Moscow, 1935.

Marcel Cachin and Georgi Dimitrov, Moscow, 1935.

Dimitrov and the Comintern leaders: (from left) seated, Georgi Dimitrov, Palmiro Togliatti, Wilhelm Florin, Wang Ming; standing, Otto Kuusinen, Klement Gottwald, Wilhelm Pieck, Dmitry Manuilsky, Moscow, 1935.

Dimitrov with the Kostroma voters, 19 December 1937.

Tito (left) and Dimitrov in Meshcherino, 15 April 1945.

Mikhail Kalinin, chairman of the presidium of the Supreme Soviet of the USSR, awards Dimitrov the Order of Lenin for his struggle against fascism, Moscow, 27 June 1945.

G. Dimitrov, with S. S. Biriuzov and Marshal F. I. Tolbukhin, commander of the Third Ukrainian Front, which entered Bulgaria on 8 September 1944, at the Sofia railway station, 22 February 1946.

Traicho Kostov and Georgi Dimitrov, 26 May 1946.

Dimitrov, chairman of the Council of Ministers of Bulgaria, in his office, 30 April 1948.

Dimitrov, general secretary of the BKP, delivers a report at the fifth party congress, Sofia, December 1948.

Georgi Dimitrov.

Dimitrov with wife Rosa and children Fania and Boyko in Meshcherino, 1948.

Dimitrov and son Boyko in Barvikha, 1948.

Georgi and Rosa Dimitrov in Barvikha, 18 June 1949.

Inauguration of a monument to Dimitrov (sculpted by K. and M. Merabishvili), Moscow, 16 June 1972.

· 27 JANUARY 1945 ·
[. . .]

—*Vyshinsky* and I talked over the text of the draft treaty for an alliance between Bulgaria and Yugoslavia.

—Drew *Molotov's* attention to Article 4 of the draft treaty, on Macedonia. Pointed out to him the need to correct this article of the treaty.

[. . .]

· 28 JANUARY 1945 ·

—Sunday.

At Stalin's dacha. Yugoslavs were invited: *Moša Pijade, Hebrang,* and the Yugoslav ambassador *Simić;*[518] and Bulgarians: beside myself, Premier *Kimon Georgiev,* Minister of Internal Affairs *Yugov,* Bulgarian political representative Prof. *Mihalchev* and Secretary of the CC of the Workers' Party (Communists) *Traicho Kostov. Molotov, Malenkov, and Beria* were present.

Exceptionally cordial atmosphere. It was noted that the draft of the treaty between Bulgaria and Yugoslavia that has been produced has been reconciled in both delegations and there are no disagreements between them. They have arranged for the chairman-ministers of the Bulgarian and Yugoslav governments to exchange letters (not for publication!) committing both countries to take measures to establish a federation of Bulgaria and Yugoslavia without predetermining the nature of that federation—whether a coequal one between Bulgaria and Yugoslavia or a united federation of Bulgars, Serbs, Croats, Slovenes, Montenegrins, and Macedonians.

Many toasts proposed. Stalin emphasized in his toasts that the alliance between Bulgaria and Yugoslavia is something revolutionary in the history of Europe and has enormous historical significance. This act lays the foundation for a union of all Slavic peoples. These peoples ought to assist and defend one another. Germany will be routed, but the Germans are a sturdy people with a great number of cadres; they will rise again. The Slavic peoples should not be caught unawares the

518. Stanoje Simić (1893–1970), Yugoslav diplomat; envoy of the Yugoslav government-in-exile to the USSR; resigned in 1944 and placed himself at the disposal of Tito's authorities; subsequently president of the People's Front of Serbia, ambassador to the USA, foreign minister, and minister without portfolio.

next time they attempt an attack against them, and in the future this will probably, even certainly, occur. The old Slavophilism expressed the aim of tsarist Russia to subjugate the other Slavic peoples. Our own Slavophilism is something completely different—the unification of the Slavic peoples as equals for the common defense of their existence and future. We have no wish to impose anything on the other Slavic peoples. We do not interfere in their internal affairs. Let them do what they can. The crisis of capitalism has manifested itself in the division of the capitalists into two factions—one *fascist,* the other *democratic.* The alliance between ourselves and the democratic faction of capitalists came about because the latter had a stake in preventing Hitler's domination, for that brutal state would have driven the working class to extremes and to the overthrow of capitalism itself. We are currently allied with one faction against the other, but in the future we will be against the first faction of capitalists, too.

Perhaps we are mistaken when we suppose that the Soviet form is the only one that leads to socialism. In practice, it turns out that the Soviet form is the best, but by no means the only, form. There may be other forms—the democratic republic and even under certain conditions the constitutional monarchy . . .

(Stalin's remarks at this remarkable evening meeting contained a great deal else that was important and interesting!)

[. . .]

· 5 FEBRUARY 1945 ·

—Major General *Davydov,* Major General *Artiomov* and Colonel Prudnikov about operations of Institute 100; Morozov handed over operations to the new director of the institute, Davydov, and so on.
—Conference on the bulletin with staff from Institute 205 (Friedrich [Geminder], Glaubauf, Lang, Toboso, and others).

[. . .]

· 6 FEBRUARY 1945 ·
[. . .]

—Meeting with deputies to plan department operations for February through April; Institute 100 and Institute 205; budget estimate for Institute 99; distribution of work in my absence.

[. . .]

· 9 FEBRUARY 1945 ·

—Received following encoded telegram from Ercoli [Togliatti] (through the NKID [People's Commissariat for Foreign Affairs]):

Public attention is turning to the question of Trieste and its future status, partly because the question is being exploited by our enemies to create a nationalist movement and isolate the Communist Party. Undoubtedly, the majority of Italians regard Trieste as an Italian city. The city's population is indeed made up of Italians for the most part, but it would accept the status of a free city, especially if that status were proposed by our party. However, Italian parties would object strenuously to this—perhaps the socialists would as well—and I do not know whether Yugoslavia would accept it. To date we have not submitted and not discussed any concrete decision. We are fighting against those who are exploiting the Trieste question in order to create dissension within the Italian people and between the Italian and Yugoslav peoples. We are arguing that the essential task is to fight alongside Yugoslavia against Hitler and fascism, that we must expose and demonstrate the crimes of fascism and Italian imperialism against the Yugoslav peoples, and that all disputes between the two countries ought to be settled by a joint accord, and so on. We have issued our organization in Trieste a directive to work with Tito's units to drive out the Germans and fascists and to establish people's power in the city.

I urge you to provide me with your advice in order to orient our future endeavors as regards this issue, which may become one of the most crucial issues of Italian politics.

· 10 FEBRUARY 1945 ·

[. . .]

—Sent the following encoded telegram to the CC in Sofia the day before yesterday (in reply to their inquiry!):

It would be inadvisable to allow the queen to leave the country at present. Her departure would be seen as flight from the country and would certainly be maliciously exploited abroad to portray the new regime in Bulgaria as supposedly incapable of providing for the needs of the queen and her son. What is more, once she was outside Bulgaria, she would be used as the focus of political intrigues of every sort for the purpose of damaging the country's international standing.

[. . .]

· 16 FEBRUARY 1945 ·

—Spoke with Molotov about the conference in the Crimea [Yalta Conference]—in particular, about its decision regarding the Balkans and the planned treaty of alliance between Bulgaria and Yugoslavia. All in all, nothing essential is changed. It is just that there will be a number of difficulties concerning the alliance between Bulgaria and Yugoslavia. The British and the Americans are clearly against it. They regard Bulgaria as a state under foreign control and not possessing the right to conclude such an alliance . . .

[. . .]

· 20 FEBRUARY 1945 ·

—Gave the courier mail for the CC (letter for Traicho [Kostov] on the Crimean conference, on Slavic rally in Sofia, on relations with the socialists and Agrarians and our ideological work against corrupted "Marxism" and agraro-syndicalism, on measures against the anarchists, on the CC plenum and the Fatherland Front and Trade Union conferences, and so on).

[. . .]

· 22 FEBRUARY 1945 ·

—Sent Sofia the following encoded telegram in connection with the forthcoming plenum of the Bulgarian party CC:

I have the following comments on the draft political resolution of the plenum:

1. The first paragraph should also indicate the exceptionally significant role played by the partisan movement organized and led by our party;

2. The eleventh paragraph should say that closer ties, cooperation, and alliance among Slavic peoples is the paramount (not the sole!) means of defending against potential resumption of hostilities by Germany and of securing our own freedom, independence, and prosperity;

3. As for Macedonia, we must welcome the equality of national rights accorded the Macedonians in the framework of the new federative Yugoslavia; we need not shrink from stating that our party is fully in favor of recognizing the Macedonians as a people in their own right and in favor of national self-determination for the Macedonian people;

4. A paragraph should be added about party education and Marxist-Leninist education, about raising the level of our party members' theoretical and political sophistication, about a serious and accelerated program for train-

ing party cadres, about cohesion between senior and junior party cadres, about work on the ideological and cultural front, which in terms of its importance for the immediate future yields nothing to the military and economic fronts;

5. Another paragraph should be added about maintaining the strictest vigilance against infiltration of the party and the entire Fatherland Front by covert enemy agents and provocateurs, and the need for decisive struggle against any and all promoters of the demoralization of party, public, and state cadres; against careerism, the pursuit of sinecures, the abuse of authority for personal gain, alienation from the masses, condescension toward the masses, arrogance, and vulgar bureaucratism. All these things create the perfect opening for the fascist enemy to undermine the party's combat readiness and discredit it in the eyes of the people.

I urge you to examine this last point at the plenum very seriously, making the greatest use possible of the available concrete facts, so that all our people—whatever their past contributions, however high their rank—straighten up and brace themselves and do not succumb in the slightest to the temptations that inevitably arise now that the party has a share in running the country.

· 23 FEBRUARY 1945 ·

—Admiral Papanin[519] and Marshal Fyodorenko[520] gave a luncheon in honor of the Red Army at the sanatorium. Attending, along with Rozi, were *Dolores* [Ibárruri], Gallego,[521] and Uribes[522] (they'd come to see me regarding their party affairs, in connection with Dolores's departure for France).

At my request, *Stalin* received Dolores [Ibárruri] tonight (together with Gallego and Uribes). Afterward they returned here to continue our discussion. They had been struck by the way Stalin had given them advice on all major issues that was *entirely in agreement* with the ad-

---

519. Ivan Dmitrievich Papanin (1854–1946), Soviet admiral and Arctic explorer.

520. Yakov Nikolaevich Fyodorenko (1896–1947), Soviet marshal; commander of the tank units of the Red Army; deputy people's commissar for defense (1941–1943).

521. Pseudonym of Jesús Garota, Spanish Communist; member of the PCE CC.

522. José Antonio Uribes, Spanish Communist; alternate member of the PCE Politburo.

vice I had given them before they met with him. After we'd gone over everything, including issues having to do with Dolores's forthcoming work in France and with the work of Uribes and the other Spanish comrades in the USSR, Dolores and I said our good-byes. She's flying out tomorrow morning, together with her daughter and Gallego.

· 24 FEBRUARY 1945 ·

—*Paniushkin* and *Khvostov* (head of our Central European sector) to see me. Finalized proposal on political work and propaganda in Germany in connection with the Red Army's advance on German territory. Shtern typed out my letter to Molotov and Malenkov containing these proposals.

[. . .]

· 12 MARCH 1945 ·

—Received for my review from Molotov the following encoded telegram, which was sent to Belgrade (to Kiselev, for Tito, Kardelj, Hebrang):

> In the interest of avoiding misunderstandings, we consider it necessary to inform you that the Russian friends of Yugoslavia in Moscow were stunned to learn that the new Yugoslav government was to include such figures as Grol,[523] [something] which had not been talked about earlier. The inclusion of persons such as Grol could not fail to meet with incomprehension in the ranks of the national-liberation movement. That incomprehension is compounded by the fact that Simić has been excluded from the government, although his sympathy for the national-liberation movement is beyond any doubt. Since we had no opportunity earlier to know of these changes in the Yugoslav government, we find it necessary to inform you, if only at this late date, that we consider these changes to be an error fraught with potential political complications. In our view, there was no compelling necessity for these changes.

523. Milan Grol (1876–1952), Yugoslav politician; theater critic and historian; member of the Serbian Independent Radical Party, later the Democratic Party (DS) of Ljuba Davidović; parliamentary deputy (1925–1929); president of the DS (after 1940); part of Simović's cabinet (1941); minister in the government-in-exile (1941–1943). He returned to Yugoslavia in 1945 and became a vice president in Tito's first cabinet (1945). After refusing to enter the People's Front, he resigned from the cabinet (August 1945) and was thereafter in the opposition; his newspaper *Demokratija* was quickly banned in November 1945.

· 13 MARCH 1945 ·

—*Gottwald, Kopecký,* and *Baranov* to see me regarding Czechoslovak issues. Consulted with me about the platform of the new Czechoslovak government, the makeup of that government, and the state structure of the new Czechoslovakia (in connection with Beneš's forthcoming visit to Moscow).

[. . .]

· 16 MARCH 1945 ·
[. . .]

—Pointed out to *Pieck* (speaking over the hot line) the impracticability of the various appeals being made over their radio broadcasting (Deutsche Volkssender), such as to reestablish free trade unions in Germany, and so on, at the present time. Gave him assorted advice regarding their propaganda henceforward.

[. . .]

· 1.7 MARCH 1945 ·
[. . .]

Audience with *Stalin* tonight, together with *Molotov.* Discussed issues pertaining to Germany. The British want to dismember Germany (Bavaria and Austria, the Rhine region, etc.). They are using every means available to destroy *their competitor.* Viciously bombing German factories and plants. We are keeping their air forces out of our zone of Germany. But they are doing everything they can to bomb there as well. The Germans are stubbornly continuing to fight. They are choosing certain death. Hitler senses that his end is near, and he is dragging the German populace down with him into the abyss. What they need is for some Germans to appear who are capable of salvaging what could still be salvaged for the survival of the German people. Organize the municipality [local urban council], reestablish the economy, etc., on the German territory taken and occupied by the Red Army. Establish local government agencies out of which would eventually develop a German government.

—He elaborated his plan, which was in the main approved. . . .

———————————

—Silesia will go to Poland, along with Pomerania and Danzig.

———————————

—Line of demarcation between our zone and the Anglo-American zone runs through *Berlin*. Berlin divided into three parts (northeast goes to the Red Army). Entire city under joint control.
—Dresden, Leipzig, etc. (Saxony)—Red Army.
—Stalin pointed out, among other things, that Bulgarian units are not distinguishing themselves in the fighting . . .

[. . .]

· 28 MARCH 1945 ·

—Had a talk with Molotov regarding the treaty of alliance between Bulgaria and Yugoslavia.

[. . .]

· 29 MARCH 1945 ·

—Sent *Molotov* a list of German prisoners of war who could be used in the work of establishing government agencies, etc., on Red Army–occupied territories, as well as a proposal for establishing such agencies, publishing a German people's newspaper, and organizing German radio broadcasting.

[. . .]

· 30 MARCH 1945 ·

—Received *Gottwald*, *Široký*,[524] and *Šverma* (*Maria*) in connection with their departure for Czechoslovakia (Košice), together with Beneš. Gottwald reported on the Communist Party's agreement with Beneš on the future provisional Czechoslovak government, its composition and platform, as well as the measures it will take as regards the party. President-minister *Fierlinger;* four vice presidents, two of them being *Gottwald* and *Široký*. Minister of Internal Affairs Nosek[525] (Com-

524. Viliam Široký (1902–1971), Czechoslovak Communist; secretary of the Slovak CP in the 1920s; member of the KSČ CC (from 1929) and Politburo (1931–1963); secretary of the KSČ CC (from 1935); Communist deputy in the Czechoslovak parliament (from 1935 on). In Moscow after 1940, he was sent to Slovakia to reorganize the party in 1941, arrested, and sentenced to a long prison term. He escaped in February 1945 and made his way to the USSR; deputy prime minister in the Košice government; chairman of the Slovak CP (after 1945); minister of foreign affairs and deputy prime minister (after 1950); prime minister of Czechoslovakia (1953–1963). He was suspended from the KSČ during the reform era (1968) on account of his role in Stalinist repression but restored to full membership in 1971.

525. Václav Nosek (1892–1955), Czechoslovak Communist; member of the

munist), Minister of War General *Svoboda*[526] (close to the Communists).

—Platform is mainly as developed by Gottwald and coordinated with me. My corrections to the draft of the platform were incorporated. It has been decided to commence negotiations with the Soviet government concerning *Transcarpathian Ukraine.*

—Gottwald consulted with me regarding his future governmental and party work.

—Agreed on party liaison between the CC of the Czechoslovak Communist Party and the CC of the VKP(b), and so on.

[. . .]

· 1 APRIL 1945 ·

—Sunday. Invited *Pieck, Ulbricht, and Ackermann* to have a more detailed discussion with them about their work in Germany, particularly on territory occupied by the Red Army. Showed them the Lenin museum (Gorky), where he died. Afterward, we had lunch together and watched a film.

· 2 APRIL 1945 ·

—*Moved back to the city* (the Pakhra is running very high and carrying a lot of ice; bridge must be dismantled. Temporarily impossible to live at the dacha).

—Received *Koplenig* (and Khvostev from the department) on Austrian affairs. (Stalin called me and advised selecting a few suitable Austrians to send to the Third Ukrainian Front. "We want Austria restored to its status quo as of 1938.")

KSČ CC (1929–1936, 1945–1954); minister of internal affairs (1945–1953) who was instrumental in the Communist coup in 1948.

526. Lukvík Svoboda (1894–1979), Czechoslovak general and statesman; office of the prewar Czechoslovak army. In 1939, with his unit, he fled to Poland and then the USSR, where he and his men were in fact interned; after the German attack on the USSR he organized and commanded Czechoslovak units within the Red Army (1941–1945). Minister of defense (1945–1950); member of the KSČ CC presidency (1968–1976); president of Czechoslovakia (1968–1975).

· 3 APRIL 1945 ·

—*Two years since Mitia died!*
—A hard day for Rozi and me . . . Visited the cemetery (Mitia's grave).

———————————

—Received Koplenig on Austrian business.
—*Kasatkin* reported on budget estimates for the special institutes and other administrative and economic matters.

[. . .]

—Sent *Stalin* my list of Austrians (along with character references for them).

· 4 APRIL 1945 ·

—Received Bulgarian comrade Nikola *Minchev*[527] (he's done NKVD work to date). Reported on his work in Bulgaria. Instructed him to transfer to Bulgarian-area work (under Yugov).
—Received Colonel *Braginsky*[528] (PUR [Red Army Political Directorate]) and *Kozlov*[529] (Institute 99) on work in the area of the Free Germany national committee and among prisoners of war.
—Koplenig, Wieden (Fischer), and *Khvostev*. Examined list of Austrians slated for transport to Austria, as well as problems of the restoration of Austria (national assembly, government, and so on).

[. . .]

· 7 APRIL 1945 ·

—Briefed and instructed *Koplenig* and *Wieden* for their transport to Austria tomorrow (together with Dekanozov from the NKVD).
—Had a detailed discussion with Major General *Kiselev* (head of Soviet military mission to Yugoslavia), who arrived together with Tito.[530] His impressions of the Yugoslav leadership's performance are not encouraging.

527. Nikola Minchev (1904–1974), Bulgarian Communist; political émigré to the USSR who was in the state security apparatus.
528. Yosif Samuilovich Braginsky (b. 1905), Soviet Communist; officer in the Political Directorate of the Red Army; liaison with the ECCI.
529. Sergei Sergeevich Kozlov (b. 1898), Yugoslav Communist; director of the Comintern school (beginning in 1939).
530. Tito visited the USSR from 5 to 20 April 1945 as a head of a delegation

—Arranged to meet with Tito tomorrow.

· 8 APRIL 1945 ·

—Sent *Stalin* the following letter:

I urge you while Comrade Tito is in Moscow to find time to consider the problem of Yugoslav-Bulgarian relations. Specifically, it would be advisable to devise an appropriate form for implementing the planned political agreement between the two countries before the war is over, since afterward there will probably be far more obstacles to contend with.

It must be noted that a considerable number of Yugoslav comrades are evidently subject to unhealthy sentiments, a certain degree of "dizziness with success" and an inappropriate, condescending attitude toward Bulgaria and even toward the Bulg[arian] Com[munist] Party.

Your assistance and influence in this regard would be most welcome.

(7 April 1945)

—Received *Tito* this evening at my apartment in the city. Had a long talk about the situation in Yugoslavia, about relations with the British and the Americans, about a possible treaty of alliance (or some other arrangement) between Yugoslavia and Bulgaria, and so on. General impression: *underestimation* of the complexity of the situation and the impending difficulties, *too arrogant,* heavy dose of conceit and sure signs of "dizziness with success." To hear him talk, of course, you would think everything was under control . . .

—Koplenig and Wieden took off for Austria today.

[. . .]

· 12 APRIL 1945 ·

—*With Tito at Stalin's.*

Tito and I met with *Stal[in]* (present were Molotov, Beria, Malenkov, Bulganin). Concerning relations between Bulgaria and Yugoslavia, the following agreements were reached: 1) As a *first step,* restore *diplomatic relations* between Bulgaria and Yugoslavia in the immediate future, and thus put the past to rest (eliminating prior hostility, issues of

that included Foreign Minister Ivan Šubašić, KPJ Politburo member Milovan Djilas, and others.

reparations, etc.). After a certain period, as a second step: conclude an agreement on *cooperation* and mutual assistance in the reconstruction of both countries and defense against possible renewed aggression from Germany. As a *third step:* after concluding such an agreement, prepare grounds for merging the two states into a *common federation.*
—*Stal[in]* advised us that after a certain period the Soviet government, too, would raise the question with the Allies of recognizing Bulgaria as an [Allied] belligerent country and would restore its own diplomatic relations with Bulgaria.
—*Stal[in]* criticized the self-confidence of Bulgarian Communists, their failure to take difficulties into account, their wish to see everything go smoothly, and so on. He believes that the Com[munist] Party's position in the country is still too weak, that the Agrar[ian] Union holds sway with the peasant masses, and that there should be no rush to hold elections and so on. Issues have to be found on which the peasants could be won over to the Com[munist] Party.

· 13 APRIL 1945 ·

—Attended the All-Slavic Committee's reception in honor of *Tito.* I was given a seat in the presidium near Tito. Many toasts. I, too, had to make a speech; the All-Slavic Committee is after all a public organization . . .

· 14 APRIL 1945 ·
[. . .]

—*Djilas* to see me. Told me about his visit to Bulgaria. Thinks the situation is good. Party is strong. Detailed discussion on relations between Bulg[arian] and Yugosl[av] Com[munist] parties—liaison, sharing of information, reaching agreement on major issues.
[. . .]

· 15 APRIL 1945 ·

—Sunday.
   I held a reception for Tito here at the dacha. [. . .]
Extremely cordial atmosphere, party lasted until four in the morning. Performers reported to me one at a time on the work they had done and their impressions of Yugoslavia and Bulgaria.
[. . .]

· 19 APRIL 1945 ·

—Received the daughter of the regent [Todor] *Pavlov* (with her husband). Both had studied in the same program, become doctors, worked for the NKGB [People's Commissariat for State Security], and been assigned to the rear, to different part[isan] detachments. Pavlova recounts various episodes of drunkenness and dissipation in the detachments in which she worked as a doctor . . . Wants to go to Bulgaria and won't hear of going without her husband. He (Major Davydov) is a Soviet subject, can go only if sent on official assignment.
—Arranged with *Sudoplatov* (NKGB) for him to have both of them relieved of their duties and assigned to me.

[. . .]

· 24 APRIL 1945 ·
[. . .]

—*Bulganin, Vyshinsky,* and I selected group of Germ[an] Communists who are to be sent to work in Germany together with the antifasc[ist] prisoners of war.

· 25 APRIL 1945 ·

—*Pieck, Ulbricht, Ackermann* to see me (together with Major Gen[eral] Shikin[531] and Lieutenant-Col[onel] Sapozhnikov). Instructed them on the work of the group of German personnel being sent to Germany.

[. . .]

· 28 APRIL 1945 ·
[. . .]

—*Stal[in]* called about the German comrades being sent to Germany. He approved the list of people I proposed.

[. . .]

· 7 MAY 1945 ·
[. . .]

—Spoke over the HF with *Biriuzov* and *Kostov* in Sofia in connection with the Agrar[ian] Union's national conference. Gave them my per-

531. Yosif Vasilievich Shikin (1906–1973), Soviet general; deputy chief (1942–1945) and chief (1946–1949) of the Red Army Political Directorate.

sonal message for *N. Petkov,* that he is to distance himself from the Gemetists,[532] participate actively in the confer[ence], remain head of the Agr[arian] Union and remain in the government, etc. Warned him that if he supports the Gemetists either directly or indirectly, then the party and I will have no choice but to publicly condemn this sort of conduct, which is harmful to our people.

· 8 MAY 1945 ·
[. . .]

—*A document of unconditional surrender by Germany* has been signed in Berlin.
   —The war in Europe is over!
   —Wiesław [Gomułka] (secretary of the PPR CC) to see me tonight.

· 9 MAY 1945 ·

—Day off. A day of national celebration. Victory Day!

—Radio address by Stalin.
—Thousand-gun salute!
[. . .]

· 10 MAY 1945 ·
[. . .]

—Spoke with *Biriuzov* and *Traicho* [Kostov] in Sofia (over the HF). Traicho informed me about the nat[ional] conference of the Agrar[ian] Union. Results entirely satisfactory. Resolution they adopted is top-notch. Members of the Admin[istrative] Council are reliable. Petkov, however, failed to appear at the conference. Although he was elected to the union leadership, he continues to waver.
[. . .]

532. Followers of Georgi M. Dimitrov (Gemeto, 1903–1972), who was a Bulgarian politician, leader of the BZNS Pladne, and secretary-general of the BZNS (1944–1945). After being expelled from the Fatherland Front in May 1945, he emigrated to the USA.

· 17 MAY 1945 ·

—Boris Hristov on Bulgarian trade issues.
—Spoke with Molotov about Italian affairs, specifically the arrival of Ercoli [Togliatti] in connection with telegram.
—Wrote *Stal[in]* about *Trieste:* argued for the necessity and justice of giving Trieste to Yugoslavia.

[. . .]

· 23 MAY 1945 ·
[. . .]

—Sent Molotov draft telegram to Ercoli [Togliatti] on Trieste in the spirit of my letter to Stalin (about why Trieste should go to Yugoslavia).

[. . .]

· 26 MAY 1945 ·

—Marshal *Voroshilov* to see me at the CC. We discussed the situation in Hungary and the tasks of the Com[munist] Party. He is pleased with the Hungarian leadership comrades, particularly Rákosi and Gerő.
—Marshal *Tolbukhin* to see me tonight at the CC. We discussed the situation in Austria and the activities of the Austrian government, specifically the tasks of our Communist ministers. Lengthy discussion of various issues as regards Bulgaria, since from now on he will be in the Bulgarian and Romanian Allied Control Commission.

[. . .]

· 28 MAY 1945 ·
[. . .]

—Sent encoded telegram to *Ercoli* [Togliatti] concerning Trieste. Stalin approved my point of view on this issue.

[. . .]

· 6 JUNE 1945 ·

—*Pieck, Ulbricht, Ackermann, Sobotka*[533] to see me. Examined their draft appeal to the German people by the CC of the Germ[an] Com-

533. Gustav Sobotka (1886–1953), German Communist who was on the staff

[munist] Party and their proposal to form a workers' party of Germany.

—Also to see me today, from PUR, were Major General Shikin, Major General Burtsev, and another colonel, regarding their work involving Germany.

—Sent Stalin edited text of the appeal.

[. . .]

· 7 JUNE 1945 ·

—Held conference in the department, at which *Ackermann, Ulbricht, and Sobotka* reported on the situation in Germany (the Soviet Zone).

—Shikin, Burtsev, the German comrades, and I determined what the R[ed] Army Political Directorate needs to do in Germany.

—Saw St[alin] (and Mol[otov]) this evening. Discussed draft appeal by the KPD. Substantial changes were introduced. (Pieck, Ulbricht, Ackermann, and Sobotka participated.)

—Stalin proposed: declare categorically that the path of imposing the Sov[iet] system on Germany is an incorrect one; an antifascist democratic parliamentary regime must be established.

—The Com[munist] Party proposes a bloc of antifascist parties with a common platform.

—Don't speak so glowingly of the Sov[iet] Union, and so on.

· 8 JUNE 1945 ·

—Germans and I finalized text of the German CP appeal (in German and Russian).

—Sent *St[alin] and Mol[otov]* the appeal in corrected form (tonight St[alin] informed me that he had approved this text).

[. . .]

· 9 JUNE 1945 ·

—Conference with German comrades (Pieck, Ackermann, Ulbricht, Sobotka) about their forthcoming work as leaders of the German CP in Berlin. Refined the German text of the party appeal. We added the following to the passage about confiscation of major landowners' and Junker estates:

---

of the Profintern (1933–1936). He worked for the German-language radio station in the USSR (1939–1945) and was a member of the KPD CC (1945–1946).

"It stands to reason that these measures do not apply in the slightest to land ownership and farming activities by the *Großbauer* [large farmers]."

[...]

· 11 JUNE 1945 ·

—Sent Stal[in] concrete proposals and requests from the German comrades (Pieck) concerning the work of the German CP CC.

[...]

· 25 JUNE 1945 ·

—Professor Nejedlý[534] (Czechoslov[ak] minister of education) to see me. Informed me of the situation in Czechoslovakia. Passed along various assignments and requests from Gottwald. Was especially insistent about helping resolve problems in relations with Poland (specifically the Poles' demands to retain *Tetschen* [Děčín] which Poland had received at one point from Hitler).

—Magnificent reception at the Kremlin tonight for participants in victory parade. Exceptionally solemn and at the same time cordial atmosphere.

· 26 JUNE 1945 ·

—Serov[535] (NKVD) to see me (on Zhukov's instructions) regarding composition of provincial governments of Brandenburg, Saxony, and Mecklenburg.

---

534. Zdeněk Nejedlý (1878–1962), Czechoslovak scholar and politician; historian of music and of the Hussite movement; follower of Masaryk, drifted to communism; political émigré to the USSR (1939–1945); deputy chairman of the All-Slavic Committee; minister of education of Czechoslovakia (from 1945); member of the KSČ CC (from 1946); president of the Czechoslovak Academy of Sciences (1952–1962).

535. Ivan Aleksandrovich Serov, Soviet security operative who was in the NKVD from 1939 on and directed the deportation of Chechens, Ingush, Kalmyks, and Crimean Tatars in 1944; deputy director of the Soviet military administration in Germany (1945–1947); deputy people's commissar/minister for internal affairs (state security, 1941–1954); chairman of the KGB and general of the army (1954–1958); led Soviet state security operations in Hungary (October–November 1956); chairman of military intelligence (GRU, 1958–1962). He was demoted in 1963 and expelled from the KPSS in 1965 for committing violations of legality in the security apparatus.

—Zelensky (NKGB) regarding his assignment to help Yugov and the Bulgarian Directorate of State Security.

[. . .]

· 29 JUNE 1945 ·
[. . .]

—Sokolov (NKGB) on Albania and the Albanians who have arrived, *Xoxe*[536] and *Spahiu*.[537] Suggests I receive *Xoxe* regarding Albanian part[y] and stat[e] issues.
—At the Kremlin (Kalinin awarded me the Order of Lenin). Very heartfelt, exchanged kisses!
—Sent *Stalin* congratulations on being awarded the Order of Victory, the title of Hero of the Soviet Union, and the supreme military rank of generalissimus.

[. . .]

· 30 JUNE 1945 ·

—Received Bulg[arian] *minister of war,* Velchev, at my *apartment* in the city. He complained about the lack of composure and confidence among military personnel and industrialists, who are fearful of persecution. Had a lengthy discussion with him, specifically on reorganization, rearmament, and democratic education of the army.

[. . .]

· 3 JULY 1945 ·
[. . .]

—Tonight (at city apartment) received delegation of the Bulgarian church (Exarch Stefan I, Bishop Nikodim, Bishop Parteny, Archimandrite Metody, the priest Georgiev, Senior Deacon Grigoriev). Long dis-

---

536. Koçi Xoxe (1911–1949), Albanian Communist leader; member of the Communist Party of Albania (PKSH) CC and organizational secretary; Albania's minister for internal affairs; pro-Yugoslav member of the PKSH leadership. After the Cominform split Enver Hoxha had him arrested as a Titoist, sentenced to death, and executed.

537. Bedri Spahiu (1908–1998), Albanian Communist; general of the Albanian partisan army. He was dismissed from all positions in 1955 and imprisoned until 1990.

cussion about the Bulgarian church and Bulgarian clergy, about their tasks and duties in Fatherland Front Bulgaria, and so on. Sat together conversing until almost morning in quite a cordial atmosphere . . .

[. . .]

· 9 JULY 1945 ·

—Stayed home to work.

—Spoke with V[iacheslav] Mikh[ailovich Molotov] about the forthcoming reconstruction of the Bulgarian cabinet. (Petkov has put out an illegal circular against the resolutions of the Agrar[ian] Union's national conference and the perm[anent] presence the conference elected. Ministers Asen Pavlov and Derzhanski sided with him. It's becoming impossible for them to continue in the cabinet.)

—Sent inquiry to CC (Sofia) regarding candidates being considered for new ministers, the new distribution of ministerial posts, and so on. Gave instructions on how to effect necessary change in the government quickly and decisively and explain this to the people.

· 10 JULY 1945 ·
[. . .]

—Regarding proposed ministerial shifts in Bulgaria, *Stal[in]* conveyed (through V. M. [Molotov]) that in the current circumstances he considers it inappropriate to remove Petkov and his Agrar[ian] comrades from the cabinet, and he finds the Communists' approach to be sectarian; recommends that the Bulg[arian] party show greater caution and tolerance, and so on. I passed on his opinion and considerations to the CC (Sofia).

· 11 JULY 1945 ·

—For a second time I had the Bulgarian exarch to my city apartment. We sat together until almost morning. Talks forever . . . Gave me his most solemn assurances that he supports and will steadfastly support the Fatherland Front and its policies . . . Quite the cunning fox . . .

[. . .]

· 14 JULY 1945 ·
[. . .]

—Spoke by way of HF to Sofia with *Kirsanov*,[538] *Chervenkov, and Kostov* regarding negotiations with the Petkov group. Gave instructions to seek a decisively positive outcome and bring negotiations to a rapid conclusion.

[. . .]

· 19 JULY 1945 ·
[. . .]

—The courier Polishchuk[539] arrived from Sofia. Brought mail, newspapers, and materials. Letters from Kostov and Chervenkov quite alarming in connection with elections (enemy intrigues, sabotage efforts, and so on).

—Gave new additional instructions to the CC in this regard: *allow separate participation in the elections by the Petkov group.*

· 20 JULY 1945 ·
[. . .]

—Spoke with Gener[al] *Biriuzov* in Sofia regarding the current situation with upcom[ing] elections of deput[ies]. Suggested to him that he advise our friends to agree to separate participation in the elections by the Petkov group (the Agrar[ian] Union), while exposing the divisive role that group is playing.

[. . .]

· 26 JULY 1945 ·
[. . .]

—Spoke by way of HF with *Molotov* (in Potsdam). Particularly about Bulg[arian] affairs. "The Allies were always proposing forming Alli[ed] obser[vers'] commissions for the elections of deputies in Bulgaria, Romania, Greece, and other countries. But we firmly rejected that proposal" (Molotov).

[. . .]

538. Stepan Pavlovich Kirsanov (1908–1967), Soviet diplomat; counselor to the Soviet mission in Bulgaria (1943–1944); envoy to Bulgaria (1945–1948).

539. Comintern and OMI courier.

—Spoke by way of HF with Kirsanov (in Sofia) in connection with the Agrar[ian] ministers' intention to quit the cabinet.

[...]

· 30 JULY 1945 ·

—Sorted out a dispute between the Hungarians (Rákosi) and the Czechoslovaks (Gottwald) regarding the Hungarian population in Czechoslovakia. The Czechs really are going overboard. Sent Molotov for coordination an encoded telegram to Gottwald indicating the need for a *different* approach to the Hungarian question in Czechoslovakia.

[...]

—Spoke with Biriuzov in Sofia over direct line. The letter from *N. Petkov* to the Alli[ed] Cont[rol] Commission requesting that the legisl[ative] elections be postponed and that Allied control be established over the election process was received by the Engl[ish] and the Amer[icans], too, but they've taken no action. Biriuzov believes that the electoral campaign is so far proceeding "well" in all respects.

[...]

· 4 AUGUST 1945 ·
[...]

—*Lavrishchev* to see me. Reported on the Berlin conference, particularly about the decisions regarding the Balkans and Bulgaria. He concurs that the decisions adopted change nothing essential as regards the leading role of the Soviet representative to the Allied Control Commission in Bulgaria.

[...]

· 6 AUGUST 1945 ·
[...]

—Spoke with Molotov about the Berlin [Potsdam] conference, and in particular about the decisions affecting Bulgaria and the Balkans. Basically, these decisions are to our advantage. In effect, this sphere of influence has been recognized as ours.

[...]

· 7 AUGUST 1945 ·
[. . .]

—Regarding my running as a candidate in the Bulg[arian] deputies' elections, Mol[otov] consulted with Stal[in] and told me that since I am currently a deputy to the USSR Supr[eme] Soviet and a Soviet citizen, my candidacy ought to be withdrawn. He insisted that we meet in person to discuss a different option: *tendering my resignation to the Supr[eme] Soviet* in order to be a Bulgarian deputy, which is more advantageous as far as future prospects are concerned.

[. . .]

· 8 AUGUST 1945 ·

—Molotov informed me that he had served the Japanese ambassador a diplomatic note in which the Sov[iet] Union declared war on Japan. An announcement from the Sov[iet] gov[ernment] is to be published this evening.

[. . .]

—In response to my proposal to maintain my candidacy to be a deputy in Bulgaria while submitting my resignation as a deputy to the USSR Supreme Soviet, *Stalin* informed me of his consent.

· 9 AUGUST 1945 ·

—*War between the USSR and Japan has commenced!*
[. . .]

· 14 AUGUST 1945 ·
[. . .]

—Regarding report from the CC (Sofia) on the *Americans' diplomatic note* with its threat to the Bulg[arian] government that if this is the way elections are held, then the US will not reestablish diplomat[ic] relations with Bulgaria—I spoke with Molotov about this.

The result: reestablishment of the USSR's diplomat[ic] relations with Bulgaria immediately, rather than after the elections, as originally planned.

—Gave the CC (Sofia) instructions on how to react to the Amer[icans'] note and to the possible boycott of elections by the opposition.

[. . .]

· 18 AUGUST 1945 ·
[. . .]

—*Paniushkin* and I drafted a telegram to *Mao Zedong* recommending to the Chinese Communists that they change their line as regards the Chiang Kai-shek government, since the situation is radically changed.

· 19 AUGUST 1945 ·
[. . .]

—Molotov approved text of telegram to Mao Zedong.

· 20 AUGUST 1945 ·

—Stayed home to work. Sent *Molotov* draft report of presidium of the Supreme Soviet on my being relieved of my duties as a deputy and re-nouncing Soviet citizenship in view of my nomination as a candidate to the National Assembly of Bulgaria.

Mol[otov] told me late tonight that the report would appear in the press tomorrow.

—Regarding [Ernest] Bevin's[540] attack on Bulg[arian] elect[oral] law and the forthcoming elections, I recommended to the CC (Sofia) that it organize the publication of a reply to *Bevin* (along with the US secre-tary of st[ate]) over the signatures of the Fath[erland] Front nat[ional] committee and representatives of all public organizations.

· 21 AUGUST 1945 ·

—*Stal[in] and Mol[otov]* advised me not to make a speech to the vot-ers of Bulgaria, in order not to irritate the Americans and English still further before the actual elections. Do it after the elections.

[. . .]

· 24 AUGUST 1945 ·

—Surprise announcement from *Stainov* that the government is willing to comply with the Amer[ican] and Engl[ish] gov[ernm]ents' demand

540. Ernest Bevin (1881–1951), British politician; trade union leader; general secretary of the Transport and General Workers' Union; Labourite MP (from 1940 on); foreign minister in Attlee's Labour cabinet (1945–1951).

to *postpone* the elections if England and America make arrangements with the Sov[iet] Union and furnish their instructions through the Allied Control Commission. Outrageous! This scandalous, capitulationist announcement has inevitably led to the postponement of the elections from 26 August to some other, later date . . .

————————

—Spoke by way of HF with the CC (Sofia) and transmitted various encoded telegrams with instructions for reorganizing and recovering from this severe setback for the party and the Fatherland Front.
—Professor *Mihalchev* came to see me. He informed me of his discussion with *Vyshinsky* but never said a word about this announcement by Stainov. Another double-dealer!

————————

· 25 AUGUST 1945 ·

—Gave Sofia various new, additional advice in connection with the temporary postponement of elections.
—Received leader of Albanian youth delegation, *Nako Spiru*[541] (studied in Italy, lived in Paris for a few months before the war, and was active in the partisan movement in Albania, starting in 1941). Had a lengthy discussion with him about Albanian affairs in connection with the general international and Balkan situation.

[. . .]

—At a press conference in Stockholm, the Labourite [Harold] *Laski* spoke out harshly against Bulgaria and specifically *against me!* . . .

[. . .]

· 27 AUGUST 1945 ·

—*Took sick*. Stayed home. Late tonight Molotov called and asked me to come to the Kremlin to discuss Bulg[arian] affairs with Stalin. Could not make the trip. Had to postpone that discussion. Settled various issues over the telephone.

541. Nako Spiru (1919–1947), Albanian Communist; member of the PKSH Politburo responsible for economic policy. He signed a series of unequal deals with Yugoslavia. His suicide precipitated the early phases of the Soviet-Yugoslav split.

· 28 AUGUST 1945 ·

—Stayed home. Getting better. Looks as though there won't be complications.

—Received a report that *Kostov* and *Chervenkov* are flying out of Sofia tomorrow to discuss the situation in view of the postponement of legisl[ative] elections.

—Gave instructions to the director of TASS to publish the Declaration of the Nat[ional] Committee of the Fatherland Front of 24 August 1945 in the press.

· 29 AUGUST 1945 ·

—*Kostov and Chervenkov* have arrived.

—Late tonight: met with Stalin and Mol[otov] (Kostov, Chervenkov, Kolarov, and I). Discussion with Stal[in] was exceptionally important in view of the situation in Bulgaria. Also settled the question of Kolarov's traveling to Bulgaria, with my own trip to follow.

· 30 AUGUST 1945 ·

—Second meeting with Stal[in] (Kostov, Chervenkov, and I).

—Present were Molotov, Khrulyov,[542] Bulganin, and Biriuzov. It was decided to relieve the Bulg[arian] gov[ernm]ent of obligations to supply the Re[d] Army with meat, sugar, and various other provisions. The balance owed was reduced for September from the prior 700 [million] leva to 420 million leva. Authorization for providing Bulgaria with forage. Stalin instructed Konev in Vienna to send [Bulgaria] two hundred tons of capt[ured] newsprint and to export a rotary press for the Bulg[arian] Com[munist] Party, and so on.

Stal[in] admonished Biriuzov: "The elections are postponed—that was a minor concession. From now on, no concessions whatsoever. No changes in the composition of the government."

542. Andrei Vasilievich Khrulyov (1892–1962), Soviet general; deputy people's commissar for defense (1941–1945); deputy minister of armed forces (1945–1951).

—Among ourselves discussed final issues with Kost[ov] and Cherv[enkov]. I gave them the necessary instructions. Tomorrow they and Biriuzov are flying out together.

[. . .]

· 1 SEPTEMBER 1945 ·
[. . .]

—Spoke with Biriuzov in Sofia. Negotiations with Kimon [Georgiev], Velchev and Stainov are proceeding favorably.

[. . .]

· 2 SEPTEMBER 1945 ·

—Sunday. Capitulation signed by Japan.
—Speech by Stalin.

[. . .]

· 4 SEPTEMBER 1945 ·
[. . .]

—I am systematically involving *Paniushkin* in the business of running the department, so that he will be able to replace me.

· 5 SEPTEMBER 1945 ·

—Received Colonel *Braginsky* and *Kozlov* (Institute 99) regarding the Fr[ee] Germany nat[ional] committee. Gave instructions to cease radio broadcasting on behalf of the nat[ional] committee and to convert *Fr[ee] Germany* into a newspaper for German prisoners of war.
—Approved new recruitment for the antifascist prisoner-of-war school.

[. . .]

· 6 SEPTEMBER 1945 ·
[. . .]

—Received mail from Rákosi. He is glad of my forthcoming departure for Bulgaria: "You'll be closer to us, and then our affairs will go even better."
—Spoke with Biriuzov in Sofia. Representatives of the opposition refused to appear at the session of the nat[ional] committee—did not rec-

ognize either the n[ational] c[ommittee] or the gov[ernment], and would agree to speak only with the regents . . .

Party and masses are in good spirits. Hostility toward the opposition is becoming even stronger.

[. . .]

· 7 SEPTEMBER 1945 ·

—Received *Gheorghiu-Dej*. Reported on the situation in Romania, the Com[munist] party and the forthcoming part[y]conference, concrete state questions which the Groza[543] government is raising with the Sov[iet] gov[ernm]ent.

During this personal conversation, at his request, I gave him various advice. Asked for second meeting before his departure for Romania.

[. . .]

· 8 SEPTEMBER 1945 ·
[. . .]

—Had a detailed discussion with Kolarov about Bulg[arian] affairs. Stipulated what he is to do in the CC of the party in the nat[ional] committee of the Fatherland Front.

—He's flying out to Sofia tomorrow. I am also sending a courier with letters for the CC. He'll be accompanied on the same flight by Baskakov, who is to bring Kostov to pass along to Zahariadis[544] $75,000 US in aid for the Communist Party.

[. . .]

543. Petru Groza (1884–1958), Romanian politician; leader of the Transylvanian-based Ploughmen's Front; minister in two prewar cabinets; prime minister (1945–1952) and president of national assembly (1952–1958) of Romania.

544. Nikos Zahariadis (1903–1973), Greek Communist leader who studied at the Communist University for Eastern Workers (KUTV); member of the KKE CC (1924–1927); studied at the Comintern's Leninist school (1929–1931); member KKE Politburo (1931–1935); KKE secretary-general (1935–1936, and again beginning in 1945); deputy in the Greek parliament (1936). Arrested during the Metaxas dictatorship (1936–1941), he was transferred by the German occupation authorities to Dachau (1941–1945). A member of the ECCI (1935–1943), he emigrated to the East European bloc countries after the Communist defeat in the Third Round (1946–1949). He was removed from his positions after Khrushchev's secret speech (1956) and was expelled from the KKE (1957). He died in the USSR.

· 13 SEPTEMBER 1945 ·
[. . .]

—Spoke with Biriuzov in Sofia: "Things are going well. Our positions are becoming stronger. Stainov was going to issue another statement to foreign countries like the one he made before elections were postponed, but that statement was stopped in time. As for Petkov, it is useless. The man is nothing but a scoundrel!" Passed on to him certain instructions for Kostov.

[. . .]

· 17 SEPTEMBER 1945 ·

—Received Prof[essor] Samodumov.[545] He recounted in detail the work of the Ministry of Education, the Council on Higher Education, and so on. Complains of improper treatment of the intelligentsia by the part[y] leader[ship], indiscriminate categorizing as fascists of everyone who did not resist fascism . . . Many excesses and improper actions on the part of the national police. Citizens' outrage is growing. Reaction is exploiting this . . .

[. . .]

· 19 SEPTEMBER 1945 ·
[. . .]

—Received personal encoded telegram from Mihalchev to *Stainov* in which he gives biased information and declares, "Under these circumstances, I don't believe that the rescheduled elections can be held!"

[. . .]

· 20 SEPTEMBER 1945 ·
[. . .]

—Went to see *Malenkov*. Settled on the arrangements for my trip to Bulgaria. It is being considered a temporary business trip (formally); everything at the department, the material base, etc., is being kept the way it is. We shall reach a final decision later about what comes next.

[. . .]

---

545. Todor Samodumov (1878–1957), Bulgarian Communist; president of the education workers' trade union.

· 27 SEPTEMBER 1945 ·
[. . .]

—Received Boris Hristov and chancellor of the Bulg[arian] legation regarding the situation in the legation and the conduct of Professor Mihalchev.

—At the apartment tonight received adviser to the Bulg[arian] legation *Nikolaev*, leaving tomorrow to deliver a report in Sofia. He characterizes the Bulg[arian] ambassador as a man inimical to the Sov[iet] Union [who is] maintaining suspicious connections with British and American agents in Moscow.

[. . .]

· 1 OCTOBER 1945 ·

—Worked at home. Regarding the CC (Sofia) decision on economic issues, sent my own suggestions, which ought to correct for the one-sidedness and insufficiency of the decision. Since Kolarov's arrival there has been a tendency in the CC to go from one extreme to another.

[. . .]

· 4 OCTOBER 1945 ·
[. . .]

—Spoke with Biriuzov and Kolarov in Sofia about the situation (the American representative Barnes[546] announced to Kimon [Georgiev] that unless N. Petkov is included in the cabinet, "it would be bad for Bulgaria").

[. . .]

· 15 OCTOBER 1945 ·

—*Saw Molotov.* Informed me in greater detail about relations with the Allies in general and the Balkans in particular. Harriman[547] came to him today with a personal letter from Truman for Stalin . . .

[. . .]

546. Maynard B. Barnes, US diplomat; representative to the Allied Control Commission in Sofia.

547. William Averell Harriman (1891–1986), American banker, politician, and diplomat; US ambassador to the USSR (1943–1946); US ambassador to Great Britain (1946); US secretary of commerce (1946–1948); governor of New York (1955–1959); undersecretary of state for political affairs (1963–1965); ambassador-at-large (1965–1968).

· 25 OCTOBER 1945 ·
[...]

—Spoke with *Molotov* on proposed force reductions in the Bulg[arian] army. Mihalchev had reported to Stainov tendentiously on his discussion with Molotov.

[...]

· 26 OCTOBER 1945 ·
[...]

—Regarding the Bulg[arian] exarch's visiting the ecumenical patriarch of Constantinople, spoke with *Karpov*[548] on the need for more concrete consideration and planning of our church policy line in the Balkan countries.

[...]

· 30 OCTOBER 1945 ·
[...]

—Had a lengthy discussion with Mikoyan about possibilities for the development of Bulgarian-Soviet economic relations. "The USSR is capable of supplying essentially everything Bulgaria needs for its agriculture and industry. Bulgaria could therefore do without any particular trade relations with America and Britain." We determined that it would be entirely feasible to establish *Bulgarian-Soviet companies* 1) for shipyard in Varna; 2) for local extraction and processing of ore; 3) for uranium production. Cooperative-based production of butter, cheese, and so on must be developed (must have our own factories); no expansion of rose oil production. Produce soy and other industrial crops. Discussed fundamentals of future trade agreement between Bulgaria and the USSR, and so on.

· 31 OCTOBER 1945 ·

—*Saw Molotov.* Discussed international situation in the Balkans. The Sov[iet] side has issued a proposal to convoke a conference on peace treaties with Italy, Finland, Romania, Bulgaria, Hungary, but a final

---

548. Georgy Grigorievich Karpov, Soviet official responsible for religious affairs.

decision must be adopted by the three countries that signed the armistice terms . . .

[. . .]

· 3 NOVEMBER 1945 ··

—Sent a letter to *Stalin* in Sochi, informing him of my departure, expressing my gratitude, and so on.

Dear Comrade Stalin,

Departing for Bulgaria in connection with the deputies' elections, I would like to express to you my most profound gratitude for the opportunity accorded to me for many years to work under your direct leadership and to learn so much from you, and also for the confidence that you have placed in me.

Naturally I will in future continue to make every effort to justify your confidence. But I beg you to provide me the opportunity in future to avail myself of your valuable advice, which is exceptionally valuable.

From the bottom of my heart I wish you good health and long life, for the benefit of the great Soviet homeland and toilers the world over.

Your ever devoted,

3 October 1945   G. D[imitrov]

—Held conference with my deputies (Panyushkin, Baranov, Ponomarev) regarding operations of the Department in my absence.

—Said my farewells to Molotov, Malenkov, Beria, Merkulov, Vyshinsky, Dekanozov, Fitin and so on.

—Packed late tonight for my early morning flight (4 November).

CHAPTER THREE

BULGARIA

AFTER his return to Bulgaria, Dimitrov immediately threw himself into the electoral campaign, which the Fatherland Front won in mid-November, aided by the Communist control of the state agencies and the opposition boycott. There commenced a prolonged cat-and-mouse game with the Bulgarian opposition, in which the Agrarians of Nikola Petkov and the Social Democrats were most contentious. The Communists rallied thanks to the dependent parties, particularly the *Zveno* (Link) of Kimon Georgiev and Damian Velchev, but had to consider the foreign-policy implications of their moves, as the Bulgarian peace treaty was not yet signed. They, Dimitrov included, were constantly prodded by contradictory Soviet directives, sometimes critical of the Bulgarians' lack of boldness and on other occasions decrying their sectarianism.

As a consequence, by the end of March 1946 Bulgaria got a Communist-dominated cabinet, headed by Kimon Georgiev, and free of overt opposition influence. By the summer the Communists were on an offensive against the opposition, arresting certain opposition figures and purging the army. By September they carried out a referendum that sealed the fate of the monarchy, the People's Republic being proclaimed on 15 September. By the end of October they undertook elections for the Grand National Assembly, a Bulgarian constitution-making institution, thereby legitimating their power. Dimitrov became the premier of Bulgaria on 22 November.

Throughout the period Dimitrov carried on a special relationship with the Yugoslav Communists, whose policies (such as the "Serbianization" of Macedonia) were not always welcome. Nevertheless, Dimitrov and

Tito entertained land swaps (of Bulgaria's Pirin Macedonia for the "western borderlands," probably the Caribrod and Bosilegrad salients, transferred from Bulgaria to Yugoslavia by the Treaty of Neuilly in 1919) and unification schemes.

It was Stalin and the Soviet policy, however, that continued to preoccupy Dimitrov after his return to Bulgaria. The diary documents the exact mechanics of control of the satellite countries. During this period, from June to November 1946, Dimitrov visited the Soviet Union no fewer than four times, once on Balkan business (Stalin's meeting with Dimitrov and Tito in June), once on the resolution of internal Bulgarian policy (November), and twice for health reasons (August and October). His health failing, increasingly susceptible to the flu, Dimitrov was still savoring the memories of the Leipzig days, to which he intermittently returned.—I.B.

· 4 NOVEMBER 1945 ·

—Early this morning (8:30) we took off from *Vnukovo* airport.
—Landed at Sofia airport *at 4:00 in the afternoon*. Met by Biriuzov. Shared the ride to Kniazhevo (once the dacha of Gen[eral] Zhekov). *After twenty-two years I am again on Bulgarian soil.*

—Visits tonight from *Kostov, Yugov, Chervenkov*. Discussed issues connected with my arrival and my possible meetings with Kimon Georgiev, etc.

· 5 NOVEMBER 1945 ·

—Settling down. Session of the Politburo. I noticed some confusion among our comrades related to the negotiations (behind the scenes!) of some *Zveno* members and Petkov's supporters; many rumors about the resignation of Kimon [Georgiev] and other ministers, turning down of offers for government posts on the verge of elections, etc. I decided that it is necessary to take the very first occasion to clarify in public our position and to stress the need to be firmly convinced that the elections will be held on November 18. They will be conducted by the present government, and any changes in the future cabinet can be effected by the future National Assembly, etc.

[. . .]

· 25 NOVEMBER 1945 ·
[. . .]

—Received two coded messages from Alekseev (M[olotov]):

1. It has been decided to grant to the Bulg[arian] gov[ernment] thirty thousand tons of corn and twenty thousand tons of wheat.

2. (At my proposal) it was decided to provide an additional hundred thousand tons to "our southern neighbors" [the Greek Communists].

[. . .]

· 28 NOVEMBER 1945 ·

—Session of the Politburo (G. D. [Georgi Dimitrov], Tr[aicho] K[ostov], V[ŭlko] Cher[venkov], V[asil] Kolarov, G[eorgi] Damianov):

1. On military questions (with the participation of Gen[eral] Kinov);[549]

2. Organizational questions (inner-party campaign—account reports—and elections of the new leadership);

3. Distribution of work within the secretariat and improvement of its organization;

4. Kolarov read his speech for the meeting on the occ[asion] of the nat[ional] day of Yugoslavia. We made some corrections of substantial importance.

—*Martulkov,*[550] from Macedonia, informed us about the situation there. He pointed out the dangerous tendencies of *Serbianization* of language, culture, and public life.

—*Moshetov*[551] and a courier (Adilov) arrived from Moscow. Moshetov brought $100,000 US for the Greek comrades.

—*Moshetov* awarded me with a *Medal* for Exceptional Achievement in the Fatherland War, 1941–1945, on the instructions of the presidium of the Sup[reme] Soviet of the USSR.

—Sent to Marshal Tito a political greeting on the occasion of the Yu-

---

549. Ivan Kinov (1893–1967), Bulgarian Communist; political émigré to the USSR (1925–1944) who was arrested during the Stalinist purges (1938–1939); chief of the general staff of the Bulgarian People's Army (1944–1949); member of the BRP(k)/BKP CC (1945–1962).

550. Aleksandŭr Martulkov, veteran of the Macedonian movement.

551. Vasily Vasilievich Moshetov, Soviet Communist; VKP(b) CC specialist on Greece and Yugoslavia; deputy chief of the foreign policy section in the VKP(b) CC.

goslav nat[ional] holiday and the opening of the constit[uent] assembly.

[. . .]

· 2 December 1945 ·

—Sent the following letter to *Tito* with the ambassador to Yugoslavia, Kovačević:[552]

Dear Friend Tito,

First of all, I would personally like to congratulate you most cordially on the historic occasion of the proclamation of Yugoslavia as a *Federal People's Republic.* One can hardly imagine the enormous impact of that event on Bulgaria's political development. It will greatly ease our task of declaring Bulgaria a *People's Republic.*

The National Assembly will now summon a Grand National Assembly, which will change the constitution in this spirit. The transformation of Bulgaria into a people's republic will not encounter any serious resistance among the people or in the National Assembly. Our situation is more complicated than the one in your country (for obvious reasons), but now, after the elections, it *is rapidly becoming more stable.* The Fatherland Front (our party in the first place), despite all the difficulties, firmly holds in its hands the administration of the country. It is certainly true that Bulgaria's international situation is much more difficult and complicated than that of Yugoslavia, but I have no doubts whatsoever that we will be able to overcome the existing difficulties in that respect, too!

It is my conviction that today we should consolidate, broaden, and deepen the fraternal ties between Bulgaria and Yugoslavia in all possible spheres—between governments, parliaments, the Yugoslav People's Front, and the Bulgarian Fatherland Front, and of course, between the Yugoslav and the Bulgarian Com[munist] parties.

I believe it would be necessary to agree in the immediate future and in more concrete and precise terms on how better to react to the hostile and subversive activity of the *external reaction,* which makes use, whenever possible, of the reactionary groups inside our countries.

We should also discuss in detail the issue of a treaty of alliance between Yugoslavia and Bulgaria and seek the advice of *our great friends* on *the time and the way* this extremely significant event should take place.

I would suggest that the *initiative* on all these matters should belong *to you,* with respect to the Yugoslav side.

552. Nikola Kovačević (1890–1970), Yugoslav Communist; envoy to Bulgaria (1945–1948); president of the assembly of Montenegro.

Could you, please, think all that over and inform me about your opinion and considerations.

I look forward to hearing from you soon.

I clasp your hand firmly!

Yours,

G. Dim[itrov].

Sofia

2 Dec. 1945

[. . .]

· 10 DECEMBER 1945 ·

[. . .]

—Spoke to *Dekanozov* (Moscow). He informed me that the agenda of the foreign ministers' meeting includes the following item on Bulgaria: "Conditions for the recognition of the Bulgarian government." He asked me to give my opinion on the *compromise formula* that the Sov[iet] side is preparing to propose.

· 11 DECEMBER 1945 ·

—Received the Yugoslav ambassador, *Kovačević*. He brought a letter from Tito (his answer to my letter). Offered to meet with me personally in his palace, with a guarantee of complete confidentiality.

· 11 DECEMBER 1945 ·

Translation from Serbian:

To Georgi Dimitrov,

Dear Comrade,

Thank you very much for your greetings on the occasion of the 29 November holiday.

I sincerely rejoice in your great electoral victory. We were all very much concerned about the treacherous activities of the opposition in your country and about the constantly increasing activities of the foreign reactionaries targeted at hindering the normal development of your country on the path of democracy. It was your firmness that blocked all their attempts. Nowadays, the international reaction is incredibly arrogant and aggressive because, after the defeat of fascism, it is desperately trying to save anything that can be saved. This arrogance can be defeated only by the firmness and the stability of small peoples who can rely on the protector of the small peoples, the Soviet Union.

I think you would agree that today we have moved away from the peace we enjoyed immediately after the victory over Germany in May of this year. International affairs are in a very confused state, and there are quite a number of fireplaces where the spark of provocation can kindle a flame. It is also quite disturbing that in some countries the leaders of the workers' movement cannot understand the essence of things, and they tail the bourgeoisie in their countries or blindly try to copy the methods of the progressive movements, say in the Balkan countries, and, of course, they encounter failures.

I support your idea for a future consolidation and deepening of the relations between Bulgaria and Yugoslavia, for there are many reasons for such a development, especially if we consider the state of confusion in the world. It might be a good idea if we could meet and discuss these and some other issues in greater detail. If you consider this possible, I would gladly welcome you as my guest, and our meeting can be kept in secret.

If you have a message for me, you can send it with the envoy Kovačević. Shaking your hand firmly,

6 December 1945   J[osip] B[roz] T[ito].

[. . .]

· 23 DECEMBER 1945 ·

—*Stal[in]* called me on the HF. His message:

I have met with the for[eign] mini[ster] of the United States, who suggested, for the purpose of the recognition of the Bulg[arian] government, the reorganization of the government through the inclusion of representatives of the opposition. My answer was that for me the issue of the reorganization of the Bulgarian government is *non-negotiable.* That government will depend on the National Assembly after the elections. The composition of the Bulg[arian] gov[ernment] is a matter for the N[ational] A[ssembly]. We consider it unnecessary to interfere in the internal affairs of Bulgaria. As far as the opposition is concerned, as is well known, the opposition can be *loyal or disloyal.* The Bulgarian opposition is *disloyal.* It has boycotted the elections. There is an opposition in America, too, the Repub[licans], but after their defeat in the elections their leader announced that he would support your government. The Bulg[arian] opposition acted in the opposite way. There is also a *disloyal* opposition in your country. Would you let the representatives of that opposition take part in your government? (He started laughing . . .) Why then would you demand that from the Bulgarians? Our conversation ended on that. In order to be sure, however, that the Bulgarian question will be solved, think whether you could include one or two ministers from opposit[ion] circles, by tearing them away from that opposition. Assign some insignificant ministry to them. Of course, I do not mean Petkov. You can find somebody else, though not so prominent. Discuss that with your comrades and inform me of your opinion. I will expect your call tomorrow.

I called our people (Traicho, Kolarov, Vŭlko) and later *Kimon* [Georgiev]. Discussed the issue and came to the conclusion that it is appropriate to undertake such an arrangement. Agreed on some possible candidacies, *Bumbarov* and Dr. *Pashev*. Gave orders to start the necessary inquiries.

[. . .]

· 24 DECEMBER 1945 ·
[. . .]

—Talked to *Stal[in]* (with the mediation of Poskr[ebyshev]). I told him about our agreement. He asked me to name promptly the possible candidacies.

[. . .]

· 6 JANUARY 1946 ·

—The talks with opposition groups were not a success. An official government statement has been published.

—A delegation for Moscow is preparing to leave (Kimon, Stainov, Yugov).

· 7 JANUARY 1946 ·

—*Kimon [Georgiev], Stainov, Yugov* flew to Moscow. R[osa] Yul[ievna Dimitrova] was with them too. I accompanied them to the airport.

In the evening, *Chankov*[553] *and Hristozov*[554] and their wives came to visit me.

553. Georgi Chankov (b. 1909), Bulgarian Communist; secretary of the Bulgarian Young Communist League (1933–1934, 1935–1938); member of the BRP CC (from 1943 on); secretary of the BRP(k)/BKP CC (1944–1949), president of the state control commission (1948–1949).

554. Rusi Hristozov, Bulgarian Communist; chief of the people's militia (after 1944); deputy minister, and later minister, of internal affairs; member of the BKP CC (beginning in 1948).

· 8 JANUARY 1946 ·

Vyshinsky arrived. We had a meeting at Biriuzov's. Discussed the stand he must take concerning the opposition. At night, he received *Lulchev.*[555] Fruitless discussion.

· 9 JANUARY 1946 ·

Official reception in the Union Club in honor of *Vyshinsky*.
Vyshinsky had a fruitless discussion with Petkov.
Vyshinsky met with the regents.

· 10 JANUARY 1946 ·

The delegation returned from Moscow. Consultation with *Vyshinsky*.
They informed us about talks with Stal[in] and Molotov.

· 11 JANUARY 1946 ·
[. . .]

Session of the Politburo. Yugov reported on the conversations in Moscow and the planned strategy with regard to the opposition.
Reception at the Military Club in honor of Vyshinsky.
Vyshinsky's departure.

· 12 JANUARY 1946 ·

Meeting of the secretariat. Gave instructions for the work of the CC concerning the Vyshinsky and the Moscow decisions.
Did not keep a record of a number of important events during this period.

· 7 FEBRUARY 1946 ·

Received the Yugoslav youth delegation with its leader *Slavko Komar.*[556]

555. Kosta Lulchev (1882–1965), Bulgarian politician; leader of the Bulgarian Social Democrats, who was in opposition after 1945.
556. Slavko Komar (b. 1918), Yugoslav Communist; student leader at the Uni-

Kovačević presented a draft project of the Yugoslav government on the settlement of the problems related to the Bulgarian army occupation during the war. The draft—unaccept[able].

[. . .]

· 9 FEBRUARY 1946 ·

Received an answer from "Alekseev" [Molotov] to a question posed by the Greek comrades—Shall they prepare for an armed uprising against the react[ionary] monarchist regime, or shall they organize their self-defense, combined with the political mobilization of the pop[ular] masses? The second is recommended.

Meeting with the members of Zveno—Members of Zveno: Kimon [Georgiev], Kulishev,[557] Harizanov, Popzlatev, Yurukov. Prolonged elucidative discussion. Agreed upon the following issues: 1) no encouragement of the opposition by "Izgrev" and individual members of Zveno; 2) firm position against the sabotage activities of the opposition; 3) discussion and solution of specific disputed issues; 4) permanent contacts between our two leaderships.

[. . .]

· 13 FEBRUARY 1946 ·

Received the cent[ral] leaders of the Thrac[ian] organization. Advised them for now not to make a lot of noise about the Thrac[ian] problem; to send a special memorandum on the situation of Thrac[ian] immigrants in Bulgaria to the ministers of the three Gr[eat] Powers.

[. . .]

· 19–28 FEBRUARY 1946 ·
[. . .]

Molotov's instructions on how the N[ational] Assem[bly] should constitute the govern[ment].

---

versity of Zagreb who became active in diversionary activities after the occupation; member of the SKOJ Bureau (1942–1947); member of the KPH CC Politburo (from 1948); member of the SKJ CC (from 1952); Yugoslavia's ambassador to India.

557. Georgi Kulishev (1885–1974), Bulgarian politician active in the Macedonian movement; NZSU leader; minister for foreign affairs (1946).

· 5 MARCH 1946 ·
[. . .]

Molotov sent a note to dismiss Mihalchev from his position in Moscow, on the accusation of being an enemy to the Sov[iet] Union.

Offered an article to RD [*Rabotnichesko delo*] on Pastuhov's arrest.[558]

[. . .]

· 13 MARCH 1946 ·

—To D[imitrov].

In a discussion with Kirsanov, Foreign Minister Stainov expressed his dissatisfaction with Krŭstyu Pastuhov's arrest. Stainov also declared that the Social Democrats, who are members of the government, were also unhappy with Pastuhov's arrest. I would like to ask you to find out who ordered the arrest. The inquiry is being made at the request of Com[rade] Dekanozov.

13 March 1946

· 15 MARCH 1946 ·

A telegram from Alekseev (M[olotov]).

To Dimitrov and Kostov,

Concerning the formation of the new Bulg[arian] gov[ernme]nt, we would like to direct your attention to the following issues:

First. It is necessary to make some changes in the distribution of ministers' portfolios among the various parties. The situation that we face nowadays could have been tolerated before the general elections, but the current distribution of portfolios among parties does not correspond to the results of the elections and to the representation of each party in parliament. It is necessary to appoint a new foreign minister to replace Stainov, whom we do not trust. It could be somebody from the Workers' Party or somebody else affiliated with it, Obbov, for example.[559] Stainov's people working abroad are opponents of good relations with the USSR. We will not tolerate this any longer, because it would harm the interests of Bulgaria.

Second. It is necessary, instead of a minister without portfolio, to appoint

558. Krŭstyu Pastuhov (1874–1949), Bulgarian politician; leader of the Social Democrats. He was arrested and tried in a rigged trial (1946) and killed in prison by a criminal inmate.

559. Aleksandŭr Obbov (1887–1975), Bulgarian politician; leader of the BZNS Pladne group; political secretary of the BZNS (1946–1947); deputy premier and minister of agriculture (1946–1947).

two deputy prime ministers, and one of them should be a Communist. In Yugoslavia, Poland, Czechoslovakia, Romania, and Hungary they have deputy prime ministers.

Third. Your deputy ministers should be Communists. It would not be bad if the other parties also had deputy ministers [in cases] where the ministers are Communists.

Fourth. You could give the ministry of justice to Zveno, and the Communists can have the ministry of finance.

We would like to hear from you as soon as possible.

Alekseev

· 16–20 MARCH 1946 ·

Discussed mainly budget issues.

Talks with K[imon] G[eorgiev] on how to proceed with the government resignation.

Strictly confidential:

To Alekseev [Molotov],

Received your advice on the formation of the new government. We consider it quite possible to achieve the following:

1. To appoint two deputy prime ministers; one of them would be a Communist.

2. To appoint deputy ministers in the major ministries—the ministries of internal affairs, finance, justice, agriculture, utilities, railroads, industry, electrification, and natural resources (the ministry of defense already has a deputy minister).

3. Make changes in the distribution of portfolios among the parties in favor of our party and the Agrarian Union. In a preliminary discussion with Kimon Georgiev we agreed on the above three points.

As far as Stainov's replacement is concerned, there are a few problems, which Kimon Georgiev pointed out: the possibility that the right wing of Zveno might split off and join the [anticommunist] opposition. Our view is that the premier should take the ministry of foreign affairs and have a deputy who would be a Communist. Obbov is not suitable for foreign minister.

We would like to follow your advice on the ministry of justice.

The government will resign next Wednesday after the final vote on the budget and appropriate preparations. Then the premier will propose to both opposition groups that they put forward their candidates in agreement with the Moscow decision, in accordance with the memorandum of the Soviet government.

16 March 1946

D[imitrov], K[ostov].

To Ivanov [Dimitrov] and Kostov,

Received your answer. We consider your suggestions acceptable, should Stainov be dismissed from the post of foreign minister. You have not given any answer concerning the replacement of the minister of finance, and it is advisable to think about it. The proportion of parties in the Bulgarian parliament is such that it enables the Workers' Party to have four to five major portfolios. We are surprised by your modesty and lack of initiative in the matter. Compared with you, the Yugoslav Communists are much more active and energetic.

Druzhkov [Stalin], Alekseev [Molotov]

18 March 1946

· 21 MARCH 1946 ·

The government has resigned.

The Nat[ional] Assembly appointed K[imon] G[eorgiev] as premier.

· 22 MARCH 1946 ·

Visited the regents, together with Traicho [Kostov]. I presented our viewpoint on the constitution of the new gov[ern]ment.

Meeting of the parliament[ary] group.

My speech on the government's resignation (the summary is going to be published on Sunday).

· 23 MARCH 1946 ·

Kimon [Georgiev] at my place. We made decisions on how to handle the talks with the OF [Fatherland Front] parties and with the representatives of the Agrar[ian] and the Social D[emocratic] opposition.

Session of the Politburo. Discussed our plan.

Talks with *Obbov and Dragnev.*[560]

· 24 MARCH 1946 ·

My speech has been published in the *O[techestven] F[ront]* [Fatherland front].

---

560. Georgi Dragnev (1886–1955), Bulgarian politician in the BZNS leadership; minister of public works (1945–1947).

Our meeting.

Boswell[561] has announced the memorandum of the Engl[ish] government in support of the Amer[ican] gov[ern]ment's interpretation.[562]

· 25 MARCH 1946 ·

Kimon [Georgiev] informed us about the talks with the OF parties and the oppos[ition] representatives.

We agreed to wait until tomorrow for the opposition's answer and then to constitute the new government. Course—not to drag out this question.

Talks with *Dragnev and Tonchev*[563]—discussed Genovski's[564] exclusion from the new government because he is not suitable to be a minister.

· 26 MARCH 1946 ·

Talks with *Kimon* [Georgiev] about the discussions with the opposition groups.

Politburo's session on our plan for the new government.

· 27 MARCH 1946 ·

Barns visited Kimon [Georgiev] and the regents.

Memorandum from *Byrnes*[565] in favor of the opposition.

Kimon's last meeting with the opposition. They have once again put forward their unacceptable demands.

· 28 MARCH 1946 ·

The discussions with the opposition *were canceled.*

Together with *Kimon,* we wrote an official statement on the progress and the results of the talks with the opposition.

561. British political representative to the Allied Control Commission.

562. The State Department memorandum supported the introduction of two opposition politicians into the government.

563. Stefan Tonchev, NZSU leader; minister.

564. Mihail Genovski (1903–1996), Bulgarian jurist; NZSU leader.

565. James F. Byrnes (1879–1972), American politician and jurist; congressman and senator from South Carolina; associate justice of the Supreme Court (1941–1942); secretary of state (1945–1947).

We have reached an agreement with *Kimon* to start the process of constituting the new government by selecting only the representatives of the OF parties.

Sent to *Molot[ov]* the following coded message:

Concerning the formation of the new government, we did our best to attract representatives of the Agrarian and Social Democratic opposition groups, in agreement with the Moscow decisions. The group of Petkov, as well as that of Lulchev, presented their absolutely unacceptable conditions: 1) immediate dissolution of the parliament until the new government is formed; 2) the new government should organize elections for a National Assembly by 15 July; 3) the ministry of internal affairs should be drawn from the Communists; 4) amnesty for the cabinet of Muraviev, which was sentenced by a people's court; 5) all political prisoners should be released from prisons and camps.

As you can see, it was again not possible to implement the Moscow decisions.

Tomorrow Kimon Georgiev will start the formation of the new government selecting its members only from the representatives of the Fatherland Front parties.

Later in the evening called Molot[ov]. Discussed with him our situat[ion]. He and St[alin] approved our line. Requested that the Sov[iet] gov[ern]ment offer support to our gov[ernment].

Kirsanov and Biriuzov met with Kimon Georgiev and announced that the Sov[iet] gov[ernm]ent considers the demands of the opposition unacceptable and approves K[imon] Georgiev's actions.

A message to Dimitrov from the Great Friend [Stalin]:

Considering the refusal of the opposition to have their representatives in the government, despite the decision of the three ministers, we would recommend to you the following policy:

1. Ignore the opposition in every possible way; do not negotiate with it any more.

2. Undertake a series of well-considered and skillfully organized measures to stifle the opposition.

3. Make Byrnes realize from a number of transparent hints in the press that the Bulgarians consider him to blame for the failure of the decisions of the Moscow conference on Bulgaria. Your attitude toward Byrnes should be strictly formal and cold. Acknowledge receipt of this message.

Alekseev [Molotov]

· 29 MARCH 1946 ·

Together with *Kimon* [Georgiev], prepared the first draft of the new cabinet.

Joint meeting with the Agrarians.

Informed *Molotov* about the basic personnel composition of the cabinet.

· 30 MARCH 1946 ·

Private talks with individual leaders of the part[ies].

Joint meeting with the Agrar[ian] leaders to settle their internal squabbles over their future ministers.

In the evening, together with *Kimon*, made a final decision on composition of the new government:

1. Prime minister—K. Georgiev
2. Vice president and minister of electrification—Tr[aicho] Kostov
3. Vice president and minister of agriculture—Al[eksandŭr] Obbov
4. Minister of foreign affairs—G[eorgi] Kulishev
5. Minister of internal affairs—Ant[on] Yugov

[The names of the other ministers follow.]

At night the regents signed the decree on the new government as listed above. Came home from the Nat[ional] Assembly at 3:30 a.m..

[. . .]

· 2 APRIL 1946 ·

Zahariadis visited us. He informed us about the situation in Greece in relation to the elections and about the situation in the party and EAM [National Liberation Front].

[. . .]

· 3 APRIL 1946 ·
[. . .]

We decided to halt publication of the *Green Agr[arian] Banner* because of its ant[i-Soviet] articles.[566]

[. . .]

· 15 APRIL 1946 ·

Kovačević (and his son) with me.

Tito has sent the following message:

566. Refers to Nikola Petkov's newspaper *Narodno zemedelsko zname* (People's Agrarian Banner).

1. He thinks it is not the right moment to initiate the making of the alliance treaty between Yugoslavia and Bulgaria as long as the international status of Bulgaria is not settled.

2. The question of the western borderlands has to be resolved *simultaneously* with the unification of Pir[in] Macedonia and federal Macedonia. He suggests that we meet in person to discuss all problems of concern to the two countries.[567]

[. . .]

· 20 MAY 1946 ·

Meeting with Kimon [Georgiev] and Kulishev.
Session of the Politburo.

In the evening, meeting with the people from Sta[te] Security and the RO [military counterintelligence] with the purpose of clarifying their activities and determining the sphere of their actions.

Measures to be taken against the antigovernment and terrorist groups.

Protection of the borders—to stop possible riots from the outside.

[. . .]

· 22 MAY 1946 ·
[. . .]

Kovačević came to my place. He is leaving for Belgrade to settle problems concerning the population in the western border regions.

[. . .]

· 1 JUNE 1946 ·

Talked to Molotov about my arrival in Moscow at the time when Tito is there.

[. . .]

· 3 JUNE 1946 ·

Molotov said I could leave for Moscow.

---

567. Tito evidently wanted to exchange Bosilegrad and Tsaribrod (Dimitrovgrad) for Pirin Macedonia.

· 4 JUNE 1946 ·

A visit to Kimon [Georgiev], together with Kolarov and Kulishev.

We discussed specific problems related to the conference of the ministers of foreign affairs in Paris.

Received 147 *Yugosl[av]* students from the special school for teachers in Belgrade.

Session of the Politburo.

We decided that I would leave for Moscow together with Kolarov and Kostov.

· 5 JUNE 1946 ·

At 4:00 a.m. (Sofia time) we were on board the plane, together with Roza, and at 12:00 noon (Moscow time) landed in Moscow. Had a nice flight.

At 1:00 p.m., in Meshcherino.

In the evening, Tito, Ranković,[568] and Dr. Nešković[569] (presid[ent] of the Council of Min[isters] of Serbia) visited me.

Discussed the relations between Bulgaria and Yugoslavia. Warm, comradely atmosphere.

Agreed to discuss these issues together with Stalin.

---

568. Aleksandar Ranković (pseudonym: Marko, 1909–1983), Yugoslav Communist leader, active in the Young Communist League (SKOJ) in Belgrade, who was imprisoned from 1929 to 1935; secretary of the regional committee of the KPJ for Serbia (1937); member of the KPJ CC (from 1938); KPJ Politburo political secretary (from 1940 on). He was arrested and tortured by the Gestapo (June 1941) in Belgrade but freed by a Communist action group. As KPJ CC organizational secretary, he was responsible for cadre policy and security. Yugoslavia's minister of internal affairs (1946–1953); vice president of the Yugoslav government (1948–1963); vice president of Yugoslavia (1963–1966). In 1966, at the fourth plenum of the SKJ CC, Ranković was denounced for violations of legality and misappropriation of state security agencies. After resigning his positions, he was expelled from the SKJ.

569. Blagoje Nešković (1907–1984), Yugoslav Communist; physician by profession; veteran of the International Brigades in Spain; secretary of the KPJ regional committee for Serbia (1941–1945) and of the Communist Party of Serbia (KPS) CC (1945–1949); member of the KPJ CC (from 1940) and Politburo (1948–1952); president of the council of ministers of Serbia (1945–1949); expelled from the SKJ in 1952 on charges of wavering in his anti-Stalinist stance.

· 6 JUNE 1946 ·

Paniushkin informed me about the progress of work at the CC Department.

Kuusinen—spoke with him about the establishment of an ideological center for the Commun[ist] parties in Paris.

Biriuzov's visit. We discussed the situation in the Bulgarian army, and in particular the behavior of D[amian] Velchev.

Sergeev [Kolev] and Blagoeva, informed me about Bulgarian affairs in Moscow.

In the evening, at the Kremlin—*Stalin and Molotov.* A warm welcome. A long discussion on the peace treaty, the situation in the country, the future republic (elections for the Grand Nat[ional] Assembly), the situation in the army, the people's militia, economic cooperation, mutual assistance between Bulgaria and Yugoslavia, the alliance treaty with the USSR, etc.

Late at night, at Stalin's dacha. Snacks. Stayed till morning (7:00 a.m.!). Discussed our tactics with regard to our allies, and in particular with regard to *D[amian] Velchev.*

Stalin criticized us for the lack of decisive actions.

Recommended that we be more resolute in our activities and pay less attention to the opinion and the mood of the Engl[ish] and Ameri[cans] and their agents in Bulgaria . . .

· 7 JUNE 1946 ·

Once again at *Stalin's place.*

Present: Molotov, Zhdanov, Beria. Also, Tito, Ranković, Nešković.

Discussed our relations with Yugoslavia.

Agreed to postpone the completion of the alliance treaty until the peace treaty is signed; very close cooperation between the Bulg[arian] and Yugosl[av] for[eign] ministries. Joint party commission (Bulg[arian] and Yugosl[av] CC) on the problems of the western borderlands and Pirin Macedonia. The final decisions on the fate of both regions should be taken *simultaneously.* The Fath[erland] Front should be maintained at the forthcoming elections. It is preferable to nominate common lists of Fatherland Front candidates if the following basis can be agreed on: 40 percent Communists, 30 percent Agrarians, 15 percent Zveno, 10 percent Social D[emocrats] and a few percent Radicals. If that plan fails, then the Communists would partic[ipate] with a sep[arate] list, but everything must be done for them to become the *first party*. Exchanged opinions on many other issues. After that we had dinner together. Stayed till morning, *a very cordial atmosphere*.

· 8 JUNE 1946 ·

Took off at 9:00 a.m. from Moscow airport. A nice flight. At 4:00 p.m. landed at Sof[ia] airport.

Yugov, Damianov, Chervenkov, and Kolarov at my place.

Informed them about work accomplished in Moscow. Discussed the concrete action we should undertake in the future.

· 13 JUNE 1946 ·
[. . .]

In the evening, I listened to the information on st[ate] security and the peo[ple's] militia presented by the Sov[iet] instructors Strudnikov[570] and Zalakis.[571]

[. . .]

· 17 JUNE 1946 ·

Yugov and the leaders of st[ate] security and the militia gathered together with the Russian instructors for a meeting.

A detailed critical analysis of the work of various offices and their respective activities.

[. . .]

D[amian] Velchev swore allegiance to me: "I will always be loyal!"

[. . .]

· 19 JUNE 1946 ·
[. . .]

Biriuzov was reported to be coming back to Sofia with new instructions from Moscow concerning the situation in the Bulg[arian] army. I

---

570. Soviet instructor in the ministry of foreign affairs.
571. Soviet instructor in Bulgarian state security.

spoke with Tolbukhin on that issue. He is also going to be in Sofia on 21 June 1946.

[...]

· 21 JUNE 1946 ·

Discussion with Tolbukhin and Biriuzov on the activities to be carried out in the army.

· 22 JUNE 1946 ·

Meeting with *Agr[arian] leadership* to discuss our plan for the army and the reactionary elements in Zveno.

Discussion with *Kimon Georgiev and D[amian] Velchev* (very important and serious conversation).

[...]

· 24 JUNE 1946 ·

Tolbukhin and Biriuzov came to me to discuss the law on command and control in the army.

[...]

· 29 JUNE 1946 ·

Session of the Politburo.

Planning our offensive against reactionary elements.

The issue of the purge in the army and Damian Velchev.

[...]

· 8 JULY 1946 ·

[...]

In the evening, a sess[ion] of the PB. After that, talks with Biriuzov and Kirsanov. Discussed the issue of the necessity of a purge in the army and all the related activities.

· 9 JULY 1946 ·

Received a delegation of the *Thrac[ian] committee*—[Nikola] Spirov, Nikola Hristov, Vŭlcho Angelov, Petko Karabelkov, Pancho Iliev, Aleksandŭr Panaiotov.

The issue of sending a delegation of the Thrac[ian] organization to the peace conference in Paris (some other Thrac[ian] problems).

Received Minister Popov.[572] He made a declaration of loyalty of the Social Democrats to our party.

[...]

· 11 JULY 1946 ·

Kimon [Georgiev] and Kulishev came to me. Present also Kostov, Yugov, and Chervenkov. Kolarov presented a detailed report about his mission in Paris.

Sess[ion] of the Council of Min[isters]—the first resolution of the government commission for the firing of 180 officers has been discussed and accepted (with the exception of only a few cases).

Tsola Dragoicheva came back. Reported on the work of the executive body of the International Women's Federation in Paris.

Zhivkov[573] reported on the work of the committee for the purge in the Ministry of Foreign Affairs.

Edited the final version of Kolarov's speech for the press.

[...]

· 16 JULY 1946 ·

Session of the Politburo.

Decisions:

1. Parl[iamentary] session will be prolonged until Sept[tember] 15.

2. 9 September—referendum for a republic.

3. 27 October—elections to the Grand Nat[ional] Assembly.

Decisions should be made by the Nat[ional] Assembly before the opening of the peace conference in Paris.

Kolarov's birth[day]—sixty-nine!

[...]

572. Georgi Popov, Bulgarian politician; Social Democratic leader and minister for social policy (1945–1946); deputy chairman of the council of ministers (1946–1949).

573. Todor Zhivkov (1911–1998), Bulgarian Communist leader; participant in the partisan movement; after the war commander of the people's militia; member of the BKP Politburo (from 1951); first secretary of the BKP CC (from 1954); premier (1962–1971) and president (1971–1989) of Bulgaria. Having resigned his positions in November 1989, he was expelled from the BKP in December 1989, arrested in January 1990, convicted of embezzlement in 1992, and sentenced to a term of seven years but permitted to serve his sentence under house arrest.

· 21 JULY 1946 ·

Sent a coded message to Molotov on the inappropriateness of a new collective *démarche* vis-à-vis the Bulgarian government to carry out the Moscow decision.

Also, to have the draft agreement on the peace with Bulgaria sent to us.

Session of the parl[iamentary] group.

[. . .]

· 26 JULY 1946 ·
[. . .]

In the evening, at my place K[imon] Georgiev, Kulishev, Harizanov, and our people—Kolarov, Kostov, Damianov.

Important conversation on the replacement of D[amian] Velchev.

[. . .]

· 30 JULY 1946 ·

Talks with Kimon [Georgiev] on the necessity of replacing Damian [Velchev] with a new minister of war.

Talks with Biriuzov and Kirsanov.

· 31 JULY 1946 ·

Lekarski[574] and Toshev[575] came to discuss the problems of the Ministry of War and the army.

Vranchev[576] on the disclosures of a secret military union.

· 1 AUGUST 1946 ·

Session of the Politburo.

574. Krum Lekarski (1898–1981), Bulgarian politician; deputy minister of defense (1944–1947).

575. Todor Toshev (1899–1976), Bulgarian Communist general; former activist of the Military League (1919–1944); member of BKP central military commission (1942–1943) and the partisan main staff (1943–1944); commander of the first infantry division (1944–1945).

576. Petŭr Vranchev (1901–1970), Bulgarian Communist general; partisan veteran (1942–1944).

Separate meeting with Yugov, Kostov, and Damianov.

Session of the parliament[ary] committee on the Ministry of Foreign Affairs.

· 2 AUGUST 1946 ·

K. Georgiev with me. Also present: Yugov, Kostov, and Damianov. Reached an agreement with Kimon [Georgiev] on the Damian [Velchev] problem, on the leadership of the Ministry of War and the army, the replacement of Gen[eral] Stanchev[577] (Second Army) with Gen. As[en] Grekov,[578] etc.

1. GENERAL KIRIL STANCHEV is dismissed as commander of the Second Army and is replaced by General ASEN GREKOV.

General Stanchev is under house arrest until the trial against him as the organizer of the secret military league starts.

2. General Lekarski is delegated to take over the leadership of the Ministry of War and the command of the army.

3. The head of the office, General Genchev from the Ministry of War, is temporarily appointed inspector of infantry.

4. Minister of War Damian Velchev is on holiday until the government delegation returns from Paris. He has no relations with the Ministry of War, and upon his return he will be replaced by a new minister.

In the Council of Ministers the minister of war is represented by the prime minister and, in his absence, by the first vice president of the Council of Ministers.

5. The restructuring of the Ministry of War, the appointment of new commanding officers and some other military staff as a replacement for those dismissed, should start immediately under the direct leadership of General Lekarski. Necessary actions should be undertaken immediately to stabilize the situation in the army.

6. Measures should be taken to clarify the necessity of the purge.

7. The investigation of the military union is extended, so that these procedures will complete it in the shortest possible period.

2 August 1946, Sofia.

Signed:　　　　　　　　　1. K. Georgiev

　　　　　　　　　　　　　2. G. Dimitrov

[. . .]

577. Kiril Stanchev (1895–1968), Bulgarian general; activist in the Military League who was sentenced to life imprisonment in 1947.

578. Asen Grekov (1893–1954), Bulgarian Communist general; political émigré to the USSR (1926–1944); member of the BRP(k)/BKP CC (1945–1954).

· 9 August 1946 ·
[. . .]

Gen[eral] Toshev and Gen[eral] Vranchev on the issue of the suspic[ious] activities of D[amian] Velchev in Varna.

[. . .]

· 11 August 1946 ·
[. . .]

We decided with Kimon [Georgiev] to give instructions to Damian [Velchev] to leave Varna because of rumors that he was preparing to leave Bulgaria illegally.

[. . .]

· 15 August 1946 ·

Flew to Moscow early in the morning. Stopped in Kiev, and *at 1:00 p.m. we were in Meshcherino. Everything is fine.*

[. . .]

· 17 August 1946 ·

Wrote to Stal[in] that I have arrived semi-incognito to take care of my health.

Also wrote to him about the request by the Bulg[arian] gov[ern]ment for a loan of one million dollars, security being the *gold* in the Bulg[arian] Nat[ional] Bank. Went to Mitia's grave and to the flat in the city.

[. . .]

· 1 September 1946 ·

Sunday.
Yesterday Molotov arrived in Moscow for two or three days.

· 2 September 1946 ·

Talked to Molotov. He said: "All is a matter of struggle. Not everything will be solved, even in Paris. The decisive part is what follows." But despite all that, he is an optimist.

First page of entry dated 2 September 1946.

Agreed on a meeting with Stalin.

In the evening, visited Stalin (in the Kremlin). Present: Molotov, Zhdanov, Beria, Malenkov, Mikoyan; later Bulganin came.

Concerning *Byrnes's* suggestion to the representatives of the opposition that they discuss and solve the Bulgarian question, *Stalin* declared that *the Soviet government will not give its consent.*

Concerning the question whether it is possible to reckon on the signing of a separate treaty with the USSR in case the English and the Americans refuse to sign the peace treaty with Bulgaria with the present Bulgarian government, *Stal[in]* declared that it will hardly come to that, because in the end *they must sign the peace treaty.*

(Molotov: If they refuse to conclude peace with Bulgaria, we shall then refuse to sign peace with Italy. They are more interested in concluding peace than we are.)

On the question whether Kimon [Georgiev] should event[ually] resign, whether we could put forward our premier, *Stalin* explained that *this is now not expedient,* because it would only create new foreign policy problems for Bulgaria. It would be better to appoint somebody from among the Agrarians who would be loyal to you.

The best thing to do would be to try to exert influence on Kimon to act more decisively against the right wing of Zveno, up to the point of the right wing's split from Zveno, while he would remain with you.

On the question of the new constitution, *Stal[in]* unfolded the following thoughts: Your constitution should be a *people's constitution,* with as few details as possible, a constitution of a people's republic with a parliamentary system; avoid frightening the *strata who do not belong to the working class;* draw up a constitution that is more to the right than the Yugoslav one. (He promised to review the first draft I sent to him and then write his remarks.)

In connection to the above, *Stalin* said: You have to establish a *Labour Party* [original in English] in Bulgaria. Unite within such a party your own party and the other parties of the working people (for example, the Agrarian Party). It is not an advantage to have a *workers' party* and then call it Communist. Earlier, the Marxists had to isolate the working class within a separate workers' party. At that time, they were in the opposition. Now you participate in governing the country. You must unite the working class and the other working strata on the basis of a *minimal program,* and later there will be time for the *maximal program.* Peasants consider the workers' party as alien, but they will look at a *labor party* as their own. *I strongly recommend that you do that.* A labor party or a *worker-peasant party* is very suitable for a country like Bulgaria. That would be a *people's party*. I can assure you that *you would lose nothing;* on the contrary, *you would only gain*. From the point of view of the country's international position, that would only make your tasks easier for you. In character the party will be Communist, but it will have a broader basis and a *convenient mask* for the present period. All this will contribute to your peculiar transition to socialism—without *a dictatorship of the proletariat*. The situation since the outbreak of our revolution has changed radically, and it is necessary to use different methods and forms and *not copy the Russian Communists,* who in their time were in an entirely different position.

Do not be afraid that you might be accused of *opportunism*. This is not opportunism, but rather the application of Marxism to the present situation.

To the remark that the Yugoslavs look down on us and that in the Balkans the Soviet Union relies more on Yugoslavia and neglects Bulgaria, *St[alin] said that this was not true: Yugoslavia is a serious country, but we consider that* Bulgaria and Yugoslavia will unite in a common state and play a unified role in the Balkans.

On the question of Thrace, St[alin] said: Bulgaria's claims to western Thrace will provide it [Bulgaria] with a [good] position for the future. Another war is needed to solve such matters completely . . .

On the tactics of the Gree[k] Com[munist] Party, *St[alin]* stressed the fact that the Greek Communists earlier made an error with the boycott of the parliamentary elections. "Boycotting makes sense when it brings about the failure of elections. Otherwise, a boycott is a foolish thing."

Stal[in] supported the idea of training the Bulgarian officers in Bulgaria rather than in the USSR. "We have many difficulties here in that respect. And also, our type of education is not so suitable for the Bulgarian army. We might help with lecturers, programs, etc., but it is better to have your own schools in the country."

Stalin considers it unfavorable for us to have Soviet instructors in our army. The enemies will make good use of this. There will be more harm than profit. Besides, the presence of instructors often prevents the independent development of your own officers. "It would be better if they studied without baby-sitters."

Stalin agreed to instruct *Biriuzov* to choose a few Soviet officers who would, under his leadership, help the Bulg[arian] army unofficially and without making too much noise.

[. . .]

· 4 SEPTEMBER 1946 ·

With Zhdanov at the CC. We discussed the international situation.

Zhd[anov]: Comrade Stal[in] thinks that a new war in the immediate future is out of the question. He is completely calm about the way things are developing. If in our analysis of the present situation we base our judgment *not on form* but *on the content of what is going on,* we can say with confidence that from our point of view *everything is in order.* All the noise made by the Anglo-Ameri[cans] and the threats of a new war are nothing but blackmail. They want to discredit the Soviet Union in the eyes of their workers. But this is already evidence that our influence in their countries is strong enough. The contradictions between England and America are still to be felt. The social conflicts in America are increasingly unfolding. The Labourites in England have promised the English workers so much concerning socialism that it is hard for them now to step back. They will soon have conflicts not only with their bourgeoisie, but also with the American imperialists. It was not by chance that [Harold] *Laski* came to us with his delegation. All the time he was justifying himself and the Labour Party and reported what they had done. He declared that they would not give in to the imperialists. They will follow their own parliamentary path to socialism. Stal[in] told him: We consider the Soviet way to be a better one, but if you think that the parliamentary way is more suitable for England, we will not object to that. It is obvious that Laski was trying to find out whether Moscow would conduct a policy of "sovietizing" England . . . It was also clear that the Labourites wanted to prepare the ground for the moment when, should they be in a tight spot, they would have some support from the Sov[iet] Union . . .

[. . .]

· 5 SEPTEMBER 1946 ·

Took off from Moscow at 7:30 Moscow time; at 1:30 Moscow time, was back in Sofia.

Yugov, Chervenkov, Damianov, and others met us at the airport.

All came to my summer house. Listened to the information on the election campaign and told the others about my Moscow discussions.

Started work immediately.

Sent a *telephone message* to Roza.

[. . .]

· 7 SEPTEMBER 1946 ·

Speech on the radio.

Last directions on how to organize the campaign (mainly the practical side of the voting—maximum participation of vot[ers] in the referendum).

Kovačević with me. Told him (so that he could pass it on to Tito) about our discussion with Stalin.

[...]

· 13 SEPTEMBER 1946 ·
[...]

Talks with Kimon [Georgiev] about sending the former royal family to Cairo.

At my place, discussed the issue of awards in relation to the proclamation of the republic.

· 14 SEPTEMBER 1946 ·

Gave Kovačević, leaving for Belgrade, the information for Tito on my talks in Moscow.

· 15 SEPTEMBER 1946 ·

Official proclamation of the Peop[le's] Republic by the National Assembly.

In the evening, reception at the Council of M[inisters].

[...]

· 14 OCTOBER 1946 ·

Dekanozov announced that the question of financial support for the Agrarians (eight mil[lion] leva) had been resolved in a positive manner.

[...]

· 19 OCTOBER 1946 ·

Session of the Politburo. Discussed the election campaign. Gave orders to carry out a more aggressive election campaign during the last week we have and also to accelerate the propaganda carried out by individuals.

[. . .]

· 27 OCTOBER 1946 ·

Election day.

No serious accidents.

For[eign] journalists confirm the peaceful nature of the elections.

All night long we received information from the country on the results of elections.

(Kolarov, Kostov, Chankov, Yugov, Chervenkov, Damianov, and others were at our place.)

· 28 OCTOBER 1946 ·

A brilliant victory of the Fath[erland] Front (mainly of our party —2,270,000 votes, 264 deputies out of 465). The opposition— 1,199,000, 101 deputies. Zveno, Social Democrats, and Radicals, a complete failure. Our Agrarians—64 deputies.

Parades and torch processions all over the country to celebrate the Fath[erland] Front victory.

· 29 OCTOBER 1946 ·

Session of the Politburo. Preliminary estimate of the election results.

Gave an article on that issue to *RD* [*Rabotnichesko delo*].

· 30 OCTOBER 1946 ·

Discussion with K[imon] Georgiev and Kulishev. They are terribly bitter about their failure and about not being elected as deputies.

Talked to them about their prospects.

[. . .]

· 5 NOVEMBER 1946 ·

At five, in *Moscow.*

At nine at *Zhdanov's* place. (Stal[in] is in Sochi.) Zhdanov sent the following coded message to Stalin:

In accordance with the position of the Bulgarian CC, as presented in the coded message of Biriuzov and Kirsanov, it is obvious that Dimitrov and others refuse all negotiations with the representatives of the opposition on the formation of the government. Such a position cannot be viewed as flexible and circumspect.

Of course it would follow that we should compose a government without the opposition. But should the opposition approach the Fatherland Front with a proposal to start negotiations for the formation of a coalition government, the Fatherland Front would be making a mistake if it refused to negotiate. It is possible that the opposition will not try to negotiate for a coalition government. In that case it would be possible to spit in the face of the opposition, while blaming it for not taking into consideration the possibility for a coalition. But if the opposition officially offers a coalition government, it would be senseless to refuse all negotiations. What is also essential is that these negotiations should be carried out in such a way that the opposition is forced to cancel them and you can put the whole blame on it. How could that be achieved? This is a practical issue, and it can be successfully solved by the Bulg[arian] CC.

Of course, the most important portfolios should be in the hands of the Workers' Party [Communists]. You should not, however, reject your allies, such as the Agrarians and others. You should try to preserve the Fatherland Front. There is a danger that the Workers' Party, after the electoral victory, might put on airs and, thinking that it can do without its allies, become dizzy with its success. That would be completely wrong.

As for the possible interference of the USA in the analysis of the Bulgarian practice of attracting the USSR—we should reject this by stating that we [the Soviet Union] cannot interfere in the internal affairs of Bulgaria.

Had a long discussion.

[...]

· 21 NOVEMBER 1946 ·

Meeting of the Grand National Assembly:
Resolution on the Greek claims to the southern border, reparations, etc.

Kimon Georgiev informed us about the government resignation.

The presidency of the republic authorized me to form the new cabinet.

Received Generals *Lekarski and Toshev* to discuss the problem of the *minister of war.*

They consider it correct to appoint G. Damianov.

Talks with the Agrarians about their ministers in the new government.

· 22 NOVEMBER 1946 ·

After long inquiries and discussions with the representatives of the parties, I finally formed the new cabinet. Went to the presidency of the republic. The decrees were signed and released for publication.

[...]

From November 1946 to January 1948 Dimitrov settled into the governmental routine, dominated by ceremonial events, interviews, speeches, and the rest. His diary is increasingly a threadbare account of events without any commentary. Important events, such as the signing of the Bulgarian peace treaty in Paris, are hardly mentioned (10 February 1947: "Meetings and demonstrations connected with the signing of the peace treaty"). The arrest of the Agrarian deputy Nikola Petkov (June 6 1947) is recorded without any comment. Dimitrov's general demeanor is more imperious: 29 April 1947: "Visited the art exhibition intended for abroad. Not quite satisfactory. Suggested considerable changes in the selection of pictures." The number of illnesses mounts. Weeks go by without any entries (28 February–20 March 1947).

The Petkov trial represented an important sharpening of internal repression. The trial was prepared by the top leadership with the help of the Soviet advisers. It was preceded by an important state visit to Yugoslavia and the signing of a protocol by two state delegations at Bled (Slovenia) on 1 August 1947. From 8 August to 16 November Dimitrov was in the USSR for medical treatment. During this period he strongly argued for the execution of Petkov (carried out on 24 September), notwithstanding the unfavorable comparisons to his treatment by the Nazis. He also agreed to revisit the Bled treaty in line with Stalin's objections. His health seriously impaired (diabetes, liver problems, heart sclerosis), he desperately held on to decision-making tasks—for example, communicating with Kostov and others in Sofia and urging a tougher stand toward the opposition. He took no serious part in the preparations for the meeting of the European Communist parties in Szklarska Poręba, Poland, in September 1947, where the Cominform was formed, but he was cheered by the meeting, which he regarded as "the best response to the anticommunist offensive of the American imperialists."

After the uneventful Evksinograd meeting and the signing of the treaty of friendship and mutual assistance between Bulgaria and Yugoslavia during Tito's visit to Bulgaria (2–28 November 1947), Dimitrov settled into the usual leadership routine. Still, the communization of the country, which grew increasingly more intense (with nationalization promulgated in late December 1947), did not seem to hint at the storm that was to come.—I.B.

· 19 JULY 1947 ·

Discussed the draft for the indictment in the N[ikola] P[etkov] trial. (The Sov[iet] comrades, Kolarov, Yugov, Tr[aicho] Kostov, Hristozov, Vranchev, Vlado Poptomov, took part.)

[...]

· 1 AUGUST 1947 ·

Agreed with Tito and the presid[ent] of the Mac[edonian] gov-[ern]ment on a single common line in Mac[edonian] matters. We should not work for a dir[ect] joining of the Pir[in] region to the Mac[edonian] republic.[579]

[...]

· 4 AUGUST 1947 ·
[...]

Session of the Politburo.
1. The situation in the country
2. The trial against Petkov
3. The visit to Yugoslavia and the decisions of the conference in Bled

[...]

· 5 AUGUST 1947 ·

The trial against Petkov started.

[...]

579. From 30 July to 1 August 1947 the delegations of Yugoslavia and Bulgaria, headed by Tito and Dimitrov, met at Bled, the lake resort in Slovenia, and arrived at the text of a friendship and cooperation treaty. They also reached an agreement on trade cooperation, customs regime, and border regime. Yugoslavia waived its right to the war reparations incurred by Bulgaria, and Dimitrov concurred with Yugoslav demands for a new policy in Pirin (Bulgarian) Macedonia, whereby teachers from Vardar (Yugoslav) Macedonia were imported into Bulgarian schools with de-Bulgarized textbooks that promoted Macedonian language and culture across the border.

· 8 AUGUST 1947 ·

[. . .]

At 12:00 noon (Bulg[arian] time) or 1:00 p.m. (Mosc[ow] time), at the airport in Moscow.

From there, directly to Meshcherino.

At 11:00 p.m., at St[alin's] dacha. Started discussing the issue of securing our Black Sea border. He is ready to give us a few more patrol boats (one squadron in all). He also thinks we could get support for establishing a good naval base and fleet. It is essential to send our sailors to Odessa to train them to operate these ships. It is also possible that we be granted the arms we requested for the army and the border troops. He called Bulganin and instructed him on these issues. Decided to call the chief of staff of the army and the chief of the navy immediately to Moscow to deal with the details of resolving all these problems. Bulganin gave orders for these arrangements through Gen[eral] Cherepanov[580] in Sofia.

As far as the decisions of the Bled conference are concerned, he thinks that the agreement on the text of the treaty should not have been announced—all the more so since the text has not been made public. He criticized the reference to a treaty of *unlimited duration;* such a thing is not accepted in international relations. In general, it is quite inappropriate to have done all that before the ratification of the peace treaties. The Americans and the English would exploit that fact to expand military aid for Greece and Turkey. Generally, "you acted hastily, you got carried away. Made too much fuss about it. You could have achieved the same goals without noise, especially having in mind the fact that Bulgaria is still considered to have been a satellite country in the Second [World] War."

For Bulgaria and Yugoslavia *the external threat is decisive, not the internal.*

"As far as aid from the USSR is concerned, it is complicated by the fact that Bulgaria was in the war on Hitler's side, and we cannot ignore that fact by *openly* rendering such aid; it would often be better to look for other, roundabout ways. But we shall nevertheless help."

Discussed the building of a nitrogen fertilizer plant, the trade agree-

580. Aleksandr Ivanovich Cherepanov (1895–1984), Soviet general; military adviser in Canton (1923–1927) and Nanjing 1938–1939); aide (1944), vice chairman (1945–1947) and chairman (1947–1948) of the Allied Control Commission in Bulgaria; chief Soviet adviser to the Bulgarian army (1947–1948).

ment, the exchange rate of the ruble, the German enterprises in Bulgaria, etc. When I complained that the Sov[iet] officials in Bulgaria act mainly as departmental bureaucrats, not taking into consideration the peculiar political situation and Bulgaria's role, he said that much of this was new to him and that in the future in such cases I should turn to him directly.

Discussed in detail the situation of various Communist parties, especially those in France and Italy. Considers the policy of the Fr[ench] party entirely wrong. Its leaders have fallen prey to the fear that France would collapse without American credits. The Communists should have left the government with the explanation that they are against the betrayal of France's independence, instead of waiting to be thrown out. And still more awkward to declare that they will support the government conditionally.

He was also quite critical of the Ital[ian] Communist Party, led by Ercoli [Togliatti].

Had a long discussion on a number of issues. With Bulganin, in my presence, talked about some military problems and the retraining of the army. "We should not only be proud of our victory, but also examine carefully the mistakes we made during different periods and stages of the war."

Stayed till five in the morning, eating and raising little glasses in toasts to one another. We had a cordial parting and will meet again.

"The victors too must not be immune from judgment for their errors!"

(Referring to errors committed by Zhukov, etc.)

[. . .]

· 12 AUGUST 1947 ·

Sent three letters to *Druzhkov* [Stalin] on our economic problems.

In the evening, at *Druzhkov's* [Stalin's]. Showed me the following decision of the Soviet government:

USSR
Chairman of the Council of Ministers
12 August 1947
Moscow, the Kremlin
To Comrade Dimitrov:
The Soviet government considers it its duty to inform the fraternal republics, Yugoslavia and Bulgaria, about its attitude toward the treaty of unlimited duration between Yugoslavia and Bulgaria.

The opinion of the Soviet government is that both governments have made a mistake, having made a treaty, moreover, of unlimited duration, before the peace treaty starts to function, despite the warnings of the Soviet government. The Soviet government considers that the impatience of these two governments has facilitated the actions of reactionary Anglo-American elements, giving them an additional excuse to intensify the military intervention in Greek and Turkish affairs against Yugoslavia and Bulgaria.

It is certainly true that the Soviet Union is bound by alliance to Yugoslavia and Bulgaria because it has a formal agreement of alliance with Yugoslavia, and with Bulgaria—an effective alliance, which is equal to a formal treaty of alliance. The Soviet government must be given advance notice, as it cannot take responsibility for agreements of great importance in the area of foreign policy that are signed without consultation with the Soviet government.

Chairman of the Council of Ministers of the USSR
J. Stalin

The military and some additional issues remained for tomorrow.

· 13 August 1947 ·

Sent to Belgrade the following coded message:

To Walter [Tito]: Concerning the message of our Great Friend, we should admit that we were carried away in the matter of the agreement. To correct this committed mistake, it is necessary, to my mind, to annul this act and, when more favorable times come, and after consultations with our Soviet friends, to sign the treaty and make it public.

Ivan. [Dimitrov]

In the evening, at the Kremlin. Stalin reviewed our military and economic problems. Present: St[alin], Beria, Malenkov, Zhdanov, Voznesensky, Bulganin, Antonov,[581] Yumashev[582] (navy), and from our side (on military issues), Kinov, Halachev.[583]

Everything concerning armament and suggestions on military issues was accepted. We would pay only *half* price in five years' time, for a period of ten years.

581. Aleksandr Inokentievich Antonov (1896–1962), Soviet general; chief of the supreme staff of the Red Army (1945–1946).

582. Ivan Stepanovich Yumashev (1895–1972), Soviet admiral; commander of the Black Sea (1938–1939) and Pacific (1939–1947) fleets; minister of the navy (1947–1951); alternate member of the VKP(b) CC.

583. Hristo Halachev (1885–1952), Bulgarian Communist; political émigré to the USSR (1926–1948) who worked in various news and publishing capacities.

Economic issues:

1. Reduction of fares for passengers and cargo on planes
2. Considerable reduction in price on Soviet literature
3. Covering by the Soviet government of half the costs for our students studying in the USSR

The debt to Bulgaria for former German property to be paid in a lump sum of nine million dollars. The money would be used for the expansion of Bulgarian enterprises. A possible shortening of the terms for the equipment of plants.

The properties managed by our party to be turned over to us (free or at a very low price).

To sign the already negotiated agreements.

[. . .]

· 20 AUGUST 1947 ·

Vyshinsky sent Vlasov [Vlahović] with a message about the necessity for Bulgaria to ratify the peace treaty.

Sent a telegram to Kostov on that issue.

Gave instructions for dissolving Petkov's alliance before the decisions of the court of appe[als]. The Nat[ional] Assembly—in one of its coming sessions should invalidate the mandates of the deputies.

· 21 AUGUST 1947 ·

Sent a number of instructions to the CC concerning the summoning of the Gra[nd] Nat[ional] Assembly and the dissolution of Petkov's alliance [party].

[. . .]

· 25 AUGUST 1947 ·
[. . .]

The Gra[nd] Nat[ional]. Assembly ratif[ied] the peace treaty.

· 26 AUGUST 1947 ·
[. . .]

To Spiridonov [Kostov] and Vladimirov [Chervenkov]:
Using all possible channels, we should immediately reinforce and make

more convincing our reaction to the hostile campaign from abroad against the verdict. We should attack the claim that Petkov was sentenced because of his relations with the West. It is necessary to try to get a letter written and signed by Petkov himself addressed to the prime minister, in which he would completely admit his guilt and repent and point to his relations with foreign advisers. He should also stress his and Lulchev's antipopular activity—i.e., they acted as a united opposition against the people's power. A copy of the letter should be published after that in our country and abroad.

22 August 1947
Ivanov [Dimitrov]

[. . .]

To Spiridonov [Kostov] and Vladimirov [Chervenkov]:
I am of the opinion that Petkov's alliance should be completely dissolved, both its central leadership and the regional branches. His youth union should also be dissolved. Half measures are out of place now. It is necessary to act radically and close one page in the history of the internal political development of our country, thereby clearing the way for future progress. We should not be bothered by the noise from abroad.

22 August 1947
Ivanov [Dimitrov]

[. . .]

· 7 SEPTEMBER 1947 ·

Sent the following recommendations on Traicho's [Kostov's] report:

Urgent message to Spiridonov [Kostov]
Since this is a report made by the government, the personal address of the prime minister is not necessary. I will recommend the following in the report:

1. In the part concerning foreign policy, that the gradual improvement of the relations with France, Italy, Belgium, and Sweden also be mentioned
2. In the paragraph on Yugoslavia, that the part about the agreement signed at Bled be skipped and that it instead be mentioned only that a treaty of friendship, cooperation, and mutual assistance with Yugoslavia will be concluded
3. On the issue of Soviet aid, that it be stressed that this year we have already received Soviet oats, etc., a fact that contradicts the hostile rumors about the export of Bulgarian grain
4. That a special paragraph be written on the need for a very strict economic regime and a decisive attack on wastefulness; that it also be mentioned that we should rely only on ourselves and our resources in all respects

5. As far as the opposition is concerned, that it be clearly stressed that the people and the people's power would show no mercy toward saboteurs, wreckers, spies, and traitors—no matter what their social standing—involved in activities against the national independence and state sovereignty of the people's republic. No defense or threats from abroad would save the saboteurs, wreckers, spies, and traitors from severe legal punishment by sovereign Bulgarian justice

6. In relation to minorities, that mention be made of the special concerns of the Fatherland Front and its government as regards the Turkish population and the Bulgaro-Mohammedans, thereby countering the treacherous and hostile campaign of the Turkish press and organs of Turkish government

7. When determining the most important future tasks, that the fact be strongly stressed that in today's unstable international situation, in which various new aggressors and adventurers are trying to fish in troubled waters, our major task, which should take precedence over all other tasks of government, is to undertake all possible actions and fight for the final endorsement of national independence, state sovereignty, and the security of our country. Without all that, the country would turn into a plaything in the hands of foreign imperialists and invaders, and the people would suffer from political injustice and enslaving labor. The slogan to hold on to our independence as to the apple of our eye, not to allow any foreign interference, to provide full freedom and safety for people's peaceful work and for the development of our people's republic, should these days become the common people's slogan, to which everything else should be subordinated.

The report needs some editing and clarification. I am sure that you can manage that yourself.

Ivanov [Dimitrov]

7 September 1947

[. . .]

· 8 SEPTEMBER 1947 ·

[. . .]

Sent to Chervenkov the following message: "You should bear in mind the fact that the meeting (in Poland) will be closed.[584] No information on its beginning and participants should be given to anybody."

[. . .]

584. Refers to the founding meeting of the Communist Information Bureau (Cominform, Informburo) at Szklaska Poręba, Poland, in September 1947, where a regional type of coordination, not quite a new Comintern, was agreed on. The Soviet delegation, headed by Zhdanov, evidently wanted to signal a new international Communist offensive, with which the Yugoslavs concurred. Represented

· 14 September 1947 ·

Received the following coded message:

On 16 September [. . .], the peace treaties will come into effect. It is our opinion that the Bulgarian and the Yugoslav governments can start work on the treaty for peace and mutual assistance.
Druzhkov [Stalin], Alekseev [Molotov].

[. . .]

· 15 September 1947 ·

Sent the following coded messages to Spiridonov [Kostov]:

The peace treaties would go into effect on 16 September. Druzhkov [Stalin] informed me that we could now start preparations for the realization of the treaty between Yugoslavia and Bulgaria. Take the necessary measures for the meeting and the accommodation of the Yugoslav delegation arriving in the middle of October.

[. . .]

We should already be starting the trial of the Military Union. The less noise, the better. Death sentences are not necessary in this case. It would be better to recall Velchev for consultations before the trial starts.

Please inform us immediately about the reaction to the carrying out of the verdict on the part of our allies in the government and in the local organizations of the Fatherland Front.

[. . .]

· 17 September 1947 ·

Sent the coded message on the issue of Petkov's verdict to Kostov and Kolarov .

Urgent:
To Spiridonov [Kostov] and Venelin [Kolarov]:
After the Anglo-Americans interfered and demanded the rescinding of the death sentence, the issue has acquired new dimensions in light of our domestic and foreign politics and calls for change of our initial plans. All

---

were the nine Communist parties of the USSR, Poland, Czechoslovakia, Hungary, Romania, Bulgaria, Yugoslavia, Italy, and France. It was agreed that the headquarters of the Cominform would be in Belgrade. Significantly, the parties of Germany, Greece, and Albania were not invited.

that has a direct influence on Bulgaria's sovereignty and also encourages the activities of the reaction in our country. If we do not carry out the sentence, it would be considered, both in the country and abroad, a surrender to outside interference and would undoubtedly encourage renewed intervention. The time has come now to give a good lesson to those who are trying to undermine the people's power and to interfere in our internal affairs. The unavoidable unpleasant consequences as a result of carrying out the sentence will be temporary, and, besides, they will be less than those from rescinding the sentence. We should ask for confirmation of the sentence by the court of appeal. The sentence should be carried out no matter what declarations the condemned man makes. Any wavering on this issue, to judge from the standpoint of the current situation in our country and abroad, might only cause damage. You should act firmly, with long-term state interests in mind. This is also the opinion of our friends.

Ivanov [Dimitrov], 17 September 1947.

[. . .]

· 20 SEPTEMBER 1947 ·

Cherv[enkov] and Tomov [Poptomov] took off for the session of the European Communist parties.

[. . .]

· 24 SEPTEMBER 1947 ·
[. . .]

To be delivered to Banchev![585]

(For Traicho Kostov)

1. In an attempt to defend Petkov, foreign journalists would quite often refer to the Leipzig trial and the verdict proclaiming Dimitrov not guilty. It is necessary to find a suitable strategy to do away with this manipulation of the facts by pointing out the basic difference between the Leipzig trial and the trial against Petkov. We could do this when we mark the fourteenth anniversary of the Leipzig trial, September 1933.

[. . .]

· 27 SEPTEMBER 1947 ·
[. . .]

To Spiridonov [Kostov]:

It is highly advisable to start the trial soon on the Military Union. It is necessary to present solid explanations of the fact that Gen[eral] Stanchev, who

585. Tsviatko Banchev, Dimitrov's secretary.

participated in the war on the side of Germany, later on, owing to his Bonapartist ambitions and his inflated pride, crossed over to the side of the enemies of people's power. There are a number of other such cases in world history. We should give examples of some of the most typical cases.

To Chervenkov:

Everything that needs to be done for our southern friends is done here. Grozev[586] should give them only what it is within our ability to give.

[. . .]

· 5 OCTOBER 1947 ·

Sunday.
The documents of the Communist meeting in Poland were published in *Pravda*.
For the time being, this is our "atomic bomb," which will explode thunderously over the world. This is the best response to the anticommunist offensive of the American imperialists.

· 6 OCTOBER 1947 ·

Received a coded message from Kostov—Tito suggested a visit to Sofia for three days between 20 and 25 October.

· 7 OCTOBER 1947 ·

To Spiridonov [Kostov]. My health is still not quite right. It is most probable that my treatment will last longer than I have thought. Bearing that in mind, we should ask Tito to postpone his visit till November, maybe 15–20. Of course, this is extremely inconvenient and unpleasant, but still it is much better than accepting the proposed date, on which I will not be able to come.

[. . .]

· 9 OCTOBER 1947 ·

Sent Molotov the draft treaty, offered by the Czechs, in order to ask the opinion of the Sov[iet] government. "To Spiridonov [Kostov]: It

586. Gocho Grozev (1900–1966), Bulgarian Communist; member of the BRP CC (from 1936 on), alternate member of the Politburo (from 1945 on).

would be a very good thing to publish the treaty with Yugoslavia. We could publish an official statement that the text of the treaty on which we agreed in Bled was recognized by the two governments. The exchange of ratification documents could be connected with Tito's visit in November."

[...]

· 11 OCTOBER 1947 ·
[...]

To Spiridonov [Kostov]:

All evidence from the trial related to Velchev should be recorded. We will need it. At this point we should not start prosecuting Velchev, but rather expose him by means of documents. After the trial, by use of the evidence against him, Velchev should be deprived of any government positions and dismissed from the post of diplomatic representative.
Ivanov [Dimitrov]

[...]

· 13 OCTOBER 1947 ·
[...]

To Spiridonov [Kostov]:

It would be better not to sentence Stanchev to death. I do not find anything illogical in that, since Petkov was the major instigator and organizer of the coup d'état, whereas Stanchev actually played only a secondary role. Please discuss the issue of the sentence seriously, while bearing in mind my opinion.
Ivanov [Dimitrov].

[...]

· 16 OCTOBER 1947 ·
[...]

Molotov called to say that the Sov[iet] government supports our point of view on the Bulgarian-Czechoslovak agreement—i.e., that mutual cooperation should be directed against every aggression, and not only against German aggression. He emphasized that the situation now is completely different. The USSR would not be opposed to signing the peace treaty first with Romania and then with Czechoslovakia.

The opinion of the Soviet government is that treaties should be signed between the small countries (Bulgaria, Romania, Hungary, Albania) and after that between them and the Soviet Union. Otherwise, it could appear as if the smaller countries are signing peace treaties under instructions from Moscow.

Sent the following coded messages:

Urgent.
To Spiridonov [Kostov]
The Soviet government supports our point of view on the Bulgarian-Czechoslovak agreement. Now the situation is completely different from the time when we signed the last peace treaties. Now our mutual cooperation should be directed against every aggression, and not only against German aggression. The Soviet government considers that the government of Czechoslovakia will accept this position concerning the treaty with Bulgaria. Please inform Comrade [Zdeněk] Nejedlý before his departure from Sofia, so that he can give this message to Comrade Gottwald.
Ivanov [Dimitrov]
16 October 1947

[. . .]

· 18 OCTOBER 1947 ·
[. . .]

To Spiridonov [Kostov]

Druzhkov [Stalin] recommended that Tito and I define the duration of the treaty with Yugoslavia. We have to do this. It would be good if the treaty were longer-lasting than usual—for example, twenty-five or thirty years.
Ivanov [Dimitrov]
18 October 1947

[. . .]

· 20 OCTOBER 1947 ·
[. . .]

To Spiridonov [Kostov]
In order to avoid any possible surprises from Damian Velchev in relation to the disclosures at the trial, we should immediately dismiss him and temporarily appoint Secretary Boris Popov head of the embassy. The Swiss government and the press have to be informed about this. It is advisable for Ki-

mon [Georgiev] to warn Velchev to avoid any interviews in the foreign press.
Ivanov [Dimitrov]
20 October 1947

[. . .]

· 24 OCTOBER 1947 ·

[. . .]

To Spiridonov [Kostov]
Waiting for Velchev to undertake some actions and after that to take the necessary measures would hardly be the best thing. He should at least be informed of the severe consequences—i.e., trial, verdict, and confiscation of his property, in case he does not return to Bulgaria or dares to undertake any hostile activities or make hostile statements abroad.
Ivanov [Dimitrov].
24 October 1947

[. . .]

· 28 OCTOBER 1947 ·

Sent the following coded message:

To Vladimirov [Kostov]
I agree to send [Vladimir] Poptomov to Belgrade.
Please inform me of your suggestions concerning the appointment of our two representatives to the Cominform.
Ivanov [Dimitrov]
28 October 1947

[. . .]

· 31 OCTOBER 1947 ·

[. . .]

Reached an agreement with Druzkov [Stalin] and Alekseev [Molotov] that the publication of signed treaties between Bulg[aria] and Yu[goslavia] would be dated 1 August at Bled and that they would be given a copy of the act of signing.

[. . .]

· 25 NOVEMBER 1947 ·

Meeting Tito's delegation.[587]
An enormous rally in front of the Council of Ministers.
Tito's speech and my speech in response.
In the evening, a reception at the Council of Ministers.
After that, departure for Varna.

· 26 NOVEMBER 1947 ·

We spent the night at the *Kurilo* train station.
The train started early in the morning. Everywhere people were welcoming us enthusiastically. Small rallies in Mezdra, Cherven Briag, Pleven, Gorna Oriahovitsa, Shumen, Kaspichan, Provadiia, Varna. In the evening, in Evksinograd.
Dinner.

· 27 NOVEMBER 1947 ·

Evksinograd.
Delegation conference.
The results of the specific agreements in Bled and the new initiatives were discussed.
Exchange of opinions on the international situation and on the situation on the Balkans in particular.
Complete unanimity on all issues.
Signing of the treaty of alliance in the afternoon.
In the evening, a friendly dinner. My toast. Tito's toast.
Tito's delegation and some of our ministers are leaving for southern Bulgaria at twelve.

· 28 NOVEMBER 1947 ·

Flight to Sofia of two hours and ten minutes.
We had a good flight.

587. On 25 November 1947 Tito and Dimitrov met at Sofia and then traveled to the Evksinograd resort, near Varna, to sign the Yugoslav-Bulgarian friendship treaty. The meeting took place at a time when Stalin was becoming increasingly annoyed about Yugoslav policies in Albania, the Albanian Politburo member Nako Spiru having committed suicide on 20 November.

In the evening, a reception at the Military Club organized by the Yugoslav embassy.

Seeing the delegation off at the train station.

At 11:30 Tito and his people departed, accompanied by Yugov and other Bulgarian comrades.

[. . .]

On 24 January 1948 Stalin sent Dimitrov a strongly worded letter of protest against the "rash and injudicious" statements that Dimitrov had made at a press conference during a visit to Romania. Although Stalin did not elaborate, he was not just furious at "unauthorized" references to the federal and confederative plans in Communist Eastern Europe; he was especially alarmed at Dimitrov's inclusion of Greece among the "people's democracies." Yugoslav penetration into Albania was becoming an additional cause of alarm for Stalin, who saw Yugoslav expansionism as opening the way to armed confrontations with the West in neighboring Greece, itself in the throes of civil war. Dimitrov and Tito were summoned to Moscow in late January. In an affront to Stalin, Tito sent his second-in-command, Edvard Kardelj.

The tongue-lashing at the Kremlin by Stalin and Molotov was in many respects the beginning of Dimitrov's political eclipse. His health rapidly deteriorated and, concentrating on various ceremonial duties, he offered no personal perspective on the increasingly serious dispute between Stalin and the Yugoslavs. Dimitrov remained loyal to Stalin (one of his letters to Tito is touted as a "remarkable Stalinist document") and courteous to Tito (sending him birthday greetings in May 1948). This posture became impossible after the Cominform resolution of 28 June 1948, in which the Communist Party of Yugoslavia (KPJ) was expelled from the Cominform by all the other member parties, including the Bulgarian party.

By the summer of 1948, Dimitrov was no longer involved in everyday decisions. From 15 September to 21 November he was treated in the USSR, his condition having only marginally improved. Again at Moscow in early December, he basked in Stalin's attention to his views on the possibility of transition from capitalism to socialism without a dictatorship of the proletariat. But he could only be alarmed by Stalin's references to Traicho Kostov as somebody who was repeating Tito's mistakes. Reconciled to increasingly bad health, petulant on occasion (Kolarov's voyage to Paris in September 1948 he saw as "a big mistake"), he stumbled through the party congress in December 1948. The last entry in his diary (increasingly telegraphic in 1949) was made on 6 February 1949: "I am gradually getting better." Dimitrov died on 2 July 1949 during medical treatment in Moscow.—I.B.

· 24 January 1948 ·
[. . .]

Received the following coded message:

To Ivanov [Dimitrov]

We consider it our duty to bring to your attention the fact that the part of your statement at the press conference in Romania (in Sofia) concerning the federation or confederation of people's democracies, including Greece, Poland, Czechoslovakia, etc., is viewed by the Moscow friends as harmful, causing detriment to the countries of the new democracy and facilitating the struggle of the Anglo-Americans against these countries.

We consider your statement about a customs union between allied countries—i.e., between countries having treaties of mutual assistance—equally careless and harmful. It might be interpreted to mean that you include the Soviet Union, which has or will have in the near future treaties of mutual assistance with these countries.

It is hard to figure out what could have made you make such rash and injudicious statements at the press conference.

24 January 1948

Druzhkov [Stalin]

The following response was sent:

To Druzhkov [Stalin]:

I confirm the receipt of your telegram. I am grateful to you for your remarks. I shall draw the proper conclusions.

Ivanov [Dimitrov]

· 25 January–3 February 1948 ·

Preparation and holding of the congress of the Fatherland Front.

Report, statute, program, election of the Nat[ional] Council.

Coordination with our allies.

Talks with foreign delegations at the reception in the Council of Ministers (2 February).

Received invitation for our delegation for an unofficial visit to Moscow, together with a delegation from Yugoslavia.

V[ery?] urgent

To Comrade Druzhkov [Stalin]

As soon as the announcement published in the *Pravda* was broadcast on the Moscow radio, hostile rumors about an existing disagreement between Bulgarian and the Soviet governments and about Moscow's disapproval of the policies of our party and the Fatherland Front government spread with unusual speed at home and abroad. To neutralize these rumors, which are extremely harmful to our country at the present moment, on the eve of the congress of the Fatherland Front, we are publishing the *Pravda* announcement with some explanations, stressing our agreement with the basic idea expressed in *Pravda* on that issue. It is hardly necessary to state once again that nobody in our party, and least of all I, would take any step in either our domestic or our foreign policy that would contradict the position of the VKP(b) or would be harmful to our common cause. Please do take into consideration that even the slightest hint concerning disagreements between our party and the VKP(b), between the Bulg[arian] and Sov[iet] governments, encourages our malicious enemies in the country and abroad and may cause confusion and a feeling of insecurity among people.

As far as some of my improper statements are concerned, I will remember your remarks, and I can assure you that in the future I shall not be so careless and inattentive.

30 January 1948

Ivanov [Dimitrov].

[. . .]

· 9 FEBRUARY 1948 ·

We took off for Moscow at 6:30 a.m., Bulgarian time. (Roza and I, Kolarov with his wife, Yugov's wife, Dr. Simeonov, a nurse, and Grŭbchev (st[ate] security). Arrived at 3:30 p.m. Moscow time at the central airport. (Stopped for fifteen min[utes] at the airport in Odessa.) It was a good flight.

It is winter in Moscow, -20 C°.

[. . .]

· 10 FEBRUARY 1948 ·

At the Kremlin. Stalin, Molotov, Zhdanov, Malenkov, Zorin.[588]

From our side: G[eorgi] D[imitrov], V[asil] K[olarov], Tr[aicho] K[ostov].

---

588. Valerian Aleksandrovich Zorin (1902–1985), Soviet diplomat; Soviet envoy to Czechoslovakia (1945–1947); deputy minister for foreign affairs (1947–1955, 1956–1965); Soviet representative to the UN Security Council (1952–1953, 1960–1962); Soviet envoy to West Germany (1955–1956) and France (1965–1971); candidate-member (1956–1962) and member (after 1962) of the KPSS CC.

From Yugoslavia: Kardelj, Djilas, Bakarić.[589]

The Bled treaty.

Interview of G[eorgi] D[imitrov].

The relations between Yugoslavia and Albania.

Had a long discussion. Criticism. I cleared away the misunderstandings. (Tr[aicho] Kostov took shorthand notes on the greater part of the discussion.)

Result: *statement on the mutual consultations* between Bulgaria and the USSR, Yugoslavia and the USSR, on the most important international issues regarding both countries.

Extremely confidential:

X [Molotov]: Between the Sov[iet] government on the one hand and the Bulgarian and Yugoslav governments on the other, there are serious differences, which became clear in relation to three major issues: the Bulgarian-Yugoslav treaty, Comrade Dimitrov's interview, and the introduction of the Yugoslav troops into Albania.

1. Concerning the Bulg[arian]-Yugoslav treaty of Bled we had a few remarks, which were conveyed to comrades Dimitrov and Tito in time. The Sov[iet] government considers that the signing of a treaty, moreover of unlimited duration, before the coming into effect of the peace treaty was a mistake. By acting rashly, both governments played into the hands of react[ionary] elements from England and America, thus providing them with a pretext to increase their intervention in Greece against Bulgaria and Yugoslavia. The Sov[iet] government must warn you that it cannot take responsibility for treaties in the realm of high policy that are concluded without consultations with the USSR.

You had previously agreed with us and then acted in a different way without notifying us. The relations between our two countries and parties should not take this improper and intolerable course. It was necessary to correct the mistake later on.

2. It seems to us that Com[rade] Dimitrov has gone a little bit too far with his press conferences and interviews, allowing others to challenge him about issues that may not be widely discussed. We consider this wrong and improper. A plan going much too far was presented in the interview, and

---

589. Vladimir Bakarić (1912–1983), Yugoslav Communist leader; political commissar at the main staff of Croatia (1941–1943); secretary of the KPH CC (from 1944); member of the KPJ CC (from 1948 on); member of the SKJ presidency (after 1966); premier and president of federal Croatia (1945–1953); president of the Croatian parliament (1953–1963); member of the presidency of Yugoslavia (from 1974); Marxist theoretician; specialist on the problems of land rent.

not a single attempt was made to coordinate it with anybody. The issues of a federation or a confederation, of a customs union, were put forward with Poland, Czechoslovakia, and Greece to be included in it. Com[rade] Dimitrov spoke for all these parties, without having been officially authorized by anybody to do so. This is essentially wrong and tactically very harmful. All that facilitates the job of the founders of the Western bloc. We could not ignore this fact. Comrade Dimitrov was given advance warning about this by Comrade Druzhkov [Stalin] through party channels: "Your presentation at the press conference concerning the establishment of a federation or confederation is considered harmful, causing detriment to the countries of the new democracy and helping the Anglo-Americans. Your statement about the customs union is harmful and careless, for it may be understood that the Soviet Union, which will soon have treaties of mutual assistance with these countries, might also be included. It is hard to figure out what could have made you make such injudicious statements at the press conference."

When we spoke with the Polish comrades, they said: "We thought that this was your position." This is what all think: if Dimitrov or Tito talks about some other countries, this certainly comes from the USSR. The Polish comrades mentioned that basically they are against Com[rade] Dimitrov's idea and consider it incorrect.

We had to take a stand because everybody—both enemies and friends—thought that this was our viewpoint. We consider such things absolutely incorrect and inadmissible for the future. Dim[itrov's] explanation did not help and on the contrary added to the confusion. The conclusion from it is that earlier it was Germany which prevented a federation with Serbia, and now it is the USSR.

D[imitrov]: We had no such thought.

S[talin]: You are a politician, and you should think not only of your intentions but also of what can come of your statements. We do not object at all to the customs union between Bulgaria and Yugoslavia, on the contrary.

M[olotov]: Beneš's newspaper in Czechoslovakia reported on the spot that "Dimitrov revealed the Communist plans—now let the Czech communists respond."

On the other hand, Com[rade] Dimitrov's position is at odds with the declaration of the nine Communist parties.

S[talin]: Your interview, containing a different message from the one presented at the conference of the nine Com[munist] parties, is distracting attention from internal issues.

M[olotov]: We consider that such things should not happen in the future.

3. We learned by chance that at the end of January one Yugoslav division was going to be introduced into Albania, to the Greek-Albanian border, to prevent an attack from the Greek side under the patronage of the Anglo-Americans. The Yugoslav comrades did not inform us in advance about

this. When we asked Tito, he confirmed it: a Yugoslav military base was going to be established in Albania for a joint protection of the border. The Albanians said that they had been assured that this was taking place with our consent.

It follows from this that we evaluate the situation in Albania in a different way. This is again a disagreement that cannot be ignored. We have to speak openly on these questions, to see how you evaluate the situation. We think that such things should not be allowed to happen in the future. We have to bring the existing disagreements out into the open; if there are different views, they should be presented and discussed. For the sake of our cause and mutual agreement, no action should be undertaken without due consultation on such issues.

In the future Com[rade] Dimitrov should spare himself and us the risk of making similar statements.

D[imitrov]: As far as Bled is concerned, I explained earlier that there we did not sign a treaty but agreed upon the text of a future treaty between Bulgaria and Yugoslavia. I made a special statement about the interview at the congress of the OF, emphasizing that the criticism of the PB was correct. To increase the economic and defense capability of our country, we need the cooperation of the other friendly countries of the new democracy.

S[talin]: You wanted to say something new. The Poles and the Czechs laughed at your idea of a federation. Why don't you ask them whether they want it or not?

D[imitrov]: This was harmful and incorrect in its essence. My clarification was targeted at all those who would like to use my statement against us and the USSR. At present there are no disagreements between us. Such statements will not be repeated in the future.

S[talin]: We do not understand each other; therefore, there are disagreements between us. And you are trying to conceal this.

M[olotov]: These are serious disagreements; they are not trifles.

S[talin]: You are a veteran politician. What are the mistakes we are talking about? You have some different assumptions, and maybe you are not completely aware of them. You should not give interviews so often. You want to say something new and impress the world! You speak as if you were still general secretary of the Comintern giving an interview for a Commun[ist] newspaper. You provide ammunition to the reactionary elements in America for convincing public opinion that America would not be doing anything extraordinary in creating a Western bloc, since in the Balkans there already exists not only a bloc but also a customs union. Right now, a great electoral struggle is going on in America. For us, it is of great importance to see what the future government there will be, because America is a powerful country, well armed. Its government is headed not by intellectuals but by moneybags who hate us terribly and look for any pretext to do us harm. They might lose in the elections if by our actions we provide arguments to the progressive elements. But our actions might also be helpful to the reaction. The American government is facing the elections and is anxious about the outcome. But if the same financial tycoons are elected once again to the government, it will be our fault, to a large extent. They will say: "Not only are you trying to establish a bloc, but you are unifying a whole group of countries—against whom?" Why do you need such a bloc? After all, if you want to unite, why make so much fuss about it? You are either inexperienced or getting carried away like the Komsomol activists who fly like butterflies right into the burning flames. What do you need all this for? Why make things easier for your enemies in England, America, and France?

And concerning Albania: The Yugoslav comrades have solved the problem so easily! During the war the three Allied powers declared Albania's independence and supported its independence. Of all the tangles in the struggle between reaction and democracy, the Albanian knot is our weakest point. Albania is still not admitted into the UN; the British and the Americans do not recognize it. This question is still open. There is no other such weak point. Albania alone is not protected legally in the international arena. If Tito sends a division or even a single regiment to Albania, it will not remain hidden from America and England. They will immediately claim that Albania has been occupied. Has Albania officially asked for any help from Yugoslavia? And these scoundrels from England and America will pretend to be the defenders of Albanian independence. Only irrational people would try to establish a front that would be hopeless. Nowadays, we should try to improve the organization of the Albanian army, to provide instructors and arms. And then, if Albania is attacked, it could ask for help from Yugoslavia. Otherwise, Yugoslavia would be accused of occupying an independent country. Then a military intervention would be entirely possible. The American ships and bases are nearby. And this would be the most convenient situation and a noble pretext for America to intervene. When you are going to fight a war, you have to build up your front the way it is most advantageous for you, and in this case you would only expose your back to be beaten by the Americans.

Consider the scale of the war in China. It took on enormous dimensions. There is not a single soldier from our country there.

The Albanians are not worse than the Chinese, are they? You could train them, provide them with arms, and then they would be able to defend themselves. It is much better if they defend their independence themselves. In this case, the Americans would hardly attack first, but otherwise their task would be much easier. You offer very simple solutions to these issues, but they are much more complicated.

If the Greek partisans were defeated, would you start a war?

K[arde]lj.: No.

S[talin]: I base my conclusions on analysis of the possibilities available to the partisans and to their opponents. Recently I started to doubt that the partisans could win. If you are not sure that the partisans would win, the partisan movement should be restricted. The Americans and the English have a very strong interest in the Mediterranean. They would like to have their bases in Greece. They would use all possible means to support a government that would be obedient. This is an international issue of great importance.

If the partisan movement is halted, they will have no excuse to attack you. It is not so easy to start a war now, when they lack the pretext that you are organizing civil war in Greece.

If you are confident that the partisans have good chances of winning, it is a different matter. But I have some doubts about this.

D[imitrov]: We receive little information from here too.

S[talin]: You have the right to ask to be informed by us. Let us then make an agreement for obligatory consultations on all important international questions.

D[imitrov]: We will keep to this agreement.

S[talin]: We will not delay the treaty with Bulgaria by much. On the fifteenth of this month the Hungarians will be here. Then we will turn to the Finns, and after that to you.

M[olotov]: In one of the treaties it is said that all hotbeds of aggression should be destroyed. These are only fine words that provide gratuitous ammunition to our enemies. Why do you say things that are not included in the other treaties? Are you going to wage a preventive war?

S[talin]: These are leftist infatuations.

M[olotov]: Not all UN initiatives against aggression should be supported. They could be directed against us. Weren't we denounced as aggressors by the League of Nations because of the conflict with Finland?

The Yugoslav comrades did not allow Albania to buy five thousand tons of oats from us, and they sent it [Albania] to look for it in Argentina!

S[talin]: Obviously, the Yugoslavs are afraid that we would take away Albania from them. You should take Albania, but wisely.

The decree for the coordination of the economic plans restricts your and Romania's sovereignty.

Only three federations appear to be possible and natural: 1) Yugoslavia and Bulgaria; 2) Romania and Hungary; 3) Poland and Czechoslovakia. These are the real possibilities. The confederation among these is a concoction.

Tr[aicho] [Kostov]: Can we consider that we might direct our efforts toward accelerating the establishment of a federation between Bulgaria and Yugoslavia?

S[talin]: You can establish it even tomorrow if you want to. This is a natural process, and we are not against it. We are only against Komsomol methods of unification. You should prepare the people in these countries and public opinion abroad to accept the idea of federation.

K[ardelj]: We are of the opinion that even in the case of Bulgaria you should not hurry, mainly because of the international implications. Any acceleration of the process could put you in a difficult situation.

S[talin]: I think you are making a mistake here. The unification process between Yugoslavia, Bulgaria, and Albania should not be delayed. The National Assemblies of these countries should make their decision and instruct their governments to start negotiations for unification. It is better to start with political unification and then send troops to Albania. Then this would not be a pretext to attack you. Establishing a federation before signing the peace treaty with Bulgaria would have been premature. But now Bulgaria is a normal country enjoying full international rights. In my opinion, you should not delay these issues any longer—you had better speed up. If you can arrange the unification through the National Assemblies, everything will be fine. The federation resolves all issues. Bulgarians and Yugoslavs are very close both racially and in their way of life, and everyone would understand [the reasons for] this unification. And the Albanians would also gain from a future federation because a new, united Albania would be created with almost double the population.

All efforts should be concentrated on forming such a natural federation: develop its economy; develop your national culture; strengthen the army. Otherwise Poland would be relying on you [to do something], you on Poland, and nothing would come of it. There is no need to deviate from the decisions of the nine Com[munist] parties.

M[olotov]: If it is necessary to destroy the hotbeds of aggression, about which Com[rade] Dimitrov spoke, destroy them, but why all this fuss about it? Nowadays, people tend to be picky about every word you say.

Tr[aicho] [Kostov]: We think that if the partisan movement in Greece fails, it would create a very difficult situation for the rest of the Balkan countries.

S[talin]: Of course, the partisans should be supported. But if the prospects for the success of the partisan movement in a certain country are declining, it is better to postpone the struggle until a more favorable time. You cannot replace what is missing from the balance of the opposing forces through mere exclamations and worrying. A sober analysis of the balance of forces is needed. If it proves that at some moment we are not doing well, we should not be ashamed to admit this. The activities of partisan movements have been halted in the past when the situation has been unfavorable. If it cannot be done today, it can be done tomorrow. You are afraid to put the question straightforwardly. You feel bound by the "moral responsibility." But if you cannot carry some burden that you wanted to carry, you have to admit this to yourself. You should not be afraid of any "categorical imperative" regarding moral responsibility. We are not bound by any "categorical imperatives." The key issue is the balance of forces. If you are strong, then strike a blow. If not, do not enter the fray. We agree to fight not when the adversary wants us to, but when it is in our interests to do so.

K[ardelj]: It will become clear in a few months what the chances of the partisans are.

S[talin]: Fine, then wait. Maybe you are right.

I also doubted that the Chinese could succeed, and I advised them to come to a temporary agreement with Chang Kai-shek. Officially, they agreed with us, but in practice they continued mobilizing the Chinese people. And then they openly put forward the question: Will we go on with our fight? We have the support of our people. We said: Fine, what do you need? It turned out that the conditions there were very favorable. The Chinese proved to be right, and we were wrong. Maybe in this case it can also turn out that we are wrong. But we want to be certain about what we are doing.

K[osto]v: Will the Americans allow the victory of the partisans?

S[talin]: No one will ask them. If there are enough forces to win and if there are people capable of utilizing the people's forces, then the struggle should be continued. But one shouldn't think that if nothing comes up in Greece, everything else is lost.

The neighboring countries have to be the last to recognize the government of General Markos.[590] First, let the others recognize it.

M[olotov]: Com[rade] Dimitrov's statement against the Lulchev opposition was also incorrect and is now widely used by our enemies. Was it necessary to make this statement?

D[imitrov]: It was motivated rather by internal necessity, to discourage them from making trouble again.

S[talin]: Let Yugov negotiate with the opposition: he knows how to do this.

K[ardelj]: We think that there are no essential disagreements between us. It's only a matter of certain errors.

S[talin]: These are not certain errors but a system.

In the treaty with Czechoslovakia you can use the Czech formula—if there is an attack from Germany or some of its allies. If there is a threat from some other country, then the article on mutual consultations will be applied.

590. Markos Vafeiadis (1906–1992), Greek Communist leader; head of the KKE in Salonika; political commissar of an ELAS division during the war; commander of the Macedonian corps; supreme commander of the Democratic Army of Greece (October 1946); prime minister of the KKE-sponsored provisional democratic government of Greece (1947–1948) during the Third Round of the Greek civil war. He was expelled from the KKE in 1948 after a series of military defeats; after a period of exile in Albania and the USSR after 1949, he returned to Greece in 1986 after the general amnesty and, having joined the PASOK Socialist Party of Andreas Papandreou, became its parliamentary deputy in 1989.

We support the emigration of Jews to Palestine in accordance with the decision of the UN to allow up to four hundred thousand people into Palestine. The UN took a positive attitude toward the Jewish demands. So the Englishmen have no right to protest.

Tr[aicho] [Kostov]: It is very hard in a small and backward country. If we constantly raise the issue of economic cooperation among the Balkan countries, of coordinating our plans, it is because we need to help each other accelerate our economic development.

S[talin]: You can sign a customs agreement with Yugoslavia and even become one common state. But I cannot see what the use would be in signing a customs agreement and coordinating your plans with Romania. The Romanians will sell their goods wherever they make better profits.

· 11 FEBRUARY 1948 ·
[. . .]

With Molotov (Kremlin). We signed a written statement with Molotov for mutual consultations.

Presented to Stalin (a copy to Molotov) a number of memos with our appeals on economic problems, on issues concerning the army and the people's militia, on the transmitter and the movie center.

Before that, we had lunch with the Yugoslav comrades in Meshcherino.

We agreed that the Yugoslav CC and the Bulgarian CC would analyze the possibilities for a quick unification of Bulgaria and Yugoslavia in a federation.

[. . .]

· 14 FEBRUARY 1948 ·

Meeting: G[eorgi] D[imitrov], V[asil] K[olarov], Yugov, Chankov, Chervenkov. A report on the discussion in Moscow and the memorandum.

Discussed the conclusions. We decided that the Politburo would consider the issue of unification with Yugoslavia.

[. . .]

· 16 FEBRUARY 1948 ·

The chief prosecutor with me. I warned him about the *inappropriate timing* of the publication of the indict[ment] against Gichev. Such mistakes should not be repeated. Everything concerning polit[ical] trials has to be coordinated with us.

[. . .]

· 25 MARCH 1948 ·

Introduced Vŭlko [Chervenkov], Yugov, Chankov to the documents of the session of the Yugosl[av] CC (Trotskyite and anti-Soviet statements!).

[. . .]

· 4 APRIL 1948 ·

Sunday.

[. . .]

Levichkin[591] gave me a document from Moscow (stric[tly] conf[idential]) with Stal[in's] and Molotov's answers to two letters written by Tito relating to the withdrawal of the military and civ[il] (Soviet) specialists from Yugoslavia.

[. . .]

· 7 APRIL 1948 ·

Meeting of the secretariat, together with Yugov, Kolarov, Vlado Poptomov.
Besides all the other issues, the answers of Mol[otov] and Stal[in] to Tito and the Yugosl[av] CC that were severely critical of the anti-Soviet position of the latter concerning the relations between Yugoslavia and the USSR were read and discussed.

[. . .]

· 16 APRIL 1948 ·
[. . .]

The courier from Moscow brought from Zhdanov the decision of the Hungarian Politburo concerning the leadership of the Yugosl[av]

591. Kliment Danilovich Levichkin (b. 1907), Soviet diplomat; counselor at the Allied Control Commission in Bulgaria.

Com[munist] Party (in relation to Molotov and Stalin's letter to Tito and his friends).

[. . .]

· 18 APRIL 1948 ·
[. . .]

Edited our decision on the letter of the CC of the VKP(b) to the CC of the Yugoslav C[ommunist] P[arty].

· 18 APRIL 1948 ·

At 11:40 left for Prague.
In the evening, Belgrade (Topčider).
Djilas and Simić came to see us on the train.

[. . .]

· 10 MAY 1948 ·

Discussed the new letter of the CC of the VKP(b) to the Yugoslav Com[munist] Party (a marvelous Stalinist document).

Sent to Molotov our letter concerning the above:

To Comrade Alekseev [Molotov]:

I would like to confirm receipt of the letter of 4 May 1948 from the CC of VKP(b) to the Central Committee of the KPJ [Communist Party of Yugoslavia]. Our Politburo has discussed the letter and has come to the opinion that this remarkable Stalinist document should help not only the Yugoslav Com[munist] Party find its way out of the deadlock into which it was led by egoistic, painfully ambitious, and thoughtless leaders. This letter has exceptional meaning for other Communist parties, including our party, especially in its treatment of issues of principle. We completely agree with your suggestion that the whole problem be discussed at the next meeting of the Cominformburo, for this is the only correct strategy for coping with the deeds of the Yugoslav leaders.

We are of course afraid that Tito and his friends will try to find various excuses not to attend such a meeting—or at least to postpone it as long as possible. But then we would consider it proper to inform the *aktiv* of the Yugoslav Com[munist] Party of the content of your letter or even to reveal in the press the views of the leaders of the Yugoslav Com[munist] Party.
10 May 1948
Ivanov [Dimitrov]

[. . .]

· 24 MAY 1948 ·
[. . .]

Sent a congratulatory telegram to *Tito* on the occasion of his fifty-sixth birthday.

[. . .]

· 5 JUNE 1948 ·
[. . .]

Asked for a meeting with Zahariadis to discuss the Greek problems.

Sent an invitation to the CC of the C[ommunist] P[arty] of Y[ugoslavia] for a meeting between the Yugosl[av] representatives and ours on the same issue.

[. . .]

· 7 JUNE 1948 ·

Received Levichkin. He asked on behalf of Moscow whether we would agree to hold the *Danube conference* in Sofia. I gave a positive answer. He informed me that Moscow agrees with us about not hurrying recognition of the Jewish state of *Israel.*

[. . .]

· 11 JUNE 1948 ·

Received a message from Zhdanov informing us that our delegates for the Informburo sess[ion] should be in Bucharest on June 18–19, and then they would go to the meeting.

We informed him that Tr[aicho] Kostov and V[ŭlko] Chervenkov will be in Bucharest on June 19.

[. . .]

In the evening, discussion with *Zahariadis* on the situation in Greece.

There are favorable conditions for continuing the struggle.

Our help will be necessary in the future.

Discussed how to improve the exchange of information and our communication with the Greek comrades.

[. . .]

· 14 JUNE 1948 ·
[. . .]

Prepared a letter to the part[y] committee in the Pirin region concerning the speech of the Maced[onian] prime minister, Koliševski,[592] which was used in a hostile way against Yugoslavia and us by the Amer[ican] and English press. I am proposing to explain that Koliševski's message was ungrounded and harmful.

[. . .]

· 27 JUNE 1948 ·
[. . .]

Traicho's [Kostov] report, discuss[ions], my final speech, and a unanimous decision to approve the resolution of the Informburo[593] and the measures concerning the clarification work.

[. . .]

· 28 JUNE 1948 ·

Meeting of the Execut[ive] Committee of the Nat[ional] Council on the Yugoslav question.

592. Lazar Koliševski (1914–2000), Yugoslav Communist leader; Macedonian who entered the KPJ in Kragujevac, Serbia, where he worked in the arms factory. He was sent by the KPJ to Macedonia in 1941 to reestablish the KPJ's authority after Metody Šatorov (Šarlo), the secretary of the KPJ organization in Macedonia, attempted, after the beginning of Bulgarian occupation, to bring the Macedonian party organization under the authority of the BRP. Koliševski was arrested by the Bulgarian authorities in November 1941, tortured, and sentenced to death. Although the sentence was not carried out, he remained in prison, mainly in Pleven, Bulgaria, until the arrival of the Red Army and the coup of September 1944. While in prison, Koliševski was appointed the secretary of the Macedonian CP CC (March 1943). First premier (1945–1953) of People's Republic of Macedonia (within Yugoslavia); president of the National Assembly of Macedonia (1953–1962); member of the KPJ/SKJ CC (from 1948 on); member of the SKJ CC Executive Committee (1952–1969) and of the SKJ presidency (1974–1978); member and, after Tito's death, chairman (1980–1981) of the presidency of Yugoslavia.

593. On 21 June 1948, the Cominform member parties, except the KPJ, which refused to attend, met at Bucharest, Romania, and arrived at the notorious Cominform resolution on the "situation in the KPJ," which included a section calling for the overthrow of Tito's leadership. This resolution was then adopted by each of the eight signatories and publicly announced on 28 June 1948.

Unanimous approval of the resolution of the Informburo and the measures concerning the clarification work.

[. . .]

· 19 AUGUST 1948 ·

Received the following coded message from Moscow:

To Comrade Dimitrov:
We have received the message of the doctors who are insisting on your two-month leave and treatment in Barvikha. Our advice is not to postpone the treatment.
Sending our greetings to you,
Druzhkov [Stalin], Alekseev [Molotov]

[. . .]

To Comrades Druzhkov [Stalin] and Alekseev [Molotov].
Thank you very much for your concern, attention, and greetings. As soon as I feel well enough to fly by plane, I will come to Moscow for my treatment in Barvikha. I send you, with deepest gratitude, my warmest regards,
21 August 1948.
Ivanov [Dimitrov]

[. . .]

· 5 OCTOBER 1948 ·
[. . .]

Kuusinen with me. We discussed the situation—in particular, the situation in the people's democracies. He is inclined, like me, to accept the argument that thanks to the powerful support of the Sov[iet] Union on the one hand and the leading role of the work[ing] class and its Communist vanguard [on the other], people's democracies can accomplish the building of socialism without the dictatorship of the proletariat that was the inevitable necessity in the USSR.

[. . .]

· 23 OCTOBER 1948

Kuusinen was with me. Had a long discussion on the character and the perspectives of people's democracy, on the peasant question in the people's democracies, the kulak question and the nationalization of land, etc.

As far as the dictatorship of the proletariat is concerned, nowadays the issue is viewed *in a different manner* in the people's democracies.

It is possible to make the transition from capitalism to socialism without a direct dictatorship of the working class. But this is only a possibility, and the possibility is desirable.

Such development is possible thanks to the existence of a powerful socialist country (a stronghold providing technical, political, and moral support; the country's great and reliable experience in the building of socialism) and also thanks to the taking of the *leading role* by the working class and of its Com[munist] vanguard.

This does not quite mean that the question of the implementation of the dictatorship of the proletariat has disappeared entirely. The working class, which is leading social development on the road to socialism, will not give up the implementation of the dictatorship of the proletariat should countervailing internal and external forces make it necessary to resort to it as the necessary means for the transition from capitalism to socialism (kulaks and capit[alist] owners in the country, imperialist pressure from abroad!).

The dictatorship of the proletariat is not *an aim* in itself but *a means* for the realization of socialism. The aim is *one*—socialism. *The means* can be *different.* If *the peop[le's] democracy* proves impossible, then *the dictatorship of the proletariat. But socialism must be realized.*

[. . .]

· 6 DECEMBER 1948 ·

We took off from Bucharest at 7:30 a.m. (Sofia time). Arrived in Moscow at 3:15 p.m. (Sofia time). Had a good flight.

In the evening, at *Stalin's* dacha. There we met Bierut, Minc, Berman. Had dinner with Stalin and Molotov. Stalin made important remarks concerning my letter on peop[le's] democracy and the dict[atorship] of the proletariat, as well as on some other fundamental issues. (Traicho took short[hand] notes of the whole discussion.)

> Top secret, five copies
> Two possibilities or two forms of the dictatorship of the proletariat have been outlined in the history of Marxist thought. We consider it an axiom that the transition from capitalism to socialism without dictatorship of the proletariat is impossible. Two forms of the dictatorship of the proletariat are known. The first is the democratic republic, which Marx and Engels saw as in the Paris Commune, in claiming that the democratic republic and the majority of the proletariat is the best form of the dictatorship of the pro-

letariat. They meant a democratic republic in which the proletariat had a dominant role, rather than the republics in America or Switzerland. Lenin formulated the Soviet form of the dictatorship of the proletariat as a better match for our conditions. Here in Russia, where the proletariat took power by means of an uprising (when an uprising begins, everything collapses), the Soviet form proved to be the most appropriate one. In your country, where the working class seized power not by means of an uprising but with help from outside—with the help of the Soviet army, in other words—the seizure of power was easier; you can do without the Soviet form, going back to the model of Marx and Engels—i.e., the people's democratic parliamentary form. We are of the opinion that you can do without the Soviet regime. In your case, you will be able to carry out the transition from capitalism to socialism by means of a people's democracy. The people's democracy will play the role of the dictatorship of the proletariat.

We deprived the kulaks and the bourgeoisie of the right to vote. In our country, only the working people had this right. We had to relocate two million kulaks to the north, and when we abolished the kulaks as a class, we granted suffrage to all people. The capitalists and the landowners fought against us for four years during the Intervention, whereas in your country they just fled and surrendered without fight. In our case, there was no other country that could help us the way we are helping you now. That is why we needed a different form to establish the power of the working class and the working people. You can do without the Soviet regime. But the regime you have now is playing the role of a dictatorship of the proletariat. Where there are antagonistic classes and the working class has the power, dictatorship is indispensable. But you have the legal arguments to defeat your enemies. There are still some signs of a civil war going on in your country. Only after you destroy the exploiting classes completely will you be able to claim that you no longer have a dictatorship of the proletariat.

A democratic republic in which the working class has a substantial role to play—this is what Marx and Engels considered the most appropriate form of dictatorship of the proletariat. Instead, we had a Soviet system rather than a parliamentarian one, and there were workers', peasants', and soldiers' deputies in the Soviets, whereas all non-working-class elements were excluded. The advantage of the Soviet form is that it solves the problems quickly—by shedding blood; but you can do without it because the capitalists in your country surrendered immediately. In other words, you were lucky, and we are responsible for your luck, as we readily admit.

As long as there are antagonistic classes, there will be dictatorship of the proletariat. But in your country it will be a dictatorship of a different type. You can do without a Soviet regime. However, the regime of the people's republic can fulfill the major task of the dictatorship of the proletariat, both in terms of abolishing classes and in terms of building socialism. The people's democracy and the Soviet regime are two forms of dictatorship of the proletariat.

Stalin severely criticized *Traicho* [Kostov] for his refusal to permit the Soviet representatives in Sofia [to get information] about the Bulgarian economy directly from the relevant institutions. Stalin described this refusal as equivalent to the case of Tito. "This is exactly how our conflict with Tito began."

There should be only friendship and cooperation between Communists, "without cheating and boasting." Stalin spoke for a long time on this issue. He has very serious suspicions that *Traicho* is cheating and playing tricks (these suspicions are shared by Molotov too); Stalin also has some doubts about Yugov (?) . . . This was an extremely unpleasant affair for our party.

. . . We stayed till morning. Stalin was very lively and cheerful. He was treating his guests. He played some records, told us jokes, and even danced.

We arranged a new meeting for tomorrow to discuss other important issues.

· 7 DECEMBER 1948 ·

At the *Kremlin*. Stalin, Molotov, Beria, Malenkov, Voznesensky, Bulganin, Kaganovich, Kosygin.[594] (As we were already leaving, Mikoyan came; he had been with an Ital[ian] delegation, and that is why he was late.)

We discussed our econ[omic] issues. Concerning the commodity credit in the amount of $40 million that we requested for 1949, Stalin said that after their discussions with the Czech delegation, which is to come soon, they would be able to determine the amount of credit the USSR would give to each country of peop[le's] democracy. We will be informed by 14–15 December of what we can expect.

He considers correct our decisions regarding the armed forces:

An increase in our army and a relevant increase in the staff of each division.

594. Aleksei Nikolaevich Kosygin (1904–1980); Soviet Communist leader; member of the VKP(b) CC (from 1939 on); people's commissar for the textile industry (beginning in 1939); deputy chairman of the Council of People's Commissars responsible for consumer industries (1940–1953, 1960–1964); premier of the Russian Federation (1941–1945); minister of finance (1948) and light industry (1948–1953); member of the VKP(b)/KPSS Politburo/Presidium (1948–1952, 1960–1980); premier of the USSR (1964–1980); one of the ruling triumvirate, along with Leonid I. Brezhnev and Nikolai V. Podgorny, during the late 1960s and early 1970s.

Establishment of two new infantry divisions.

He thinks that we should have two or even three infantry divisions, fighter air-force and anti-aircraft defense.

So far as cavalry is concerned, he thinks that we don't need a cavalry division.

Airfields are necessary, and they are ready to help us with this.

The task of our army in case of war is to hold back the enemy—the major blow will come from the Sov[iet] army.

For the time being, we should have everything necessary to repel a partial attack against our country (especially from Turkey).

These issues will be worked out in detail with our military representatives in the near future.

We discussed a number of other issues.

[. . .]

· 9 DECEMBER 1948 ·

Meeting of the PB.

Information on the discussions in Moscow. Condemnation of Traicho's [Kostov's] error. Measures to clear up the mistrust regarding our relations with the USSR.

Preparation for the congress.

[. . .]

· 30 DECEMBER 1948 ·

[. . .]

Together with *Traicho* [Kostov] and *Yugov,* received the Greek comrade Leonidis (member of the Politburo).

He informed us about the dismissal of *Markos,* the establishment of a military council headed by *Zahariadis,* and the current situation in Greece. The general picture—*optimistic.*

Agreed on the *specific* help we will continue to provide in the future.

[. . .]

· 19 JANUARY 1949 ·

Meeting of the secretariat.

Zahariadis reported on the situation in Greece. The prospects are not bad.

General *Petrushevski's* information about our army.

[He made] some specific suggestions.

In the milit[ary] hospital, [visiting] the hopelessly ill Iv[an] Dimitrov.

· 24 JANUARY 1949 ·

Meeting at the Council of Min[isters] concerning the trial against *Evang[elical] pastors* (accused of espionage), Yugov, Neichev,[595] Chankov, Hristozov, Timev (deputy minister of justice), *Vl[adimir] Georgiev* (chief prosecutor) and *Vl [adimir] Poptomov.*

Received *Dekanozov,* together with *Iv[an] Stefanov*[596] and *D[obri] Terpeshev,* to discuss the agreement with the Soviet government concerning the Soviet property (former German property) given to Bulgaria.

[. . .]

Together with Chervenkov, received *Todor Pavlov* to discuss his proposal presented to the Union of Bulgarian-Soviet Societies and his participation in the congress.

Severe criticism of his behavior, particularly his harmful speech at the par[ty] congress on the issue of the dictatorship of the proletariat.

He recognizes his mistake and is ready to admit it in public.

595. Mincho Neichev (1887–1956), Bulgarian Communist; minister of justice (1944–1946) and of education (1946–1947); member of the BRP(k)/BKP CC (from 1945 on); alternate member (1948–1949) and member (1949–1954) of the Politburo.

596. Ivan Stefanov (1899–1980), Bulgarian Communist who was active in the KPD (1922–1925) and the PCF (1925–1927); member of the BRP CC (from 1929); minister of finance (1946–1949).

Biographical Notes

Andreev, Andrei Andreevich (1895–1971): Soviet Communist leader, from a peasant family in Smolensk Province. Member of the RSDRP(b) Petrograd Committee (from 1916 on), who was active in the trade unions; secretary of the VKP(b) Northern Caucasus Territorial Committee (from 1927 on); chairman of the VKP(b) Central Control Commission (from 1930 on); people's commissar for worker-peasant inspection and deputy chairman of the Council of People's Commissars (from 1930 on); candidate-member (1926–1930) and full member (1932–1952) of the VKP(b) Politburo; chairman of the Commission for Party Control (1939–1952) and people's commissar for agriculture (1943–1953); deputy chairman of the Council of Ministers (1946–1953). Andreev fell into disgrace with Stalin in 1952 and was criticized for his "incorrect positions" on using small teams in agricultural production. After Stalin's death he was a member of the presidium of the Supreme Soviet of the USSR (1953–1962).

Beria, Lavrenty Pavlovich (1899–1953): Soviet Communist leader from a peasant family in the Sukhumi area of Georgia, active in the Bolshevik underground organization in Baku (1915–1920) and from 1921 on in the secret police: Beria was deputy chairman of the Azerbaijan Cheka; chairman of the Georgian and Transcaucasian GPU, plenipotentiary of OGPU in the Transcaucasian federation, and member of the OGPU Collegium of the USSR; first secretary of the CC of the CP of Georgia (from 1931 on); first secretary of the Transcaucasian Territorial Committee (1932–1938); member of the VKP(b) CC (from 1934 on); people's commissar for internal affairs (1938–1945); candidate-member (1939–1946) and full member (1946–1953) of the VKP(b) Politburo. Beria was one of Stalin's closest associates after the death of A. A. Zhdanov (1948). He was arrested, tried secretly, and executed after Stalin's death in 1953.

Browder, Earl (1891–1973): American Communist; secretary-general of the CPUSA (1930–1944); member of the ICC (1924–1928); member of the ECCI (1935–1943). During the Second World War Browder pursued a line that essentially decommunized the CPUSA, which was transformed into the Communist Association. Jacques Duclos, a leading French Communist, but backed by the authority of Moscow, denounced this policy in 1945 as "Browderite revisionism." The National Convention of the CPUSA condemned Browder in July 1945. He was expelled from the CPUSA in February 1946.

Bukharin, Nikolai Ivanovich (1888–1938): Prominent Russian Bolshevik, from a teacher's family in Moscow; coopted into the RSDRP's Moscow committee (1908), he was repeatedly arrested and exiled into the Onega region and spent 1910 to 1917 in emigration. Member of the RKP(b) CC (1917–1929); candidate-member (1917–1924) and then full member (1924–1929) of the RKP(b) Politburo; member of the ECCI (1928–1929). Bukharin was Stalin's chief ally in the struggle against Trotsky and Zinoviev (1926). He succeeded Zinoviev at the helm of the Comintern in November 1926. In 1928, however, Bukharin's clash with Stalin led to the expulsion of the Bloc of Rights from their functions (1929). Having undergone self-criticism, Bukharin was appointed the editor of *Izvestiia* (1934–1937) and elected a candidate-member of the VKP(b) CC (1934). Arrested and tried in the case of the Bloc of Rights and Trotskyites (January 1937), he was sentenced to death and executed. Bukharin was an important Marxist theoretician and a member of the Academy of Sciences of the USSR (from 1929 on).

Bulganin, Nikolai Aleksandrovich (1895–1975): Soviet Communist leader from a working class family; member of the RKP(b) from 1918 on. He served in the Cheka (1918–1922) and on the Supreme Council on the National Economy (1922–1927). Chairman of the Moscow soviet (1931–1937); chairman of the Council of People's Commissars of RSFSR (from 1937 on); deputy chairman of the Council of People's Commissars (1938–1941); member of the Military Soviet of the Western Front (1941–1943); member of the Military Soviet of the Second Baltic and First Belorussian Fronts (1943–1944); member of the State Council for Defense (1944–1945); minister of defense (1947–1949, 1953–1955) and marshal ("civilian marshal") of the USSR (1947–1958); member of the VKP(b) CC (from 1934 on) and of the KPSS Politburo (1952–1958); chairman of the Council of Ministers (1955–1958). Supported the "antiparty" group in 1957. He was dismissed in 1958.

Chervenkov, Vŭlko (Vladimirov, 1900–1980): Bulgarian Communist leader; Dimitrov's brother-in-law, married to Dimitrov's sister Lena. He joined the BKP in 1919 and participated in the September 1923 uprising. Chervenkov continued underground work in Bulgaria until 1925, when, together with Lena, he escaped to the USSR. He graduated from the Leninist School and worked in the Comintern apparatus (1928–1943). Director of the KUNMZ (1937–1938); director of the Leninist School (from 1937 on); member of the Foreign Bureau of the BRP CC (1941–1944); chief editor for the Hristo Botev radio station; member of the BRP(k)/BKP Politburo (1944–1961) and CC secretary (1944–1949). After going back to Bulgaria in 1944, Chervenkov was president of the Council for Science, Art, and Culture (1947–1949) in Dimitrov's cabinet. After Dimitrov's death, he was deputy prime minister in Kolarov's government (1949–1950) and, after Kolarov's death, prime minister of Bulgaria (1950–1956); secretary-general of the BKP (1950–1954); president of the OF (from 1950 on); minister of education (until 1961). During the de-Stalinization campaign he was stripped of his positions, excluded from the CC (1962), and exiled to Varna.

Damianov, Georgi (pseudonym: Belov, 1892–1958): Bulgarian Communist leader; he joined the *tesniaks* in 1912. Damianov participated in the September 1923 uprising as a military commander and after its defeat escaped to Yugoslavia and the USSR. He graduated from the Frunze Military Academy in 1929. Afterward he worked on the BKP and Comintern staffs. Sent to Bulgaria in 1936, he purged the BRP of "leftist sectarians." Soon thereafter, he was sent to Spain, where he served as an instructor in the International Brigades. When he went back to Moscow, he headed the Comintern's Cadre Department (1937–1938). Member of the Foreign Bureau of the BRP (1937–1944). Damianov fought in the Red Army during the war, returned to Bulgaria in 1944, became a BRP(k) CC secretary, and headed the Military Department of the CC (1944–1946); minister of defense in Dimitrov's and Kolarov's cabinets (1946–1950); member of the BRP(k)/BKP Politburo (1945–1958); president of the Bulgarian national assembly (1950–1958).

Díaz, José (1894–1942): Spanish Communist leader from Seville, a baker from a baker's family, and a militant trade unionist. Originally an anarchist, Díaz joined the PCE in 1926 and, by 1927, had become head of the party organization in Andalusia. In 1932, after intense internal struggle, the Comintern appointed him secretary-general of the PCE, a post he held until his death in 1942. After heading the PCE during the Popular Front and the Civil War, he went to the USSR before the fall of the Spanish Republic; there, he served as member of the ECCI (1935–1942) and worked in the Comintern's secretariat. Mortally ill, he committed suicide in a Tbilisi clinic.

Dimitrov, Stanke (pseudonym: Marek, 1889–1944): Bulgarian Communist leader; he obtained a law degree from the University of Sofia (1919). Dimitrov was instructor to the military commission of the KKP CC (1921) and its organizational secretary (1923–1925). In the USSR (from 1925) he worked in the apparatus of the ECCI (from

1925), notably its Balkan secretariat (1932–1935) and taught at the KUNMZ and the Leninist School. Back in Bulgaria from 1935 to 1937 he worked clandestinely as the BKP secretary. From 1937 to 1943 he was in Moscow working in the ECCI apparatus, the Foreign Bureau of the BKP, and Radio Hristo Botev. He died in a plane crash on the way to Bulgaria in September 1944.

Djilas, Milovan (1911–1995): Yugoslav Communist leader and dissident; member of the KPJ Politburo (from 1940 on); organizer of the Partisan uprising in Montenegro (1941); chief of agitprop of the KPJ CC; president of the Yugoslav Federal National Assembly (1953). After conflict with the party (1954), he was expelled from the SKJ and twice imprisoned. Djilas was the author of numerous theoretical, historical, and literary works, most notably *The New Class* (1957).

Fischer, Ernst (Wieden, 1899–1972): Austrian Communist leader; prominent Social Democratic journalist. He fled to Czechoslovakia after the Austrian civil war (February 1934) and joined the KPÖ. In Moscow from 1934 to 1945, he worked in the Comintern apparatus, specializing in press and propaganda. He edited the Comintern's review *Kommunis-ticheskii Internatsional* (Communist International) and directed the wartime radio broadcasts to Austria. After going back to Austria in April 1945, he was minister of education and religious affairs in the coalition government (1945). Member of the KPÖ Politburo (1945–1969) and deputy in the parliament, he was expelled from the party in 1969 after he strongly criticized the Soviet intervention in Czechoslovakia (1968).

Florin, Wilhelm (1894–1944): German Communist leader; metalworker active in the Social Democratic youth movement who joined the KPD in 1920. Member of the KPD CC (from 1924 on) and Reichstag deputy; secretary of the KPD of the Ruhr (1925) and Berlin-Brandenburg (1932) regional committees. He emigrated to the USSR after Hitler's coming to power. Candidate-member (1931–1933) and full member (1933–1943) of the ECCI presidium; KPD representative on the Free Germany Committee. He died in Moscow in 1944.

Fürnberg, Friedl (1902–1978): Austrian Communist leader; head of the KPÖ youth organization; member of the KPÖ CC (1924–1978) and the Politburo (1933–1978); secretary of the KPÖ Vienna organization (1933–1934) during the civil war in Austria; secretary-general of the KPÖ (1945–1965); first secretary KPÖ CC (1965–1970); member of the executive committee of KIM; representative of the KPÖ in the ECCI (1937–1943). He was sent to Yugoslavia in 1944 to organize a battalion of Austrian partisans within the Yugoslav Partisan army.

Geminder, Bedřich (Friedrich, 1901–1952): Czechoslovak Communist leader, from a Moravian Jewish family. He studied at the University of Berlin and joined the KSČin 1921. In the USSR (1924–1926), he worked in the Comintern's secret apparatus and afterward took secret assignments in Czechoslovakia and elsewhere. Member of the KIM Executive Committee (from 1928 on) and of the Comintern's central apparatus (after 1938), Geminder directed the press and information service. Having gone back to Czechoslovakia after 1945, he was one of the organizers of the Communist coup in 1948. Arrested in September 1951 in the Slánský case, he was tried, sentenced to death, and executed.

Gerő, Ernő (pseudonym: Pedro, real name: Singer, 1898–1980): Hungarian Communist leader. He joined the Hungarian CP in 1919 and participated in the Hungarian Council Republic. After the fall of the Republic he emigrated, but he returned to Hungary in 1922 to conduct underground activity. Arrested and then released in 1924, he maintained his base in Moscow until 1944, although he was assigned to various duties in Western Europe: instructor in the PCF; Comintern/NKVD emissary to Spain engaged in the suppression of the Partido Obrero de Unificacíon Marxista (POUM) in Catalonia. He also served as Manuilsky's secretary. With Rákosi, Mihály Farkas, and József Révai, Gerő was a member of the Hungarian Stalinist inner leadership; he was a member of the Hungarian CP/Workers' Party Politburo (1945–1956); deputy secretary-general (1948–1951); CC secretary (1951–1953); first secretary of the CC (1956); minister of transport (1945–1949); minister of finances (1949); minister of the interior (1953–1954); deputy chairman of the Council of Ministers (1953–1956). Overthrown in the Hungarian uprising of 1956, he lived in the Soviet Union from 1956 to 1960. After going back to Hungary, he was expelled from the party (with Rákosi) in 1962.

Gottwald, Klement (1896–1953): Czechoslovak Communist leader, from a Moravian peasant family. Employed as a woodworker in Vienna, he joined the Social Democratic youth organization in 1912. Having deserted from the Austro-Hungarian army on the Dolomite front in summer 1918, he returned home, served in the Czechoslovak army, and joined the KSČ in 1921. An official of the KSČ in Slovakia (1921–1926), Gottwald was elected to the KSČ CC in 1925, directed the KSČ CC agitprop section (1926–1929), and became the KSČ secretary-general (1929–1945) and president (1945–1953); member of the ECCI (from 1928 on) and the ECCI presidium (from 1929 on); deputy in the Czechoslovak parliament (from 1929 on). In Moscow from November 1938 to the end of the war, he returned to Prague in 1945 as deputy prime minister of the new coalition government; prime minister (1946–1948) and president of Czechoslovakia (1948–1953). The preeminent Czechoslovak Stalinist, he was buried at the Vítkov national monument in Prague, his embalmed body having been cremated in 1962 as part of the de-Stalinization drive.

Heckert, Fritz (1884–1936): German Communist leader; head of the workers' and soldiers' council in Chemnitz (1918); founding member of the KPD; member of the KPD CC (1918–1936); member of the ECCI presidium (1921–1928); candidate-member (1928–1936); member of the EC of the Profintern (1921–1936). During the revolutionary action of October 1923 in Germany he was named minister of finance in the government of Saxony. Deputy in the Reichstag (1924), he emigrated to the USSR after Hitler came to power and died in Moscow in 1936.

Ibárruri, Dolores ("La Pasionaria," 1895–1989): Spanish Communist leader, from a Basque miner's family. Founding member of the PCE, Ibárruri became a member of the PCE CC in 1930 and of the Politburo/ EC in 1932 and served as its secretary (1932–1942). Candidate-member of the ECCI (1935–1943), deputy in the Cortes (1936), and ECCI vice president (1937), she went to the USSR after the fall of the Spanish Republic. Member of the ECCI presidium (1942–1943); secretary-general of the PCE (1942–1960) and its president (after 1960); vice president of the World Federation of Democratic Women (from 1945 on). Her son Rubén (1920–1942), who perished in the battle of Stalingrad, was awarded the Order of Hero of the Soviet Union. Ibárruri returned to Spain in June 1977 after the end of the Franco dictatorship to triumphant chants of "¡Sí, sí, sí, Dolores está aquí!" (Yes, yes, yes, Dolores is here!). She was briefly a member of the Cortes.

Kaganovich, Lazar Moiseevich (1893–1991): Senior Stalinist figure, from a poor Jewish family in a village near Kiev; member of the Bolshevik party after 1911; member of the RSDRP(b) committees in Kiev (1914–1916), Yekaterinoslav (1916), Yazovka (1917), and Saratov (1917). He headed the Bolshevik uprising in Homel; in the Civil War he served as a Red Army political commissar and was engaged in the provinces, notably Turkestan (1920–1922). Part of the CC apparatus, from 1922 on, he was responsible for cadre appointments. Member of the RKP(b) CC (1924–1957); candidate-member (1927–1930) and full member (1930–1957) of the VKP(b)/KPSS Politburo/presidium; secretary-general of the CP of Ukraine (1925–1928); secretary of the VKP(b) CC (1928–1939). During the 1930s Kaganovich was one of Stalin's closest associates, whose services were required for particularly difficult assignments, as in the collectivization of Ukraine and the various urban reconstruction projects in Moscow. He was the first secretary of the Moscow VKP(b) committee (1930–1935); chairman of the Commission for Party Control (1934–1935); people's commissar for railroads (1935–1937, 1938–1942), heavy industry (1937–1939), the fuel industry (1939), and the oil industry (1939–1940); deputy chairman of the Council of People's Commissars (from 1938 on). During the war he was a member of the State Council for Defense and member of the Military Soviet of the Northern Caucasus and Transcaucasian Fronts. His power on the wane after the war, he was briefly appointed the first secretary of the CP of Ukraine (1947). He served as the deputy chairman (from 1947 on) and first deputy chairman of the council of ministers of

USSR. In 1957, he joined the "antiparty group" against N. S. Khrushchev. Having been expelled from all his offices, he was sent to the Perm district to direct a potash works.

Kalinin, Mikhail Ivanovich (1875–1946): Soviet Communist leader, from a Russian peasant family in the Tver district. A member of the RSDRP from its inception, he worked as a Bolshevik agitator in St. Petersburg, Tiflis (Tbilisi), Reval (Tallin), and Moscow. Kalinin was a member of the Petrograd Bolshevik committee (1917), member of the RKP(b) CC (from 1919 on), candidate-member of the RKP(b) Politburo (1919–1926), and full member of the VKP(b) Politburo (1926–1946). Kalinin's position as chairman of the Central Executive Committee of the USSR (1922–1938) and of the presidium of the Supreme Soviet of the USSR (1938–1946) made him the nominal head of state of the USSR.

Kang Sheng (real name: Zhang Shaoqing, 1889–1975): Chinese Communist leader; member of the CPC Politburo (after 1931). He specialized in the Comintern apparatus of the USSR in security affairs (1933–1937); directed Mao Zedong's purges in Yan'an ("Rectification Campaign," 1942); served as head of the regional government of Shandong Province (1949–1954); and in Beijing after 1955 controlled the Chinese secret services and the CPC internal organizational structure. Prominent in relations with the foreign Communist parties; nominated member of the CPC CC's Cultural Revolution Group (1966); elected member of the standing committee of the CPC Politburo at the Ninth Congress of the CPC (1969); posthumously denounced as "one of those criminals most responsible for setting the Chinese revolution back fifteen years" (Hu Yaobang, 1980). He was expelled from the CPC in 1980.

Kardelj, Edvard (pseudonyms: Birk, Bevc, Sperans, 1910–1979): Yugoslav Communist leader and theoretician; member of the regional committee of the KPJ for Slovenia (from 1932 on); instructor at the KUNMZ (1934–1937). Briefly on the staff of the KPJ Politburo in Paris (1937), he participated in the founding of the CP of Slovenia (within the KPJ, 1937); served as member of the KPJ CC (from 1938 on) and the Politburo (from 1940 on); participated in the July 1941 Partisan uprising in Slovenia; and edited the KPJ organ *Borba* (Struggle) in the Užice (Serbia) liberated area (fall 1941). After going back to Slovenia, he restricted the organizational growth of the non-Communist parties in the Liberation Front (March 1943). Vice president of the AVNOJ Executive Committee (Bihać, 1942); vice president of the NKOJ (1943); vice president of the government of Yugoslavia (1945); minister of foreign affairs (1948–1953); chief theoretician of Yugoslav self-management; and principal creator of Yugoslavia's constitutional system. His theoretical activities, particularly in the 1970s, were meant to foreclose the possibility of systemic evolution in the direction of liberalism and political pluralism.

Khrushchev, Nikita Sergeevich (1894–1971): Soviet Communist leader, from a peasant family in Kursk Province. His father moved the family to the Donbas (Ukraine) in 1908, thereafter working as a miner in the coal pits. Khrushchev, who worked first as a machinist, then as a miner, joined the RKP(b) in 1918. A veteran of the Red Army and political commissar at Tsaritsyn (Volgograd) and Kuban, he climbed in the party hierarchy in the Donbas and Ukraine, moving to Moscow in 1929 as a student at the Industrial Academy. A solid supporter of Stalin, Khrushchev was promoted by Kaganovich in the Moscow hierarchy. Member of the VKP(b) CC (starting in 1934); first secretary of the Moscow city committee (1934); first secretary of the Moscow oblast committee (1935–1938, 1949–1953); member of the VKP(b) Politburo (from 1938 on); first secretary of the Ukrainian CP CC (1938–1949); first secretary of the Kiev oblast committee (from 1938 on). During the war Khrushchev was commissar of the Kiev special military district, member of Stalingrad military council, and, after the recapture of Kiev, chairman of Council of People's Commissars of Ukraine. After the war, until his removal to Moscow in 1949, he worked tirelessly to destroy the Ukrainian armed resistance. After Stalin's death Khrushchev took over the secretariat of the KPSS CC, organized the downfall of Beria, and assumed the post of the first secretary of the KPSS CC (September 1953) and chairman of the council of ministers (1958–1964). During the period of his leadership, he restored relations with Yugoslavia (1955), established the Warsaw Pact (1955), commenced the policy of de-Stalinization (in his secret speech on the "cult of personality and its consequences" at the Twentieth Congress of the KPSS in February 1956), initiated Soviet intervention in Hungary (1956), beat back the Stalinist opposition—the "antiparty" group (1957)—initiated internal reforms, and, despite occasional crises (Berlin, Cuba), pursued a policy of peaceful coexistence with the West, thereby precipitating the split with China. He was dismissed in 1964, accused of "subjectivism" and "voluntarism."

Knorin, Wilhelm (1890–1938/9?): Soviet Communist leader, from a Latvian peasant family. He joined the Bolsheviks before the First World War and directed their underground work in Riga. Among the recruits in Belorussia in February 1917, he organized the Minsk soviet of workers' deputies; he headed the Minsk RKP(b) committee after the October Revolution; member of the Belorussian CP CC (1918–1922) and the central RKP(b) apparatus (1922–1927), and secretary of the Belorussian CP (1927–1929). After the fall of Bukharin, Knorin was delegate to the Comintern; member of the ICC (from 1928 on); head of the Central European secretariat (1929–1936); candidate-member of the ECCI presidium (1931–1935); member of the VKP(b) CC (from 1927 on); director of the Institute of Red Professors; in charge of Polish CP affairs (after 1929); member of the Polish CP CC (from 1930 on). Associated with the policies of the Third Period, he was removed from the ECCI in 1935. Arrested in 1937, he died in Stalin's Gulag.

Kohn, Felix (1864–1941): Soviet Communist leader, from a Polish Jewish family. He worked in the Polish and Swiss socialist movements and went to Petrograd after the February Revolution in 1917. Member of the Ukrainian CP CC (1919–1920); member of the ECCI secretariat (1921–1922) and the ICC (1924–1935); editor of *Krasnaia zvezda* (Red Star), *Rabochaia gazeta* (Workers' Newspaper), and *Nasha strana* (Our Country); chairman of the USSR broadcasting committee (1931–1933).

Kolarov, Vasil (pseudonym: Venelin, 1877–1950): Bulgarian Communist leader from a working-class family. He studied law in Geneva and joined the Bulgarian Social Democrats in 1897, falling in with the tesniaks from the outset. Member of the BRSDP(t.s.) CC (from 1905 on); deputy in the national assembly (from 1912 on); member (1919–1950) and secretary (1919–1923) of the BKP CC; member of the ECCI (1921–1943) and the ECCI presidium (1922–1943). In emigration after the failure of the September 1923 uprising, he worked in the Comintern leadership, presided over the Executive Committee of the Krestintern (1928–1939), and directed the Comintern's Balkan secretariat (1928–1929). He returned to Bulgaria in 1945, served on the Bulgarian delegation to the Paris peace conference (1946), presided over the Bulgarian national assembly (1946), and served first as first deputy prime minister and foreign minister in Dimitrov's cabinet (1947–1949) and then as prime minister of Bulgaria (1949–1950).

Koplenig, Johann (1891–1968): Austrian Communist leader. An Austro-Hungarian soldier captured on the Russian front in 1916, he joined the pro-Bolshevik federation of foreign Communist groups at Nizhny Novgorod (1917). After going back to Austria after 1920, he served as secretary of the KPÖ organization in Styria (1922), member of the KPÖ CC (from 1922 on), KPÖ secretary (from 1924 on), and member of the ECCI (1928–1943) and its presidium (1935–1943). In the USSR from 1934 to 1945, he worked in the Comintern apparatus. After returning to Austria in 1945, he served as deputy chancellor and secretary of state without portfolio in the coalition government (1945), deputy in the Austrian parliament (1946–1959), president of the KPÖ (1945–1965), and honorary president (1965–1968).

Kostov, Traicho (pseudonym: Spiridonov, 1897–1949): Bulgarian Communist leader from a working-class family. Kostov studied law at Sofia and joined the BKP in 1919. Arrested after the failed September 1923 uprising, he was imprisoned until 1929, when he went to Moscow, worked in the ECCI apparatus, and attended the Leninist School. After returning to Bulgaria in 1931, he was a member of the BKP CC (from 1931 on). Back again in Moscow (1934–1935), he worked for the Bulgarian delegation at the Comintern's Balkan secretariat. In Bulgaria after that, he headed up the BKP's domestic activities and served as member of the BKP Politburo (from 1937 on) and secretary of the BBKP CC (from 1940 on). Arrested in 1942, he was imprisoned until the Muraviev amnesty in early September 1944. Then, after serving as secretary-general of the BKP (1944–1945) and deputy prime minister (1946–1949), he was arrested in 1949 and charged with being a "left sectarian" Trotskyite, Titoist, confidant of the Bulgarian police, and British agent. After being tried at a show trial in December 1949, he was sentenced to death and executed.

Kuibyshev, Valerian Vladimirovich (1888–1935): Soviet Communist leader from Omsk, Siberia, active in the Bolshevik organizations of St. Petersburg (from 1905 on) and Samara (1915–1920). In Moscow (from 1920 on), Kuibyshev worked on electrification projects. Chairman of the state planning commission (Gosplan); deputy chairman of the Council of People's Commissars (1930–1934); chairman of the Commission of Soviet Control; first deputy chairman of the Council of People's Commissars (1934–1935); and member of the VKP(b) Politburo (1927–1934).

Kun, Béla (1886–1939): Hungarian Communist leader, from the family of a Jewish civil servant in Transylvania. A Social Democrat from 1902 on, he took part in the organization of construction workers' and miners' unions in Transylvania and studied law at the universities of Kolozsvár (Cluj) and Budapest. A leading organizer of strike actions in Transylvania in 1905, Kun was imprisoned for his role in the movement. Recruited into the Austro-Hungarian army during the First World War, he was captured in 1916 on the Russian front and sent to a POW camp in Tomsk, where he established contacts with the Bolsheviks. After the February Revolution he worked in the Tomsk provincial committee of the RSDRP(b). After the October Revolution he moved to Petrograd, organized the Hungarian Communist group, worked on the mobilization of Hungarian POWs within the Red Army, and participated in the early battles of the Civil War. On his return to Hungary in November 1918, he organized the Hungarian CP. After having been briefly arrested in 1919, he headed the Hungarian Council Republic after 21 March 1919, his official title being commissar for foreign affairs. Following the fall of the republic in the summer of 1919, he fled to Austria and, after time in internment, made his way to Soviet Russia. Afterward, during the conflict with the Wrangel forces, he was a member of the military-revolutionary soviet of the southern front. As a member of the ECCI presidium (1921–1922), he was sent to Germany to direct the abortive March Action (1921). Thereafter in Yekaterinburg (1921–1923) as a member of the Urals RKP(b) bureau, he returned to the Comintern in 1924, heading its agitprop; candidate-member of the ECCI (from 1924 on) and the ECCI presidium (from 1926 on), he headed the Balkan secretariat and became a full member of the ECCI presidium in 1931. His influence grew during the Third Period but declined thereafter. Arrested in 1937, he was liquidated in the Stalinist purges.

Kuusinen, Otto Wilhelm (1881–1964): Finnish Communist active in Soviet and Comintern affairs. The son of a tailor, he studied history and philology at Helsingfors (Helsinki), and joined the Finnish Social Democrats in 1904. Active in the party's left wing, he commanded a Red Guard unit in the Revolution of 1905, edited two party newspapers, and served in the Finnish parliament (1908–1917) and on the executive committee of the party (1911–1917). In 1918, Kuusinen was among the founders of the SKP and took part in the Finnish Soviet government, where he was responsible for education. After the collapse of the Finnish Soviet Republic he moved to Soviet Russia, where he worked in the Comintern. He was Comintern secretary (1921), member of the ECCI and its presidium (1922–1943), and head of many ECCI commissions. During the Soviet-Finnish war (1939–1940) he was named the head of the puppet Finnish government at Terijoki; he was also chairman of the Karelo-Finnish SSR (1940–1956) and member of the VKP(b)/KPSS CC (from 1941 on) and its Politburo/presidium (1952–1953, 1957–1964).

Lin Biao (pseudonym: Li Tin, 1907–1971): Chinese Communist leader and military strategist; participant in the failed Nanchang uprising (August 1927), after which he retreated with Zhu De's forces to join Mao Zedong's base area in Jinggang Mountains (1928). Member of the Jianxi Soviet central executive committee in 1931, Lin commanded the First Chinese Red Army, which seized Zunyi during the early stages of the Long March. In the Yan'an years he became president of the Red Academy (1936) and commanded the 115th division of the Eighth Route Army (1937). Wounded and stricken with tuberculosis, he went to the USSR, where, from 1938 to 1942, he represented the CPC in the ECCI. Upon returning to China, he headed the CPC Central School and became a CC member in 1945. In the civil war of 1945–1949, Lin commanded the People's Liberation Army (PLA) in Manchuria, winning the northeast (by 1948), Tianjin and Beijing (January 1949), and, at the head of the Fourth Army, Changsha and Canton (August–October 1949). After the Communist victory he headed the CPC's Southern Bureau and commanded the southern China military region; member of the CPC Politburo and third-ranked marshal of the PLA (1955), he succeeded Peng Dehuai as the minister of defense after the Lushan plenum (1959). During the Cultural Revolution he became Mao's deputy and wrote the strategic Maoist document "Long Live the Victory of the People's War!" (1965), in which he argued that "contemporary world revolution also presents a picture of the encirclement of cities [North

America and Western Europe] by the rural areas [Asia, Africa, Latin America]." Proclaimed "Chairman Mao's closest comrade-in-arms and successor" at the Ninth Congress of the CPC (1969), he was purged and died under mysterious circumstances in 1971.

Malenkov, Georgy Maksimilianovich (1902–1988): Soviet Communist leader and one of Stalin's closest associates after the death of Zhdanov (1948). Roy Medvedev has remarked that it is "difficult to write even a minimal sketch of Malenkov, for he is a man without a biography. His was a life of special departments and privy councils" (*All Stalin's Men,* 1983). Malenkov worked on the VKP(b) Moscow committee (1930–1934) and became director of the Department of Leading Party Organs at the VKP(b) CC—that is, the personnel section (1934–1939). After serving as member of the VKP(b) CC (1939–1957), the CC secretariat (from 1939 on), candidate-member (from 1941 on) and full member (from 1946 on) of the Politburo, and member of the State Committee for Defense (1941–1945), Malenkov fell briefly into disfavor (1949) and was exiled to Tashkent. He rebounded and conducted a purge of A. A. Zhdanov's adherents in the Leningrad VKP(b) organization. After Stalin's death he was briefly the highest ranking leader as chairman of the Council of Ministers. After being dismissed from that position in 1955, he was purged with the "antiparty" group in 1957, directed a hydroelectric power station in Kazakhstan (1957–1961), and was expelled from the KPSS in 1961.

Manuilsky, Dmitry Zakharovich (1883–1959): Son of a priest from rural Volhynia (western Ukraine), he became a Bolshevik as a student at the University of St. Petersburg. During the revolution of 1905 and in its aftermath he was a party operative in Petersburg, Dvinsk, and Kronstadt. Arrested in 1906, he escaped and joined the Kiev Bolshevik organization and, after its collapse, fled abroad in 1907. He joined the Bolshevik Otzovist faction, which favored the recall of Bolshevik deputies from the Duma, and wrote for its émigré organ *Vpered* (Forward). A socialist-internationalist during the Great War, he collaborated with Trotsky on *Nashe slovo* (Our Word), which Lenin decried as centrist. After returning to Russia in 1917, Manuilsky belonged to Trotsky's *mezhraiontsii* (In-betweeners), who stood halfway between the Mensheviks and Bolsheviks but were admitted into the Bolshevik party in August 1917. Sent by the Soviet government on a first foreign mission in 1919, he served in the Bolshevik government of Ukraine (1920) and was a secretary of the Ukrainian CP (1921). Once back in Moscow in 1922, he represented the Comintern at the congresses of foreign CPs. Member of the VKP(b) CC (1923–1952); member of the ECCI and its presidium (1924–1943); chief Soviet operative in the Comintern from 1929 to 1935 and its informal head. After the dissolution of the Comintern he worked in the apparatus of the VKP(b) CC. Reassigned to Ukraine after the war, he served as deputy prime minister of the Ukrainian SSR and

Ukraine's minister of foreign affairs (1944–1953), and he represented Ukraine at the founding of the United Nations in San Francisco (1946) and at several meetings of the General Assembly.

Marty, André (1886–1956), French Communist leader, son of an 1871 Communard. He was a naval machinist and a participant in a naval squadron rebellion on the Black Sea (November 1918). Sentenced to a term of twenty years by the French war council, he was released in 1923, joined the PCF, and was elected to the parliament in 1924. Member of the PCF CC (1925–1952) and its Politburo (1931–1952); PCF representative to the Comintern (1932–1943); member of the ECCI (1932–1943) and its presidium (1935–1943); commander-in-chief of the International Brigades in Spain; member of parliament (1924–1928, 1929–1955). Marty spent the war in Moscow, going to Algiers in 1943 to join the French provisional assembly as a PCF representative. Accused of provoking factional conflicts in the PCF on behalf of the police, Marty was removed from the PCF leadership in 1952 and expelled from the party in 1953.

Mao Zedong (1893–1976): Chinese Communist leader and theoretician, from a peasant family in Hunan. He organized a Marxist group in Changsha (Hunan, 1920) and was among the twelve founders of the CPC (Shanghai, 1921). Member of the CPC CC (1923–1925); representative of the CPC at the first Guomindang congress (1924). He was elected a candidate-member of the Guomindang Central Executive Committee. As secretary of the CPC CC peasant movement committee, Mao started arguing for the leading role of peasantry in the Chinese revolution (*Report on the Peasant Movement in Hunan,* 1927) and in favor of the use of violence. He became a candidate-member of the CPC CC after the fall of Chen Duxiu (1927) and directed the Autumn Harvest Uprising in Hunan and Jiangxi (1927). After its defeat, he established a revolutionary base at Jinggangshan in Jiangxi. Increasing Communist regional power from there, Mao presided over the Jiangxi Soviet Republic (1931). After the Chiang Kai-shek encirclement campaigns, the Jiangxi Soviet was abandoned, and Mao headed the Long March of Communist troops that ultimately established a new base area at Yan'an (Shaanxi, 1936). On the way, at Zunyi (Guizhou, January 1935), Mao became the chairman of the CPC CC military commission and member of the standing committee of the CPC Politburo, thereby obtaining full control of the CPC. After being elected member of the ECCI (1935), he argued for a "new democracy"—a bloc of workers, peasants, intelligentsia, and sections of the petty bourgeoisie (1940). In 1945, on the eve of the final conflict with the Guomindang, he was elected the chairman of the CPC. Presiding over the establishment of the People's Republic (1949) and directing it in various stages, Mao was frequently inspired by his radical vision—notably, the Great Leap Forward (1958) and the Cultural Revolution (1966). Aloof from Moscow since the mid-1950s, he challenged the "Soviet revisionists" in the great split (1959).

Mikoyan, Anastas Ivanovich (1895–1978): Soviet Communist leader from an Armenian working-class family in Tbilisi, Georgia; member of the RSDRP(b) from 1915 and of its Baku committee (1917). After the fall of the Baku Commune (1918), Mikoyan survived the execution of the Baku commissars. He headed the Bolshevik underground organization until the taking of the city by the Soviets. Afterward he was secretary of the RKP(b) provincial committee in Nizhny Novgorod (1920–1922) and of the Northern Caucasus territorial committee (1922–1926), member of the RKP(b) CC (from 1922 on), and candidate-member (from 1926 on) and full member (1935–1966) of the VKP(b) Politburo. A person who had Stalin's and Khrushchev's trust, Mikoyan was the senior Soviet authority on trade matters. He was people's commissar for internal and foreign trade (1926–1930), supply (1930–1934), food production (1934–1938), and foreign trade (1939–1940, 1946–1949); deputy chairman of the Council of People's Commissars (1937–1946); member of the State Committee for Defense (1942–1945); deputy chairman (1946–1955) and first deputy chairman of the Council of Ministers; chairman of the Supreme Soviet of the USSR (nominal head of state, 1964–1965) and then a member of the Supreme Soviet (1965–1974).

Molotov, Viacheslav Mikhailovich (real name: Skriabin, 1890–1986): Soviet Communist leader, from a lower-middle-class family near Nolinsk, Viatsk Province. Molotov joined the Bolsheviks in 1906 as a student at Kazan. Exiled to Siberia in 1915, he escaped and made his way to Petrograd, where he joined the Bolshevik underground bureau, edited *Pravda* (after February 1917), and served as member of the military-revolutionary committee in the October Revolution. After the Bolshevik seizure of power, Molotov worked in Nizhny Novgorod, the Donbas, and Ukraine. Member and secretary (1921) of the RKP(b) CC; candidate-member of the RKP(b) Politburo (1921–1926); member of the VKP(b)/KPSS Politburo and presidium (1926–1957); chairman of the Council of People's Commissars (1930–1941). Molotov stood briefly at the helm of the Comintern (1929) and served as the Soviet people's commissar and minister for foreign affairs (1939–1949, 1953–1956) during the dramatic wartime period. His name is associated with the nonaggression pact with Germany (Molotov-Ribbentrop pact) and the Finnish war (Molotov cocktails). After being expelled from the KPSS leadership with the "antiparty" group (1957), he served as Soviet ambassador to Mongolia (1957–1960). After being expelled from the KPSS in 1962, he was reinstated in 1984.

Moskvin, Mikhail Abramovich (real name: Trilisser, 1883–1940): Soviet Communist active in the secret police and the Comintern. Born into a

Jewish family in Astrakhan, he joined the Bolsheviks and was imprisoned and exiled to Siberia. After the Revolution he worked under Piatnitsky in the OMS, reorganized the Turkish CP, and proposed a plan for the Comintern's Far Eastern Bureau. Chief of the GPU foreign department in the 1920s; assistant to the OGPU chief V. R. Menzhinsky (1928). Suspected of sympathy for the "Rights," he was temporarily removed from the OGPU, only to resume his activities. Head of the OMS in 1935; member of the presidium of the ECCI; alternate member of the Comintern secretariat (1935–1938). He was liquidated in the Stalinist purges.

Münzenberg, Willi (1889–1940): German Communist leader; secretary of the KIM (1919–1921); member of the ECCI (from 1921 on). In charge of propaganda for Communist front organizations, he directed the campaign on behalf of the starving in Russia and subsequently directed work among the antifascist intellectuals. Deputy to the Reichstag (1924) and member of the KPS CC (1927–1938), he directed the campaign for the defense of Dimitrov and in support of the Spanish Republic. After being expelled from the KPD in 1938, he was interred in France after the beginning of the war. He vanished near Montagne (France) in 1940, probably liquidated by the NKVD.

Neumann, Heinz (1902–1937?): German Communist leader from a bourgeois family; philology student at the University of Berlin; KPD representative to the Comintern (1925); member of the KPD secret apparatus (1923) and the KPD CC and Politburo (until 1932). Stalin sent him to China to organize the abortive Canton Commune (1927). Member of the Reichstag (1930); candidate-member of the ECCI presidium (1931–1932). He underwent self-criticism in 1932. After serving as delegate to Spain (1932–1933), he went to the USSR after 1935. He was liquidated in the Stalinist purges.

Ordzhonikidze, Grigory (Sergo) Konstantinovich (1886–1937): Soviet Communist leader, from the family of a petty nobleman in western Georgia. He joined the Bolsheviks in 1903 and was active in revolutionary work, mainly in Baku. A member of the RSDRP(b) CC (from 1912 on), he was arrested in St. Petersburg in 1912, imprisoned, and then exiled to Siberia, from where he returned to Petrograd in June 1917. After the October Revolution he served as a commissar in Ukraine, southern Russia, and the Northern Caucasus. A close associate of Stalin, Ordzhonikidze was a candidate-member (1926–1930) and full member (1930–1937) of the VKP(b) Politburo and served as deputy chairman of the Council of Ministers (from 1927 on), chairman of the Supreme Council on the National Economy (1930–1937), and people's commissar for heavy industry (1932–1937). He committed suicide in February 1937.

Pauker, Ana (1893–1960): Romanian Communist leader, from a rabbi's family in Moldavia. Wife of Marcel Pauker, a leading Romanian Communist, who was repressed in the Stalinist purges, Ana Pauker was a member of PCR CC (from 1922 on). After a second imprisonment she departed for Germany, Austria, and, in 1928, the USSR, where she entered the Leninist School and, together with her husband, worked in the Comintern apparatus and undertook various assignments abroad, notably France. Having returned to Romania, where she was in charge of PCR underground activities (1934), she was arrested in 1935 but was exchanged in 1940 for a Soviet-held Romanian. On the Comintern staff during the war, she directed the Romanian-language broadcasts and worked with the Romanian POWs. Pauker returned to Romania in 1944 and became a member of the PCR CC and Politburo, organizational secretary (1945–1948), agriculture secretary (1948–1952), and foreign minister (1947–1952). She was stripped of her functions in 1952, expelled from the party, and placed under house arrest.

Piatnitsky, Iosif (Osip) Aronovich (real name: Tarshis, pseudonyms: Piantnitsa, Freitag, 1882–1939): Soviet Communist leader, Bolshevik from 1903 on. He organized communications between Russia and the party apparatus abroad and carried out party work in Berlin, Odessa (1905), and Saratov Province (1912). Member of the Moscow Bolshevik committee in 1917 and secretary of the committee (1920); treasurer of the Comintern and head of the OMS (from 1921 on); member of the ECCI secretariat (from 1923 on); alternate member of the ECCI (1923–1935); member of the Profintern's Executive Committee (from 1930 on); member of the VKP(b) CC and CCC in the 1920s and early 1930s; director of the Administrative-Political Department of the VKP(b) CC (1935–1937). He was liquidated in the Stalinist purges.

Pieck, Wilhelm (1876–1960): German Communist leader with the longest career in the leadership; one of the two chairmen at the KPD founding congress; member of the KPD CC (1918–1960); member of the Prussian diet (1921–1928); member of the ECCI (1928–1931) and the ECCI presidium and secretariat (1931–1943); secretary-general of the KPD (1933–1946); secretary of the SED (1946–1960); president of the German Democratic Republic (1949–1960).

Pollitt, Harry (1890–1960): British Communist leader, from an English working-class family. A boilermaker by profession, he joined the Independent Labour Party in 1906. Founding member of the British CP and a militant trade unionist; member of the British CP and Politburo (from 1922 on); member of the ECCI and candidate-member (1924–1931) and full member (1931–1943) of the ECCI presidium; secretary-general of the British CP (1929–1939, 1941–1956). Demoted for his opposition to the Comintern's defeatist line after the beginning of the war in

Europe (September 1939), he was reinstated after the German attack on the USSR; president of the British CP (1956–1960).

Ponomarev, Boris Nikolaevich (1905–1995): Soviet Communist leader, from a family of a civil servant in the Moscow region. Active in the Komsomol (1920–1923), in party work in the Donbas and Turkmenia (1926–1928), and in the ECCI apparatus (1937–1943). Deputy director of the Marx-Engels-Lenin Institute (1943–1944); member of the VKP(b) apparatus (1944–1961); secretary of the KPSS CC (1961–1986); candidate-member (1961–1956) and full member (from 1956 on) of the KPSS CC; candidate-member of the KPSS Politburo (1972–1986); head of the KPSS Department for Relations with the Foreign Communist Parties (1955–1957), or International Department (1957–1986). He was a leading party historian and theoretician.

Radek, Karl Berngardovich (1885–1939): Middle-class Jewish Socialist of Polish culture from Galicia. Radek was active in the socialist movements of Poland, Germany, and Russia. A participant in the internationalist Socialist conferences at Zimmerwald (1915) and Kienthal (1916), he joined the Bolshevik party in 1917 and arrived in Petrograd after the October Revolution. Active in the Central European section of the Commissariat for Foreign Affairs, he was involved in the Comintern's operations in Germany. Radek was a member of the RKP(b) CC (1919–1924) and of the ECCI (1920–1924) and its presidium (1921–1924). Despite the fact that he had sided with the Left Opposition (1923–1924), he was appointed head of the Comintern's Sun Yat-sen University (1926–1927). Expelled from the RKP(b) in 1927, he was sent into exile. After recanting in 1929, he was readmitted but thenceforth concerned himself mainly with commentaries on international affairs. Expelled for a second time in 1936, he was tried in January 1937, together with Y. L. Piatakov and others, in the case of the "Parallel Center" and sentenced to ten years of penal servitude. He died in prison.

Rákosi, Mátyás (1892–1971): Hungarian Communist leader, from a Jewish trader's family. He joined the Hungarian Social Democrats in 1910 as a radical student. Afterward he studied in Hamburg and London, but he was drafted into the Austro-Hungarian army in 1914 and then captured on the Russian front in 1915. Won over as a POW by the Bolsheviks, he returned to Hungary in 1918 and joined the Hungarian CP. During the Hungarian Council Republic (1919) he served in various administrative capacities—deputy commissar for commerce, commissar for production, commander-in-chief of the Red Guards. Afterward, in Austria and Soviet Russia, he served in the Comintern apparatus and as the member of the ECCI secretariat (1921–1923) in charge of the Italian commission. As a member of the Hungarian CP CC, he was sent on an underground mission to Hungary in December 1924. Arrested in

1925, he was imprisoned by the Hungarian authorities and held until the exchange of prisoners with the USSR in October 1940. In Moscow until 1945, he resumed work in the ECCI and Hungarian CP. On his return to Hungary after the war, Rákosi was the secretary-general and first secretary of the Hungarian CP or Workers' Party (1945–1956), as well as deputy prime minister (1945–1952) and prime minister of Hungary (1952–1953). As Hungary's preeminent Stalinist, he was a target of popular hostility in 1956. Dismissed in July 1956, he emigrated to the USSR, where he died. He was expelled from the Hungarian Workers' Party in 1962.

Shvernik, Nikolai Mikhailovich (1888–1970): Soviet Communist leader, from a working class family in St. Petersburg; member of the party committees in Petersburg (1905, 1915–1917), Nikolaev (1910–1911), Tula (1911), and Samara (1917); chairman of the Samara city soviet (1917). After a stint in the Red Army during the Civil War, member of the presidium of the CCC and people's commissar for worker-peasant inspection of the RSFSR (1923–1925); member of the VKP(b) CC (from 1925 on); secretary of the Leningrad regional committee (1925); secretary of the VKP(b) CC (1926); secretary of the Ural regional committee (1927–1928); first secretary (1930–1944) and chairman (1953–1956) of the All-Union Central Council of Trade Unions (VTsSPS); chairman of the Commission for Party Control (1956–1962); candidate-member of the VKP(b)/KPSS Politburo and presidium (1939–1952, 1953–1957); member of the KPSS presidium (1952–1953, 1957–1966); chairman of the Council of Nationalities of the Supreme Soviet of the USSR (1938–1946); chairman of the Supreme Soviet of the USSR (1946–1953)—that is, nominal head of state.

Šmeral, Bohumír (1880–1941): Czechoslovak Communist leader, journalist, and ideologue, from a Prague teacher's family. Šmeral studied law at Charles University in Prague, joined the Czech Social Democrats in 1897, and edited the party's newspaper *Práva lidu* (People's Rights); president of the Czechoslovak Social Democratic Party CC (1916–1917) he had moved leftward by the end of the First World War and became president of the newly founded KSČ in 1921. A member of the KSČ CC (1921–1929, 1936–1938) and its Politburo (1924–1929), he was also a member of the ECCI and its presidium (1922–1935). Šmeral was demoted in 1928 and was accused of "Social Democratic tendencies" during the Third Period. He served as deputy in the Czechoslovak parliament (1920–1921) and also as senator (1935–1938). He moved to Moscow after the Munich treaty.

Stalin, Joseph (Iosif) Vissarionovich (real name: Dzhugashvili, 1879–1953): Supreme leader of the Communist movement from 1922 on; secretary-general of the Russian/Soviet CP (1922–1952); chairman of the Council of People's Commissars (ministers, 1941–1953); people's commissar for defense (1941–1947); chairman of the State Committee for Defense and the supreme commander of the armed forces of the USSR (1941–1945); member of the ECCI presidium (1924–1943).

Thälmann, Ernst (1886–1944): German Communist in the leadership of the KPD after 1920, part of the party's left wing; member of the KPD CC (from 1923 on); candidate-member of the ECCI (1924–1925) and vice chairman of the Comintern (1924–1925); chairman of the KPD (from 1925 on); deputy in the Reichstag (from 1924 on); member of the presidium (from 1925 on) and secretariat (from 1931 on) of the ECCI. Thälmann followed sectarian Stalinist politics in Germany that contributed to the rise of Nazism. After Hitler came to power, he was arrested (March 1933) and held in various prisons. Executed by the Nazis in the Buchenwald concentration camp in August 1944.

Thorez, Maurice (1900–1964): French Communist leader. A miner and a socialist militant, he joined the PCF and became a professional functionary in 1923. He joined the Politburo in 1925 and was a member of the ECCI beginning with the Sixth Congress of the Comintern (1928) and a deputy in the French parliament from 1939 on. Arrested in 1929, he became secretary of the PCF CC in 1930 and a member of the ECCI presidium in April 1931. After the debacle of the Third Period and the rise of Hitler, Thorez became the main spokesman for a "broad united front" and ultimately for the Popular Front, which would include the "middle classes." At the Seventh Congress of the Comintern (1935) he headed the French delegation and sat on Stalin's right at the opening session. At the Eight Congress of the PCF, in January 1936, he was elected the party's general secretary, a post that he held until 1964. After the beginning of the war in Europe, Thorez deserted from the French army and made his way to Moscow. He was sentenced in absentia to five years in prison and deprived of his citizenship. Amnestied in October 1944, he returned to France and became a minister in de Gaulle's cabinet; he continued to serve in subsequent cabinets until May 1947. A stalwart follower of the Moscow line, he defended Soviet positions to the end, being a "particularly energetic" participant, according to the Chinese party organ *Renmin ribao* (People's Daily, 27 February 1963), in the "anti-Chinese chorus."

Tito (real name: Josip Broz, pseudonym: Walter, 1892–1980): Yugoslav Communist leader; secretary-general (later president) of the KPJ/SKJ (1939–1980); president (1953–1980) and marshal of Yugoslavia. Trained as a metalworker, Tito served in the Austro-Hungarian army in the First World War. Having been captured by the Russians, he became acquainted as a POW with Bolshevik literature and, after the October Revolution, served in a Red Guard unit in Omsk, Siberia. After going back to Yugoslavia in 1920, he joined the KPJ and became the political secretary of its Zagreb organization (1928). Arrested in 1928 and charged with preparing terrorist attacks, he was sentenced to a term of five years, which he served during King Aleksandar's dictatorship (1929–1934). After his release he was summoned by the émigré KPJ leadership to Vienna and coopted into the KPJ Politburo. He represented the KPJ in the Comintern (1935–1936) and was a KPJ delegate at the Seventh World Congress of the Comintern. Increasingly involved in underground organizational work in Yugoslavia, he was the only senior member of the KPJ leadership to survive the Stalinist purges. As a favorite of Dimitrov, he became the leader of the KPJ in 1937, his status as secretary-general being confirmed in 1939. A leftist, suspicious of Popular Front coalitions, he organized the Partisan insurrection in occupied Yugoslavia (summer 1941) and steered a course toward power, frequently at odds with the wishes of the Soviet leadership. The military successes of the Partisans prompted British recognition and support, ultimately opening the way to total power. By 1945, Yugoslavia had undergone a domestic revolution that established a regional and very militant Communist center. Stalin evidently saw great danger in Tito's militancy and in 1948 attempted to dislodge him from the KPJ leadership. This produced a split with the Soviets and the Communist movement under their control. After Stalin's death, relations with the USSR improved, although occasional crises marred these relations, in which the Soviet leaders never again established supremacy. Titoism consisted of an "independent road" to socialism, attempts to establish Communist legitimacy through the pursuit of "workers' self-management," and nonalignment with either bloc in foreign policy. In internal affairs Tito favored a balance of federal and republican interests in the Yugoslav federation and significant liberalization in cultural policy, but he was never open to political pluralism.

Togliatti, Palmiro (pseudonyms: Ercoli, Alfredo, 1893–1964): Italian Communist leader from a middle-class family; graduate, with a degree in law, of the University of Turin; editor-in-chief of the Socialist organ *Avanti* (Forward) and a founder of the pro-Comintern weekly *L'Ordine Nuovo* (The New Order, 1919); member of the PCI CC (from 1922 on) and Executive Committee (from 1923 on); editor of *Il Comunista* (The Communist), the organ of the Rome PCI organization (1922–1924); member of the ECCI and its presidium (from 1924 on) and secretariat (from 1926 on). Arrested after the beginning of Mussolini's dictatorship, he went abroad and participated in the struggle against the PCI leader Amadeo Bordiga (1926). Secretary-general of the PCI (from 1927 on), though mostly in the USSR after 1928; head of the Central European secretariat after the fall of Knorin (1936); Comintern representative to the PCE CC during the Civil War; head of Italian-language broadcasts from the USSR during the Second World War. After going back to Italy in April 1944, Togliatti directed the transformation of the

PCI into a mass-based party ready for participation in governance. He himself served briefly as minister in the governments of Badoglio, Bonomi, and de Gasperi (1944–1947) and was repeatedly elected to parliament. After the Twentieth Congress of the KPSS, Togliatti argued for an "Italian road to socialism" and introduced the concept of "polycentrism" into the previously unicentric and monolithic structure of the Communist movement.

Trotsky, Leon (Lev) Davidovich (real name: Bronstein, 1879–1940): Russian Marxist, son of a Jewish colonist in Kherson Province (southern Ukraine), who was second only to Lenin in the October days and the early period of Soviet power. After the party split of 1903 Trotsky, who was in exile in Western Europe from 1902 to 1905, and again from 1906 to 1917, was closer to the Mensheviks and did not enter the Bolshevik party until July 1917. Member of the Bolshevik CC (from August 1917 on); chairman of the Petrograd Soviet (after September 1917); member of the RKP(b) Politburo (1919–1926); people's commissar for foreign affairs (1917–1918) and war (1918–1925); organizer of the Red Army and mastermind behind its victorious strategy in the Civil War; alternate member (1920–1921, 1924–1927) of the ECCI and member in the intervening years (1921–1924); leader of the Left Opposition. In his writings, particularly in *Uroki Oktiabria* (Lessons of October, 1924) he defended the leftist concept of "permanent revolution" against the Stalinist program of building socialism in the USSR. After being expelled from the VKP(b) in 1927, Trotsky was sent into internal exile and then in February 1929 expelled from the USSR. As his adherents and others were being exterminated in the Stalinist purges, Trotsky's international followers formed the stillborn Trotskyist Fourth International (founded in Périgny, near Paris, in September 1938). He was assassinated by a Stalinist agent in Mexico (August 1940).

Ulbricht, Walter (1893–1973): German Communist leader; founding member of the Spartakusbund and the KPD; district KPD secretary in Saxony; member of the KPD committees for Halle-Merseberg and Leipzig; member of the KPD CC (1923–1924, and 1927 on); part of the Comintern apparatus (1924–1927); deputy in the Reichstag (after 1928); candidate-member of the ECCI (1928–1943); secretary of the Berlin KPD organization (1929–1933). After Hitler came to power, Ulbricht joined the KPD leadership in Paris. He was in Spain during the Civil War (1936–1937) and then in the USSR beginning in January 1938, as part of the Comintern apparatus until 1945, when he returned to Germany. Vice chairman of the SED and member of its Politburo (beginning in 1946); secretary-general (1950–1953) and first secretary (1953–1971) of the SED; deputy chairman of the East German Council of Ministers (1949–1960); chairman of the German Democratic Republic Council of State (that is, head of state) from 1960 on.

Varga, Jenő (pseudonyms: Eugen, Yevgeny, 1879–1964): Hungarian Communist exile and eminent Soviet economist. Varga received a doctorate from the University of Budapest (1906), wrote in the socialist press, taught at the University of Budapest (1918–1919), and joined the Hungarian CP in 1919. After serving as people's commissar for finance and chairman of the Supreme Economic Council in the government of the Hungarian Council Republic (1919), he emigrated to the USSR, joined the RKP(b), and worked for the Comintern apparatus as a specialist in economic affairs; director of the Institute of World Economy and Politics; member of the Academy of Sciences of the USSR (1939); candidate-member of the ECCI (1928–1943). In 1946 he published a book *Izmeneniia v ekonomike kapitalizma v itoge vtoroi mirovoi voiny* (Changes in the Economy of Capitalism as a Result of the Second World War), which implied that wartime planning in capitalist economies would be retained after the war, thereby strengthening the world capitalist system. Although Stalin apparently shared some of Varga's views, he permitted the sharp attacks against the culprit that were launched in 1947 by, among others, Politburo member N. A. Voznesensky. Varga underwent self-criticism, but, with the fall of Voznesensky (March 1949), the pressures against him diminished. Reinstated and much decorated, he wrote the *Pravda* article (February 1956) that rehabilitated Béla Kun.

Voroshilov, Kliment Yefremovich (1881–1969): "Red Marshal" of the Soviet Union, from a working class family in Yekaterinoslav Province. During the revolution of 1905 Voroshilov headed the Bolshevik committee and the soviet of workers' deputies in Lugansk (later Voroshilovgrad) in the Donbas; he worked with Stalin on the Baku Bolshevik committee (1908). After going back to Lugansk after the February revolution, he headed the RSDRP(b) city committee and was elected the mayor and chairman of the city soviet. After serving briefly in the Cheka, Voroshilov was assigned to the Red Army. He commanded the Ukrainian army group that, after numerous reversals, joined the defense of Tsaritsyn (Stalingrad), a city under Stalin's command, where Voroshilov became close to the future Soviet leader. Dismissed from the command of the Tenth Army by Trotsky because of his stubborn opposition to the use of tsarist officers, he was appointed people's commissar for internal affairs in Ukraine (1919). Having gone back to the Red Army in the fall of 1919, Voroshilov commanded the First Cavalry against the forces of Denikin, Makhno, Petliura, and Wrangel. He commanded the Northern Caucasus military district (1921–1924) and the Moscow military district (1924–1925). After the death of M. V. Frunze (1925), Voroshilov became people's commissar for military and naval affairs (later defense) and held that position until 1940, when he left after criticisms that stemmed from the reversals in the Finnish war. In

1935, he became the first marshal of the Soviet Union. He was appointed deputy chairman of the Council of People's Commissars in 1940. During the war he was a member of the State Council for Defense and, after commanding the feeble defense of the northwest (Leningrad) in 1941, was assigned to less exacting tasks (training reservists, commanding the partisan movement, directing the committee for captured enemy property, and arranging armistice commissions with Finland, Hungary, and Romania). Once out of the army, after 1945, Voroshilov headed the Allied Control Commission in Hungary (1945–1947) and the Cultural Bureau of the Council of Ministers. He was a member of the VKP(b) CC (1921–1961) and the Politburo (from 1926 on); from 1953 to 1960 he was the chairman of the Supreme Soviet of the USSR (that is, nominal head of state). Attacked at the Twenty-Second Congress of the KPSS (1961) as an adherent of the "antiparty" group of Molotov, Malenkov, and Kaganovich, Voroshilov underwent self-criticism and was not expelled from the KPSS. During the partial rehabilitation of Stalin in the Brezhnev era, Voroshilov was readmitted to the KPSS CC (1966).

Wang Ming (real name: Chen Shaoyu, 1907–1974): Chinese Communist leader, from a rich peasant family in Anhui Province. As a student at Shanghai University he participated in the 30 May Movement and joined the CPC in 1925. During the same year he was among the fifty students sent to Moscow to study at the newly opened Sun Yat-sen University. In May 1938, Pavel Mif, the Comintern China expert, went to China with the so-called returned students or twenty-eight Bolsheviks, Wang among them. The "returned students" opposed the leadership of Li Lisan. In 1931 Wang became the new CPC secretary-general, heading the "third leftist deviation," as Maoist historiography had it later. He held the post until his return to Moscow in 1931, but only nominally thereafter. He represented the CPC in the Comintern (1931–1937) and was elected in absentia to the Central Executive Committee of the Jiangxi Soviet Republic (1931). A member of the Comintern, he was elected to the ECCI presidium (1933) and participated in the work of the Seventh World Congress of the Comintern (1935). After returning to China in 1937, he was appointed the head of the CPC's department in charge of united front work and sent to the nationalist capital of Hankow in 1938, where he also headed the CPC Yangzi Department. At Yan'an beginning in the fall of 1938, he became a target of Mao's rectification campaign (1942) and was charged with "foreign formalism." After being elected a member of CPC CC (1945), he held minor posts after the establishment of the People's Republic and, after the mid-1950s, lived in veritable exile in Moscow, where he died. He participated in the Soviet anti-Maoist campaign after the great split, writing, among other works, a book titled *Predatel'stvo Mao Tze-duna* (Mao

Zedong's Betrayal, 1974). His daughter Fania was adopted by Dimitrov.

Yezhov, Nikolai Ivanovich (1895–1940): Soviet secret police chief who lent his name to the worst period of Stalinist terror—the *Yezhovshchina* of 1937. Born in Mariampol, in Suvalki Province (Poland), he joined the Bolsheviks as a worker in Petrograd (1917). Active in party work during the 1920s, he was brought to Moscow at the end of the 1920s and started working in the CC Cadre (personnel) Department. Highly placed at the time of the party purge of 1933, he was already connected by then with the OGPU. Member of the VKP(b) CC (1934–1939); deputy chairman (1934–1937) and chairman (1934–1939) of the Party Control Commission; people's commissar for internal affairs (1937–1938); candidate-member of the VKP(b) Politburo (1937–1939). Arrested in April 1939, he was accused of being a Polish and British spy. He defended himself before the military collegium of the supreme court of the USSR (February 1940) by saying that "during the twenty-five years of my party work I have fought honorably against enemies and have exterminated them. I have committed crimes for which I might well be executed. [. . .] But I have not committed and am innocent of the crimes which have been imputed to me by the prosecution in its bill of indictment." He was executed shortly thereafter.

Zhdanov, Andrei Aleksandrovich (1896–1948): Soviet Communist leader and ideologist, from a bureaucrat's family in Mariupol on the Sea of Azov; member of the RSDRP(b) from 1915 on; member of the Tver committee of the RSDRP (1916); party leader during the Revolution and Civil War in the Urals and in Tver (1919–1922); secretary of the Nizhny Novgorod regional committee; first secretary of the Leningrad oblast and city VKP(b) committees (1934–1944); chairman of the Allied Control Commission in Finland (1944–1945); candidate-member (1925–1930) and full member (from 1930 on) of the VKP(b) CC; candidate-member (1935–1939) and full member (1939–1948) of the VKP(b) Politburo; member of the VKP(b) apparatus (1944–1948) responsible for ideology. In 1946 Zhdanov initiated a campaign against ideological deviations and "formalism" in Soviet literature. The *Zhdanovshchina,* however inimical to the freedom of art, had bureaucratic roots and was aimed at Malenkov and Beria. By 1947, the course of several party debates over philosophy, biology (Lysenko), and economics (Varga) demonstrated that Zhdanov's forces were being beaten by Stalin-backed ultraconservatives. Zhdanov represented the KPSS in September 1947 at the founding meeting of the Cominform in Szklarska Poręba (Poland), where his keynote speech suggested a more aggressive Soviet foreign policy. The split with Yugoslavia was a setback for Zhdanov, and his public activities were negligible during his illness in the second half of 1948.

Zhou Enlai (1898–1976): Chinese Communist leader from a mandarin family. In France from 1920 to 1924, he participated in the establishment of the Chinese Communist group. Member of the CPC regional committee for Guangzhou (Canton, 1924) and head of the Political Department at the Whampoa (Huangpu) military academy under Chiang Kai-shek; political commissar of the 1st division of the First Chinese Army of Guangzhou (1925). Having headed the CPC's underground political work in Shanghai (1926), he was obliged to flee after Chiang Kai-shek commenced his attack on the Communists. He was a member of the CPC Politburo (from 1927 on). As head of the CPC Front Committee, responsible for providing guidance to military units, he ordered the abortive Nanchang uprising (Jiangxi, April 1927). In Moscow from 1928 to 1929 and in 1930, he was elected candidate-member of the ECCI, took part in the Long March, and served as the CPC's chief liaison with the Guomindang. Member of the ECCI (1935–1943); prime minister (1949–1976) and foreign minister (1949–1958) of the People's Republic of China.

Zinoviev, Grigory Yevseevich (real name: Radomilsky, 1883–1936): leading Bolshevik, from a lower-middle class Jewish family in Kherson Province (southern Ukraine). Zinoviev joined the Bolsheviks after the party split of 1903. He was a member of the RSDRP committee in St. Petersburg (1906–1908), which he represented at the Fifth Congress of the RSDRP in London (1907). In emigration from 1908 to 1917, he was at Lenin's side during Bolshevik organizational and propaganda efforts. Member of the RSDRP(b)/RKP(b)/VKP(b) CC from 1912 on, he opposed Lenin on the decision to seize power in October 1917 and to establish the government without other Socialist parties. Zinoviev was a candidate-member (1919–1921) and full member of the RKP(b) Politburo (1921–1926), chairman of the Petrograd Soviet (1917–1926), and chairman of the ECCI (1919–1926). After Lenin's death Zinoviev was one of the ruling "troika" (with Stalin and Kamenev). He broke with Stalin in 1925, organized the Leningrad Opposition, and joined forces with Trotsky. Stripped of his functions in 1926 and expelled from the VKP(b) in 1927, Zinoviev underwent self-criticism in 1928 and was readmitted. After being expelled again in 1932, reinstated in 1933, and expelled again at the end of the year, he was imprisoned in 1935, sentenced to a term of ten years, then tried publicly (with L. B. Kamenev) in the case of the "Trotskyite-Zinovievite United Center," sentenced to death, and executed.

Index

Berman, J., 292, 296, 297, 450

Béron, E., 95

Bevin, E., 379

Bianco, V., 223

Bierut, B., 328, 450

Bilen, İ., 101

Biriuzov, S. S., 340, 369–70, 376, 377, 381–82, 384, 385, 389, 395, 401, 405–07, 418

BKP. *See* Bulgarian Communist Party (BKP)

Blagoev, D., xvii, xviii, xx, xxii, 20, 98, 216, 225, 269

Blagoeva, S., 20, 108, 178, 240, 269, 336

Bled conference and agreement, xl, 419, 420, 421–23, 425, 430, 432–33, 437, 439

Blinov, 199, 210

Bliukher, V. K., 46

Bloch, J. R., 164

Blum, L., 32, 38, 43, 80, 86

Boboshevski, T., xliv–xlv, 334

Bogdanov, 97, 184

Bogomolov, A. Y., 40, 57, 250–51, 311

Bolívar, C., 31–32

Bolshakov, Col., 204, 226, 256, 279, 293

Boris III, xx, xxiv, 54–55, 141, 144, 173–74, 286

Borkenau, F., xlvi *n* 24

Bortnowski, B., 47

Bosnia, 213

Botev, H., xvii

Bozhilov, D., 317

Bradley, O., 236

Braginsky, Y. S., 366, 382

Brandler, H., xxvi

Brecht, B., xlv

Bredel, W., 242

Brezhnev, L. I., 452 *n* 594

British Communist Party, 35, 67, 77, 107, 117, 134, 156, 167–69, 202–03, 212, 214–15, 217–19, 234–35, 243–44, 275–76, 415

Browder, E., 59, 79–82, 93, 94, 272, 285, 299, 305–07, 456

BRSDP. *See* Bulgarian Workers' Social Democratic Party (Narrow Socialists)

Bubnov, A. S., 46

Budenny, S. M., 46, 64, 88, 121, 124, 130, 145, 189–90

Bukharin, N. I., xxvi, xxxi, 18, 36, 39, 54, 55, 56 *n* 129, 66, 72, 456

Bulganin, N. A., 46, 64, 88, 124, 130, 134, 136–37, 338, 354, 367, 369, 381, 413, 422, 423, 452, 456

Bulgaria: and Ottoman Empire, xvi, xviii;

in World War I, xix–xxi; Radomir republic in, xx; strikes of 1919–1920 in, xxi, xxii; and Treaty of Neuilly, xxi, xl, 348, 389; September uprising of 1923 in, xxii–xxiii, xxv, 21 *n* 22; and Stalin, xxx, xxxv, 18, 59, 184, 187, 286–87, 328, 330–31, 340, 343, 349, 352, 354, 356–58, 367–68, 375, 380, 381, 393–94, 399, 401, 405, 411, 413–14, 417–18, 421–24, 436, 441–42, 444, 452–53; transition to socialism in, xxxiv; and Thrace, xxxv, 158–59, 161–62, 297, 300, 337, 338, 340, 396, 407–08, 414; Dimitrov's return to, in 1945, xxxix, 339–40, 378, 379, 382, 384, 387–89; and Macedonia, xxxix–xl, 158–59, 161–62, 297, 300, 303, 314, 326, 337, 338, 340, 341, 347–48, 360, 388–89, 403, 405, 420, 448; union and friendship treaty between Yugoslavia and, xxxix–xl, 337, 343, 347–49, 352–58, 360, 364, 367–68, 391, 393, 403–05, 419, 421–23, 425, 427, 430–33, 437, 439, 441–42, 444; and Bled conference and agreement, xl, 419, 420, 421–23, 425, 430, 432–33, 437, 439; and Molotov, xli, 135, 136, 139, 140, 144, 214, 318, 328, 330–31, 340, 341, 343, 349, 354, 375, 378, 380, 381, 386, 390, 396–99, 401, 402, 405, 409, 437–38, 444; Fatherland Front in, xliv, 286–87, 301–02, 317, 330, 332–37, 343–44, 346–47, 351, 360, 361, 375–84, 388, 391, 399–401, 405–06, 417, 418, 426, 427, 435–36; and Petkov trial and execution, xliv–xlv, 419, 420, 424–25, 427–28, 430; and Romania, 123; relations with Yugoslavia in 1940, 125; and World War II, 134–41, 144, 154, 158–59, 161–62, 173–74, 184, 186, 189, 206, 215, 225–26, 315, 316, 318, 330–32, 338–41, 364; and mutual assistance pact with Soviet Union, 135–39; preparations for uprising in (1941), 187; and Turkey, 229; radio broadcasts in, 248, 325; Soviet plans for Bulgaria's withdrawal from Germany, 294; and All-Slavic Committee, 296–297; military assistance to, 300–302, 308–09, 325; sovietization of, 301–02; military in, 309–10, 405–11, 414, 421, 423, 444, 452–54; Bozhilov resignation in, 317; Bagrianov government in, 320–21, 324–25; Muraviev government in, 330 *n* 466, 331; queen of, 359; church in, 374–75, 386; Dimitrov as candidate in

diary of, 63, 131, 412; concern of, for reputation, 75, 104, 151; and theses on social democracy, 150–52; in Kuibyshev and Ufa during World War II, 165, 197–202; and dissolution of Comintern, 257–58, 270–80; U.S. journalist's request for interview of, 318; as candidate in Bulgarian deputies' elections (1945) in, 378, 379, 387–88; on dictatorship of the proletariat, 434, 449–50

Dimitrov, I., 454

Dimitrov, K., xvii

Dimitrov, N., xvii

Dimitrov, S., 31, 75, 159, 201, 302, 304, 316, 317, 325, 327, 329, 457

Dimitrov, T., xvii

Dimitrova, E. (Lena), xvii, 113, 170, 177, 179, 201

Dimitrova, M. (Lina), xvii, 17

Djilas, M., xxx–xxi, xli, xliii, xliv, xlvii–xlviii n37, 209, 316, 368, 437, 446, 457–58

Dolanský, J., 139

Dong Biwu, 311

Donovan, W., 216n341

Doriot, J., 1, 22

Dragnev, G., 399–400

Dragoicheva, Ts., 161, 355–56, 408

Dramaliev, K., 309

Duclos, 208, 236, 246–47, 272, 316

Duff Cooper, A., 86

Dutt, R. P., 35

Dzierżyńska, Z., 211

Dzierżyński, F., 211

East European federation, xli, 434–40

Eberlein, H., 29

ECCI. *See* Executive Committee of the Communist International (ECCI)

Eden, A., 235, 241–42, 340

Eisenhower, D., 247n386

Eitingon, L. A., 187

Engels, F., xvii, xxxiii, 450–51

England. *See* Great Britain

Ercoli, A. *See* Togliatti, P.

Executive Committee of the Communist International (ECCI), xxii–xxiii, xxv, xxvii, xxix, 9, 10, 12, 14, 16, 17, 22, 29, 58, 67, 70, 87, 91–93, 107, 112, 124, 129, 150, 156–57, 162–64, 167, 185, 192, 194, 198–200, 261, 266, 271–79. *See also* Comintern

Falcón, I., 103, 201, 223

Farkas, M., 254, 257, 272, 340

Fascism, xxvi, xxviii–xxix, 13, 45, 61, 74–75, 81, 85–87, 167, 169, 359. *See also* Germany; Italy

Fedeev, A. A., 192

Feierstein, 185

Ferdinand I, xviii–xx, xxiii

Ferguson, A., 35

Feuchtwanger, L., 44, 51

Fierlinger, Z., 288, 364

Filov, B., 137

Finder, P., 178, 192, 205, 206, 253–54, 263, 272, 287

Finland, xxxii–xxxiii, 107, 121–24, 127–29, 132, 134, 149, 206, 212, 260–63, 265–66, 386, 441

Fischer, E., 49, 59, 366, 367, 458

Fischer, R., xlvii$n$25

Fitin, P. M., xxxvii, 161, 181, 187, 190, 220, 235, 242, 246, 265, 272, 279, 285–86, 288, 292, 300–302, 308, 324, 387

Fleischmann, B., 113

Fleischmann, H., 113

Fleischmann, R., xliii, 2, 10, 23, 25, 27, 29, 134, 165, 177, 180, 184–86, 196, 199, 200, 268–69, 271, 272, 280, 307, 361, 366, 415, 436

Florin, W., 33, 93, 201, 222, 287, 458

Fornalska, M., 253

Foster, W. Z., 57, 285, 299, 305–07

France, 22, 23, 52, 61, 83, 114, 129, 193, 322, 425; Soviet relations with, in 1930s, xxvii, xxviii, 70–71, 110, 116; Popular Front in, 26n36, 32–33, 71, 80, 86; Blum government in, 32, 38, 41, 43, 80; and Spanish civil war, 33, 93–94, 114; Socialist Party in, 67, 71, 80; and Czechoslovakia, 74, 76, 78, 114; and Munich Pact (1938), 74, 78, 79, 80; and World War II, 115, 117, 123, 147–48, 159, 164, 181, 236, 238, 244, 247, 304–05, 321–22. *See also* De Gaulle, C.; French Communist Party

Franco, F., 61, 74, 241, 304

French Communist Party, 25, 30n49, 32–34, 36, 38, 41, 67, 70, 77, 80, 88, 100, 107, 109, 117, 123, 134, 147, 158, 167–69, 177, 193, 202–03, 204, 207–08, 246–47, 255, 259, 278, 304–05, 322, 342–43, 422, 426–27n584. *See also* France

Fried, E., 30, 33–35, 100, 139, 180, 202

Frinovsky, M. P., 65, 88

Fürnberg, F., 59, 170, 212, 222, 267, 272, 275–77, 458

Fyodorenko, Y. N., 361

Gábor, A., 345
Gallacher, W., 35
Gamarnik, Y. B., 46
Ganev, D., 336, 338
Ganev, V., xliv–xlv, 334
Garaux, 236, 238, 255, 261–63
Garota, J., 361
Gaus, F., 113
Gavrilović, M., 188
Gemetists, 370
Geminder, B., 82–83, 89, 170, 207, 222, 254, 257, 260, 267, 269–70, 275, 277, 283, 289, 329, 358, 458
Genchev, I., 27, 265
General Federation of Trade Unions (ORSS), xviii, xix, xxi
Genov, G., xxiii
Genovski, M., 400
Georgiev, K., 332, 344, 354, 355–57, 382, 385, 388, 389, 394, 396, 398–404, 407–11, 413, 416–18, 431–32
Georgiev, V., 454
German Communist Party (KPD), xxvi, xxxi, xlvii$n$25, 107, 124, 134, 156, 177, 191, 196–97, 211–13, 221, 222, 226, 249, 275, 276–77, 279, 287, 352, 369, 371–73, 426–27n584
Germanov, Col., 227
Germany: Nazi Party in, xv–xvi, xxvi–xxvii, xlvii$n$25, 1–8, 13–14, 134, 249; Reichstag fire case in, xv–xvi, xxv, xxvi–xxvii, xxx, xlvii$n$25, 2–8, 16, 17, 21, 24 n28, 89, 284; aggressiveness and remilitarization of, in 1930s, xxviii, 75–79; nonaggression pact between Soviet Union and, xxxiv–xxv, 107, 112–14, 115; invasion of Soviet Union by, xxxvi, 165–69, 171; Dimitrov's diary entries from, 1–8; and Knorin, 23; Goebbels's speech at Nuremberg party rally (1936), 30; and Trotsky and Trotskyites, 43, 51n124; and Spanish Civil War, 45, 74; Soviet commission on German issues, 52, 54, 57, 212; plans of, for attack on Russia in 1937, 70; and Munich Pact (1938), 74, 78, 79, 80, 85–86; Manuilsky on aggression of, 75, 85–87; and Jews, 82, 89, 134, 237, 270; and Soviet-Finnish war, 129; military forces of, 133, 138, 159–60; strength of German people, 256; working class in, 257; and Free Germany committee, 279–82, 284, 382; Soviet plans for Bulgaria's withdrawal from, 294; division of, following World War II, 363–64, 372; radio broadcasts in, 363,

364; surrender of, 370; and Serbia, 438; and peace treaty after World War II, 443. *See also* German Communist Party; Hitler, A.; Nazi Party; World War II
Gerő, E., 47, 76, 165, 201, 276, 340, 344, 371, 458–59
Gheorghiu-Dej, G., 350, 383
Gichev, D., 286, 444–45
Gide, A., 44n96
Giorla, L. C., 108
Giral, J., 28
Girginov, A., 173
Glaubauf, F., 275, 358
Goebbels, J., xvi, xxvi–xxvii, 2, 30
Golikov, F. I., 141–42, 149, 150, 192
Gomułka, W., 253, 328, 370
González Peña, R., 71
Gopner, S. I., 60
Göring, H., xvi, xlii, xlvi$n$23, 2
Gorkić, M., 34
Gorky, M., 17, 25
Gottwald, K., xxix, xxxv, 29, 30, 34, 36, 49, 50, 93, 101, 162, 165, 170, 202, 212, 223, 252, 274, 289, 327, 329–30, 350, 363–65, 373, 377, 431, 459
Gramsci, A., 182
Great Britain, 68, 83, 93–94, 114, 129, 235, 251, 324, 360, 363, 413, 415, 437, 439, 440; and Czechoslovakia, 74, 76, 78; and Munich Pact (1938), 74, 78, 79, 80, 85–86; Soviet negotiations with, 105, 110–11, 116, 174–75; and World War II, 115, 117, 123, 133, 137, 152, 159, 164, 167, 169, 174–76, 179, 181, 203, 205, 208, 217–18, 221, 224–25, 228, 230, 233–36, 238, 300–301, 319, 321–22, 338–39, 363; and Yugoslavia, 210, 298–301; and Anglo-Soviet pact, 224–25, 228; and Bulgaria, 379–80, 386, 405, 413, 421, 437, 448. *See also* Chamberlain, N.; Churchill, W.
Greece, xl, xli, xlviii$n$37, 134, 137, 138, 154, 155, 158, 284, 285, 291–92, 316, 326, 327, 337, 345, 352–53, 390, 396, 402, 414, 418, 421, 423, 426–27n584, 434, 437–43, 447, 453
Grekov, A., 410
Grenier, F., 266, 267
Grol, M., 362
Gross, B., xlvii$n$25
Groza, P., 383
Grozdanov, 31, 72
Grozev, G., 429
Guliaev, P. V., 198

Lukanov, T., xxii
Lukianov, V. V., 28
Lulchev, K., 395, 425, 443

Macedonia, xvi, xxxix–xli, 21 n22, 111,
158–59, 161, 189, 239, 285, 291, 297,
300, 303, 314–15, 317, 326, 329, 337,
338, 340, 341, 347–48, 353, 360, 388–
90, 403, 405, 420, 448
Maddalena, M., 24
Maisky, I. M., 149–50, 180
Málaga, 31–32
Malenkov, G. M., xli, 130, 150, 155, 166,
171, 172, 178, 183, 189, 195, 197, 209,
213, 271, 274, 277, 279–80, 282, 354,
357, 362, 384, 387, 413, 423, 436, 452,
466
Manchuria, 72, 140–42, 188, 194
Mandalian, 28, 40, 42
Manuilska, V. P., 202
Manuilsky, D. Z., xxix, xxxii, xxxvii, 9–
17, 22, 26–28, 35, 37, 39, 42, 46, 47, 53,
57, 59, 61, 72–88, 93, 98, 99, 104–07,
110, 115, 118, 134, 146, 150–51, 162,
167, 174, 195, 201–02, 205, 207, 208,
221, 222, 226, 255, 258, 268–75, 279–
87, 292, 293, 296, 301, 303, 308, 311,
315, 317, 318, 322–24, 330–31, 466
Mao Zedong, xxxvii, 42, 96, 147, 164,
165, 176, 183, 193, 204, 212, 227, 228,
231–32, 256–59, 272, 285, 289–90,
293–301, 306–07, 311–13, 326, 379,
467
Martulkov, A., 390
Marty, A., xxix, 32, 34, 55–60, 74, 109,
135, 147, 158, 174, 180, 181, 193, 195,
207, 223, 236, 238, 240, 244, 255, 257,
259, 261–63, 266–67, 271, 272, 282,
285–286, 304–05, 467
Marx, K., xvii, xxxiii, xxxviii, 17, 19, 156,
271, 274, 275, 450–51
Matsuoka, Y., 153, 155
May Day celebrations, 17–18, 106–07,
154–55, 339
Mayakovsky, 125, 144
Mednikarov, A., 98
Mekhlis, L. Z., 47, 88, 127–28, 166, 191
Melchor, F., 102
Mercader, C. del R., 237–38
Meretskov, K. A., 145, 146
Merkulov, V. N., 90, 93, 145, 148, 177,
179, 181, 281, 387
Mexico, 185, 316–17
Mezhlauk, V. I., 46, 64
Miaja, J., 99, 101

Michael I, 328 n463
Mif, P., 295
Mihailović, D., 212, 214, 218–19, 221,
233, 239–40, 242, 244, 255, 264
Mihalchev, D., 333, 346–47, 355, 357,
380, 384–86, 397
Mije, A., 316–17
Mikhailov, N. A., 146, 198, 294
Mikołajczyk, S., 324
Mikoyan, A. I., xlii, 15, 17, 18, 46, 54, 59,
64, 65, 88–89, 104, 121, 130, 155, 183,
198, 274, 279–80, 341, 354, 386, 413,
467–68
Minc, H., 297, 450
Minchev, N., 366
Minev, S., 101, 103, 109, 147, 195, 201,
207, 223, 272, 285
Mirov–Rozkin, Y. T., 328, 334
Mirza, S., 205
Modesto, J., 102, 316, 342
Mołojec, B., 192, 205, 206, 249, 253–54
Molotov, V. M., xxxvii, 14, 17–18, 38, 39,
45, 55, 56, 59, 64, 88, 105, 110–11,
116, 127, 130, 149–50, 177, 181, 261,
360, 385, 397, 403, 449, 450; and
Czechoslovakia, xxv, 288; and Lenin,
xxxi, 66, 122–23; and Bulgaria, xli, 135,
136, 139, 140, 144, 214, 286–87, 294,
316, 318, 328, 330–31, 340, 341, 343,
349, 354, 356, 357, 375, 378, 380, 381,
386, 390, 396–99, 401, 402, 405, 409,
413, 437–38, 444, 452; and Yugoslavia,
xli, 152, 193, 206, 209–10, 214, 221–
22, 232–33, 239–40, 266, 293–94,
313–15, 343, 349, 354, 356, 357, 438–
39, 445–46; and Dimitrov's membership
in ECCI, 9, 15; and Spain, 28, 58, 73,
99–100; and France, 32–33; and China,
42, 48, 52, 73, 172, 180, 182, 183, 250,
379; and Sudeten Communists, 97; and
German-Soviet nonaggression treaty,
113; and World War II, 114, 117, 119,
124, 135–36, 166–68, 171, 172, 174–
75, 182, 183, 189, 193–97, 209–10,
221–22, 263, 266; on Red Army's crossing border into Belorussia and Ukraine,
117; praise for Stalin by, 122–23; and
Iceland, 179; and radio broadcasts, 180,
263, 266; and Poland, 184, 293, 294,
296–98, 307–08; and German Communist Party, 196–97, 372–73; and Iran,
206; and Comintern dissolution, 257–
58, 270, 278; and Italy, 298, 303, 331,
371; and Greece, 327, 345, 396; and
union and friendship treaty between Bul-

Molotov (continued)
   garia and Yugoslavia, 343, 349, 354,
   356, 357, 360, 364, 427, 430, 432, 437;
   and Potsdam Conference, 376–77; on
   Paris peace conference (1946), 411; and
   Bulgarian-Czechoslovak agreement
   (1947), 429–30; criticisms of Dimitrov
   by, 437–39, 443; biographical sketch on,
   468
Mongolia, 31, 128, 251
Morozov, I. A., 226, 238, 257, 265, 275,
   277, 283, 287–88, 316, 342, 358
Moshetov, V. V., 390
Moskvin, M. A., xxxvii, 26–29, 32, 35, 37,
   42, 45, 47, 58, 59, 72–85, 82, 87, 90, 91,
   468–69
Munich Pact (1938), 74, 78, 79, 80, 85–86
Münzenberg, W., xxxvii, xlvii n 25, 69, 469
Muraviev, K., 330 n 466, 331
Mushanov, N., 286, 294
Mussolini, B., 78, 81, 207, 257, 303 n 434

Nagy, I., 344–45
Natanson, S., 211, 222
Nationalism, xxxiv–xxxv, 163
Nazi Party, xv–xvi, xxvi–xxvii, xlvii n 25,
   1–8, 13–14, 134, 249. *See also* Fascism;
   Germany; Hitler, A.
Nedić, M., 221, 240
Negarville, C., 322
Negrín, J., 91, 103
Neichev, M., 332, 454
Neikov, D., 333
Nejedlý, Z., xxxv, 373, 431
Nenni, P., 323
Nešković, B., 404, 405
Netherlands, 88, 107, 114, 167, 180, 202,
   212, 229, 246, 278
Neumann, H., 19, 469
Nevsky, A., 128
Nikolaev, A. K., 91, 385
Nikoliš, G., 352 n 510
North Africa, 247
Norway, 88, 123, 175, 180, 265
Nosek, V., 364
Novella, A., 322
Nowotko, M., 178, 192, 205, 206, 212,
   224, 232, 245–46, 249, 253–55
Nygaardsvold, J., 175

Obbov, A., 397, 398, 399, 402
Ordhzonikidze, Z. G., 268
Ordzhonikidze, G. K., 17, 18, 28, 36, 42,
   45, 53–54, 118, 469
Ordzhonikidze, Z. G., 268, 269

ORSS. *See* General Federation of Trade
   Unions (ORSS)
Osten, M., 44, 51
Ottoman Empire, xviii–xix. *See also* Turkey
Ovakimian, G., 219

Palau, J., 109
Palestine, 265, 444
Panaiotov, A., 407
Panfilov, Gen., 140–42, 181, 194, 215–16,
   227
Paniushkin, A. S., 249, 250, 260, 342, 344,
   362, 379, 382, 387, 405
Papandreou, G., 352–53
Papanin, I. D., 361
Papen, F. von, 230
Paris peace conference (1946), 411, 419
Parliamentarianism, xxxiii–xxxiv, 12–13
Pashov, I., 309
Pastuhov, K., 397
Pauker, A., xxxviii, 134, 165, 268, 272,
   276, 282–83, 328, 329, 331, 335, 350,
   470
Paulus, F., 212, 281–82
Pavelić, A., 240
Pavlov, A., 375
Pavlov, T., 126, 158, 159, 161, 334, 346,
   369, 454
Peace treaties after World War II, 386–88,
   409, 413, 419, 424, 427, 430–31, 443–
   44
Pétain, P., 147, 164, 305
Peter II, 269–70, 284, 298–99
Péti, Gen., 244, 255, 259
Petkov, N., xliv–xlv, 334, 370, 375–77,
   385, 388, 394, 402 n 566, 419, 420, 424–
   25, 427–28, 430
Petkova, S., xlv
Piatakov, Y. L., 38, 39, 43, 48–50, 62, 132
Piatakov–Radek trial, 48–51
Piatnitsky, I. A., 9, 12, 14, 15, 16, 22, 23,
   24, 470
Pieck, W., xxix, xlvii n 25, 22, 72, 159, 165,
   191, 201, 212, 222, 256, 271–73, 276,
   279, 281–82, 287, 296, 334, 352, 363,
   365, 369, 371, 372, 470
Pijade, M., 356–57
Pivertists, 83
Pladne Agrarians, xliv
Plekhanov, G. V., xvii
Plyshevsky, I. P., 238, 257
Pock, F., 184
Podgorny, N. V., 452 n 594
Poland, xxvii, xxxv, 29, 33, 47, 75–76,
   107, 110–11, 114, 116, 174, 184, 188,

191, 192, 205, 206, 211, 212, 216, 218–19, 224, 232, 245–46, 249, 251, 253–55, 263, 264, 285, 292–94, 296–98, 307–08, 323–24, 363, 373, 438, 439, 441, 442. *See also* Polish Communist Party

Poliachek, L. M., 91

Polikarpov, 196, 255–56

Polish Communist Party, 44–45, 72, 75, 76, 88, 150, 172, 176–79, 181, 191–92, 205, 216, 218, 226, 246, 253–55, 263, 278, 287–88, 296–99, 303–04, 426–27 n584. *See also* Poland

Pollitt, H., 22, 32–35, 215, 217–19, 234–35, 272, 470

Ponomarev, B. N., 28, 36, 49, 53, 201, 205, 254, 267, 342, 387, 471

Popov, A., 215

Popov, B., xv–xvi, xxv, xxvii, 2, 431

Popov, G., 408

Popović, K., 209

Poptomov, V., xxxix, 111, 225, 291, 313–14, 336, 420, 428, 432, 445, 454

Popular Front, xxviii–xxix, xxxvi, 26n36, 27n37, 31–34, 45, 60, 71, 80, 86, 93–95, 116, 147

Poskrebyshev, A. N., 148, 166, 211, 394

Potsdam Conference, 339, 376–77

POUM. *See* Workers' Party of Marxist Unification (POUM)

Prestes, L. C., 230

Prisoners of war, 165, 181, 186, 187, 208, 252, 258, 267–68, 276–77, 282, 364, 382

Pritt, D. N., 25

Procházka, J., 223

Próchniak, E., 61

Proletariat, dictatorship of, 434, 449–51

Propaganda work. *See* Radio broadcasts

Psarros, D., 291

PSUC. *See* United Socialist Party (PSUC)

Pushkin, A. S., 52

Qin Bangxian, 97

Radek, K. B., xxii, 36, 43, 48–51, 471

Radio broadcasts, xxxvii, 22, 53, 165, 170, 176, 178, 180–82, 185, 186, 193, 194, 196, 201, 206–08, 212, 222, 228, 244–45, 248, 255–56, 262–64, 266, 269–70, 277, 279, 282, 289, 309, 318, 329, 331, 334, 335, 363

Radionov, T., 215

Rákosi, M., xxxii, xxxv, 101, 130, 134, 165, 170, 186, 207, 233–234, 248, 249,

251, 272, 276, 280, 282, 283, 287, 329, 338, 340, 344, 352, 371, 377, 382, 471–72

Rakovsky, C., 62

Ramette, A., 342

Ranković, A., 404, 405

Razumova, A. L., 47, 53

Reale, E., 311, 319

Redens, S. F., 65

Reese, M., xlvii$n$25

Reichstag fire case, xv–xvi, xxv, xxvi–xxvii, xxx, xlvii$n$25, 2–8, 16, 17, 21, 24 n28, 89, 284

Relecom, X., 53

Ren Bishi, 96, 126

Révai, J., 340

Ribar, I., 209

Ribbentrop, J. von, 112–13, 137n254

Ribnikar, V., 293

Robeson, P., 284

Roca, B., 230

Romania, xxxviii, 75, 86, 110, 123, 134, 185, 206, 282–85, 328, 329, 330, 332, 335, 337, 350–51, 371, 383, 386, 398, 426–27n584, 430–31, 434, 435, 441, 444

Roosevelt, F. D., 81, 94, 195–96, 225, 311, 312

Ross, J., 236

Rousos, P., 345

Rozenberg, M. I., 38, 40

Rudas, L., 179

Rudzutak, J. E., 46

Russia. *See* Soviet Union

Russian tsars, 65

Rydz-Śmigły, E., 29, 33

Rykov, A. I., xxxi, 36, 39, 54, 55, 56n129, 66

Saburov, M. Z., 198

Sadoul, J., 23

Sakŭzov, Y., xviii

Salaj, Dj., 254, 267

Samodumov, T., 384

Sarafis, S., 291

Schulenberg, F. W. von der, 166

Schutzbund insurrection, 9–12, 16, 19

Scoccimarro, M., 322

September uprising (1923), xxii–xxiii, xxv, 21n22

Serbia, xliii, 285, 337, 404, 438

Serebriakov, L. P., 38

Serov, I. A., 373

Shakhurin, A. I., 193

Shaposhnikov, B. M., 64, 88, 195, 197

BOOKS IN THE ANNALS OF COMMUNISM SERIES

The Fall of the Romanovs: Political Dreams and Personal Struggles in a Time of Revolution, by Mark D. Steinberg and Vladimir M. Khrustalëv

The Last Diary of Tsaritsa Alexandra, introduction by Robert K. Massie; edited by Vladimir A. Kozlov and Vladimir M. Khrustalëv

The Unknown Lenin: From the Secret Archive, edited by Richard Pipes

Voices of Revolution, 1917, by Mark D. Steinberg

Stalinism as a Way of Life: A Narrative in Documents, edited by Lewis Siegelbaum and Andrei K. Sokolov

The Road to Terror: Stalin and the Self-Destruction of the Bolsheviks, 1932–1939, by J. Arch Getty and Oleg V. Naumov

The Diary of Georgi Dimitrov, 1933–1949, introduced and edited by Ivo Banac

Enemies Within the Gates? The Comintern and the Stalinist Repression, 1934–1939, by William J. Chase

Stalin's Letters to Molotov, 1925–1936, edited by Lars T. Lih, Oleg V. Naumov, and Oleg V. Khlevniuk

Dimitrov and Stalin, 1934–1943: Letters from the Soviet Archives, edited by Alexander Dallin and Fridrikh I. Firsov

Spain Betrayed: The Soviet Union in the Spanish Civil War, edited by Ronald Radosh, Mary R. Habeck, and G. N. Sevostianov

The Secret World of American Communism, by Harvey Klehr, John Earl Haynes, and Fridrikh I. Firsov

The Soviet World of American Communism, by Harvey Klehr, John Earl Haynes, and Kyrill M. Anderson

Stalin's Secret Pogrom: The Postwar Inquisition of the Soviet Jewish Anti-Fascist Committee, edited by Joshua Rubenstein and Vladimir P. Naumov